GW00702065

HARDEN'S

UK
Restaurants
2003

RÉMY MARTIN

FINE CHAMPAGNE COGNAC

Rémy Martin is launching the Restaurant Rémy Awards in association with Harden's to recognise the rising stars of the UK restaurant scene.

The skill, passion and dedication required to make Rémy Martin Cognac are also the qualities which are found in the greatest chefs.

For centuries Rémy Martin Cognac has been enjoyed as a perfect complement to food. In the past decade the British appetite for new taste experiences has altered forever our ideas of good food and dining out in particular.

Standards have risen dramatically and diners now expect that innovation will be at the heart of every menu.

We want the Restaurant Rémys to recognise and encourage those chefs and restaurateurs who constantly strive to bring these new taste experiences to our tables.

Taste is also at the heart of what we do. Enjoy Rémy Martin on ice as an aperitif, in a long drink with your favourite mixer, served chilled with your starter or dessert, or even as a traditional digestif.

Rémy Martin
The Taste of Excellence

THE RESTAURANT RÉMYS

In selecting the 20 winners of the first Restaurant Rémys we have tried to draw out rising stars from the restaurant world which, on the basis of feedback from their customers – thousands of regular diners – stand out for excellence.

It's clear that there is no single route to this level of achievement. It may involve simply making the very best of the freshest ingredients, or it may involve injecting creative 'twists' to surprise and delight the diner. It may be found in the heart of the capital, in a major provincial city, or in a tiny Scottish fishing port. It may be driven by a display of culinary fireworks, or it may be the creation of a good all-round experience, where good food is but an important part of a package whose point is that it takes diners on an adventure outside their daily existence.

What is evident from talking to many of our rising stars is that the secret of their success is simply that they seek to do what they do very well, and take infinite pains to do so. As that's what we've been doing at Rémy Martin for almost 300 years now, it's something we understand very well.

THE REGIONAL WINNERS

EE USK – OBAN

At his portside bistro, Callum McLeod aims to take full advantage of the impeccably fresh seafood available. "We want to get the people to come to the source of the seafood rather than the other way round," he says. "but equally we've tried to bring a bit of city life to a coastal location."

HOTEL DES CLOS – NOTTINGHAM

In their conversion of these Victorian farm buildings, Dan Ralley and Sat Baines have avoided period clichés with a view to creating "a complete experience that does more than satisfy people's hunger". "We serve classic dishes with a 'twist' that aim both to excite visually, while paying attention to the joy of classic food combinations."

LOUNGE 10 – MANCHESTER

Phil Yates has had the courage to do something completely different in the conversion of what used to be a tapas bar. No lesser designer than Vivienne Westwood was used to design the 'Edwardian' loos, and this innovative streak doesn't end with the plumbing…

L'ORTOLAN - READING

It's a brave chef who takes over a restaurant whose status as a 'destination' was established by one of the industry's big names. Alan Murchison – who in his early career worked as a junior under John Burton-Race here – has shown himself unfazed by the challenge, and has worked to develop a menu where ethnic influences add excitement to what is essentially a classical approach.

RESTAURANT BAR & GRILL – MANCHESTER

This comfortable, stylish and central restaurant is an 'all-rounder' that makes a suitable champion for a city whose restaurant scene is emerging strongly. And it has a management who've realised that quality food – and value – is important too.

RIVERSIDE BRASSERIE – BRAY

"I am fascinated by the science of cooking and the psychology of eating and want to share that excitement." So speaks famed "culinary alchemist" Heston Blumenthal, famed for his unique brand of 'molecular gastronomy'. This 'high-wire' performance requires a rock-solid understanding of the 'basics' of cooking, displayed to brilliant effect at his charmingly-located, new 'number 2' restaurant.

SEAHAM HALL – DURHAM
This "super luxurious" new hotel with spa, on the edge of the North Sea has been hailed as "the most exquisite modern retreat in the UK". Head chef John Connell is determined that his food is not going to be eclipsed by the setting – "we use the finest, freshest ingredients in an eclectic yet original style."

SEAFOOD CAFÉ – ST. IVES
A bit of humility does no harm in a town with a well-developed restaurant scene. "We don't think we're the best restaurant but what we do is the best and that's reflected by our customers," says chef Ken Humphries, whose philosophy for this new venture is "simple and seasonal."

60 HOPE STREET – LIVERPOOL
In a city without a 'grand dining culture', Gary and Colin Manning's stylish yet unpretentious café/bar/brasserie is winning an ever more widespread following by offering quality across the board.

VANILLA POD – MARLOW
Let's be grateful it's not called the Garlic Pod – Michael McDonald attempts to infiltrate his trademark flavour into every course at his new operation. Otherwise, the creed here is admirably straightforward: "fresh produce comes in in the morning and is used that day – we don't over-elaborate, we don't complicate, we let good quality ingredients speak for themselves."

THE LONDON WINNERS

CHAMPOR-CHAMPOR
"The name means 'mix and match', but we are careful to make sure it is not a case of 'mix and mis-match'", according to owner Charles Tyler. This eclectic philosophy – shared by chef Adu Amran Hassan – is winning fame for his small Borough establishment – "If our guests leave us feeling that they have been on an exotic holiday, we are getting close to achieving our goal."

THE DRAPER'S ARMS
This hidden gem of a Georgian pub was derelict for years before being rescued by Paul McElhinney, who has installed chef Mark Emberton to preside over the cooking. Their aim is clear: "we're not doing anything terribly different – it's the quality of what we do that distinguishes us."

E&O

Will Ricker's aim was to serve "the best dishes from China, Japan and Thailand", while creating a "neighbourhood place that was affordable and buzzy" too. As the neighbourhood in question was Notting Hill, it's no surprise that it's instantly become one of the most fashionable places in the capital.

EALING PARK TAVERN

"Homeliness without forsaking quality" – that's the philosophy that's made Vincent Morse's stylish west London gastropub an instant success in an area crying out for a decent eatery. "Atmosphere is absolutely key", he says, but he also aims to serve "traditional, rustic food at its very best."

1837 AT BROWN'S

"Certain simple combinations can totally change the way you think about food", says Andrew Turner, Head Chef at this grand Mayfair dining room, where the list of wines by the glass is legendary. "They don't have to be particularly fancy or complicated but in their own way they can provide you with the fascinating alchemy that is cooking."

LOCANDA LOCATELLI

"To Italians, food is the most important thing in their lives" – that's the credo which enabled Giorgio Locatelli to estabish Zafferano as the best Italian restaurant in London for many years. He's now repeating his magic – under his own name, this time – at this stylish new establishment, just north of Oxford Street.

THE OAK

"In a locality it's important to keep ideas fresh and creative so our menu changes regularly": so say Mark Broadbent and Jasper Gorst, proprietors of this Bayswater gastropub. "We are committed to using fresh, seasonal produce from eclectic sources, but making excellent food that offers value for money."

RACINE

It may have only just opened, but the assured style of this Knightsbridge newcomer makes it feel like a long-established veteran. Henry Harris and Eric Garnier have a very simple philosophy: "providing the best food and the best service in the best possible surroundings."

RESTAURANT ONE-O-ONE

"Pure dedication" and "the freshest and most natural ingredients, using newly caught fish arriving daily." That's the formula which chef Pascal Proyart brings to this Knightsbridge hotel restaurant (where "cuisine de la mer" is the speciality). He's not yet famous, but judged on the feedback from restaurant-goers, he deserves to be.

LA TROMPETTE

This increasingly famous French restaurant in Chiswick has made waves well beyond west London, but the aspiration that's driven it to success couldn't be easier to understand – "to provide an excellent standard of food and wine in a convivial, warm, honest environment."

RATINGS & PRICES

We see little point in traditional rating systems, which generally tell you nothing more than that expensive restaurants are 'better' than cheap ones because they use costlier ingredients and attempt more ambitious dishes. You probably knew that already. Our system assumes that, as prices rise, so do diners' expectations.

Prices and ratings are shown as follows:

£ Price
The cost of a three-course *dinner* for one person.
We include half a bottle of house wine, coffee and service (or a 10% tip if there is no service charge).

Food
The following symbols indicate that, *in comparison with other restaurants in the same price-bracket*, the cooking at the establishment is:

★★ **Exceptional**
★ **Very good**

We also have a category for places which attract a notably high proportion of adverse comment:

✗ **Disappointing**

Ambience
Restaurants which provide a setting which is very charming, stylish or 'buzzy' are indicated as follows:

𝔸 **Particularly atmospheric**

Small print

Telephone number – *All numbers in the London section are (020) numbers. Dublin numbers are shown for dialling within the Republic (the international code for which is + 353).*

Sample dishes – *these dishes exemplify the style of cooking at a particular establishment. They are merely samples – it is unlikely that these specific dishes will be available at the time of your visit.*

Value tip – *if we know of a particularly good-value set menu or some similar handy tip, we note this. Set lunch deals are for weekdays, unless stated. Details change, so always check ahead.*

Details – *the following information is given where relevant:*

Directions – *to help you find the establishment.*

Website – *if applicable.*

Last orders time – *at dinner (Sun may be up to 90 mins earlier).*

Opening hours – *unless otherwise stated, restaurants are open for lunch and dinner seven days a week.*

Credit and debit cards – *unless otherwise stated, Mastercard, Visa, Amex and Switch are accepted.*

Dress – *where appropriate, the management's preferences concerning patrons' dress are given.*

Smoking – *cigarette smoking restrictions are noted. Pipe or cigar smokers should always check ahead.*

Children – *if we know of a specified minimum age for children, we note this.*

Accommodation – *if an establishment has rooms, we list how many and the minimum price for a double.*

Publisher's announcements

At last... Hardens on your PDA

Harden's London Restaurants and *Harden's UK Restaurants* are now available for use on your PDA (both Pocket PC and Palm OS).

Other Harden's titles

London Restaurants 2003
Good Cheap Eats in London 2003
London Bars & Pubs
London Food Shops 2002/03
London Baby Book 2002/03
Party Guide for London 2001/02
London for Free (new edition Spring 2003)

The ideal corporate gift

Harden's London Restaurants, *Harden's UK Restaurants* and *Harden's London Bars & Pubs* are available in a range of specially customised corporate gift formats.

For further information on any of the above, please call (020) 7839 4763 or visit www.hardens.com.

© Harden's Limited 2002

ISBN 1-873721-52-8 (paperback)
ISBN 1-873721-53-6 (bonded leather)

British Library Cataloguing-in-Publication data:
a catalogue record for this book is available from
the British Library.

Printed and bound in Finland by
WS Bookwell Ltd

Editorial Manager: Antonia Russell
Production Manager: Elizabeth Warman
Research assistant: Frances Gill

Harden's Limited
14 Buckingham Street
London WC2N 6DF

The views expressed in the editorial section of this guide are exclusively those of Harden's Limited.

The contents of this book are believed correct at the time of printing. Nevertheless, the publisher can accept no responsibility for errors or changes in or omissions from the details given.

CONTENTS

HOW THIS BOOK IS ORGANISED

This guide begins in *London*, which, in recognition of the scale and diversity of its restaurant scene, has an extensive introduction and indexes, as well as its own maps. Thereafter, the guide is organised strictly alphabetically, without regard to national divisions– Ballater, Beaumaris, Belfast and Birmingham appear together under 'B'.

For *cities and larger towns*, you should therefore be able to turn straight to the relevant section. Cities which have significant numbers of restaurants also have a brief introductory overview, as well as entries for the restaurants themselves.

In *less densely populated areas*, you will generally find it easiest to start with the map of the relevant area at the back of the book, which will guide you to the appropriate place names.

HOW THIS BOOK IS RESEARCHED

This book is the result of a research effort involving thousands of 'reporters'. These are 'ordinary' members of the public who share with us summary reviews of the best and the worst of their annual dining experiences. This year, some 7000 people gave us approximately 100,000 reviews in total.

The density of the feedback on London (where many of the top places attract several hundred reviews each) is such that the ratings for the restaurants in the capital included in this edition are almost exclusively statistical in derivation. We have, as it happens, visited all the restaurants in the London section, anonymously, and at our own expense, but we use our personal experiences only to inform the standpoint from which to interpret the consensus opinion.

In the case of the more commented-upon restaurants away from the capital, we have adopted an approach very similar to London. In the case of less-visited provincial establishments, however, the interpretation of survey results owes as much to art as it does to science.

In our experience, smaller establishments are – for better or worse – generally quite consistent, and we have therefore felt able to place a relatively high level of confidence in a lower level of commentary. Conservatism on our part, however, may have led to some smaller places being under-rated compared to their more visited peers.

HOW YOU CAN JOIN THE SURVEY

Register for a free update – at www.hardens.com or by writing to us – and you will be invited, in the spring of 2003, to participate in our next survey. **If you take part you will, on publication, receive a complimentary copy of *Harden's UK Restaurants 2004*.**

FROM THE EDITORS

We have been in the business of publishing restaurant guides (to London) for the past twelve years, but this is only the fifth edition of our guide to the UK as a whole.

To an extent that we believe is unique in the UK, this guide is written 'from the bottom up'. That is to say, its composition is driven by the restaurants which people across the country – as represented by our diverse reporter base – talk about. It does not, therefore, concentrate on hotel restaurants (as is the case with one of our 'independent' competitors, which does a big business in hotel inspections). Nor – unlike all the other major UK restaurant guides – does it (by their relative omission) give the impression that 'ethnic' cuisines are somehow second-rate, or of less interest than 'proper' European ones.

The effects of London's restaurant revolution of the '90s are now spreading across the whole of the UK. The task of following the growing number of restaurants proper – as well as the gastropubs, the hotel dining rooms, the bistros and the quality café/bars – grows annually. We know – as any honest publisher must acknowledge – that all guide books are imperfect. There will be deserving places missing, and opinions will be repeated that the passing of time has rendered redundant. However, we believe that our system – involving the careful processing of tens of thousands of reports – is the best available.

Given the growing scale of our task, we are very grateful for the support we have received from Rémy Martin in the publication of this guide. With their help, we hope to make this the most comprehensive, as well as the most diverse, guide available to the restaurants of the UK.

Assembling a large number of reporters interested to contribute their views on restaurants is no easy task, and thanks go to Berry Bros. & Rudd, the wine merchant, for inviting their account customers to take part in the survey. We are no less grateful to the growing band of our 'own' reporters who also participated.

All restaurant guides are the subject of continual revision. This is especially true when the restaurant scene is undergoing a period of rapid change, as at present.

Please help us to make the next edition even more comprehensive and accurate: sign up to join the survey by following the instructions opposite.

Richard Harden   **Peter Harden**

LONDON
INTRODUCTION
& SURVEY RESULTS

LONDON INTRODUCTION

Introduction

In practically every respect, London today is an incomparably more interesting city to eat out in than it was ten years ago. For quality *and* range, London now has only one serious competitor in the world, New York, and the diversity has become so great that the choice can seem bewildering.

With its many maps and indexes – in particular the Survey results (pages 19-22) and Area overviews (pages 82-93) – this guide is designed to provide numerous ways of locating the restaurant you're seeking for any particular occasion. But, if you're new in London – or just an occasional visitor – you may find the following a handy introduction.

Which is London's best restaurant?

In the sense people usually mean this question – that is, money-no-object, probably French – the answer is clearly *Gordon Ramsay* (in Chelsea). Or, for a more traditional atmosphere, head for *Le Gavroche* – London's longest established 'temple of gastronomy'. *Pétrus* has recently emerged to claim a place in the first rank, though its ambience is rather 'businessy'. *The Square* is similarly a favourite place to entertain top clients.

For first-rate cooking, hotel dining rooms are rarely the best option, but two are of note. If you like fish, *Restaurant One-O-One*, in Knightsbridge, is now the second highest-rated restaurant in town overall. If you're looking for a more all-round 'classic' experience, *1837* in Mayfair would be the place.

Other names of note include Mayfair's *Nobu* (see below), Chelsea's *Aubergine* and – on the basis of the quality of cooking alone – *Tatsuso*, a City Japanese.

What's 'in' at the moment?

The Ivy and, to a lesser extent, its sibling *Le Caprice* are always 'in' – they make a 'can't-go-wrong' choice for pretty much any occasion… if you can get a booking. The *Mirabelle* is slowly building a similar reputation. The hottest ticket of recent years has been, and probably remains, *Nobu*, which has the advantage that the food is as notable as the clientèle. As a star magnet, *San Lorenzo* has a timeless – and to the uninitiated, quite inexplicable – appeal. For the fashion world, *Asia de Cuba* remains quite a place.

Among recent arrivals, *Zuma* stands out, as, for a slightly younger crowd, does *Hakkasan*. In groovy Notting Hill, trustafarians fall over themselves to get seats at *E&O* and the *Electric Brasserie*. If the launch to any extent lives up to the pre-launch hype, then *Sketch* – part owned by the man behind the ever-fashionable *Momo* – will enjoy at least its 15 minutes in the sun.

I'm not fussed about fashionable scenes – where can I find a really good meal without spending the earth?

The Ivy and *Le Caprice* are not that expensive, and neither is their emerging stablemate *J Sheekey*. If you want a bit of glamour plus a decent meal in the heart of town, they are hard to beat. Though more remote, three establishments run by low-profile restaurateur Nigel Platts-Martin are also top choices – *Chez Bruce* in Wandsworth, *La Trompette* in Chiswick and *The Glasshouse* in Kew.

For French cooking of utmost quality, but without great formality, two names stand out – *Monsieur Max* in distant Hampton Hill, and the trendier *Club Gascon*, on the fringe of the City. Shepherd's Bush's quirky *Chinon* has long been producing modern (Anglo-)French cooking on a par with many places that charge twice as much.

Other names which have stood the test of time include *Clarke's* (Kensington), *Monkeys* (Chelsea) and – at a very affordable price level – *Andrew Edmunds* (Soho).

What if I want the best of British tradition?

Because Britain is a 'pub culture', there are very few 'traditional' restaurants of note, and fewer which can be recommended. *The Dorchester Grill* and *Wilton's* are the grandest native flag bearers. The venerable (but cheaper) *Rules* may be a mite touristy, but it offers an excellent combination of good cooking with charming period style. The City preserves some extraordinary olde-worlde places such as *Sweetings* or *Simpson's Tavern*, and the famous pub *Ye Olde Cheshire Cheese*. Other ancient taverns include the *Grenadier*, the *Queen's Head*, the *Trafalgar Tavern* and the *Windsor Castle*. (For more on modern pubs see below.)

For afternoon tea, the *Basil Street Hotel*, *Brown's Hotel* or *The Ritz* are best. Tea (or any light meal) at *Fortnum's Fountain* is also pleasant. For good old fish 'n' chips, the best chippy, *Faulkner's*, is in the heart of the East End. Smithfield's *St John* has made quite a name for its exploration of traditional British cooking, including lots of offal (served in an uncompromising modern setting).

Isn't London supposed to be a top place for curry?

There are – it is said – more Indian restaurants in London than in India. What's more, London is leading the way with a new style of Indian-fusion cooking that, for many, has taken the cuisine out of the 'ethnic' category altogether. Leading exponents are *Tamarind*, *Zaika*, *Vama* and *The Cinnamon Club*.

At the other end of the scale – but famous for the quality of its food – lies the legendarily scruffy *Lahore Kebab House*. In between, good places are legion – see page 21 for a few more suggestions. Note that many of the best names – *Rasa* and *Kastoori*, for example – are veggie. As you will see, what good Indian restaurants tend to have in common is that they are not located in the West End.

What are gastropubs?

In the past ten years, many pubs have re-invented themselves as informal restaurants – you order at the bar, and your meal is brought to you. *The Eagle* was the original, and is still often credited as the best.

The trend goes from strength to strength, and is pushing the pub upmarket to an extent that would once have been inconceivable even five years ago. Some arrivals of recent years – the *Admiral Codrington*, *The Perseverance*, *The Ealing Park Tavern*, *St Johns*, *Oak* and *The Waterway*, for example – are much superior to many restaurants.

You said diverse: what about other cuisines?

London has good representations of most major cuisines (with the possible exception of Latin American ones).

Italian cooking has long been a popular choice for relaxed neighbourhood dining, especially in the more affluent parts of town, and there is an enormous variety of trattorias and pizzerias. In recent years, some excellent high-level Italians have emerged – see the list on page 21.

When it comes to oriental cuisines, the capital is quite well provided for. There are many Chinese restaurants, but the best of them – with the exception of *Fung Shing* and *Yming* – are not in or near Chinatown. The biggest concentration of excellent Chinese restaurants is, in fact, in Bayswater – *Royal China*, *Four Seasons* and *Mandarin Kitchen*. Thai cooking is also widespread but strongest in west London. A few years ago, London was weak in Japanese restaurants, especially at lower price-levels, but there have been many improvements in recent years, and the cuisine is now becoming fashionable in a way which has long been the case in some US cities. See the lists on page 21 for the top places in each category.

Are there any sharp practices I should look out for

Yes: the 'blank credit card slip trick'– a fraud practised to a shocking extent, even by many top places.

If you are presented with a credit card slip with a blank line for a gratuity, don't assume that a tip is appropriate. Often, 10% or 12.5% service has already been included but the restaurant is hoping that you will inadvertently 'double up'.

If you are not sure – and especially if the bill has not been brought back so you can check – ask if service was included. If so, don't add a further tip unless the staff have been amazing. You may also wish to write "please don't leave this blank" on the slip.

SURVEY – MOST MENTIONED

These are the restaurants which were most frequently mentioned by reporters. (Last year's position is given in brackets.) An asterisk* indicates the first appearance in the list of a recently-opened restaurant.

1   The Ivy (1)
2   J Sheekey (6)
3   Mirabelle (3)
4   Oxo Tower (Brasserie) (2)
5   Nobu (4)
6   Pétrus (10)
7   Gordon Ramsay (8)
8   Le Caprice (5)
9   Chez Bruce (7)
10   Gordon Ramsay at Claridge's*

11   Bleeding Heart (27)
12= La Poule au Pot (16)
12= Blue Elephant (9)
14   Club Gascon (15)
15   The Square (14)
16   Zafferano (12)
17   Andrew Edmunds (17)
18   Smiths of Smithfield (Dining Rm) (26)
19   Moro (23)
20   Hakkasan*

21   Bank Aldwych (11)
22   The River Café (17)
23   Le Gavroche (20)
24   Le Pont de la Tour (-)
25   The Sugar Club (19)
26   The Cinnamon Club*
27   Tas (36)
28   La Trompette*
29   Incognico (32)
30   Rules (34)

31   Bluebird (21)
32   Coq d'Argent (23)
33   City Rhodes (25)
34   Quaglino's (29)
35   Joe Allen (35)
36   L'Oranger (-)
37   1 Lombard Street (39)
38   L'Escargot (-)
39   Royal China W2 (-)
40   The Criterion Grill (21)

LONDON – HIGHEST RATINGS

These are the restaurants which received the best average food ratings. All of the restaurants listed here are in the London directory which starts on page 26.

We have divided the most represented restaurant cuisines (opposite page) into two price-brackets – under and over £40 a head.

Where the less represented cuisines (below) are concerned, just the best three performers in the survey are shown, regardless of price-bracket.

British, Traditional

1. Monkeys
2. Wiltons
3. The Dorchester Grill

Burgers, etc

1. Gourmet Burger Kit'n
2. Black & Blue
3. Lucky Seven

East/West

1. Nobu
2. Ubon
3. Champor-Champor

Fish & Chips

1. Faulkner's
2. North Sea Fish
3. Brady's

Greek

1. Halepi
2. The Real Greek
3. Lemonia

Turkish

1. Tas
2. Gallipoli
3. Pasha N1

Vegetarian

1. The Gate
2. Blah! Blah! Blah!
3. Food for Thought

Pizza

1. Pizza Metro
2. Basilico
3. Pizzeria Castello

Thai

1. Talad Thai
2. Chiang Mai
3. Thai Bistro

Fish & Seafood

1. Rest. One-O-One
2. Mandarin Kitchen
3. J Sheekey

Spanish

1. Cambio de Tercio
2. Rebato's
3. El Rincón Latino

Lebanese

1. Ranoush
2. Al Hamra
3. Maroush

British, Modern

£40 and over
1 Chez Bruce
2 The Glasshouse
3 Clarke's
4 Lindsay House
5 Alastair Little

Under £40
1 Chinon
2 Thyme
3 The Havelock Tavern
4 Alastair Little W11
5 The Stepping Stone

French

£40 and over
1 Gordon Ramsay
2 Monsieur Max
3 Le Gavroche
4 Pétrus
5 Club Gascon

Under £40
1 Les Associés
2 Café du Marché
3 French House
4 Soulard
5 L'Estaminet

Italian/Mediterranean

£40 and over
1 Zafferano
2 Assaggi
3 Locanda Locatelli
4 Tentazioni
5 Teca

Under £40
1=Made in Italy
1=Osteria Basilico
3 Olivo
4 Caraffini
5 Aglio e Olio

Indian

£40 and over
1 Tamarind
2 Zaika
3 The Cinnamon Club
4 Rasa Samudra
5 La Porte des Indes

Under £40
1 Lahore Kebab House
2 Kastoori
3 Vijay
4 Vama
5 Sarkhel's

Chinese

£40 and over
1 Ken Lo's SW1
2 Dorchester, Oriental
3 Ken Lo's W8
4 Kai
5 Hakkasan

Under £40
1 Hunan
2 Royal China
3 Mandarin Kitchen
4 Yming
5 Gung-Ho

Japanese

£40 and over
1 Tatsuso
2 Shogun
3 Matsuri
4 Suntory
5 Defune

Under £40
1 Café Japan
2 Kulu Kulu
3=Inaho
3=Yoshino
5 K10

SURVEY – NOMINATIONS

Ranked by the number of reporters' votes for:

Top gastronomic experience

1. Gordon Ramsay (1)
2. Nobu (3)
3. Chez Bruce (4)
4. Gordon Ramsay at Claridge's*
5. Pétrus (5)
6. The Ivy (2)
7. Club Gascon (7)
8. Mirabelle (6)
9. The Square (8)
10. Le Gavroche (9)

Favourite

1. The Ivy (1)
2. Le Caprice (2)
3. Chez Bruce (3)
4. Gordon Ramsay (6)
5. J Sheekey (-)
6. Mirabelle (5)
7. Moro (7)
8. Nobu (4)
9. Zafferano (8)
10. La Trompette*

Best for business

1. City Rhodes (1)
2. 1 Lombard Street (3)
3. The Square (6)
4. Bank Aldwych (2)
5. Coq d'Argent (4)
6. Oxo Tower (5)
7. Savoy Grill (7)
8. The Ivy (8)
9. Bleeding Heart (10)
10. Pétrus (-)

Best for romance

1. La Poule au Pot (1)
2. Andrew Edmunds (2)
3. The Ivy (3)
4. Bleeding Heart (9)
5. Le Caprice (7)
6. Oxo Tower (5)
7. Julie's (4)
8. Chez Bruce (-)
9. Mirabelle (-)
10. Blue Elephant (8)

OPENINGS AND CLOSURES

Restaurants in **bold** are included in the London section of this guide – for the full selection, see *Harden's London Restaurants 2003* (£8.99), available in all good bookshops.

OPENINGS

Adam Street
Al Bustan
The Almeida
Annie's
Armadillo
El Asado
Bacio
Bar Spice
Benares
Bistrot SW6
Bonds
Brasserie Roux
Bug
Busaba Eathai WC1
Cabanon
Café Crêperie de Hampstead
Carpaccio's
La Chaumière
Chelsea Mandarin
China Dream
Chowki
The Clerkenwell Dining Room
The Coach & Horses
The Commissary
The Connaught (Angela Hartnett's Menu)
Corum
The Crinnigan Rooms
Cru
Dartmouth Arms
Deca
Dexter's Grill
The Dining Room
The Drapers Arms
Dumela
E&O
Ealing Park Tavern
East
ECapital
Eddalino
Edera
Electric Brasserie
Embassy
Errays
The Evangelist
Fabrizio
Field & Forest
Fifteen

Fish Hoek
Fish Shop
Fishbar
500
La Galette
Giardinetto
Gourmet Burger Kitchen NW6, SW15
Grand Union
Harry's Social Club
Horse
Ifield NW3
The Independence
Infuzion
Inside
kare kare
Lan Na Thai
Lay & Wheeler
Lightship Ten
Little Bay EC1
Locanda Locatelli
Lucky Seven
The Market Brasserie
The Marquee
Matriciano
Mirch Masala SW17
MVH
Myna Bird
Need The Dough!
Nosh
Notting Grill
O'Zon
The Oak
One
One-Seven-Nine
The Open Page
Ophim
The Painted Heron
Paolo
Paul W1
Petit Auberge
The Pilot
Il Posto
QC
Racine
Raks
La Rascasse
Red Veg
The Refectory
Rick's Café

OPENINGS (cont'd)

Les Sans Culottes
Sabbia
Sapori
Sketch
Sophie's Steakhouse
Sugar Hut
Sumosan
The Sutton Arms
Taka
Tartine
Tartuf SW4
Tendido Cero
Thai Noodle Bar

Thai Square
 SW7, EC3, N1
Thomas' Restaurant
Thyme
Timo
Tipico
Tomato
Tsunami
Walnut
The Waterway
Wheeler's of St James's
Zamzama
Zuma

CLOSURES

Aix*
Babe Ruth's
Bah Humbug
Bali Sugar
Bangkok Brasserie
Black Truffle
Le Bon Choix
I Cardi*
Cassia Oriental
Chezmax
cheznico
Christian's
The Connaught
Conrad Gallagher*
Cranks (all branches)
DK's
Empire †
Exhibition
FireBird
Hanover Square
Helter Skelter
The House
Hujo's
Idaho (later
 Highgate Hill †)
Julius
Lemon Thyme
The Lexington
Marché Mövenpick
The Marquis
Mash Mayfair*
Mongolian Barbecue W4
Montana
Morton's
MPW Brasserie*
Neat*
Nico Central
Noto EC4

Oak Room
 Marco Pierre White
L'Odéon
Organic Cafe
 (both branches)
The Orient
Passion*
Paulo's
Le Potiron Sauvage*
Quincy's
Raccolto*
Rain
Riviera (E14)
Saints*
Sauce
Shi Hon Mei †
Six Degrees (now a bar)
Soup Works (all branches)
Soviet Canteen
Springbok Café
Station Grill
Tabla*
Titanic
Topsy-Tasty
Turner's
Verandah
The White Onion
Wiz
Wok Wok (all branches)
Zen SW3
Zucchina*

* was a newcomer last year; † came and went during year

for updates visit www.hardens.com

LONDON DIRECTORY

Abeno WC1 £29 ★

47 Museum St 7405 3211 1–1C

A "fun" and "different" central stand-by – this "very friendly" fixture near the British Museum serves okonomi-yaki ("Japanese-style omelettes") "cooked on the table in front of you". / **Sample dishes:** Japanese fish salad; pancakes with pork, squid & prawns; tropical fruit salad. **Details:** 10 pm; closed Wed L.

Adam Street WC2 £40 Ⓐ

9 Adam St 7379 8000 3–4D

With its "convenient location", near the Savoy, and "great atmosphere", this "cosy" cellar dining room of a "discreet" new club (open to non-members for lunch) is a "discovery" worth making; the "uncomplicated" food is "well prepared", and a "very interesting" wine list is a highlight. / **Sample dishes:** crispy duck salad with watercress; saffron risotto with artichokes; banana & raisin crumble. **Details:** www.adamstreet.co.uk; L only (open for D to members only), closed Sat & Sun.

Adams Café W12 £24

77 Askew Rd 8743 0572

"Interesting" North African couscous dishes make this "very friendly" BYO Shepherd's Bush café an evening destination that's perennially "good at what it does"; by day, it's a greasy spoon. / **Details:** 11 pm; D only, closed Sun.

Admiral Codrington SW3 £38

17 Mossop St 7581 0005 4–2C

The smart and "buzzy" rear dining room of this once-(in)famously Sloaney Brompton Cross boozer is a "relaxed" destination nowadays, well-known for offering "decent value" in a pricey part of town. / **Sample dishes:** mussels with thyme & shallots; honey & ginger chicken with kaffir lime rice; banana tarte Tatin. **Details:** 11 pm.

Aglio e Olio SW10 £30 ★

194 Fulham Rd 7351 0070 4–3B

"First-class pasta" and "outstanding value, for Chelsea" make this "fast 'n' fun" Italian an "always reliable" destination; "don't forget your earplugs", though. / **Sample dishes:** beef carpaccio & rocket salad; spaghetti with lobster; pannacotta. **Details:** 11.30 pm.

Al Duca SW1 £38 ★

4-5 Duke Of York St 7839 3090 2–3D

This "dependable" modern Italian has a "handy" St James's location, and its affordable prices have won it a widespread following; the "spare" setting can get rather "noisy". / **Sample dishes:** smoked goose ham with Mozzarella; pan-fried salmon with fennel salad; coconut sorbet withchocolate leaves. **Details:** www.alduca-restaurant.co.uk; 10.15 pm, Fri & Sat 10.45 pm; closed Sun L.

Al Hamra W1 £44 ★

31-33 Shepherd Mkt 7493 1954 2–4B

An "authentic", "upmarket" Mayfair Lebanese, long touted by some as "the best in town"; inside, the atmosphere can seem "leaden", but the outside tables are charming. / **Details:** www.alhamrarestaurant.com; 11.30 pm.

Alastair Little W1 £47 ★★

49 Frith St 7734 5183 3–2A

"Vibrant" and "skillful" Mediterranean cooking is – after a decade In the wilderness – again putting this "informal" and "sparse" Soho venture back on the capital's culinary map. / **Sample dishes:** spring nettle & ricotta risotto; calves liver with button onions & pancetta; apple tart with praline ice cream. **Details:** 11 pm; closed Sat L & Sun.

Alastair Little, Lancaster Rd W11 £39 ★★

136a Lancaster Rd 7243 2220

"Simple, very high-quality" cooking (with a Mediterranean slant) and "knowledgeable" and "welcoming" staff make this Notting Hill restaurant "excellent value" nowadays; only the "cramped" and "uninspired" setting discourages the following it would otherwise enjoy. / **Sample dishes:** sizzling prawns in parsley & garlic; duck cassoulet with sausage & borlotti beans; chocolate brownies with fudge sauce. **Details:** 11 pm; closed Sun D.

Alba EC1 £34 ★

107 Whitecross St 7588 1798 5–1B

"Cracking pizzas", "the best pasta" and "quality regional wines" make this "thoughtful" Piedmontese seem a "real" and "different" sort of Italian; it's handy for the Barbican too. / **Sample dishes:** calamari with aubergine caponata; braised rabbit wth olives & polenta; pannetone with chocolate mousse. **Details:** 10.30 pm; closed Sat & Sun.

The Almeida N1 £40 ★

30 Almeida St 7354 4777

With its consistently-realised "'70s-French" menu and its "friendly" staff, this "smooth" (if perhaps "unmemorable") new Conran venture in Islington stands "head and shoulders above most others in the group". / **Sample dishes:** foie gras terrine; coq au vin; nougat glacé. **Details:** www.almeida-restaurant.co.uk; 11 pm.

Andrew Edmunds W1 £29 A★

46 Lexington St 7437 5708 2–2D

This "characterful" Soho townhouse "just goes on and on being delightful", and is hugely popular for any "relaxed" occasion, especially romance; "unpushy" staff offer an "eclectic menu" of simple, "bistro" food and "top-notch" wines, all at "good-value" prices. / **Sample dishes:** courgette & rocket pesto cake; gnocchi with bacon & sausage; tarte Tatin. **Details:** 10.45 pm.

Angel of the North N1 £29 A

353 Upper St 7704 8323

This "lovely, little restaurant", near Islington Antiques Market, is a "fun" destination with an eclectic menu. / **Sample dishes:** prawns in filo pastry with lemongrass dressing; jerk chicken with sweet potato & carrot mash; chocolate brownie. **Details:** www.aotn-restaurant.co.uk; 11 pm; Mon-Thu L only, Fri-Sun open L&D; no Amex.

The Anglesea Arms W6 £29 A★★

35 Wingate Rd 8749 1291

"Get there early" – "there's no chance of a table later on" – at this "bustling" Hammersmith "gastropub par excellence"; even fans concede that service can be "impossibly slow", but the "reasonably-priced" and "stunningly-good" food is "a joy". / **Sample dishes:** goujons of sole & scampi; papardelle with lamb's sweetbreads & lardons; Knickerbocker Glory. **Details:** 10.45 pm; no Amex; no booking.

Antipasto e Pasta SW4 £25 ★

31 Abbeville Rd 8675 6260 6–2D

"Consistently good" cooking makes this "friendly" Italian probably the top culinary choice on Clapham's 'Restaurant Row'. / **Sample dishes:** beef carpaccio; grilled squid; tiramisu. **Value tip:** set weekday L £15(FP). **Details:** 11.30 pm.

Aperitivo W1   £27   A

41 Beak St   7287 2057   2–2D

"Unusual and well-executed Italian tapas" at "reasonable prices"
– and "charming" service too – help make this "cool" venture
a "noisy but fun" Soho rendezvous. / **Sample dishes:** fennel, walnut &
Pecorino salad; polenta with Gorgonzola & pancetta; dark chocolate mousse.
Details: 11 pm; closed Sun.

Aquasia
Conrad International SW10   £40   A

Chelsea Harbour   7823 3000   4–4B

The style may be a touch "Footballers' Wives", but this Chelsea
Harbour dining room is "glamorous" in its way, and has a "lovely"
waterside location; the Asian/Mediterranean cooking can be
"variable", but generally satisfies (and on Sundays, there's
a great-value champagne buffet brunch). / **Sample dishes:** seared
scallops with smoked duck; Thai monkfish with sweet potato mash & crab spring
rolls; Bramley apple tart. **Details:** www.conradlondon.com; 10.30 pm; no smoking
area.

Arancia SE16   £24   A★

52 Southwark Park Rd   7394 1751

"Great food" served in a "café-like" setting wins much support for
this "unpretentious" Bermondsey Italian; this year, however, saw
a few more misfires than usual. / **Sample dishes:** minestrone soup;
seared tuna with balsamic vinegar dressing; chocolate semi-freddo.
Details: www.arancia-london.co.uk; 11 pm; closed Mon L & Tue L; no Amex.

Archipelago W1   £56   A★

110 Whitfield St   7383 3346   1–1B

"Croc' on a rock and a lovebug salad anyone?"; this tiny and
"enchantingly bizarre" Fitzrovian – with its "completely different"
cuisine and its "unforgettable" décor – delivers "an explosion for
the senses"; food quality can vary, but "when it's good, it's very
good". / **Sample dishes:** peacock & tropical fruit satay; smoked open lasagne;
ginger brûlée with nashi pears. **Value tip:** set weekday L £35(FP).
Details: 10.30 pm; closed Sat L & Sun; no smoking area.

Armadillo E8   £32   ★

41 Broadway Mkt   7249 3633

"Strange tastes that surprisingly work" have won a lot of interest
for this "cool Latino", recently opened in Hackney – a "quirky"
experience, which most reporters think "worth the trip".
/ **Sample dishes:** baked courgettes with sweetcorn & Parmesan crust; salt cod,
curly kale & potato stew; Mayan chocolate ice cream & almond pastry.
Details: www.armadillorestaurant.co.uk; 10.30 pm.

Asia de Cuba
St Martin's Lane WC2   £62

45 St Martin's Ln   7300 5500   3–4C

Even some critics concede that this "impressively-designed" venue
(part of a hip Covent Garden boutique hotel) is "good fun";
"shocking" prices, "bizarre" fusion cooking and "chaotic" service,
however, lead many to dismiss it as a "rip-off".
/ **Sample dishes:** rock shrimp salad with sweet chilli sauce; Latino-spiced chicken
with coconut rice in tamarind sauce; roast pineapple & chocolate sushi.
Details: www.asiadecuba-restaurant.com; midnight, Sat 1 am; closed Sun L.

for updates visit www.hardens.com

Assaggi W2 £47 A★★
39 Chepstow Pl   7792 5501
The setting is "basic", so it can be "a wonderful surprise" to find "perfectly-executed Italian" food – the best in London, for many – in this dining room above a Bayswater boozer; it's undeniably "noisy" ("they need carpets and curtains!"), but "superb", if rather OTT, service soothes most reporters; book well ahead. / **Sample dishes:** pan-fried Pecorino with Parma ham; rack of lamb with spring vegetables; fig & almond tart. **Details:** 11 pm; closed Sun.

Les Associés N8 £34 A★
172 Park Rd   8348 8944
"Like being in a small bistro in France"; this tiny Crouch End "classic" wins rave reviews for its "genuine, beautifully-prepared food", its "cosy, down-to-earth style" and, above all, its "jolly" staff who show real "pride in standards". / **Sample dishes:** skate salad with caper sauce; quail stuffed with pork; lemon tart. **Details:** 10 pm; D only, except Sun open L only.

The Atlas SW6 £27 A★
16 Seagrave Rd   7385 9129   4–3A
"Great-value Mediterranean food" is helping win ever higher acclaim for this "ideal gastropub", hidden away in the backstreets near Earl's Court 2; it does get rather "crowded", though. / **Sample dishes:** broccoli & sweet onion soup with Parmesan crisps; Turkish style lamb with couscous salad; lemon polenta cake with poached pears. **Details:** 11 pm; no Amex; no booking.

Aubergine SW10 £69 ★
11 Park Walk   7352 3449   4–3B
William Drabble's "outstanding" cooking, and "great" service win solid praise for this eminent Chelsea fixture; prices strike some as very high, though, and what is an "intimate" ambience to some is just rather "lifeless" to others. / **Sample dishes:** crab & cauliflower salad with avocado purée; poached turbot with red wine sauce; cherry beignet soufflé. **Value tip:** set weekday L £43(FP). **Details:** 10.30 pm; closed Sun; jacket required.

Aurora W1 £36 A
49 Lexington St   7494 0514   2–2D
"A romantic night is guaranteed" at this "candlelit, casual and buzzy" Soho venture (which has the additional benefit of a "fantastic, small walled garden"); the cooking is "unpretentious, but well executed". / **Sample dishes:** yellow pepper soup; pork with spiced red cabbage & caramelised pears; sticky toffee pudding. **Details:** 10.30 pm; closed Sun; no Amex.

L'Aventure NW8 £41 A★★
3 Blenheim Ter   7624 6232
This small St John's Wood fixture has a formidable reputation both for romance – especially in summer, "under the stars" – and for its "good, traditional Gallic cuisine"; service is normally "charming", but off-nights are not unknown. / **Sample dishes:** snail & oyster mushroom fricasée; rabbit confit with lemon & dried tomatoes; apricot compote with creme anglaise. **Value tip:** set weekday L £26(FP). **Details:** 11 pm; closed Sat L & Sun.

Babur Brasserie SE23 £28 ★
119 Brockley Rise   8291 2400
"Very inventive" cooking (with "excellent regional specialities") can make this Brockley Indian an "unexpected" find; it's "always crowded". / **Details:** www.babur-brasserie.com; 11 pm; closed Fri L; no smoking area.

sign up for the survey at www.hardens.com

Back to Basics W1 £36 ★★
21a Foley St 7436 2181 1–1B
"Book, or turn up early" to this "excellent" Fitzrovia gem, whose "amazing" blackboard menu offers some of "the best-prepared fish" in town; the setting is "unpretentious", but there is "great pavement eating" in summer. / *Sample dishes:* monkfish & spicy prawn couscous; deep-fried Dover sole with tartare sauce; bananas & rum baked in foil. *Details:* www.backtobasics.uk.com; 9.45 pm; closed Sat & Sun.

Baltic SE1 £33 Ⓐ★
74 Blackfriars Rd 7928 1111 5–4A
"The space is stunning", at this "cool, hip and happening" conversion of a Victorian workshop, by Southwark tube, but that's not all – the Eastern European cooking is unexpectedly "subtle" and "delicious"; a "superb choice of vodkas" completes a winning package. / *Sample dishes:* Polish black pudding with pickled cabbage & pear purée; paprika chicken with garlic yoghurt; vodka-marinated berry compote. *Value tip:* set pre-theatre menu £20(FP). *Details:* www.balticrestaurant.co.uk; 11 pm; closed Sat L.

Bam-Bou W1 £36 Ⓐ
1 Percy St 7323 9130 1–1C
"Dark and atmospheric", this "stylish" Fitzrovia townhouse makes a "great cocktail venue"; the "pretty" Vietnamese cooking seems to be bucking up its ideas, too, but the "achingly hip" staff can still be "stroppy". / *Sample dishes:* marinated squid with bitter lemon dressing; pan-fried duck with crispy greens; banana spring rolls with chocolate sauce. *Details:* www.bam-bou.co.uk; 11.30 pm; closed Sat L & Sun.

Bank Aldwych WC2 £44
1 Kingsway 7379 9797 1–2D
Taste moves on, and this "big and noisy" Theatreland brasserie (est. 1996) strikes many reporters as rather a "harsh" place to eat nowadays; it's still "just right for power breakfasts", though, and "good for most business occasions". / *Sample dishes:* tuna with miso dressing; calves liver with bubble & squeak; honey nougat with iced cherries. *Value tip:* set pre-theatre menu £24(FP). *Details:* www.bankrestaurants.com; 11 pm.

Bar Capitale £32 ★
The Concourse, 1 Poultry, EC2 7248 3117 5–2C
Bucklersbury Hs, 14 Walbrook, EC4 7236 2030 5–3C
For a fast and pretty authentic pizza, try this hard-edged venture, near Mansion House, where "nothing is too much trouble"; there's now a new branch nearby. / *Sample dishes:* pasta with clams & garlic; four cheese pizza; tiramisu. *Details:* www.mithrasbars.co.uk; 10pm; closed Sat & Sun; no smoking area; EC4 no booking at L.

Bar Gansa NW1 £22 Ⓐ
2 Inverness St 7267 8909
With its "bustling" atmosphere, "reliable" and "good-value" grub, and "very friendly" staff, this "happy" tapas bar remains a happening Camden Town hang-out. / *Sample dishes:* garlic prawns; seafood platter; cinnamon & chocolate ice cream. *Details:* midnight; no Amex.

Bar Italia W1 £10 Ⓐ
22 Frith St 7437 4520 3–2A
"The best coffee bar in the world, bar none" – this "unfailing" 24/7 Soho linchpin is "always buzzing" with those in need of a "caffeine hit" or "a good panini". / *Sample dishes:* ham & tomato panini; four cheese pizza; tiramisu. *Details:* open 24 hours Mon-Sat, Sun 4 am; no booking.

The Basil Street Hotel SW3 £39 Ⓐ
8 Basil St 7581 3311 4–1D
*"Nothing is too much trouble", for the "old-fashioned and
cosseting" staff at this "lovely", creaky Knightsbridge hotel
("whose interior is a bit like a country house"); it's "ideal for
Sunday lunch", or an "excellent afternoon tea". / **Sample
dishes:** deep-fried whitebait with lemon; roast beef with Yorkshire pudding; bread &
butter pudding. **Details:** www.thebasil.com; 9.45 pm; no smoking area.*

Basilico £27 ★★
690 Fulham Rd, SW6 0800 028 3531 6–1B
175 Lavender Hill, SW11 0800 389 9770 6–2C
178 Upper Richmond Rd, SW15 0800 096 8202 6–2B
*"Out-of-this-world" pizza – "there's a reason it costs more" –
makes this a "superb" take-away chain (with a few seats in some
branches); it's sad that service can be "inefficient" and "grumpy".
/ **Sample dishes:** Caesar salad; smoked haddock & spinach pizza; bittersweet
chocolate tart. **Details:** www.basilico.co.uk; 11pm; no Amex; no booking.*

Beirut Express W2 £17 ★★
112-114 Edgware Rd 7724 2700
*You get "great food at great prices" at the Maroush group's
budget Bayswater outlet, whose "tasty" menu includes "excellent
shawarmas and fruit juices". / **Sample dishes:** mezze; chicken & lamb
kebabs; baklava. **Details:** www.maroush.com; 1.45 am; no credit cards.*

Bellamys SE11 £35 Ⓐ
332 Kennington Ln 7582 9569 6–1D
*"A sophisticated and relaxed atmosphere" has made this bistro
yearling – with its "variable but well-meaning cooking" –
an "excellent opening" in "an unlikely location", on the
Vauxhall/Kennington border; "most inconveniently, it shuts at
weekends!" / **Sample dishes:** pan-fried squid with Denhay ham; sirloin steak
with salsify & green beans; meringues with strawberry syrup. **Details:** 10 pm; closed
Sat & Sun; no Amex.*

Belvedere W8 £55 Ⓐ
Holland Park, off Abbotsbury Rd 7602 1238
*"The best possible location" ("especially in summer") makes
Marco Pierre White's "beautiful" Holland Park fixture a classic
"romantic" destination; the Gallic cooking is somewhere between
"dependable" and "uninspiring". / **Sample dishes:** tarte Tatin of endive &
foie gras; smoked haddock with poached egg & colcannon; caramel soufflé. **Value
tip:** set pre-theatre menu £31(FP). **Details:** www.whitestarline.org.uk; 10.45 pm.*

Bibendum SW3 £63 Ⓐ
81 Fulham Rd 7581 5817 4–2C
*"Much improved" this year, this "lovely" and "spacious" Brompton
Cross landmark dining room is praised by most reporters for its
"good, all-round standards" (although the "excellent fixed-price
lunch" gets a more consistent press than dinner); "a wine list that
strikes fear into the heart" is a major feature – "thank heavens
for the sommelier". / **Sample dishes:** sea bass tartare with dill crostini; steak
with foie gras pithivier; tarte Tatin. **Value tip:** set Sun L £41(FP).
Details: www.bibendum.co.uk; 11.30 pm.*

Black & Blue W8 £39 ★
215-217 Kensington Church St 7727 0004
*"Good steaks and burgers" are helping to make this "smarter
version of Tootsies" – which had the same founder – a popular
Kensington destination; some find it slightly "antiseptic".
/ **Sample dishes:** artichoke & spinach dips; char-grilled fillet steak with French fries;
chocolate mousse. **Details:** 11 pm; no Amex; no smoking area; no booking.*

Blah! Blah! Blah! W12   £25   ★★
78 Goldhawk Rd   8746 1337
"Vegetarian food at its best" – *"alive with flavours"* and *"at a great price"* – wins a big thumbs-up for this *"cosy"*, *"perennial favourite"* on a Shepherd's Bush highway; BYO.
/ **Sample dishes:** *warm mushroom salad; pasta with asparagus; blueberry & amaretti tart.* **Details:** *11 pm; closed Sun L; no credit cards.*

Blakes Hotel SW7   £90   🄰
33 Roland Gdns   7370 6701   4–2B
"Dark, secretive and exotic" – this notoriously *"sexy"* South Kensington basement has long been a seducer's dream; given the *"not-great"* cooking, it's easy *"to feel fleeced afterwards"*, but romantics say that *"love justifies such a cost"*.
/ **Sample dishes:** *ginger soup with prawn gyoza; rack of lamb with rosemary; tamarillo sorbet with biscuits.* **Details:** *www.blakeshotels.com; 11.30 pm.*

Bleeding Heart EC1   £40   🄰★
Bleeding Heart Yd, Greville St   7242 8238   5–2A
This *"charming"*, ever more popular *"hideaway"* – a rambling warren of rooms and basements *"in an historic yard"*, off Holborn – combines a bistro, brasserie and restaurant; it offers *"a fantastic all-round experience"*, combining *"true French cuisine"*, *"super wines"* and an *"intimate"* setting that suits business or romance.
/ **Sample dishes:** *scallops with fennel & ginger; Welsh lamb with rosemary jus; blueberry & blackberry mousse.* **Details:** *10.30 pm; closed Sat & Sun.*

Blue Elephant SW6   £44   🄰★
3-6 Fulham Broadway   7385 6595   4–4A
"Like being in a Disney movie, with impeccable food"; despite prices almost as *"lavish"* as the décor, enthusiasm remains very high for the *"delicious"* Thai cooking and *"attentive"* service at this vast Fulham *"special occasion place"*. / **Sample dishes:** *citrus fruit, chicken & prawn salad; sweet & sour pork with mushrooms & baby corn; sour mango & roasted coconut.* **Value tip:** *set weekday L £27(FP).* **Details:** *www.blueelephant.com; 11.30 pm; closed Sat L.*

Bluebird SW3   £47   ✗
350 King's Rd   7559 1000   4–3C
"The most lamentable Conran"?; though potentially stylish, this *"bland"* Chelsea landmark – with its *"unbelievably average"* and *"totally overpriced"* food, and often *"appalling"* service – is dismissed as *"pathetic"* by many reporters. / **Sample dishes:** *spring pea soup; sautéed kidneys & bacon in mustard sauce; apricot clafoutis.* **Value tip:** *set pre-theatre menu £30(FP).* **Details:** *www.conran.com; 11 pm.*

Bohème Kitchen & Bar W1   £37   🄰
19 Old Compton St   7734 5656   3–2A
"Zippy" décor and *"a chilled-out vibe"* make this offshoot of Soho's nearby Café Bohème a *"hip and very funky"* hang-out; the straightforward food is *"surprisingly good, given how busy the place often is"*. / **Sample dishes:** *asparagus & Gruyère tart; char-grilled tuna with couscous & salsa verde; orange cheesecake.* **Details:** *www.bohemekitchen.co.uk; 11.45 pm.*

Boiled Egg & Soldiers SW11   £17   🄰
63 Northcote Rd   7223 4894   6–2C
"It does a great brunch, but there are always too many brats", at this celebrated café – the buzzing social hub of Wandsworth's 'Nappy Valley'; *"be prepared to queue"*. / **Sample dishes:** *egg, ham & cheese muffin; vegetable pie; carrot cake.* **Details:** *L & afternoon tea only; only Switch; no booking.*

Boisdale SW1   £40   A

13-15 Eccleston St   7730 6922   1–4B

"A great game, haggis and steak menu", a "wonderful range of malt whiskys" and a "staggering wine list" make this "unique and buzzy" Belgravian ideal for "a boys' night out"; there's sometimes "cool jazz" too. / **Sample dishes:** Hebridean lobster bisque; roast haggis with mash & bashed neeps; gooseberry & fig syllabub. **Details:** www.boisdale.uk.com; 10.30 pm; closed Sat L.

Bombay Bicycle Club SW12   £34   A ★

95 Nightingale Ln   8673 6217   6–2C

"My idea of a good Indian"; this "amazingly consistent" "old favourite" – long at the vanguard of "ungreasy" subcontinental cuisine – remains one of the most popular restaurants south of the river. / **Details:** 11 pm; D only, closed Sun.

Bombay Palace W2   £35   ★

50 Connaught St   7723 8855

"Very good" cooking and "very attentive" service make this Bayswater subcontinental well worth seeking out; sadly the interior is "totally uncharismatic" – but you can always take away! / **Details:** www.bombay-palace.co.uk; 11.30 pm; no smoking area; booking essential at D.

Il Bordello E1   £33   A ★

75-81 Wapping High St   7481 9950

"Gigantic portions" of pizza and other "down-to-earth stuff" win high enthusiasm for this "great-value" Wapping Italian; it's "brash", "loud", "cramped" and – "if you're in the right mood" – "always good fun". / **Sample dishes:** avocado & prawns wrapped in salmon; seafood pizza; tiramisu. **Details:** www.ilbordello.com; 11 pm; closed Sat L.

Brady's SW18   £19   ★

513 Old York Rd   8877 9599   6–2B

"Upper-class fish 'n' chips" have long made this "non-greasy" Wandsworth bistro a very popular local stand-by; praise this year was particularly consistent. / **Sample dishes:** salmon fishcakes; battered plaice with chips & mushy peas; apple crumble. **Details:** 10.30 pm; D only, closed Sun; no credit cards; no booking.

Brasserie St Quentin SW3   £37   ★★

243 Brompton Rd   7589 8005   4–2C

Standards at this Gallic Knightsbridge fixture have shot up under new ownership (in fact a re-purchase by one of the founders), and an early (April 2001) visit found some of the best-value classic brasserie fare in town; a growing following may well pep up the atmosphere. / **Sample dishes:** Burgundy snails in garlic butter; rabbit cassoulet with polenta; tarte Tatin. **Details:** www.brasseriestquentin.co.uk; 10.30 pm.

Brick Lane Beigel Bake E1   £ 4   ★★

159 Brick Ln   7729 0616

Did they really "make Mariah Carey go to the back of the queue"? – more power to this "all-hours East End institution", whose "incredible", "cheap" bagels are always in demand. / **Sample dishes:** cream cheese & tomato beigel; salt beef sandwich; no puddings. **Details:** open 24 hours; no credit cards; no smoking; no booking.

(The Court)
British Museum WC1   £34   A✗
Great Russell St   7323 8990   1–1C
*"A smashing location, now all they need is a good chef" – it's only
the striking mezzanine setting, in the wonderful Great Court,
which raises the BM's restaurant above the level of a cafeteria.*
/ **Sample dishes:** salmon with minted tabbouleh; chicken & artichokes with pesto
mash; mango & passion fruit crème brûlée. **Details:** www.digbytrout.co.uk; 5 pm,
Thu-Sat 9 pm; L only, Thu-Sat open L & D; no Amex; no smoking.

La Brocca NW6   £27   A
273 West End Ln   7433 1989
*An "easy-going" atmosphere is the best feature of this "bustling
and fun, but too crowded" West Hampstead local, where "hearty"
pizza and pasta dishes are the menu mainstay.*
/ **Sample dishes:** garlic & Mozzarella bread; gnocchi with blue cheese; tiramisu.
Details: 11 pm; booking: max 8.

Brown's Hotel W1   £27
Albemarle St   7493 6020   2–3C
*"The best tea in London", say fans of the "wide variety of cakes"
and infusions served every afternoon in the Drawing Room of this
creaky Mayfair institution; as a concession to early 21st century
mores, jacket and tie are no longer required; (the price given is for
afternoon tea – see also 1837 at Brown's).*
/ **Details:** www.raffles-brownshotel.com; 10 pm (tea daily 3 pm-5.45 pm); closed
Sat L & Sun; no booking at weekends.

Bug SW2   £31   A
The Crypt, St Matthew's Church   7738 3184   6–2D
*The atmospheric Brixton church crypt formerly occupied by Bah
Humbug (RIP) has now been elegantly revamped as a moderately
ambitious (and no longer exclusively veggie) restaurant; standards
were consistently good on an early (August 2002) visit, but prices
seemed on the high side.* / **Sample dishes:** aubergine masala with onion
bhaji; peppered monkfish with cardamom sauce; cinnamon doughnuts with red
cherries. **Details:** www.bugbrixton.co.uk; 11 pm; D only.

Burnt Chair TW9   £39   A
5 Duke St   8940 9488
*"The owner puts on a great show with your wine selection" –
from a "fantastic" list – at this "small but sophisticated"
Richmond fixture; moderately interesting cooking plays
a supporting role.* / **Sample dishes:** Morrocan-style stuffed squid with lime
coulis; beef with pearl barley risotto & black olives; roasted pears with ginger crisps.
Details: www.burntchair.com; 11 pm; D only, closed Mon & Sun; no Amex;
no smoking.

Busaba Eathai   £23   A★
106-110 Wardour St, W1   7255 8686   2–2D
22 Store St, WC1   1–1C
*"Horrendous queues" advertise the appeal of this "trendy" Soho
Thai, where "fresh, well-cooked" grub is served up in what –
considering the "great-value" prices – is a "chic" and "gorgeous"
setting; the new Bloomsbury branch listed is to open in late-2002.*
/ **Details:** 11 pm, Fri & Sat 11.30 pm; no smoking; no booking.

Café 209 SW6   £21   A
209 Munster Rd   7385 3625   6–1B
*"Insane" service – from the "delightful" owner Joy – ensures this
"noisy" BYO Fulham café is always "good for a laugh"; the Thai
scoff it offers is "cheap" and "tasty" too.* / **Details:** 10.45 pm; D only,
closed Sun; no credit cards.

Café Bagatelle
Wallace Collection W1 £36 A

Manchester Sq 7563 9505 2–1A

"The sense of space" in the Wallace Collection's covered courtyard makes it a "charming" place (if sometimes "too hot in summer"); the food is only "OK", though, and service can be "very slow". / **Sample dishes:** Dolcelatte with walnut bread crostini; lemon sole in ham with fennel gratin; vanilla & liquorice parfait.
Details: www.wallace-collection.com; L only; no smoking.

Café Bohème W1 £34 A

13 Old Compton St 7734 0623 3–2A

Open round-the-clock, this "hugely laid-back" (but "crowded") Soho café/bar/restaurant makes "a good venue at any time of the day or night"; the grub (from snacks to a full meal) used to be good, but is increasingly "bog-standard". / **Sample dishes:** poached egg & smoked salmon salad; rabbit & pappardelle with mustard sauce; glazed strawberry crepes. **Details:** 2.45 am, Thu-Sat open 24 hours, Sun 11.30 pm; booking: max 6, Fri & Sat.

Café du Marché EC1 £38 A★

22 Charterhouse Sq 7608 1609 5–1B

"A wonderful secret hideaway on the fringe of the City"; few restaurants are as "excellent all-round" as this Smithfield "taste of France", with its "fine" food, "jolly" staff and "marvellous" atmosphere. / **Sample dishes:** fish soup; prawn & herb risotto; cherry sorbet. **Details:** 10 pm; closed Sat L & Sun; no Amex.

Café Japan NW11 £27 ★★

626 Finchley Rd 8455 6854

The "marvellous and varied sushi" still draws fans from across town to this "friendly" but "worn" Japanese, near Golders Green tube; some "miss the hot dishes", though (now that they no longer serve yakitori or tempura). / **Details:** 10.30 pm; closed Mon & Tue L; no Amex; no smoking area.

Café Laville W2 £30 A

453 Edgware Rd 7706 2620

"The food is average but the canal view is outstanding", at this Maida Vale café; it's best for brunch or a light bite.
/ **Sample dishes:** goats cheese crostini; smoked haddock & salmon fishcakes with dill sauce; chocolate fudge cake. **Details:** www.cafelaville.co.uk; 10 pm; no Amex; no smoking area.

Café Portugal SW8 £26 A

5a-6a Victoria Hs, South Lambeth Rd 7587 1962 6–1D

"A smoky bar, with all eyes glued to the TV football" is a typical scene at this "authentically Portuguese" Vauxhall fixture; its serves "good-value tapas" and other "inexpensive", "traditional" fare.
/ **Sample dishes:** Portuguese-style octopus; pork with clams & sautéed potatoes; crème Catalan. **Value tip:** set weekday L £17(FP).
Details: www.outworld.ision.co.uk/cafe; 11 pm; no Amex; no smoking area.

Cambio de Tercio SW5 £38 A★

163 Old Brompton Rd 7244 8970 4–2B

"London's best Spanish restaurant by far", on the fringe of South Kensington, has it all – "delicious and inventive" cooking, a "fine wine list", "excellent" service and a "buzzing" atmosphere.
/ **Sample dishes:** octopus with paprika & olive oil; roast suckling pig; gin & tonic sorbet. **Details:** 11.30 pm.

Camden Brasserie NW1 £33 ᵉ

216 Camden High St 7482 2114

*No change (fortunately) at this "well-run" and "bustling" Camden Town fixture, which delivers "consistently good" grills (steaks and fish) with "superb chips". / **Sample dishes:** Caesar salad; fish with roasted beetroot; tiramisu. **Details:** 11.30 pm; no Amex.*

Canyon TW10 £38 ✕

Riverside 8948 2944

*This "beautiful", "Californian-style" venture, overlooking the Thames near Richmond Bridge, is – for many reporters – "redeemed only by its setting"; for "sunny Sunday brunching" it's great – otherwise it's "pretentiousness personified". / **Sample dishes:** salt & pepper squid with sesame red chard; garlic-roasted poussin with sage & bacon jus; chocolate tart with orange cream. **Details:** www.canyonfood.co.uk; 11 pm; no smoking area.*

Le Caprice SW1 £48 ᵉ★

Arlington Hs, Arlington St 7629 2239 2–4C

*"It just keeps on delivering" – a "great balance of food, service and ambience" maintains the extraordinary enduring appeal of this "elegant" brasserie behind the Ritz; it's "accessible" too... as long as you "book six weeks ahead". / **Sample dishes:** Chinese crispy duck; squid with chorizo & figs; Scandinavian iced berries. **Details:** midnight.*

Caraffini SW1 £36 ᵉ★

61-63 Lower Sloane St 7259 0235 4–2D

*"All-round consistency" – with "superb service" a highlight – has won a vast fan club for this small trattoria, near Sloane Square; it's "cramped" and "impossibly noisy", though – some tip sitting outside as preferable. / **Sample dishes:** antipasti; scallops with spinach & mushrooms; crème brûlée. **Details:** www.caraffini.co.uk; 11.30 pm; closed Sun.*

Carnevale EC1 £27 ★

135 Whitecross St 7250 3452 5–1B

*"Imaginative ideas for veggies" maintain the popularity of this "tiny and intimate" spot, near the Barbican. / **Sample dishes:** tagliatelle with Taleggio & wild garlic; okra & red pepper casserole with falafel; apple & date bread pudding. **Details:** www.carnevalerestaurant.co.uk; 10.30 pm; closed Sat L & Sun; no Amex.*

Carpaccio's SW3 £36 ᵉ★

4 Sydney St 7352 3433 4–2C

*"Relaxed, but chic too"; if you're looking for a pretty much perfect 'Chelsea Italian', you won't do better than this "simple but good" newcomer, from the people behind Ziani and Como Lario. / **Sample dishes:** smoked Mozzarella, aubergine & anchovy salad; warm monkfish carpaccio with rosemary oil; fruit strudel. **Details:** 11.15 pm; closed Sun.*

Casale Franco N1 £34 ᵉ★

rear of 134-137 Upper St 7226 8994

*This "busy" Islington Italian, hidden down an alleyway, has a strong following for its "excellent pizza" and other good "rustic" fare. / **Sample dishes:** grilled squid with chilli & rocket; lobster ravioli; white & dark chocolate layer cake. **Details:** 11 pm, Sun 9 pm; closed Mon, Tue-Fri D only, Sat & Sun open L & D; no smoking area; need 6+ to book.*

for updates visit www.hardens.com 36

Champor-Champor SE1 £33 A★★

62 Weston St
7403 4600 5–4C
"Weird and wonderful" – this *"bizarre"* Borough yearling wins
nothing but 'bravos' for its *"extraordinary"* Asian/eclectic food,
its *"really friendly"* service and its *"funky but calming"*
surroundings. / **Sample dishes:** chicken satay with steamed Indian bread;
smoked cobra dumplings in vermicelli broth; black rice pudding with durian ice cream
Details: www.champor-champor.com; 10.30 pm; closed Mon L, Sat L & Sun;
booking: max 8.

La Chaumière SW3 £50

50 Cheyne Walk 7376 8787 4–3C
This retro-conversion of an old Chelsea boozer is the new venture
of a Gallic chef of some note; on an early-days (July 2002) visit,
the £45 prix-fixe extravaganza included too much food for local
tastes – ratings are on the basis that a forthcoming revised menu
will offer food in the quantities most Londoners actually want to
eat! / **Sample dishes:** Parma ham with aubergine caviar; char-grilled fillet steak
with dauphinoise potatoes; crème brûlée. **Details:** 11.30 pm; Mon-Fri D only, Sat
open L&D, Sun L only.

Chelsea Mandarin SW3 £33 ★

257-259 Fulham Rd 7351 7823 4–2C
This smart, very welcoming oriental newcomer could hardly be
in sharper contrast to its dismal (and short-lived) predecessor
Shi Hon Mei (RIP); the menu doesn't attempt fireworks, but –
on an early (July 2002) visit – everything was well done.
/ **Details:** 11 pm; closed Sun L.

Chez Bruce SW17 £46 A★★

2 Bellevue Rd 8672 0114 6–2C
"Still the most satisfying gastronomic experience" – Bruce Poole's
"fabulous", straightforward cooking and super service again
makes this consistently *"excellent"* dining room by Wandsworth
Common one of the most popular destinations in town; it is a bit
"squashed". / **Sample dishes:** asparagus frittata with ham & Manchego; rabbit
with stuffed cabbage & polenta; cherry & almond tart. **Details:** 10.30 pm; closed
Sun D; booking: max 6 at D.

Chez Liline N4 £30 ★★

101 Stroud Green Rd 7263 6550
"Amazing to find something of this quality here!" – the *"tatty"*
exterior gives no hint of the *"really outstanding fish and shellfish"*
on offer at this *"cramped"* Mauritian, long established in Stroud
Green. / **Sample dishes:** tuna & pesto with rocket salad; snapper in Creole sauce;
coconut & passion fruit sorbet. **Details:** 10.30 pm; closed Mon L & Sun L.

Chez Lindsay TW10 £31 ★

11 Hill Rise 8948 7473
"Good", *"simple"* Breton cuisine – *"wonderful crêpes"*, *"great
fruits de mer"*, *"delicious cider"* – wins a more than local following
for this *"pleasant"* bistro, near Richmond Bridge.
/ **Sample dishes:** mussels; seafood pancake; crepes Suzette. **Value tip:** set brunch
menu £20(FP). **Details:** 11 pm; no Amex.

sign up for the survey at www.hardens.com 37

Chez Moi W11 £40 A★
1 Addison Ave 7603 8267
"Impeccable service" and often "excellent" cooking have made
this a vintage year for Holland Park's "delightfully old-fashioned"
and "romantic" French "favourite" – over 30 years in business,
and still improving! / **Sample dishes:** borscht with cream & horseradish; roast
venison with Parmesan gnocchi; pink grapefruit & Campari sorbet. **Value tip:** set
menu always available £25(FP). **Details:** www.chezmoi-restaurant.co.uk; 10.30 pm;
closed Mon L, Sat L & Sun; booking: max 8.

Chiang Mai W1 £30 ★★
48 Frith St 7437 7444 3–2A
"Grotty but superb" – many think this "soulless" Soho
"old-favourite" still offers "the best Thai food in London".
/ **Details:** 11 pm; closed Sun L; no smoking area.

China Dream NW3 £32 A★
68 Heath St 7794 6666
With its "terrific dim sum", "very friendly" service and a "great"
atmosphere, this tastefully-converted Hampstead boozer – now
a trendy oriental – wins a unanimous thumbs-up from reporters.
/ **Value tip:** set weekday L £20(FP). **Details:** 10.30 pm, Thu-Sat 11.30 pm.

Chinon W14 £38 ★★
23 Richmond Way 7602 4082
"Why help pay off Gordon Ramsay's mortgage?", when you can
eat "huge portions" of "amazingly delicious", "innovative" food at
"unbeatable" prices, at this "hidden" and "charming" Shepherd's
Bush fixture. / **Sample dishes:** prawn tempura with lemon & raisin chutney;
roast duck with apple sauce; crème brûlée with passionfruit sorbet.
Details: 10.30 pm; D only, closed Sun.

Chowki W1 £25 ★★
2-3 Denman St 7439 1330 2–2D
Mela is one of the best-value Indians in the West End, and its new
sibling near Piccadilly Circus does not let it down; indeed – on the
evidence of an early-days (July 2002) visit – this chic little
hide-away may become the preferred destination.
/ **Details:** www.chowki.com; 11.30 pm; no smoking area.

Chutneys NW1 £19 ★
124 Drummond St 7388 0604
A "budget" south Indian stalwart, near Euston, whose "consistent
and tasty" veggie fare is "very good value" (especially the
"excellent lunch buffets"). / **Details:** 11 pm; no Amex or Switch; no smoking
at L; need 4+ to book.

Cicada EC1 £33 A★
132-136 St John St 7608 1550 5–1B
"Funky", "cool" and "fun" – there's little but praise for this
Clerkenwell bar/restaurant, with its "interesting pan-Asian
cooking" and its "slick and friendly" service. / **Details:** www.cicada.nu;
10.45 pm; closed Sat L & Sun; no smoking area.

Cinnamon Cay SW11 £29 A★
87 Lavender Hill 7801 0932 6–1C
"A great local restaurant"; this "really enjoyable" Battersea
"all-rounder" is winning an enthusiastic following for its "fantastic"
service, its "innovative fusion food" and its "relaxed" atmosphere;
"book ahead". / **Sample dishes:** shiitake mushrooms with spiced tofu &
noodles; pistachio-crusted sea bass with salsa verde; lemongrass & ginger
pannacotta. **Details:** www.cinnamoncay.co.uk; 11 pm; closed Sun.

The Cinnamon Club SW1 £42 A★
Great Smith St 7222 2555 1–4C
"A superb modernisation of Indian food" is hailed by the many
fans of Iqbal Wahhab's *"different and very refreshing"* yearling;
housed in a *"stylish"* conversion of a former Westminster library,
it's more a venue for business than romance. / **Sample dishes:** smoked
lamb kebabs; mustard tandoori prawns with saffron kedgeree; coconut cake with
cumin yoghurt. **Details:** www.cinnamonclub.com; 11 pm; closed Sat L & Sun D;
no smoking area; booking: max 8.

City Miyama EC4 £55 ★★
17 Godliman St 7489 1937 5–3B
The place is *"drab"* and prices are *"silly"*, but this grand City
Japanese serves *"about the best sushi in London"*, and there's also
"excellent teppan-yaki". / **Details:** 9.30 pm; closed Sat D & Sun; no booking
at L.

City Rhodes EC4 £60 ★
New Street Sq 7583 1313 5–2A
The office block setting, just off Fleet Street, is a mite *"grim"*,
but Gary R's *"slick"* establishment remains the capital's most
popular destination for a business lunch, thanks to its
"professional" staff and its *"very impressive"* British cooking.
/ **Sample dishes:** foie gras & pigeon terrine with quince jelly; halibut with shellfish
linguine; raspberry shortbread pannacotta. **Details:** 9 pm; closed Sat & Sun.

Clarke's W8 £60 A★★
124 Kensington Church St 7221 9225
"Outstanding fresh, seasonal creations" from a deceptively simple
menu (which, in the evening, offers zero choice) win the usual
bouquets for Sally Clarke's *"congenial, if low-key"* Kensingtonian;
"serious wines" and *"incredible"* staff – and also now *"a classy,
affordable brunch"* – are further attractions. / **Sample dishes:** onion
puff pastry with tomatoes & Mozzarella; salmon with courgette flower fritters; vanilla
cream pot with lemon thyme shortbread. **Details:** www.sallyclarke.com; 10 pm;
closed Sat & Sun (open for Sat brunch); no smoking area at L, no smoking at D;
no booking at brunch.

Club Gascon EC1 £42 A★★
57 West Smithfield 7796 0600 5–2B
"Foie gras in all its glory" is the menu mainstay of this
extraordinarily popular Smithfield dining room, where the
"regional cuisine in a tapas format" combines *"superb ingredients,
faultlessly prepared"* with an *"amazing wine list"*.
/ **Sample dishes:** foie gras consommé with oysters; steamed white fish with chorizo;
French cheese selection. **Details:** 10 pm, Fri & Sat 10.30 pm; closed Sat L & Sun.

Le Colombier SW3 £37 A
145 Dovehouse St 7351 1155 4–2C
A rather mature local fan club maintains the crush at this popular
"traditional" bistro in Chelsea (and younger souls are attracted to
the smart terrace on sunny days); it's *"so French it could be in
Paris"*, but some find the cooking a bit *"safe"*. / **Sample dishes:** foie
gras terine with salad; shepherds pie; vanilla ice cream with hot chocolate sauce.
Details: 11 pm.

Como Lario SW1 £33
22 Holbein Pl 7730 2954 4–2D
"A warm welcome" is guaranteed at this *"solid"*, *"busy"* and
"old-fashioned" trattoria, near Sloane Square.
/ **Sample dishes:** deep-fried smoked Mozzarella with spicy tomato sauce; roast
duck in black cherry sauce; tiramisu. **Details:** 11.30 pm; closed Sun.

sign up for the survey at www.hardens.com 39

Il Convivio SW1 £44 A★

143 Ebury St 7730 4099 1–4A

Sometimes "startling" modern Italian cooking and very "friendly" service are winning growing respect for this "very pleasant" all-rounder; critics say it's too "pricey" – but then where in Belgravia isn't? / **Sample dishes:** Jerusalem artichoke soup with Parmesan crisps; roast duck with fig sauce; candied lime cake.
Details: www.etruscagroup.co.uk; 10.30 pm; closed Sun.

Coq d'Argent EC3 £47

1 Poultry 7395 5000 5–2C

"Sit outside in the lovely 'grounds'", and you might forget you were on a rooftop near Bank, at this sixth-floor Conran venture; the cooking is no more than "quite nice", but it suffers badly from "City overpricing", and service is often, er, "cocky". / **Sample dishes:** veal sweetbreads with pea purée; lamb with goat's cheese crust; peach gratin. **Details:** www.conran.com; 10 pm; closed Sat L & Sun D.

The Cow (Bar) W2 £29 A★

89 Westbourne Park Rd 7221 0021

"You can always people-watch while you wait for a table" – there's usually quite a crush for the "consistently good pub grub" (seafood the speciality) at Tom Conran's "trendy-in-an-olde-worlde-way" Notting Hill boozer. / **Sample dishes:** risotto nero with cuttlefish; grilled Dover sole with parsley & cockles; chocolate & Amaretto torte.
Details: 10.30 pm; no Amex; no booking.

The Criterion Grill W1 £50 A

224 Piccadilly Circus 7930 0488 2–3D

"The setting is stunning", but these days "they trade on location and décor" at Marco Pierre White's "unique" neo-Byzantine dining room; fans do say the classic cuisine is "fabulous", but others find it "disappointing at the price", and "very poor service" is a recurrent problem. / **Sample dishes:** vichyssoise; roast pheasant with quince purée; lemon tart. **Value tip:** set pre-theatre menu £31(FP).
Details: www.whitestarline.org.uk; 11.30 pm; closed Sun L.

Daphne NW1 £21 A

83 Bayham St 7267 7322

"An old favourite" – this family-run Camden Town Greek is liked for its "very friendly" service, its "cosy" and "down-to-earth" atmosphere, and its "good food at reasonable prices"; there's a nice roof terrace, too. / **Sample dishes:** spinach & feta filo parcels; lamb baked with cumin; baklava. **Details:** 11.30 pm; closed Sun; no Amex.

Deca W1 £54 A★

23 Conduit St 7493 7070 2–2C

Now that Chez Nico has closed, this Gallic Mayfair townhouse newcomer (on the site of Firebird, RIP) has become the Ladenis family's flagship; an early-days (July 2002) visit found a coolly classical venue, whose accomplished cuisine was well into its stride. / **Sample dishes:** foie gras with oranges; John Dory with olive oil & thyme sauce; pear tart with crème anglaise. **Value tip:** set pre-theatre menu £26(FP).
Details: 11 pm; closed Sun.

Defune W1 £55 ★

34 George St 7935 8311 1–1A

"More comfortable, but less atmospheric" is the verdict on this re-located Japanese veteran (which moved a couple of years ago within Marylebone); its "melt-in-the-mouth" sushi is "so fresh it practically swims", but even some fans think it "way overpriced". / **Sample dishes:** salmon roe sushi; chicken teriyaki; green tea ice cream.
Details: 10.45 pm; closed Sun L.

Delfina Studio Café SE1   £32   A★
50 Bermondsey St   7357 0244   5–4D
"Well worth the trip"; "interesting cooking" is making this "spacious" Bermondsey gallery a popular destination for businessmen as well as arty types; "shame it's only open for lunch". / **Sample dishes:** *pea & mint soup with feta croutons; cinnamon-crusted pork with fennel & orange salad; rhubarb streusel tart.* **Details:** *www.delfina.org.uk; L only, closed Sat & Sun.*

The Depot SW14   £32   A
Tideway Yd, Mortlake High St   8878 9462   6–1A
"Wonderful view" – "shame about the food"; the trade-off is as clear as ever at this "buzzing" local, which overlooks the Thames near Barnes Bridge; it's "great for families on Sunday". / **Sample dishes:** *poached langoustine with tomato consommé; roast duck with braised cabbage & berry jus; strawberry pavlova with raspberry coulis.* **Details:** *10.30 pm; no smoking area.*

Ditto SW18   £36   A
55-57 East Hill   8877 0110   6–2B
"Lots of comfy sofas" set the tone at this "relaxing" Wandsworth bar/restaurant; with its "cheerful" staff and "good modern cooking", it's established itself as the "easy local choice" for many hereabouts. / **Sample dishes:** *crab & vegetable samosas; twice-cooked lamb with basil mash; gingerbread pudding with butterscotch sauce.* **Value tip:** *set weekday L £19(FP).* **Details:** *www.doditto.co.uk; 11 pm; closed Sat L & Sun D; no Amex.*

The Don EC4   £45   A★
20 St Swithin's Ln   7626 2606   5–3C
The location – in a backstreet near Bank – is hidden away, but "good" Gallic cooking (with a "nice" wine list), a "lovely" ambience, and "exceptional" service have made this year-old Bleeding Heart-offshoot an "excellent find" for City cognoscenti. / **Sample dishes:** *scallops en croute with lime; venison with roasted figs & port mash; banana tarte Tatin.* **Details:** *10 pm; closed Sat & Sun.*

don Fernando's TW9   £24   A
27f The Quadrant   8948 6447
"Quick service, even when packed" adds to the attractions of this large and lively tapas bar, by Richmond BR. / **Sample dishes:** *monkfish & Spanish ham skewers; lamb & pork meatballs with tomato sauce; deep-fried cheese with cranberry sauce & cream.* **Details:** *www.donfernando.co.uk; 11 pm; no booking.*

Don Pepe NW8   £28
99 Frampton St   7262 3834
The "real Spanish feel" (aided by "very friendly staff") is the special point of London's longest-established tapas bar, near Lords; as so often with such places, "go for the bar, not the restaurant". / **Sample dishes:** *merluza a la gallega (flan); salt-baked sea bass; pancakes with honey.* **Details:** *midnight; closed Sun.*

Dorchester Hotel, Grill Room W1   £67   A
53 Park Ln   7629 8888   2–3A
"Everything clicks" at this "wonderful", "spacious" Spanish-Baronial-style dining room in Mayfair, where "attentive, but not overbearing" staff deliver a "well cooked" menu in traditional grand British style; (the bread trolley is a feature – "the choice is out of this world"). / **Sample dishes:** *smoked Norfolk duck with onion compote; Aberdeen beef with sautéed goose liver; flambéed peppered peaches.* **Value tip:** *set weekday L £42(FP).* **Details:** *www.dorchesterhotel.com; 11 pm.*

Dorchester Hotel, Oriental W1   £75
53 Park Ln   7629 8888   2–3A
"On a par with Hong Kong"; "superb materials and skill" are used to sometimes "awesome" effect at this "luxurious" and "incredibly expensive" Mayfair dining room; perhaps when it's re-launched in September 2002, the rather "clinical" ambience will have been put to rights. / Sample dishes: spicy scallops, prawns & jellyfish; pork & bamboo shoots in sea spice sauce; sweet water chestnuts in lemon juice. Value tip: set weekday L £32(FP). Details: www.dorchesterhotel.com; 11 pm; closed Sat L & Sun; no jeans or trainers; booking: max 8.

The Drapers Arms N1   £34   A★★
44 Barnsbury St
7619 0348
This "wonderfully-renovated", "hidden gem" in an Islington side street has made an "excellent start"; it offers "very good food" and – unusually for a gastropub – "very good service too". / Sample dishes: smoked duck & beetroot with Brie croutons; chilli-roasted fish with Asian coleslaw; pannacotta with raspberries. Details: 10.30 pm; no Amex.

E&O W11   £32   A★★
14 Blenheim Cr
7229 5454
Instantly "fashionable", this new "linchpin" of the Notting Hill set has "a great buzz" (and it's "excellent for star-gazing", too); the surprise is that its "oriental tapas-with-a-slant" menu is "surprisingly cheap and innovative". / Sample dishes: pan-fried squid with chilli & salt; black cod with sweet miso; chocolate pudding with green tea ice cream. Details: www.eando.nu; 11 pm.

The Eagle EC1   £24   A★
159 Farringdon Rd   7837 1353   5–1A
London's original gastropub, established in Farringdon in 1991, is just "as good as ever"; yes, it's "scruffy", "cluttered" and "crowded", but – thanks to its "rustic, well-prepared" Mediterranean grub – the chief gripe is still the "difficulty of finding a table". / Sample dishes: stuffed aubergine with cracked wheat salad; sea bass with fennel & orange salad; Portuguese custard tart. Details: 10.30 pm; closed Sun D; only Switch; no booking.

Ealing Park Tavern W5   £29   ★
222 South Ealing Rd
8758 1879
"Newly-converted from a dodgy old local", this "excellent gastropub" (sibling to Archway's St Johns) is "a great addition to a barren area"; "top-quality" food – of above-average ambition for a pub – comes at "affordable prices". / Sample dishes: apple, apricot & pigeon terrine; Toulouse cassoulet; apple & pear crumble. Details: 10.30 pm.

**1837
Brown's Hotel W1**   £65   A★★
Albemarle St
7408 1837   2–3C
Andrew Turner's "superb" modern French cuisine and an amazing wine list (including over 250 choices by the glass) are beginning to win acclaim for this "richly-furnished and spacious" (but oft-overlooked) Mayfair dining room; ("the grazing menu plus he Sommelier's Choice" is a top tip). / Sample dishes: Chilled gazpacho, langoustines and courgette; Roast breast and confit leg of challans duck with foie gras, green celery; Raspberry soufflé, bitter chocolate sorbet. Value tip: set weekday L £44(FP). Details: www.raffles-brownshotel.com; 10.30 pm; closed Sat L & Sun; no smoking area.

El Rincón Latino SW4   £29   𝔸

148 Clapham Manor St   7622 0599   6–2D

"What a laugh" – this "lively bit of Spain" off Clapham High Street wins rave reviews for its "fun", "friendly" spirit and "good" tapas; "great set menu for groups". / **Sample dishes:** *goats cheese croquettes; Colombian chorizo with fried plantain; Manchego with quince jelly.* **Details:** *11.30 pm.*

Electric Brasserie W11   £42   𝔸

191 Portobello Rd   7908 9696

A landmark location – attached to a famous old Notting Hill cinema – has helped make this brasserie newcomer an instant smash hit with the local trustafarians; no surprise, then, that the standard Gallic fare comes at OTT prices. / **Sample dishes:** *sautéed mushroom gnocchi with tomato sauce; duck cottage pie; Drambuie bread & butter pudding.* **Details:** *www.electricbrasserie.com; 10.45 pm.*

Elena's L'Etoile W1   £46   𝔸★

30 Charlotte St   7636 7189   1–1C

The "special welcome" from Elena Salvoni – doyenne of London's maîtresses d'hotel – plays no small part in the success of this "old-fashioned" Fitzrovia institution; the cooking – "traditional French with a modern twist" – is "surprisingly good".
/ **Sample dishes:** *crab & salt cod fritters with sweetcorn butter; sage-crusted calves liver with mustard mash; vanilla pod crème brûlée.* **Value tip:** *set pre-theatre menu £28(FP).* **Details:** *www.trpplc.com; 10.30 pm; closed Sat L & Sun.*

Elistano SW3   £34   𝔸★

25-27 Elystan St   7584 5248   4–2C

"Only go if you can take the noise", says one of the many fans of this "cheerful" Chelsea "ristorante" – "attentive" staff, plus "great" pasta and other "completely reliable" grub, ensure it's always "really buzzing". / **Sample dishes:** *artichoke salad; pasta with aubergine & Mozzarella; tiramisu.* **Details:** *10.45 pm.*

Enoteca Turi SW15   £42   ★

28 Putney High St   8785 4449   6–2B

The "really extensive and exciting wine list", notably "attentive" staff and some "delicious" Italian cooking has made a big name for this Putney fixture; even some fans, though, note that it is becoming "pricey". / **Sample dishes:** *Mozzarella with sardines & pine nuts; roast lamb; peach tart with lime sorbet.* **Details:** *11 pm; closed Sun.*

L'Escargot W1   £42   𝔸★

48 Greek St   7437 2679   3–2A

"Very impressive in every respect"; this characterful Soho "classic" is an unsung star of the Marco Pierre White empire, where staff "who anticipate your needs" serve up "slick and dependable" Gallic fare – both in the brasserie (price shown) and in the more expensive Picasso Room. / **Sample dishes:** *foie gras & green peppercorn terrine; caramelised skate wing with winkles; Grand Marnier soufflé.* **Details:** *www.whitestarline.org.uk; 11.30 pm; closed Sat L & Sun (Picasso Room also closed Mon).*

L'Estaminet WC2   £38   𝔸★

14 Garrick St   7379 1432   3–3C

As a "great pre-theatre" venue, this "pleasing corner of France" in Covent Garden has long had its admirers; it has "improved over the last couple of years", and its "calm" and "reliable" virtues are making it an increasingly useful central destination.
/ **Sample dishes:** *warm herring & potato salad; roast lamb with honey & rosemary sauce; crème caramel.* **Value tip:** *set pre-theatre menu £23(FP).* **Details:** *11 pm; closed Sun.*

Faulkner's E8   £21   ★★
424-426 Kingsland Rd   7254 6152
For "fresh, fresh fish with delicious chips and mushy peas" – and in "massive" portions, too – you just can't beat this "real, old-fashioned" Dalston institution. / **Sample dishes:** fish soup; rock salmon & chips; pistachio ice cream. **Details:** 10 pm; no Amex; no smoking area.

Feng Shang NW1   £29   Ⓐ
Opposite 15 Prince Albert Rd   7485 8137
"They really know how to do it", when it comes to "friendly and attentive" service at this attractive Chinese barge – moored near Regent's Park Zoo; the food is "consistently good" on most reports, but there were a few "let-downs" this year. / **Details:** 11 pm.

Ffiona's W8   £32   Ⓐ
51 Kensington Church St   7937 4152   4–1A
It's "the proprietor's personal touch" that generally makes this "homely" Kensington bistro a "perfect destination for comfort food"; "if Ffiona's not in the mood, though…"
/ **Sample dishes:** duck & port pâté with rye bread; steak & kidney pie; bread & butter pudding. **Details:** 11 pm; closed Mon, Tue-Sat D only, Sun open L & D.

Fish Hoek W4   £39   ★★
6-8 Elliot Rd   8742 0766
"A wide variety of unusual fish" – "simply, but well prepared" – has made this "surprising newcomer" (from the team behind the Springbok Café, now Dumela) a "welcome addition to Chiswick"; the setting is "noisy" and "very cramped", but "cheery and knowledgeable" staff help create a "fun" atmosphere.
/ **Sample dishes:** giant prawns in garlic cream; grilled barracuda with seasonal vegetables; chocolate mealie meal pudding. **Details:** 10.30 pm; closed Mon (except Aug); no smoking area.

Foliage
Mandarin Oriental SW1   £60   ★
66 Knightsbridge   7201 3723   4–1D
With "beautifully presented" modern French cooking, and often "excellent" service, this Knightsbridge dining room – with its "super views over Hyde Park" – almost has it all; the "classy" refurb of a couple of years ago, however, left it feeling rather "sterile". / **Sample dishes:** cauliflower & spiced quail salad; roast bream with pumpkin ravioli; Cuban chocolate fondant. **Details:** www.mandarinoriental.com; 10.30 pm; no smoking area; booking: max 6.

Food for Thought WC2   £15   ★
31 Neal St   7836 0239   3–2C
"Excellent, hearty vegetarian fare" at "good-value" prices maintains the long-standing appeal of this "cramped" Covent Garden basement; "there are never enough seats".
/ **Sample dishes:** carrot & coriander soup; Ethiopian vegetable wrap; strawberry crunch. **Details:** 8.15 pm; closed Sun D; no credit cards; no smoking; no booking.

Fortnum's Fountain W1   £36   Ⓐ
181 Piccadilly   7734 8040   2–3D
For "a British breakfast at its best", or "a perfect cream tea and cucumber sandwiches", this "spacious" and "comfy" buttery (attached to the famous grocers) makes a "great location"; "there can be lengthy queues". / **Sample dishes:** smoked salmon with light rye bread; Aberdeen Angus cottage pie; pear & blackberry crumble.
Details: www.fortnumandmason.co.uk; 7.45 pm; closed Sun; no smoking area; no booking at L.

The Four Seasons W2 £22 ★
84 Queensway 7229 4320
"Some dishes are exceptional" – in particular *"the best roast
duck in the UK!"* – at this *"very authentic"* (and rather
"brusque") Bayswater Chinese. / **Details:** 11.15 pm.

Frederick's N1 £39 A ★
106 Camden Pas 7359 2888
"The beautiful conservatory" is the star of the show at this
Islington *"old-favourite"*; that said, while neither the Gallic cooking
nor the service is at the cutting-edge, the place consistently
provides a *"very good all-round experience"*. / **Sample dishes:** smoked
haddock & new potato salad; roast duck with French beans; fruit crudités with Greek
yoghurt. **Value tip:** set menu always available £26(FP).
Details: www.fredericks.co.uk; 11.30 pm; closed Sun; no smoking area.

French House W1 £36 A ★
49 Dean St 7437 2477 3–3A
"A gem in the heart of Soho"; new management has reinvigorated
the *"small"*, *"cosy"* and *"intimate"* dining room above this famous
boozer, now serving a *"good, if basic"* menu. / **Sample dishes:** chicken
liver & foie gras pâté; seared scallops with gazpacho sauce; nougat glacé with
passion fruit coulis. **Details:** 10.30 pm; closed Sun; booking: max 8.

Fung Shing WC2 £34 ★★
15 Lisle St 7437 1539 3–3A
It's *"best to be adventurous"*, at this *"dowdy"* Cantonese, whose
long-term reputation as *"the best Chinese in Chinatown"*
continues to be well deserved; it's *"very good for fish"* (with
"excellent crab" also winning particular praise).
/ **Details:** www.fungshing.co.uk; 11.15 pm.

Gallipoli £21 A
102 Upper St, N1 7359 0630
120 Upper St, N1 7226 8099
These *"cosy"* and *"crowded"* Islington Turks have *"loads of
atmosphere"*, and staff who remain amazingly *"friendly"* and
"quick", given the weight of custom; the food is *"dependable"*,
"tasty" and *"cheap"*. / **Details:** 11 pm, Fri & Sat 11.30 pm; no Amex.

Gastro SW4 £30 A
67 Venn St 7627 0222 6–2D
A *"gritty"* but *"cosy"* location, opposite the Clapham Picture
House, contributes much to the *"fabulous French atmosphere"*
of this *"tucked-away"* café, popular as a breakfast destination;
the *"great home-cooking"* is on an up, but *"non-existent"* service
remains a problem. / **Sample dishes:** salmon & scallop terrine with rosemary
dressing; pan-fried turbot with mango salsa & rice; chocolate & pear tart.
Details: midnight; no credit cards; mainly non-smoking.

The Gate £31 A ★★
51 Queen Caroline St, W6 8748 6932
72 Belsize Ln, NW3 7435 7733
"The best vegetarian restaurant in town" – the *"delightful"*
Hammersmith original of this veggie duo is *"inventive"* enough to
interest carnivores too; it draws far more (and more favourable)
commentary than its Belsize Park offshoot. / **Sample dishes:** courgette
flower & feta salad; teriyaki aubergine with rice noodles; banana brûlée.
Details: www.gateveg.co.uk; 10.45 pm; W6 closed Sun – NW3 closed Sun D;
smoking restrictions at NW3; W6 booking: max 10.

Le Gavroche W1 £92 *A*★★

43 Upper Brook St 7408 0881 2–2A

Michel Roux Jr's "superb", "classical" Gallic cuisine is still "tops", say the many advocates of this famous Mayfair basement, where the "phenomenal" service and vast wine list are also highly esteemed; prices, as ever, strike some as "unreal"; (note – the salon privé is no more). / **Sample dishes:** artichoke heart with foie gras & chicken mousse; roast grouse with bread sauce; millefeuille with Mascarpone & mango. **Value tip:** set weekday L £63(FP).
Details: www.le-gavroche.co.uk; 11 pm; closed Sat L & Sun; jacket required at D.

Geeta NW6 £15 ★★

57-59 Willesden Ln 7624 1713

As ever, this "friendly" Kilburn veteran wins no prizes for décor, but its "freshly cooked", "flavoursome" and "cheap" South Indian cooking "never fails". / **Sample dishes:** hot lentil curry; prawn curry with lemon rice; gulab jamon. **Details:** 10.30 pm, Fri & Sat 11.30 pm; no Switch.

The Glasshouse TW9 £41 *A*★★

14 Station Pde 8940 6777

"Fantastic" cooking and service that's "attentive but not overbearing" win the highest praise for Nigel Platts-Martin's venture by Kew Gardens station; a major refurb' in summer 2002, aims to curb residual criticisms of its "bright" and "crowded" "fish-bowl" setting. / **Sample dishes:** salt cod fishcake with pickled cucumber; roast pork with black pudding & grainmustard; rhubarb & yoghurt ice creams. **Details:** 10.30 pm.

Globe Restaurant NW3 £33

100 Avenue Rd 7722 7200

"Very pleasant" service and the "excellent Thursday cabaret" are undoubted highlights at this "easy-going", modernistic Swiss Cottage spot; the cooking can be "erratic", but it "can be inspired" too. / **Sample dishes:** smoked salmon mousse with Parmesan crostini; chicken with tarragon polenta & porcini sauce; rice pudding with elderflower & gooseberry compote. **Details:** www.globerestaurant.co.uk; 11 pm; closed Sat L & Sun L; no Amex; no smoking area.

Gordon Ramsay SW3 £83 *A*★★

68-69 Royal Hospital Rd 7352 4441 4–3D

"London's ultimate"; "exquisite attention to detail" has made Gordon Ramsay's Chelsea "temple of gastronomy" – with its "inspirational" and "intensely flavoured" modern French cooking – unchallengeable as the capital's top culinary destination; the main quibble, as ever, is service that's "so efficient it can be suffocating". / **Sample dishes:** hot foie gras with lentils; lobster & langoustine tortellini in shellfish bisque; blood oranges in jelly. **Value tip:** set weekday L £49(FP). **Details:** www.gordonramsay.com; 11 pm; closed Sat & Sun; jacket required; booking: max 6.

Gordon Ramsay at Claridge's
Claridge's Hotel W1 £73

55 Brook St 7499 0099 2–2B

"Not a patch on Royal Hospital Road" – the much-hyped revamp of this Deco Mayfair dining room performs no better than many other "forgettable" hotel restaurants; yes, some did report "world-class" cuisine and "impressive" new décor, but much more striking is the high proportion of reporters for whom "soulless" cooking and "smug" service made the place "a real disappointment". / **Sample dishes:** scallops with cauliflower purée & beetroot crisps; roast duck with celeriac fondant & confit leeks; chocolate savarin with champagne granita. **Value tip:** set pre-theatre menu £45(FP). **Details:** 11 pm; booking: max 8.

Gordon's Wine Bar WC2   £23   𝔸 ✕
47 Villiers St   7930 1408   3–4D
"So good it still exists" – this *"gloomy"*, ancient wine bar is *"one
of central London's most atmospheric locations"*; it's often *"busy"*
and *"smoky"*, and the *"plain"* food is too *"expensive"*, but most
say it's *"worth the struggle"*; (there's also a great terrace for
summer). / **Sample dishes:** duck pâté & French bread; sausages, mash & onion
gravy; apple pie. **Details:** 10 pm; no Amex; no booking.

Goring Hotel SW1   £53   𝔸
15 Beeston Pl   7396 9000   1–4B
"Impeccable, low-key service" is the hallmark of this *"timeless"*,
family-run *"bastion of England"* – an *"oasis of calm"* near
Victoria, which serves *"reliable"* traditional cuisine; for business or
breakfast (or both), it is a top recommendation.
/ **Sample dishes:** watercress soup; Norfolk duck with caramelised apple; chocolate
millefeuille with coffee ice cream. **Value tip:** set breakfast £31(FP).
Details: www.goringhotel.co.uk; 10 pm; closed Sat L; no smoking area.

Gourmet Burger Kitchen   £20   ★
331 West End Ln, NW6   7794 5455
44 Northcote Rd, SW11   7228 3309   6–2C
333 Putney Bridge Rd, SW15   8789 1199   6–2B
"Big, thick, delicious, juicy hamburgers that force you to dribble" –
and in *"massive variety"* too – are winning this Battersea diner
(and its new West Hampstead and Putney siblings) a reputation
as the home of *"London's best burger"*; *"who cares if it feels like
a transport café?"* / **Sample dishes:** chunky chips with salsa; Jamaican burger
with mango & ginger sauce; no puddings. **Details:** 11 pm; no smoking (except at
outside tables); no booking.

The Grapes E14   £38   𝔸 ★
76 Narrow St   7987 4396
A *"characterful"* and *"unpretentious"* tavern (near the Limehouse
Link), whose *"small"* upstairs dining room provides *"picturesque"*
views over the Thames, plus *"lovely fresh fish that's not been
messed about with"*; (there's also *"good-value"* pub grub in the
downstairs bar). / **Sample dishes:** Greek salad; deep-fried fish & chips;
bread & butter pudding. **Details:** 9.15 pm; closed Sun D.

Great Nepalese NW1   £20
48 Eversholt St   7388 6737
"Ignore the area" (Euston Station's east flank) and you can find
some *"fresher-tasting-than-normal curries"* at this *"quiet"* and
"exceptionally friendly" *"old-favourite"*; *"non-standard"* dishes are
best. / **Details:** 11.30 pm.

The Green Olive W9   £38   𝔸 ★
5 Warwick Pl   7289 2469
"A comfortable atmosphere", *"enjoyable"* cooking and *"very
good"* service win praise at this *"upmarket"* *"neighbourhood"*
Italian in Maida Vale; steer clear of the *"drab"* basement, though.
/ **Sample dishes:** tuna carpaccio with raspberry vinaigrette; roast pork wrapped in
Parma ham with lentils; blood orange terrine with lemon sorbet. **Details:** 10.45 pm.

Green's SW1   £47   𝔸
36 Duke St   7930 4566   2–3D
"Classy food for St James's gentlemen" – *"with prices to match"* –
is the stock-in-trade of this *"clubby"* fixture, where the *"discreet
booths"* are particularly popular. / **Sample dishes:** spiced prawns with
papaya & mango relish; pan-fried lemon sole with truffled leeks; rhubarb crème
brûlée. **Details:** www.greens.org.uk; 11 pm; closed Sun, May-Sep.

Grenadier SW1 £35 Ⓐ
18 Wilton Row   7235 3074   4–1D
*"A beautiful Belgravia location" helps make this ultra-"quaint"
mews pub Madonna's (and many other visiting Americans')
favourite 'local'; no surprise, then, that its restaurant charges
"ridiculous prices for standard grub" – "sausages and Bloody
Marys" at the bar are a much smarter choice.*
/ **Sample dishes:** Stilton tart with red wine & port jam; beef Wellington;
blackberry & apple crumble. **Details:** 9 pm.

Gung-Ho NW6 £26 Ⓐ★
328-332 West End Ln   7794 1444
*This "great neighbourhood Chinese" in West Hampstead is
consistently praised for its "clean and light-tasting" cooking,
its "polite" staff and its "nice", "relaxing" surroundings.*
/ **Details:** 11.30 pm; no Amex.

Hakkasan W1 £50 Ⓐ★
8 Hanway Pl   7927 7000   3–1A
*"Very cool, but very expensive" – five words sum up this "sexy"
(but "smug") "modern Chinese" basement, which, despite its
grungy location off Tottenham Court Road, is a magnet for "hip
and happening" thirtysomethings; lunchtime dim sum offers the
chance to check out the often "excellent" cooking at more
reasonable cost.* / **Sample dishes:** steamed scallops with tobiko caviar;
deep-fried Tienging bun stuffed with chicken & prawn; mango spring roll.
Details: 11 pm; no smoking area.

Halepi £36
18 Leinster Ter, W2   7262 1070
48-50 Belsize Ln, NW3   7431 5855
*"Dark", "intimate" and old-fashioned (Bayswater) or "trendy and
white" (Belsize Park) – this Greek duo could hardly seem more
different, but their "good", if "pricey", fare is pretty consistent
throughout.* / **Details:** W2 12.30 am – NW3 11 pm.

Harry's Social Club W2 £40 Ⓐ✕
30 Alexander St   7229 4043
*"I didn't expect much, and got worse" – good thing the food is
"not the point" of this "hip and trendy" Bayswater club dining
room; romantics may find consolation in the
"dark-enough-for-anything" ambience.* / **Sample dishes:** tuna & salmon
carpaccio; jerk chicken Caesar salad; banana split with fudge sauce.
Details: 10.30 pm; D & Sun brunch only, closed Mon; booking: max 8.

The Havelock Tavern W14 £29 Ⓐ★★
57 Masbro Rd   7603 5374
*"Prepare to share a table, and catch as catch can", at this
"trendy" ("crowded" and "smoky") Olympia backstreet
gastropub, which draws hordes of fans with its "seriously tasty"
and "well-priced" cooking; the staff, though, can be "a bit
preoccupied with their own importance".* / **Sample dishes:** pork & duck
terrine; lamb shank with mash; sticky toffee pudding. **Details:** 10 pm; no credit
cards; no booking.

Hellenik W1 £29 Ⓐ★
30 Thayer St   7935 1257   1–1A
*"Completely unchanged for decades", this Greek taverna in
Marylebone is "a delight"; "give it a go".*
/ **Sample dishes:** taramasalata & pitta bread; kleftiko; baklava.
Details: 10.30 pm; closed Sun.

Home EC1 £38 𝔸

100-106 Leonard St 7684 8618 5–1D
*Given this Clerkenwell venue's "cool" and "informal" vibe
(particularly in the "funky" but "comfy" basement bar) the
cooking in its "relaxing" ground floor dining room is surprisingly
"imaginative and well-executed". / Sample dishes: butternut squash
ravioli; roast chicken with chorizo mash & salsa; gooseberry sponge pudding.
Details: www.homebar.co.uk; 10 pm; closed Sat L & Sun; no smoking area.*

Hunan SW1 £35 ★★

51 Pimlico Rd 7730 5712 4–2D
*"Definitely let the owner choose for you" – the "wacky" Mr Peng's
"masterful" guidance is much valued by regulars at this
"excellent-value" (but "cramped") Chinese fixture, near Pimlico
Green. / Details: 11 pm; closed Sun; no smoking area.*

I Thai
The Hempel W2 £70 𝔸

31-35 Craven Hill Gdns 7298 9001
*"Beautiful presentation in a stunning setting" can make dining in
this "theatrical", "low-lit" Bayswater townhouse hotel basement
a "Zen-like" experience; despite the "outrageous" cost,
its "amazing" fusion fare found somewhat more favour this year.
/ Details: www.the-hempel.co.uk; 10.45 pm; closed Sat L & Sun.*

Imperial City EC3 £36 ★

Royal Exchange, Cornhill 7626 3437 5–2C
*A "decent Chinese for a business lunch", this well-run City oriental
benefits from an interesting setting in the cellars of the Royal
Exchange; the food is "improving again", after a rather rough
patch. / Details: www.imperial-city.co.uk; 9.30 pm; closed Sat & Sun.*

Inaho W2 £29 ★★

4 Hereford Rd 7221 8495
*"Incredibly cheap and delicious food" – including arguably
"the best sushi in town" – wins a disproportionate following for
this "tiny" Bayswater shack; service, though, can be "poor".
/ Details: 11 pm; closed Sat L & Sun; no Amex or Switch.*

Incognico WC2 £48 ★

117 Shaftesbury Ave 7836 8866 3–2B
*"A stylish brasserie, in both cooking and surroundings";
the Ladenis family's "professional" Gallic two-year-old continues to
establish itself as one of Theatreland's key destinations.
/ Sample dishes: goat's cheese & roast pepper open ravioli; crispy salmon in ginger
cream sauce; warm chocolate mousse. Value tip: set pre-theatre menu £27(FP).
Details: midnight; closed Sun.*

Indigo
One Aldwych WC2 £50 𝔸★

1 Aldwych 7300 0400 1–2D
*"There are no surprises in the food, but it's consistently good", at
this "efficient" and "very comfortable" Covent Garden-fringe
"haven" (on the mezzanine of a boutique hotel); with its
"spacious" and "relaxing" setting, it's "great for a business lunch"
(and also "good pre-theatre"). / Sample dishes: monkfish carpaccio woth
mango salsa; roast lamb with vegetable caviar; crunchy chocolate praline tart.
Details: www.onealdwych.co.uk; 11.15 pm.*

Inside SE10 £35 ★

19 Greenwich South St   8265 5060

This Greenwich newcomer is loudly hailed locally as a "great neighbourhood restaurant" on account of its "always good" cooking, its "fantastic" service and its "chatty" atmosphere.
/ **Sample dishes:** Indonesian chicken satay; grilled tuna with yellow pepper salad; apple & strawberry crumble. **Details:** www.inside.org.uk; 11 pm; closed Mon & Sun D; no Amex.

Itsu £25 A★

103 Wardour St, W1   7479 4794   2–2D
118 Draycott Ave, SW3   7584 5522   4–2C

Purists may sneer – "sushi for people who don't like sushi!" – but these "funky" conveyor-belt operations in Soho and Chelsea win much praise for their "creative" and "delicious" dishes; they offer "good people-watching" too. / **Details:** www.itsu.co.uk; 11 pm; smoking in the bar only; no booking.

The Ivy WC2 £47 A★

1 West St   7836 4751   3–3B

"It never fails to make an impression"; the problem is that "mere mortals can't get in" to this discreet Theatrelander which – with its "slick" cooking and "impeccable" service ("even to non-glitterati") – is yet again the survey's No 1 Favourite Restaurant. / **Sample dishes:** rock shrimp linguine; braised beef in Guinness with carrot mash; chocolate pudding soufflé. **Value tip:** set Sun L £30(FP). **Details:** midnight.

Iznik N5 £24 A

19 Highbury Park   7354 5697

"The atmosphere is still A1", at this "cosy" and "delightful" Highbury Turk; the "affordable" food, however, is becoming increasingly "disappointing". / **Sample dishes:** courgette & feta fritters; lamb with stuffed aubergines; baklava. **Details:** 11 pm; no Amex.

Jin Kichi NW3 £30 ★★

73 Heath St   7794 6158

"Great yakitori from the grill" – plus "super sushi" and other Japanese fare – win high esteem for this "small Hampstead hide-away", where "helpful and friendly" service helps make up for the basic setting. / **Sample dishes:** prawn & asparagus spring rolls; grilled chicken & pork skewers; green tea ice cream. **Details:** 11 pm; closed Mon, Tue-Fri D only, Sat & Sun open L & D.

Joe Allen WC2 £36 A

13 Exeter St   7836 0651   3–3D

The food – "fantastic" off-menu burgers aside – isn't anything to write home about, but the "convivial" atmosphere of this Covent Garden basement (which has an identical NYC twin) continues to win it a huge following nonetheless; book ahead for a late table.
/ **Sample dishes:** salmon & smoked haddock chowder; lamb & mint sausages with red lentil purée; banana cream pie. **Details:** www.joeallen.co.uk; 12.45 am; no smoking area.

Julie's W11 £48 A

135 Portland Rd   7229 8331

"You could fall in love, even with Dracula", at this "dark, sexy, private and comfortable" Gothic Holland Park fixture – a subterranean "labyrinth of exotic rooms"; the food is "not the main strength" – indeed, some think it plain "ghastly".
/ **Sample dishes:** prosciutto & Parmesan summer salad; rack of lamb with garlic bean mash; meringue with red berries. **Details:** www.juliesrestaurant.com; 10.45 pm; closed Sat L.

Julie's Wine Bar W11 £38 𝔸
137 Portland Rd   7727 7985
As with its similarly "charming" restaurant neighbour, "it's the intimate interior that is the draw" at this ground-floor wine bar – its food is far too "bland". / Sample dishes: peppered ricotta salad; grilled lamb with Moroccan tajine; chocolate & mint liqueur mousse.
Details: www.juliesrestaurant.com; 10.45 pm.

K10 EC2 £20 ★
20 Copthall Ave   7562 8510   5–2C
"The best conveyor-belt sushi" – and an "interesting selection of other hot and cold dishes" – makes this modernistic basement venture "a neat venue for simple City lunches"; "be there by noon – the queues can be huge". / Sample dishes: courgette tempura; seared tuna with miso vinaigrette; ginger mousse. Details: www.k10.net; 10 pm; closed Sat & Sun; no smoking; no booking.

Kai W1 £48 𝔸★
65 South Audley Street   7493 8507   2–3A
"Very good food and highly professional service" come together to make this "chic" (going-on-"stuffy") Mayfair spot one of the capital's leading orientals; some say it's "overpriced" ("but where else can you get soup with gold in it?"). / Sample dishes: deep-fried soft shell crab; Szechuan chicken with cashews & crispy seaweed; green tea.
Details: www.kaimayfair.co.uk; 10.45 pm.

Kastoori SW17 £20 ★★
188 Upper Tooting Rd   8767 7027   6–2C
"Still worth the trip to Tooting"; this Indo-African vegetarian certainly isn't chic, but its "out-of-this-world" dishes offer "such good value for money". / Sample dishes: samosas; mushroom & spinach curry; Indian cheesecake. Details: 10.30 pm; closed Mon L & Tue L; no Amex or Switch.

Ken Lo's Memories SW1 £48 ★★
67-69 Ebury St   7730 7734   1–4B
"The benchmark Chinese, against which all others should be judged" – at the top end of the market, this "consistent" Belgravia veteran has few rivals; "the new décor is a big improvement". / Sample dishes: courgettes stuffed with prawns; stewed lamb with lemongrass; toffee apple & banana. Details: 11.30 pm; closed Sun L.

Ken Lo's Memories of China W8 £48 𝔸★
353 Kensington High St   7603 6951
Considering its no-man's-land Kensington/Olympia location, this upmarket oriental can seem "very expensive"; its "very refined" cooking, though, is highly praised for its "consistently high quality". / Details: 11.15 pm.

Kennington Lane SE11 £34 𝔸★
205-209 Kennington Ln   7793 8313
"Maintaining high standards in an unlikely setting" – this "slick" and "friendly" Kennington venture provides "serious cooking at fabulous prices"; the atmosphere's good too, "particularly in summer, when the courtyard is in use". / Sample dishes: buffalo Mozzarella salad; sea bream with raspberry vinegar sauce; almond tart. Details: www.kenningtonlanerestaurant.com; 10.30 pm; closed Sun L.

Khan's of Kensington SW7 £27 ★
3 Harrington Rd   7581 2900   4–2B
"Healthy (organic and low-fat) Indian food" and "pleasant" service make this well-established, "upmarket" curry house by South Kensington tube a local worth remembering. / Value tip: set weekday L £14(FP). Details: 11.15 pm, Fri & Sat 11.45 pm; no smoking area.

Konditor & Cook £23 ★★

10 Stoney St, SE1 7407 5101 5–4C
66 The Cut, SE1 7620 2700 5–4A

"Super, snacky soups", "an excellent selection of sandwiches"
and some "blissful pâtisserie" are amongst the "top-quality,
simple grub" on offer at these "cramped" South Bank cafés
(at the Young Vic, and Borough Market). / *Sample dishes:* salad
Niçoise; salmon with green beans & béarnaise sauce; chocolate cake with vanill ice
cream. *Details:* The Cut 8 pm – Stoney St 6.30pm; breakfast, L & early evening
only; closed Sun; no Amex.

Kulu Kulu W1 £19 ★★

76 Brewer St 7734 7316 2–2D

"A great variety" of "fantastic", "really fresh" sushi and sashimi –
and "at affordable prices" too – makes this "always-full" Soho
café "the pick of the conveyor-belt operators" for many reporters.
/ *Details:* 10 pm; closed Sun; no Amex; no smoking; no booking.

Lahore Kebab House E1 £17 ★★

2 Umberston St 7488 2551

This celebrated East End Pakistani is "a complete dive", but –
"if you can put up with the surroundings" – the food is
"excellent", and "amazing value" too. / *Details:* midnight;
no credit cards.

The Lanesborough SW1 £60 Ⓐ

Hyde Park Corner 7259 5599 4–1D

"So pretty" and "so discreet"; the "fantastic" setting of the
conservatory restaurant at this landmark hotel has many fans –
for breakfast, lunch and tea, or for a business discussion; as
a serious dinner venue, however, it "doesn't measure up".
/ *Sample dishes:* foie gras with apple & raisin Tatin; lamb shank with Swiss chard;
plum tart with cinnamon ice cream. *Details:* www.lanesborough.com; midnight;
jacket required at D.

Langan's Bistro W1 £32 Ⓐ

26 Devonshire St 7935 4531 1–1A

"The best of the Langan's" – this "good, if cramped" Marylebone
bistro offers "well-cooked French food", and "promptly" too.
/ *Sample dishes:* salmon mousse with spinach sauce; pan-fried lambs kidneys with
mustard sauce; profiteroles. *Details:* www.langansrestaurants.co.uk; 11 pm; closed
Sat L & Sun.

The Langley WC2 £31 Ⓐ

5 Langley St 7836 5005 3–2C

"A fabulous atmosphere", in a series of intriguing cellars, is key to
the success of this retro Covent Garden hang-out; "good basic
food" helps soak up the alcohol that's really its raison d'être.
/ *Sample dishes:* smoked trout hash with eggy bread; chicken & mushroom pie;
mango & white chocolate mousse. *Details:* www.latenightlondon.co.uk; 1 am, Sun
10.30 pm.

Laughing Gravy SE1 £37 Ⓐ

154 Blackfriars Rd 7721 7055 5–4A

It's "a bit isolated", but this "tucked away" Southwark local – with
its "good straightforward cooking" and friendly service – "seldom
fails to be a thoroughly enjoyable experience".
/ *Sample dishes:* scallops in Guinness & bacon; chicken biryani with coconut dahl;
honey & saffron poached pears. *Details:* 10.30 pm; closed Sat L & Sun; no Amex.

Launceston Place W8   £45   A★

1a Launceston Pl   7937 6912   4–1B
*A location "off the beaten track", and "professional" service
contribute much to the "quiet" and "romantic" charms of this
civilised Kensington townhouse; its deft modern European cooking
is "solid" and "reliable".* / **Sample dishes:** deep-fried oysters with tartare
sauce; Dover sole with parsley butter; apple soufflé.
Details: www.launcestonplace.co.uk; 11.30 pm; closed Sat L & Sun D.

Lemonia NW1   £24   A

89 Regent's Park Rd   7586 7454
*"Huge fun, and very lively" – this "classic", "cheap and cheerful"
Primrose Hill Greek continues to enjoy an enormous north London
following; the cooking is "consistent", but unremarkable.*
/ **Sample dishes:** deep-fried aubergine; lamb baked with lemon & herbs; Greek
yoghurt with honey & nuts. **Value tip:** set weekday L £15(FP). **Details:** 11.30 pm;
closed Sat L & Sun D; no Amex.

Levant W1   £34   A

Jason Court, 76 Wigmore St   7224 1111   2–1A
*"Fantastic belly dancers" and "funky" décor create a "fab"
atmosphere at this "hip and trendy" basement North African
near Selfridges, where the cooking is incidental.* / **Value tip:** set
weekday L £19(FP). **Details:** www.levantrestaurant.co.uk; 11.30 pm.

Lightship Ten E1   £37   A

5a Katharine's Way, St Kath's Dock   7481 3123   5–3D
*"Great novelty-value" and a "cosy" atmosphere won praise for
this "romantic" old hulk, newly docked by the City; its "simple"
fare was also generally approved – we're with the reporter,
though, who found "it didn't match the ambience".*
/ **Sample dishes:** mussels cooked in beer & wild garlic; Scandinavian meatballs;
passion fruit crème brûlée. **Details:** www.lightshipten.com; 10 pm; closed Sun;
smoking discouraged.

Lindsay House W1   £70   A

21 Romilly St   7439 0450   3–3A
*"Hearty British cooking at its finest" and a "delightful
late-Georgian interior" can make a visit to Richard Corrigan's
"romantic" Soho townhouse "an amazing sensory experience";
even some fans say it's "too expensive", though, and staff "don't
stand on ceremony" – sometimes to a fault.* / **Sample dishes:** crayfish
gazpacho; stuffed guinea fowl with Madeira jus; banana soufflé. **Value tip:** set
weekday L £44(FP). **Details:** www.lindsayhouse.co.uk; 11 pm; closed Sat L & Sun.

Lisboa Patisserie W10   £ 5   ★★

57 Golborne Rd   8968 5242
*"Fast", "furious" and "dirt-cheap"; this North Kensington
institution is "perfect for brekkie and people-watching";
"outstanding Portuguese custard tarts" and "great coffee"
are highlights.* / **Sample dishes:** cheese croissant; vegetable rissoles; custard
tarts. **Details:** 8 pm; no Amex; no booking.

LMNT E8   £26   A

316 Queensbridge Rd   7249 6727
*The "outlandish" Egyptian décor "has to be seen to be believed",
say fans of this "extraordinary and unexpected" Dalston
pub-conversion; what's more it serves Mediterranean food that's
"tasty" and "reasonably priced".* / **Sample dishes:** goats cheese &
beetroot terrine with walnut bread; baked sea bass with olive & lemongrass dressing;
tarte Tatin with green apple sorbet. **Details:** www.lmnt.co.uk; 11 pm; no Amex.

Lobster Pot SE11 £36 ★

3 Kennington Ln   7582 5556

A "mad" venture, on an unlovely Kennington highway – this "old-fashioned" Gallic fish restaurant is decked out with "bizarre" and "kitsch" nautical décor; sceptics say it's "a bit overpriced", but most reporters are full of praise for its "well-cooked" fare.
/ **Sample dishes:** frogs legs with Cajun spices; monkfish with wild mushrooms & Pernod sauce; ice cream profiteroles. **Value tip:** set weekday L £23(FP).
Details: www.lobsterpotrestaurant.co.uk; 11 pm; closed Sun & Mon.

Locanda Locatelli Churchill InterContinental W1 £46  A★★

8 Seymour St
7935 9088   1–2A

"Fantastic… and Madonna to boot!"; it doesn't get much better than Giorgio Locatelli's "sophisticated" new dining room near Portman Square, where "warm and friendly" staff provide "classical Italian cooking with real panache".
/ **Sample dishes:** cabbage stuffed with sausage & saffron risotto; sea bream with braised fennel & anchovies; iced gingerbread mousse with mandarins.
Details: www.locandalocatelli.com; 11 pm; closed Sun; no Switch.

Lucky Seven W11 £30

127 Westbourne Park Rd   7727 6771

"You may have to share a table" (if you can get one, that is) at Tom Conran's trendy new "American-retro" diner in Notting Hill, where "great burgers with yummy toppings" and breakfast are the highlights; "over-pressed" service is "charming, but slow".
/ **Sample dishes:** clam chowder; cheeseburger & fries; triple chocolate fudge brownies. **Details:** 11 pm; closed Sun D; no credit cards; no booking.

Lundum's SW7 £40 A★

119 Old Brompton Rd   7373 7774   4–2B

"London's best Scandinavian" is a "very friendly" place, serving a "good, traditional Danish menu" (which tends to major in fish); its "quaint and old-fashioned" South Kensington premises are nominated by some as "possibly the most charming in town".
/ **Sample dishes:** marinated herrings; cured duck with radishes & honey sauce; crème brûlée. **Details:** 10.30 pm; closed Sun D.

Ma Goa SW15 £29 ★

244 Upper Richmond Rd   8780 1767   6–2B

"Every mouthful is guaranteed tasty" at this "authentically different" and "relaxing" family-run Putney Indian, known for its "unusual and appealing Goanese dishes". / **Details:** www.magoa.co.uk; 11 pm; closed Mon, Tue–Sat D only, Sun open L & D.

Made in Italy SW3 £32 A★

249 King's Rd   7352 1880   4–3C

"Fabulous slabs of pizza" – "just how Mamma makes it" – win high praise for this classic "cheap and cheerful" Chelsea destination, though the "volatile" service veers from "friendly" to "surreally bad". / **Sample dishes:** ravioli with sage butter; seafood platter; cream-filled liqueur sponge. **Details:** 11.30 pm; closed weekday L; no credit cards.

Madhu's Brilliant UB1 £22 ★

39 South Rd   8574 1897

With its "plentiful" and "different" dishes, this smart (for Southall) Indian retains a high reputation in this curry-mad suburb.
/ **Details:** 11.30 pm; closed Tue, Sat L & Sun L.

Maggie Jones's W8 £39 _A_

6 Old Court Pl   7937 6462   4–1A

"A must on a rainy day" – this "camp" and "rustic" Kensington veteran is a wonderfully "cosy" and "intimate" place, where old-fashioned, "wintery" fare is served up in "huge portions". / **Sample dishes:** haddock mousse; grilled chicken with cucumber hollandaise; bread & butter pudding. **Details:** 11 pm.

Maghreb N1 £24 ★

189 Upper St   7226 2305

This unassuming Moroccan bistro in Islington attracts surprisingly little commentary; it offers "good" and reasonably-priced food, and its atmosphere (better at the weekends) is "good for groups". / **Details:** www.maghrebrestaurant.co.uk; 11.30 pm; D only.

Maison Bertaux W1 £ 9 _A_ ★

28 Greek St   7437 6007   3–2A

"Where would we be without its idiosyncratic charms and almond croissants?" – London's oldest coffee house, in Soho, offers "outstanding pastries" and "evokes a different era" (circa 1871). / **Sample dishes:** no starters; ham & cheese croissant; plum & almond cake. **Details:** 8.30 pm; no credit cards; no smoking area.

Malabar W8 £28 _A_ ★

27 Uxbridge St   7727 8800

This "convivial" Indian, just off Notting Hill Gate – which looks more like a trattoria than a curry house – is one of the most consistent restaurants in town; the cooking is "well above average", and service is "friendly" and "professional". / **Details:** www.malabar-restaurant.co.uk; 11.15 pm; no Amex.

Malabar Junction WC1 £33 _A_ ★

107 Gt Russell St   7580 5230   1–1C

With its "pleasing conservatory atmosphere", "helpful waiters" and "authentic" south Indian food, this "elegant" Bloomsbury venture is a surprisingly good all-rounder. / **Details:** 11.30 pm; no smoking area.

Mandalay W2 £18 ★★

444 Edgware Rd   7258 3696

"Incredible-value" food plus "the friendliest service in town" wins many fans for this "excellent" Burmese ("a cross between Indian and Chinese"), occupying a simple shop-conversion north of Edgware Road tube. / **Value tip:** set weekday L £11(FP). **Details:** 10.30 pm; closed Sun; no smoking.

Mandarin Kitchen W2 £28 ★★

14-16 Queensway   7727 9012

"Having to wait, even when you've booked" may be annoying, but most visitors to this "weird" and "dingy" Bayswater oriental find ample compensation in "the best Chinese seafood in town" (not least "the most delicious lobster"). / **Details:** 11.15 pm.

Maroush £38 ★

I) 21 Edgware Rd, W2   7723 0773

II) 38 Beauchamp Pl, SW3   7581 5434   4–1C

III) 62 Seymour St, W1   7724 5024   1–2A

The settings are "glitzy" and the service can be so-so, but, if you're looking for a "top Lebanese", this long-established group still has many admirers; for "late-night munchies", "the Rolls-Royces of kebab shops" – the smart café/takeaways at I and II – are very popular. / **Details:** W1 1 am – W2 2 am – SW3 5 am.

Matsuri SW1   £52   ★
15 Bury St   7839 1101   2–3D
"The food's certainly not inexpensive but always of very good quality" at this *"hospitable"* St James's teppan-yaki, where the *"delight of watching the chefs at work"* improves the *"slightly staid"* atmosphere; it also offers *"wonderful"* sushi and sashimi. / **Value tip:** set pre-theatre menu £29(FP). **Details:** www.matsuri-restaurant.com; 10.30 pm.

McClements TW1   £43   ★
2 Whitton Road, Twickenham   8744 9610
"Wasted in this location" – *"an unlovely strip of shops near Twickenham Station"* – this *"comfortable"* French fixture offers professional service and some *"superb"*, *"traditional"* Gallic cooking. / **Sample dishes:** scallops with cep risotto; roast pigeon & foie gras wrapped in spinach; baked lime & rhubarb mousse. **Value tip:** set pre-theatre menu £26(FP). **Details:** www.mcclementsrestaurant.com; 11 pm; closed Sun D; no smoking area.

Mediterraneo W11   £35   𝔸★
37 Kensington Park Rd   7792 3131
It may seem *"chaotic"*, but this *"trendy"* Notting Hill Italian does almost everything right (and it's *"always bursting"*); as at its sibling (Osteria Basilico), only the *"stupid"* 'sittings' system causes any real complaint. / **Sample dishes:** pan-fried mussels & clams; veal with deep-fried courgettes; tiramisu. **Value tip:** set weekday L £18(FP). **Details:** 11.30 pm; booking: max 8.

Meson don Felipe SE1   £24   𝔸
53 The Cut   7928 3237   5–4A
A *"marvellous buzz"* is the hallmark of this *"scrum"* of a tapas bar opposite the Young Vic, where a *"familiar"* selection of dishes is *"well done"*. / **Sample dishes:** chick pea, spinach & potato soup; baby red peppers stuffed with prawns; profiteroles. **Details:** 11 pm; closed Sun; no Amex; no booking after 8 pm.

Metrogusto   £39   ★
13 Theberton St, N1   7226 9400
153 Battersea Park Rd, SW8   7720 0204   6–1C
"Consistently charming" service, *"good-quality"* cooking (if not in enormous portions) and an *"interesting wine selection"* help maintain the popularity of this *"trendy"* Italian duo. / **Sample dishes:** grilled pear & Pecorino salad; sea bream & root vegetables with saffron sauce; nougat parfait with orange sauce. **Details:** 10.30 pm – SW8 Fri & Sat 10.45 pm; SW8 closed Sun – N1 closed Mon; no Amex; no smoking area.

Mirabelle W1   £56   𝔸★
56 Curzon St   7499 4636   2–4B
With its *"lovely, '30s glamour"*, its *"classic"* Gallic menu, and its *"extraordinary"* wine list, Marco Pierre White's *"sexy and romantic"* Mayfair classic still exudes plenty of *"wow factor"*. / **Sample dishes:** warm salad of smoked eel & bacon; steak & kidney pudding with swede purée; peppered pineapple tarte Tatin. **Value tip:** set Sun L £36(FP). **Details:** www.whitestarline.org.uk; 10.45 pm; no smoking area.

Mirch Masala   £13   ★★
1416 London Road, SW16   8679 1828   6–2C
213 Upper Tooting Rd, SW17   8672 7500   6–2D
"The best Indian grub you could wish for" – and at *"rock-bottom prices"* – is served at this *"fantastic"* Norbury canteen and its *"great"* new Tooting sibling. / **Details:** midnight; SW17 no credit cards.

Mitsukoshi SW1 £53 ★★
14-20 Lower Regent St 7930 0317 2–3D
*"Awful décor", but "the best sushi and sashimi there is";
the trade-off is the same as ever at this "tired" and sterile
Japanese department store basement. / **Value tip:** set Sun L £26(FP).*
Details: *9.30 pm; closed Sun D; no smoking area.*

Mju
Millennium Knightsbridge SW1 £60 ★
17 Sloane St 7235 4377 4–1D
*"Exquisite" Japanese fusion fare and "excellent" service win loud
applause for this year-old Knightsbridge hotel dining room; even
supporters can find the setting "lifeless", though, and there are
critics for whom the whole performance is just "stunningly
overpriced". / **Sample dishes:** lobster mousse with wasabi jelly; rack of lamb
with miso & water chestnuts; orange, honey & black pepper sorbet.* ***Details:*** *10 pm;
closed Sat L & Sun L; no smoking.*

Momo W1 £44 🄰
25 Heddon St 7434 4040 2–2C
*"Exotic and bustling, and with great pillows to relax on" – this
"vibrant" Mayfair Moroccan scores full marks for its "brilliant",
"party" ambience; the grub is "only good-to-average", though,
and the "beautiful" staff come complete with "attitude".
/ **Sample dishes:** cod carpaccio with alfalfa & caviar; seared tuna with chickpea
polenta; quince & clementines with rose water.* ***Details:*** *11.30 pm.*

Mon Plaisir WC2 £38 🄰
19-21 Monmouth St 7836 7243 3–2B
*A "petit coin de Paris", on the fringe of Covent Garden; this
rambling, "fabulously intimate" veteran wins solid praise for its
"reliable bourgeois cooking", and an "exceptional-value
pre-theatre menu" is a highlight. / **Sample dishes:** onion, black olive &
anchovy tart; confit duck in red wine sauce; cocobut mousse with pineapple gratinée.
Value tip: set pre-theatre menu £18(FP).* ***Details:*** *www.monplaisir.co.uk;
11.15 pm; closed Sat L & Sun.*

Monkeys SW3 £55 🄰★
1 Cale St 7352 4711 4–2C
*"The best game in London" is the menu highlight, at this
"charming", old-style Anglo-French restaurant, on Chelsea
Green; its "amusing" host "runs it rather like a private club",
and a "keenly-priced wine list, strong on vintage claret" is
a special attraction. / **Sample dishes:** lobster & leek terrine; roast partridge
with traditional trimmings; sorbet.* ***Details:*** *10 pm; closed Sat & Sun; no Amex.*

Monsieur Max TW12 £54 🄰★★
133 High St, Hampton Hill 8979 5546
*"Still the greatest suburban secret"; this Hampton Hill fixture is
an outstanding "oasis", on account of its "top-notch" service and
its "absolutely fantastic" French cooking – "calorific, rich and
creamy" and with a cheeseboard "to die for".
/ **Sample dishes:** foie gras & duck terrine with Sauternes jelly; John Dory with
champagne & sorrel risotto; liqorice meringue.* ***Details:*** *10 pm; closed Sat L.*

Moro EC1 £36 🄰★★
34-36 Exmouth Mkt 7833 8336 5–1A
*"Creative" Moorish cooking (with some "wonderful and unusual
flavours"), "professional" service and a "very bustling" ("noisy")
atmosphere has made this "understated" Clerkenwell venture one
of the major ongoing success-stories of recent years.
/ **Sample dishes:** Russian salad with smoked anchovies; lamb with roast beetroot &
parsley sauce; chocolate & apricot tart.* ***Details:*** *10.30 pm; closed Sat L & Sun.*

Naked Turtle SW14   £35   A

505 Upper Richmond Rd   8878 1995   6–2A

*"Singing waitresses add to the outstanding atmosphere" of
this "welcoming and cheerful" Sheen wine bar, where live
entertainment is a regular feature; the food is "average, and
not cheap".* / **Sample dishes:** sweet chicory tart; wild boar with sweet potato
mash & four-berry sauce; peach & vanilla trifle. **Details:** www.naked-turtle.com;
11 pm; Mon-Thu D only, Fri-Sun open L & D; no smoking area.

Nam Long SW5   £33   A

159 Old Brompton Rd   7373 1926   4–2B

*"Killer cocktails" (not least the now infamous 'Flaming Ferrari')
fuel the "fun" at this stylish but "cramped" South Kensington
bar/restaurant; the Vietnamese nosh is "pleasant enough",
if rather "overpriced".* / **Details:** 11.30 pm; closed Sat L & Sun.

Nobu
Metropolitan Hotel W1   £57   A★★

Old Park Lane   7447 4747   2–4A

*"All the hype is fair!"; "awesome" Japanese/South American
fusion cuisine helps make this "sexy" Mayfair celebrity haunt
a continuing success, even if it is "very, very overpriced".*
/ **Sample dishes:** 'new-style' sashimi; black cod with miso; chocolate Bento box.
Details: 10.15 pm, Fri & Sat 11 pm; closed Sat L & Sun L; no smoking area.

North Sea Fish WC1   £27   ★

7-8 Leigh St   7387 5892

*The "huge portions" of "simple, but very well-cooked" fish "have
been good for over fifteen years" at this "friendly", "glorified
chippy" in Bloomsbury.* / **Sample dishes:** smoked cods roe salad; battered
cod & chips; sherry trifle. **Details:** 10.30 pm; closed Sun.

Noura SW1   £37   ★

16 Hobart Pl   7235 9444   1–4B

*"At last, a cosmopolitan place to enjoy Lebanese food" – this
"spacious" restaurant near Victoria Station is making quite
a name for its "delicious" fare in "generous portions"; service
is "friendly", too.* / **Details:** www.noura-brasseries.co.uk; 11.30 pm.

The Oak W2   £29   A★

137 Westbourne Park Rd
7221 3599

*"Hip, but not OTT", this new Notting Hill boozer, which offers
"slightly different" pub grub (with "yummy pizzas" a highlight) in
its mellow downstairs bar, quickly acquired quite a following;
a more ambitious upstairs dining room (formula price £37)
opened post-survey.* / **Sample dishes:** spiced aubergine salad; char-grilled
longhorn beef; apple tart. **Details:** 10.30 pm; closed weekday L.

Odette's NW1   £41   A★

130 Regent's Park Rd   7586 5486

*"Mirrors and candles everywhere delight the eye", at this
"intimate" Primrose Hill "old favourite"; it remains a splendid
all-rounder, offering "consistently good" and "interesting" cooking.*
/ **Sample dishes:** sea scallop risotto; roast lamb with tempura courgettes; chocolate
mousse. **Value tip:** set Sun L £26(FP). **Details:** 11 pm; closed Sat L & Sun.

Odette's Wine Bar NW1 £29   𝔸
130 Regent's Park Rd   7722 5388
The "cute" and "relaxed" cellars below the restaurant benefit
from both the aura and the wine list from upstairs; a "limited but
good" menu is dependably realised. / **Sample dishes:** smoked salmon,
avocado & tiger prawns; roast lamb with courgette & mint salad; apple, honey &
cinnamon tart. **Details:** 11 pm; closed Sun D.

Odin's W1 £41   𝔸
27 Devonshire St   7935 7296   1–1A
This "classy" and "comfortable" Marylebone fixture – beautified
by the late Peter Langan's "fabulous" art collection – maintains
a "discreet" and "charming" air that equally suits business or
romance; the generally "enjoyable" English cooking can be rather
"bland". / **Sample dishes:** smoked eel mousse with horseradish; Cumberland
sausages with mash & onion sauce; date & ginger pudding.
Details: www.langansrestaurants.co.uk; 11 pm; closed Sat & Sun; no smoking area.

Ye Olde Cheshire Cheese EC4 £25   𝔸
145 Fleet St   7353 6170   5–2A
"For a trencherman's lunch in front of a blazing fire" –
Dr Johnson-style – you still can't beat this "classic" City inn; yes,
it's corny, but "visitors love it". / **Sample dishes:** duck & port pâté with
Cumberland sauce; roast pork with apple & cranberry stuffing; treacle sponge &
custard. **Details:** www.yeoldecheshirecheese.com; 9.30 pm; closed Sun D;
no smoking at L.

Olivo SW1 £39   ★
21 Eccleston St   7730 2505   1–4B
Some find this Belgravia-fringe venture a touch "variable"
(especially the atmosphere), but many of its customers "have
known it for years", and it is generally a safe bet for "very good
Sardinian food" at a "fair price". / **Sample dishes:** Mozzarella with
marinated aubergines; seafood risotto; lemon tart. **Details:** 11 pm; closed Sat L &
Sun L.

1 Lombard Street EC3 £48
1 Lombard St   7929 6611   5–3C
"A useful position" – right by Bank – helps make this "slick"
former banking hall by far the most popular business venue in the
heart of the Square Mile, though the food is no more than
"acceptable" given the prices; the brasserie (price indicated) is
generally preferred to the restaurant. / **Sample dishes:** smoked haddock
with quail's eggs & mustard sauce; veal with caramelised artichokes & truffles;
liquorice crème brûlée with blackcurrant coulis. **Details:** www.1lombardstreet.com;
10 pm; closed Sat & Sun.

Ophim W1 £34   ★
139 Wardour St   7434 9899   2–2D
Some rate the cheaper "buffet concept on the ground floor"
(formula price £24) above the pricier basement restaurant at this
stylish new "nouvelle Indian" in Soho; both venues, though,
provide "friendly" service and "interesting" food.
/ **Details:** www.ophim.com; 11 pm, Fri & Sat 11.30 pm; closed Sun; no smoking
area.

Opium W1 £56   𝔸
1a Dean St   7287 9608   2–1D
"Boudoir-esque décor" creates a "fun" and "romantic" vibe in this
Soho "oriental den" (which becomes a club as the evening
progresses); neither the "mediocre" Vietnamese cooking, however,
nor the "how-beautiful-am-I" service is a particular attraction.
/ **Sample dishes:** chicken satay; Vietnamese noodles with monkfish; banana
spring rolls. **Details:** 9.30 pm; closed Sun.

L'Oranger SW1 £61 A★

5 St James's St   7839 3774   2–4D

"A very polished operation"; with its "delicious, classic French cooking", this "elegant", "intimate" and "well-spaced" St James's establishment remains a top choice for business or pleasure; service is "relaxed but attentive". / **Sample dishes:** salt cod & potato tartlet; roast pork with bacon & sage; hazelnut soufflé. **Details:** 10.45 pm; closed Sat L & Sun.

Orrery W1 £61 A★

55 Marylebone High St   7616 8000   1–1A

"Best of all the Conran places"; some do find prices "extortionate", but this "very smart" and "discreet" Marylebone dining room – with a daytime view over a quiet churchyard – offers some "fantastic" modern French cooking, and "impeccable" service. / **Sample dishes:** Bayonne ham with celeriac; seared tuna with coco beans; peach soufflé. **Value tip:** set Sun D inc glass of champagne £35(FP). **Details:** www.orrery.co.uk; 10.30 pm.

Oslo Court NW8 £46 A★

Prince Albert Rd   7722 8795

A "unique" institution – oddly-located at the foot of a Regent's Park apartment block – many of whose grey-haired regulars know the "fabulously attentive" staff by name; its "classic European" menu (with an "exceptional" sweet trolley) offers "great old-fashioned value". / **Sample dishes:** scallop & bacon salad; sea bass; raspberry tart with apple pancakes. **Details:** 11 pm; closed Sun.

Osteria Antica Bologna SW11 £35 A★

23 Northcote Rd   7978 4771   6–2C

Enthusiasm is reviving for this "busy", "cosy" and "packed" Battersea favourite, whose "very realistic, rustic Italian cooking" has "recovered from a slump". / **Sample dishes:** battered frogs legs with grilled semolina; Sicilian-style goat with almond pesto; chocolate & date tart. **Value tip:** set weekday L £21(FP). **Details:** www.osteria.co.uk; 11 pm, Fri & Sat 11.30 pm.

Osteria Basilico W11 £34 A★

29 Kensington Park Rd   7727 9957

"A great example of a successful rustic Italian"; "distinctive", "sensibly-priced" and "consistently reliable", this Notting Hill spot is an almost unanimous crowd-pleaser; the "two-sittings-a-night policy" is the only real complaint. / **Sample dishes:** beef carpaccio with pesto & Parmesan; pan-fried swordfish with sun-dried tomatoes; chocolate cake with hot chocolate sauce. **Details:** 11 pm; no booking, Sat L.

Oxo Tower (Brasserie)
Oxo Tower Wharf SE1 £44 A✗

Barge House St   7803 3888   5–3A

"I'd rather go to the Eye" – even fans of the "fabulous" and "romantic" views from Harvey Nichols's eighth-floor South Bank eyrie say they "don't compensate" for the "dull" food and sometimes "appalling" service. / **Sample dishes:** snails with mushrooms and smoked bacon; roast pheasant with caramelised endive; lemon parfait with rhubarb. **Details:** www.harveynichols.com; 11.15 pm.

Ozer W1 £33 A

4-5 Langham Pl   7323 0505   2–1C

With its "comfy" setting and "attentive" service, this modern Turkish restaurant, just north of Oxford Circus, has won a fair following; the "predictable" fare may not set the world alight, but it is "good value" and "well presented". / **Sample dishes:** parsley salad; lamb kofte; yoghurt with honey & nuts. **Value tip:** set menu always available £17(FP). **Details:** midnight; no jeans.

The Painted Heron SW10 £34 ★★
112 Cheyne Walk 7351 5232 4–3B
"Wonderful" and *"imaginative"* cooking makes it well worth
seeking out this new Chelsea Indian (on the site of Busabong Tree,
RIP); in the early days at least, it wasn't winning the following it
deserved. / **Details:** 11 pm.

Pan-Asian Canteen
Paxton's Head SW1 £23 ★
153 Knightsbridge 7589 6627 4–1D
"Very fresh" Thai dishes that are *"super for the price"* make it
well worth knowing about this *"relaxing"* communal dining room
above a Knightsbridge pub; service can be *"excellent"* too.
/ **Details:** 10.30 pm; no smoking area.

Parade W5 £37 ★
18-19 The Mall 8810 0202
"A godsend in the Ealing culinary desert", this *"excellent"* modern
brasserie (sibling to Sonny's) offers *"consistent"* and *"well-priced"*
contemporary cooking in a *"minimalist"* (*"echoey"* when empty)
setting. / **Sample dishes:** chicken, black pudding & egg salad; skate with borlotti
beans; baked egg custard tart. **Details:** 10.30 pm; closed Sun D.

Paradise by Way
of Kensal Green W10 £29 Ⓐ★
19 Kilburn Ln 8969 0098
With its *"thoroughly reliable"* cooking and *"conservatory-like"*
setting, this *"spacious"* gastropub has long been a key local
destination; *"nice garden"*, too. / **Sample dishes:** crispy fried squid with
coriander salsa; monkfish with chorizo & mussels; banoffi pie.
Details: www.paradise.co.uk; 10.30 pm; no Amex.

The Parsee N19 £31 ★★
34 Highgate Hill 7272 9091
The *"brilliant and exotic flavours"* of Cyrus Todiwala's
"fascinating" Parsee cooking help make his *"pleasant"*, Highgate
yearling *"a most atypical Indian dining experience"*; service is
"wonderful" too. / **Details:** www.theparsee.com; 10.45 pm; D only, closed Sun;
no smoking area.

Pasha SW7 £40 Ⓐ
1 Gloucester Rd 7589 7969 4–1B
"Step off the street, and into the souk", at this *"exotic"*, *"dark"*
and *"romantic"* South Kensington Moroccan; authenticity can be
undermined, though, by *"pricey"* and *"average"* food, and *"poor"*
service. / **Sample dishes:** mezze; chicken with preserved lemons; Turkish delight
crème brûlée. **Details:** www.pasha-restaurant.co.uk; 11.15 pm; closed Sun L;
booking: max 10 at weekends.

Pasha N1 £27 Ⓐ
301 Upper St 7226 1454
This *"dependable"* Islington fixture may be a touch *"cramped"*,
but it wins a lot of support for its *"obliging"* service, its *"lively"*
atmosphere and *"decent"* mezze, all at *"good-value"* prices.
/ **Sample dishes:** courgette fritters; kleftiko; rosewater rice pudding.
Details: 11.30 pm, Fri & Sat midnight; no Switch.

Patara   **£37**   ★
3&7 Maddox St, W1   7499 6008   2–2C
181 Fulham Rd, SW3   7351 5692   4–2C
9 Beauchamp Pl, SW3   7581 8820   4–1C
For "value for money" – in Chelsea and, now, Mayfair – these
"crushed", but "civilised" and "consistent", Thais have many
admirers. / Value tip: set weekday L £24(FP). Details: 10.30 pm;
no smoking areas.

Paul   **£12**   𝔸★
115 Marylebone High St, W1   7224 5615   1–1A
29-30 Bedford St, WC2   7836 3304   3–3C
"It's very difficult to restrain yourself", at these "real French-style
pâtisseries", what with their "great coffee", "delicious tarts" and
"good savouries"; if you want to eat in, you may have to queue.
/ Sample dishes: soup with sourdough bread; leek & lardon tartlet with salad;
citron tart. Details: 8pm; no smoking; no booking.

The Pen SW6   **£35**   𝔸★
51 Parsons Green Ln   7371 8517   6–1B
"Refreshingly good, for Fulham"; this "airy" but "intimate" dining
room, over a stylish bar, offers "confident" cooking and "very
good" service. / Details: www.thepenrestaurant.co.uk; 11 pm; closed Sun D;
no Amex.

The Pepper Tree SW4   **£17**   𝔸
19 Clapham Common S'side   7622 1758   6–2D
"Worth the trip to Clapham", say fans of the "fast Thai food at
low prices", served refectory-style at this ever-popular canteen.
/ Details: 11 pm, Mon & Sun 10.30 pm; no Amex; no smoking area;
no booking at D.

The Perseverance WC1   **£28**
63 Lamb's Conduit St   7405 8278   1–1D
"White linen tablecloths" set a grander-than-average tone at this
year-old Bloomsbury gastropub; its "good" food is quite
"grown-up" by boozer standards too, though service can be
"sloppy". / Sample dishes: Catalan-style baby octopus salad; chicken with
rosemary & potato fondant; iced coconut soufflé with kiwi coulis. Details: 9 pm;
closed Sat L & Sun D.

Pétrus SW1   **£75**   ★★
33 St James's St   7930 4272   2–4C
Marcus Wareing's "fantastic talent" has made this Gallic dining
room in St James's one of the most notable in town; even fans
say it's becoming "hugely expensive", though – especially the
"intimidating" wine list – and the atmosphere can be rather
"rigid". / Sample dishes: tuna carpaccio with coriander salad; pork belly with wild
mushrooms; peach clafoutis. Value tip: set weekday L £43(FP).
Details: www.petrus-restaurant.com; 10.45 pm; closed Sat L & Sun; booking:
max 6.

Phoenix Bar & Grill SW15   **£38**   𝔸★
Pentlow St   8780 3131   6–1A
This "buzzy" Putney all-rounder remains "everything a suburban
local should be"; however, the much-reported-on spring 2002
appointment of the celebrated Franco Taruschio as consultant
chef created false expectations for some reporters, who found it
"pleasant enough, but disappointing after all the hype".
/ Sample dishes: cod goujons with Thai dipping sauce; pan-fried sweetbreads with
mushrooms & marsala; pannacotta with baked figs. Value tip: set D £25(FP).
Details: 11 pm; no smoking area.

Phoenix Palace NW1 £27 ★★

3-5 Glentworth St 7486 3515 1–1A

"The very high proportion of Asian customers" attests to the "very authentic" cooking at this comfortable Chinese, near Baker Street tube; "excellent, fresh dim sum" is among "the best in town". / **Details:** 11.45 pm.

Pied à Terre W1 £55 ★

34 Charlotte St 7636 1178 1–1C

"Improved by refurbishment" – there's a brighter look and prices have been moderated at this eminent Fitzrovian; some find Shane Osborne's modern French cuisine "over-elaborate", but most say it's "sensational". / **Sample dishes:** celeriac, chive & salt cod soup; braised lamb with deep-fried tongue & olives; mandarin parfait with lemon curd. **Value tip:** set weekday L £33(FP). **Details:** www.pied.a.terre.co.uk; 11 pm; closed Sat L & Sun; no smoking area; booking: max 8.

Pizza Metro SW11 £29 𝔸★★

64 Battersea Rise 7228 3812 6–2C

A "typical Neapolitan joint" that somehow ended up in Battersea; "the best pizza in town" ("served by the metre"), "an authentic buzz" and "reliable" service ensure this "noisy" "Mecca" is "always packed". / **Sample dishes:** antipasti; pizza with salami & olives; tiramisu. **Details:** 11 pm; closed Mon, Tue-Fri D only, Sat & Sun open L & D.

Pizzeria Castello SE1 £21 𝔸★

20 Walworth Rd 7703 2556

"Pizza as you would expect it in Italy", "friendly service" and a "cheerful" atmosphere have long made this "always-reliable" destination worth braving Elephant & Castle for; watch out for an address-change in early-2003, when the bulldozers are scheduled to roll in. / **Sample dishes:** prawns in garlic; four cheese pizza; cheesecake. **Details:** 11 pm, Fri & Sat 11.30 pm; closed Sat L & Sun.

Poissonnerie de l'Avenue SW3 £53 ★

82 Sloane Ave 7589 2457 4–2C

The "fresh" and "simple" Gallic fish cookery at this "legendary" Brompton Cross old-timer retains many admirers; the setting can seem "cramped" and "stuffy", though, and prices give nothing away. / **Sample dishes:** lobster & salmon ravioli in cream sauce; seared tuna with salsa; lemon tart. **Details:** 11.30 pm; closed Sun.

The Polish Club SW7 £32 𝔸

55 Prince's Gate, Exhibition Rd 7589 4635 4–1C

For "faded grandeur", it's hard to beat the "elegant" dining room of this "fascinating" South Kensington émigrés' club, which offers "solid" but inexpensive Polish fare; in summer, the "peaceful" terrace is "a top alfresco spot". / **Sample dishes:** beetroot soup with rye bread; pork with red & white cabbage; chocolate & almond cheesecake. **Details:** 11 pm.

Pomegranates SW1 £42 𝔸

94 Grosvenor Rd 7828 6560 1–4C

"The charm of the proprietor" adds much to the atmosphere at this "dark", "dated" and – some think – "romantic" old Pimlico basement; its "eclectic" cooking has been "consistent for decades". / **Details:** 11.15 pm; closed Sat L & Sun.

Le Pont de la Tour SE1   **£61**

36d Shad Thames   7403 8403   5–4D
"Good views of Tower Bridge, but how you pay for them";
Conran's attractive South Bank flagship showed less "volatility of
food and service" this year, but many reporters still found it
"disappointing, for a supposedly top restaurant".
/ *Sample dishes: Dorset crab & avocado with gazpacho dressing; pot-roasted lamb*
with cumin & carrots; vanilla & gingerbread parfait. Details: www.conran.com;
11 pm; closed Sat L.

La Porte des Indes W1   **£46**   A★

32 Bryanston St   7224 0055   1–2A
"The flamboyant décor" – complete with waterfall – is almost
matched by the "very good posh curries" (with a French influence)
at this large West End subcontinental; it's not cheap – "think of it
as a mini holiday". / Details: www.la-porte-des-indes.com; midnight; closed
Sat L.

The Portrait
National Portrait Gallery WC2   **£38**   A

St Martin's Place   7312 2490   3–4B
"Marvellous views" can help make a visit to this top-floor gallery
restaurant, in the heart of the West End, a positively "decadent"
experience; both cooking and service, however, could be much
improved. / Sample dishes: black pudding & poached egg with apple sauce;
broccoli & Stilton tart with hazelnut salad; cranberry cheesecake with port syrup.
Details: 8.30 pm; L only, except Thu & Fri open L & D; smoking in bar only;
booking: max 8.

La Poule au Pot SW1   **£40**   A★

231 Ebury St   7730 7763   4–2D
"You can't beat it for atmosphere" – this "cosy", "country
auberge"-style Pimlico old-timer was for the umpteenth year
running reporters' top choice for a romantic encounter;
"authentic" cooking and "entertaining" Gallic service complete its
"timeless" appeal. / Sample dishes: pork & foie gras terrine; roast lamb with
green beans; chocolate mousse. Details: 11.15 pm.

(Tapa Room)
The Providores W1   **£30**   A★

109 Marylebone High St   7935 6175   1–1A
"Good-value", "unusual" and "interesting" light bites make this
"really relaxed" street-level bar much more consistently popular
than the upstairs restaurant; "excellent" breakfasts and brunches
are a highlight. / Sample dishes: tamarind laksa with prawn dumplings; crispy
pork with chorizo mash & lotus root; chocolate mousse cake with wattleseed cream.
Details: www.theprovidores.co.uk; 10.30 pm.

Putney Bridge SW15   **£58**   A★

Embankment   8780 1811   6–1B
"Wonderful views over the bridge" are a special plus of this
striking modern landmark; most reporters find the "creative"
Gallic cooking "impressive" too, but many think it "expensive"
for what it is, and service can be "fussy". / Sample dishes: roast quail
wrapped in vine leaves; sea bass with Jabugo ham & truffles; black fig tart with
almond milk sorbet. Value tip: set weekday L £38(FP).
Details: www.putneybridgerestaurant.com; 11 pm; closed Mon & Sun D.

Quaglino's SW1 £47 X
16 Bury St   7930 6767   2–3D
"They don't even try"; this once-celebrated Conran mega-brasserie in St James's – with its "duff" and "overpriced" fare and sometimes "actively rude" staff – is now "well past the sell-by date". / Sample dishes: foie gras terrine with fig jam; roast guinea fowl with buttered spinach; pineapple with ginger & basil. Value tip: set menu always available £27(FP). Details: www.conran.com; midnight, Fri & Sat 1 am.

Queen's Head W6 £22
13 Brook Grn   7603 3174
The "excellent" beer garden is the star feature at this ancient Brook Green tavern (which – without the dead hand of big brewery ownership – could be a truly amazing place); it serves a "huge menu", realised with varying degrees of success. / Sample dishes: spiced tomato soup; fillet steak with mushroom & brandy sauce; banana toffee crumble. Details: 10 pm; no smoking area; no booking.

Quiet Revolution £28 A★
28-29 Marylebone High St, W1   7487 5683   1–1B
49 Old St, EC1   7253 5556   5–1B
"You leave feeling refreshed", from these simple cafés; they're "nice places to be", serving "great organic omelettes, salads, soups and pasta". / Sample dishes: French onion soup; roasted pepper omelette & salad; apricot & almond cake. Details: www.quietrevolution.co.uk; W1 6 pm – EC1 9 pm; W1 closed Sat – EC1 closed Sat & Sun; no smoking.

Racine SW3 £33 ★
239 Brompton Rd
7584 4477   4–2C
An early (July 2002) trip to this stylishly-muted new brasserie found simple but sophisticated French cooking (from former Fifth Floor chef Henry Harris) and a notably charming welcome; this could well become a key Knightsbridge destination. / Sample dishes: garlic & saffron mousse; rabbit with mustard & smoked bacon; Mont Blanc dessert. Details: 10.30 pm.

Rani N3 £23 ★
7 Long Ln   8349 4386
"Fresh and inventive vegetarian Indian cooking, that's inexpensive too" wins little but praise for this North Finchley fixture. / Details: www.raniuk.com; 10 pm; D only; no smoking area.

Ranoush W2 £22 ★
43 Edgware Rd   7723 5929
"The best late-night place in town", say fans of this "Lebanese-style bar", north of Marble Arch; it serves "great kebabs" and "fabulous juices". / Sample dishes: houmous & crudités; grilled meat skewers; baklava. Details: www.maroush.com; 2.45 am; no credit cards.

Rasa £31 ★★
6 Dering St, W1   7629 1346   2–2B
55 Stoke Newington Church St, N16   7249 0344
"Explosions of unexpected tastes and textures" – both at the "cramped" Stoke Newington original and the classier Mayfair offshoot – win a wide following for "the best vegetarian Indians in town". / Details: www.rasarestaurants.com; 10.30 pm; N16 closed Mon L-Thu L – W1 closed Sun; no smoking.

Rasa Samudra W1 £42 ★
5 Charlotte St 7637 0222 1–1C
*"Delicious combinations of spicy seafood flavours" win high
praise for this rambling Fitzrovia Indian (which also serves some
"unusual and exciting" veggie fare); the "intimate" ambience can
be a little underwhelming. / Value tip: set weekday L £24(FP).*
Details: www.rasarestaurants.com; 10.30 pm; closed Sun L; no smoking area.

Rasa Travancore N16 £25 ★
56 Stoke Newington Church St 7249 1340
*"Another great addition to the Rasa chain", say fans of this Stoke
Newington yearling, acclaiming the "singular" flavours of its
"satisfying" and inexpensive fare (here including meat dishes);
not everyone is convinced. / Details:* www.rasarestaurants.com; 10.45 pm;
D only, ex Sun open L & D; no smoking.

The Real Greek N1 £42
15 Hoxton Market 7739 8212 5–1D
*"Food like it never was in Greece" – "creative" and "delicious" –
still impresses at this "buzzy" Hoxton two-year old; prices have
rocketed since opening though, much dimming its 'golden glow'.
/ Sample dishes: pork, leek & prune terrine; pork stuffed with spiced peaches &
feta; baklava with peaches & ouzo sorbet. Details:* www.therealgreek.co.uk;
10.30 pm; closed Sun; no Amex.

Rebato's SW8 £25 Ⓐ
169 South Lambeth Rd 7735 6388 6–1D
*"Viva España", say fans of this "old-fashioned" Vauxhall tapas
bar, loved for its "great staff", "buzzing" atmosphere and
"stupendously cheap" grub; the restaurant at the rear is "less
atmospheric". / Sample dishes: stuffed roast piquillo peppers; kidneys in sherry
with mushrooms & bacon; crema Catalan. Details:* www.rebatos.com; 10.45 pm;
closed Sat L & Sun.

Redmond's SW14 £43 ★
170 Upper R'mond Rd West 8878 1922 6–1A
*"The new décor creates a better atmosphere", at the Redmond
family's "very well-run" Sheen fixture; with its "careful" cooking,
quality wine, and "charming" and "attentive" service, it could
become quite a destination. / Sample dishes: leek & ginger soup with
scallops; roast pigeon with thyme polenta & seared foie gras; berry trifle with blood
orange sorbet. Details:* 10.30 pm; closed Sat L & Sun D.

Restaurant One-O-One
Sheraton Park Tower SW1 £68 ★★
William St, 101 Knightsbridge
7290 7101 4–1D
*"Pascal Proyart is a truly great chef", and his "magnificent"
cooking – with fish the mainstay of the menu – is beginning to
win the acclaim this slightly "stark" Knightsbridge dining room
deserves. / Sample dishes: salmon carpaccio; peppered fillet steak; strawberry
cheesecake. Value tip: set weekday L £39(FP). Details:* 10.30 pm.

Rhodes in the Square SW1 £53 ★
Dolphin Sq, Chichester St 7798 6767 1–4C
*"Superb" British cooking (not least some "historic" puds) is loudly
acclaimed at Gary R's polished dining room in a Pimlico
apartment complex; the "ocean liner" décor inspires slightly mixed
feelings, but the "well-spaced" tables are certainly well suited to
business. / Sample dishes: scallops & prawns with fennel marmalade; pork with
morels & sage cream; apple tart with blackberry ice cream. Value tip: set
weekday L £34(FP). Details:* 10 pm; closed Mon, Sat L & Sun.

The Ritz W1   £80   Ⓐ
150 Piccadilly   7493 8181   2–4C
"Frivolous, fantastic, a frothy folly" – this Louis XVI dining room is so famously "beautiful" that it's a shame that the cooking is so resolutely "average"; breakfast here, though, is "a fabulous way to start the day". / **Sample dishes:** *spiced potted lobster; monkfish with potato cakes & pancetta; prune & armagnac parfait.* **Details:** *www.theritzlondon.com; 11 pm; jacket & tie required.*

The River Café W6   £56
Thames Whf, Rainville Rd   7386 4200
"Joke" prices inspire ever-greater antipathy to this fantastically famous – and "noisy and crowded" – Hammersmith Italian; some do still find it "very special", but the complaints that it's "tired, pretentious and poor value" are now becoming deafening. / **Sample dishes:** *asparagus risotto; crispy Bresse pigeon; chocolate nemesis.* **Details:** *9.30 pm; closed Sun D.*

Rocket W1   £30   Ⓐ
4-6 Lancashire Ct   7629 2889   2–2B
"Hidden" it may be – in a mews, just off Bond Street – but the word's well and truly out about this "fun" and "busy" pizzeria; as "a cheap and entertaining venue", it has few rivals in the West End. / **Sample dishes:** *prosciutto & Parmesan salad; Gorgonzola & spinach pizza; strawberry cheesecake.* **Details:** *11.30 pm; closed Sun.*

Roussillon SW1   £51   ★★
16 St Barnabas St   7730 5550   4–2D
"At last, starting to get the reputation it deserves" – thanks to M. Gauthier's "fabulous" Gallic cooking, this Pimlico side street spot Is no longer a "secret"; even some fans, though, note a continuing "absence of buzz". / **Sample dishes:** *millefeuille of asparagus & morels; crunchy-skin sea bass with salsify in ham; blood orange tart.* **Details:** *www.roussillon.co.uk; 10.45 pm; closed Sat L & Sun; no smoking area.*

Royal China SW15   £30   ★★
3 Chelverton Rd   8788 0907   6–2B
"Excellent dim sum" is a highlight at this "reliable" Putney oriental; it's unrelated, except by history and '70s décor, to the larger group of the same name, but similar in its appeal. / **Details:** *11 pm; only Amex; need 7+ to book, Sun L.*

Royal China   £34   ★★
40 Baker St, W1   7487 4688   1–1A
13 Queensway, W2   7221 2535
68 Queen's Grove, NW8   7586 4280
30 Westferry Circus, E14   7719 0888
"There are long queues but it's worth the wait", for the "immaculate" lunchtime morsels at these "time-warp", '70s orientals – "London's Number 1 for dim sum"; the food is notably a cut-above at the older branches – Bayswater and Marylebone. / **Details:** *10.45 pm, Fri & Sat 11.30 pm.*

Rules WC2   £48   Ⓐ
35 Maiden Ln   7836 5314   3–3D
"Splendid" historic surroundings help make London's oldest restaurant (est. 1798) the hit you'd expect with foreign visitors (and popular for business, too); the English cooking – strong in beef and game – is "actually rather good". / **Sample dishes:** *Stilton & celeriac soup; rabbit casserole with broad beans & mustard mash; champagne sabayon.* **Details:** *www.rules.co.uk; 11.30 pm; no smoking.*

Rusticana W1 £29

27 Frith St   7439 8900   3–3A

*With its "quick, smiley and hands-on service" and its "unflagging good standards", this still little-known Soho pizza-and-pasta stop is an under-used central stand-by. / **Sample dishes:** wild mushroom bruschetta; mussell & king prawn risotto with tomato sauce; tiramisu. **Details:** 11.30 pm.*

Sabras NW10 £22 ★★

263 High Rd   8459 0340

*"Why have you left it out, it should be in!" – it was in fact a processing error which caused this "old-favourite" Indian café (in far-off Willesden Green) to be omitted last year; it offers "fabulous vegetarian food" and "friendly service". / **Details:** 10.30 pm; D only, closed Mon; no smoking area.*

St John EC1 £43 ★

26 St John St   7251 0848   5–1B

*"Robust flavours and offal" make this champion of "bold" British cooking a notable foodie destination; the setting in a former Smithfield smokehouse, however, strikes many as "stark" and "sterile". / **Sample dishes:** duck broth; roast quail with lentils & broad beans; blood orange jelly & shortbread. **Details:** www.stjohnrestaurant.co.uk; 11 pm; closed Sat L & Sun.*

St Johns N19 £32 A★

91 Junction Rd   7272 1587

*"A gastropub extraordinaire", is hailed by fans of the "large and very comfortable" dining room behind this "buzzy" Archway boozer; it wins high praise all-round, not least for its "really high-quality food". / **Sample dishes:** chicken liver terrine with chutney; grilled black bream; apple crumble. **Details:** 11 pm; closed Mon L; booking: max 10.*

Sakonis HA0 £18 ★★

129 Ealing Rd   8903 9601

*"There's not much in the way of décor", but this "real Indian hang-out" in Wembley makes up for it with an "almost overwhelming" variety of "excellent and tasty" dishes, and all at bargain prices. / **Details:** 9.30 pm; no Amex; no smoking.*

Sale e Pepe SW1 £38 A★

9-15 Pavilion Rd   7235 0098   4–1D

*This "wonderfully chaotic" Knightsbridge trattoria of long standing offers surprisingly "reliable" cooking; a few find it all a bit too much. / **Sample dishes:** beef carpaccio & Parmesan salad; veal chops with sautéed mushrooms & peppers; frozen tiramisu. **Details:** 11.30 pm; closed Sun.*

San Lorenzo SW3 £50 ✗

22 Beauchamp Pl   7584 1074   4–1C

*"Non-celebs are non-entities" at this undeservedly famous Knightsbridge trattoria, where "dreadful" food at "shocking" prices is delivered by "surly and disinterested" staff. / **Details:** 11.30 pm; closed Sun; no credit cards.*

Sarastro WC2 £33 A✗

126 Drury Ln   7836 0101   1–2D

*"Sod the food" (it's "awful" anyway) – this OTT-operatic Theatreland Turk is the "campest, craziest room in town". / **Sample dishes:** grilled sardines; kofte lamb meatballs with rice; cassata ice cream. **Details:** www.sarastro-restaurant.com; 11.30 pm.*

Sarkhel's SW18   £28   ★★

199 Replingham Rd   8870 1483   6–2B

Udit Sarkhel's "fabulous updates of classic dishes" (with "added interest from regional menus") make this unremarkable-looking Southfields curry house a well-known destination; it's "keeping up standards despite expansion". / **Details:** www.sarkhels.com; 10.30 pm, Fri & Sat 11 pm; closed Mon; no smoking area.

(Savoy Grill)
Savoy Hotel WC2   £75   𝔸

Strand   7420 2066   3–3D

"A great place to impress, that's perfect for business"; it's the "spacious", panelled setting and "old-world" service that maintain the standing of this celebrated power scene – the "well-executed" traditional fare is pretty "dull". / **Sample dishes:** seared tuna with coriander couscous; roast chicken with truffles & port sauce; apple & rhubarb crumble. **Value tip:** set pre-theatre menu £44(FP). **Details:** www.savoygroup.com; 10.30 pm; closed Sat L & Sun; jacket & tie required.

Scalini SW3   £47   𝔸

1-3 Walton St   7225 2301   4–2C

"You always leave with a smile", say fans of this ever-"buzzy" Italian near Harrods – it's "expensive", but "great fun if you like 'em packed and noisy". / **Sample dishes:** spaghetti with lobster; veal escalope with rosemary; tiramisu. **Details:** midnight.

Serafino W1   £37   ★

8 Mount St   7629 0544   2–3B

"Good-quality (if somewhat formulaic) dishes" and "attentive service" have proved a winning combination at this "reliable" Italian; it makes "a cheap stand-by", at least by Mayfair standards. / **Sample dishes:** grilled Italian cheeses with radiccio; veal with Parma ham & sage; tiramisu. **Details:** 10.45 pm; closed Sat L & Sun.

Seven Stars W12   £30   𝔸

243 Goldhawk Rd   8748 0229

A large Shepherd's Bush boozer that's been very stylishly converted (by some of the backers of the 'in'-crowd club, Soho House); its location – on a mini-roundabout – is hardly glamorous, but it draws a "lively" crowd nonetheless, and serves "reasonable" gastropub fare. / **Sample dishes:** seared scallops with pear purée; sea bass with roasted courgettes; pineapple tarte Tatin. **Details:** 10.15 pm; no Amex.

Shanghai E8   £23   𝔸

41 Kingsland High St   7254 2878

When visiting this "friendly" Dalston Chinese, ensure you "get one of the tiled booths at the front" – they retain the "beautiful" décor of the premises' former incarnation as a pie 'n' eel shop; the Sunday buffet is particularly good. / **Details:** 11 pm; no Amex.

J Sheekey WC2   £48   𝔸★★

28-32 St Martin's Ct   7240 2565   3–3B

"Absolutely first-class" fish and "discreetly efficient and attentive" service have completely re-energised this "intimate" and "unusually laid-out" Theatreland old-timer – it's now second only to its stablemate, The Ivy, in the sheer volume of feedback it generates. / **Sample dishes:** seared tuna; Dover sole with asparagus; spotted dick. **Value tip:** set Sun L £30(FP). **Details:** midnight.

sign up for the survey at www.hardens.com   69

Shogun W1 £50 ★★
Adam's Row 7493 1255 2–3A
"Excellent", "delicate" sushi and sashimi, as well as other "reliably delicious" dishes, again win praise for this top-notch Mayfair Japanese; some like the "weird" basement setting — others find it "a bit dark" and "in need of redecoration". / **Details:** 11 pm; D only, closed Mon; no Switch.

Signor Sassi SW1 £48 Ⓐ
14 Knightsbridge Grn 7584 2277 4–1D
"Madcap" service and "surprisingly good food" have made this "noisy, but great fun" Knightsbridge trattoria of long standing "a favourite since the day it opened". / **Sample dishes:** avocado & crab baked in lobster sauce; beef, bacon & mushrooms in red wine sauce; tiramisu. **Details:** 11.30 pm; closed Sun.

Simpson's Tavern EC3 £23 Ⓐ
38 1/2 Cornhill 7626 9985 5–2C
They've served "simple, good-quality lunches for over 250 years" at this "great British pit stop" in a Dickensian City alleyway — "an absolute time-warp classic". / **Details:** 3 pm; L only, closed Sat & Sun; no booking.

Sketch W1
9 Conduit St 0870 777 4488 2–2C
If it half lives up to its hype, this autumn-2002 Mayfair newcomer — a collaboration between Parisian super-chef Pierre Gagnaire and Momo-founder Mourad Mazouz — will be one of the biggest openings of recent years; at press time details are vague, but both a mega-pricey fine dining room and a brasserie are promised.

(Dining Room)
Smiths of Smithfield EC1 £32 Ⓐ
67-77 Charterhouse St 7251 7997 5–1A
The "stylish", "lively" and "very noisy" second-floor brasserie of this "upbeat" Manhattan-style Smithfield complex receives a huge amount of commentary; its steak and simple grill dishes are "solid", if a touch "uninspiring". / **Sample dishes:** Thai-style omelette with tiger prawns; roast Welsh black beef with ratatouille; chocolate fondant with strawberry ice cream. **Details:** www.smithsofsmithfield.co.uk; 10.45 pm; closed Sat L & Sun.

(Top Floor)
Smiths of Smithfield EC1 £48 Ⓐ★
67-77 Charterhouse St 7251 7950 5–1A
The "spacious" rooftop fine-dining room of this three-floor warehouse complex outshines those below and — with its "fantastic views" — it's "a great place to make clients feel well treated"; "superlative steaks" — served by "fast" and "discreet" staff — are the menu mainstay. / **Sample dishes:** lobster omelette with star anise; roast Old Spot pork with crackling & apple sauce; Sauternes custard with armagnac prunes. **Details:** www.smithsofsmithfield.co.uk; 11 pm; closed Sat L (café open all day).

Sonny's SW13 £38 Ⓐ★
94 Church Rd 8748 0393 6–1A
With its "inventive" menu, its "friendly" service and its "lively" atmosphere, Barnes's "very good local restaurant" of many years' standing is "always a winner". / **Sample dishes:** duck liver parfait with sweet pickle; salmon with red lentils & samphire; apple & sultana tart. **Details:** 11 pm; closed Sun D.

Sotheby's Café W1 £37 A★
34 New Bond St   7293 5077   2–2C
"Unfailingly good" light dishes, "excellent" service and a "handy" location – no wonder you "need to book ahead" for the "classy", if "cramped", café of the Mayfair auctioneers; also a "tea oasis".
/ **Sample dishes:** *roast smoked salmon with horseradish cream; pan-fried scallop & lentil salad with salas verde; dark chocolate filo pastry with white chocolate sauce.* **Details:** *L only, closed Sat & Sun; no smoking.*

So.uk SW4 £32 A
165 Clapham High St   7622 4004   6–2D
"Fab", "funky" Clapham Moroccan full of "Eastern promise"; it makes a "fun place for drinks and nibbles" – the more substantial food is "fairly expensive" for what you get.
/ **Details:** *9.45 pm; closed weekday L; no booking.*

Souk WC2 £26 A
27 Litchfield St   7240 1796   3–3B
A "low-lit and exotic interior" (complete with "cushions and belly-dancing") and modest prices makes this "fun" but "cramped" Moroccan, near The Ivy, a top budget party venue; the food "could be tastier", though, and the odd service mishap is not unknown. / **Details:** *11.30 pm.*

Soulard N1 £30 A★
113 Mortimer Rd   7254 1314
As a host, "Philippe is second to none", and his "cosy" and "wonderful" bistro on the Islington/Hackney fringe has a huge local following, not least for its "simple French food, done well".
/ **Sample dishes:** *grilled goats cheese with honey; smoed haddock with saffron sauce; crème brûlée.* **Details:** *10 pm; D only, closed Mon & Sun; no Amex.*

Sporting Page SW10 £29 A
6 Camera Pl   7349 0455   4–3B
This superior Chelsea boozer enjoys a tranquil backstreet location; despite sometimes "erratic" food, it retains a younger local fan club. / **Sample dishes:** *Welsh rarebit with crispy bacon; Cumberland sausages with grain mustard mash; syrup sponge pudding.* **Details:** *www.frontpagepubs.com; 10 pm; closed Sat D & Sun D.*

Spread Eagle SE10 £25 A
2 Stockwell St   8853 2333
It looks like a tourist-trap, so it's a surprise to find that this "old and woody", "converted Greenwich tavern" is capable of some "beautifully presented" (and surprisingly up-to-date) Gallic cooking. / **Sample dishes:** *deep-fried oysters & mussels; rabbit stuffed with herbs & black pudding; spiced pear tart with caramel sauce.* **Details:** *www.spreadeagle.org; 10.30 pm; closed Sun D.*

The Square W1 £72 ★
6-10 Bruton St   7495 7100   2–2C
Phillip Howard's accomplished cooking at this grand Mayfair dining room "continues to impress"; some find the atmosphere "rather like a bank", though, and service can be "way over the top" – "I did not appreciate the waiter trying to sell me Ch. Pétrus…" / **Sample dishes:** *pea & ham soup with morels; sea bass with risotto; blood orange soufflé with chocolate ice cream.* **Value tip:** *set weekday L £38(FP).* **Details:** *www.squarerestaurant.com; 10.45 pm; closed Sat L & Sun L.*

Sree Krishna SW17 £19 ★★
192-194 Tooting High St   8672 4250   6–2D
"There's never a bad meal" at this "unpretentious" Tooting spot, which is "loved by all devotees of south Indian cuisine", and "always crowded". / **Details:** *www.sreekrishna.co.uk; 10.45 pm.*

Star of India SW5　　　　　　　　**£36**　　★★
154 Old Brompton Rd　7373 2901　4–2B
This "renaissance Indian" – actually one of the country's oldest curry houses – delivers "stimulating" dishes that are "surprisingly light and very good"; the "rich" décor of its Earl's Court premises isn't everyone's cup of chai. / **Details:** www.starofindia.co.uk; 11.45 pm.

The Stepping Stone SW8　　　　**£37**　　Ⓐ★★
123 Queenstown Rd　7622 0555　6–1C
"Always a delight", this "stylish" Battersea fixture is "a great neighbourhood restaurant" – staff are "charming" and the cooking can be "quite stunningly good". / **Sample dishes:** smoked salmon & balsamic grapes; roast duck with chorizo & chickpeas; orange & bay leaf pannacotta. **Details:** 11 pm, Mon 10.30 pm; closed Sat L & Sun D; no Amex; no smoking area.

Stratford's W8　　　　　　　　**£37**　　★
7 Stratford Rd　7937 6388　4–2A
An impressively "consistent" traditional fish restaurant in a Kensington backwater – "it does nothing new or exciting, but the food is good nonetheless". / **Sample dishes:** grilled calamari; swordfish with roasted garlic; chocolate mousse. **Value tip:** set pre-theatre menu £23(FP). **Details:** www.stratfords-restaurant.com; 11 pm, 11.30 Thu-Sat.

The Sugar Club W1　　　　　　**£45**　　★
21 Warwick St　7437 7776　2–2D
"A challenging range" of "innovative" and "excellently-executed" fusion dishes makes this Spartan but "buzzy" venture, off Regent Street, the "favourite trendy restaurant" for many reporters. / **Sample dishes:** Indian prawn fishcakes with mango; venison with apple & pistachio pancakes; banoffi pie with galangal sorbet. **Details:** www.thesugarclub.co.uk; 11 pm; no smoking area.

Sugar Hut SW6　　　　　　　　**£41**　　Ⓐ
374 North End Rd　7386 8950　4–3A
Sultry décor helps create a special, very romantic atmosphere at this dimly-lit Fulham oriental newcomer; service is efficient and welcoming, and the cooking is very competent – we agree with the early reporter, though, who found it "overpriced". / **Details:** www.sugarhutfulham.com; 11.30 pm; D only.

Suntory SW1　　　　　　　　　**£70**
72 St James's St　7409 0201　2–4D
Some feel that punishing prices and a "dreadful" atmosphere make this St James's veteran "fit only for visiting Japanese businessmen"; the luxurious cuisine is "of a consistently good standard", though, and supporters feel it's "expensive, but worth it". / **Value tip:** set Sun L £38(FP). **Details:** 10 pm.

Sushi-Say NW2　　　　　　　　**£31**　　★
33b Walm Ln　8459 7512
"It's worth the drive", says a (Chelsea) fan of this "simple, family-run Japanese", in the culinary wastelands of Willesden Green; it's "a touch pricey" for a local, but then "fresh" and "fantastic" sushi rarely comes cheap. / **Sample dishes:** clear soup with picked vegetables; salmon, tuna & eel sushi; ice cream. **Value tip:** set weekday L £16(FP). **Details:** 10.30 pm; closed Mon, Tue-Fri D only, Sat & Sun open L & D; no smoking area.

Sweetings EC4   £38   A ★

39 Queen Victoria St   7248 3062   5–3B

"An unbeatable relic of a bygone age"; this "eccentric" Victorian
City seafood parlour – most famous for its "great grilled fish" –
has survived an almost seamless recent change of ownership,
but now "they even take credit cards!" / **Sample dishes:** crab cocktail;
deep-fried halibut & chips; baked jam sponge. **Details:** L only, closed Sat & Sun;
no booking.

Talad Thai SW15   £20   ★ ★

320 Upper Richmond Rd   8789 8084   6–2A

"You can't beat the prices" – or the "starburst" flavours – of the
"utterly authentic" cooking at this "very basic" canteen, which is
part of a Thai supermarket in Putney. / **Details:** 10 pm; no credit cards;
no smoking; no booking.

Tamarind W1   £44   A ★ ★

20 Queen St   7629 3561   2–3B

"Eye-opening" cuisine "in a different class" made this 'nouvelle
Indian' in Mayfair – with its "attentive" service and
"sophisticated" setting – reporters' best in town; it lost its two top
chefs in the summer of 2002, though – let's hope it keeps up
standards. / **Sample dishes:** prawn & scallop tandoori with sour grapes; curried
lamb shank with paratha bread; mango kulfi.
Details: www.tamarindrestaurant.com; 11.15 pm; closed Sat L.

Tandoori Lane SW6   £24   ★

131a Munster Rd   7371 0440   6–1B

Superior curries ("well-spiced, and not run-of-the-mill") and
service that's "very keen to please" make it worth seeking out this
"cramped" Fulham subcontinental. / **Details:** 11 pm; no Amex.

Tartine SW3   £29   A

114 Draycott Ave   7589 4981   4–2C

"Light meals beautifully presented in a chic setting" have won
instant acclaim for this "smart and affordable" concept – a diner
serving 'posh toasties', with bread from the celebrated baker
Poilâne. / **Sample dishes:** Caesar salad; tartine with sardines & tomato salsa;
chocolate fondant. **Details:** www.tartine.co.uk; 11 pm.

Tartuf   £19   ★

88 Upper St, N1   7288 0954
169 Clapham High St, SW4   7622 8169   6–2D

"Excellent" service and "interesting Alsatian pizzas" (technically
speaking, Flammkuchen) win a wide following for these
"consistent" and "fun" snackeries in Islington and, now, Clapham.
/ **Sample dishes:** no starters; smoked ham & cheese tarte flambée; crème brûlée.
Details: midnight; no Amex.

Tas   £22   A ★

33 The Cut, SE1   7928 2111   5–4A
72 Borough High St, SE1   7403 7200   5–4C

They may be "a bit noisy when full (ie always)", but that does
little to dent enthusiasm for this amazingly popular South Bank
Turkish duo; service is "prompt", and the "hearty" fare is "great",
"inexpensive" and "always reliable". / **Details:** 11.30 pm.

sign up for the survey at www.hardens.com

(Level 7 Café)
Tate Modern SE1 £32 🄰
Bankside 7401 5020 5–3B
"Fabulous views of the wobbly bridge and St Paul's" are the
star attraction at this seventh-floor "canteen" of the world's
most-visited modern art museum – arrive early or expect a big
queue; simple fare (burgers, pasta and so on) is tolerably well
*executed. / **Sample dishes:** beetroot-cured salmon with soda bread; lamb steak*
with soft Parmesan polenta; Indian mango & lime ice cream.
***Details:** www.tate.org.uk; 5.30 pm, Fri & Sat 9 pm; L only, except Fri & Sat open*
L & D; no smoking.

Tatsuso EC2 £68 ★
32 Broadgate Circle 7638 5863 5–2D
"Outstanding-quality food" – both in the ground-floor teppan-yaki
and the basement restaurant (which serves some "excellent
sushi") – wins continued praise for this "impressive" City oriental;
it's the top-rated Japanese in town, but prices can seem
*"ridiculous, even on expenses". / **Details:** 9.45 pm; closed Sat & Sun;*
no smoking area.

Teca W1 £48 ★★
54 Brooks Mews 7495 4774 2–2B
"Outstanding" north Italian cuisine, a "tremendous" wine list and
"excellent" service are winning ever-greater recognition for this
"stylish" and "bustling" outfit, off Bond Street; gripes include
a somewhat elusive atmosphere, and portions which can be
*"annoyingly small". / **Sample dishes:** foie gras terrine with cherry bread;*
*bream with red pepper sauce & fried basil; tiramisu. **Details:** 10.30 pm; closed Sun.*

Tentazioni SE1 £43 ★★
2 Mill St 7237 1100
"If it was in W1, there would be queues around the block", say
fans of this "hidden gem", near Tower Bridge, where "welcoming"
staff serve "authentic northern Italian cooking" that's among the
best in town; the only real criticism is that "the place needs more
*buzz". / **Sample dishes:** gnocchi with tomatoes & smoked ricotta; pan-fried*
calves liver with aubergine purée; Gorgonzola with figs & walnuts.
***Details:** www.tentazioni.co.uk; 11 pm; closed Mon L, Sat L & Sun.*

The Tenth
Royal Garden Hotel W8 £52 🄰
Kensington High St 7361 1910 4–1A
Considering it has "remarkable" park views ("from the window
seats"), the surprise is how "competent" the cooking is at this
elevated Kensington dining room, which comes recommended for
*both business and romance. / **Sample dishes:** quail with black truffles;*
monkfish, tiger prawn & coconut broth with rice; chocolate pudding with Bailey's ice
*cream. **Details:** www.royalgardenhotel.co.uk; 10.45 pm; closed Sat L & Sun;*
no smoking area.

The Terrace W8 £43 🄰
33c Holland St 7937 3224 4–1A
This "pretty little local restaurant", in a Kensington backwater,
offers "friendly" service and some "delicious, if not inexpensive"
cooking; the "cosy" interior is "cramped", but there's a "lovely"
*summer terrace. / **Sample dishes:** clam risotto with salmon carpaccio; chicken*
with lemon & Burrata cheese; sweet cannelloni with coffee ice cream.
***Details:** 10.30 pm.*

Thai Bistro W4 £26 ★
99 Chiswick High Rd 8995 5774
"It's not a place to relax", but this "noisy and cramped" Chiswick "canteen" reliably offers "authentic and tasty" Thai grub.
/ **Details:** 11 pm; closed Tue L & Thu L; no Amex; no smoking.

Thailand SE14 £28 ★★
15 Lewisham Way 8691 4040
"Too busy, but unique" – this "very small", family-run Lewisham destination retains its name for "Thai food better than many places in Thailand!" / **Value tip:** set weekday L £16(FP). **Details:** 11 pm; closed Mon, Sat L & Sun L; no Amex; no smoking.

3 Monkeys SE24 £36 🇦 ★
136-140 Herne Hill 7738 5500
An "original" menu of "posh Indian" nosh "gets the palate going" at this "subcontinental with a twist"; its modernistic décor is "pretty swanky, for Herne Hill". / **Details:** www.3monkeysrestaurant.com; 11 pm; D only; smoking in bar only.

Thyme SW4 £37 ★★
14 Clapham Park Rd 7627 2468 6–2D
"Awesome-value" Gallic cooking has won instant acclaim for this Clapham newcomer (on the obscure site that was Moxon's, RIP); there's no denying, though, that the "interesting concept" of presenting all dishes tapas-style "just doesn't quite work" for some people. / **Sample dishes:** cauliflower soup with truffle butter; peppered beef fillet with red onion confit; honeycomb nougat glacé. **Details:** www.thymeandspace.com; 10.30 pm; closed Sun; no smoking area; booking: max 8.

Timo W8 £30 ★
343 Kensington High St 7603 3888
"Excellent-value" prices for very competent cooking ("wonderful pasta", especially) have made this well-run Italian newcomer "a great addition to W8"; if the styling was not so forgettable, this could be a notable destination. / **Sample dishes:** ham, celeriac & rocket salad; tomato-crusted monkfish with Sardinian couscous; saffron pannacotta with honey & apple sauce. **Details:** 11 pm; booking: max 8.

Toto's SW1 £48 🇦 ★
Lennox Gardens Mews 7589 0075 4–2C
It's "not well-known" (especially given its handy Knightsbridge location), but for its fans this "grand" Italian is "the best in London", thanks in particular to its "lovely", "spacious" setting and "wonderful" service. / **Sample dishes:** lamb carpaccio; monkfish with artichokes & pesto; mango mousse. **Details:** 11 pm.

The Trafalgar Tavern SE10 £28 🇦
Park Row 8858 2437
"The views over the Thames are worth paying for", at this grand and "beautiful" Greenwich tavern; the pub grub is only OK.
/ **Details:** www.trafalgartavern.co.uk; 9 pm; closed Mon D & Sun D; no Amex; no booking at weekends.

Les Trois Garçons E1 £55 🇦
1 Club Row 7613 1924
"Fabulously glamorous" décor – complete with "bejewelled stuffed animals" – makes this "bizarre" East Ender quite a "wow" experience; shame about the "ordinary" cooking and the increasingly "abrupt" service, though, and prices which are becoming seriously off-putting. / **Sample dishes:** snails in garlic butter; steak with red wine jus and greens; French cheese platter.
Details: www.lestroisgarcons.com; 10 pm, Thu-Sat 10.30 pm; D only, closed Sun.

sign up for the survey at www.hardens.com

La Trompette W4 £45   A★★
5-7 Devonshire Rd
8747 1836

Nigel Platts-Martin's "very classy" neighbourhood yearling can come as something of "a surprise" in Chiswick; "top-quality" French cooking at "stunning-value" prices, "stimulating wines" and "excellent staff" make it a worthy stablemate to the celebrated Chez Bruce. / Sample dishes: grilled sardine tart with gremolata; duck with foie gras & madeira sauce; chocolate profiteroles. Details: 11 pm; smoking discouraged; booking: max 6.

Troubadour SW5   £24   A
265 Old Brompton Rd   7370 1434   4–3A

This "eccentric" Earl's Court coffee shop may have "lost some intimacy" now it's expanded, but most reporters are still enraptured by its "Bohemian" charm; it's as a breakfast and all-day hang-out that it excels – evenings aren't as good. / Sample dishes: crab & melon salad; bangers & mash; crème brûlée. Details: 11 pm; no Amex.

Ubon E14   £58   ★★
34 Westferry Circus   7719 7800

"Stunning textures, inspired flavours, and the best sushi ever" – some claim Nobu's Canary Wharf cousin is "actually better than the original"; it doesn't have Mayfair's atmosphere, of course, but "superb views" help overcome its "office block" location. / Sample dishes: toro tartare with caviar; rock shrimp donburi (one-pot rice dish); fresh fruit Bento box. Details: 10.15 pm; closed Sat L & Sun; no smoking area.

Uli W11   £23   ★
16 All Saints Rd   7727 7511

"The cheerful host always gives a warm welcome" at this "tiny", but increasingly popular, Notting Hill eatery; it serves "an interesting range of oriental dishes" in a "cramped but atmospheric" setting. / Details: www.uli-oriental.co.uk; 11 pm; D only, except Sun open L & D; no Amex.

The Vale W9   £28
99 Chippenham Rd   7266 0990

"Consistent standards" win many admirers for this "imaginative" Maida Hill local; "very friendly" service is a highlight. / Sample dishes: spicy lamb koftes with minted yoghurt; char-grilled squid with tomato risotto; buttermilk pudding. Details: 11 pm; closed Mon L, Sat L & Sun D; no Amex; no smoking area.

Vama SW10   £38   A★★
438 King's Rd   7351 4118   4–3B

"Refined", "distinctive" and "delightful" cooking makes for "a very different experience" at this "high-class" World's End Indian, whose fame continues to grow. / Value tip: set weekday L £19(FP). Details: www.vama.co.uk; 11 pm.

Veeraswamy W1   £38   A★
Victory House, 99 Regent St   7734 1401   2–3D

Even traditionalists think London's oldest Indian restaurant "was much improved" by its late-'90s "minimalist" refurbishment; it now offers "stylish" dishes in a "light and airy setting". / Details: www.realindianfood.com; 11.30 pm.

for updates visit www.hardens.com

Vegia Zena NW1 £34 ★
17 Princess Rd   7483 0192
Though it's been "hit-and-miss" over the years, the "good Genoese cooking" is back "on top form" at this "homely" ("cramped") Primrose Hill local; "the garden is bliss on a summer night".
/ **Sample dishes:** black tagliatelle with scallops & broccoli; grilled Argentinean beef with sautéed leeks; ice cream with hot espresso. **Value tip:** set weekday L £16(FP).
Details: www.vegiazena.com; 11 pm.

Vertigo
Tower 42 EC2 £60 🅐
Old Broad St   7877 7842   5–2C
"It's good for views of the City, and as a venue for meeting clients", so hardly surprising that the former NatWest Tower's 42nd-floor bar offers a menu which is as "incidental" as it is "hideously expensive". / **Sample dishes:** scallop & pancetta brochettes; Cajun beef fajitas; pannacotta with passionfruit & mango.
Details: www.vertigo42.co.uk; 9.15 pm; closed Sat & Sun; booking essential.

Vijay NW6 £20 ★★
49 Willesden Ln   7328 1087
"Excellent for more than 20 years"; this Kilburn local is "a real find" for new customers, thanks to its "cheap" but "outstanding" south Indian food, and service that's "charming, despite being really busy". / **Details:** www.vijayindia.com; 10.45 pm, Fri & Sat 11.45 pm; no smoking area.

Vong SW1 £62 ★
Wilton Pl   7235 1010   4–1D
It never hits the headlines these days, but this "original" Knightsbridge French/Thai establishment – which has a twin in NYC – continues to deliver "fabulous" fusion cooking to a "chic" crowd; as ever, some find the ambience rather "flat".
/ **Sample dishes:** chilled tomato, cucumber & watermelon soup; steak with gingered mushrooms & soy caramel sauce; Valrhona chocolate cake. **Value tip:** set pre-theatre menu £42(FP). **Details:** www.jean-georges.com; 11.30 pm; closed Sun L; no smoking area.

Vrisaki N22 £26 ★
73 Myddleton Rd   8889 8760
"Unbelievable amounts" of "excellent mezze" make this "fun" institution – in a quiet Bounds Green backwater – "London's best Greek by far", for some reporters. / **Sample dishes:** smoked trout & pitta bread; moussaka; Greek yoghurt with honey. **Details:** midnight; closed Sun.

Wapping Food E1 £39 🅐
Wapping Pumping Hs, Wapping Wall   7680 2080
"The exciting setting" can make for a "memorable" meal at this converted East End pumping station; it offers "simple, fresh modern British cooking" and an "excellent range of Australian wines"; a "great Sunday brunch" is a further highlight.
/ **Sample dishes:** pork with Manchego cheese & sherry vinegar; fillet steak with leeks & pancetta; lavender pannacotta. **Details:** 10.30 pm; closed Sun D.

The Waterway W9 £31 🅐
54 Formosa St   7266 3557
This ultra-sleek, new bar/restaurant in Little Venice – improbably converted from a hellish old boozer – has a fantastic canalside terrace; on our early (June 2002) visit, the attractions of the good, light dishes were undercut by high prices and service that was slow – so, so slow. / **Sample dishes:** duck foie gras with caramelised pears; fillet steak with truffle oil mash; capuccino & praline brûlée. **Details:** 10.45 pm; no Amex; booking: max 12.

sign up for the survey at www.hardens.com

The Well EC1 £32 A ★
180 St John St   7251 9363   5–1A
Good standards across the board (not least the "short, but well executed" menu) are winning a strong local following for this "relaxed" modern wine bar on a Clerkenwell corner site – "it's hard to get a table if you don't book". / **Sample dishes:** sweet potato, chilli & ginger soup; roast guinea fowl with lemon & herb risotto; cranberry crème brûlée. **Details:** www.downthewell.com; 10.30 pm.

The Westbourne W2 £31 A
101 Westbourne Park Villas   7221 1332
"There's a great atmosphere, but not enough room", at this trendy and "overcrowded" Bayswater boozer, which is "best in summer", if you can nab a seat on the terrace; the food's "not bad", but the service is "slow" and "disinterested". / **Sample dishes:** roast cauliflower soup with Parmesan; confit duck with sage mash & bacon; chocolate tart. **Details:** 10 pm; closed Mon L; need 4+ to book.

The White Horse TW10 £29
Worple Way   8940 2418
"A good gastropub, in the back streets of Richmond"; it's a "busy" (and fashionably "shabby") place, but its "Anglo-Med" cooking is "reliable" and "well done". / **Sample dishes:** smoked chicken salad with rocket & olive tapenade; pan-fried salmon with potato & swede mash; chocolate bread & butter pudding. **Details:** 9.45 pm; no smoking area.

The White House SW4 £29 A
65 Clapham Park Rd   7498 3388   6–2D
The "hip and happening" atmosphere at this Clapham bar/nightclub is easily its best feature, so it's no great surprise that some find the tapas-style scoff "patchy" and "overpriced". / **Sample dishes:** straw mushroom spring rolls with chilli sauce; roast lamb with leek & potato cakes; blueberry ice cream crumble. **Details:** www.thewhitehouselondon.co.uk; 11 pm; D only.

William IV NW10 £29 A ★
786 Harrow Rd   8969 5944
"Everything a gastropub should be" – this "cool" and "spacious" Kensal Green "hang-out" offers "good-value food", "great beer" and "a wonderful beer garden". / **Sample dishes:** smoked duck & Asian vegetable salad; steamed trout with salsa verde; Greek yoghurt with fruit & honey. **Value tip:** set weekday L £15(FP). **Details:** www.william-iv.co.uk; 10.30 pm, Fri & Sat 11 pm.

Willie Gunn SW18 £32 A
422 Garratt Ln   8946 7773   6–2B
"A gem in the Earlsfield desert" – this "simple", "honest" bar/restaurant has a huge fan club locally for its "reliable and easy dining". / **Sample dishes:** duck spring rolls with spiced plum sauce; Lincolnshire sausages with mash & onion gravy; banoffi glacé with baked bananas. **Details:** 11 pm.

Wiltons SW1 £63 A ★
55 Jermyn St   7629 9955   2–3C
It may appear "wonderfully fossilised", but this "club-like" St James's bastion is quietly raising its game; Jerome Ponchelle's arrival from The Connaught seems likely only to add lustre to the "quintessentially English" menu, on which seafood of "incomparable quality" is a highlight. / **Sample dishes:** duck, pork & foie gras terrine; braised Scottish turbot with champagne sauce; raspberry crème brûlée. **Value tip:** set Sun L £43(FP). **Details:** www.wiltons.co.uk; 10.30 pm; closed Sun D; jacket & tie required.

Windows on the World
Park Lane Hilton Hotel W1   **£80**   𝔸 ✗
22 Park Ln   7208 4021   2–4A
"Absolutely no redeeming features except the view" – there's little
but dismay about the "appalling" food, "dreadful" service and
"crazy" prices at this 24th-floor Mayfair dining room.
/ **Sample dishes:** chicken soup with curry glaze; roast lamb with coconut rice &
citrus sauce; cherry clafoutis. **Value tip:** set weekday L £54(FP).
Details: 10.30 pm, Fri & Sat 11.30 pm; closed Sat L & Sun D; jacket & tie
required at D; no smoking at breakfast.

Windsor Castle W8   **£25**   𝔸
114 Campden Hill Rd   7243 9551
A "lovely", "leafy" garden is arguably the lead attraction of this
"charming" Kensington boozer, though its "Dickensian" interior is
also particularly "cosy" and characterful; it serves "simple food,
properly done". / **Sample dishes:** oysters; steak & ale pie; chocolate sponge
pudding. **Details:** www.windsor-castle-pub.co.uk; 9.30 pm; no smoking area at L;
no booking.

The Wine Library EC3   **£17**   𝔸
43 Trinity Sq   7481 0415   5–3D
"Brilliant wine is the focus" – "you pick your own bottle and just
pay retail plus corkage" – at these "cramped" but atmospheric
City vaults; the food is a buffet of "simple pâté and cheese";
book ahead. / **Sample dishes:** liver pâté & toast; quiche lorraine & salad; fresh
fruit. **Details:** 8 pm; L & early evening only, closed Sat & Sun.

Wódka W8   **£37**   𝔸
12 St Alban's Grove   7937 6513   4–1B
"The authentic Polish fare fills you up" – a necessity if you're to
take full advantage of the "fantastic list of vodkas" at this
"consistent" and "fun" Kensington fixture. / **Sample dishes:** herrings
with apple & dill cucumber; cabbage stuffed with pork & wild rice; white chocolate
& poppyseed cheesecake. **Value tip:** set weekday L £20(FP).
Details: www.wodka.co.uk; 11.15 pm; closed Sat L & Sun L.

Yming W1   **£28**   𝔸 ★★
35-36 Greek St   7734 2721   3–2A
With its "masterful" and "unusual" cooking, its "polite", "genial"
service and its "calm" interior, this long-established Soho Chinese
couldn't be much further from the stereotype prevalent in nearby
Chinatown; it is winning ever-wider recognition.
/ **Details:** www.yming.com; 11.45 pm; closed Sun.

Yoshino W1   **£34**   ★★
3 Piccadilly Pl   7287 6622   2–3D
"A hidden gem in the centre of town" – this small, "quiet" and
"completely authentic" Japanese outfit, just off Piccadilly, has
"warm and professional" service, and provides "perfect sushi"
(and sashimi). / **Details:** 10 pm; closed Sun; no smoking.

Zafferano SW1   **£48**   𝔸 ★★
15 Lowndes St   7235 5800   4–1D
"Magnificent" Italian cooking – "the best in town" – and
"genuinely friendly and courteous" service wins rave reviews for
this "lively" Belgravian; "pity about the closeness of the tables".
/ **Sample dishes:** saffon risotto; monkfish with walnuts & caper sauce; figs with
mint sorbet. **Details:** 11 pm.

sign up for the survey at www.hardens.com   79

Zaika W8 £44 ★★
1 Kensington High St 7795 6533 4–1A
"Inspired" and "subtle" dishes still make this "chic" Kensington Indian one of London's very best; reporters "preferred the old location", though – the new one is rather "boring", and service isn't yet back up to the previous (very high) level.
/ **Sample dishes:** tamarind chicken with milk fritters; crab & spiced scallops with Indian risotto; deep-fried stuffed dates. **Details:** www.cuisine-collection.co.uk; 10.45 pm; closed Sat L.

Zaika Bazaar SW3 £28 Ⓐ★
2a Pond Pl 7584 6655 4–2C
"Relatively undiscovered", this offshoot of one of London's top subcontinentals serves up a tapas-style menu in a "Bombay-hip" Brompton Cross basement; service is erratic. / **Sample dishes:** tandoori broccoli & cauliflower; lamb with cinnamon & cloves; cardamom rice pudding. **Details:** www.cuisine-collection.co.uk; 10.45 pm; D only, closed Sun.

Zamzama NW1 £20 Ⓐ
161-163 Drummond St 7387 6699
It's hard to imagine anything less in keeping with its neighbours than this high-tech newcomer in Euston's Little India; on our early-days (Feb 2002) visit, the cooking was rather less cutting-edge than the décor. / **Details:** www.zamzama.co.uk; 11.30 pm; closed Sat L.

Ziani SW3 £36 Ⓐ★
45-47 Radnor Walk 7352 2698 4–3C
"Great fun, but bring your ear-plugs", say fans of this "friendly" Chelsea backstreet trattoria, whose "simple" fare – including an "excellent Sunday lunch" – is consistently praised.
/ **Sample dishes:** scallop & rocket salad; macaroni with wild boar sausage & aubergine; pannacotta. **Value tip:** set Sun L £21(FP). **Details:** 11.30 pm.

Zilli W11 £39 ★
210 Kensington Park Rd 7792 1066
Fans say you get "the best pasta" – and in "large portions", too – at this "fun" Notting Hill Italian, where fish dishes are a speciality; it's "not one for claustrophobics", though. / **Sample dishes:** tuna carpaccio with lime dressing; Italian sausages with garlic mash & red onion gravy; pannacotta with caramel sauce. **Details:** www.zillialdo.com; 11.30 pm.

Zuma SW7 £59 Ⓐ
5 Raphael St 7584 1010 4–1C
Gossip columns say it's a smash hit, but our June 2002 visit to this new Knightsbridge Japanese (on the former site of the Chicago Rib Shack, RIP) left us in two minds – the food's good (sushi was excellent) and the setting's chic, but it's a pricey place, and the overall experience was more slick than it was memorable. / **Details:** www.zumarestaurant.com; 10.45 pm.

LONDON
AREA OVERVIEWS

CENTRAL

Soho, Covent Garden & Bloomsbury
(Parts of W1, all WC2 and WC1)

£70+	Lindsay House	*British, Modern*	𝔸
	Savoy Hotel (Grill)	*British, Traditional*	𝔸
£60+	Asia de Cuba	*East/West*	-
£50+	Indigo	*British, Modern*	𝔸★
	The Criterion Grill	*French*	𝔸
	Opium	*Vietnamese*	𝔸
£40+	Alastair Little	*British, Modern*	★★
	Bank Aldwych	*"*	-
	The Ivy	*"*	𝔸★
	Adam Street	*"*	𝔸
	Rules	*British, Traditional*	𝔸
	L'Escargot	*French*	𝔸★
	Incognico	*"*	★
	The Sugar Club	*East/West*	★
	J Sheekey	*Fish & seafood*	𝔸★★
£35+	Aurora	*British, Modern*	𝔸
	The Portrait	*"*	𝔸
	L'Estaminet	*French*	𝔸★
	French House	*"*	𝔸★
	Mon Plaisir	*"*	
	Bohème Kitchen	*International*	𝔸
	Joe Allen	*American*	𝔸
£30+	British Museum	*British, Modern*	𝔸
	The Langley	*British, Traditional*	𝔸
	Café Bohème	*French*	𝔸
	Sarastro	*International*	𝔸
	Fung Shing	*Chinese*	★★
	Malabar Junction	*Indian*	𝔸★
	Ophim	*"*	★
	Chiang Mai	*Thai*	★★
£25+	Andrew Edmunds	*British, Modern*	𝔸★
	The Perseverance	*"*	-
	Aperitivo	*Italian*	𝔸
	Rusticana	*"*	-
	North Sea Fish	*Fish & chips*	★
	Souk	*North African*	𝔸
	Yming	*Chinese*	𝔸★★
	Chowki	*Indian*	★★
	Itsu	*Japanese*	𝔸★
	Abeno	*"*	★
£20+	Gordon's Wine Bar	*International*	𝔸
	Busaba Eathai	*Thai*	𝔸★
£15+	Food for Thought	*Vegetarian*	★
	Kulu Kulu	*Japanese*	★★
£10+	Paul	*Sandwiches, cakes, etc*	𝔸★
	Bar Italia	*Sandwiches, cakes, etc*	𝔸
£5+	Maison Bertaux	*Sandwiches, cakes, etc*	𝔸★

Mayfair & St James's (Parts of W1 and SW1)

£90+	Le Gavroche	*French*	𝔸★★
£80+	The Ritz	*French*	𝔸
	Windows on the World	*"*	𝔸
£70+	Pétrus	*French*	★★
	The Square	*"*	★
	G Ramsay at Claridges	*"*	-
	Dorchester, Oriental	*Chinese*	-
	Suntory	*Japanese*	-
£60+	Wiltons	*British, Traditional*	𝔸★
	Dorchester Grill	*"*	𝔸
	1837	*French*	𝔸★★
	L'Oranger	*"*	𝔸★
£50+	Rhodes in the Square	*British, Modern*	★
	Deca	*French*	𝔸★
	Mirabelle	*"*	𝔸★
	Nobu	*East/West*	𝔸★★
	Hakkasan	*Chinese*	𝔸★
	Mitsukoshi	*Japanese*	★★
	Shogun	*"*	★★
	Matsuri	*"*	★
£40+	Le Caprice	*British, Modern*	𝔸★
	Quaglino's	*"*	-
	Green's	*British, Traditional*	𝔸
	Teca	*Italian*	★★
	Momo	*Moroccan*	𝔸
	Al Hamra	*Lebanese*	★
	Kai	*Chinese*	𝔸★
	Tamarind	*Indian*	𝔸★★
£35+	Sotheby's Café	*British, Modern*	𝔸★
	Fortnum's Fountain	*"*	𝔸
	Al Duca	*Italian*	★
	Serafino	*"*	★
	Veeraswamy	*Indian*	𝔸★
	Patara	*Thai*	★
£30+	Rocket	*Mediterranean*	𝔸
	Levant	*Middle Eastern*	𝔸
	Rasa	*Indian*	★★
	Yoshino	*Japanese*	★★
£25+	Brown's Hotel	*Afternoon tea*	-

Fitzrovia & Marylebone (Part of W1)

£60+	Orrery	*French*	𝔸★
£50+	Pied à Terre	*French*	★
	Archipelago	*East/West*	𝔸★
	Defune	*Japanese*	★
£40+	Odin's	*British, Traditional*	𝔸
	Elena's L'Etoile	*French*	𝔸★
	Locanda Locatelli	*Italian*	𝔸★★
	La Porte des Indes	*Indian*	𝔸★
	Rasa Samudra	*"*	★
£35+	Café Bagatelle	*French*	𝔸
	Back to Basics	*Fish & seafood*	★★
	Maroush	*Lebanese*	★
	Bam-Bou	*French-Vietnamese*	𝔸
£30+	Langan's Bistro	*French*	𝔸
	Providores (Tapa Room)	*East/West*	𝔸★
	Ozer	*Turkish*	𝔸
	Royal China	*Chinese*	★★
£25+	Hellenik	*Greek*	𝔸★
	Quiet Revolution	*Organic*	𝔸★
£10+	Paul	*Sandwiches, cakes, etc*	𝔸★

Belgravia, Victoria & Pimlico (SW1, except St James's)

£60+	The Lanesborough	*British, Modern*	𝔸
	Foliage	*French*	★
	Mju	*East/West*	★
	Vong	*"*	★
	Restaurant One-O-One	*Fish & seafood*	★★
£50+	Goring Hotel	*British, Traditional*	𝔸
	Roussillon	*French*	★★
£40+	La Poule au Pot	*French*	𝔸★
	Zafferano	*Italian*	𝔸★★
	Il Convivio	*"*	𝔸★
	Toto's	*"*	𝔸★
	Signor Sassi	*"*	𝔸
	Boisdale	*Scottish*	𝔸
	Pomegranates	*International*	𝔸
	Ken Lo's Memories	*Chinese*	★★
	The Cinnamon Club	*Indian*	𝔸★
£35+	Grenadier	*British, Traditional*	𝔸
	Caraffini	*Italian*	𝔸★
	Sale e Pepe	*"*	𝔸★
	Olivo	*"*	★
	Noura	*Lebanese*	★
	Hunan	*Chinese*	★★
£30+	Como Lario	*Italian*	-
£20+	Pan-Asian Canteen	*Pan-Asian*	★

WEST

Chelsea, South Kensington, Kensington, Earl's Court & Fulham (SW3, SW5, SW6, SW7, SW10 & W8)

£90+	Blakes Hotel	*International*	Ⓐ
£80+	Gordon Ramsay	*French*	Ⓐ★★
£60+	Clarke's	*British, Modern*	Ⓐ★★
	Aubergine	*French*	★
	Bibendum	*"*	Ⓐ
£50+	The Tenth	*British, Modern*	Ⓐ
	Monkeys	*French*	Ⓐ★
	Belvedere	*"*	Ⓐ
	La Chaumière	*"*	-
	San Lorenzo	*Italian*	-
	Poissonnerie de l'Avenue	*Fish & seafood*	★
	Zuma	*Japanese*	Ⓐ
£40+	Launceston Place	*British, Modern*	Ⓐ★
	The Terrace	*"*	Ⓐ
	Bluebird	*"*	-
	Lundum's	*Danish*	Ⓐ★
	Scalini	*Italian*	Ⓐ
	Pasha	*Moroccan*	Ⓐ
	Ken Lo's Memories	*Chinese*	Ⓐ★
	Zaika	*Indian*	★★
	Aquasia	*Pan-Asian*	Ⓐ
	Blue Elephant	*Thai*	Ⓐ★
	Sugar Hut	*"*	Ⓐ
£35+	The Pen	*British, Modern*	Ⓐ★
	Admiral Codrington	*"*	-
	The Basil Street Hotel	*British, Traditional*	Ⓐ
	Maggie Jones's	*"*	Ⓐ
	Brasserie St Quentin	*French*	★★
	Le Colombier	*"*	Ⓐ
	Carpaccio's	*Italian*	Ⓐ★
	Ziani	*"*	Ⓐ★
	Wódka	*Polish*	Ⓐ
	Cambio de Tercio	*Spanish*	Ⓐ★
	Stratford's	*Fish & seafood*	★
	Black & Blue	*Steaks & grills*	★
	Maroush	*Lebanese*	★
	Vama	*Indian*	Ⓐ★★
	Star of India	*"*	★★
	Patara	*Thai*	★
£30+	Ffiona's	*British, Traditional*	Ⓐ
	Racine	*French*	★
	Elistano	*Italian*	Ⓐ★
	Made in Italy	*"*	Ⓐ★
	Aglio e Olio	*"*	★
	Timo	*"*	★
	The Polish Club	*Polish*	Ⓐ
	Chelsea Mandarin	*Chinese*	★
	The Painted Heron	*Indian*	★★
	Nam Long	*Vietnamese*	Ⓐ

£25+	Tartine	French	𝔸
	The Atlas	Mediterranean	𝔸 ★
	Sporting Page	International	𝔸
	Windsor Castle	"	𝔸
	Basilico	Pizza	★★
	Malabar	Indian	𝔸 ★
	Zaika Bazaar	"	𝔸 ★
	Khan's of Kensington	"	★
	Itsu	Japanese	𝔸 ★
£20+	Troubadour	Sandwiches, cakes, etc	𝔸
	Tandoori Lane	Indian	★
	Café 209	Thai	𝔸

Notting Hill, Holland Park, Bayswater, North Kensington & Maida Vale (W2, W9, W10, W11)

£70+	I Thai	East/West	𝔸
£40+	Harry's Social Club	British, Modern	𝔸
	Julie's	"	𝔸
	Chez Moi	French	𝔸 ★
	Assaggi	Italian	𝔸 ★★
	Electric Brasserie	International	𝔸
£35+	Alastair Little	British, Modern	★★
	Julie's Wine Bar	"	𝔸
	Halepi	Greek	-
	The Green Olive	Italian	𝔸 ★
	Zilli	"	★
	Mediterraneo	Mediterranean	𝔸 ★
	Maroush	Lebanese	★
	Bombay Palace	Indian	★
£30+	The Waterway	British, Modern	𝔸
	The Westbourne	"	𝔸
	Osteria Basilico	Italian	𝔸 ★
	Café Laville	International	𝔸
	Lucky Seven	American	-
	Royal China	Chinese	★★
	E&O	Pan-Asian	𝔸 ★★
£25+	The Oak	British, Modern	𝔸 ★
	Paradise, Kensal Green	"	𝔸 ★
	The Vale	"	-
	The Cow (Bar)	Fish & seafood	𝔸 ★
	Mandarin Kitchen	Chinese	★★
	Inaho	Japanese	★★
£20+	Ranoush	Lebanese	★
	The Four Seasons	Chinese	★
	Uli	Pan-Asian	★
£15+	Beirut Express	Lebanese	★★
	Mandalay	Burmese	★★
£5+	Lisboa Patisserie	Sandwiches, cakes, etc	★★

Hammersmith, Shepherd's Bush, Chiswick & Olympia (W4, W5, W6, W12, W14)

£50+	The River Café	*Italian*	-
£40+	La Trompette	*French*	𝔸★★
£35+	Chinon	*British, Modern*	★★
	Parade	*"*	★
	Fish Hoek	*South African*	★★
£30+	Seven Stars	*British, Modern*	𝔸
	The Gate	*Vegetarian*	𝔸★★
£25+	The Anglesea Arms	*British, Modern*	𝔸★★
	The Havelock Tavern	*"*	𝔸★★
	Ealing Park Tavern	*"*	★
	Blah! Blah! Blah!	*Vegetarian*	★★
	Thai Bistro	*Thai*	★
£20+	Queen's Head	*British, Traditional*	-
	Madhu's Brilliant	*Indian*	★
	Adams Café	*Moroccan*	-

NORTH

Hampstead, West Hampstead, St John's Wood, Regent's Park, Kilburn & Camden Town (NW postcodes)

£40+	Odette's	*British, Modern*	A★
	L'Aventure	*French*	A★★
	Oslo Court	*"*	A★
£35+	Halepi	*Greek*	-
£30+	Globe Restaurant	*British, Modern*	-
	Camden Brasserie	*French*	A
	Vegia Zena	*Italian*	★
	The Gate	*Vegetarian*	A★★
	Royal China	*Chinese*	★★
	China Dream	*"*	A★
	Jin Kichi	*Japanese*	★★
	Sushi-Say	*"*	★
£25+	William IV	*British, Modern*	A★
	Odette's Wine Bar	*"*	A
	La Brocca	*Italian*	A
	Don Pepe	*Spanish*	-
	Phoenix Palace	*Chinese*	★★
	Gung-Ho	*"*	A★
	Feng Shang	*"*	A
	Café Japan	*Japanese*	★★
£20+	Daphne	*Greek*	A
	Lemonia	*"*	A
	Bar Gansa	*Spanish*	A
	Gourmet Burger Kitchen	*Burgers, etc*	★
	Vijay	*Indian*	★★
	Zamzama	*"*	A
	Great Nepalese	*"*	-
	Sabras	*Indian, Southern*	★★
£15+	Geeta	*Indian*	★★
	Sakonis	*"*	★★
	Chutneys	*"*	★

Islington, Highgate, Hoxton, Crouch End, Stoke Newington, Finsbury Park, Muswell Hill & Finchley (N postcodes)

£40+	The Almeida	*French*	★
	The Real Greek	*Greek*	-
£35+	Frederick's	*British, Modern*	A★
	Metrogusto	*Italian*	★
£30+	The Drapers Arms	*British, Modern*	A★★
	St Johns	*British, Traditional*	A★
	Les Associés	*French*	A★
	Soulard	*"*	A★
	Casale Franco	*Italian*	A★
	Chez Liline	*Fish & seafood*	★★
	The Parsee	*Indian*	★★
	Rasa	*"*	★★

£25+	Vrisaki	Greek	★
	Angel of the North	International	𝔸
	Pasha	Turkish	𝔸
	Rasa Travancore	Indian, Southern	★
£20+	Maghreb	Moroccan	★
	Gallipoli	Turkish	𝔸
	Iznik	"	𝔸
	Rani	Indian	★
£15+	Tartuf	Alsatian	★

SOUTH

South Bank (SE1)

£60+	Le Pont de la Tour	*British, Modern*	-
£40+	Tentazioni	*Italian*	★★
	Oxo Tower (Brasserie)	*International*	Ⓐ
£35+	Laughing Gravy	*International*	Ⓐ
£30+	Baltic	*Polish*	Ⓐ★
	Delfina Studio Café	*International*	Ⓐ★
	Tate Modern (Level 7)	*"*	Ⓐ
	Champor-Champor	*East/West*	Ⓐ★★
£20+	Konditor & Cook	*British, Modern*	★★
	Meson don Felipe	*Spanish*	Ⓐ
	Pizzeria Castello	*Pizza*	Ⓐ★
	Konditor & Cook	*Sandwiches, cakes, etc*	★★
	Tas	*Turkish*	Ⓐ★

Battersea, Clapham, Wandsworth, Barnes, Putney, Brixton, Greenwich & Lewisham
(All postcodes south of the river except SE1)

£50+	Monsieur Max	*French*	Ⓐ★★
	Putney Bridge	*"*	Ⓐ★
£40+	Chez Bruce	*British, Modern*	Ⓐ★★
	The Glasshouse	*"*	Ⓐ★★
	Redmond's	*"*	★
	McClements	*French*	★
	Enoteca Turi	*Italian*	★
£35+	The Stepping Stone	*British, Modern*	Ⓐ★★
	Thyme	*"*	★★
	Phoenix	*"*	Ⓐ★
	Sonny's	*"*	Ⓐ★
	Inside	*"*	★
	Bellamys	*"*	Ⓐ
	Burnt Chair	*"*	Ⓐ
	Ditto	*"*	Ⓐ
	Ost. Antica Bologna	*Italian*	Ⓐ★
	Metrogusto	*"*	★
	Naked Turtle	*International*	Ⓐ
	Lobster Pot	*Fish & seafood*	★
	Canyon	*American*	-
	3 Monkeys	*Indian*	Ⓐ★
£30+	Kennington Lane	*British, Modern*	Ⓐ★
	The Depot	*"*	Ⓐ
	Willie Gunn	*"*	Ⓐ
	Chez Lindsay	*French*	★
	Gastro	*"*	Ⓐ
	Bug	*International*	Ⓐ
	So.uk	*North African*	Ⓐ Ⓐ
	Royal China	*Chinese*	★★
	Bombay Bicycle Club	*Indian*	Ⓐ★

£25+	The White Horse	British, Modern	-
	The Trafalgar Tavern	British, Traditional	A
	Spread Eagle	French	A
	Antipasto e Pasta	Italian	★
	Café Portugal	Portuguese	A
	El Rincón Latino	Spanish	A
	Rebato's	"	A
	The White House	International	A
	Cinnamon Cay	East/West	A ★
	Pizza Metro	Pizza	A ★★
	Basilico	"	★★
	Sarkhel's	Indian	★★
	Babur Brasserie	"	★
	Ma Goa	"	★
	Thailand	Thai	★★
£20+	don Fernando's	Spanish	A
	Arancia	Italian	-
	Gourmet Burger Kitchen	Burgers, etc	★
	Kastoori	Indian	★★
	Talad Thai	Thai	★★
£15+	Tartuf	Alsatian	★
	Brady's	Fish & chips	★
	Boiled Egg & Soldiers	Sandwiches, cakes, etc	A
	Sree Krishna	Indian	★★
	The Pepper Tree	Thai	A
£10+	Mirch Masala SW16	Indian	★★

EAST

Smithfield & Farringdon (EC1)

£40+	Smiths (Top Floor)	*British, Modern*	𝔸★
	St John	"	★
	Club Gascon	*French*	𝔸★★
	Bleeding Heart	"	𝔸★
£35+	Home	*British, Modern*	𝔸
	Café du Marché	*French*	𝔸★
	Moro	*Moroccan*	𝔸★★
£30+	The Well	*British, Modern*	𝔸★
	Alba	*Italian*	★
	Smiths (Dining Room)	*Steaks & grills*	𝔸
	Cicada	*Pan-Asian*	𝔸★
£25+	Quiet Revolution	*Organic*	𝔸★
	Carnevale	*Vegetarian*	★
£20+	The Eagle	*Mediterranean*	𝔸★

The City & East End
(All E and EC postcodes, except EC1)

£60+	City Rhodes	*British, Modern*	★
	Vertigo	*Fish & seafood*	𝔸
	Tatsuso	*Japanese*	★
£50+	Les Trois Garçons	*French*	𝔸
	Ubon	*East/West*	★★
	City Miyama	*Japanese*	★★
£40+	The Don	*British, Modern*	𝔸★
	1 Lombard Street	"	-
	Coq d'Argent	*French*	-
£35+	Lightship Ten	*Danish*	𝔸
	Wapping Food	*International*	𝔸
	The Grapes	*Fish & seafood*	𝔸★
	Sweetings	"	𝔸★
	Imperial City	*Chinese*	★
£30+	Il Bordello	*Italian*	𝔸★
	Armadillo	*South American*	★
	Bar Capitale	*Pizza*	★
	Royal China	*Chinese*	★★
£25+	LMNT	*British, Modern*	𝔸
	Ye Olde Cheshire Cheese	*British, Traditional*	𝔸
£20+	Simpson's Tavern	*British, Traditional*	𝔸
	Faulkner's	*Fish & chips*	★★
	Shanghai	*Chinese*	𝔸
	K10	*Japanese*	★

£15+	The Wine Library	British, Traditional	Ⓐ
	Lahore Kebab House	Indian	★★
£1+	Brick Lane Beigel Bake	Sandwiches, cakes, etc	★★

LONDON INDEXES

The Grapes
Smiths (Top Floor)
Wapping Food
The Well

BUSINESS

Central
Adam Street
Al Duca
Bank Aldwych
Boisdale
Le Caprice
The Criterion Grill
Deca
Dorchester Grill
Dorchester, Oriental
1837
Elena's L'Etoile
L'Escargot
Foliage
Le Gavroche
Goring Hotel
Green's
Indigo
The Ivy
Ken Lo's Memories
The Lanesborough
Lindsay House
Locanda Locatelli
Mirabelle
Mitsukoshi
Mon Plaisir
Odin's
L'Oranger
Orrery
Pétrus
Pied à Terre
Quaglino's
Restaurant One-O-One
Rhodes in the Sq
The Ritz
Rules
Savoy Hotel (Grill)
J Sheekey
The Square
The Sugar Club
Suntory
Veeraswamy
Vong
Wiltons
Windows on the World
Zafferano

West
Aubergine
Bibendum
Bluebird
Clarke's
Gordon Ramsay
Launceston Place
Poissonnerie de l'Avenue
The Tenth

North
Frederick's
Odette's

South
Brasserie
Delfina Studio Café
Le Pont de la Tour
Putney Bridge

East
Bleeding Heart
Café du Marché
City Miyama
City Rhodes
Coq d'Argent
Imperial City
Moro
1 Lombard Street
Sweetings
Tatsuso

BYO
(Bring your own wine)

Central
Food for Thought

West
Adams Café
Blah! Blah! Blah!
Café 209
Paradise by Way of
  Kensal Green
The Terrace

South
Basilico: *SW11*
Mirch Masala: *all branches*
Monsieur Max
Spread Eagle
Talad Thai

East
Faulkner's
Lahore Kebab House

CHILDREN
(h – high or special chairs
m – children's menu
p – children's portions
e – weekend entertainments
o – other facilities)

Central
Abeno *(hp)*
Al Hamra *(h)*
Alastair Little *(h)*
Asia de Cuba *(p)*
Back to Basics *(p)*
Bank Aldwych *(hm)*
Bar Italia *(h)*
Brown's Hotel *(h)*
Café Bagatelle *(hm)*
Le Caprice *(hp)*
The Cinnamon Club *(h)*
Como Lario *(h)*
Il Convivio *(p)*
The Criterion Grill *(h)*
Dorchester Grill *(hm)*
Dorchester, Oriental *(h)*
1837 *(hp)*

INDEXES

Elena's L'Etoile (p)
L'Escargot (h)
Foliage (hm)
Food for Thought (p)
Fortnum's Fountain (hm)
Fung Shing (h)
Gordon Ramsay at
  Claridge's (h)
Goring Hotel (hm)
Grenadier (p)
Hakkasan (p)
Indigo (hp)
The Ivy (hp)
The Lanesborough (hm)
Langan's Bistro (p)
Levant (m)
Locanda Locatelli (hp)
Malabar Junction (h)
Maroush: all branches (p)
Matsuri (h)
Mirabelle (h)
Mitsukoshi (h)
Mju (h)
Momo (o)
Nobu (h)
Noura (hp)
Orrery (h)
Ozer (h)
Paul: WC2 (he)
La Porte des Indes (h)
The Portrait (h)
La Poule au Pot (h)
Quaglino's (hm)
Restaurant One-O-One (h)
Rhodes in the Sq (h)
The Ritz (hm)
Royal China: W1 (h)
Rules (h)
Rusticana (h)
Sarastro (p)
Savoy Hotel (Grill) (h)
J Sheekey (hp)
Signor Sassi (h)
Souk (h)
Suntory (h)
Tamarind (h)
Providores (Tapa Room) (h)
British Museum (hp)
Toto's (hp)
Veeraswamy (hm)
Vong (h)
Windows on the World (h)
Zafferano (hp)

West

Admiral Codrington (h)
Aglio e Olio (h)
Alastair Little W11 (hp)
The Anglesea Arms (hp)
Aquasia (hm)
Assaggi (p)
Aubergine (p)
The Basil Street Hotel (hm)
Beirut Express (h)
Belvedere (h)
Bibendum (h)
Blakes Hotel (h)

Blue Elephant (he)
Bluebird (hmo)
Bombay Palace (hp)
Brasserie St Quentin (hm)
Café 209 (hp)
Carpaccio's (hp)
Chez Moi (p)
Le Colombier (hp)
E&O (hp)
Ealing Park Tavern (h)
Electric Brasserie (h)
Elistano (p)
The Gate: W6 (h)
Halepi: W2 (hp)
The Havelock Tavern (hp)
I Thai (h)
Itsu: SW3 (p)
Julie's (ho)
Julie's Wine Bar (hm)
Khan's of Kensington (p)
Lucky Seven (h)
Lundum's (p)
Made in Italy (h)
Madhu's Brilliant (h)
Maggie Jones's (h)
Malabar (hp)
Mandalay (hp)
Mandarin Kitchen (h)
Maroush: all branches (p)
Mediterraneo (h)
Osteria Basilico (h)
The Painted Heron (hp)
Parade (he)
Paradise by Way of
  Kensal Green (hm)
Poissonnerie
  de l'Avenue (p)
The Polish Club (p)
Queen's Head (m)
Racine (h)
Ranoush (m)
The River Café (hp)
San Lorenzo (h)
Scalini (h)
The Tenth (h)
Timo (h)
La Trompette (h)
Troubadour (h)
The Vale (hp)
Vama (hp)
William IV (h)
Zaika Bazaar (h)
Zilli (hm)
Zuma (he)

North

The Almeida (h)
Angel of the North (hp)
Les Associés (m)
L'Aventure (h)
Bar Gansa (h)
La Brocca (p)
Camden Brasserie (h)
Casale Franco (p)
China Dream (hp)
Chutneys (m)
Daphne (hp)

ENTERTAINMENT
(Check times before you go)

Central
Bank Aldwych
  (jazz, Sun)
Bohème Kitchen
  (band, Sun pm)
Boisdale
  (classic jazz, Mon-Sat)
Café Bohème
  (jazz, Tue-Fri & Sun)
Le Caprice
  (pianist, nightly)
The Criterion Grill
  (magician, Wed-Thurs)
Foliage
  (jazz, Mon-Sat in bar)
Goring Hotel
  (piano, nightly)
Hakkasan
  (DJ, Fri & Sat)
Indigo
  (film brunches, Sat & Sun)
Joe Allen
  (pianist, nightly (not Sun))
Kai
  (harpist, Thu & Sat nights)
The Lanesborough
  (supper dances, Fri & Sat; jazz Sun brunch)
The Langley
  (DJ, Thu-Sat)
Mirabelle
  (Pianist Tue-Sat D & Sun L)
Momo
  (live world music, Mon-Wed)
Opium
  (DJ, Thu-Sat; cabaret, Tue & Wed)
La Porte des Indes
  (jazz, Sun brunch)
Quaglino's
  (jazz, nightly in bar; pianist at brunch Sat-Sun)
The Ritz
  (band, Fri & Sat pm (every night in Dec))
Rusticana
  (jazz, Mon D)
Sarastro
  (opera, Mon & Sun)
Souk
  (belly dancer & DJ, Thu-Sat)
British Museum
  (musicians, nightly)
Windows on the World (dinner
  dance, Fri & Sat; jazz, Sun brunch)

West

Aquasia
(singer & pianist, 4 times a week)
The Basil Street Hotel
(pianist, nightly)
Bluebird
(DJ in bar, Fri & Sat pm)
Maroush: *W2*
(music & dancing, nightly)
The Tenth
(pianist, Sat)
Troubadour
(club downstairs)
Vama
(jazz, Sun)
William IV
(DJ, Fri & Sat)

North

Les Associés
(accordion, 1st Fri of month)
Bar Gansa
(flamenco, Mon)
La Brocca
(jazz, Thu in bar)
Don Pepe
(singer & organist, nightly)
Globe Restaurant
(cabaret, Thu pm)
Halepi: *NW3*
(live music, Sat)

South

Baltic
(jazz, Sun)
Ditto
(big screen sports TV)
Laughing Gravy
(jazz, Thu pm)
Meson don Felipe
(flamenco guitarist, nightly)
Naked Turtle
(jazz, nightly & Sun L, magician Sun D)
Pizzeria Castello
(salsa, Mon pm)
Rebato's
(music, Tue-Sat nights)
So.uk
(DJ, Wed-Sat)
Tas: *Borough High St SE1*
(guitarist, nightly); The Cut SE1
(music, nightly)
3 Monkeys
(jazz, Sun pm)
The Trafalgar Tavern
(bands, Fri or Sat pm)
The White House
(DJ, Wed-Sun D)

East

Café du Marché
(pianist & bass, nightly)
Coq d'Argent
(pianist Sat D: jazz Fri pm & Sun L)

LATE

(open till midnight or later as shown; may be earlier Sunday)

Central

Asia de Cuba *(midnight, Sat 1 am)*
Bar Italia *(4 am, Fri & Sat open 24 hours)*
Café Bohème *(2.45 am, Thu-Sat open 24 hours)*
Le Caprice
Incognico
Itsu: *W1 (midnight, Fri & Sat)*

The Ivy
Joe Allen *(12.45 am)*
The Lanesborough
Maroush: *W1 (1 am)*
Ozer
La Porte des Indes
Quaglino's *(midnight, Fri & Sat 1 am)*
Rasa: *all branches (Fri & Sat only)*
J Sheekey

West

Beirut Express *(1.45 am)*
Blue Elephant
Halepi: *W2 (12.30 am)*
Maroush: *W2 (2 am); SW3 (5 am)*
Ranoush *(3 am)*
Scalini

North

Bar Gansa
Don Pepe
Pasha *(Fri & Sat only)*
Rasa: *all branches (Fri & Sat only)*
Tartuf: *all branches (midnight)*
Vrisaki

South

Gastro
Tartuf: *all branches (midnight)*

East

Brick Lane Beigel Bake *(24 hours)*
Lahore Kebab House

NO-SMOKING AREAS

(* completely no smoking)

Central

Abeno
Archipelago
Busaba Eathai: *W1**
Café Bagatelle*
Chiang Mai
The Cinnamon Club
Defune*
1837
Foliage
Food for Thought*
Hakkasan
Hunan
Joe Allen
Kulu Kulu*
Maison Bertaux
Malabar Junction
Mirabelle
Mju*
Nobu
Odin's
Pan-Asian Canteen
Paul: *WC2**
The Portrait*
Rasa: *all branches**
Rasa Samudra
Roussillon
Rules*
Sarastro
Signor Sassi
Sotheby's Café*

The Sugar Club
British Museum*
Vong
Yoshino

West
Aquasia
The Basil Street Hotel
Bombay Palace
Café Laville
Itsu: SW3*
Khan's of Kensington
Mandalay*
Patara: Beauchamp Pl SW3
Queen's Head
The Tenth
Thai Bistro*
La Trompette
The Vale

North
Café Japan
Casale Franco
Frederick's
The Parsee
Rani
Rasa: all branches*
Rasa Travancore*
Sabras
Sushi-Say
Vijay

South
Babur Brasserie
Burnt Chair*
Canyon
The Depot
Gastro
Gourmet Burger Kitchen: SW11*
Konditor & Cook: Stoney St SE1*
Tate Modern (Level 7)*
Metrogusto: SW8
Naked Turtle
The Pepper Tree
Sarkhel's
The Stepping Stone
Talad Thai*
Thailand*
3 Monkeys*

East
Brick Lane Beigel Bake*
Cicada
Faulkner's
Home
K10*
Ubon

OUTSIDE TABLES
(* particularly recommended)

Central
Al Hamra*
Andrew Edmunds
Archipelago
Aurora*
Back to Basics
Bam-Bou

Bar Italia
Bohème Kitchen
Boisdale
Café Bohème
Caraffini
Il Convivio
Elena's L'Etoile
Gordon's Wine Bar*
Hellenik
Hunan
Langan's Bistro
Maison Bertaux
Mirabelle*
Momo
L'Oranger
Orrery
Ozer
The Perseverance
La Poule au Pot*
Quiet Revolution: all branches
The Ritz*
Rocket
Sarastro
Souk
Providores (Tapa Room)
Toto's*

West
Admiral Codrington*
Alastair Little W11
The Anglesea Arms
Aquasia*
The Atlas*
Belvedere*
Black & Blue
Bombay Palace
Brasserie St Quentin
Café Laville*
Cambio de Tercio
Chez Moi
Chinon
Le Colombier*
E&O
Ealing Park Tavern
Electric Brasserie
Elistano
The Gate: W6*
The Havelock Tavern
Julie's
Julie's Wine Bar*
Khan's of Kensington
Lisboa Patisserie
Lucky Seven
Lundum's
Made in Italy
Mediterraneo
Osteria Basilico
The Painted Heron
Paradise by Way of
  Kensal Green
Poissonnerie
  de l'Avenue
The Polish Club*
Queen's Head
The River Café*
Seven Stars
Sporting Page

INDEXES

LONDON MAPS

MAP 1 – WEST END OVERVIEW

MAP I – WEST END OVERVIEW

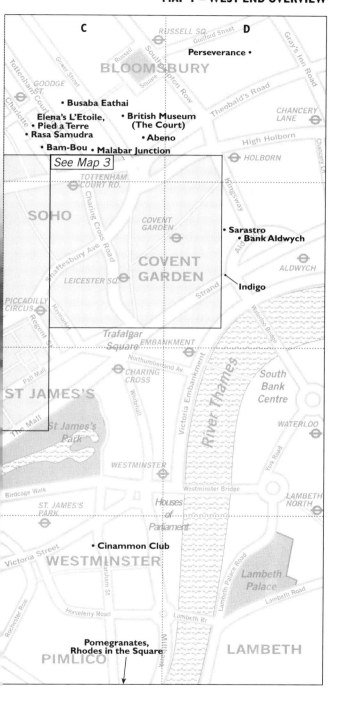

MAP 2 – MAYFAIR, ST JAMES'S & WEST SOHO

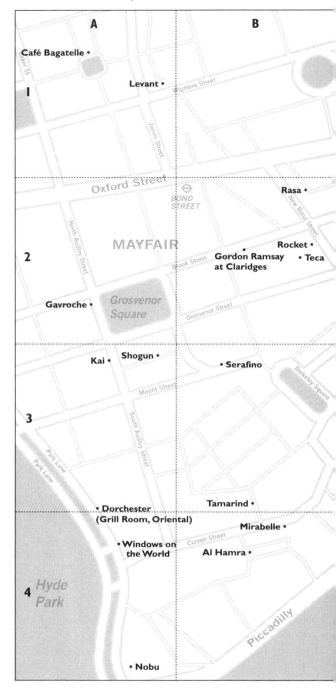

MAP 2 – MAYFAIR, ST JAMES'S & WEST SOHO

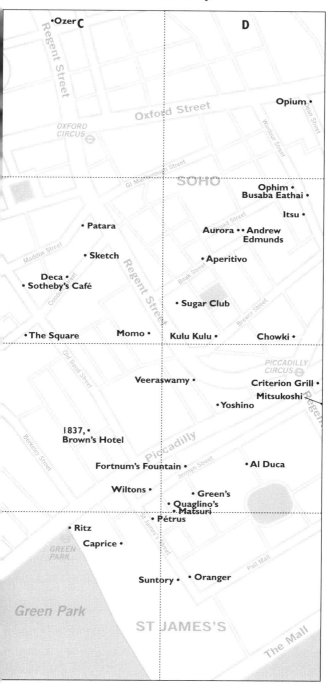

MAP 3 – EAST SOHO, CHINATOWN & COVENT GARDEN

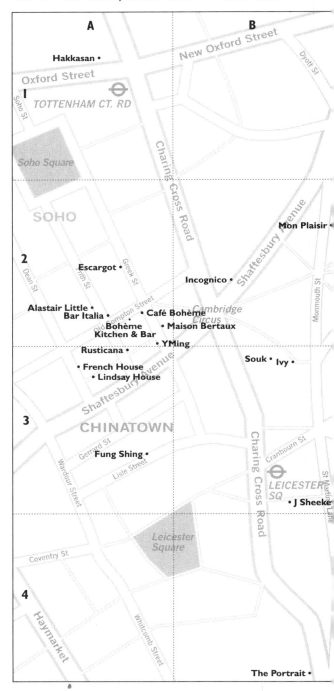

MAP 3 – EAST SOHO, CHINATOWN & COVENT GARDEN

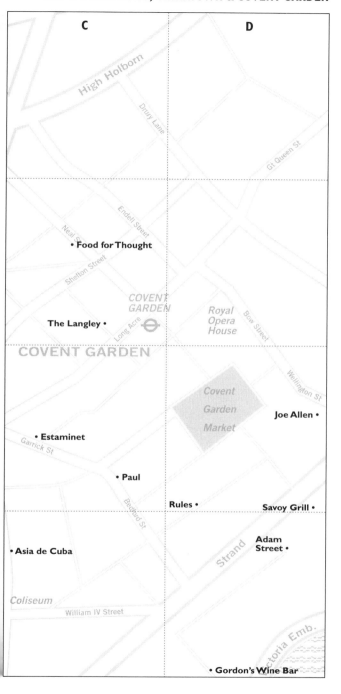

MAP 4 – KNIGHTSBRIDGE, CHELSEA & SOUTH KENSINGTON

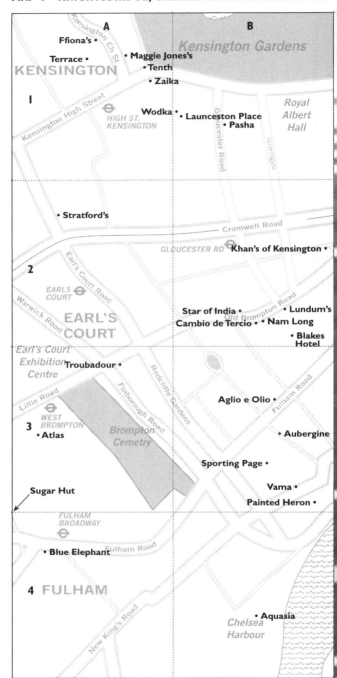

MAP 4 – KNIGHTSBRIDGE, CHELSEA & SOUTH KENSINGTON

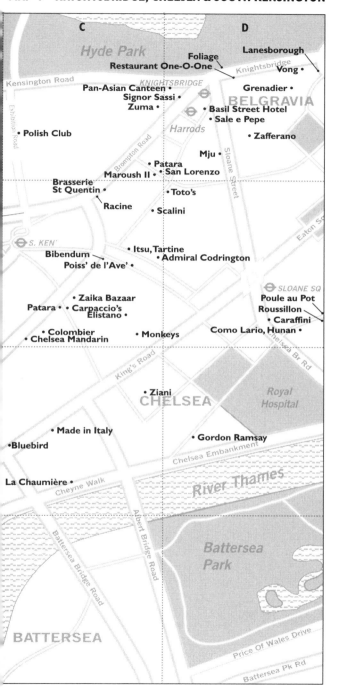

MAP 5 – THE CITY

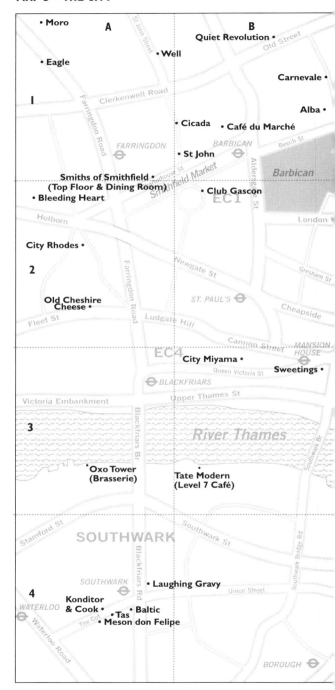

MAP 5 – THE CITY

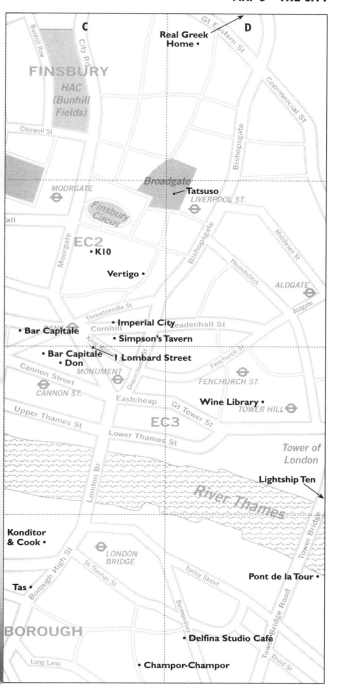

MAP 6 – SOUTH LONDON (& FULHAM)

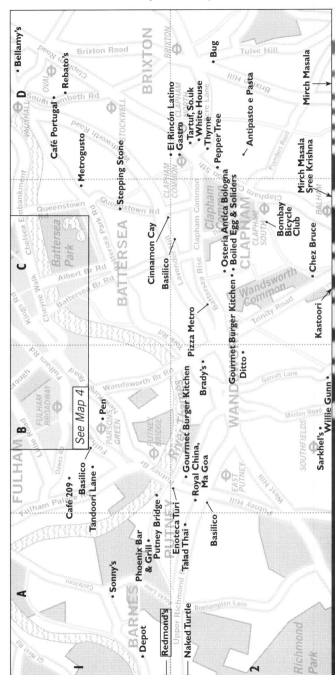

UK SURVEY RESULTS
& TOP SCORERS

PLACES PEOPLE TALK ABOUT

These are the restaurants outside London that were mentioned most frequently by reporters (last year's position is shown in brackets). For the list of London's most mentioned restaurants, see page 19.

1	Manoir aux Quat' Saisons (1)	Great Milton, Oxon
2	Seafood Restaurant (4)	Padstow, Cornwall
3	Waterside Inn (5)	Bray, Berks
4	Yang Sing (2)	Manchester
5	Fat Duck (11)	Bray
6	Magpie (18)	Whitby
7	Le Petit Blanc (3)	Oxford
8	Terre à Terre (6)	Brighton
9	Le Petit Blanc (7)	Birmingham
10	The Lime Tree (11)	Manchester
11	The Angel (9)	Hetton, N Yorks
12=	Sharrow Bay (11)	Ullswater
12=	Harts (16)	Nottingham
14	Le Petit Blanc (20)	Manchester
15	Whitstable Oyster (–)	Whitstable, Kent
16	The Witchery (–)	Edinburgh
17	Croma (–)	Manchester
18	Chaing Mai (14)	Oxford
19	Drum & Monkey (–)	Harrogate
20	Merchant House (17)	Ludlow

TOP SCORERS

All restaurants whose food rating is ★★; plus restaurants whose price is £50+ with a food rating of ★.
(Dublin restaurant prices have been converted to £.)

£100+	Le Manoir aux Quat' Saisons *(Great Milton)*	★A
£80+	Gidleigh Park *(Chagford)*	★A
	Restaurant Patrick Guilbaud *(Dublin)*	★
£60+	Sharrow Bay *(Ullswater)*	★★A
	Winteringham Fields *(Winteringham)*	★★A
	Amaryllis *(Glasgow)*	★★
	Harry's Place *(Great Gonerby)*	★★
	Bath Priory Hotel *(Bath)*	★A
	Fischers at Baslow Hall *(Baslow)*	★A
	Hambleton Hall *(Hambleton)*	★A
	Longueville Manor *(Jersey)*	★A
	Manor House, Bybrook Rest. *(Chippenham)*	★A
	Seafood Restaurant *(Padstow)*	★
£55+	L'Ortolan *(Shinfield)*	★★A
	Northcote Manor *(Langho)*	★★
	Charlton House *(Shepton Mallet)*	★A
	Chewton Glen *(New Milton)*	★A
	Number One *(Edinburgh)*	★
	One Paston Place *(Brighton)*	★
	White Hart *(Nettlebed)*	★
£50+	Seaham Hall *(Seaham)*	★★A
	Tylney Hall *(Hook)*	★★A
	Underscar Manor *(Applethwaite)*	★★A
	Ynyshir Hall *(Eglwysfach)*	★★A
	Old Chesil Rectory *(Winchester)*	★★
	The Priory House *(Stoke sub Hamdon)*	★★
	Shanks *(Bangor)*	★★
	Hotel des Clos *(Nottingham)*	★A
	Kaifeng *(Harrow)*	★A
	Kinnaird House *(Dunkeld)*	★A
	Sundial *(Herstmonceux)*	★A
	Three Chimneys *(Dunvegan)*	★A
	36 on the Quay *(Emsworth)*	★
	L'Ecrivain *(Dublin)*	★
	Horn of Plenty *(Gulworthy)*	★
	Lake Country House *(Llangammarch Wells)*	★
	Moss Nook *(Manchester)*	★
£45+	Morston Hall *(Morston)*	★★A
	Plas Bodegroes *(Pwllheli)*	★★A
	Summer Isles *(Achiltibuie)*	★★A
	Champignon Sauvage *(Cheltenham)*	★★

TOP SCORERS

Hibiscus *(Ludlow)* ★★
Markwick's *(Bristol)* ★★

£40+ Fairyhill *(Reynoldston)* ★★A
Gilpin Lodge *(Windermere)* ★★A
The Plumed Horse *(Castle Douglas)* ★★A
Bosquet *(Kenilworth)* ★★
Cellar *(Anstruther)* ★★
Merchant House *(Ludlow)* ★★
Restaurant Martin Wishart *(Edinburgh)* ★★

£35+ The Angel *(Hetton)* ★★A
Jeremys at Borde Hill *(Haywards Heath)* ★★A
22 Mill Street *(Chagford)* ★★A
Three Acres *(Shelley)* ★★A
Braidwoods *(Dalry)* ★★
Nutter's *(Cheesden)* ★★
Roly's Bistro *(Dublin)* ★A

£30+ Chiang Mai *(Oxford)* ★★A
Crannog *(Fort William)* ★★A
Nantyffin Cider Mill *(Crickhowell)* ★★A
Quince & Medlar *(Cockermouth)* ★★A
Rowan Tree *(Askrigg)* ★★A
Star Inn *(Harome)* ★★A
Terre à Terre *(Brighton)* ★★A
Black Chapati *(Brighton)* ★★
Crooked Billet *(Newton Longville)* ★★
The Fish Café (Ee-Usk) *(Oban)* ★★
Gingerman *(Brighton)* ★★
Riverside *(Bridport)* ★★

£25+ Olive Branch *(Clipsham)* ★★A
Tomlins *(Cardiff)* ★★A
Drum & Monkey *(Harrogate)* ★★
Leela's *(Newcastle upon Tyne)* ★★
Little Yang Sing *(Manchester)* ★★
Koh Samui *(Manchester)* ★★
Wheeler's Oyster Bar *(Whitstable)* ★★
Yang Sing *(Manchester)* ★★

£20+ New Emperor *(Manchester)* ★★
Magpie Café *(Whitby)* ★★
The Mermaid Café *(Hastings)* ★★
Nawaab *(Bradford)* ★★
Rajput *(Harrogate)* ★★

£15+ Gurkha Grill *(Manchester)* ★★
Mumtaz Paan House *(Bradford)* ★★
Punjab Tandoori *(Manchester)* ★★

OPENINGS & CLOSURES

The following lists contain restaurants which have opened or closed since the publication of *Harden's UK Restaurants 2002*. Those marked with an asterisk (*) are notable re-openings under new ownership.

OPENINGS

Aird's Hotel*	*Port Appin, Argyll & Bute*
Amba	*Hale, Cheshire*
Blinis	*Bath*
Brazz	*Bristol*
Browns	*Leeds*
Café Royal	*Newcastle upon Tyne*
Denial	*Birmingham*
East	*Manchester*
The Fish Café (Ee-Usk)	*Oban, Argyll & Bute*
The Forth Floor	*Edinburgh*
French Table	*Surbiton*
Hide Café Bar & Grill	*Durham*
Hotel du Vin et Bistro	*Brighton*
Izzi	*Edinburgh*
Kooky @ Whytes	*Brighton*
Living Room	*Birmingham*
Lords of the Manor*	*Upper Slaughter, Gloucs*
Masons Arms	*Cartmel Fell, Cumbria*
McCoys at the Baltic	*Newcastle upon Tyne*
Melton's Too	*York*
Milsoms	*Dedham, Essex*
Le Mont	*Manchester*
Mumbo	*Manchester*
Oloroso	*Edinburgh*
L'Ortolan*	*Shinfield, Berkshire*
La Potinière*	*Gullane, East Lothian*
Riverside Brasserie	*Bray*
Savannah	*Oxford*
Scallops	*Cardiff*
Scotsman	*Edinburgh*
The Seafood Café	*St Ives, Cornwall*
Seven Dials	*Brighton*
Simply Heathcote's	*Leeds*
Simply Heathcote's	*Liverpool*
Slammers	*Sheffield*
Spice Box*	*Boston Spa, West Yorks*
Thackeray's House	*Tunbridge Wells*
Vanilla Pod	*Marlow, Bucks*
Vermilion	*Edinburgh*
Victoria Hotel	*Holkham, Norfolk*
Waterfront Place	*Chelmsford, Essex*
White Hart	*Nettlebed, Oxon*
Zinc	*Birmingham*

CLOSURES

Becher's Brook	*Liverpool*
Boheme	*Nottingham*
Buttery	*Glasgow*
Chez Julien	*Solihull, West Midlands*
Cooke's Café	*Dublin*
Croque en Bouche	*Malvern Wells, Worcs*
Darbar	*Manchester*
Dining Room 2	*Haywards Heath, West Sussex*
Eurasia	*Glasgow*
Gousse D'Ail	*Oxford*
Hullaballoos	*Bristol*
Marsh Goose	*Moreton-in-Marsh, Gloucs*
Michael's Nook	*Grasmere, Cumbria*
Milano	*Sheffield*
Old Beams	*Waterhouses, Staffs*
Old Rectory	*Campsea Ashe, Suffolk*
Peacock Alley	*Dublin*
Plough Inn	*Saxton, North Yorks*
Rascasse	*Leeds*
Rhodes & Co	*Edinburgh*
Rococo at The Crown	*Wells-next-the-Sea, Norfolk*
La Terrasse	*Sandgate, Kent*
Thirteenth Note	*Glasgow*
Tico Tico	*Bristol*

UK DIRECTORY

Comments in "double quotation-marks" were made by reporters.

ABERDEEN, ABERDEEN   9–2D

Foyer
Trinity Church   £ 26   𝔸 ★
82a Crown Street AB11 6ET   (01224) 582277
"Superb food from a restaurant which gives aid to the homeless"
may sound odd, but the "consistently good" standards of this
"trendy" café in a converted church (run by a local charity) are
attested to by all reporters; expansion is scheduled for late-2002.
/ *Sample dishes:* gnocchi with Gorgonzola & spinach; pan-fried chicken with
smoked bacon & sage risotto; pecan pie with banana ice cream. **Details:** 10 pm;
closed Mon & Sun; no Amex; no smoking area; children: 14+ after 8 pm.

Royal Thai   £ 29
29 Crown Ter AB11 6HD   (01224) 212922
"Good Thai food" makes this northerly oriental a destination of
some note locally. / **Details:** 11 pm; closed Sun L.

Silver Darling   £ 46   𝔸
Pocra Quay, North Pier AB11 5DQ   (01224) 576229
"An old lighthouse, at the end of the harbour wall" provides the
"superb" and "lively" setting for "the best fish restaurant in the
city"; even some fans find it a touch "overpriced", though.
/ *Sample dishes:* prawn ravioli with Parma ham & lobster oil; sea bass with
tapenade & aniseed butter; tarte Tatin with green apple sorbet. **Details:** 9.30 pm;
closed Sat L & Sun; no smoking in dining room.

Simpsons   £ 34
59 Queens Rd AB15 4YP   (01224) 327799
Decked out in "impressive" (if not particularly cosy) modern style,
this hotel brasserie – convenient for the AECC – is praised by
locals for its "great-value" Mediterranean cooking.
/ *Sample dishes:* black pudding with apple croquettes; pork with haggis & spring
onion frittata; chocolate orange tart. **Details:** 9 pm; no smoking area.
Accommodation: 50 rooms, from £85.

ABERDYFI, GWYNEDD   4–3C

Penhelig Arms   £ 30   𝔸 ★
LL35 0LT   (01654) 767215
"Great plates" of "superb food using local produce" and "a
wonderful wine list" win high praise for this "unpretentious" inn,
on the seafront overlooking the Dyfi estuary.
/ *Sample dishes:* spinach & cream cheese lasagne; char-grilled lamb with roast
aubergines; raspberry frangipane tart. **Value tip:** set 2-crs L £9.95.
Details: www.penheligarms.com; 9 pm; no Amex; no smoking in dining room.
Accommodation: 14 rooms, from £70.

ABERGAVENNY, MONMOUTHSHIRE   2–1A
Walnut Tree   £ 43
Llandewi Skirrid NP7 8AW   (01873) 852797
"Not the same since Franco retired" – bizarrely, Michelin finally
chose to recognise this famous "tightly-packed" gastropub the
year after its great chef moved on (after 37 years), when Stephen
Terry's much less impressive regime moved in; reports strongly
suggest that – especially at the price – the Italian cooking is
"nothing special" nowadays. / *Sample dishes:* endive, pancetta &
Dolcelatte salad; corned beef hash with spinach & fried egg; steamed treacle sponge
pudding. **Value tip:** set 2-crs L £16.50. **Details:** www.thewalnuttreeinn.com;
3m NE of Abergavenny on B4521; 10.30 pm; closed Mon & Sun D; no Amex.

ACHILTIBUIE, HIGHLAND 9–1B
Summer Isles £47 A★★
IV26 2YG (01854) 622282
"We'll be going back soon, even though it took us nine hours to get there"; as "a wonderful place to relax and get away from it all", this remote hotel (looking out onto the islands for which it is named) has many loyal devotees, and its "fantastic" cooking rarely lets it down. / **Sample dishes:** grilled mushrooms with Parmesan croutons; grilled turbot with lime & capers; lemon soufflé crêpes.
Details: www.summerisleshotel.co.uk; 25m N of Ullapool on A835; 8 pm; no Amex; no smoking in dining room; booking essential; children: 6+. **Accommodation:** 13 rooms, from £98.

ALDEBURGH, SUFFOLK 3–1D
152 £29
152 High St IP15 5AX (01728) 454152
"Some unusual dishes" add interest to a visit to this small and "friendly" bistro, which offers "reliably good food".
/ **Sample dishes:** carrot, tomato & ginger soup; lamb with pea purée & red pepper relish; cappucino crème brûlée. **Details:** www.lawsons152.co.uk; 10 pm (9 pm in winter); closed Tue (& Mon in winter); no Amex; no smoking area; children: before 8 pm only.

Lighthouse £28
77 High St IP15 5AU (01728) 453377
"Welcoming" service "even when the place is packed" and "consistent" fish cookery underpin the success of this "jolly" bistro; it's still by far the best-known place locally, even if fans concede it "sometimes misses". / **Sample dishes:** celery & blue cheese soup; Aldeburgh sole with lime butter; boozy banana pancakes. **Details:** 10 pm; open L & D all week; closed for 2 weeks in Jan & 1 week in Oct; no smoking area.

Regatta £28
171 High St IP15 5AN (01728) 452011
"They've kept a good standard for years now" at this informal spot; it offers "a limited selection of fresh and well-prepared fish".
/ **Sample dishes:** smoked prawns; duck with French beans; crème brûlée.
Details: www.regattaaldeburgh.com; 10 pm; closed Mon-Wed in Nov-Mar; no smoking area.

ALDERMINSTER, WARWICKSHIRE 2–1C
The Bell Inn £28
CV37 8NY (01789) 450414
"Above-average" cooking wins nothing but praise for this "reliable" 18th-century coaching inn; (it's handy if you're staying overnight after a visit to Stratford, too). / **Sample dishes:** duck liver parfait with toast; steak & kidney pudding; English cheese platter. **Details:** www.thebellald.co.uk; 9.30 pm; smoking in bar only. **Accommodation:** 6 rooms, from £40.

ALDFORD, CHESHIRE 5–3A
The Grosvenor Arms £31 A
Chester Rd CH3 6HJ (01244) 620228
A "comfortable" country village pub (near the gates to Eaton Hall), liked for its "cheerful", "lively" atmosphere and "good 'home' cooking", served in "large portions" from an ever-changing blackboard menu. / **Sample dishes:** corned beef & black pudding hash cake; pork chops with Stilton rarebit topping; chocolate bread & butter pudding.
Details: 6m S of Chester on B5130; 10 pm; no smoking area; children: 14+ after 6 pm.

AMBERLEY, WEST SUSSEX
3–4A

Amberley Castle
£ 48   Ⓐ

BN18 9ND   (01798) 831992

"It makes you feel regal", dining at this *"beautiful"*, story-book castle – 900 years old this year – especially if you take *"a pre-prandial stroll around the battlements"*; even those who say the cooking is *"superb"*, though, find it *"pricey"* for what it is, and service can be *"indifferent"*. / **Sample dishes:** game terrine with plum chutney; salmon pavé with celeriac cream; roast pears with champagne sorbet. **Value tip:** set 2-crs L £12.50. **Details:** www.amberleycastle.co.uk; N of Arundel on B2139; 9.30 pm; jacket & tie required; no smoking; booking: max 8; children: 12+. **Accommodation:** 19 rooms, from £145.

AMBLESIDE, CUMBRIA
7–3D

Drunken Duck
£ 34   Ⓐ

Barngates   LA22 0NG   (01539) 436347

A *"stunning"* setting and *"above-average pub grub"* help make this pub/restaurant/brewery *"lovely in all respects"*, for most reporters; *"book early for dinner, unless you want to sit at the bar"*. / **Sample dishes:** chicken with sugar snap peas; quail stuffed with prune risotto; lemon torte with spiced oranges. **Details:** www.drunkenduckinn.co.uk; 3m from Ambleside, towards Hawkshead; 9 pm; no smoking. **Accommodation:** 15 rooms, from £90.

The Glass House
£ 29   Ⓐ ★

Rydal Rd   LA22 9AN   (01539) 432137

"Something of a find in a tourist town" – this popular fixture offers *"excellent modern cuisine"* in a *"very interesting old-mill setting"*. / **Sample dishes:** tomato & Parmesan tart; roast monkfish with Parma ham & vegetable crêpes; mint chocolate chip soufflé. **Value tip:** set 2-crs menu £10. **Details:** www.theglasshouserestaurant.co.uk; behind Little Bridge House; 10 pm; closed Tue (& all of Jan); no Amex; no smoking; children: 5+ at D.

Lucy's on a Plate
£ 33   Ⓐ ★

Church St   LA22 0BU   (01539) 431191

"A local treasure"; a *"jolly"* atmosphere plus a *"fantastic"* range of simple but *"interesting"* dishes make this 'evolved tearoom' an ideal venue *"for coffee and cakes, a snack lunch or an informal dinner"*. / **Sample dishes:** scallops with cream & dill; roast lamb with minted bacon jus; Belgian chocolate bread & butter pudding. **Details:** www.lucys-on-a-plate.co.uk; 9 pm; no Amex; no smoking.

Rothay Manor
£ 32

Rothay Bridge   LA22 0EH   (01539) 433605

This Regency country house hotel (run by the same family for over 30 years) has *"nice surroundings"*, and is a popular destination for those with kids in tow; the food can be *"very good"*, but can also disappoint. / **Sample dishes:** grilled sardines with rosemary; roast duck with red cabbage & juniper sauce; pavlova with summer fruits. **Details:** www.rothaymanor.co.uk; 9 pm; no smoking in dining room; children: 7+ at D. **Accommodation:** 17 rooms, from £126.

Sheila's Cottage
£ 30

The Slack   (01539) 433079

"For a tasty snack after walking", fans recommend the *"simple"* cooking, *"nicely"* served at this *"cheerful"* tea shop (which moonlights as a restaurant); it *"did not live up to expectations"* for everyone, though. / **Sample dishes:** salmon mousse with roasted tomatoes; roast pheasant with walnut & spinach risotto; treacle tart with custard. **Details:** www.amblesideonline.co.uk; 9 pm; closed Tue D & Wed D in winter; no Amex; no smoking; children: 8+ after 6 pm.

Zeffirelli's £ 22 Ⓐ ★
Compston Rd LA22 9DN   (01539) 433845
*"Quite a find for the Lakes!"; this "not-to-be-missed" institution –
a quirky combination of café, cinema and wholefood pizzeria –
offers "excellent pizza and pasta" in "generous helpings".*
/ **Sample dishes:** pesto & cherry tomato bruschetta; red chilli bean & Cheddar
pizza; tiramisu. **Value tip:** set 2-crs pre-theatre (incl film ticket) £14.
Details: www.zeffirellis.co.uk; 9.45 pm; D only; no Amex; no smoking.

AMERSHAM, BUCKINGHAMSHIRE 3–2A

Famous Fish £ 31
11 Market Sq HP7 0DF   (01494) 728665
*The setting is "cramped", "crowded" and "smoky" – and service
is "variable", too – but "fresh fish cooked with style" ensures high
local popularity for this BYO spot.* / **Sample dishes:** grilled prawn tails
with avocado; Cajun cod with tomato concasse; crème brûlée. **Details:** in Old
Amersham; 10 pm; closed Sun; no smoking; booking essential.

Gilbey's £ 32
1 Market Sq HP7 0DF   (01494) 727242
*"Wines sold at retail prices" and "friendly" service are highlights
at this well-established fixture, near the old clock tower; cooking
some find "reliable" is merely "predictable" to others.*
/ **Sample dishes:** crab cakes with lime pickle; braised lamb with mint mash & red
wine jus; rhubarb oat crumble. **Value tip:** set 2-crs Sun L £10.95.
Details: www.gilbeygroup.com; in Old Amersham; 9.45 pm; appreciated if guests try
to refrain from smoking.

Kings Arms £ 32
30 High St HP7 0DJ   (01494) 726333
*For fans of this ancient town-centre tavern, a visit here is "always
a pleasure", and some tip its upstairs dining room as a venue for
romance; culinary standards, though, can be "variable".*
/ **Sample dishes:** pheasant terrine; salmon & monkfish brochettes with ginger
dressing; chocolate & hazelnut galettes. **Value tip:** set 2-crs L £12.50.
Details: www.kingsarmsamersham.co.uk; in Old Amersham; 9.30 pm; closed
Mon & Sun D.

Santhi £ 24 Ⓐ
16 Hill Ave HP6 5BW   (01494) 432621
*"Best in the area" – the "good atmosphere" is a special strength
of this pleasant, unusually-decorated Indian, near the terminus of
the Metropolitan line.* / **Details:** www.santhirestaurant.co.uk; 10.45 pm;
no smoking area.

ANSTRUTHER, FIFE 9–4D

Cellar £ 44 ★ ★
24 East Grn KY10 3AA   (01333) 310378
*"Eat your heart out, Rick Stein!"; "terrific fresh seafood" and
"lovely fish" make the Jukes's "welcoming" and "convivial" cellar-
restaurant – part of a 17th-century building behind the Scottish
Fisheries Museum – "the real fishy thing".*
/ **Sample dishes:** asparagus & leek soup; roast pesto-crusted cod; hazelnut praline
parfait. **Details:** 9.30 pm; closed Mon L & Tue L; no smoking area; children: 8+.

sign up for the survey at www.hardens.com

APPLECROSS, HIGHLAND 9–2B

Applecross Inn £28 ★
Shore St IV54 8LR (01520) 744262
"Sitting outside enjoying 'just-caught' seafood" can make a visit to
this remote waterside tavern – with its "superb views" – a
"wonderful" experience. / **Sample dishes:** hot-smoked salmon; venison
sausages with mash & onion gravy; chocolate brûlée. **Value tip:** set 2-crs L £12.
Details: www.applecross.net; off A896, S of Shieldaig; 9 pm; no Amex; no smoking.
Accommodation: 7 rooms, from £50.

APPLETHWAITE, CUMBRIA 7–3C

Underscar Manor £53 A★★
CA12 4PH (01768) 775000
Robert Thornton's "superb" cooking makes this small country
house hotel "a real rival to Sharrow Bay" for those who comment
on it, and its location, "overlooking Derwent Water", is "equally
glorious". / **Sample dishes:** Swiss cheese soufflé with buttered spinach; roast
lamb with moussaka gateau; mini citrus desserts. **Details:** on A66, 17m W of M6,
J40; 8.30 pm; jacket required; no smoking; children: 12+. **Accommodation:** 11
rooms, from £180, incl D.

ARDEN, ARGYLL & BUTE 9–4B

Duck Bay Hotel & Marina £33 A
Duck Bay G83 8QZ (01389) 751234
It's not just the "great location" – with wonderful views of the loch
– which wins praise for this waterside dining room; fans say the
cooking is "great", too (but the level of feedback is unfortunately
rather limited). / **Sample dishes:** kromesky (deep-fried meat parcels); roast
lamb; mocha chocolate mousse. **Value tip:** set 2-crs L £10 (Sun £12).
Details: www.duckbayhotel.com; off A82; 10 pm. **Accommodation:** 18 rooms,
from £79.

ASCOT, BERKSHIRE 3–3A

Ascot Oriental £34 A★
London Rd SL5 0PU (01344) 621877
You might expect a restaurant near Ascot to be "upmarket",
but the "really excellent standards" of this attractive oriental –
with its "very good mix of Asian cuisines" – can come as
something of a surprise. / **Details:** 2m E of Ascot on A329; 10.30 pm.

The Thatched Tavern £36
Cheapside Rd SL5 7QG (01344) 620874
This part-thatched 17th-century building is liked for its "amiable
service and good, simple cooking"; for doubters, though,
it's "just a pub with restaurant prices". / **Sample dishes:** crispy oriental
duck salad; steak & kidney pie; lemon & ginger crunch. **Details:** 2m from Ascot,
signed to Cheapside village; 10 pm.

ASENBY, NORTH YORKSHIRE   8–4C

The Crab & Lobster   £38   𝔸
Dishforth Rd YO7 3QL (01845) 577286
An "eclectic warren" of "bric-a-brac"-infested rooms creates a
"wonderful atmosphere" at this "quirky" thatched pub (recently
enlarged with a conservatory); it's also known for its "super fish"
and "excellent seafood" – let's hope its new (August 2002)
owners keep up the good work. / **Sample dishes:** Irish oysters on ice;
crab-crusted salmon with saffron mash; chocolate torte. **Value tip:** set 2-crs L
£11.50. **Details:** www.crabandlobster.co.uk; at junction of Asenby Rd & Topcliffe Rd;
9 pm; no smoking in dining room. **Accommodation:** 11 rooms, from £130.

ASHBURTON, DEVON   1–3D

Holne Chase Hotel   £46
TQ13 7NS (01364) 631471
All agree this well-reputed country house hotel – a converted
Dartmoor hunting lodge – makes an "enjoyable", "quiet"
destination; although the odd reporter "expected better",
most rated the cooking as very satisfactory. / **Sample dishes:** creamy
sweetcorn soup with chive oil; calves liver & bacon with sage butter; steamed
chocolate sponge. **Details:** www.holne-chase.co.uk; 8.45 pm; no Amex; children:
12+ at D. **Accommodation:** 17 rooms, from £130.

ASKRIGG, NORTH YORKSHIRE   8–4B

The King's Arms   £32
Market Pl DL8 3HQ (01969) 650817
This "old coaching inn" may be best known for its role as
'The Drovers Arms' in 'All Creatures Great and Small', but its
"wide range" of pub fare is of "good quality". / **Sample dishes:** spicy
salmon fishcakes; chicken & cheese wrapped in smoked bacon; sticky toffee pudding.
Details: 9 pm; no Amex; no smoking.

Rowan Tree   £31   𝔸★★
Market Pl DL8 3HT (01969) 650536
"A friendly couple convey their love and knowledge of food",
at this "intimate" and "cosy" 22-seater; once again, it was highly
rated by reporters for its "welcoming" style and its "careful and
delicious" cooking. / **Sample dishes:** Louisiana prawn & okra gumbo;
lamb cutlets with colcannon & Shiraz jus; coffee, chocolate & cardamom truffle
torte. **Details:** 4m from Aysgarth falls; 8.30 pm; D only Wed-Sat, L only Sun; closed
Mon & Tue; no credit cards; no smoking at D; children: 7+.

ASTBURY, CHESHIRE   5–3B

Pecks   £37   ★
Newcastle Rd CW12 4SB (01260) 275161
Lunch is 'normal', dinner is a pre-booked, one-sitting-at-eight affair
at this attractive modern establishment; it generates limited
feedback, all to the effect that it offers an "excellent experience".
/ **Sample dishes:** broad bean & goats cheese risotto; braised lamb with black olive
mash; rum & raisin cheesecake. **Value tip:** set 3-crs L £12.
Details: www.pecksrest.co.uk; off A34; 8 pm (one sitting only); closed Mon &
Sun D; no smoking at D; booking essential.

AUCHTERARDER, PERTH & KINROSS   9–3C

Gleneagles
Gleneagles Hotel   £80
(01764) 662231
Andrew Fairlie's year-old dining room in the bowels of this grand and famous hotel generates fewer reports than one might expect – their general tenor is that, with its "impeccable attention to detail", it is a destination that's "expensive, but worth it".
/ **Sample dishes:** foie gras terrine with caramelised apple; roast venison with wild mushrooms; chocolate orange pudding. **Details:** www.gleneagles.com; 10 pm; closed Sun; children: 14+. **Accommodation:** 275 rooms, from £305.

AYLESBURY, BUCKINGHAMSHIRE   3–2A

Hartwell House   £59   𝔸
Oxford Rd HP17 8NL   (01296) 747444
For a "splendidly luxurious" experience, some would recommend the dining room at this imposing part-Jacobean stately home; the cooking is "very expensive" for what it is, though, and some find the atmosphere "stuffy". / **Sample dishes:** smoked chicken & spring onion sausage; sea bass with spinach & port wine sauce; mango mousse with pineapple crisps. **Value tip:** set 2-crs L £22. **Details:** www.hartwell-house.com; 2m W of Aylesbury on A418; 9.45 pm; jacket & tie required; no smoking in dining room; children: 8+. **Accommodation:** 46 rooms, from £225.

BABINGTON, SOMERSET   2–3B

Babington House   £38   𝔸
BA11 3RW   (01373) 812266
This "old country estate" has been "funked up for the London set" by the team at Soho House; the food is quite good, but it's just one part of a whole "informal but welcoming" experience that wins high praise; (note: you have to be a member or hotel resident to eat here). / **Sample dishes:** smoked duck, dandelion & hazelnut salad; monkfish with clams & bacon; trio of chocolate puddings.
Details: www.babingtonhouse.co.uk; 11 pm; open to residents & members only for L & D all week; booking essential. **Accommodation:** 28 rooms, from £210.

BAKEWELL, DERBYSHIRE   5–2C

Aitch's Wine Bar   £32   ★
4 Buxton Rd DE45 1DA   (01629) 813895
"A popular venue with an interesting menu" – the dishes at this "welcoming" wine bar are eclectic and "good-quality".
/ **Sample dishes:** spicy Thai fishcakes; crispy duck with stir-fried vegetables; champagne cheesecake with cassis ice cream. **Details:** www.aitchswinebar.co.uk; 10 pm; closed Sun (open Sun D in summer); no Amex; no smoking.

Renaissance   £30   ★
Bath St DE45 1BX   (01629) 812687
"Competent" cooking and "friendly" service make this cottagey and comfortable Gallic restaurant a popular destination, though some find its style a little "middle-aged". / **Sample dishes:** French onion & shallot soup; chicken stuffed with crab mousse; chocolate & pear terrine with claret sauce. **Details:** 9.30 pm; closed Mon & Sun D; no Amex; no smoking.

BALLATER, ABERDEEN   9–3C
Green Inn   £ 42   ★
9 Victoria Rd AB35 5QQ   (01339) 755701
*Jeff & Carol Purves's "superb" partnership makes this friendly and
"professional" restaurant with rooms quite a gastronomic
destination. / Sample dishes: duck with black pudding & sweet soy sauce;
turbot with leek risotto & Arbroath smokie; treacle tart with liquorice ice cream.
Value tip: set 2-crs D £27.50. Details: www.green-inn.com; 9.30 pm; D only;
no smoking at D. Accommodation: 3 rooms, from £119, incl D.*

BANBURY, OXFORDSHIRE   2–1D
Thai Orchid   £ 27
56 Northbar St OX16 0TL   (01295) 270833
*A "greenhouse-like" setting adds interest to a visit to this popular
oriental. / Details: 10.30 pm; closed Sat L; no smoking area.*

BANGOR, COUNTY DOWN   10–1D
Shanks   £ 52   ★★
150 Crawfordsburn Rd BT19 1GB   (028) 9185 3313
*This ambitious Conran-designed dining room — oddly-located in a
golf club — produced surprisingly little feedback this year;
such reports as there were confirmed a continuation of the high
standards of previous years, and of cooking that "never fails to
impress". / Sample dishes: smoked salmon blinis; peppered pork with Parmesan
mash; chocolate mousse with raspberries. Value tip: set 2-crs L £17. Details: A2
to Bangor, follow signs for Blackwood golf centre; 10 pm; closed Mon, Sat L & Sun.*

BANGOR, GWYNEDD   4–1C
The Fat Cat Café Bar   £ 22
161 High St LL57 1NU   (01248) 370445
*This café/bar — the first branch of a northerly chain — is "always
friendly", and its "good food and atmosphere" make it a
destination worth knowing of hereabouts. / Sample dishes: chicken
quesadillas; tuna with stir-fried vegetables in oyster sauce; Caribbean banana
charlotte. Details: www.fatcat.to; 10 pm; no smoking area; children: 18+ only.*

BARTON UPON HUMBER, NORTH LINCS   6–2A
Rafters   £ 26   ★
24 High St DN18 5PD   (01652) 660669
*"Imaginative" cooking wins praise for this "cheap and cheerful"
market town restaurant. / Sample dishes: antipasti with avocado; curried
pork with dried fruits; chocolate Scotch pancakes. Value tip: set 2-crs L £7.50.
Details: www.rafters.co.uk; just S of Humber Bridge off A15; 10 pm; closed Mon &
Sun D; smoking in bar only.*

BARWICK VILLAGE, SOMERSET   2–3B
Little Barwick House   £ 43   🄰 ★
BA22 9TD   (01935) 423902
*"An excellent country house hotel restaurant, serving the very best
straightforward country fare" — reporters speak nothing but good
of this "friendly" family-run enterprise, in a "beautiful" Georgian
dower house. / Sample dishes: pink-roasted quail with mushroom risotto;
Cornish brill with baby leeks & girolles; hot plum soufflé.
Details: www.littlebarwickhouse.co.uk; 9 pm; closed Mon, Tue L & Sun D;
no smoking in dining room. Accommodation: 6 rooms, from £46.50.*

sign up for the survey at www.hardens.com

BASINGSTOKE, HAMPSHIRE   2–3D

Hees Chinese   £31
23 Westminster Hs RG21 7LS   (01256) 464410
"Good" ("no-slop") Chinese cooking makes this long-established oriental a useful option in this under-provided town.
/ *Details:* 10.30 pm; closed Sun L; children: 6+.

BASLOW, DERBYSHIRE   5–2C

Fischers at Baslow Hall   £60   A★
Calver Rd DE45 IRR   (01246) 583259
A "beautiful location" (bordering the Chatsworth Estate), "charming" décor, "unfussy" service and "first-class" modern British cooking make this country house hotel "excellent all-round" for most reporters; the minority, though, who find its whole style unduly "pompous" can't entirely be overlooked. / **Sample dishes:** sea bream with butternut squash ratatouille; pigs trotter with morels & truffle mash; passion fruit soufflé. **Value tip:** set 2-crs L £20.
Details: www.fischers-baslowhall.co.uk; 9.30 pm; closed Sun D; jacket required at D; no smoking in dining room; children: 12+ after 7 pm. **Accommodation:** 11 rooms, from £150.

BATH, BATH & NE SOMERSET   2–2B

Given that many would regard this as England's most civilised city, it's a shame that in culinary terms Bath is currently – in spite of its plethora of places to eat – something of an 'also-ran' destination.

The closure of the excellent Lettonie hasn't helped this position: *pace* Michelin, Martin Blunos's new venture *Blinis* has come nowhere near compensating for the loss of his old one. The *Olive Tree* and the *Moody Goose* are both worthy ventures, but neither's showing in the survey this year was up to past best. The *Hole in the Wall* is a well-known old favourite, but does not excel.

Bath Priory – a very grand (and expensive) hotel restaurant – is of a very high standard and the town has an excellent, and extremely popular, veggie in the shape of *Demuths*. As a 'practical' mid-price destination, the handily-located *Moon & Sixpence* stands out. There are, of course, always the famous Pump Rooms (not listed) – you can queue, or book ahead on 01225 444477.

Bath Priory Hotel   £65   A★
Weston Rd BA1 2XT   (01225) 331922
Set in a "beautiful" location (amidst "lovely gardens", a short stroll from the centre), this "comfortable and discreet" establishment has it all – not least "excellent" and "imaginative" cuisine, and "superlative" service. / **Sample dishes:** crab & ginger ravioli with langoustine sauce; roast guinea fowl with lemon & sage; caramelised lemon tart.
Details: www.thebathpriory.co.uk; 1m W of city centre, past Victoria Park; 9.30 pm; jacket & tie required; no smoking; children: 7+ in restaurant. **Accommodation:** 28 rooms, from £210.

Blinis £ 50
16 Argyle St BA2 4BQ   (01225) 422510
"Not a patch on Lettonie"; though many do praise "out of this world" cuisine at Martin Blunos's new venture – a basement café with river views (below a street-level deli) – those who say it's a "comedown" from his previous venture are also numerous, especially given the "indifferent" ambience and "lacklustre" service; his backers are looking to sell as we go to press.
/ **Details:** 9.30 pm; closed Mon & Sun; no Amex; no smoking.

Browns £ 29 ✗
Old Police Station, Orange Grove BA1 1LP
(01225) 461199
Like its siblings nationwide, this potentially attractive branch of the fading British brasserie chain generates reports of "yuck" cooking and indifferent all-round standards. / **Sample dishes:** buffalo Mozzarella & plum tomato salad; steak, mushroom & Guinness pie; sticky toffee pudding. **Details:** www.browns-restaurants.com; 11 pm; no smoking area; no booking.

Café Fromage £ 14 ★
1 John St BA1 2JL   (01225) 313525
"Brilliant for a quick rustic snack and a glass of wine"; this "welcoming" café offers "great coffee" and "fresh and simple" dishes, which fans say are "tremendous value".
/ **Sample dishes:** no starters; grilled goats cheese salad with olives; cheesecake. **Details:** L & afternoon tea only; closed Sun; no credit cards; no smoking.

Demuths £ 30 ★
2 North Parade Passage BA1 1NX   (01225) 446059
The style is "colourful" – both the "stylish" cooking and the "bright and warm" décor – at this "quality veggie" in the heart of the city; service, though, can be "a bit slow and inattentive".
/ **Sample dishes:** feta, mint & pea pâté with walnut bread; goats cheese soufflé with tomato salsa; Indonesian black rice pudding. **Details:** www.demuths.co.uk; 10 pm; no smoking; booking: max 4 at D, Fri & Sat; children: 6+ after 7 pm.

The Eastern Eye £ 26 ★
8a Quiet St BA1 2JS   (01225) 422323
A "posh" central Indian, which offers "good curries" in "a large and splendid Georgian room". / **Details:** www.easterneye.co.uk; 11 pm; no smoking area.

Firehouse Rotisserie £ 35
2 John St BA1 2JL   (01225) 482070
It's on the "pricey" side for what's essentially a pizzeria – albeit one in a "great building" – but this California-style joint is a "fun" destination that many reporters think is "worth it".
/ **Sample dishes:** Brie & grape quesadillas; Pacific crab & smoked salmon fishcakes; chocolate pecan pie. **Details:** www.firehouserotisserie.co.uk; 11 pm; closed Sun.

Fishworks £ 42
6 Green St BA1 2JY   (01225) 448707
"Perfect fish" – the sort you'd hope for from a place with an integral fish shop (and seafood bar) – is praised by fans of this original branch of an expanding West Country mini-chain; some, however, feel it's "not as good as it used to be". / **Sample dishes:** crab salad with tarragon mayonnaise; cod with mash & parsley sauce; Sicilian lemon tart. **Details:** www.fishworks.co.uk; 10 pm; closed Mon & Sun D; no smoking.

sign up for the survey at www.hardens.com

Hole in the Wall   £ 33
16 George St BA1 2EN   (01225) 425242
This "old-favourite" basement (decked out in cheerful modern
style) has many admirers who tip it for an "excellent light lunch";
given that this was one of the England's seminal post-war
restaurants, though, it's hard to avoid the conclusion that it's "a
tiny bit boring" nowadays. / **Sample dishes:** warm scallop & bacon salad;
guinea fowl with beetroot & garlic sauce; caramelised pears with coffee ice cream.
Value tip: set 2-crs L £9.50. **Details:** 10 pm; closed Sun; no smoking area.

Loch Fyne   £ 33
24 Milsom St BA1 1DG   (01225) 750120
This "large and bustling fish café" in an old bank – part of the
growing national chain – makes a handy stand-by, and most
proclaim it a "good-value" destination. / **Sample dishes:** lobster bisque
with garlic rouille; rosemary-infused bream with tomatoes & black olives; lemon
sorbet. **Details:** www.loch-fyne.com; 10 pm; no smoking in dining room.
Accommodation: 8 rooms, from £from Jan 2003.

Mai Thai   £ 24   ★
6 Pierrepont St BA1 1LB   (01225) 445557
"The best of the city's Thais", this "cosy" central spot is a
"very friendly" place offering "tasty" dishes that are
"well presented". / **Value tip:** set 2-crs L £9. **Details:** 10.30 pm, Fri & Sat
10.45 pm; no smoking area; children: 9+.

Moody Goose   £ 42
74 Kingsmead Sq BA1 2AB   (01225) 466688
Stephen Shore's esteemed but low-key basement restaurant
generated surprisingly up-and-down feedback this year;
many reporters still hailed his cooking as "exceptional" and
"imaginative", but for a significant minority results were "good but
unmemorable". / **Sample dishes:** smoked haddock ravioli with goats cheese;
chicken with crayfish & artichoke mousse; passion fruit soufflé. **Value tip:** set 2-crs
L & pre-theatre £12. **Details:** www.moody-goose.com; 9.30 pm; closed Sun;
no smoking in dining room.

Moon & Sixpence   £ 33   A★
6a Broad St BA1 5LJ   (01225) 460962
"A central refuge from the crowds"; this "excellent" bistro/wine
bar (set back from the street) is well worth knowing about for its
"very good" cooking and "lively" atmosphere. / **Sample dishes:** guinea
fowl & pistachio ballotine; sea bass with pak choi & sweet chilli; white, milk & dark
chocolate mousses. **Details:** www.moonandsixpence.co.uk; 10.30 pm; no smoking
area.

No 5 Bistro   £ 37
5 Argyle St BA2 4BA   (01225) 444499
This convivial (and smoke-free) bistro, just off the Pulteney Bridge,
has been in business for a good few years now; it remains,
on most accounts, a "reliably good" destination.
/ **Sample dishes:** goats cheese mousse with grapefruit salad; pan-fried sea bass
with aubergine caviar; chocolate truffle & pineapple cake. **Details:** 10 pm,
Fri 10.30 pm, Sat 11 pm; closed Mon L & Sun; no smoking.

Olive Tree
Queensberry Hotel   £41
Russel St BA1 2QF   (01225) 447928
*Fans of this basement dining room hail its "intimate" ambience
and its "continuing high standards" (especially the "beautifully
prepared and imaginative food"); as ever, feedback is mixed,
though, and some find this a "soulless" place that's rather "over-
rated".* / **Sample dishes:** red mullet & roast aubergine salad; braised pork with
morels & savoy cabbage; roast peach tart. **Value tip:** set 3-crs L £15.50.
Details: www.batholivetree.com; 10 pm; closed Sun L; no Amex; no smoking.
Accommodation: 29 rooms, from £135.

Rajpoot   £26
4 Argyle St BA2 2BA   (01225) 466833
*A "great setting", in impressive cellars, helps make this
"a standard Indian offering with a twist" for most reporters;
for a small minority, however, it's "an over-rated tourist trap".*
/ **Value tip:** set 3-crs L £7. **Details:** www.rajpoot.com; 11 pm, Fri & Sat 11.30 pm.

Richmond Arms   £24   ★
7 Richmond Pl BA1 5PZ   (01225) 316725
*"Very good food for a pub, at sensible prices" makes this culinarily
creative Lansdown boozer perennially popular; "the sunny little
garden is a bonus".* / **Sample dishes:** Indonesian-spiced prawns with coconut
milk rice; duck with plum & tamarind sauce; moist orange cake with mango coulis.
Details: 8.30 pm, Fri & Sat 9 pm; closed Mon & Sun D; children: 14+.

Sukhothai   £24
90a Walcot St BA1 5BG   (01225) 462463
*"Good food and happy service" make this well-established Thai a
"firm favourite".* / **Details:** 10.30 pm; closed Sun L; no smoking in dining room.

Tilley's Bistro   £26   Ⓐ
3 North Parade Pas BA1 1NX   (01225) 484200
*In a charming pedestrian alley in the heart of the town, this small
and "friendly" bistro offers simple French dishes (and an
"excellent veggie selection"), which are generally "good"
(but which can be "bland").* / **Sample dishes:** Caesar salad;
pork Dijonnaise; warm banana pancake with toffee sauce. **Value tip:** set 2-crs L
£7.50. **Details:** www.tilleysbistro.co.uk; 11 pm; closed Sun; no Amex; no smoking
area.

Woods   £34
9-13 Alfred St BA1 2QX   (01225) 314812
*"I've been going for years, it never fails" – this Gallic brasserie of
over two decades' standing is an ever-popular destination, thanks
to its "good-value" food, "friendly" service and "spacious",
"relaxed" setting.* / **Sample dishes:** roasted tomato & basil soup; lamb & roast
garlic casserole; chocolate torte. **Value tip:** set 2-crs L £9.50.
Details: www.bathshopping.co.uk; 10.30 pm; closed Sun D; no Amex.

BAWTRY, SOUTH YORKSHIRE   5–2D

China Rose   £30   ★
16 South Parade DN10 6JH   (01302) 710461
*"Large" and "classy" – this "excellent" Chinese is acclaimed by
local supporters for its "great" food.* / **Details:** 10.30 pm; D only;
no smoking in dining room.

BEACONSFIELD, BUCKINGHAMSHIRE 3–3A

Leigh House £31
53 Wycombe End HP9 1LX (01494) 676348
"Popular and welcoming", this consistent Chinese restaurant is *"above-average in terms of both cuisine and comfort"*. / **Value tip:** set 2-crs L £13. **Details:** 10 pm; no smoking area.

Loch Fyne £33
70 London End HP9 2JD (01494) 679960
A handy pit stop off the A40, this *"bright warehouse-type"* branch of the national seafood chain is hailed as a *"noisy, but fun"* place offering *"a good range of fish and shellfish"*; culinary results, however, can be *"very average"*. / **Sample dishes:** Loch Fyne oysters; hot smoked salmon salad; toffee pudding. **Details:** www.loch-fyne.com; 10 pm; no smoking in dining room.

BEAUMARIS, ISLE OF ANGLESEY 4–1C

Ye Olde Bull's Head £43 *A* ★
Castle St LL58 8AP (01248) 810329
"A modern eating experience behind the façade of an olde-worlde pub" – this *"cosy"* veteran (whose past customers have included Dickens and Dr Johnson) is roundly praised by all who comment on it for its *"imaginative"*, *"good value"* food and *"surprisingly trendy décor"*. / **Sample dishes:** lettuce soup with smoked goose ravioli; Welsh beef with horseradish crust; clementine sponge with Grand Marnier ice cream. **Details:** www.bullsheadinn.co.uk; 9.30 pm; closed Sun; no smoking; children: 7+. **Accommodation:** 15 rooms, from £85.

BEETHAM, CUMBRIA 7–4D

The Wheatsheaf £30
LA7 7AL (01539) 562123
"A steady standard of cooking" makes this pretty old rural pub a *"safe bet"*, so far as the locals are concerned. / **Sample dishes:** gateau of black pudding & goats cheese; pork, leek & Stilton pie; ginger & banana sponge. **Details:** 5m N of A6, J35; 9 pm; no Amex; no smoking. **Accommodation:** 4 rooms, from £60.

BELFAST, COUNTY ANTRIM 10–1D

Belfast's dining scene is modest in scale, but includes a couple of good-quality places. *Aldens* is the best (to which the alternative is a trip to Bangor's *Shanks*). In the city centre, *Nick's Warehouse* – the 'grand-daddy' of Belfast's contemporary restaurant scene – remains a key destination.

The two establishments which dominate in terms of sheer volume of feedback are *Cayenne* and *Deanes*. Both are backed by 'personalities', and both attract accusations of complacency.

Aldens £37 A★
229 Upper Newtownards Rd BT4 3JF   (028) 9065 0079
*"A real treat"; it may have a "poor location" (a converted
supermarket in an un-smart part of town) but there's a
"good atmosphere" at this four-year old venture – with its
"quality" service, "imaginative modern cooking" it's rated as
"Northern Ireland's best restaurant" by reporters.*
/ **Sample dishes:** beetroot & herring salad; roast cod with Parma ham butter;
rhubarb granita with apple brandy. **Value tip:** set 1-crs L £8.95. **Details:** 2m from
Stormont Buildings; 10 pm, Fri & Sat 11 pm; closed Sat L & Sun; no smoking area.

The Apartment £21 A
2 Donegal Square West BT1 6JA   (028) 9050 9777
*"Funky décor and good food" have won a warm welcome for this
newcomer near City Hall; fans hail it as a "brilliant
bar/bistro/café" whose "young and old" clientèle make it "great
for people-watching".* / **Sample dishes:** crostini with Brie & roast tomatoes;
cured cod with leek & tarragon risotto; pecan pie with honeycomb ice cream.
Details: beside City Hall; 9 pm, Sun 6 pm; no Amex; no smoking area; no booking;
children: before 6 pm only.

Cayenne £31
7 Ascot Hs, Shaftesbury Sq BT27 7DB   (028) 9033 1532
*Many hail this "fun" and "interesting" city-centre fusion restaurant
(once called Roscoff) as "Belfast's best"; for a significant minority
of reporters, though, TV-chef Paul Rankin's "celeb status" is an
excuse for "overpriced food".* / **Sample dishes:** Caesar salad with tobacco
croutons; salmon with coconut rice & black bean vinaigrette; spiced ginger pudding.
Value tip: set 2-crs L & pre-theatre £10.50. **Details:** near Botanic Railway Station;
11.15 pm; closed Sat L & Sun; no smoking area.

Deanes £36
34-40 Howard St BT1 6PF   (028) 9056 0000
*Fans praise the "decadent" and "relaxed" atmosphere and
"sophisticated" cooking at Michael Deane's central brasserie
(with a fine-dining room upstairs, formula price £53); for too
many critics, though, it may be "trendy" but it's just a "banal"
place that's "trading on its reputation".* / **Sample dishes:** goats cheese
with salami & asparagus; ground beef with onion mash & spiced ketchup; steamed
pineapple pudding. **Details:** www.deanesbelfast.com; near Grand Opera House;
11 pm; closed Sun.

Nick's Warehouse £36 A★
35 Hill St BT1 2LB   (028) 9043 9690
*"There's a tremendous buzz at lunch" at this long-established
wine bar when it's "still the most consistent and best-value place
in town"; it's also a reliable choice at other times.*
/ **Sample dishes:** lemon & chilli chicken tempura; salmon & roast tomatoes with
rocket mayonnaise; white peach cheesecake. **Details:** www.nickswarehouse.co.uk;
behind St Anne's Cathedral; 10 pm; closed Mon D, Sat L & Sun; children: before
9 pm only.

Shu £30
253 Lisburn Rd BT9 7EN   (028) 9038 1655
*Support is ebbing for this trendy two-year-old bar/restaurant;
some do still praise its "vibrant" ambience and "very good"
modern British grub, but even fans say it's "overpriced",
and increasingly it's written off as "pretentious".*
/ **Sample dishes:** salt & chilli squid; roast cod with pak choi & green curry; coconut
rice spring rolls with ginger. **Value tip:** set 2-crs L £11.50.
Details: www.shu-restaurant.com; by Windsor Park; 10 pm; closed Sun; children:
12+.

BERKHAMSTED, HERTFORDSHIRE 3–2A

Nicholl's £29
163-165 High St HP4 3HB (01442) 879988
Standards are "decent (if not great)", and this "local brasserie" (part of a small Chilterns chain) can make a useful stand-by. / **Sample dishes:** *onion bread bruschetta with Greek salad; fillet steak with pepper sauce; crème brûlée.* **Details:** *www.nichollsonline.com.*

BERKSWELL, WARWICKSHIRE 5–4C

Bear Inn £22
Spencer Ln CV7 7BB (01676) 533202
"Good pub food" (with "great beer", too) maintains the popularity of this classic country boozer. / **Sample dishes:** *fishcakes; minted lamb with lime sauce; caramel tart.* **Details:** *off A45 through Meriden; 10 pm; no smoking area; no booking; children: 14+ in bar.*

BEVERLEY, EAST RIDING OF YORKSHIRE 6–1A

Copperfields Bistro 22 £31 Ⓐ
22 N Bar Within HU17 8AX (01482) 887624
It's the "romantic" setting of this "quaint" bistro which generates most support, though the "good (if expensive)" standards of its fish (and other) dishes are also well-acclaimed locally. / **Sample dishes:** *crab salad; stir-fried tiger prawns with smoked bacon & garlic; tiramisu.* **Details:** *9.30 pm; closed Sun; no smoking area.*

Wednesdays £29
8 Wednesday Mkt HU17 0DG (01482) 869727
"You can bring your own wine on Wednesdays", but the "imaginative" cooking is "good any day of the week" at this popular local restaurant. / **Sample dishes:** *Thai fishcakes with sweet & sour cucumber sauce; lamb shank in pearl barley broth; spicy date & ginger pudding.* **Value tip:** *set 2-crs L £10.* **Details:** *near Beverley Minster; 9.30 pm; closed Sun.*

BIDDENDEN, KENT 3–4C

Three Chimneys £33
Hareplain Rd TN27 8LW (01580) 291 472
"A wide choice of pub food from blackboard menus" and good real ales win unanimous recommendations for this cosy, beamed country boozer. / **Sample dishes:** *baked mushrooms with goats cheese; sea bass with sweet potato & coconut chowder; lemon tart with plum compote.* **Details:** *A262 between Biddenden and Sissinghurst; 9.45 pm; no Amex; no booking, Sun L.*

BIGBURY, DEVON 1–4D

Oyster Shack £26 Ⓐ★
Millburn Orchard Farm, Stakes Hills TQ7 4BE
(01548) 810876
It's "a complete experience" to visit this small seafood restaurant, which enjoys splendid views towards Burgh Island (and has "fantastic" seats outside); the simple seafood is "excellent quality". / **Sample dishes:** *grilled oysters with cream; smoked fish medley with salad; raspberry pavlova.* **Details:** *L only in summer (closed Tue & Wed, but open Sat D in winter); no Amex; no smoking; booking essential; children: only at L.*

BIRCHOVER, DERBYSHIRE 5–3C

Druid Inn £26

Main St DE4 2BL (01629) 650302

This "busy" Victorian pub generated mixed reviews this year (presumably not helped by a fire in the kitchen at New Year); it serves a "vast menu" that's "good for veggies", but which some feel needs "spicing up" – fingers crossed for a return to form in 2003. / **Sample dishes:** port & Stilton pâté; rack of lamb with redcurrant & gooseberry sauce; date & ginger pudding with butterscotch sauce. **Details:** www.birchovervillage.co.uk; NE of Ashbourne off B5056; 9 pm; no smoking area; children: 10+.

BIRKENHEAD, MERSEYSIDE 5–2A

Capitol £26 ★

24 Argyle St CH41 6AE (0151) 647 9212

Overlooking Hamilton Square Gardens, this long-established Chinese fixture still wins praise from locals for its "authentic" chow. / **Details:** www.capitol-restaurant.co.uk; 2m from Liverpool city centre; 11 pm; no smoking area.

BIRMINGHAM, WEST MIDLANDS 5–4C

Five years ago, there wasn't much of a restaurant scene in "England's second city" – the situation is changing rapidly, and much new restaurant space has been created in the major developments which have transformed the townscape. The sheer scale of many such places – *Bank, fish!* and *Le Petit Blanc* – has been such that they have efficiently met a need without creating anything terribly distinctive or of great quality. The recently-arrived *Hotel du Vin et Bistro* is similar in generating a lot of interest, without 'hitting the heights'.

As is invariably the pattern in London, the places which are emerging as of greatest distinction are by and large not those run by 'major restaurant operators' – *Metro*, the city's leading modern European-style restaurant, and *Thai Edge* are cases in point, and *La Toque d'Or* is also emerging with credit.

Of the longer-established places, *San Carlo* remains the best-known, but put in a very mixed performance this year. The giant Chineses – *Chung Ying* and *Chung Ying Garden* – as ever offer a solid performance, if not one with great personality. Though less well known, *The Bucklemaker* put in a good showing in the survey this year.

Brum's most famous contribution to world gastronomy probably remains the balti, with the greatest concentrations to be found in Moseley and Sparkbrook.

Adils £14 ★

148-150 Stoney Ln B12 8AJ (0121) 449 0335

Some still hail this "home of the balti" as "the first, and the best" of this Brum-based phenomenon; even many who say it's "still good value for money", though, say its cooking has "lost some of its edge" in recent times. / **Details:** www.adilbalti.co.uk; 3m from city centre on A41; 12.30 am; no smoking area.

Bank £ 37

4 Brindleyplace B1 2JB (0121) 633 4466

This "efficient" city-centre mega-brasserie rivals the nearby Petit Blanc (which reporters rate slightly more favourably overall); fans praise its "stylish modern British cooking" and "trendy" style, but it also has a fair number of critics for whom it's "pretentious" and "sterile". / **Sample dishes:** *five-onion soup with cheese croutons; calves liver & bacon with red onion confit; rum & raisin cheesecake.* **Value tip:** *set 3-crs L & pre-theatre £12.50 (Sun £15.50).* **Details:** *www.bankrestaurants.com; 11 pm, Fri & Sat 11.30 pm; no smoking area.*

The Bucklemaker £ 33   A ★

30 Mary Ann St, St Paul's Sq B3 1RL (0121) 200 2515

Seventeenth-century cellars provide a civilised setting for this "friendly and unpretentious" wine bar/restaurant of long standing; "good fish" is the highlight of the extensive menu. / **Sample dishes:** *halloumi with truffle oil & cardamom couscous; veal stuffed with ratatouille; bitter chocolate cake with strawberry cream.* **Details:** *www.thebucklemaker.co.uk; 10.30 pm; closed Sat L & Sun.*

Café Ikon £ 21

Ikon Gallery B1 2HS (0121) 248 3226

For "great snacks with style", this "chic" gallery café still has a sizeable and devoted fan club; even some reporters who say it "tried hard", though, found their experience this year rather underwhelming. / **Sample dishes:** *cured Spanish meats; seared tuna with roasted vegetables; baked custard flan.* **Details:** *10.30 pm; closed Mon & Sun D; no smoking area; children: before 9 pm only.*

Chez Jules £ 28

5a Ethel St, off New St B2 4BG (0121) 633 4664

No one pretends the "simple cuisine" at this "very buzzy, city-centre French-style canteen" is art, but the "very good prices" (especially from the set menus) win it numerous "cheap and cheerful" nominations. / **Sample dishes:** *chicken liver & mushroom pâté; pork in honey & grain mustard sauce; crème brûlée.* **Value tip:** *set 2-crs L £5.90.* **Details:** *11 pm; closed Sun L; no smoking area.*

Chung Ying Garden £ 28   ★

17 Thorp St B5 4AT (0121) 666 6622

Some favour the older Chung Ying (16-18 Wrottesley St, B5, tel 0121 622 5669) over the slightly newer and smarter Chung Ying Garden, when it comes to this huge Chinatown duo; service can be "sullen" and the setting is "mediocre", but the "authentic" menu offers a "fabulous variety" of dishes (and at lunch there's "the best dim sum"). / **Details:** *www.chungying.co.uk; 11.30 pm.*

Denial £ 35

120-122 Wharfside St B1 1RB (0121) 643 3080

Some "interesting" dishes and a "relaxed" ambience help win praise for this "cleverly-designed" hang-out in the upmarket Mailbox shopping centre – a top brunch and snack venue. / **Sample dishes:** *seared scallops with rocket & chorizo; semi-dried beef with pink peppercorn béarnaise; cheesecake with blackcurrant & lime compote.* **Details:** *www.denial.ltd.uk; 10 pm.*

52 Degrees North   £32
Arcadian Centre, Hurst St B5 4TD   (0121) 622 5250
*Twenty- and thirtysomething reporters hail this "cool"
bar/restaurant opposite the Hippodrome as a "stylish" destination
for a date; one reporter who has outgrown such things, however,
dismisses the place as "an expensive way of insulting all six
senses".* / **Sample dishes:** *black pudding & pancetta salad; lamb with cardamom
sauce & basil mash; raspberry crème brûlée.*
Details: *www.fiftytwodegreesnorth.co.uk; 2 am; D only.*

fish!   £30
Mailbox, 156-158 Wharfside St B1 1RQ   (0845) 100 4555
*A "wide range" of "honest-to-goodness fish" cooked "to your
preference" has made this "lively" canalsider a pretty "reliable"
destination, even if the cooking does tend to be rather "average".*
/ **Sample dishes:** *devilled whitebait; grilled monkfish with olive oil dressing; bread &
butter pudding.* **Value tip:** *set 2-crs weekday menu £10.*
Details: *www.fishdiner.co.uk; 10.30 pm; closed Sun D; no smoking area.*

Giovanni's   £29
27 Poplar Rd B14 7AA   (0121) 443 2391
*This "quirky" Italian near Highbury Park is "too cramped" for
some reporters, but its "excellent specials" (with fish a highlight)
generally find favour.* / **Sample dishes:** *spinach & ricotta cannelloni;
red snapper with vegetables; tiramisu.* **Details:** *10.30 pm; closed Mon, Sat L & Sun.*

The Green Room   £35
A208 Arcadian Centre, Hurst St B5 4TD   (0121) 605 4343
*This "imaginative bar/brasserie", opposite the Hippodrome,
doesn't try to scale culinary heights; it's "handy pre-theatre",
though, and "a good place to take teenagers".*
/ **Sample dishes:** *deep-fried broccoli; spicy chicken with curly fries & coleslaw;
poached pears.* **Details:** *11 pm, Thu midnight, Fri & Sat 2 am; no smoking area.*

Henry's Cantonese   £25
27 St Paul's Sq B3 1RB   (0121) 200 1136
*"Top-notch, basic Chinese cooking" makes this "noisy" city-centre
spot a handy destination.* / **Details:** *www.henrysrestaurant.co.uk; 11 pm.*

Hotel du Vin et Bistro   £40
Church St B3 2NR   (0121) 236 0559
*"A great addition to Brum's hotels"; the latest member of the
growing national boutique-hotel chain "may not be quite as good
as in Bristol or Winchester", but it is "an oasis in what is still
something of a desert", offering "pretty good" food in a
"convivial" setting.* / **Sample dishes:** *curried cauliflower soup; calves liver &
bacon with mash; butterscotch cheesecake with chocolate sauce.*
Details: *www.hotelduvin.com; 10 pm.* **Accommodation:** *66 rooms, from £110.*

Imran's   £11   ★
264-266 Ladypool Rd B12 8JU   (0121) 449 6440
*"An old Sparkbrook favourite" – in business for over 30 years –
famed for serving "lovely baltis" and "huge naans".*
/ **Details:** *www.imrans.co.uk; midnight; no smoking area.*

sign up for the survey at www.hardens.com

Jonathans £39
16-24 Wolverhampton Rd B68 OLH   (0121) 429 3757
*This long-established Victorian-style restaurant is "much-touted
locally", and it can be quite a "fun" destination; it inspires every
flavour of feedback, however, from "superb", via "variable but
honest", to plain "shoddy". / Sample dishes: 'Market day' broth; wild berry
chicken; bread & butter pudding. Value tip: set 3-crs D £15.90.
Details: www.jonathans.co.uk; 10 pm; closed Sat L & Sun D; no smoking area.
Accommodation: 48 rooms, from £80.*

Jyoti £15 ★
569-571 Stratford Rd B11 4LS   (0121) 766 7199
*Standards are "a bit hit-and-miss", but the "wonderfully cheap
veggie fare" of this BYO Gujerati commends it to most reporters.
/ Details: 8.30 pm; closed Mon & Tue L-Thu L; no Amex; no smoking.*

Kababish £21 ★
29 Woodbridge Rd B13 8EH   (0121) 449 5556
*The "spruced-up décor now matches the very good food",
says one of the fans of this popular Moseley balti house.
/ Details: 11.15 pm; D only.*

Lime & Chilli House £30
25 Woodbridge Rd B13 8EH   (0121) 449 4498
*This "compact" and brightly-decorated Moseley venture is "always
packed" – say locals – thanks to its "innovative" food which is
"Mexican-ish" in style. / Sample dishes: garlic & olive tapenade; rib-eye
steak; treacle tart. Details: 10 pm; no Amex.*

Living Room £28
Regency Whf, Broad St B1 2DS   (0121) 616 6820
*A "buzzy", "see-and-be-seen" outpost of a growing national chain
of piano-bar/restaurants – given that one wouldn't really expect
the cooking to be the main point, reports are in fact surprisingly
positive. / Sample dishes: salt & pepper squid; cheese & bacon burger;
hot chocolate fudge cake. Details: www.thelivingroom.co.uk; 11 pm, Wed & Thu
11.30 pm, Fri & Sat midnight .*

Maharaja £24 ★
23 Hurst St B5 4SA   (0121) 622 2641
*Some find this city-centre Indian (est. 1972) a little "dated",
but fans say its "reliable" performance puts it "in a class of its
own". / Details: 11 pm; closed Sun.*

Malt Shovel £16
1 Newton Rd B43 6HN   (0121) 357 1148
*This "enthusiastically-run" boozer (in Great Barr, just north of the
city) offers "well-prepared" tucker in a "lively" setting; it can get
"tremendously busy" – "get there early" if you want to eat in the
pub, or "book for the more formal restaurant".
/ Sample dishes: melon; roast pork & traditional trimmings; ice cream selection.
Details: 8.30 pm, Fri & Sat 9 pm; no Amex; no smoking; need 10+ to book.*

Metro £35 🅐 ★
73 Cornwall St B3 2DF   (0121) 200 1911
*It's not just the fact that it's "in the centre of the business district"
that makes this "the place for Brum's movers and shakers" –
it has an "elegant" setting, where an "ever-changing" menu is
realised to "consistently high" standards. / Sample dishes: deep-fried
squid with peanut butter & mango salsa; minted lamb with summer vegetables;
apricot & nectarine crumble. Details: www.themetrobar.co.uk; 9.30 pm; closed Sun.*

Le Petit Blanc £31
9 Brindleyplace B1 2HS   (0121) 633 7333
As a "good everyday restaurant", this "classy but noisy" brasserie
by the canal wins a big thumbs-up from Brummies and visitors
alike (and it's "always full"); some are "dubious" about the level of
Monsieur Blanc's involvement, though, finding the cooking "good,
but not as good as expected". / *Sample dishes:* smoked chicken & chilli
linguine; Thai-baked sea bass with coriander rice; sticky toffee pudding.
Value tip: set 2-crs L & pre-theatre £12.50. *Details:* www.lepetitblanc.co.uk;
11.30 pm; no smoking area.

Rajdoot £24
78-79 George St B3 1PY   (0121) 236 1116
"Delicately spiced" Indian dishes are "pleasingly presented" at this
"calm" and "courteous" city-centre Indian, which moved from its
old Albert St premises in July 2002. / *Details:* www.rajdoot.co.uk;
11.15 pm; closed Sat L & Sun L.

Royal Naim £14 ★
417-419 Stratford Rd B11 4JZ   (0121) 766 7849
Not many reporters comment on this "café-like" Sparkhill curry
house, but those who do hail "exceptional quality" cooking that
"sets the standard for balti". / *Details:* 2 mins from city centre on A34;
midnight.

San Carlo £38
4 Temple St B2 5BN   (0121) 633 0251
"Resting dangerously on its laurels", this "smart" and "shiny" city-
centre Italian – where "a wide choice of fish" is a highlight –
seems to have hit a rough patch; "slapdash" or even "aggressive"
service was at the root of a number of the more unhappy reports
this year. / *Sample dishes:* barbecue spare ribs; veal in wine & mushroom sauce;
coffee bean ice cream. *Details:* 10.45 pm; children: 5+.

Shimla Pinks £29
214 Broad St B15 1AY   (0121) 633 0366
Some still say "it's the place to go", but this "beautiful,
if pretentious" curry house draws more brickbats than bouquets
these days; "mostly appalling, arrogant service" is the chief
complaint, though "uninteresting" and "overpriced" cooking isn't
far behind. / *Details:* www.shimlapinks.com; 11 pm; closed Sat L & Sun L.

Thai Edge £31 A★
Brindleyplace B1 2HS   (0121) 643 3993
With its "calm and relaxing" atmosphere and "efficient and
friendly" service, this "polished" canalside yearling is the most
popular Thai in town – indeed, it's one of the more consistent
recommendations of any type. / *Value tip:* set 2-crs L £9.90.
Details: 11 pm, Fri & Sat 11.30 pm.

La Toque d'Or £35 ★
27 Warstone Ln B18 6JQ   (0121) 233 3655
This "discreet", "intimate" and "unpretentious" Jewellery Quarter
"gem" (on the former site of Gilmore, RIP) has quickly become
"deservedly popular", thanks to its "very good" Gallic cooking and
"charming" service. / *Sample dishes:* rainbow trout with lemon dressing;
marinated lamb with vegetables; vanilla crème brûlée.
Details: www.latoquedor.co.uk; 9.30 pm; closed Mon, Sat L & Sun (& 2 weeks in
Aug).

sign up for the survey at www.hardens.com

Zinc   £ 33   ✕
Regency Whf, Gas Basin St B1 2SD   (0121) 200 0620
"Clinical" décor, service which "goes through the motions" and cooking which is "OK but unexceptional" – this "typically Conran" newcomer displays all the traits that Londoners have come to associate with the capital's 'leading' multiple restaurant operator. / **Sample dishes:** chilli squid; wild mushroom & spinach linguine; lemon tart. **Details:** www.conran-restaurants.co.uk; 10.30 pm.

BISHOPS STORTFORD, HERTFORDSHIRE   3–2B

The Lemon Tree   £ 37   𝔸★
14-16 Water Ln CM23 2JZ   (01279) 757788
"I am amazed you left it out" – we are pleased to rectify last year's deficiency concerning this "excellent all-round" restaurant, housed in a Georgian terrace, as it offers "delightful" cooking and "great" service. / **Sample dishes:** cured salmon with avocado salsa; chicken with Mediterranean vegetables; rhubarb & apple sponge. **Details:** www.lemontree.co.uk; 9.30 pm; closed Mon & Sun D; no Amex; no smoking in dining room.

BISHOPS TACHBROOK, WARWICKSHIRE   5–4C

Mallory Court   £ 59
Harbury Ln CV33 9QB   (01926) 330214
New chef Simon Haigh is "getting into his stride", say reporters on the new regime at this "elegant", and notably "friendly", hotel, in an impressive inter-war country house. / **Sample dishes:** goats cheese ravioli with caramelised walnuts; sea bass with tarragon mousse; raspberry soufflé. **Value tip:** set 2-crs L £19.50 (Sun £23). **Details:** www.mallory.co.uk; 2m S of Leamington Spa, off B4087; 10 pm, Sat 10.30 pm; no smoking in dining room; children: 9+. **Accommodation:** 18 rooms, from £185.

BISPHAM GREEN, LANCASHIRE   5–1A

Eagle & Child   £ 26
Maltkiln Ln L40 3SG   (01257) 462297
An "interesting menu" and an "attractive interior" distinguish this popular country pub; veggie options are "poor or non-existent", though, and service can be "slow". / **Sample dishes:** deep–fried goats cheese; toasted chicken & red pepper panini; sticky toffee pudding. **Details:** M6, J27; 8.15 pm; no Amex; no smoking area.

BLACKPOOL, LANCASHIRE   5–1A

September Brasserie   £ 31
15-17 Queen St FY1 1PU   (01253) 623282
"Standards are always high", say supporters of this "unexpected" first-floor bistro, long hailed as "the best place for miles around"; its ratings drifted this year, though. / **Sample dishes:** pumpkin & goats cheese soufflé; braised pork knuckle; sticky date pudding. **Value tip:** set 2-crs L £11. **Details:** just past North Pier, opp Cenotaph; 10 pm; closed Mon & Sun.

BLAIR ATHOLL, PERTH & KINROSS 9–3C

The Loft £23
(01796) 481377
*The youngest head chef in the UK (16), it is claimed, has recently been installed at the stoves of this locally-popular destination, in an ancient building which now boasts such mod cons as a conservatory bar and roof terrace; let's hope the formerly impressive standards can be maintained! / **Sample dishes:** roasted cherry tomato tartlet; green Thai chicken curry with lemongrass rice; pineapple tarte Tartin. **Details:** www.theloftrestaurant.co.uk; 9.30 pm; closed Mon; no smoking in dining room; children: 12+ (except in conservatory).*

BLAIRGOWRIE, PERTH & KINROSS 9–3C

Kinloch House £41 ★
PH10 6SG (01250) 884237
*A small but rapturous following acclaims the "fabulous" (and "reasonably-priced") Scottish cooking at this Victorian country house hotel. / **Sample dishes:** wild mushroom, chicken & sweetbread terrine; fillet steak with Lanark Blue cheese; chocolate truffle cake with mint cream. **Value tip:** set 3-crs L £12.50. **Details:** www.kinlochhouse.com; 9.15 pm; jacket & tie required at D; no smoking; children: 7+ at D. **Accommodation:** 20 rooms, from £200.*

BLAKENEY, NORFOLK 6–3C

The White Horse Hotel £35 Ⓐ
4 High St NR25 7AL (01263) 740574
*This "fun" and "friendly" old inn has a "gorgeous" location a little way from the quayside; all reports testify to the "reliable" nature of its straightforward cooking (in both restaurant and bar). / **Sample dishes:** smoked cod, leek & Parmesan tartlet; roasted black bream with chilli & fennel dressing; raspberry tart. **Details:** www.blakeneywhitehorse.co.uk; 9 pm; D only, closed Mon & Sun; no smoking in dining room; children: 6+. **Accommodation:** 10 rooms, from £60.*

BLANCHLAND, COUNTY DURHAM 8–2B

Lord Crewe Arms £38 Ⓐ
DH8 9SP (01434) 675251
*Restaurant and pub settings don't come much more historic than this 12th &17th-century building, which started off life as an abbey; it's now a "stately" inn, offering "good pub food" in the ancient cellars, and "reasonable-value" fare in the dining room. / **Sample dishes:** tomato & Mozzarella salad with basil dressing; sirloin steak in green peppercorn & brandy sauce; sticky toffee pudding. **Details:** www.lordcrewehotel.com; 9.15 pm; D only, except Sun open L & D; children: small children discouraged. **Accommodation:** 19 rooms, from £110.*

BOLLINGTON, CHESHIRE 5–2B

Church House Inn £25
Church St SK10 5PY (01625) 574014
*"Recently changed hands, but the food's still good"; this traditional boozer makes a handy destination in this pretty part of the world. / **Sample dishes:** garlic mushrooms; steak diane with Dijon mustard sauce; hot almond tart. **Details:** close to Shrigley Hall Hotel; 9.30 pm; no Amex; no smoking area; no booking in main bar. **Accommodation:** 5 rooms, from £48.*

BOLTON ABBEY, NORTH YORKSHIRE 8–4B

Devonshire Arms £ 62 𝖸

Grassington Rd BD23 6AJ (01756) 710441

A "breathtaking" setting makes a visit to this grand and "comfortable" country inn (owned by the Devonshires for over 250 years) quite a special event; "food quality can vary", though, so the modern brasserie (£31) may be a better bet than the restaurant. / **Sample dishes:** goose, mango & smoked foie gras salad; roast cod with fennel & olive sauce; chocolate & Turkish Delight soufflé. **Value tip:** set 3-crs Sun L £19.50. **Details:** www.devonshirehotels.co.uk; on A59, 5m NE of Skipton; 10 pm; D only, except Sun open L & D; no smoking. **Accommodation:** 41 rooms, from £195.

BOLTON, LANCASHIRE 5–2B

Strawbury Duck £ 19 𝖸

Overshores Rd, Turton BL7 OLU (01204) 852013

This "agreeable" pub enjoys a "great location", on the way to the Pennines, and serves "simple" but "tasty" food at "good-value" prices. / **Sample dishes:** black pudding tower; lamb Devonshire; Italian trifle. **Details:** 100 yds from Entwistle railway station; 9.30 pm, Sat 10 pm; no Amex. **Accommodation:** 4 rooms, from £39.50.

BOSTON SPA, WEST YORKSHIRE 5–1C

Spice Box £ 28 ★

152 High St LS23 6BW (01937) 842558

"Under new owners it's still very good" – that's the consensus on the "innovative but unpretentious" fish and seafood cooking at this brasserie-style restaurant (which changed hands at the end of 2001). / **Sample dishes:** fishcakes with Thai sauce; duck with bacon & thyme potatoes; chocolate truffle. **Details:** www.spiceboxrestaurant.co.uk; 2m E of A1, on A659; 9.30 pm; closed Mon L & Sun; no smoking.

BOUGHTON LEES, KENT 3–3C

Eastwell Manor £ 48

Eastwell Pk TN25 4HR (01233) 213000

This Elizabethan manor house has a "beautiful setting"; the past year has seen changes of chef and management, though, so this must be in the nature of a 'holding' entry – there is now a brasserie (£34) as well as the restaurant. / **Sample dishes:** white bean soup with langoustine & truffles; chicken supreme with mustard cream sauce; apple & rhubarb crumble. **Value tip:** set 2-crs weekday L £10. **Details:** www.eastwellmanor.co.uk; 3m N of Ashford on A251; 9.30 pm; no smoking in dining room; booking: max 12. **Accommodation:** 62 rooms, from £200.

BOURNEMOUTH, DORSET 2–4C

Bistro on the Beach £ 35 𝖸★

Solent Promenade BH6 4BE (01202) 431473

"An unusual beach café that transforms itself into a candlelit bistro at night"; fans say "the food is amazing and the views perfect", and everyone says the cooking is at least "competent" and "good value". / **Sample dishes:** smoked salmon & prawn terrine; braised lamb with mint mash; bread & butter pudding. **Details:** 9.30 pm; D only, closed Sun-Tue; no smoking.

Chez Fred   £15   ★
10 Seamoor Rd BH4 9AN   (01202) 761023
"Cheap, fresh and fun" – reporters only have good things to say
about this *"excellent seaside chippy"*. / **Sample dishes:** no starters;
cod & chips with mushy peas; treacle sponge & custard.
Details: www.chezfred.co.uk; 1m W of town centre; 9.45 pm; closed Sun L;
no Amex; no smoking; no booking.

Clarks   £39   ★
350-352 Charminster Rd BH8 9RX   (01202) 240310
*Ex-Dorchester chef, Gary Clark, is cooking up a storm at his small
"oasis" of quality cooking on the outskirts of town, where the food
is "well presented and full of flavour"; the setting, though,
is "somewhat lacking in atmosphere".* / **Sample dishes:** asparagus &
truffle tart; roast lamb & sweetbreads with summer vegetables; banana pannacotta
with walnut praline. **Details:** 10 pm; closed Mon, Tue L, Sat L & Sun; no smoking
before 10 pm; children: 10+.

Mandarin   £24   ★
194-198 Old Christchurch Rd BH1 1PD   (01202) 290681
"Lovely" Chinese food and *"superb"* service makes this
"consistently good" Chinese restaurant a destination of some note
locally. / **Details:** www.themandarin.net; 11 pm.

Ocean Palace   £27   ★
8 Priory Rd BH2 5DG   (01202) 559127
*A "very good Chinese" near the Bournemouth International
Centre; it's a competent performer across the board.*
/ **Details:** www.oceanpalace.co.uk; 11 pm.

BOWNESS, CUMBRIA   7–3D
Miller Howe   £53   Ⓐ
Rayrigg Rd LA23 1EY   (01539) 442536
"Not as good as in John Tovey's heyday, but well worth a visit" –
that was the survey's verdict on this destination hotel (famed for
its *"staggering views over the lake"*); let's hope new chef Paul
Webster can earn a more ringing endorsement from next year's
survey! / **Sample dishes:** warm chicken liver salad; roast halibut with sage mash;
sticky toffee pudding & toffee sauce. **Value tip:** set 3-crs L £17.50 (Sun £20).
Details: www.millerhowe.com; on A592 between Windermere & Bowness; 8 pm;
closed for 2 weeks in Jan; no smoking in dining room; children: 8+.
Accommodation: 15 rooms, from £80, incl D.

Porthole   £40   Ⓐ★
3 Ash St LA23 3EB   (01539) 442793
*"A brilliant family-run Italian"; Judy & Gianni Berton's veteran
institution, which occupies a charming 17th-century house at the
heart of the village, remains as popular as ever.*
/ **Sample dishes:** antipasto; veal with mushrooms; sticky toffee pudding.
Details: www.porthole.fsworld.co.uk; near Old England Hotel; 10.30 pm; closed
Mon L, Tue & Sat L.

BRADFORD, WEST YORKSHIRE   5–1C
Aagrah   £23
483 Bradford Rd LS28 8ED   (01274) 668818
*As you'd expect from a branch of this prominent Yorkshire chain,
results at this "modern" subcontinental are "always good".*
/ **Details:** www.aagrah.com; on A647, 3m from city centre; 11.30 pm, Fri & Sat
midnight; D only; no smoking area.

sign up for the survey at www.hardens.com

Akbars Balti £ 20 🅐★
1276 Leeds Rd BD3 3LF (01274) 773311
"A real find in an area with plenty of good Indians" –
this *"very busy"* Balti house wins high praise for its *"fabulous, freshly cooked dishes"*, *"efficiently"* served in a *"smart"* setting.
/ **Details:** www.akbars.co.uk; midnight; D only; no credit cards; no smoking area.

Clarks £ 26
46-50 Highgate BD9 4BE (01274) 499890
This rare Bradford non-subcontinental is *"popular"* with the locals
– it's a reasonably-priced bistro that's *"always enjoyable"*.
/ **Sample dishes:** pea & mint soup; bacon chop with Cheddar mash & parsley sauce; treacle tart. **Value tip:** set 2-crs L £7.95.
Details: www.clarksrestaurant.co.uk; 5 mins from city centre on A650 to Shipley;
10 pm; closed Sat L & Sun L; no smoking area.

Karachi £ 9 ★
15-17 Neal St BD5 OBX (01274) 732015
"So much food for so little money", at this basic (*"no-cutlery"*)
Indian veteran, in the centre of town. / **Details:** I am, Fri & Sat 2 am;
no credit cards.

Kashmir £ 11 ★
27 Morley St BD7 1AG (01274) 726513
For *"a real bargain"*, you won't do much better than this
"very authentic" and *"consistent"* curry house (the oldest in town);
gripes about *"rising prices"* have to be put in context – *"you don't
get much change from a fiver nowadays"*. / **Details:** 3 am; no Amex;
no smoking area.

Mumtaz Paan House £ 15 ★★
Great Horton Rd BD7 3HS (01274) 571861
"Brilliant, authentic Pakistani food at rock-bottom prices" makes
this *"rapidly expanding"* star still *"the best 'Indian' restaurant in
England"* for its army of fans; *"wonderful smells"* and *"no booze"*
add to the *"multicultural experience"*. / **Details:** www.mumtaz.co.uk;
I am; no smoking area.

Nawaab £ 22 ★★
32 Manor Rw BD1 4QE (01274) 720371
"A legend, and deservedly so", this city-centre Indian offers an
"amazing" menu, which includes many *"top-quality specials"*.
/ **Details:** www.nawaab.com; 11 pm; closed Sat L & Sun L; no smoking area.

BRANCASTER, NORFOLK 6–3B

White Horse £ 30 🅐★
Main Rd PE31 8BY (01485) 210262
"Stunning view, great food" – four words say it all about this
popular sea-view inn, where *"excellent local produce"* (crab and
mussels are top recommendations) comes *"well presented"*.
/ **Sample dishes:** char-grilled sardines with aubergine caviar; roast chicken with
pearl barley & beetroot risotto; strawberry shortcake.
Details: www.whitehorsebrancaster.co.uk; 9 pm; no smoking in dining room.
Accommodation: 15 rooms, from £68.

BRANSCOMBE, DEVON   2–4A

Masons Arms   £27
Main St EX12 3DJ   (01297) 680300
"A pub for all seasons", say devotees of this rustic country inn
with views to the coast, which is praised for its "pub grub with
imagination"; service "varies". / *Sample dishes:* smoked duck with
pineapple pickle; grilled plaice with garlic & prawns; chocolate truffle torte.
Details: www.masonsarms.co.uk; 9.15 pm; D only; no Amex; no smoking.
Accommodation: 27 rooms, from £44.

BRAY, WINDSOR & MAIDENHEAD   3–3A

The Fat Duck   £80
High St SL6 2AQ   (01628) 580333
Heston Blumenthal's "fantastically inventive" brand of 'molecular
gastronomy' was rated more highly this year, with those hailing his
concoctions as a "super-stimulation of the senses" outnumbering
those who found them "bizarre, and occasionally horrifying";
neither service nor ambience, however, really measures up.
/ *Sample dishes:* cuttlefish cannelloni with duck & maple syrup; slow-cooked lamb
with lambs tongue & onion purée; tarte Tatin with bay leaf & almond foam.
Value tip: set 3-crs L £28. *Details:* 9.30 pm, Sat 10 pm; closed Mon & Sun D;
closed 2 weeks at New Year; no smoking area.

Fish   £31   ✕
Old Mill Ln SL6 2BG   (01628) 781111
Fans hail "consistently good cooking" at this former pub where
fish is the highlight (no relation to the fish! chain);
some "very poor dishes" were reported this year, however,
and some reporters find service "supercilious" and the
atmosphere "cold". / *Sample dishes:* oysters; char-grilled tuna with black olive
mash; chocolate truffle cake. *Value tip:* set 3-crs L £12.95.
Details: www.thefishatbray.com; 9.15 pm; closed Sun D; no smoking area.

Riverside Brasserie   £37   ★
Monkey Island Ln, Bray Marina
SL6 2EB   (01628) 780553
This "wooden shed" in a Thameside marina may be "difficult to
find", but ownership by Heston Blumenthal has won it immediate
fame; "if you expect a budget Fat Duck, you may be
disappointed", but prepare yourself for something "cheaper and
less mucked-about", and you should have a "delicious" meal.
/ *Sample dishes:* sardine tart; rib-eye steak & chips with marrowbone sauce;
strawberry soup with butter biscuits. *Details:* follow signs for Bray Marina off A308;
10.15 pm; no Amex.

Waterside Inn   £103   Ⓐ
Ferry Rd SL6 2AT   (01628) 620691
Michel Roux's "awesome" gastronomy and a "very beautiful"
Thames-side location makes this a "breathtaking" experience for
many traditionalists; at the "astonishingly high prices", though,
quite a number judge the cooking "not bad, but not notable" and
find the place unduly "full of itself". / *Sample dishes:* spiced foie gras
terrine with poached figs; grilled rabbit with glazed chestnuts; golden plum soufflé.
Value tip: set 3-crs L £36 (Sun £52.50). *Details:* www.waterside-inn.co.uk;
off A308 between Windsor & Maidenhead; 10 pm; closed Mon & Tue (open Tue D
Jun-Aug); children: 12+. *Accommodation:* 9 rooms, from £150.

BREARTON, NORTH YORKSHIRE   8–4B
The Malt Shovel   £20   ★
HG3 3BX   (01423) 862929
"Good pub nosh without pretensions" (plus *"excellent ale"*) proves
a winning formula for this *"quaint"* venture, which occupies a
former barn. / **Sample dishes:** goats cheese & leek tart; steak & ale pie; treacle
tart. **Details:** off A61, 6m N of Harrogate; 9 pm; closed Mon & Sun D; no credit
cards; no smoking area; no booking.

BRIDPORT, DORSET   2–4B
Riverside   £34   ★★
West Bay   DT6 4EZ   (01308) 422011
"Cult status amongst West Country fish aficionados" elevates the
regard for this humble-looking café to giddy heights; *"there's no
finer place for oysters on a sunny day"*, but *"wonderfully-fresh fish,
carefully cooked"* is an attraction at any time. / **Sample dishes:** warm
oysters with laverbread; halibut with rarebit topping; limoncello pannacotta.
Value tip: set 2-crs L £12.50. **Details:** www.dorset-seafood-restaurant.co.uk; 9 pm;
closed Mon & Sun D; no Amex; smoking discouraged.

BRIGHTON, EAST SUSSEX   3–4B

Brighton has always had lots of restaurants, but until recently
they were generally rather more notable for their variety
than their quality. But this is beginning to change.

At the top end of the market, *One Paston Place* has stood
unchallenged for a number of years, but a 'second tier' of
contenders is now becoming established, most notably
Gingerman, but also *Blanch House* and *Strand*. As long as
you're willing to brave the service, the quirky but very
interesting *Black Chapati* continues to offer some highly
original cooking.

Vegetarians are especially well catered for, with *Terre à Terre*
– probably the best place of its type in the country – being
the most commented-on establishment in town. For
quintessential seaside seafood, the *Regency* is hard to beat.

In *English's*, Brighton boasts one of the UK's few true period
restaurants. It fails to impress consistently, however.

Those looking for the more obvious ethnic cuisines will find
an unusually wide choice of relatively inexpensive
establishments of good quality. The Lanes and the trendier
'hang-out' districts of North Laine and Kemptown continue
to boast a host of decent-enough mid-range places.

Al Duomo   £20
7 Pavilion Building BN1 1EE   (01273) 326741
*Though it looks a bit like a tourist trap, this huge fixture by the
Royal Pavilion is rated as a "genuine" destination by many locals,
and its "simple Italian food (including great wood-fired pizzas)"
wins little but praise; look out for a major expansion in 2003.*
/ **Sample dishes:** calamari; fusilli with tomatoes & anchovies; tiramisu.
Value tip: set 2-crs L & D £8.50. **Details:** www.alduomo.co.uk; near the Royal
Pavilion; 11 pm.

Aumthong Thai £25 ★

60 Western Rd BN3 1JD (01273) 773922
*The setting is "noisy" and "cramped", but "authentic" Thai food
makes this Hove spot a consistently popular destination.
/ **Details:** www.aumthong.com; 10.45 pm; closed Mon L.*

Black Chapati £30 ★★

12 Circus Pde, New England Rd BN1 4GW
(01273) 699011
*"Stunning", "Asian/fusion" cuisine can "make up for" the failings
of the staff ("sour") and the setting (like "a shoe shop store-
room") at this celebrated but "hard-to-find" location.
/ **Details:** 10 pm; D only, closed Mon, Tue & Sun; management declined to provide
further information.*

Blanch House £38 ★

17 Atlingworth St BN2 1PL (01273) 645755
*It's a bit "self-consciously trendy" for some tastes, but fans say
the décor is "lovely" at this refurbished small hotel, on the edge
of Kemptown, praised for its "wonderful" restaurant
(plus a "fabulous" cocktail bar). / **Sample dishes:** celeriac ravioli with
goats cheese; juniper-crusted lamb with ratatouille & rosemary polenta;
pink peppercorn meringue with strawberries. **Details:** www.blanchhouse.co.uk;
10.30 pm; closed Mon, Tue L, Wed L, Sat L & Sun D. **Accommodation:** 12 rooms,
from £100.*

Bombay Aloo £14 ★

39 Ship St BN1 1AB (01273) 771089
*This celebrated "buffet-style vegetarian" offers "excellent value",
and fans find it "authentic", too – "just like India", according to
one. / **Details:** near the Lanes; 11 pm; no Amex; no smoking area; need 6+ to
book; children: under 6s eat free.*

Browns £29

314 Duke St BN1 1AH (01273) 323501
*Standards at this (the original) outlet of the well-known British
brasserie chain have sunk so far that even some fans concede
"food is really the last thing one visits for"; the setting is
"nice enough" and can still make "a good meeting place".
/ **Sample dishes:** smoked salmon with soda bread; chicken & leek pie; sticky toffee
pudding. **Details:** www.browns-restaurants.com; 11.30 pm; no smoking area;
no booking.*

China Garden £29

88-90 Preston St BN1 2HG (01273) 325124
*"Wonderful dim sum" is the undoubted highlight at this large,
café-style oriental near Preston Park; otherwise, it's generally held
to be a reasonable "value-for-money" destination. / **Details:** on
seafront near Grand Hotel & Metropole Hotel; 11 pm.*

Donatello £30

1-3 Brighton Pl BN1 1HJ (01273) 775477
*"OK" Italian fare at reasonable prices makes this "busy" and
"noisy" Lanes spot a "reliable" stand-by for most who report on it;
it's "a fast in-and-out kind of place" – sometimes to excess.
/ **Sample dishes:** grilled sardines; tagliatelle with smoked salmon & cream; cherries
in liqueur with ice cream. **Value tip:** set 3-crs L £9.25.
Details: www.donatello.co.uk; 11.30 pm; no smoking area.*

The Dorset Street Bar   £25   A
28 North Rd BN1 1YB   (01273) 605423
"A top place for a hearty brekkie with the papers…", "perfect for summer lunches…" – this *"chilled"* café bar (a converted North Laine pub) offers *"fresh"* and *"simple"* fare, and *"friendly"* service. / **Sample dishes:** salmon fishcakes; grilled chicken with salami & Camembert; chocolate brioche. **Details:** 10 pm; no smoking area; booking: max 8.

English's   £38   ✕
29-31 East St BN1 1HL   (01273) 327980
There are some – even among the locals – who acclaim this venerable venture in the Lanes as a "charming" institution with "nice old-fashioned fish"; the denigrators – and there are many – say it should be "left to day-trippers with more money than sense". / **Sample dishes:** avocado, feta & nectarine salad; Dover sole & prawns with sorrel & lobster sauce; apple Bakewell. **Value tip:** set 2-crs D £7.95. **Details:** www.englishs.co.uk; 10 pm.

Food for Friends   £17   ★
17-18 Prince Albert St BN1 1HF   (01273) 202310
A "very varied menu" of veggie fare in "good portions" makes this "cheap", "fun" and "crowded" stalwart in the heart of the Lanes perennially popular; "you have to get used to the service", though. / **Sample dishes:** Jerusalem artichoke soup; Cheddar & mushroom risotto with spicy tomato sauce; Bramley & blackberry crumble. **Details:** www.foodforfriends.com; 10 pm; no smoking area.

La Fourchette   £33
101 Western Rd BN3 36H   (01273) 722556
"Shame about the very close tables" – and also the unreliable service – at this small and "busy" Gallic restaurant; the "interesting" menu sometimes includes "wonderful" fish dishes, and the place has won quite a following. / **Sample dishes:** spinach, asparagus & Mozzarella lasagne; confit duck with mash & veal sauce; citron tart. **Value tip:** set 3-crs L £10. **Details:** 10.30 pm; closed Mon L & Sun. **Accommodation:** 8 rooms, from £70.

Gars   £26
19 Prince Albert St BN1 1HF   (01273) 321321
Feedback was slightly mixed this year regarding this "friendly" oriental near the seafront; it remains quite a popular destination, though, serving "a wide variety of Chinese food". / **Value tip:** set 2-crs L £6.50. **Details:** near the Lanes; 11 pm; children: 7+ after 7 pm.

The George   £21   ★
5 Trafalgar St BN1 4EQ   (01273) 681055
"Really top-quality vegetarian food" ensures that this "cool" hang out near the station is "always packed"; "long waits" are sometimes the result. / **Sample dishes:** tomato & Mozzarella bruschetta; smoked Applewood rarebit with leeks & salsa; tarte Tatin. **Details:** 9.30 pm, Fri-Sun 8 pm; no smoking area; no booking, Fri-Sun; children: before 7 pm only.

Gingerman   £34   ★★
21a Norfolk Square BN1 2PD   (01273) 326688
Ben McKellar's "uncompromisingly good" and "inventive" cooking continues to win rave reviews for this small (and rather "cramped") venture), on the Hove/Brighton border. / **Sample dishes:** beetroot & anchovy salad; swordfish with plum tomato tart; passion fruit soufflé. **Value tip:** set 2-crs L £12.95. **Details:** off Norfolk Square; 10 pm; closed Mon & Sun.

The Grand £ 53 ✗
97-99 Kings Rd BN1 2FW   (01273) 224300
"Tea at The Grand can't be beaten", say fans of this famous five-star landmark; full meals come at "high prices", though, and too many judge results "pretty mediocre". / **Sample dishes:** prawns in garlic & coriander butter; duck with oriental noodles; raspberry crème brûlée. **Value tip:** set 3-crs Sun L £22. **Details:** www.grandbrighton.co.uk; 10 pm; jacket & tie required at D; no smoking before 9 pm. **Accommodation:** 200 rooms, from £220.

Harry's £ 25
41 Church Rd BN3 2BE   (01273) 727410
"Fantastic burgers", "great club sandwiches" and a top all-day breakfast – the food at this "casual but friendly" Hove diner may have no great aspirations, but the place does what it does very well, and it's "always full". / **Sample dishes:** prawn cocktail; cheese & chilli burger; banoffi pie. **Details:** www.harrysrestaurant.co.uk; 10.30 pm.

Havana £ 44
32 Duke St BN1 1AG   (01273) 773388
"The food and service don't live up to the décor", at this "beautiful" and "spacious" Lanes venue, which critics say just "pretends to be hip and trendy", and charges "silly prices"; a new chef was installed during 2002, so let's hope for better reports next year. / **Sample dishes:** haddock & poached egg tartlet; roast venison; Baileys parfait with biscuits. **Details:** www.havana.uk.com; 10 pm, Sat 11 pm; children: 6+ after 7 pm.

Hotel du Vin et Bistro £ 42
Ship St BN1 1AD   (01273) 718588
This popular shabby-chic hotel chain is opening its fifth branch – in one of the intriguing buildings which have become its forte – in late-2002; performance elsewhere suggests it will at the very least be a useful addition to the local scene.
/ **Details:** www.hotelduvin.com; 9.45 pm. **Accommodation:** 36 rooms, from £115.

Kooky @ Whytes £ 36
33 Western St BN1 2PG   (01273) 776618
Formerly Whytes, this small restaurant on the Hove border now has new owners and a 'kooky' theme – the aim, however, is a serious one, and diners are promised a table for the whole evening. / **Sample dishes:** oriental smoked duck salad; salmon fondant with confit fennel & saffron broth; lime & tequila tart with sweet chilli sorbet. **Details:** www.whytesrestaurant.com; 10 pm; D only, closed Mon & Sun; no Amex.

Latin in the Lanes £ 32 ★
10-11 Kings Rd BN1 1NE   (01273) 328672
"Top Italian food" – in particular "wonderful fresh seafood" – wins high praise for this "friendly" Lanes fixture.
/ **Sample dishes:** avocado & crab cocktail; linguine with clams; profiteroles. **Details:** 11 pm.

One Paston Place £ 55 ★
1 Paston Pl BN2 1HA   (01273) 606933
For a "serious" gastronomic experience, this grand Kemptown townhouse – with its "fine" and "careful" Gallic cuisine – is without equal in these parts; it's quite "expensive" for what it is, though, and the ambience can seem rather "austere".
/ **Sample dishes:** skate stuffed with potted shrimps & fennel; duck with balsamic jus & butternut squash; caramel soufflé. **Value tip:** set 2-crs L £16.50. **Details:** between the pier & marina; 9.45 pm; closed Mon & Sun; children: 2+.

sign up for the survey at www.hardens.com

Regency £19 ★
131 Kings Rd BN1 2HH (01273) 325014
"A classic Brighton experience" – for *"great fish and chips by the sea"*, this *"fast and friendly"* spot has many admirers.
/ **Sample dishes:** oysters; dressed crab salad; peach Melba.
Details: www.theregencyrestaurant.co.uk; opp West Pier; 11 pm; no smoking area.
Accommodation: 30 rooms, from £50.

The Saint £35 ★
22 St James's St BN2 1RF (01273) 607835
Thanks to the quality of its "limited but daily-changing menu of fresh food", this "friendly", white-walled Kemptown newcomer is "already making a name for itself". / **Sample dishes:** 'Saintly' antipasti; roast duck with courgette cakes & liquorice sauce; trio of brûlées. **Details:** 10 pm; closed Mon.

Sanctuary Café £21
51-55 Brunswick Street East BN3 1AU (01273) 770002
A trendy Kemptown local (with changing displays of "cool" art), which is tipped as a good place for "coffee, bagels and cakes", and "large portions" of other "healthy and tasty" fare.
/ **Sample dishes:** vegetarian pâté with pitta bread; aubergine lasagne; carrot cake.
Details: www.thesanctuarycafe.co.uk; 10 pm; no smoking area.

Saucy £30
8 Church Rd BN3 2FL (01273) 324080
Many reporters have a "top time" at this "funky" Hove brasserie, liking its "great seafood (in particular)" and "amiable" service; there are some, though, who feel the cooking's "good, but missing something". / **Sample dishes:** crayfish tails with linguine; beef with smoked anchovy tapenade; banana & butterscotch steamed pudding.
Details: www.saucyrestaurant.com; 10.30 pm; closed Sun D; no smoking area; booking: max 6, Fri & Sat.

Seven Dials £42
1-3 Buckingham Pl BN1 3TD (01273) 885555
A former bank provides the setting for this ambitious new restaurant; verdicts span the whole range from "indifferent" to "very good" – let's hope the reporter who says it "probably needs time" has it right. / **Sample dishes:** herb-crusted goats cheese salad; stuffed quail with pancetta & truffle jus; lavender pannacotta. **Details:** 10.30 pm; closed Mon, Tue L & Wed L; no smoking area.

Strand £28 A★
6 Little East St BN1 1HT (01273) 747096
This "lovely", "fun" fixture, near the Royal Pavilion, maintains a trendy following for its "really tasty" dishes, from a menu in which fish and veggie dishes figure large. / **Sample dishes:** Dolcelatte gnocchi; Thai fish wrapped in leeks; banana cream pie with honeycomb ice cream.
Details: 10 pm, Fri & Sat 10.30 pm; closed Mon L.

Terre à Terre £34 A★★
71 East St BN1 1NQ (01273) 729051
"Gourmet meat-free cooking" – *"sufficient to convert any carnivore"* – won rave reviews this year for this famous Lanes café; its claim to be *"the best veggie in the UK"* – shaky last year – is now looking more assured. / **Sample dishes:** fried corn cakes with salsa; asparagus wrapped in pasta with sun-dried tomato pesto; rhubarb & rosehip sorbet. **Details:** 10.30 pm; closed Mon L; no smoking area.

for updates visit www.hardens.com

Trogs £33 ★
124 Kings Rd BN1 2FA (01273) 204655
This "upmarket" basement veggie attracts nothing but praise for
its "wonderful" dishes (from organic ingredients), and its
"very friendly" staff. / **Sample dishes:** Thai coconut, chilli & lime patties;
steamed wild mushroom pudding; passion fruit brûlée. **Details:** opp West Pier,
by Metropole Hotel; 9.30 pm; no smoking. **Accommodation:** 24 rooms, from £75.

Tsing Tao £26 ★
33 Preston St BN1 2HP (01273) 202708
"Very good dim sum" is the highlight at this "authentic" Chinese,
near the West Pier. / **Details:** 11 pm.

BRIMFIELD, SHROPSHIRE 5–4A
The Roebuck Inn £34 ★
SY8 4NE (01584) 711230
"Well cooked food" and "cheerful" service make this "cramped"
but "excellent" gastropub a destination that's "vaut le voyage".
/ **Sample dishes:** gin-soused salmon with dill crème fraiche; steak & mushroom
suet pudding with ale gravy; pear, rhubarb & ginger charlotte.
Details: www.roebuckinn.demon.co.uk; 9.30 pm; no Amex; no smoking.
Accommodation: 3 rooms, from £60.

BRINKWORTH, WILTSHIRE 2–2C
The Three Crowns £29
The Street SN15 5AF (01666) 510366
"Arrive early" to nab a seat in the dining conservatory of this
"popular" boozer – thanks to its ample portions of "rich",
traditional-ish cooking, it's "always busy"; no wonder – "where else
can you find food like this around Swindon?" / **Sample dishes:** no
starters; grilled kangaroo, venison & ostrich with vegetables; sticky toffee pudding.
Details: www.threecrowns.co.uk; 9.30 pm; no smoking area; no booking.

BRISTOL, CITY OF BRISTOL 2–2B

In *Markwick's*, Bristol has one of the UK's few provincial city
restaurants of outstanding quality. *Harveys* is the town's other
gastronomic 'heavy hitter', but though it generates a fair
amount of feedback, it is rather mixed.

The city tends to specialise in interesting-looking restaurants
where food is not the main thing. In one short year, the *Hotel
du Vin et Bistro* has become THE place locally. The design
attractions of *riverstation* continue to stand it in very good
stead, while *Bell's Diner* remains a well-liked local favourite.

Fishworks is the most notable newcomer and stands high
amongst the town's foodie destinations. (*Fishers* is also quite
a recent arrival in a not dissimilar vein, and has generated a
fair amount of interest.) Other worthwhile locations include
Red Snapper (another seafood place), *Sands* (a good
Lebanese) and *A Cozinha* (one of the UK's few good quality
Portuguese restaurants).

A couple of smartish Indians aside, 'ethnic' restaurants are of
less importance at the smarter end of the market than in
most major English cities, though at the inexpensive end of
the market, *Teohs* and *Budokan* are well-liked oriental mini-
chains.

Anthem £ 28 A
27-29 St Michaels HI BS2 8DZ (0117) 929 2834
Set in a "fascinating old building", this "hippyish" venture makes a "chilled-out" venue; some reporters find the fusion cooking a mite "incoherent", but for the most part it's judged "unusual and tasty". / **Sample dishes:** smoked duck with gin & orange dressing; chicken with pine nut stuffing in Sauternes sauce; chocolate truffle terrine. **Details:** 10.30 pm; D only, closed Mon & Sun; no Amex.

Bell's Diner £ 32 A
1 York Rd BS6 5QB (0117) 924 0357
"A long-established favourite in a quiet back street" – this "atmospheric" Montpelier fixture offers "simple" but quite "imaginative" cooking, and "good if laid-back" service. / **Sample dishes:** braised octopus with black pudding; monkfish, saffron & broad bean risotto; Muscat jelly with Granny Smith sorbet. **Details:** www.bellsdiner.co.uk; 10 pm; closed Mon L, Sat L & Sun D; no smoking.

Blue Goose £ 28 ★
344 Gloucester Rd BS7 8TP (0117) 942 0940
This "friendly" Horfield bistro is all the more "pleasant" for being in an area without a huge number of competing attractions; "dishes both classic and unusual" receive favourable reports. / **Details:** 9 pm; D only, except Sun open L & D; management declined to provide further information.

Bocanova £ 29
90 Colston St BS1 5BB (0117) 929 1538
"Interesting" cooking (from a native chef) has made this groovy Brazilian a generally welcome city-centre arrival; live Bossa Nova music enlivens Wednesday nights. / **Sample dishes:** goats cheese salad with raspberry dressing; Scottish salmon with prawn & lime leaf sauce; pannacotta with plums & whisky syrup. **Details:** 10.30 pm, Fri & Sat 11 pm; closed Sun; no Amex; no smoking.

Boston Tea Party £ 19 A
75 Park St BS1 5PF (0117) 929 8601
For "cosy coffee and a chat on a sofa", it's hard to beat this celebrated café, whose attractions include an "excellent choice of sandwiches" and a "great garden". / **Sample dishes:** carrot & coriander soup; Spanish chicken; rum & raisin cheesecake. **Details:** 10 pm, Sun 7 pm; closed Mon D & Sun D; no smoking in dining room.

Brazz £ 28
85 Park St BS1 5PJ (0117) 925 2000
The third branch of Kit Chapman's ambitious West Country chain of brasseries, on the site that used to be Hullaballoos, RIP; if standards elsewhere are any guide, it will be a useful destination, rather than a foodie one. / **Sample dishes:** mushrooms & spinach on toast; fishcakes with tartare sauce; chocolate Cathedral pudding.
Details: www.the-castle-hotel.com/brazz.htm; 10.30 pm, Thu-Sat 11 pm; closed Sun.

Brunel Raj £ 23
Waterloo St BS8 4BT (0117) 973 2641
This cosy Indian in the heart of Clifton provides freshly-cooked dishes that are "not bad at all". / **Details:** 11.30 pm.

Budokan £ 20
31 Colston St BS1 5AP   (0117) 914 1488
Serving "a variety of Japanese, Thai, Malaysian, Singaporean and Indian dishes", these "trendy" Pan-Asian pit stops (there's also a Clifton branch on Whiteladies Rd, tel 0117 949 3030) still enjoy a high degree of local popularity; they're "a bit sterile", though, and some think "all image and no substance".
/ **Details:** www.budokan.co.uk; 10.30 pm; closed Sun; no Amex; no smoking; need 10+ to book.

Byzantium £ 39 Ⓐ
2 Portwall Ln BS1 6NB   (0117) 922 1883
It's the "superb, darkly mysterious atmosphere" which is the star feature of this theatrical Moroccan-style venue; of the limited feedback it generates, opinions are split as to whether the food lives up, or is "overpriced". / **Sample dishes:** crab, chilli & coriander tart; smoked lamb with Swiss chard gratin; chocolate & Grand Marnier mousse. **Details:** www.byzantium-restaurant.co.uk; near Temple Meads, opp St Mary's Redcliffe church; 11 pm; D only, closed Sun (open for L in Dec); no smoking area.

A Cozinha £ 32 ★
40 Alfred Pl BS2 8HD   (0117) 944 3060
"The simple rustic charm" of Bristol's only Portuguese establishment helps win hearts, as do "large portions" of "freshly prepared" dishes, complemented by a "simple but excellent wine list". / **Sample dishes:** salt cod & chick pea salad; Catalan pork, fish & seafood stew; honey & cinnamon cake. **Value tip:** set 1-crs express lunch £7.50. **Details:** 9.30 pm; closed Mon, Sat L & Sun; no Amex; children: 14+ at D.

Fishers £ 32
35 Princess Victoria St BS8 4BX   (0117) 974 7044
"Delightful for those fish lovers" – locals generally look kindly on this relatively new outpost of the popular Oxford bistro, with its "pleasant" staff and "good" cooking. / **Sample dishes:** grilled sardines with parsley & lemon; beer-battered fish & chips; banana fritters with Amaretto ice cream. **Details:** www.fishers-restaurant.com; 10.30 pm; closed Mon L; no Amex; no smoking.

Fishworks £ 42 ★
128 Whiteladies Rd BS8 2RS   (0117) 974 4433
"Better than the Bath original" – "a wonderful array of the freshest fish, impeccably cooked" have made this "informal" and "buzzy" (if slightly "cramped") newcomer a great local success story. / **Sample dishes:** spaghetti with crab & chilli; grilled plaice with black butter; lemon tart. **Details:** www.fishworks.co.uk; 10.30 pm; closed Mon & Sun D; mainly non-smoking.

Glasnost £ 27 Ⓐ
1 William St BS3 4TU   (0117) 972 0938
An "inventive" and "varied" menu (with lots for veggies) makes this popular backstreet restaurant a continuing "beacon of excellence", for most reporters; "too many customers" can be a problem, though, with standards suffering accordingly.
/ **Sample dishes:** mushrooms stuffed with Stilton; pork in Parma ham with peach compote; chocolate & praline soufflé. **Details:** www.glasnostrestaurant.co.uk; 10 pm; D only, closed Mon & Sun; no Amex; no smoking.

sign up for the survey at www.hardens.com

The Glass Boat £34
Welsh Back BS1 4SB (0117) 929 0704
This barge anchored in the city-centre docks enjoys an "idyllic setting"; even some who find it "a nice place for entertaining", though, say the food is "unadventurous", and detractors find it "pricey" and "ill-conceived". / **Sample dishes:** *goats cheese with radish & chive salad; roast duck with duck spring rolls & mango; Szechuan-peppered crème brûlée.* **Value tip:** *set 2-crs L £14.50.* **Details:** *www.glassboat.co.uk; below Bristol Bridge; 9.30 pm; closed Sat L & Sun; no smoking area.*

Harveys £62
12 Denmark St BS1 5DQ (0117) 927 5034
"The cosiest cave in England"; the "posh" cellar of the famous sherry shipper provides the home for this "well-established fine dining room"; reports of "high prices" for "disappointing" cooking remain far too common, however, though an "amazing" wine list is some consolation. / **Sample dishes:** *warm tomato tart with crab salad; veal cutlet with macaroni gratin & truffles; lavender soufflé with peach sorbet.* **Value tip:** *set 2-crs L £18.* **Details:** *www.j-harvey.co.uk; 9.30 pm; closed Sat L & Sun; no smoking at D.*

Hope & Anchor £20 Ⓐ
38 Jacobs Wells Rd BS8 1DR (0117) 929 2987
"Continuing good value" is the theme of all reports on this jolly boozer, where the "great garden" is a leading attraction; it's "always busy". / **Sample dishes:** *crayfish tail & anchovy salad; lamb & rosemary pie; sticky toffee pudding & custard.* **Details:** *10 pm; no credit cards; no booking; children: 14+ in bar.*

Hotel du Vin et Bistro £43 Ⓐ
The Sugar House, Narrow Lewins Mead BS1 2NU
(0117) 925 5577
"A beautifully restored warehouse" provides the "buzzy" setting for this "popular" outpost of the boutique-hotel chain; the wines are "exceptional", and the "yummy French provincial food" is also generally (but by no means universally) approved. / **Sample dishes:** *gravadlax with citrus oil; braised lamb shank with olive jus; banana tarte Tatin.* **Details:** *www.hotelduvin.com; 9.45 pm; booking: max 10.* **Accommodation:** *40 rooms, from £109.*

Howards £33
1a-2a, Avon Cr BS1 6XQ (0117) 926 2921
It's "small" and "cramped", but this long-established Hotwells stalwart remains "very busy"; one or two locals voice fears, though, that it's "losing its edge". / **Sample dishes:** *chicken, asparagus & leek terrine; seafood tagliatelle; lemon meringue pie.* **Details:** *11 pm; closed Sat L & Sun.*

Johns £26
27 Midland Rd BS2 0JT (0117) 955 0333
Fans still praise the "consistent quality" and "relaxed atmosphere" of John Wright's quirky Thai restaurant (which goes English for puddings and Sunday lunch); a couple of very disappointing meals, however, were reported this year. / **Sample dishes:** *Balinese pork satay; tiger prawns stir-fried with tomato & chilli; raspberry crème brûlée.* **Details:** *10 pm; closed Mon & Tue, D only Wed-Sat, L only Sun; no Amex; no smoking in dining room.*

Markwick's £ 47 ★★
43 Corn St BS1 1HT (0117) 926 2658
"Faultless" results are often reported from this former Merchant Quarter bank vault, where Stephen Markwick uses *"the finest ingredients"* for his *"precise"* cooking; with its *"professional"* approach, it's perfect *"for a classy business lunch"*, but some find the setting a mite *"dull"*. / **Sample dishes:** sea trout tartare with cucumber pickle; spring vegetable risotto with Pecorino; baked pears with blue cheese fondant. **Details:** 10 pm; closed Sat L & Sun; no smoking in dining room.

Melbournes £ 29 ✕
74 Park St BS1 5JX (0117) 922 6996
"You know what to expect", say supporters of these *"busy"* BYO bistros (also at 217a Gloucester Rd, Bishopston, 0117 924 6000); there are those, however, who feel they've *"rather lost their way"*. / **Sample dishes:** salmon & sweet potato fishcakes; pork with apple & sage stuffing; jam roly poly & custard. **Details:** 10.30 pm; D only, closed Sun.

Mud Dock £ 27
40 The Grove BS1 4RB (0117) 934 9734
The *"great view from the balcony"* is an undoubted strength of this waterside café (over a cycle shop); *"slow"* and *"don't-care"* service, however, is a major handicap. / **Sample dishes:** spinach, yoghurt & mint soup; grilled tuna with olive oil mash; banoffi pie. **Details:** www.mud-dock.com; close to the Industrial Museum & Arnolfini Gallery; 10 pm; closed Mon D; no smoking area; no booking.

Primrose Café £ 27 Ⓐ
1 Boyces Ave BS8 4AA (0117) 946 6577
This popular café-by-day (where *"exceptional breakfasts"* are a highlight) becomes an *"intimate"*, if rather *"ad hoc"*, BYO bistro at night; *"well-prepared fish dishes"* are a highlight.
/ **Sample dishes:** crab risotto with avocado ice cream; curried Welsh mutton with black pepper rice; brown sugar meringues with grilled bananas. **Details:** 9.30 pm; closed Mon D & Sun D; no Amex; no smoking area; no booking at L.

Quartier Vert £ 36
85 Whiteladies Rd BS8 2NT (0117) 973 4482
This *"pretentiously organic"* Clifton tapas bar (once known as Rocinantes) gets a wide but very mixed press from reporters; prices which can seem *"simply absurd"* explain much of the disgruntlement. / **Sample dishes:** pan-fried scallops with pea purée; pork chops with smoked pimento mash; lemon & almond polenta cake. **Value tip:** set 2-crs L £14.50. **Details:** www.quartiervert.co.uk; 10.30 pm; closed Sun D (in winter only); no Amex.

Rajdoot £ 25 ★
83 Park St BS1 5PJ (0117) 926 8033
A much smarter-than-average – if rather *"muted"* – central curry house, with a *"consistently good"* standard of cooking.
/ **Details:** www.rajdoot.co.uk; 11.30 pm; closed Sun L.

Rajpoot £ 30 ★
52 Upper Belgrave Rd BS8 2XP (0117) 973 3515
"Expensive for an Indian, but worth it" – this superior subcontinental attracts nothing but praise. / **Details:** 11 pm; closed Sun; no smoking.

sign up for the survey at www.hardens.com

Red Snapper £ 35 ★

1 Chandos Rd BS6 6PG (0117) 973 7999

"Wondrous" and "unusual" fish dishes have won quite a following for this "consistent" backstreet venture, near Clifton.
/ **Sample dishes:** *Stilton & bacon salad; skate with sprouting broccoli & anchovy butter; mango & muscat crème brûlée.* **Value tip:** *set 2-crs L £10.50.*
Details: *10 pm; closed Mon L & Sun; no smoking before 9.30 pm.*

riverstation £ 34 Ⓐ

The Grove BS1 4RB (0117) 914 4434

"A great setting by the harbour" and "sharp design" help make this "airy" venture still an "enjoyable" destination for many reporters; others see it as "trendy but fading", saying its "sophisticated" dishes have become "overpriced", and that service can be "slapdash". / **Sample dishes:** *sautéed morels & asparagus; sea trout with summer vegetables & aioli; gooseberry & elderflower fool.* **Value tip:** *set 2-crs L £11.50.* **Details:** *www.riverstation.co.uk; 10.30 pm, Fri & Sat 11 pm; no Amex; no smoking area; no booking in deli bar.*

Sands £ 25 Ⓐ★

95 Queens Rd BS8 1LW (0117) 973 9734

"Very good Lebanese cuisine" helps make this cellar restaurant an "interesting" local destination, and one that's "great for a party" (especially if you go for "the monthly banquet, with music and dancing", generally on the last Thursday of the month).
/ **Sample dishes:** *fried aubergine with chick peas; Lebanese mixed grill; lemon sorbet.* **Details:** *11 pm; no smoking area.*

Severnshed £ 29 Ⓐ

The Grove, Harbourside BS1 4RB (0117) 925 1212

This strikingly-designed venture has a "lovely" riverside setting, and its "cool, chic (if slightly pretentious)" ambience has many admirers; under new ownership, the "light" Moroccan-influenced cuisine seems more reliable than of old. / **Sample dishes:** *fish mezze platter; hot chicken & rosemary salad; lemon curd tart.*
Details: *www.severnshed.co.uk; 10.30 pm; no smoking.*

Teohs £ 23

26-34 Lower Ashley Rd BS2 9NP (0117) 907 1191

"Some misses, but mainly hits" is the theme of reports on the "clean"-tasting "noodle-concoctions" at these "informal" orientals (also at The Tobacco Factory, Raleigh Rd, tel 0117 902 1122); however, given the "very cheap" prices, reporters are happy to overlook any inconsistencies. / **Value tip:** *set 2-crs menu £10.* **Details:** *100 yds from M32, J3; 10.30 pm; closed Sun; no Amex; no smoking.*

Thai Classic £ 26

87 Whiteladies Rd BS8 2NT (0117) 973 8930

"Good food" makes this "friendly" oriental (which also offers some Malaysian dishes) a useful Clifton stand-by.
/ **Details:** *11.30 pm; no smoking area.*

for updates visit www.hardens.com

BRITWELL SALOME, OXFORDSHIRE   2–2D

The Goose   £34

OX49 5LG   (01491) 612304

Chef/patron Chris Barber – former chef to the Prince of Wales – is praised for his "wholesome" organic cooking by fans of this simple country pub; others say it's "absurdly overpriced", though, and that "the owner's pedigree is the only reason it gets noted".
/ **Sample dishes:** celery soup with truffle oil; roast chicken with morels; banana crème brûlée. **Value tip:** set 3-crs L £12.50.
Details: www.thegoose.freeserve.co.uk; M40, J6 near Watlington; 9 pm; closed Mon & Sun D; no Amex; no smoking.

BROAD HAVEN, PEMBROKESHIRE   4–4B

Druidstone Hotel   £29   Ⓐ

Druid Haven SA62 3NE   (01437) 781221

A major refurbishment will keep this "eccentric" clifftop establishment closed until approximately March 2003; its "amazing views" will no doubt survive – let's hope its "relaxed" charm does too. / **Sample dishes:** Polish meat soup; sea bass & mullet with watercress cream; chocolate orange cheesecake. **Details:** www.druidstone.co.uk; from B4341 at Broad Haven turn right, then left after 1.5m; 9.30 pm; closed Sun D; no smoking in dining room. **Accommodation:** 9 rooms, from £52.50.

BROADHEMBURY, DEVON   2–4A

Drewe Arms   £39   ★

EX14 3NF   (01404) 841267

"Improbable in an isolated Devon village" – this "wonderful English pub/restaurant" generates nothing but praise for "simple fresh fish" that's "reliable" and "good value". / **Sample dishes:** mixed seafood selection; grilled turbot with hollandaise; bread pudding with whisky butter. **Details:** 5m from M5, J28, on A373 to Honiton; 9.30 pm (9 pm in winter); closed Sun D; no Amex; no smoking.

BROADWAY, WORCESTERSHIRE   2–1C

Lygon Arms   £61   ✗

High St WR12 7DU   (01386) 852255

"Expensive and nothing special"; the Savoy Group's famous Cotswold outpost is an "old favourite" for some (thanks especially to its "wonderful" Elizabethan setting), but strikes many reporters as "passé" nowadays, particularly on the cooking front.
/ **Sample dishes:** leek & mushroom lasagne with truffle oil; sea bass with creamed leeks & chorizo; plum crumble soufflé with liquorice ice-cream. **Value tip:** set 3-crs D £26.50. **Details:** www.savoygroup.com; just off A44; 9.15 pm, Fri & Sat 10 pm; closed weekday L; no smoking; children: 6+. **Accommodation:** 70 rooms, from £180.

BROCKENHURST, HAMPSHIRE   2–4C

Simply Poussin   £31

The Courtyard, Brookley Rd SO42 7RB   (01590) 623063

"A small restaurant with pretensions"; the "bistro sister of the Poussin at Parkhill" is mostly (if not unanimously) praised for its "straightforward" and "well-presented" cooking.
/ **Sample dishes:** ham hock & foie gras terrine; chicken provençale; chocolate truffle cake. **Details:** www.simplypoussin.co.uk; behind Bestsellers Bookshop; 10 pm; closed Mon & Sun; no smoking.

BRODICK, ISLE OF ARRAN 7–1A

Creelers Seafood Restaurant £34 ★
Home Farm KA27 8DD (01770) 302810
*This old "wooden hut" is a "quirky" venue that has spawned a growing national chain; "really good and very reasonably priced" fish and seafood is the general theme of reports, but the odd "stodgy" dish is not unknown. / **Sample dishes:** smoked fish pâté with Arran oatcakes; sea bass with caper & lemon butter; strawberry cheesecake.* **Details:** www.creelers.co.uk; 9.30 pm; closed Mon; no Amex or Switch.

BUCKLAND, GLOUCESTERSHIRE 2–1C

Buckland Manor £63
WR12 7LY (01386) 852626
*"Expensive, but worth it" is the general drift of comments on this "exquisite" 13th-century Cotswold manor house hotel, which offers reliably "high standards of food and service"; it also features a "huge wine list". / **Sample dishes:** smoked duck, fennel & orange salad; Angus beef with truffled lentils; pear & apple crumble with Calvados sauce.* **Value tip:** set 3-crs Sun L £24.50. **Details:** www.bucklandmanor.com; 2m SW of Broadway on B4632; 9 pm; jacket & tie required at D; no smoking in dining room; children: 12+. **Accommodation:** 13 rooms, from £225.

BUCKLAND, OXFORDSHIRE 2–2C

Lamb at Buckland £40
Lamb Ln SN7 8QN (01367) 870484
*There's "varied" and "well-prepared" cooking to be had at this "cosy" and "well-run" village gastropub; "be prepared for premium prices", though. / **Sample dishes:** lemon sole with chive butter; pan-fried skate wing; peach & almond flan.* **Details:** on A420 between Oxford & Swindon; 9.30 pm; closed Mon & Sun D; no smoking. **Accommodation:** 4 rooms, from £42.50.

BURFORD, OXFORDSHIRE 2–2C

The Lamb £37 A
Sheep St OX18 4LR (01993) 823155
*With its "Cotswold stone, lovely floors, beams, fire places and beautifully quiet setting", this "unspoilt" country inn serves "reliable" cooking that's "a cut above pub-grub expectations". / **Sample dishes:** Parma ham & Brie fritters; steak & Guinness pie; coffee profiteroles.* **Details:** 9 pm; D only, except Sun open L & D; no Amex; no smoking. **Accommodation:** 15 rooms, from £120.

BURLEY IN WHARFEDALE, WEST YORKSHIRE 5–1C

David Woolley's £34
78 Main St LS29 7BT (01943) 864602
*"Good-value" cooking – "always tasty, always unusual" – has made Mr Woolley's convivial village restaurant a popular local destination; let's hope new chef John Whaits maintains standards. / **Sample dishes:** salmon platter; blackened duck with orange & honey; brown bread parfait with butterscotch sauce.* **Details:** www.davidwoolleysrestaurant.co.uk; 10 pm; D only, except Sun L only; no Amex; no smoking area.

BURNHAM MARKET, NORFOLK   6–3B

Fishes   £32   ★
Market Pl PE31 8HE   (01328) 738588
"Tucked away, in a lovely village square" – this well-established
fish restaurant is "moving on with its new chef and new owner" –
satisfaction with its "delicious", "modernised" cooking and
"friendly, professional" service is high. / **Sample dishes:** potted brown
shrimps; monkfish with fennel & cream sauce; strawberry mousse. **Value tip:** set
2-crs L £12.50. **Details:** 9 pm, Sat 9.30 pm; closed Mon & Sun L; no smoking;
children: 5+ after 8.30 pm.

Hoste Arms   £31
The Green PE31 8HD   (01328) 738777
This "upmarket(ish)" inn has a classic "pub ambience" which
belies its reputation as a "London yuppie rendezvous";
the cooking, with fish the speciality, is "enjoyable", but critics find
the menu "limited", and say the place is "too popular and pricey"
nowadays. / **Sample dishes:** cullen skink with poached quails egg; honey-glazed
ham hock with minted mash; apple tart with cinnamon ice cream.
Details: www.hostearms.co.uk; 6m W of Wells-next-the-Sea; 9 pm; no Amex;
no smoking area. **Accommodation:** 36 rooms, from £64.

BURNSALL, NORTH YORKSHIRE   8–4B

Red Lion   £35
BD23 6BU   (01756) 720204
"A beautiful location on the River Wharfe" and a "rambling
interior" contribute to the attractions of this "historic" pub;
the cooking may be a touch "hit-and-miss", but "when it works it's
excellent". / **Sample dishes:** gravadlax & avocado with lemon dressing;
chilli-marinated chicken with spiced tomato sauce; treacle tart with candied lemon.
Details: www.redlion.co.uk; off A59; 9.30 pm; D only, except Sun open L & D;
no smoking in dining room. **Accommodation:** 13 rooms, from £100.

BURY ST EDMUNDS, SUFFOLK   3–1C

Maison Bleue   £32   ★
30-31 Churchgate St IP33 1RG   (01284) 760623
"Very friendly staff" set the tone at this "classy", "quintessentially
French" and "fairly-priced" fish restaurant (an offshoot of the
Great House at Lavenham); the set lunch is especially good value.
/ **Sample dishes:** fish soup with garlic croutons; Dover sole with pink peppercorn
butter; white chocolate & lime mousse. **Value tip:** set 2-crs L £12.95.
Details: www.maisonbleue.co.uk; 9.30 pm; closed Mon & Sun; no smoking.

BUSHEY, HERTFORDSHIRE   3–2A

St James   £35
30 High St WD2 3DN   (020) 8950 2480
"It's very good by local standards", but "there's not much
competition" for this suburban Italian, which enjoys a big
reputation in the locality – it's not hugely atmospheric, though,
and some reporters complain of "London prices".
/ **Sample dishes:** grilled vegetable antipasti; roast lamb with creamed leeks & basil
jus; Toblerone cheesecake. **Value tip:** set 2-crs L £13.95. **Details:** opp St James
Church; 9.45 pm; closed Sun; no smoking area.

CADNAM, HAMPSHIRE   2–3C
White Hart   £ 22
Old Romsey Rd SO40 2NP   (023) 8081 2277
*"A good variety" of "pub food with a twist" makes it worth
knowing about this relaxed New Forest inn.* / **Sample dishes:** dressed
crab with Mediterranean sauce; guinea fowl stuffed with couscous; crêpes Suzette.
Details: signposted off M27, J1; 9.30 pm; no Amex; no smoking area.

CALVER, DERBYSHIRE   5–2C
Chequers   £ 27   ★
Froggatt Edge, Hope Valley S32 3ZJ   (01433) 630231
*"Good pub food" ("more home-cooked than you'd expect from the
laminated menu") makes it well worth knowing about this Peak
District gastropub.* / **Sample dishes:** smoked chicken & chorizo salad;
beef goulash with paprika dumplings; sticky toffee pudding. **Details:** on road
between Sheffield & Bakewell; 9.30 pm; no smoking area. **Accommodation:** 5
rooms, from £45.

CAMBRIDGE, CAMBRIDGESHIRE   3–1B

Cambridge's time-immemorial reputation as a dismal place to
eat continues to be pretty well deserved. That its most
commented-on location is an undistinguished member of the
Loch Fyne seafood chain – joined in the top 5 places
(by volume of mentions) by a branch of the Browns brasserie
chain – speaks volumes.

Midsummer House is the city's claim to gastronomic fame,
though, as ever, its high price level is a red rag to its critics.
22 Chesterton Road is the other venue for a special meal.

The only restaurants thought star-worthy by reporters are
places for day-to-day eating: a noodle bar (*Dojo*),
an inexpensive boozer (*Wrestlers Pub*) and a budget Turk
(*Efes*).

Browns   £ 29   ✕
23 Trumpington St CB2 1QA   (01223) 461655
*"How the mighty have fallen" – fans may still vaunt this as a
"lovely" branch of the brasserie chain, but many reporters
nowadays are vitriolic in their condemnation of its "dire" and
"nasty" food, its "half-hearted" service and its "barn-like"
ambience.* / **Sample dishes:** Caesar salad; steak, mushroom & Guinness pie;
hot fudge brownie. **Details:** www.browns-restaurants.com; opp Fitzwilliam Museum;
11 pm; no smoking area; need 10+ to book.

Cafe Adriatic   £ 29
12 Norfolk St CB1 2LF   (01223) 355227
*"Good, for Cambridge" – a greasy spoon that turns into an Italian
restaurant after breakfast; it's "pleasant all-round", from most
reports, but some find its output rather "bland".*
/ **Sample dishes:** rocket, pear & Parmesan salad; char-grilled squid & spinach
risotto; Amaretti biscuits with Mascarpone. **Details:** 11 pm; closed Sun; no Amex.

Cazimir   £ 12
13 King St CB1 1LH   (01223) 355156
*This Polish-run café may be "a bit small and smoky" for some,
but it wins praise for a menu more "interesting" than most.*
/ **Sample dishes:** roast vegetable bruschetta; Polish sausage & Mozzarella salad;
chocolate cake. **Details:** L & afternoon tea only; no credit cards; no smoking area.

Curry Queen £18
106 Mill Rd CB1 2BD (01223) 351027
The fare may be "typical", but it's also "well executed" at this self-explanatory spot. / **Details:** midnight.

Dojo £13 ★
1-2 Millers Yd, Mill Ln CB2 1RQ (01223) 363471
"Cheap oriental fusion fare" in "huge portions" make this "great" budget noodle bar a consistently "buzzing" destination.
/ **Details:** www.dojonoodlebar.co.uk; off Trumpington St; 10.45 pm; no Amex; no smoking; no booking.

Efes £22 ★
78 King St CB1 1LN (01223) 500005
"Delicious char-grilled meats and exquisite gooey baklava" are the sort of "better-than-usual" fare which make this "uncomplicated" Turk well worth discovering; it's "well off the tourist trail", but local popularity can lead to an atmosphere verging on "frantic".
/ **Details:** 10.30 pm; no Amex; no smoking area.

Loch Fyne £30
37 Trumpington St CB2 1QY (01223) 362433
It may only be "half-decent", but – in this culinarily-challenged city – this "uninspiring" chain outlet "stands out"; its fish, which is the menu mainstay, is "usually good, and not too overpriced".
/ **Sample dishes:** queen scallops; lobster platter; ice cream. **Value tip:** set 2-crs L £9.95. **Details:** www.loch-fyne.com; opp Fitzwilliam Museum; 10 pm; no smoking in dining room.

Maharajah £22
9-13 Castle St CB3 0AH (01223) 358399
"A wide selection" of "consistently good" dishes makes this local curry house "the best in town", for some reporters.
/ **Details:** midnight.

Michels Brasserie £32
21-24 Northampton St CB3 0AD (01223) 353110
"A hackneyed brasserie, popular with students and their parents" – a harsh, but probably fair, view on this "basic" fixture at the back of St John's. / **Sample dishes:** charcuterie with rustic pickles; fish kebabs with samphire; chocolate bread & butter pudding. **Value tip:** set 3-crs L £9. **Details:** 10 pm; no smoking area.

Midsummer House £58 𝔸
Midsummer Common CB4 1HA (01223) 369299
Fans hail this Victorian villa-restaurant – whose "great conservatory" enjoys a "beautiful" location on a common by the Cam – as "an oasis of sophisticated cooking in the Fens"; its style can seem "fussy", though, and – for a large proportion of reporters – the menu is noticably "overpriced".
/ **Sample dishes:** deep-fried snails with bacon risotto; slow-roasted beef with mushroom gnocchi; prune & armagnac soufflé. **Value tip:** set 2-crs L £18. **Details:** www.midsummerhouse.co.uk; facing University Boathouse; 10 pm; closed Mon & Sun; no smoking.

Peking Restaurant £34
21 Burleigh St CB1 1DG (01223) 354755
Even those who find the cooking "fantastic" at this long-established Chinese, near the Grafton Centre, admit that it's "not cheap" (and some say it's just "too expensive for what it is").
/ **Details:** 10.30 pm; no credit cards; no smoking area.

Sala Thong £21
35 Newnham Rd CB3 9EY   (01223) 323178
"Cambridge's best Thai" is a pretty "basic" place, but it's generally held to be a "good-value" destination. / **Details:** 9.45 pm; closed Mon; no Amex; no smoking.

22 Chesterton Road £35 🇦
22 Chesterton Rd CB4 3AX   (01223) 351880
This "small" and "cosy" restaurant in an Edwardian house retains the feeling that it is "someone's front room"; some find the menu "too short", but it "changes regularly" and mostly wins the thumbs-up. / **Sample dishes:** pork & rabbit terrine with plum sauce; crab cakes with spring onion risotto; steamed marmalade pudding. **Details:** www.restaurant22.co.uk; 9.45 pm; D only, closed Mon & Sun; no smoking; children: 12+.

Venue £33 🇦
66 Regent St CB2 1DP   (01223) 367333
Regular jazz nights spice up the atmosphere at this "lively" joint, where the cooking is "good, if nothing to get excited about". / **Sample dishes:** Thai-style mussels; butternut squash gnocchi; dark chocolate truffle cake. **Value tip:** set 2-crs L £14.75. **Details:** www.venuerestaurant.com; 10.30 pm; closed Mon L, Tue L, Fri L & Sat L; no Amex; no smoking area.

Wrestlers Pub £18 ★
337 Newmarket Rd CB5 8JE   (01223) 566553
"Good and authentic Thai food" has made quite a name for this basic boozer, near the Cambridge United ground – "avoid on match nights"! / **Details:** www.wrestlers.co.uk; 9 pm; closed Sun (for food); no Amex.

Augustines £34 🇦★
1-2 Longport CT1 1PE   (01227) 453063
It's not yet that well-known, but the few who report on Tom & Robert Grimer's small and atmospheric establishment say it's well worth discovering for its "tip-top" cooking (and, in particular, its "excellent set-price lunch menus"). / **Sample dishes:** provençale fish soup; Romney Marsh lamb with parsley mash; lemon tart with raspberry sauce. **Value tip:** set 3-crs L £11. **Details:** near the Cathedral; 9.30 pm; closed Mon & Sun D; no smoking; booking: max 7; children: no babies.

Cafe des Amis £27 🇦
95 St Dunstan's St CT2 8AA   (01227) 464390
"Average food" plus "plenty of buzz" remains a winning formula for this "friendly" and "fun" Mexican – the most commented-on eatery in this under-served city. / **Sample dishes:** prawn & Serrano ham cakes; lamb with Merguez sausages; pineapple tarte Tatin. **Details:** by Westgate Towers; 10 pm; no smoking area; booking: max 6 at D, Fri & Sat.

Bryn Tyrch £26
LL24 0EL   (01690) 720223
"Very busy, even out of season" – this "cosy" walkers' pub (in the Snowdonia National Park) offers "imaginative" food at "reasonable" prices. / **Sample dishes:** smoked duck with orange & apricot chutney; Greek feta & spinach pie; bread & butter pudding. **Details:** on A5; 9 pm; no Amex; no smoking area. **Accommodation:** 15 rooms, from £24.50.

CAPEL GARMON, CONWY   4–2C

Tan Y Foel   £ 46   ★

LL26 0RE   (01690) 710507

"In a wonderful setting high up in the Conwy valley", this small
hotel (occupying an old stone-built house) wins praise for its
"fantastic" locally-sourced cooking including some *"amazing
vegetarian dishes"*. / **Sample dishes:** grilled mackerel with ginger soy; Welsh
beef Wellington with wild horseradish; pear & ginger upside-down pudding.
Details: www.tyfhotel.co.uk; 8.15 pm; D only (closed Dec-Mid Jan); no smoking;
booking essential; children: 7+. **Accommodation:** 6 rooms, from £120.

CARDIFF, CARDIFF   2–2A

When it comes to Cardiff's restaurant scene, there is a sense
that the Welsh capital has yet really to join the 21st century
as far as eating out is concerned. In many other cities, its top
places would be middle-rankers.

Facing one another across the road in the posh suburb of
Canton, *Le Gallois y Cymro* and *Le Cassoulet* remain the most
talked-about places in town. The former stands head and
shoulders above anywhere else in terms of the feedback it
generates, but neither it nor its neighbour scored as well as
they have in previous years.

In the centre of town, the complex incorporating *Le Monde*
and *La Brasserie* is the safest best. The Cardiff Bay
development has attracted one or two good places in the
shapes of *Woods Brasserie* and the original *Izakaya*. There are
also some fair options near the University, best-known being
the long-established *Armless Dragon* and the veggie
Greenhouse Café.

The best-rated cooking in the area is, in fact, veggie. A few
miles out of the centre in Penarth, *Tomlins* generates
outstanding reports.

Armless Dragon   £ 29

97 Wyeverne Rd CF2 4BG   (029) 2038 2357

It's "slightly off the beaten track", but chef-patron Paul Lane's
"cosy" and *"obliging"* bistro offers an *"interesting"* menu – Welsh
ingredients (including an *"excellent cheese selection"*) figure
strongly. / **Sample dishes:** liver parfait with date chutney; roast chicken with
leeks & truffle oil; crème brûlée. **Value tip:** set 3-crs L £10.
Details: www.thearmlessdragon.co.uk; 9.30 pm, Sat 10.30 pm; closed Mon & Sun;
no Amex; no smoking in dining room.

La Brasserie   £ 31

60 St Mary St CF10 1FE   (029) 2037 2164

The décor is *"very basic (sawdust on the floor and so on)"*,
but that adds to the atmosphere at this vast and *"noisy"* central
venue, where you choose your own seafood or steak for them to
prepare; most reporters find it a *"fun"* and *"good-value"* package.
/ **Sample dishes:** frogs legs with garlic mayonnaise; lemon sole with new potatoes;
apple tart. **Value tip:** set 2-crs L £5.95.
Details: www.le-monde.co.uk/brasserie.html; midnight; closed Sun; need 8+ to book.

Le Cassoulet £ 42
5 Romilly Cr CF11 9NP   (029) 2022 1905
A change of ownership in 2001 has not improved this well-established Gallic fixture in Canton, long known for its "rustic" regional French cooking; "what was once a good local now seems to compromise on quality and service". / Sample dishes: watercress soup with goats cheese ravioli; beef in red wine & pink peppercorn sauce; spiced bread soufflé. Value tip: set 3-crs L £10. Details: 10 mins W of city centre; 10 pm; closed Mon & Sun.

Cibo £ 27   Ⓐ
83 Pontcanna St CF11 9HS   (029) 2023 2226
Though the menu includes some quite substantial dishes, this "little bit of Italy" is "more a café than a restaurant"; "excellent pizzas, coffee and puddings" are singled out for praise. / Sample dishes: vegetable antipasti; salami & Mozzarella ciabatta; lemon cheesecake. Details: 9 pm; no Amex.

Le Gallois Y Cymro £ 45
6-10 Romilly Cr CF11 9NR   (029) 2034 1264
This "modern" and "vibrant" Canton venture is still proclaimed "Cardiff's best restaurant" by many reporters; "rising prices", are a turn-off for some, though, who consider it "over-rated". / Sample dishes: Roquefort soufflé with poached pears; roast pork with truffle mash & clove sauce; spiced pineapple with pepper ice cream. Value tip: set 2-crs L £12.95. Details: www.legallois.co.uk; 1.5m W of Cardiff Castle; 10.30 pm; closed Mon & Sun; no smoking area.

The Greenhouse Café £ 24   ★
38 Woodville Rd CF24 4EB   (029) 2023 5731
"Very fresh and tasty vegetarian and fish dishes" make this "innovative" café, near the University, a uniformly popular destination. / Sample dishes: potato, leek & celeriac soup; parsley-crusted salmon with saffron mayonnaise; banoffi pie. Details: near Cardiff University; 10.30 pm; closed Mon; no Amex; no smoking in dining room.

Happy Gathering £ 26
233 Cowbridge Road East CF11 9AL   (029) 2039 7531
"Very large", "informal" and "busy" – this popular Chinese restaurant continues to live up to its name. / Details: 10.45 pm.

Izakaya £ 26   Ⓐ★
Mermaid Quay CF10 5BW   (029) 2049 2939
"A beautiful setting in the Bay" adds lustre to this "authentic Japanese pub experience"; it wins uniform praise as an "interesting" concept that's consistently well realised. / Details: www.izakaya-japanese-tavern.com; 10.30 pm; no smoking area.

King Balti £ 19
131 Albany Rd CF24 3NS   (029) 2048 2890
The name deceives – the Pan-Asian menu at this "popular" and "lively" diner includes dishes that are Thai and Chinese, as well as Indian, and fans say they're "often done really well". / Details: 11.45 pm; D only; no smoking area.

Le Monde £ 27   Ⓐ
62 St Mary St CF10 1FE   (029) 2038 7376
The steak-and-seafood formula is "simple and uncomplicated", but "mouthwatering", say fans of the smarter (but still "loud") upstairs section of La Brasserie; it's "always full". / Sample dishes: marinated seafood salad; venison with port wine sauce; Welsh cheeses. Details: www.le-monde.co.uk; midnight; closed Sun; no booking.

Noble House £24
9-11 St Davids Hs, Wood St CF1 4ER   (029) 2038 8430
*Most (if not quite all) reporters proclaim the "good location and good value" of this "great-for-the-family" Chinese. / **Details:** next to Millennium stadium; 11 pm.*

Scallops £36
Unit 2 Mermaid Quay CF10 5BZ   (029) 2049 7495
*A "good if expensive" modern fish restaurant with "sea views"; reports are thinner on the ground than we'd like, but all give the place the thumbs-up. / **Sample dishes:** king scallops with roasted tomatoes; monkfish wrapped in bacon with curried mussels; Eton Mess. **Details:** 10 pm.*

Tides
St David's Hotel & Spa £43 ✕
Havannah St CF10 5SD   (029) 2031 3018
*Kinder critics see "unfulfilled potential" in the dining room of this swanky new hotel overlooking the harbour; others just say it's "expensive", "unimaginative" and "disappointing" (though as a brunch venue, it is consistently recommended).
/ **Sample dishes:** kipper pâté with whisky; smoked haddock colcannon; sherry trifle. **Value tip:** set 2-crs L £15. **Details:** www.rfhotels.com; in Cardiff Bay; 10.30 pm; no smoking. **Accommodation:** 132 rooms, from £180.*

Tomlins £26 A★★
46 Plassey St CF64 1EL   (029) 2070 6644
*"A jewel in the gastronomic wasteland of south east Wales" – "even meat-eaters flock" to David & Lorraine Tomlinson's "innovative" and "consistently excellent" vegetarian restaurant, in cheerful premises in Penarth (just a few miles from the city centre). / **Sample dishes:** won-tons with black bean sauce; black olive polenta with grilled vegetables; steamed syrup pudding. **Value tip:** set 2-crs Sun L £8.50. **Details:** www.tomlinsvegetarianrestaurant.co.uk; 10 pm; closed Mon, Tue L-Thu L & Sun D; no smoking.*

Valentino's £25 ✕
5 Windsor Pl CF10 3BX   (029) 2022 9697
*In this under-served city, this "basic" but "cheerful" central Italian has something of a following; too often, though, service appears "to make no effort to please". / **Sample dishes:** grilled olive bread with Mascarpone; penne with chicken in Dijon mustard sauce; raspberry & chocolate mousse. **Value tip:** set 2-crs L £9. **Details:** 11 pm; closed Sun.*

Woods Brasserie £39 ★
Pilotage Building, Stuart St CF10 5BW   (029) 2049 2400
*"The best eclectic food in town" is hailed by the many fans of this "bright" and "interesting" modern brasserie on the Bay; it has an "excellent location", but it can get "very crowded".
/ **Sample dishes:** crispy beef salad with Thai dressing; pan-fried John Dory with parsnip pureé; Bakewell tart with custard. **Details:** in the Inner Harbour; 10 pm; closed Mon & Sun D.*

CARTERWAY HEADS, NORTHUMBERLAND 8–3B
Manor House £25
DH8 9LX   (01207) 255268
*"The varied pub food is always competent", say fans of this "welcoming" pub, near the Derwent Reservoir.
/ **Sample dishes:** ham & lentil soup; chicken stuffed with crayfish & chives; plum & almond upside-down cake. **Details:** A68 just past turn-off for Shotley Bridge; 9.30 pm; no smoking area; children: 9+ at D. **Accommodation:** 4 rooms, from £55.*

CARTMEL FELL, CUMBRIA   7–4D

Masons Arms   £26
Strawberry Bank LA11 6NW   (01539) 568486
"Wholesome and tasty food in a great location" has made this
"snug" pub (and microbrewery) a *"very popular place to eat"* and
it's also drinker's dream, offering home-brewed damson gin and
over 150 bottled lagers; let's hope the new owner and chef
(2002) keep up standards. / **Sample dishes:** spare ribs; chicken &
mushroom pie; butterscotch crumble. **Details:** www.masonsarms.uk.com; W from
Bowland Bridge, off A5074; 9 pm; no Amex; no smoking area. **Accommodation:** 5
rooms, from £50.

CARTMEL, CUMBRIA   7–4D

Uplands   £39   𝔸★
Haggs Ln LA11 6HD   (01539) 536248
"Quality reigns" at this *"elegant old house"* in a *"pretty"* Lakeland
location; it offers a *"comfortable"* setting, *"friendly"* service and
"100%-reliable" cooking. / **Sample dishes:** hot salmon soufflé;
honey-roasted duck; chocolate Grand Marnier mousse.
Details: www.uplands.uk.com; 8 pm; closed Mon; closed Jan & Feb; no smoking;
no booking, Sat; children: 8+ at D. **Accommodation:** 5 rooms, from £81, incl D.

CASTLE DOUGLAS, DUMFRIES & GALLOWAY   7–2B

The Plumed Horse   £43   𝔸★★
Crossmicheal DG7 3AU   (01556) 670333
The *"outstanding"* cooking using *"great ingredients"* is *"worth
travelling for"*, say all who comment on this *"very special"* village
restaurant; there is the odd gripe regarding staff *"attitude"*,
however. / **Sample dishes:** smoked salmon & scallop soup; pork loin & kidneys
with candied turnips; chocolate tart with apricot sorbet. **Value tip:** set 3-crs L £16.
Details: 9 pm; closed Mon, Sat L & Sun D; no Amex; no smoking.

CASTLETON, DERBYSHIRE   5–2C

Castle Inn   £21   𝔸
Castle St S33 8WG   (01433) 620578
This *"great pub for walkers"* has an *"excellent location in the
heart of the Peak District"*; most still say its grub is *"well-cooked
and plentiful"*, but there were a couple of reports of *"poor"* meals
this year. / **Sample dishes:** field mushrooms with garlic toast; butterfly chicken
with tomato risotto; toffee bread & butter pudding.
Details: www.peakland.com/thecastle; 10 pm; no smoking area; no booking.
Accommodation: 12 rooms, from £50.

CATTERLINE, ABERDEEN   9–3D

Creel Inn   £26   ★
AB39 2UL   (01569) 750254
For *"fresh"* fish, this *"wonderfully-located"* inn (in a clifftop village)
is worth the drive from Aberdeen. / **Sample dishes:** fishcakes in smoked
haddock broth; salmon with lemon & lime; Belgian white chocolate ice cream.
Details: www.thecreelinn.co.uk; 4m S of Stonehaven on A92; 9.30 pm; closed Tue;
no Amex; no smoking. **Accommodation:** 2 rooms, from £50.

CAUNTON, NOTTINGHAMSHIRE   5–3D

Caunton Beck   £ 27

Main St NG23 6AB   (01636) 636793

*There is the odd "uninspiring" report, but most praise the "upmarket pubby food, that's generally well cooked" at this attractive country pub (related to Lincoln's Wig & Mitre); all-day opening is a feature. / **Sample dishes:** chicken laksa with pork wontons; duck with bean & chorizo cassoulet; passion fruit & ginger cheesecake. **Value tip:** set 2-crs meal £9 (not Sat D or Sun L). **Details:** 6m NW of Newark past British Sugar factory on A616; 10 pm; no smoking.*

CHADDESLEY CORBETT, WORCESTERSHIRE   5–4B

Brockencote Hall   £ 45   𝔸 ★

DY10 4PY   (01562) 777876

*If you like a "very French" style, you won't do better than this "beautifully located" – and rather château-like – country house hotel; it's an "elegant" place, and mainly generates reports of "impressive" results. / **Sample dishes:** scallops with juniper berry sauce; rabbit wrapped in Parma ham with marjoram sausages; lemon tart with Earl Grey sorbet. **Value tip:** set 3-crs L £15. **Details:** www.brockencotehall.com; on A448, just outside village; 9.30 pm; closed Sat L; no smoking. **Accommodation:** 17 rooms, from £135.*

CHAGFORD, DEVON   1–3D

Gidleigh Park   £ 80   𝔸 ★

TQ13 8HH   (01647) 432367

*"Faultless" cuisine and an "extensive" wine list help make Kay & Paul Henderson's "sumptuous" and "romantic" '30s country house hotel, on the fringe of Dartmoor, a "fantastic weekend-away venue"; a few detractors find it "too pricey", though, and the whole style "a bit OTT". / **Sample dishes:** langoustines & frogs legs with pasta in truffle cream; roast duckling with honey & spices; hot apple tart. **Value tip:** set 2-crs L £26. **Details:** www.gidleigh.com; from village, right at Lloyds TSB, take right fork to end of lane; 9 pm; no Amex; no smoking; children: 7+ at D. **Accommodation:** 15 rooms, from £400 incl D.*

22 Mill Street   £ 37   𝔸 ★★

22 Mill St TQ13 8AW   (01647) 432244

*"Really exceptional food" – "an imaginative menu every day" – and "caring" service make Duncan Walker's "small and intimate" restaurant (in the village near Gidleigh Park, where he used to cook) a "tremendous" spot for practically all who report on it. / **Sample dishes:** saffron lasagne of crab & red pepper; roast pigeon with pea purée; hot raspberry soufflé. **Details:** www.22millstreet.co.uk; 9 pm; closed Mon L, Tue L, Sat D & Sun; no Amex; no smoking area; children: 14+. **Accommodation:** 2 rooms, from £50.*

CHAPELTOWN, SOUTH YORKSHIRE   5–2C

Greenhead House   £ 44   𝔸 ★

84 Burncross Rd S35 1SF   (0114) 246 9004

*"Beautiful food, beautifully presented" – there's nothing but praise for the "consistently good" standards at the Allen family's "stylish" 17th-century house. / **Sample dishes:** rabbit rillettes with honey-pickled grapes; venison with apple & Calvados sauce; raspberry meringues. **Value tip:** set 3-crs L £18. **Details:** 1m from M1, J35; 9 pm; closed Mon, Tue, Wed L, Sat L & Sun; no smoking in dining room; children: 5+.*

sign up for the survey at www.hardens.com

CHEADLE, STAFFORDSHIRE   5–3B

Thornbury Hall Rasoi   £ 28   𝔸 ★

Lockwood Rd ST10 2DH   (01538) 750831

A former manor house provides the "fantastic" setting for Mr & Mrs Siddique's one-off subcontinental, which serves "great" Pakistani cooking. / **Details:** www.thornburyhall.co.uk; 10.30 pm; no Amex; no smoking area.

CHEESDEN, LANCASHIRE   5–1B

Nutter's   £ 38   ★★

Edenfield Rd OL12 7TY   (01706) 650167

"Close attention to detail" from TV-chef Andrew Nutter is rewarded with rave reviews for his "stylish" cooking at his family's rurally-located pub conversion; "exceptional banquets" are a highlight. / **Sample dishes:** black pudding wontons; pork with bubble 'n' squeak & tomato jus; cappuccino pannacotta. **Details:** between Edenfield & Nordon on A680; 9.30 pm; closed Tue; closed 2 weeks in Aug; no smoking.

CHELMSFORD, ESSEX   3–2C

Waterfront Place   £ 32   𝔸

Wharf Rd CM2 6LU   (01245) 252000

This "exciting new restaurant (and bar) with over 200 covers" (from the owners of Hatfield Peverel's Blue Strawberry) is part of a large canalside conference centre; some find it a touch "formulaic", but for the majority it's a "buzzy" and "welcoming" place, serving "tasty" modern fare. / **Sample dishes:** goats cheese, prosciutto & fig bruschetta; char-grilled salmon with mango & lime salsa; banoffi brûlée in chocolate. **Details:** www.waterfront-place.co.uk; 10 pm; closed Sun D; no smoking area.

CHELTENHAM, GLOUCESTERSHIRE   2–1C

Champignon Sauvage   £ 48   ★★

24-26 Suffolk Rd GL50 2AQ   (01242) 573449

"Exquisite" and "complex" French food "at incredibly reasonable prices" has long won fame for the Everitt Matthais's dining room; this year, however, its "pleasant" service and "unstuffy" atmosphere were also more consistently praised. / **Sample dishes:** eel tortellini with watercress cream; lamb with cauliflower dumplings; lemon mousse with milk sorbet. **Value tip:** set 2-crs L £16.50. **Details:** near Cheltenham Boys College; 9 pm; closed Mon & Sun; no smoking before 10.30 pm.

Daffodil   £ 36   𝔸

18-20 Suffolk Parade GL50 2AE   (01242) 700055

The "exceptional" location – a "tastefully converted" (but "noisy") Art Deco cinema – "is the star" at this "fun" destination; the place is "too pre-occupied with image", though, and neither food nor service lives up. / **Sample dishes:** rabbit confit with leek risotto; swordfish with Toulouse sausage & tomato cassoulet; lemon crème brûlée with chocolate shortbread. **Details:** www.thedaffodil.co.uk; just off Suffolk Square; 10.30 pm; closed Sun; no smoking in dining room.

Mayflower   £ 29

32-34 Clarence St GL50 3NX   (01242) 522426

"The oldest Cantonese restaurant in town" offers "consistently good" cooking, including an "excellent selection of vegetarian dishes". / **Value tip:** set 3-crs L £6.95. **Details:** 10 pm; closed Sun L.

Le Petit Blanc £31

Promenade GL50 1NN (01242) 266800

"I think they are taking the name for granted, and not delivering quality" – many reporters remain very critical of Raymond Blanc's "bleak" and "noisy" ballroom-conversion, where standards overall are judged "really average". / **Sample dishes:** twice-baked Roquefort soufflé; tuna with pine kernel crust & red pepper relish; chocolate fondant with pistachio ice cream. **Value tip:** set 2-crs L & pre-theatre £12.50.
Details: www.lepetitblanc.co.uk; 10.30 pm; no smoking in dining room.

Ruby £29

52 Suffolk Rd GL50 2AQ (01242) 250909

This "good but pricey" Cantonese vies in reporters affections for nominations as the top oriental in town. / **Details:** near Cheltenham Boys College; 11.30 pm; no smoking.

Storyteller £28 A★

11 North Pl GL50 4DW (01242) 250343

An "exotic menu" and "fascinating wine room" (where you choose from "a good range of wines, fairly priced") make this "relaxed" and "friendly" venture a thoroughly "enjoyable" concept. / **Sample dishes:** Mauritian beef skewers; roast lamb with new potatoes; chocolate mud pie. **Value tip:** set 3-crs L £10. **Details:** www.storyteller.co.uk; 10 pm; no smoking area.

CHESTER, CHESHIRE 5–2A

Albion Inn £17 A★

Park St CH1 1RN (01244) 340345

Idiosyncrasies such as 'no chips' with the "traditional pub grub" only strengthen respect for the Mercers' "characterful" backstreet boozer (near the Newgate), decorated in WW1 style. / **Sample dishes:** no starters; steak & kidney pie; bread & butter pudding. **Details:** www.albioninnchester.co.uk; 8 pm; no credit cards; no smoking before 9 pm; need 6+ to book; children: 18+ only.

Arkle
The Chester Grosvenor £70

Eastgate CH1 1LT (01244) 324024

In the North West, the "formal" dining room of this grand city-centre hotel stands out as a "special occasion" venue (not least because it costs so much); the "good wine list" is in accord with the aspiration level, but the "rich" and "luxurious" cooking is "overstated" and "overpriced". / **Sample dishes:** oxtail ravioli with langoustine tails; Gressingham duck with black fig sauce; basil blancmange with iced gingerbread. **Details:** www.chestergrosvenor.co.uk; 9.30 pm; closed Mon & Sun D; jacket & tie required; no smoking. **Accommodation:** 83 rooms, from £235.

Francs £24 A

14 Cuppin St CH1 2BN (01244) 317952

"The original bistro in town" changed hands this year; let's hope the new owners do nothing to disturb its appeal as a "crowded and useful" local favourite. / **Sample dishes:** smoked salmon, melon & avocado salad; lambs liver & bacon with mash; lemon tart. **Value tip:** set 2-crs L £6.95. **Details:** www.francs.co.uk; 11 pm; no smoking.

CHICHESTER, WEST SUSSEX
3–4A

Comme Ça £35
67 Broyle Rd BO19 4BD (01243) 788724
"Popular with the locals and theatregoers", this well-known Gallic
fixture is hailed by some as *"the only possible place to eat in the
local gastronomic wasteland"*; this year's reviews, however,
were notably less rapturous all round. / **Sample dishes:** *asparagus with
hollandaise sauce; cured Scottish salmon; summer pudding.* **Value tip:** *set 2-crs L &
pre-theatre £15.25.* **Details:** *www.commeca.co.uk; 0.5m N of city centre;
10.30 pm; closed Mon & Sun D; no smoking area.*

CHILGROVE, WEST SUSSEX
3–4A

White Horse £36
High St PO18 9HX (01243) 535219
It's "not as good since it changed ownership" (a couple of years
ago), but this South Downs pub is still a *"professional"* operation,
and its *"wonderful wine list"* (running to hundreds of bins)
remains a key attraction. / **Sample dishes:** *chicken liver salad with raspberry
dressing; braised oxtail with potato purée; warm chocolate gâteaux.* **Details:** *8m
NW of Chichester on B2141; 9.30 pm; closed Mon & Sun D; no smoking.*
Accommodation: *8 rooms, from £85.*

CHINNOR, OXFORDSHIRE
2–2D

Sir Charles Napier £39 *A*
Spriggs Alley OX9 4BX (01494) 483011
"A remote, away-from-it-all" Chilterns location and comfortable,
"eclectic" décor help make Julie Griffiths' long-established
destination (*"hardly a pub anymore"*) a *"delightful venue, both in
winter and summer"*; the cooking is *"reliable"*,
but *"very expensive"* for what it is. / **Sample dishes:** *butternut squash
soup; skate wing with capers, saffron potatoes & spinach; date cake with toffee
sauce.* **Value tip:** *set 2-crs weekday L £15.50.* **Details:** *M40, J6 into Chinnor,
turn right at roundabout; 10 pm; closed Mon & Sun D; no smoking area; children:
6+ at D.*

CHIPPENHAM, WILTSHIRE
2–2C

Manor House, Bybrook Restaurant £64 *A* ★
Castle Combe SN14 7HR (01249) 782206
"A veritable treasure"; this *"magnificent"* building (14th-century in
origin, and now a hotel and golf club) is set in *"lovely"* grounds,
and it wins unanimous endorsements for its *"wonderful"*
atmosphere and *"excellent"* cooking. / **Sample dishes:** *chicken,
artichoke & wild mushroom terrine; smoked salmon & crayfish with horseradish
potatoes; glazed lemon tart.* **Details:** *www.star.co.uk/manor/; 9 pm; no smoking.*
Accommodation: *46 rooms, from £145.*

CHIPPING CAMPDEN, GLOUCESTERSHIRE
2–1C

Eight Bells £29
Church St GL55 6JG (01386) 840371
"Above-average pub food" has established this pretty 14th-century
stone pub as a useful Cotswolds destination; there were a couple
of *"disappointing"* reports this year, though.
/ **Sample dishes:** *twice-baked cheese soufflé; braised lamb with julienne vegetables;
dark chocolate cheesecake.* **Details:** *www.eightbellsinn.co.uk; 10m S of Stratford
upon Avon; 9.30 pm, Fri & Sat 10 pm; no Amex; no smoking area.*
Accommodation: *6 rooms, from £70.*

CHOBHAM, SURREY   3–3A

Quails   £ 38   ★

1 Bagshot Rd GU24 8BP   (01276) 858491
Chris Wale's "consistent and innovative" cooking commends his family's "pleasant" town-centre fixture – of over a decade's standing – to all who comment on it. / **Sample dishes:** *chilli-glazed salt & pepper squid; BBQ chicken & smoked Gouda pizza; raisin pancakes with butterscotch bananas.* **Value tip:** *set 2-crs weekday L £12.* **Details:** *2m SE of M3, J3; 9.30 pm; closed Mon, Sat L & Sun.*

CHRISTCHURCH, DORSET   2–4C

Fishworks   £ 42

10 Church St BH23 1BW   (01202) 487000
The Bath and, more recently Bristol, branches of these combined fishmonger and restaurants have proved useful additions to the West Country dining scene; this most recent venture – which opened as our survey was closing – is the first to benefit from a seaside location. / **Sample dishes:** *spaghetti with crab & chilli; grilled plaice with black butter; lemon tart.* **Details:** *www.fishworks.co.uk; 9 pm; closed Mon & Sun; no smoking.*

Splinters   £ 42   🅐 ★

12 Church St BH23 1BW   (01202) 483454
Even those noting that prices are "quite high" endorse the unanimously positive views on this "romantic" destination near the Priory, whose cooking achieves "impressive" results.
/ **Sample dishes:** *Gorgonzola & spinach tart; sea bream with roasted vegetables; cappuccino brûlée.* **Details:** *10 pm; closed Mon & Sun; no smoking.*

CIRENCESTER, GLOUCESTERSHIRE   2–2C

Tatyan's   £ 24

27 Castle St GL7 1QD   (01285) 653529
A long-established Chinese of more than usual note; even those who say it's "not as good as it used to be" say it's "still well worth a visit". / **Details:** *www.tatyans.com; near junction of A417 & A345; 10.30 pm; closed Sun.*

CLACHAN, ARGYLL & BUTE   9–3B

Loch Fyne Oyster Bar   £ 30   ★

PA26 8BL   (01499) 600236
"Unfussy seafood" in an "excellent location", with "superb views" of the Loch, has created a big name for this unpretentious fixture – the cradle of what is now a growing UK-wide chain; some, though, fear it's becoming "so popular it doesn't have to try any more"; (it's up for sale as we go to press). / **Sample dishes:** *smoked haddock chowder; king scallops; ice cream.* **Details:** *www.loch-fyne.com; 10m E of Inveraray on A83; 5 pm, Fri & Sat 7.30 pm; open L & D all week (Nov-Mar D only); no smoking.*

sign up for the survey at www.hardens.com   175

CLANFIELD, OXFORDSHIRE 2–2C
Plough £ 43 𝔸★

Bourton Rd OX18 2RB (01367) 810222

*This (rather oddly-named) Elizabethan manor house – now an hotel – offers a "comfortable" and "friendly" (if "restrained") setting in which to enjoy cooking which its small local fan club says is simply "fantastic". / **Sample dishes:** chicken liver terrine with pink peppercorns; poached hake with gravadlax sauce; crème brûlée with figs.* **Value tip:** set 2-crs L £15. **Details:** 9 pm; no smoking; children: 12+ at D. **Accommodation:** 12 rooms, from £95.

CLAVERING, ESSEX 3–2B
The Cricketers £ 35

Wicken Rd CB11 4QT (01799) 550442

*"Now Jamie Oliver is so famous", it's "very hard to get a table" at this shrine to celebrity culture – the boozer still owned and run by his father; the cooking is not without fans, but for the critics it's just "not so pukka". / **Sample dishes:** turmeric tempura monkfish; veal with Savoy cabbage & blue cheese sauce; chocolate cheesecake.* **Details:** www.thecricketers.co.uk; on B1038 between Newport & Buntingford; 10 pm; smoking in bar only. **Accommodation:** 14 rooms, from £100.

CLAYGATE, SURREY 3–3A
Le Petit Pierrot £ 35 ★

4 The Parade KT10 0NU (01372) 465105

*"A tiny French restaurant" in "cramped" shop-conversion premises, where "carefully and knowledgeably prepared food" comes at "reasonable prices". / **Sample dishes:** pan-fried foie gras with sweetcorn galette; guinea fowl with morel risotto; sweet chestnut & prune pudding.* **Value tip:** set 2-crs L £12.25. **Details:** 9.30 pm; closed Sat L & Sun; children: 8+.

CLECKHEATON, WEST YORKSHIRE 5–1C
Aakash £ 27

Providence Pl, Bradford Rd BD19 3PN (01274) 870011

*This former congregational chapel – which claims to be the world's largest curry house – opened only last year, but has inspired remarkably few reports; well, just one actually, which says it's "an amazing building which offers disappointing food". / **Details:** www.aakashrestaurant.com; A638 towards Dewsbury from M62, J26; 11 pm; D only; no smoking area.*

CLENT, WORCESTERSHIRE 5–4B
The Fountain Inn £ 29 ★

Adams Hl DY9 9PU (01562) 883286

*"Very generous portions" of "traditional" pub grub and "good real ale", again help make this "crowded" beamed pub a very popular destination. / **Sample dishes:** deep-fried goats cheese with raspberry coulis; chicken Wellington; summer fruit cheesecake.* **Details:** 2m from Hagley by Clent Hills; 9.30 pm; no Amex; no smoking area.

CLEOBURY MORTIMER, SHROPSHIRE 5–4B
Spice Empire £ 21 ★

17 High St DY14 8DG (01299) 270419

*"An unlikely gem in deepest south Shropshire" – this above-average curry house is "deservedly popular". / **Details:** 11 pm; closed Mon.*

CLEVEDON, BATH & NE SOMERSET 2–2A

Junior Poon £29 ★

16 Hill Rd BS21 7NZ (01275) 341900

"Immaculate service and reliably good food" is a recipe which created a high satisfaction level for this *"good-quality Chinese"*, which occupies a listed Georgian building. / **Details:** www.juniorpoon.com; near Clevedon Pier; 10 pm; D only.

The Olive Garden £28 ★

91 Hill Rd BS21 7PN (01275) 341999

"A small-town restaurant that's going places" – the Murray family's establishment offers *"good rustic food"* (often organic), *"great Italian wines"* and *"super-smiley service"*. / **Sample dishes:** poached salt cod with butter beans; braised Orkney beef with bubble 'n' squeak; crème brûlée. **Details:** 10 pm; closed Mon & Sun; no smoking pre 9 pm; booking: max 8.

CLIPSHAM, RUTLAND 6–4A

Olive Branch £28 𝔸★★

Main St LE15 7SH (01780) 410355

"If all pub grub was this good, no one would leave the UK"; this *"down-to-earth"* but *"buzzing"* venture delivers a *"marvellous-value"* formula that includes *"brilliant"* and *"strongly-flavoured"* food, and an *"excellent wine list"*. / **Sample dishes:** honey-roasted parsnip soup; roast sea bream with olive mash & tomato relish; coconut rice pudding. **Value tip:** set 3-crs L £11.50 (Sun £14.50). **Details:** 2m E from A1 on B664; 9.30 pm; closed Sun D; no Amex; no smoking area.

CLITHEROE, LANCASHIRE 5–1B

Inn at Whitewell £37 𝔸★

Forest of Bowland BD7 3AT (01200) 448222

This *"gem"* of a *"rambling country pub"* offers a splendid formula that includes a *"super-picturesque"* and *"unspoilt"* location, and characterful service; there is the occasional concern that the fairly traditional cooking has *"lost a bit of its sparkle"*, but most reporters still find it *"superb"*. / **Sample dishes:** goats cheese cannelloni with sweet pepper sauce; grilled black pudding with lambs kidneys; British & Irish cheeses. **Details:** 9.30 pm; D only (bar meals only at L). **Accommodation:** 17 rooms, from £87.

CLYTHA, MONMOUTHSHIRE 2–2A

Clytha Arms £31

NP7 9BW (01873) 840206

Andrew Canning, the chef/proprietor produces *"good local grub"* at this *"friendly"* country inn. / **Sample dishes:** melon & avocado salad; roast hake with herb salsa; Sauternes cream with spiced prunes. **Value tip:** set 2-crs meal £14.95. **Details:** on Old Abergavenny to Raglan Road; 9.30 pm; closed Mon & Sun D; no smoking. **Accommodation:** 4 rooms, from £70.

COBHAM, SURREY 3–3A

La Capanna £39

48 High St KT11 3EF (01932) 862121

Entering its 25th year, this rustic, *"barn"*-like Italian completely splits the locals; fans say it's *"a steady performer"* where *"everything is first class"* — foes say it *"continues to disappoint"*. / **Sample dishes:** fresh crab salad; veal & scallops with mushroom sauce; profiteroles. **Value tip:** set 3-crs Sun L £18.95. **Details:** 10.45 pm; closed Sat L.

---

sign up for the survey at www.hardens.com

Cricketers £ 36
Downside KT11 3NX (01932) 862105
A setting by the village green helps make this "reliable" and
"child-friendly" boozer a particularly good "summer lunchtime"
destination. / **Sample dishes:** smoked haddock & salmon with poached egg;
roast lamb with garlic & rosemary; cheesecake. **Value tip:** set 2-crs L £13.50
(not Sun). **Details:** 2m from Cobham High St; 9.30 pm; closed Mon & Sun D.

COCKERMOUTH, CUMBRIA 7–3C

Quince & Medlar £31 A★★
13 Castlegate CA13 9EU (01900) 823579
Colin & Louisa Le Voi's popular fixture offers "fantastic" veggie
cooking in the "quite posh" dining room of their Georgian home.
/ **Sample dishes:** French onion tart; lentil & apricot strudel with wilted spinach;
spiced quince cheesecake. **Details:** next to Cockermouth Castle; 9.30 pm; D only,
closed Mon & Sun; no Amex; no smoking; children: 5+.

COGGESHALL, ESSEX 3–2C

Baumann's Brasserie £ 30
4-6 Stoneham St CO6 1TT (01376) 561453
Those with long memories recall the involvement of the late and
great Peter Langan in this suburban brasserie; it still has its fans,
but there are also critics nowadays, who say it's "poorly managed"
and "overpriced". / **Sample dishes:** watercress soup with crispy spring onions;
blackened beef with Worcestershire sauce butter; maple syrup custard with apple
cookies. **Value tip:** set 2-crs L £11. **Details:** www.baumannsbrasserie.co.uk;
9.30 pm; closed Mon & Tue; no smoking area.

COLCHESTER, ESSEX 3–2C

Lemon Tree £ 25 A★
48 St Johns St CO2 7AD (01206) 767337
Set into the town's Roman walls, this "simple and unpretentious"
bistro wins all-round commendations for its "lovely" atmosphere
and its "reasonably-priced" menu that's "not afraid to try
something new". / **Sample dishes:** goats cheese & red pepper tart; sea bass
with basil butter & samphire; baked black cherry cheesecake. **Value tip:** set 2-crs L
£7.95. **Details:** www.the-lemon-tree.com; 10 pm; closed Sun; no smoking.

COLERNE, WILTSHIRE 2–2B

Lucknam Park £ 68 A
SN14 8AZ (01225) 742777
An "imaginative" menu and "classy" surroundings make this
"pretty" Georgian country house "the sort of place to propose to
your spouse-to-be"; overall feedback is uniformly positive, but –
at this elevated price level – ratings fall just short of 'star' quality.
/ **Sample dishes:** spinach cappuccino with truffled quails eggs; roast venison with
game chips & spiced pears; citrus sorbets with citrus jelly.
Details: www.lucknampark.co.uk; 6m NE of Bath; 9.30 pm; D only, except Sun
open L & D; jacket & tie required; no smoking; children: 12+ at D.
Accommodation: 41 rooms, from £205.

COLN ST ALDWYNS, GLOUCESTERSHIRE 2–2C
New Inn at Coln £ 40 A★
GL7 5AN (01285) 750651
Reports speak nothing but good of this "lovely" and "romantic" Cotswold inn, where "simple modern cooking in good portions" is complemented by a "good wine list". / **Sample dishes:** wild mushroom & baby vegetable consommé; pan-fried cod with tomato fondue; rich chocolate tart. **Details:** www.new-inn.co.uk; off B4425, 2m SW of Bibury; 9 pm, Fri & Sat 9.30 pm; no smoking in dining room; children: 10+ at D. **Accommodation:** 14 rooms, from £110.

COLSTON BASSETT, NOTTINGHAMSHIRE 5–3D
Martins Arms Inn £ 51 A
School Ln NG12 3FD (01949) 81361
As you'd hope, the Stilton pot cakes are a highlight of the "good food" on offer at this "wonderful country pub". / **Details:** 2 miles off A46; 9.30 pm; closed Sun D; no Amex; children: 14+.

COMPTON, SURREY 3–3A
The Withies Inn £ 37 A
Withies Ln GU3 1JA (01483) 421158
No one doubts that this "textbook country pub, complete with beams and open fire" offers a "great environment"; for what it is, however, its restaurant is "not cheap". / **Sample dishes:** pan-fried sardines with lemon; roast lamb with rosemary; treacle tart & custard. **Details:** off A3 near Guildford, signposted on B3000; 10 pm; closed Sun D; booking essential.

CONSTANTINE, CORNWALL 1–4B
Trengilly Wartha Inn £ 37
Nancenoy TR11 5RP (01326) 340332
"Once found, never forgotten" – fans of this celebrated but obscurely-located rural fixture say it's "worth the detour" for its "vast wine list" and wide variety of eating options; service, however, can seem "laid-back to the point of indifference". / **Sample dishes:** scallops with creamed cabbage; duck with sherry & puy lentils; nougat parfait. **Details:** www.trengilly.co.uk; 1m outside village; 9.30 pm; D only. **Accommodation:** 8 rooms, from £77.

COOKHAM, BERKSHIRE 3–3A
Bel & The Dragon £ 39
High St SL6 9SQ (01628) 521263
This "good but expensive" gastropub (part of a small chain) has a "lovely" location and "interesting" décor; it has won quite a following, though it can seem "impersonal" at peak times. / **Sample dishes:** goats cheese & spinach strudel; roast lamb with herb mash & raspberry jus; banoffi cheesecake. **Details:** www.belandthedragon.co.uk; opp Stanley Spencer Gallery; 10 pm; no smoking area.

CORBRIDGE, NORTHUMBERLAND 8–2B
The Angel of Corbridge £ 32
Main St NE45 5LA (01434) 632119
It occupies one of the oldest buildings in town, but the dining room of this "newly-refurbished" old coaching inn is now "well-appointed" in modern style, and its consistent standards make it a useful option in a thin area. / **Sample dishes:** smoked salmon soufflé; roast guinea fowl; chocolate tart. **Details:** 9.30 pm; no smoking in dining room. **Accommodation:** 5 rooms, from £74.

The Valley £26
Old Station Hs NE45 5AY (01434) 633434
*For a "highly original" way to enjoy "good" curry, bag a place on
the 'Package to India' from Newcastle (whereby you order on the
train and dinner awaits you here on arrival); you could of course
just drive, but you'd miss half the fun.*
/ **Details:** www.northeastonline.co.uk/valley; 10.30 pm; D only, closed Sun;
no smoking area.

CORSCOMBE, DORSET 2–4B

Fox Inn £33 🅰
DT2 0NS (01935) 891330
*"A lovely location" adds to the atmosphere at this "cosy" and
"picturesque" thatched pub; its "fresh and classy" cooking is
widely praised, but "prices that seem more Dorchester Hotel than
Dorset" can take the shine off the experience for some.*
/ **Sample dishes:** roast aubergines with tomato & Mozzarella; chicken with celery,
red pepper & cream sauce; plum crumble. **Details:** www.fox-inn.co.uk; 5m off A37;
9 pm, Fri & Sat 9.30 pm; no smoking area. **Accommodation:** 4 rooms, from £80.

CORSE LAWN, GLOUCESTERSHIRE 2–1B

Corse Lawn Hotel £41 ★
GL19 4LZ (01452) 780771
*The dining room at this "very pleasant" hotel – set in a listed
Queen Anne building on the village green – attracts nothing but
praise, thanks to its "professional" cuisine and its "on-the-ball"
service.* / **Sample dishes:** char-grilled squid with rocket & chilli oil; pigeon with
lentils & black sausage; poached fruits with vanilla cream. **Value tip:** set 2-crs L
£16.50. **Details:** www.corselawnhousehotel.co.uk; 5m SW of Tewkesbury on B4211;
9.30 pm; no smoking; children: 6+ at D. **Accommodation:** 19 rooms, from £125.

COVENTRY, WEST MIDLANDS 5–4C

Thai Dusit £25
39 London Rd CV1 2JP (024) 7622 7788
*"Friendly and efficient staff" and "good value" grub make this
popular oriental "one of Coventry's rare culinary gems".*
/ **Value tip:** set 2-crs L £5.95. **Details:** 11 pm; no Amex.

COWBRIDGE, VALE OF GLAMORGAN 2–2A

Farthings £26
54 High St CF71 7AH (01446) 772990
*"Casual, relaxed, cosy and friendly" – Natalie & Nick Dobson's
brasserie generates limited but upbeat feedback.*
/ **Sample dishes:** French onion soup with cheese croutons; wild boar & pheasant
sausages with grain mustard mash; hazelnut & raspberry meringue.
Details: 10 pm; closed Mon D & Sun D; no Amex; no smoking area.

COWLING, WEST YORKSHIRE 5–1B

Harlequin £30
139 Keighley Rd BD22 0AH (01535) 633277
*Both fish and fowl are reported to be well prepared at this wine
bar-cum-restaurant, whose cooking attracts uniform local praise.*
/ **Sample dishes:** calamari & chorizo salad; roast duckling with rhubarb compote;
Yorkshire ginger sponge. **Value tip:** set 3-crs Sun L £13.25. **Details:** on A6068
towards Colne; 9.30 pm; closed Mon & Tue; no smoking; children: 7+ at D.

COXWOLD, NORTH YORKSHIRE   8–4C

Fauconberg Arms   £ 30
YO61 4AD   (01347) 868214
This "nice" pub in a "lovely village" uses "local produce of a high
standard"; the results are "well prepared, if not exciting".
/ **Sample dishes:** scallops with sweet chilli & lobster oil; roast duck with mash &
blackberry jus; vanilla brûlée with chocolate sauce. **Value tip:** set 3-crs Sun L £14.
Details: 9.30 pm; restaurant open only Wed D-Sat D & Sun L, pub open L & D all
week; no Amex; no smoking in dining room. **Accommodation:** 4 rooms, from £60.

CRASTER, NORTHUMBERLAND   8–1B

Jolly Fisherman   £ 13   ★
NE66 3TR   (01665) 576461
The "best crab soup in the world" is among the attractions which
make this simple inn universally popular; it has "lovely views",
too, "especially in winter". / **Sample dishes:** crab soup with whisky; Craster
kipper pâté with melba toast; blackcurrant crumble with custard. **Details:** near
Dunstanburgh Castle; 8 pm; no credit cards; no smoking area.

CREIGIAU, CARDIFF   2–2A

Caesars Arms   £ 33   ★
Cardiff Rd   CF15 9NN   (029) 2089 0486
The formula of Cardiff's La Brasserie – you choose your fish/meat,
they grill it – is happily transposed to the country at this
"very popular" and "busy" rural pub/brasserie.
/ **Sample dishes:** smoked salmon with eggs & capers; honey-roasted duckling;
raspberry pavlova. **Value tip:** set 1-crs L £5. **Details:** beyond Creigiau, past golf
club; 10.30 pm; closed Sun D.

CRICKHOWELL, POWYS   2–1A

The Bear   £ 35
High St   NP8 1BW   (01873) 810408
This "intimate" and "friendly" old coaching inn on the market
place is one of the best-known destinations in Wales; its cooking is
good, rather than remarkable, and some tip the bar food as
"better than the restaurant". / **Sample dishes:** seared king scallops with
noodles; swordfish with wild rice; summer fruit pudding. **Details:** 9.30 pm; closed
Mon, Tue-Sat D only, closed Sun D; no smoking in bar; children: 7+ in restaurant.
Accommodation: 34 rooms, from £70.

Nantyffin Cider Mill   £ 32   A★★
Brecon Rd   NP8 1SG   (01873) 810775
This "unusual venue" – an "atmospheric converted mill" –
continues to put in an impressive all-round performance;
an "interesting menu (for Wales)" is realised to "fantastic" effect
in a "happy, rustic setting". / **Sample dishes:** chicken liver parfait with red
onion confit; red mullet with saffron linguine & crab; Drambuie pannacotta with figs.
Details: www.cidermill.co.uk; on A40 between Brecon & Crickhowell; 9.30 pm;
closed Mon (& Sun D in winter); no smoking area.

CROSTHWAITE, CUMBRIA
The Punch Bowl £ 30 7–4D ★

LA8 8HR (01539) 568237

A Gavroche-trained chef adds lustre to "first-class" cooking that's "traditional with a contemporary edge" at this famous Lakeland inn; it also benefits from a "fantastic view".
/ **Sample dishes:** beetroot & goats cheese tart; slow-cooked lamb with leek & white bean stew; chocolate & ginger tart with honey ice cream. **Value tip:** set 2-crs L £9.95. **Details:** www.punchbowl.fsnet.co.uk; off A5074 towards Bowness, turn right after Lyth Hotel; 9 pm; closed Mon & Sun D; no Amex; no smoking. **Accommodation:** 3 rooms, from £55 (£97.50 incl D).

CROYDON, SURREY
Banana Leaf £ 24 3–3B ★

7 Lower Addiscombe Rd CR0 6BQ (020) 8688 0297

"Great food at reasonable prices" has made this south Indian canteen very popular locally; ambience, though, can be "lacking".
/ **Details:** near East Croydon station; 11 pm; no smoking area.

CUCKFIELD, WEST SUSSEX
Ockenden Manor £ 43 3–4B 🅐

Ockenden Ln RH17 5LD (01444) 416111

This "charming" Elizabethan country house hotel offers "a step back in time"; the cooking – if not quite an attraction equal to the atmosphere – is "well presented", too. / **Sample dishes:** truffle risotto; grilled beef with mustard sauce; warm apple fritters. **Value tip:** set 2-crs L £15.50. **Details:** www.hshotels.co.uk; 9.30 pm; no smoking. **Accommodation:** 22 rooms, from £132.

CUPAR, FIFE
Ostlers Close £ 41 9–3D ★

25 Bonnygate KY15 4BU (01334) 655574

This "excellent country restaurant" recently celebrated its 21st birthday; it remains a consistent favourite for most of the (small number of) reporters who comment on it. / **Sample dishes:** monkfish with red pepper salsa; oxtail & pigs trotter roly-poly with oxtail gravy; pineapple syrup sponge. **Details:** www.ostlersclose.co.uk; 9.30 pm; closed Mon, Tue L, Wed L, Thu L & Sun; no smoking; children: 6+ at D.

The Peat Inn £ 42 🅐

KY15 5LH (01334) 840206

Chef/patron David Wilson's "superb" cooking and a notable wine list "continue to impress" visitors to this famous former coaching inn; some are unmoved, though, and even fans concede the place is "a wee bit stuffy". / **Sample dishes:** roast scallops with leeks & smoked bacon; roe deer fillet with cocoa bean purée; trio of caramel desserts. **Details:** www.thepeatinn.co.uk; at junction of B940 & B941, SW of St Andrews; 9.30 pm; closed Mon & Sun; no smoking. **Accommodation:** 8 rooms, from £145.

DALRY, AYRSHIRE
Braidwoods £ 39 9–4B ★★

Drumastle Mill Cottage KA24 4LN (01294) 833544

"Exquisite" cooking (from a menu of modest length) is the theme of most reports on Keith & Nicola Braidwood's "small and intimate" restaurant of high ambition, located in a "very pleasant country cottage". / **Sample dishes:** curried prawn & coriander soup; honey-glazed duck with spiced beetroot; raspberry crème brûlée. **Details:** www.braidwoods.co.uk; 9 pm; closed Mon, Tue L & Sun D; closed 2 weeks in Jan & Sep; no smoking; children: 12+.

DARTMOUTH, DEVON   1–4D

Carved Angel   £ 58
2 South Embankment TQ6 9BH   (01803) 832465
"Not what it was five years ago"; it's still a "gem", for some,
but many reporters – citing "arm-and-a-leg pricing" and a
"snooty" atmosphere – feel this famous waterside fish restaurant
is "disappointing, since the new people took over"; perhaps the
new chef (2002) will pep things up. / **Sample dishes:** Dartmouth crab
with smoked pepper relish; lamb with root vegetable strudel & cherry jus; rhubarb
soufflé. **Details:** www.thecarvedangel.com; opp passenger ferry pontoon; 9.30 pm;
closed Mon L & Sun D; no smoking; children: 10+ at D.

Carved Angel Café   £ 31
7 Foss St TQ6 9DW   (01803) 834842
This "unpretentious bistro" – the first of the spin-offs from the
famed restaurant of the same name – offers "simple but
gratifying" dishes from a blackboard menu. / **Sample dishes:** avocado,
chicken & pear salad; red mullet with tagliatelle & pepper butter; grapefruit &
brandy soufflé. **Value tip:** set 2-crs L £10. **Details:** www.thecarvedangel.com;
9.30 pm; L only Mon-Wed, closed Sun; no smoking; no booking at L.

Hooked   £ 47   ★
5 Higher St TQ6 9RB   (01803) 832022
"Well worth a visit for wonderful food" – feedback on this
"pretty" modern fish and seafood restaurant is uniformly upbeat;
the occasional off-the-wall dish enlivens a generally
"straightforward" menu. / **Sample dishes:** potted shrimps with piccalilli;
poached lobster with three-cheese macaroni; coconut crumble with lemongrass
sherbert. **Details:** 8.30 pm (9.30 pm in summer); D only, closed Mon & Sun;
no smoking.

DAVENTRY, NORTHANTS   2–1D

Fawsley Hall   £ 52   Ⓐ
NN11 3BA   (01327) 892000
"Wonderful surroundings, poor food, slow service" – this Tudor
hall, recently revamped with an agreeable modern interior, makes
a very attractive destination, but its catering operations smack of
"pretentiousness". / **Sample dishes:** foie gras terrine with pickled cherries;
herbed lamb with creamed shallots; raspberry soufflé with chocolate sorbet.
Value tip: set 2-crs Sun L £16.50. **Details:** www.fawsleyhall.com; on A361
between Daventry & Banbury; 9.30 pm; no smoking in dining room.
Accommodation: 43 rooms, from £189.

DEDHAM, ESSEX   3–2C

Milsoms   £ 30
Stratford Rd CO7 6HW   (01206) 322795
This new (and "modern"), no-booking offshoot of the famous
Talbooth similarly benefits from a "beautiful rural location"
(even if it's rather near the A12); its simple dishes are generally
realised to a "good" standard, and popularity already makes it a
"buzzy" local destination. / **Sample dishes:** glass noodle & tiger prawn
salad; braised lamb with mustard mash & sage fritters; raspberry ripple cheescake.
Details: 9.30 pm; no booking. **Accommodation:** 14 rooms, from £80.

sign up for the survey at www.hardens.com

Le Talbooth   £51
Gun Hill   CO7 6HP   (01206) 323150
"A wonderfully-picturesque, old-world, truly English setting"
underpins support for the Milsom family's Constable Country
fixture; it can seem to "trade on its reputation" nowadays, though,
and many reports are of "very average food and service".
/ **Sample dishes:** foie gras terrine; seabass with braised fennel & cucumber;
hot chocolate & orange fondant. **Value tip:** set 2-crs L £14.50.
Details: www.talbooth.com; 5m N of Colchester on A12, take B1029; 9.30 pm;
closed Sun D (in winter only). **Accommodation:** 10 rooms, from £155.

DENSHAW, GREATER MANCHESTER   5–2B

Rams Head Inn   £27   A ★
OL3 5UN   (01457) 874802
The Pennines may seem "an unusual place to find an excellent
pub/restaurant specialising in fish", but this "unpretentious"
establishment attracts almost unanimous praise.
/ **Sample dishes:** smoked salmon & asparagus salad; pan-fried venison with black
cherry & orange sauce; chocolate & Bailey's cheesecake. **Details:** 2m from M63,
J22 towards Oldham; 10 pm; no Amex; no smoking area; children: no babies at D.

DERBY, DERBYSHIRE   5–3C

Darleys   £45
Darley Abbey Mill   DE22 1DZ   (01332) 364987
"An unbelievable setting overlooking river and weir" is an
undisputed highlight at this mill-conversion; but even some who
find it "improved all-round by the recent refurbishment" still say
that it "doesn't justify the price". / **Sample dishes:** scallops with crispy
crab risotto cakes; roast pork belly with black pudding & mustard mash; spiced
poached pears with cinnamon shortbread. **Value tip:** set 2-crs L £13.50.
Details: www.darleys.com; 2m N of city centre by River Derwent; 10 pm; closed
Sun D; no smoking.

DODDISCOMBSLEIGH, DEVON   1–3D

Nobody Inn   £24   A
EX6 7PS   (01647) 252394
"West Country cheeses to die for", an "amazing wine list" and "a
good choice of whisky" are part of a package which have secured
a huge reputation for this "idyllic" rural inn, a short drive from
Exeter; it's "usually packed". / **Sample dishes:** pork meatballs with sweet &
sour sauce; quail stuffed with rice & apricots; sticky toffee pudding.
Details: www.nobodyinn.com; off A38 at Haldon Hill (signed Dunchidrock); 9 pm;
closed Mon & Sun; no smoking area; children: 14+. **Accommodation:** 7 rooms,
from £55.

DOGMERSFIELD, HAMPSHIRE   3–3A

Queen's Head   £24   ★
Pilcot Ln   RG27 8SY   (01252) 613531
"Hearty helpings" of "imaginative" fare again win praise for this
upmarket rural boozer. / **Sample dishes:** potato skins with cheese & bacon;
steak & ale pie; treacle sponge & custard. **Details:** off A287 between Farnham &
Odiham; 9 pm; closed Mon.

DOLGARROG, CONWY   4–1D
Lord Newborough   £ 26   ★
Conway Rd LL32 8JX   (01492) 660549
A "varied" menu realised to a "consistent" standard helps make
this rural gastropub a "very pleasant" destination.
/ **Sample dishes:** bacon & cheese salad; pan-fried chicken with leek & mushroom
sauce; summer pudding. **Details:** 9 pm; closed Mon & Sun D; no smoking area.

DORCHESTER, DORSET   2–4B
Mock Turtle   £ 30
34 High West St DT1 1UP   (01305) 264011
Some reporters are a touch lukewarm in their praise of this
modern conversion of an old rectory; on balance, though,
it's judged a "welcoming place", with "reasonable" all-round
standards. / **Sample dishes:** smoked chicken with Waldorf salad; grilled plaice;
blueberry cheesecake. **Details:** www.themockturtle.com; 9.30 pm; closed Mon L,
Sat L & Sun; no smoking area; no booking after 9.30 pm.

DORKING, SURREY   3–3A
Partners   £ 42
2-4 West St RH4 1BL   (01306) 882826
"A very personable owner" helps to create an "intimate"
atmosphere at this beamed town-centre establishment; even those
praising the "good" modern cooking, however, can find it "pricey"
for what it is. / **Sample dishes:** whole quail; calves liver & black pudding with
mash; apple & Calvados brioche. **Details:** www.scoot.co.uk/partners; 10 pm; closed
Mon, Sat L & Sun; no smoking area.

DORRINGTON, SHROPSHIRE   5–4A
Country Friends   £ 41   𝔸 ★
SY5 7JD   (01743) 718707
"Exceptionally good" cooking from an "imaginative" menu makes
this mock-Tudor manor house well worth seeking out; it's a "cosy"
and "comfortable" place, too, with "discreet" service.
/ **Sample dishes:** twice-baked red pepper & pesto soufflé; venison with sloe gin
sauce; Queen of puddings. **Details:** 5m S of Shrewsbury on A49; 9 pm; closed Mon,
Tue & Sun; no Amex; no smoking. **Accommodation:** 1 room, at about £130.

DUBLIN, COUNTY DUBLIN, ROI   10–3D

*Though clearly not geographically within the ambit of a
guide called* **UK Restaurants,** *we have included a small
range of the best-known names in the Irish capital.*

The big news of the past year has been the closure of
Peacock Alley, and the relocation to the same site of
Thorntons, leaving behind its obscure backstreet premises.
This is now the only rival at the top for *Restaurant Patrick
Guilbaud* – long the city's most revered temple of gastronomy.

Reporters' favourites in town still tend to be as much
'atmosphere' places as they are foodie haunts. *Roly's Bistro*
remained reporters' top all-rounder, and *La Stampa* is still
the top tip for pure atmosphere. The exception proving the
rule was *Jacob's Ladder,* which achieved equal mention for its
serious culinary approach.

Temple Bar is the best known touristy area, and —
like London's Covent Garden — you will often eat better and
more cheaply elsewhere.

Clarence Hotel (Tea Rooms)   € 70
6-8 Wellington Quay   D2   (01) 670 7766
*Reports on the groovy dining room at this famous U2-owned
design-hotel were thin on the ground this year, and a bit mixed;
for dedicated fans, though, "Sunday brunch here is a must when
you're staying in Dublin". / Sample dishes: deep-fried potato & bacon cakes;
chicken with spinach & black pudding jus; chocolate clafoutis with tiramisu ice
cream. Value tip: set 3-crs L €23. Details: www.theclarence.ie; opp New
Millennium Bridge; 10.45 pm; closed Sat L; no Switch; no smoking area.
Accommodation: 50 rooms, from £285.*

L'Ecrivain   € 80   ★
109 Lower Baggot St   D2   (01) 661 1919
*"Fabulous food" and "a great wine list" is the general tenor of
commentary on Derry & Sally Anne Clarke's long-established
Gallic restaurant (which had a major revamp a couple of years
ago). / Sample dishes: baked rock oysters with cabbage & bacon; seared blue fin
tuna; summer berry truffle cake. Details: www.lecrivain.com; opp Bank of Ireland;
10.30 pm; closed Sat L & Sun; no Switch; no smoking area; booking essential.*

Eden   € 63
Meeting House Sq   D2   (01) 670 5372
*"Knowledgeable" service contributes to general satisfaction with
this sleek-looking bar/restaurant — "a Temple Bar hotspot";
not everyone is impressed, however. / Sample dishes: smoked eel salad;
organic pork & apricot stew; crème brûlée. Details: www.edenrestaurant.ie;
near Olympia Theatre; 10.30 pm; no Switch; no smoking area.*

Jacob's Ladder   € 50   ★
4-5 Nassau St   D2   (01) 670 3865
*"A special restaurant with a lovely wine list" is the unanimous view
on Adrian Roche's ambitious first-floor venture, overlooking Trinity
College, praised for its "super" contemporary cuisine.
/ Sample dishes: roast quail with quails eggs & celeriac cream; roast pigeon with
lentils; rum & raisin brûlée. Value tip: set 2-crs L €19.
Details: www.jacobsladder.ie; beside Trinity College; 10 pm; closed Mon & Sun;
no Switch; no smoking area.*

Mermaid Café   € 55   ★
69-70 Dame Street   D2   (01) 670 8236
*"Is it a café, or is it a restaurant?" — it matters little at this
relaxed, stripped-down spot, on the fringe of Temple Bar, where
"creative modern European cuisine" is complemented by "a good,
reasonably-priced selection of wines"; a bar area is a recent
addition. / Sample dishes: smoked fish chowder with celery biscuits; rabbit
fricassée with oyster mushrooms & pancetta; pecan pie with maple ice cream.
Details: www.mermaid.ie; near Olympia Theatre; 11 pm, Sun 9 pm; no Amex or
Switch; no smoking area.*

Restaurant Patrick Guilbaud   €128   ★
21 Upper Merrion St   D2   (01) 676 4192
*"On a par with any top London venue", this airy and tranquil
"gastronomic haven" — arguably the best in Ireland — receives
nothing but praise for its "perfect" Gallic cooking (albeit at a hefty
price), and its incredible wine list. / Sample dishes: lobster ravioli in
coconut cream; venison with pumpkin cream & black radishes; black fig confit with
fennel. Value tip: set 2-crs L €28 (not in Dec). Details: www.merrionhotel.com;
10.15 pm; closed Mon & Sun; no Switch; no smoking area.*

Roly's Bistro € 54 _A_ ★
7 Ballsbridge Ter   D4   (01) 668 2611
"Great craic", "fantastic food" and "excellent" service won consistent praise this year for this legendary brasserie, a "noisy" and perennially 'in' Ballsbridge favourite; "always book".
/ **Sample dishes:** _spiced crab with angel hair pasta; Dublin Bay prawns with tarragon rice; Jaffa Cake torte._ **Value tip:** _set 3-crs L €18._
Details: _www.rolysbistro.ie; near American Embassy; 9.45 pm; no Switch; no smoking area._

La Stampa € 40 _A_
35 Dawson St   D2   (01) 677 8611
This "amazing" former ballroom provides an absolutely wonderful setting for a brasserie; inevitably, the cooking has to play second fiddle. / **Sample dishes:** _pan-fried foie gras brioche; roast fillet of beef; chocolate fondant._ **Details:** _www.lastampa.ie; off St Stephen's Green; midnight, Sat 12.30 am; D only; no Switch; no smoking area._

Thorntons
Fitzwilliam Hotel € 96
119 St Stephen's Grn   D2   (01) 478 7008
Kevin Thornton has upped sticks from his recherché former backstreet premises to this prime central site; he's hoping to recreate the reputation he enjoyed in his old location, and to outshine the glory days of Peacock Alley (RIP), the previous occupant. / **Sample dishes:** _sautéed foie gras & scallops; roast suckling pig; apple tarte Tatin with butterscotch ice cream._ **Details:** _www.fitzwilliam-hotel.com; 9.30 pm; D only, except Fri when L & D; closed Mon & Sun; no Switch; no smoking area._

DUNDRUM, COUNTY DOWN 10–2D

Bucks Head £31 _A_
77-79 Main St   BT33 0LU   (028) 4375 1868
A small local fan club is generous in its praise for the cooking at this "lovely country inn", beautifully-situated in Dundrum Bay.
/ **Sample dishes:** _garlic soda bread with Parmesan; rib-eye beef with burnt onion mash; marshmallow meringue with pistachio ice cream._ **Value tip:** _set 3-crs Sun L £14.50._ **Details:** _www.thebucksheadinn.co.uk; 3m N of Newcastle; 9 pm; closed Mon (in winter only); no smoking area._

DUNKELD, PERTH & KINROSS 9–3C

Kinnaird House £51 _A_ ★
Kinnaird Estate   PH8 0LB   (01796) 482440
An "idyllic" location in the Tay valley helps to create a "relaxing" atmosphere at this small Edwardian country house hotel; "top-class" standards are praised throughout, not least the "wonderful" cuisine and "attentive and friendly" staff. / **Sample dishes:** _squab pigeon salad; pan-fried John Dory with peas & fèves; hot pear soufflé._
Details: _www.kinnairdestate.com; 8m NW of Dunkeld, off A9 onto B898; 9.30 pm; closed Mon-Wed in Jan & Feb; jacket & tie required; no smoking; children: 12+._
Accommodation: _9 rooms, from £365._

sign up for the survey at www.hardens.com

DUNVEGAN, ISLE OF SKYE 9–2A

Three Chimneys £53 A★
Colbost IV55 8ZT (01470) 511258
"Worth a detour – and it is some detour"; "exceptional use of local produce" makes Shirley & Eddie Spear's "remote" but "idyllic" former crofter's cottage a destination that's "hard to reach, but well worth the effort". / **Sample dishes:** carrot, orange & ginger soup; black pudding with leek & potato mash; warm apple & almond tart. **Value tip:** set 2-crs L £15. **Details:** www.threechimneys.co.uk; 5m from Dunvegan Castle on B884 to Glendale; 9.30 pm; closed Sun L; closed part of Jan & Feb; no smoking. **Accommodation:** 6 rooms, from £175.

DUNWICH, SUFFOLK 3–1D

The Ship £26
St James St IP17 3DT (01728) 648219
New owners took over at this popular seaside village pub too late for reporters to comment on it; let's hope the new regime maintains the "reliable" standards associated with the old one. / **Sample dishes:** deep-fried Camembert; steak & ale casserole; profiteroles. **Details:** 7m S of Southwold, follow signs from A12; 9.30 pm; no Amex; no smoking; no booking at L. **Accommodation:** 4 rooms, from £60.

DURHAM, COUNTY DURHAM 8–3B

Almshouses £19
Palace Grn DH1 3RL (0191) 386 1054
"Reliable, home-cooked" snacks (suited to lunch or a tea stop) make this "busy" and "friendly" veggie bistro – in a "beautiful position, near the Cathedral" – a consistently "pleasant" destination. / **Sample dishes:** tomato, olive & peanut butter soup; fishcakes with lemon & chive mayonnaise; orange & lemon treacle tart. **Details:** 5 pm; L only; no Amex; no smoking; no booking.

Bistro 21 £33 A★
Aykley Heads Hs DH1 5TS (0191) 384 4354
"A quaint old building" provides the "interesting" setting for this "favourite" local – an offshoot of Newcastle's Café 21 that "never fails to please"; "prices are moderate, considering", and the fare is "always reliable". / **Sample dishes:** Cheddar & spinach soufflé; slow-cooked beef with polenta & Parmesan crisps; profiteroles with pistachio ice cream. **Value tip:** set 2-crs L £12. **Details:** near Durham Trinity School; 10.30 pm; closed Sun; no smoking.

Hide Café Bar & Grill £28
39 Saddler St DH1 3NU (0191) 384 1999
This rather "inconsistent" newcomer has established itself as quite a "lively" destination (near the Cathedral and overlooking the river); it's "very good value at lunchtime" (and popular as a breakfast venue) – at other times it can seem "pricey" for what it is. / **Sample dishes:** duck spring rolls with wasabi mayo; pizza with anchovies & roasted peppers; sticky toffee pudding. **Details:** www.hidebar.com; 10.15 pm; no smoking area.

Shaheens Indian Bistro £22 ★
Old Post Office, 48 North Bailey DH1 3ET
(0191) 386 0960
"Durham's best Indian" attracts nothing but praise from the locals – "it's definitely a cut above most curry houses". / **Details:** 11 pm; D only, closed Mon; no Amex or Switch; no smoking area.

EAST CHILTINGTON, EAST SUSSEX 3–4B
Jolly Sportsman £35 ★
BN7 3BA (01273) 890400

"Affordable and improving food" makes this *"isolated"* boozer well worth seeking out; some – finding the restaurant *"lacking in ambience"* – prefer eating at the bar. / **Sample dishes:** ham, asparagus & Manchego salad; grilled halibut with crab mash & capers; apricot, walnut & ginger toffee pudding. **Value tip:** set 2-crs L £10. **Details:** NW of Lewes; 9 pm, Fri & Sat 10 pm; closed Mon & Sun D; no Amex; no smoking.

EAST GRINSTEAD, WEST SUSSEX 3–4B
Gravetye Manor £56 Ⓐ
Vowels Ln RH19 4LJ (01342) 810567

"Lovely" gardens add to the *"beautiful"* setting of this family-run Elizabethan manor house, long noted for *"high standards"* all round, including *"excellent"* cooking and a *"very good wine list"*; *"prices are hefty"*, though, and some find the approach rather *"formal"*. / **Sample dishes:** quail, black pudding & lardon salad; roast John Dory; pannacotta with rhubarb. **Value tip:** set 3-crs L £27. **Details:** www.gravetyemanor.co.uk; 2m outside Turner's Hill; 9.30 pm; no Amex; jacket & tie required; no smoking; children: 7+. **Accommodation:** 18 rooms, from £190.

EAST LINTON, EAST LOTHIAN 9–4D
Drovers Inn £31
5 Bridge St EH40 3AG (01620) 860298

This *"comfortable and cosy"* coaching inn, just off the A1, moved into new ownership this year; the chef remains, however, so the *"big helpings"* of traditional pub fare will presumably be unaffected. / **Sample dishes:** chicken liver pâté with oatcakes; Scottish beef stew with herb dumplings; raspberry trifle. **Details:** 9.30 pm; no smoking area.

EAST WITTON, NORTH YORKSHIRE 8–4B
Blue Lion £34 Ⓐ★
DL8 4SN (01969) 624273

"An utterly splendid marriage of top-hole tucker and beer" is acclaimed by the many fans of this atmospheric dining pub; some still consider it the *"best in Yorkshire"*, but its ratings slipped rather this year. / **Sample dishes:** onion & blue Wensleydale tart; chicken with smoked foie gras sauce; lemon mousse with lemon shortbread. **Value tip:** set 3-crs Sun L £16.75. **Details:** between Masham & Leyburn on A6108; 9.30 pm; no Amex. **Accommodation:** 12 rooms, from £69.

EASTBOURNE, EAST SUSSEX 3–4B
The Mirabelle
The Grand Hotel £59
King Edwards Pde BN21 4EQ (01323) 412345

Gerald Roser (known for his eponymous former restaurant in St Leonards) took over as chef in the *"first-class"* grand dining room of this huge, five star hotel in the summer of 2002 (post-survey); we've felt obliged to remove ratings, but on the past form of both chef and restaurant, it would be a surprise if it didn't merit a visit. / **Sample dishes:** salmon terrine with sweet pepper coulis; pork with Cumberland stuffing & Bramley apple sauce; warm toffee & date pudding. **Value tip:** set 2-crs L £16.50. **Details:** www.grandeastbourne.co.uk; 10 pm; closed Mon & Sun; jacket & tie required at D; no smoking; children: 14+. **Accommodation:** 152 rooms, from £159.

EDENBRIDGE, KENT 3–3B

Haxted Mill £43
Haxted Rd TN8 6PU (01732) 862914
"In summer you can sit out by the water" – and in winter in the
"cosy" interior – at this "old mill" in the leafy Edenbridge valley;
reporters divide over whether the cooking is "expensive but worth
it" or "exorbitantly overpriced". / **Sample dishes:** *grilled oysters with*
spinach; roast rack of lamb with rosemary jus; fig tarte Tatin. **Value tip:** *set 2-crs L*
£15. **Details:** *www.haxtedmill.co.uk; between Edenbridge & Lingfield; 9 pm; closed*
Mon & Sun D (& Tue in winter); no Amex; no smoking.

EDINBURGH, CITY OF EDINBURGH 9–4C

The options for eating out in Auld Reekie have improved
considerably in recent times.

Gastronomically speaking, the most important arrival was
that a couple of years ago of *Restaurant Martin Wishart*, at last
providing the Scottish capital with the modern destination
restaurant it had always so singularly lacked.

For a trendy modern experience, restaurant-goers were for
a number of years disproportionately reliant on *The Atrium*
(and the cheaper *blue bar café*). All that has changed. *The
Tower*, *Rogue*, *Oloroso* and *North Bridge* all have their critics,
but have injected some much-needed excitement into the
'scene'.

The traditional establishments are still going strong,
and some of them are really quite good – *Le Café St-Honoré*,
Dubh Prais, *Jacksons*, *Martins* and the historic *Vintners Rooms*
are the best examples. On account of the experience it
provides – even if it's not a particularly foodie one –
the *Witchery by the Castle* remains the most commented-on
place in town. The long-established Italian deli and wine
merchant *Valvona & Crolla* retains a cult following.

Leith's waterfront offers a concentration of good, mid-priced
all-rounders rarely found in the UK, including the trio of
Fisher's Bistro, *The Shore* and *Skippers*.

Edinburgh is not especially strong in ethnic restaurants,
though those in search of a budget curry are quite well
catered-for (*Kalpna*, *Khushi's*, *Suruchi*). Vegetarians (*Bann UK*,
Black Bo's) also find a fair degree of choice.

Ann Purna £18
44-45 St Patrick's Sq EH8 9ET (0131) 662 1807
This "homely" Gujerati Indian didn't please everyone this year,
but for most reporters it remains a venerable "institution", thanks
to its "wide-ranging menu" of "good vegetarian dishes".
/ **Value tip:** *set 3-crs L £4.95.* **Details:** *10.30 pm; closed Sat L & Sun L; no Amex*
or Switch; no smoking.

Apartment   £ 25
7-13 Barclay Pl EH10 4HW   (0131) 228 6456
*For its fans, this oddly-sited trendy spot (on the fringe of the Old Town) remains a "top value-for-money" destination – a "buzzing" place offering "different" food; too many, though, find it's "not worth the hype" nowadays. / **Sample dishes:** wild mushrooms with aubergine & sweet potato; peppered rib-eye steak & fries; profiteroles with Cointreau sauce. **Details:** between Tollcross & Bruntsfield; 11 pm; D only Mon-Fri, L only Sat & Sun; no Amex; no smoking area.*

The Atrium   £ 43
10 Cambridge St EH1 2ED   (0131) 228 8882
*Feedback on this trendy, rather '90s venture was again mixed this year, though ratings did improve; many still find the place "pretentious" and "stupidly expensive", but there was more praise for its "attractively presented" dishes and "sophisticated" décor. / **Sample dishes:** courgette & Parmesan soup; roast duck with cabbage & bacon; marjoram crème brûlée. **Value tip:** set 2-crs L £13.50. **Details:** www.atriumrestaurant.co.uk; by the Usher Hall; 10 pm; closed Sat L & Sun (except during Festival).*

Bann UK   £ 30
5 Hunter Sq EH1 1QW   (0131) 226 1112
*"Interesting" veggie food at "reasonable prices" has proved a successful formula for this trendy café, off the Royal Mile; founder David Bann moved on this year – let's hope the new owners maintain his standards. / **Sample dishes:** aubergine cannelloni; veggie bangers & mash; coconut & lime brûlée. **Details:** www.urbann.co.uk; 11 pm; no smoking area.*

Black Bo's   £ 29   ★
57-61 Blackfriar's St EH1 1NB (0131) 557 6136
*A "pleasingly-shabby, candlelit restaurant" (and bar), near the Royal Mile; its "original and eccentric veggie food" has a small but enthusiastic following among reporters. / **Sample dishes:** sun-dried tomato & smoked tofu roulade; aubergine & leeks with Parmesan crust; almond tart. **Details:** www.blackbos.com; 10.30 pm; D only, except Fri & Sat open L & D; no Amex.*

blue bar café   £ 33
10 Cambridge St EH1 2ED   (0131) 221 1222
*"Cheaper and more cheerful than the Atrium" (in the same building), this "bustling" first-floor brasserie is a decent all-rounder and attracts "a great mixed clientèle"; service, though, can be "slow". / **Sample dishes:** char-grilled tuna niçoise; sea bream with tomato & courgette galette; apple tart with Calvados parfait. **Details:** www.bluebarcafe.com; by the Usher Hall; 10.45 pm; closed Sun (except during Festival); no smoking area; children: before 8 pm only.*

Browns   £ 29
131-133 George St EH2 4JS   (0131) 225 4442
*Either Auld Reekians are the kindliest of Britons, or this West End branch of the UK-wide brasserie chain is better than most; locals praise it for its "lively" atmosphere, "cheerful" staff and "food that can be relied upon". / **Sample dishes:** smoked salmon & watercress salad; steak & mushroom pie; hot fudge brownie with vanilla ice cream. **Details:** www.browns-restaurants.com; 11 pm; no smoking area.*

sign up for the survey at www.hardens.com

Le Café St-Honoré   £ 37   Ⓐ
34 NW Thistle Street Ln EH2 1EA   (0131) 226 2211
"A find", tucked away in the New Town – this "unpretentious"
and highly popular brasserie generates "lots of French
atmosphere", and its "friendly" staff deliver "good Gallic provincial
*cooking" of a very "consistent" standard. / **Sample dishes:** carrot &*
ginger soup; sirloin steak with caramelised shallots; chocolate & fig steamed pudding.
***Value tip:** set 2-crs pre-theatre £13.50. **Details:** www.cafesthonore.com; between*
George St and Queen St; 10.15 pm; closed Sun; no smoking area.

La Cuisine d'Odile   £ 15   ★
13 Randolph Cr EH3 7TT   (0131) 225 5685
"Lots of savoury tarts" are the sort of "typically French" fare
which makes up the "excellent-value set lunch" on offer in the
basement café of the Institut Français; you can BYO for modest
*corkage. / **Sample dishes:** red lentil & Stilton soup; pasta with courgettes &*
*smoked salmon; pear, coffee & chocolate cake. **Value tip:** set 2-crs L £6.65.*
***Details:** between Dean Bridge & Charlotte Square; L only; closed Mon & Sun;*
no credit cards.

Daniel's   £ 28
88 Commercial St EH6 6LX   (0131) 553 5933
"Robust cooking from Alsace" at "good-value" prices makes this
"noisy" Leith bistro a consistently popular recommendation.
*/ **Sample dishes:** tarte flambé; duck confit with spring greens;*
*spicy ice cream terrine. **Value tip:** set 2-crs L £5.95.*
***Details:** www.edinburghrestaurants.co.uk/daniels.html; 10 pm; no smoking area.*

The Dial   £ 33   ★
44 George IV Bridge EH1 1EJ   (0131) 225 7179
An "awkward basement setting" does it no favours, but the
imaginative modern cooking at this Old Town venture has a small
but devoted following, which claims it's "still the best restaurant in
Edinburgh, despite the arrival of more glamorous competition".
*/ **Sample dishes:** lemon & thyme croquettes; guinea fowl with root vegetable confit;*
*apple & cinnamon crumble. **Value tip:** set 3-crs L £8.95. **Details:** 11 pm; closed*
Sun L.

The Dome   £ 38   Ⓐ
14 George St EH2 2PF   (0131) 624 8624
The "impressive" setting in a vast neo-classical converted banking
hall wins praise for this "atmospheric" bar/restaurant in the New
Town (which has no relation to the Dôme chain); the cooking –
from snacks to a full meal – is pretty "standard".
*/ **Details:** www.thedomeedinburgh.com; 11.45 pm; management declined to provide*
further information.

Dubh Prais   £ 36   ★
123b High St EH1 1SG   (0131) 557 5732
"The owner James is always welcoming", at this "cosy", cramped
cellar in the Old Town, which provides "good traditional Scottish
food" in "huge portions"; some, though, wonder "why don't they
*redecorate" the dated interior. / **Sample dishes:** kedgeree; lamb cutlets*
with tomato & rosemary sauce; lemon shortcake.
***Details:** www.bencraighouse.co.uk; 10.30 pm; closed Mon, Sat L & Sun;*
no smoking; children: 5+.

Duck's at Le Marché Noir £39

2-4 Eyre Pl EH3 5EP (0131) 558 1608

Repeat visitors may find standards "variable", but on a good day Mr Duck's ambitious (and "expensive") Gallic New Town establishment delivers some "very good" results.
/ **Sample dishes:** *seared wasabi tuna with pickled cucumber; monkfish wrapped in prosciutto with chilli sauce; flourless chocolate cake with white chocolate ice cream.* **Details:** *www.ducks.co.uk; 10 pm, Fri & Sat 10.30 pm; closed Mon L, Sat L & Sun L; no Amex; no smoking area.*

Fisher's Bistro £33 ★

1 The Shore EH6 6QW (0131) 554 5666

"Consistently excellent and adventurous" fish and seafood dishes win consistent praise for this "lively" Leith waterfront hang-out; its sister restaurant – Fisher's in the City (58 Thistle St, tel 0131 225 5109) – generates less copious, but even more enthusiastic, feedback. / **Sample dishes:** *red snapper with sweet potato & Parmesan rosti; monkfish & swordfish brochette with spinach tagliatelle; Turkish delight in brandy snaps.* **Details:** *www.fishersbistros.co.uk; 10.30 pm.*

(Fitz) Henry £37

19 Shore Pl EH6 6SW (0131) 555 6625

A "nice location", in a warehouse-conversion near the waterfront, sometimes "lovely" cooking and an impressive wine selection combine to make this trendy Leith spot a continuing success; it still has some progress to make, however, to regain quite the popularity it enjoyed under its former ownership.
/ **Sample dishes:** *pan-fried ox tongue & asparagus salad; braised lamb with polenta & Parmesan mash; pine kernel tart with honey ice cream.* **Value tip:** *set 3-crs L £16.* **Details:** *www.fitzhenrys.com; 10 pm, Fri & Sat 10.30 pm; closed Sun.*

Forth Floor
Harvey Nichols £40

30-34 St Andrew Sq EH2 3AD (0131) 524 8388

Who says retailers don't have a sense of humour? – after Harvey Nics's Fifth Floor (London) and Fourth Floor (Leeds) comes this side-splittingly-named newcomer, opened just as we were going to press; performance elsewhere would lead one to expect more style than content. / **Sample dishes:** *cured salmon with buckwheat blinis; grilled sea bass; strawberry & Mascarpone tart.* **Details:** *www.harveynichols.com; 10.30 pm; no smoking area; booking: max 6.*

Glass & Thompson £18 ★

2 Dundas St EH3 6SU (0131) 557 0909

"Half deli/half café", this "elegant" New Town establishment is "always busy"; some find prices rather elevated, but even critics concede that the food (all cold) is "fresh and tasty".
/ **Sample dishes:** *no starters; spinach & walnut pâté with rye bread; passion cake.* **Details:** *L & afternoon tea only; no Amex; no smoking.*

Hadrian's
Balmoral Hotel £29

1 Princes St EH2 2EQ (0131) 557 5000

The Balmoral's number two restaurant is a "good-value" all-rounder, and makes a useful central rendezvous; its bright modern décor, though, can seem a tad "clinical". / **Sample dishes:** *saffron risotto Milanese; sirloin steak with fries & green beans; orange & grapefruit in Sauternes jelly.* **Details:** *www.thebalmoralhotel.com; 10.30 pm; no smoking area.* **Accommodation:** *185 rooms, from £210.*

sign up for the survey at www.hardens.com

Henderson's £ 20
94 Hanover St EH2 1DR (0131) 225 2131
This "vegetarian experience" – a self-service buffet (est. 1965), in a grungy but characterful basement just off Princes Street – is "great" for some, and at least "reliable" for most others. / **Sample dishes:** vegetable soup; baked aubergine & tomato with Mozzarella; banoffi pie. **Details:** www.hendersonsofedinburgh.co.uk; 10 pm; closed Sun; mainly non-smoking.

Indian Cavalry Club £ 25
3 Atholl Pl EH3 8HP (0131) 228 3282
"Still good after all these years"; though it's not as commented-upon as once it was, this colonial-style subcontinental is still hailed as a "classic" by its fans. / **Details:** between Caledonian Hotel & Haymarket Station; 11.30 pm; no smoking area.

Indigo (yard) £ 26
7 Charlotte Ln EH2 4QZ (0131) 220 5603
It's as "a great place for a drink" that this strikingly-designed West End venue is of most note; the cooking has always been rather incidental – perhaps the new chef will pep it up. / **Sample dishes:** moules marinière; seafood tagliatelle with tomato sauce; banoffi cheesecake. **Details:** www.indigoyardedinburgh.co.uk; just off Queensferry St; 10 pm; no smoking area; children: 12+.

Izzi £ 28
119 Lothian Rd EH3 9AN (0131) 466 9888
Opened post-survey, this minimalist West End newcomer serves extensive Chinese and Japanese menus; it also claims to offer the only teppan-yaki in town. / **Details:** www.izzi-restaurant.co.uk; 12.45 am; no Amex; no smoking in bar.

Jacksons £ 37
209 High St EH1 1PZ (0131) 225 1793
This "small" and "friendly" basement, on the Royal Mile, is "a perennial favourite for a classy lunch"; there is the odd gripe of "being crammed in like sardines", though. / **Sample dishes:** potato soup with pea ravioli; lamb with spring greens & pearl barley; pear & almond tart. **Details:** www.jacksons-restaurant.com; 10.30 pm, Fri & Sat 11 pm.

Kalpna £ 19 ★
2-3 St Patrick Sq EH8 9EZ (0131) 667 9890
"Consistently a favourite" – this plain-looking Gujerati near the University remains the most-commented-on subcontinental in town, thanks to its "cheap and cheerful" – but "subtle" and "distinctive" – veggie fare. / **Value tip:** set 2-crs L £5. **Details:** 10.30 pm; closed Sun L; no Amex or Switch; no smoking.

Khushi's £ 14 ★
16 Drummond St EH8 9TX (0131) 556 8996
There are "no frills or pretensions" at this "school canteen"-style BYO Indian, near the University – a "bargain" stand-by for over 50 years now. / **Details:** next to New Festival Theatre; 9 pm; closed Sun; no credit cards.

Loon Fung £ 25
2 Warriston Pl EH3 5LE (0131) 556 1781
"The ambience and location let the place down, but the food more than makes up" at this Canonmills oriental; it's "usually full of Chinese families" (especially for "the best dim sum"). / **Details:** near Botanical Gardens; 11.30 pm, Fri & Sat 12.30 am; closed Sat L & Sun L.

Malmaison £ 32
1 Tower Place EH6 7DB   (0131) 468 5000
A recent revamp and new chef have helped buck up the stylish brasserie of this Leith waterfront design-hotel – if the improvement continues, this could re-establish itself as a really worthwhile destination. / **Sample dishes:** *black pudding & potato pancake with apple; roast lamb with minted peas & beans; crème brûlée.* **Value tip:** *set 3-crs D £11.95.* **Details:** *www.malmaison.com; 11 pm.* **Accommodation:** *60 rooms, from £110.*

The Marque £ 35 ★
19-21 Causewayside EH9 1QF   (0131) 466 6660
"Very good cooking" is the theme of almost all reports on this "small and friendly" duo of restaurants (Marque Central is in the Royal Lyceum Theatre, 30b Grindlay St, tel 0131 229 9859); "cramped" surroundings are the main complaint. / **Sample dishes:** *butternut squash & red lentil soup; baked cod with salsa & pancetta; rhubarb, ginger & apple crumble.* **Value tip:** *set 2-crs L & pre-theatre £11.50.* **Details:** *10 pm, Fri & Sat 11 pm; closed Mon; no smoking in dining room.*

Martins £ 41 ★
70 Rose St, North Ln EH2 3DX   (0131) 225 3106
"Still totally reliable after nearly two decades", this "eccentric" bastion of the New Town offers an "inventive" modern Scottish menu in "calm" (if "unatmospheric") surroundings; the "cheese experience" is not to be missed ("allow 15 minutes for the description"). / **Sample dishes:** *sea trout cannelloni with artichoke confit; guinea fowl with morel mousse; basil-marinated strawberries.* **Details:** *10 pm; closed Mon, Sat L & Sun; no smoking; children: 7+.*

Mussel Inn £ 27 ★
61-65 Rose St EH2 2HN   (0131) 225 5979
"Fantastic" mussels have helped make a big hit of this ordinary-looking bistro; success has its perils, though, and some fear it's becoming a "get-you-in, get-you-out" kind of place. / **Sample dishes:** *hot-smoked salmon Caesar salad; mussels with leeks & horseradish; sticky date pudding.* **Details:** *www.mussel-inn.com; 10 pm.*

North Bridge
The Scotsman £ 28
20 North Bridge EH1 1YT   (0131) 556 5565
This "smart" new brasserie, housed in the landmark former offices of the eponymous newspaper, has got off to a reasonable start; menu choice is "limited", though, and "sloppy" service can let the place down badly; see also Vermilion. / **Sample dishes:** *crabcakes with sweet chilli salsa; Highland beef fillet with pepper sauce; mango delice & melon sorbet.* **Details:** *www.thescotsmanhotel.co.uk; 10.30 pm.*

Number One
Balmoral Hotel £ 59 ★
1 Princes St EH2 2EQ   (0131) 557 6727
A setting with "all the atmosphere of a conference room" sours appreciation of the "good standards" at this grand hotel basement restaurant; the value offered by its lunch menu remains "one of the best-kept secrets in town". / **Sample dishes:** *crab & avocado salad with caviar; Dover sole roulade with langoustines; rice pudding with basil sorbet.* **Value tip:** *set 3-crs L £15.50.* **Details:** *www.thebalmoralhotel.com; 10 pm, Fri & Sat 10.30 pm; closed Sat L & Sun L; no smoking area.* **Accommodation:** *189 rooms, from £215.*

sign up for the survey at www.hardens.com

Oloroso £43

33 Castle St EH2 3DN (0131) 226 7614

"The view and the cocktails are brilliant" at this ambitious fourth-floor newcomer, which enjoys *"panoramic views over to Fife"* (and wins many nominations as a business rendezvous); many also hail its *"fantastic"* modern cuisine, but iffy service and *"overpricing"* limit its appeal. / **Sample dishes:** tandoori quail with pickled cucumber salad; halibut with linguine & champagne sauce; deep-fried jam sandwich with custard. **Details:** www.oloroso.co.uk; 10 pm; closed Sun (in winter only); no smoking in dining room.

Le Petit Paris £28 Ⓐ

38-40 Grassmarket EH1 2JU (0131) 226 2442

"Rustic cooking" at *"reasonable prices for the city-centre"* win recommendations for this *"very Gallic"* bistro, near the Castle. / **Sample dishes:** smoked chicken & wild mushroom pancake; broccoli-crusted salmon with lemon butter; chocolate truffle with cherries. **Details:** www.petitparis-restaurant.co.uk; near the Castle; 11 pm; closed Mon (in winter only); no Amex.

Point Hotel £22 Ⓐ

34 Bread St EH3 9AF (0131) 221 5555

Some say the minimalist dining room is *"not as cool as the rest of the set-up"* at this stylish budget hotel, but prices are still low enough to ensure *"good value for money"*. / **Sample dishes:** smoked chicken salad with pineapple salsa; courgette & broccoli frittata; champagne sorbet with raspberries. **Details:** www.point-hotel.co.uk; 10 pm; closed Sun. **Accommodation:** 140 rooms, from £95.

Restaurant Martin Wishart £44 ★★

54 The Shore EH6 6RA (0131) 553 3557

"The best in Scotland, by a mile" – Martin Wishart's *"exquisite cooking"* at his *"friendly and unsnobbish"* Leith waterfront HQ attracts little but praise; the *"rather plain"* décor was always a bit of a handicap, but a major refurbishment was being carried out in late-2002. / **Sample dishes:** guinea fowl with leek cream & veal sweetbreads; daube of beef with root vegetables; raspberry & almond tart. **Value tip:** set 3-crs L £14.50. **Details:** www.martin-wishart.co.uk; near Royal Yacht Britannia; 10 pm; closed Mon, Sat L & Sun; no Amex; no smoking before 10 pm.

Rogue £35

67 Morrison St EH3 8BU (0131) 228 2700

This *"intriguing"* yearling is praised by most reporters as a *"cool"* place, with *"imaginative"* food and *"helpful"* service; it's not without its critics, though, who think the whole approach *"tries to be too 'now'… and misses"*. / **Sample dishes:** potato, rocket & goats cheese soup; roast monkfish with black pudding & mushy peas; pineapple soup with citrus sorbet. **Details:** www.rogues-uk.com; 11 pm; closed Sun D.

Le Sept £30

7 Old Fishmarket Close EH1 1RW (0131) 225 5428

For fans, this *"sweet little bistro"* in a quaint Old Town alleyway offers *"good crêpes"* and *"simple French country cooking"*; it divides opinions, though, and critics say it's *"disappointing from start to finish"*. / **Sample dishes:** grilled goats cheese; rack of lamb with roast vegetables; banana & chocolate crêpe. **Value tip:** set 3-crs L £7.50. **Details:** www.lesept.co.uk; 10.30 pm, Fri 11 pm; no smoking area.

The Shore £ 32 Ⓐ★

3-4 The Shore EH6 6QW (0131) 553 5080

"A lovely wee dining room attached to a great bar", a short step from Leith's waterfront; the setting is "cosy" (if "cramped") and "an interesting choice of fish" is "simply presented" and sold at a "fair price". / **Sample dishes:** grilled sardines with smoked paprika sauce; grilled trevally fish with couscous; plum & orange crumble. **Value tip:** set 2-crs L £15. **Details:** www.edinburghrestaurants.co.uk/shore.html; 10 pm; no smoking in dining room.

Siam Erawan £ 30

48 Howe St EH3 6TH (0131) 226 3675

"Still going strong"; thanks to its "strong, clean flavours", this New Town basement Thai retains a small but vocal fan club. / **Value tip:** set 2-crs L £6.50. **Details:** 10.45 pm; closed Sun L; no Amex.

Skippers £ 33 Ⓐ

1a Dock Pl EH6 6LU (0131) 554 1018

"Warm, welcoming, intimate and memorable" – despite the occasional misgiving, most reporters speak nothing but good of this "unpretentious" ("cramped") fish bistro on Leith's waterfront. / **Sample dishes:** chicken liver parfait; seared salmon with prosciutto-wrapped asparagus; treacle tart. **Details:** www.skippers.co.uk; 10 pm.

Suruchi £ 26 ★

14a Nicolson St EH8 9DH (0131) 556 6583

"A crazy Scots menu" sets a "different" tone at this "classy" Indian, opposite the Festival Theatre (with a new Leith branch at 121 Constitution St, tel 0131 554 3268); its "fresh", "new-wave" curries are consistently highly rated. / **Details:** 11.30 pm; closed Sun L.

Susies £ 15

51-53 West Nicolson St EH8 9DB (0131) 667 8729

There's some "cheap and tasty veggie food" on offer at this "cheerful", self-service café, by the University; it's licensed, but you can BYO. / **Sample dishes:** falafel with houmous; chilli bean enchiladas; pear frangipane flan. **Details:** 9 pm; closed Sun (except Festival time); no credit cards; no smoking area; no booking.

Thai Orchid £ 28 ★

44 Grindlay St EH3 9AP (0131) 228 4438

"Fresh zingy flavours" make this popular Thai, off Lothian Road, of more than average note. / **Value tip:** set 3-crs L £7.95. **Details:** 10.45 pm; closed Sat L & Sun L; no smoking.

Tinelli's £ 27

139 Easter Rd EH7 5QA (0131) 652 1932

If you're looking for an "old-school Italian", you won't do much better than Signor Tinelli's twenty-year-old fixture near Leith Links; it's quite "child-friendly" too. / **Sample dishes:** snails with bacon & mushrooms; baked rabbit with cream & rosemary sauce; strawberry gelati. **Value tip:** set 2-crs L £8.95. **Details:** 11 pm; closed Mon & Sun; no Switch.

sign up for the survey at www.hardens.com

The Tower
Museum of Scotland   £ 44   ✕

Chambers St EH1 1JF   (0131) 225 3003

"Sublime" castle views and *"fresh"* Scottish cooking mean this
elevated dining room is *"worth every penny"* for fans; too many
reporters, though, find it *"lazy"* and *"overpriced"* – *"a fantastic
location, wrecked by terrible food and very average service".*
/ **Sample dishes:** lobster claw & pickled vegetable salad; chicken with cep mash &
Madeira jus; chocolate truffle torte. **Value tip:** set 2-crs pre-theatre £12.
Details: www.tower-restaurant.com; at top of Museum of Scotland; 11 pm;
no smoking.

Valvona & Crolla   £ 30   ★

19 Elm Row EH7 4AA   (0131) 556 6066

Celebrated for its *"simple but delicious"* Italian cooking (and wine
at retail prices plus modest corkage), the café attached to this
"fabulous" institution (a deli and wine merchants owned by the
Contini family since 1934) is regularly *"mobbed"*; it *"isn't cheap"*,
though, and some find it a touch *"overhyped".*
/ **Sample dishes:** pumpkin tortellini; Italian spicy sausage pizza; lemon tart.
Details: www.valvonacrolla.com; at top of Leith Walk, near Playhouse Theatre;
5.30 pm; closed Sun; no smoking.

Vermilion
The Scotsman   £ 53

North Bridge EH1   (0131) 556 5565

The fine dining restaurant at this swanky new hotel opened in
May 2002 (just after the survey had concluded); judging solely
from the menu, prices do not seem too vertiginous, considering.
/ **Sample dishes:** foie gras ballottine with white peach soup; venison with celeriac
croquettes & chocolate sauce; dark chocolate tart with orange Mascarpone.
Details: www.thescotsmanhotel.com; 9.45 pm; D only, closed Mon & Sun; smoking
in bar only; children: 12+. **Accommodation:** 68 rooms, from £120.

Vintners Rooms   £ 40   𝔸★

87 Giles St EH6 6BZ   (0131) 554 6767

The *"classy"* charms of this *"fantastic"* 16th-century dining room
include *"lighting by candles and a roaring fire"*; on the food front,
misfires are by no means unknown, but most assessments remain
somewhere between *"good"* and *"excellent".* / **Sample dishes:** smoked
salmon with sweet cucumber pickle; chicken supreme with lime & Madeira;
chocolate pecan silk with coffee sauce. **Value tip:** set 3-crs L £15.
Details: www.thevintnersrooms.demon.co.uk; 9.30 pm; closed Sun; no smoking in
dining room.

The Waterfront   £ 31

1c Dock Pl EH6 6LU   (0131) 554 7427

A *"wonderful wine list"* and *"reasonably priced"* fresh fish are
among the strengths of this well-established fixture, prominently
located on Leith's waterfront; it was totally renovated in 2002.
/ **Sample dishes:** grilled sardines with feta & chick peas; swordfish with hot & sour
sauce; white chocolate & Bailey's cheesecake. **Details:** www.sjf.co.uk; near Royal
Yacht Britannia; 9.30 pm, Fri & Sat 10 pm; no smoking area.

for updates visit www.hardens.com

The Witchery by the Castle £ 45 🅰

Castlehill, The Royal Mile EH1 2NF (0131) 225 5613

A "magical" setting – "especially at night" – makes this "amazing" Old Town institution a major destination, "particularly for romantic occasions" (and the "monster wine list" is also quite an attraction); the Scottish cooking has traditionally played a supporting rôle, but it has improved of late.

/ **Sample dishes:** home-smoked salmon with sautéed green beans; seared scallops with lobster risotto; lemon meringue pie with rhubarb sauce. **Value tip:** set 2-crs L & pre/post-theatre £9.95. **Details:** www.thewitchery.com; 11.30 pm. **Accommodation:** 6 rooms, from £195.

EGLINGHAM, NORTHUMBERLAND 8–1B

Tankerville Arms £ 26

15 The Village NE66 2TX (01665) 578444

"Reliably good food in either the bar or the restaurant" is noted in all reports on this "cosy" coaching inn; it's a "very friendly" place, and "children are welcome". / **Sample dishes:** smoked trout salad with lime dill sauce; rump steak with creamed green peppercorn sauce; fruits of the forest cheesecake. **Details:** 9 pm; no smoking in dining room.

EGLWYSFACH, CEREDIGION 4–3C

Ynyshir Hall £ 54 🅰★★

SY20 8TA (01654) 781209

"One of the great eating experiences of Wales", this "hidden gem" of a country house hotel, near the Dyfi estuary, is universally hailed by reporters for its "faultless" culinary standards and for its "wonderfully relaxed" atmosphere. / **Sample dishes:** prawn cannelloni with Avruga caviar; seared turbot with lemon potatoes; hot mango & apricot soufflé. **Details:** www.ynyshir-hall.co.uk; signposted from A487; 8.30 pm; no smoking area; booking essential at L; children: 9+. **Accommodation:** 10 rooms, from £150.

ELSTEAD, SURREY 3–3A

Woolpack £ 26

The Green GU8 6HD (01252) 703106

"Reliable" food helps make this "pleasant" pub "extremely popular"; the fare is "pricey", though, and some find it "formulaic". / **Sample dishes:** deep-fried calamari; steak & kidney pie; fruit pavlova. **Details:** 7m SW of Guildford, on village green; 9.45 pm; no Amex; no smoking in dining room; no booking.

ELTERWATER, CUMBRIA 7–3D

Britannia Inn £ 23 ★

LA22 9HP (01539) 437210

This "idiosyncratic" Lakeland inn is "the perfect pub" to its aficionados; "fantastic beers" accompany the "hearty" grub, served in an agreeably old-fashioned setting. / **Sample dishes:** potted shrimps with toast fingers; roast lamb with minted gravy & braised leeks; lemon cheesecake. **Details:** 9.30 pm; no smoking in dining room; children: before 9 pm only. **Accommodation:** 9 rooms, from £39.

sign up for the survey at www.hardens.com

ELY, CAMBRIDGESHIRE　　　　　　　　3–1B

Old Fire Engine House　　　　£ 33　　　Ⓐ
25 St Mary's St CB7 4ER　(01353) 662582
*"Honest-to-goodness 'school dinners' fare, in a lovely setting" has
made this very English restaurant, in the shadow of the Cathedral,
popular for more than 30 years now; "it gets too busy at
weekends", though. / **Sample dishes:** lovage soup; lemon sole with prawn &
dill sauce; old-fashioned sherry trifle. **Details:** 9 pm; closed Sun D; no Amex;
no smoking area.*

EMSWORTH, HAMPSHIRE　　　　　　2–4D

36 on the Quay　　　　　　£ 52　　　★
47 South St PO10 7EG　(01243) 375592
*"Exceptional food" – and "in a culinary desert", too – makes it
worth seeking out Ramon Farthing's "consistently good"
restaurant, which has a "lovely location" overlooking Emsworth
harbour. / **Sample dishes:** pan-fried mullet with pesto; scallops with chicken &
goose liver sausage; quartet of lemon desserts. **Value tip:** set 2-crs L £17.
Details: www.36onthe quay.co.uk; off A27 between Portsmouth & Chichester;
10 pm; closed Mon L, Sat L & Sun; no smoking in dining room.*

EPWORTH, NORTH LINCOLNSHIRE　　5–2D

Epworth Tap　　　　　　　£ 35
DN9 1EU　(01427) 873333
*Since new owners took over, this eminent bistro is found to be
"less amazing than it was"; it remains of above-average note in
this "remote" location, though, not least for its "delicious" wines.
/ **Sample dishes:** duck spring rolls; pork with bacon & spiced red cabbage; apple,
apricot & pecan strudel. **Value tip:** set 2-crs pre-theatre £13.50. **Details:** 3m from
M180, J2; 9.30 pm; D only, closed Sun-Tue; no Amex; no smoking.*

ERBISTOCK, CLYWDD　　　　　　　5–3A

The Boat Inn　　　　　　　£ 34　　　Ⓐ
LL13 0DL　(01978) 780666
*"On the banks of the River Dee", this ancient boozer makes a
delightful "summer evening" destination; the food, if usually
satisfactory, is generally rather less of an attraction.
/ **Sample dishes:** seared scallops & asparagus; haggis-stuffed chicken in whisky
sauce; Eton Mess. **Details:** www.theboatinn.co.uk; 9 pm; closed Sun D (in winter
only); no Amex.*

ESHER, SURREY　　　　　　　　　3–3A

Good Earth　　　　　　　£ 39
14-18 High St KT10 9RT　(01372) 462489
*Fans find "wonderful" cooking at this popular and long-established
suburban Chinese, but it's also "rather expensive" and the place
can seem "clinical". / **Details:** www.goodearthgroup.co.uk; 11 pm.*

Siam Food Gallery　　　　　£ 32　　　★
95-97 High St KT10 9QE　(01372) 477139
*"Great for an out-of-town restaurant" – this "super local" wins
applause for its "lovely" service and its Thai food that fans say is
simply "excellent". / **Details:** 11 pm.*

ETON, WINDSOR & MAIDENHEAD   3–3A

Gilbey's   £ 33
82-83 High St SL4 6AF   (01753) 855182
*Once more descriptively named 'The Eton Wine Bar',
this "welcoming" fixture (with a front bar and large rear
conservatory) makes a handy option in these parts; the food is
"variable", but there's an "excellent and good-value wine list".*
/ **Sample dishes:** Parma ham with celeriac remoulade; confit duck leg; toffee apple
with brown bread ice cream. **Value tip:** set 2-crs L £10.95.
Details: www.gilbeygroup.com; 5 mins walk from Windsor Castle; 9.45 pm, Fri &
Sat 10 pm.

EVERSHOT, DORSET   2–4B

The Acorn Inn   £ 32
Fore St DT2 0JW   (01935) 83228
*This stone-built coaching inn – under the same ownership as the
Fox Inn at Corscombe – wins praise for its "imaginative" food;
it has a "lovely" setting, too.* / **Sample dishes:** pigeon & bacon salad;
scallops with pine nuts & croutons; almond tart with ice cream.
Details: www.acorn-inn.co.uk; 9 pm, Fri & Sat 9.30 pm; no smoking in dining room.
Accommodation: 9 rooms, from £80.

Summer Lodge   £ 46   Ⓐ
Summer Lodge DT2 0JR   (01935) 83424
*"A lovely location" (an 18th-century house with walled gardens)
and staff who "make every effort to please" win generous praise
for the "elegant" dining room of this "understated" Relais &
Châteaux hotel; its "superb" cooking ("using local ingredients") is
generally praised, but misfires are not unknown.*
/ **Sample dishes:** assorted melons & ham with raspberry & mint coulis; seared cod
with orange butter sauce; iced honey parfait with seasonal berries. **Value tip:** set
2-crs L £12.50. **Details:** www.summerlodgehotel.com; 12m NW of Dorchester on
A37; 9.30 pm; jacket required; no smoking in dining room; children: 7+.
Accommodation: 17 rooms, from £135.

EVESHAM, WORCESTERSHIRE   2–1C

Evesham Hotel   £ 35
Coopers Ln WR11 1DA   (01386) 765566
*For oenophiles, there's just no place like this "privately-owned"
(and somewhat "quirky") hotel; the food is pleasant enough,
but it's the globetrotting wine list – from which France and
Germany are rigorously excluded – which is the real point of
seeking the place out.* / **Sample dishes:** smoked chicken, cherry & watercress
salad; baked cod with red wine risotto & mushrooms; lemon meringue ice cream.
Details: www.eveshamhotel.com; 9.30 pm; no smoking. **Accommodation:** 40
rooms, from £103.

EXETER, DEVON   1–3D

Brazz   £ 31
10-12 Palace Gate EX1 1JU   (01392) 252525
*With its "bubbly atmosphere (enhanced by a huge fish tank)",
this outpost of Kit Chapman's expanding West Country brasserie
chain is "a pleasant place"; "service really lets it down", though,
and the food is too often thought "nothing special".*
/ **Sample dishes:** mushroom brioche; chicken with lemon leeks & wild mushroom
sauce; chocolate brownie with white chocolate sauce.
Details: www.the-castle-hotel.com/brazz.htm; 10.30 pm, Fri & Sat 11 pm;
no smoking.

---

sign up for the survey at www.hardens.com

Carved Angel Café £26
Cathedral Yd EX1 1HB (01392) 210303
"A wonderful view of the Cathedral" distinguishes this café-offshoot of the well-known Dartmouth establishment; it otherwise seems to have had a rather muted reception. / **Sample dishes:** crab pancake with red pepper dressing; Moroccan lamb with couscous; chocolate jaffa mousse cake. **Details:** www.thecarvedangel.com; 9.30 pm; closed Sun D; no Amex; no smoking.

Double Locks £22 Ⓐ
Canal Banks, Alphington EX2 6LT (01392) 256947
"A great canalside location" is the chief draw to this popular pub, which offers a *"cheap and cheerful"* menu. / **Sample dishes:** garlic bread with Cheddar; turkey & mushroom pie; sticky toffee pudding. **Details:** through Marsh Barton industrial estate, follow dead-end track over bridges to end of towpath; 10.30 pm; no Amex.

Hotel Barcelona £33
Magdalen St EX2 4HY (01392) 281000
According to fans, the *"lively and lovely"* setting justifies the *"top prices"* at this wacky design-hotel brasserie; it's also *"good outside in summer"*. / **Sample dishes:** beef carpaccio with rocket & Parmesan; Magret duck breast with couscous; chocolate fondant pudding. **Details:** www.hotelbarcelona-uk.com.

Michael Caines
Royal Clarence Hotel £48 ★
Cathedral Yd EX1 1HD (01392) 310031
"A superb setting by the Cathedral" gives a positive initial impression of this ambitious restaurant, which is presided over from afar by the chef of Gidleigh Park; the *"high standards"* of *"imaginative, modern cooking"* encountered thereafter rarely let the side down. / **Sample dishes:** red mullet with saffron risotto; Bethan duck with roast garlic & spiced jus; chocolate nougatine with cherries. **Value tip:** set 2-crs L £16.50. **Details:** www.michaelcaines.com; 10 pm; no smoking. **Accommodation:** 56 rooms, from £85.

Thai Orchid £27
5 Cathedral Yd EX1 1HJ (01392) 214215
"Good set menus" and *"personal"* service help win praise for this popular oriental, near the Cathedral. / **Value tip:** set 2-crs L £7.50. **Details:** www.thaiorchid.co.uk; next to Exeter Cathedral; 10.30 pm; closed Sun; no Amex.

Vienna £41
112 West St GU9 7HH (01252) 722978
After two decades in business, Mr Sanders's *"small-town restaurant"* is still generally a *"solid"* performer; it's *"expensive"* though. / **Sample dishes:** deep-fried Brie; seafood risotto with sun-dried tomato jus; cappuccino brûlée. **Details:** 10.30 pm; closed Sun; no Amex or Switch; no smoking area; children: 5+.

The Dove £33 ★
Plum Pudding Ln ME13 9HB (01227) 751360
"Hard to book, but worth the effort" – this *"friendly"* gastropub offers *"a small menu, done superbly well"*; it also has *"a lovely setting, especially in summer"*. / **Sample dishes:** spring onion & crab risotto; duck with lentils & foie gras; baked chocolate pudding. **Details:** 9 pm; closed Mon, Tue D & Sun D; no Amex; booking essential.

Read's £ 58

Macknade Manor, Canterbury Rd ME13 8XE
(01795) 535344

Most agree that the new country house location is a "great improvement" on the previous (infamously grungy) converted-supermarket setting of this long-standing family-run venture; it's much more "expensive" now, though, and — though most still proclaim it "an all-round winner" — its ratings have declined. / **Sample dishes:** smoked eel with beetroot; calves liver with chive mash & melted onions; lemon & white chocolate mousse. **Details:** www.reads.com; 9.30 pm; closed Mon & Sun. **Accommodation:** 6 rooms, from £125.

FERRENSBY, NORTH YORKSHIRE   8–4B

General Tarleton £ 36

Boroughbridge Rd HG5 0PZ   (01423) 340284

It's related to the illustrious Angel at Hetton, but even some fans admit this upmarket pub/restaurant is no rival for its celebrated sibling; that said, it's still a "quality" venture and a popular "oasis" in a thin area. / **Sample dishes:** Jerusalem artichoke soup; tuna with butter bean mash & Parmesan crisps; lemon & ginger cheesecake. **Details:** www.generaltarleton.co.uk; 2m from A1, J48 towards Knaresborough; 9.30 pm; D only, except Sun when L only; no smoking. **Accommodation:** 14 rooms, from £84.90.

FISHGUARD, PEMBROKESHIRE   4–4B

Three Main Street £ 41   ★

3 Main St SA65 9HG   (01348) 874275

"An amazing find in the far reaches of the Principality" — Inez Ford and Marian Evans's harbourside restaurant with rooms has a broad following, thanks to its "innovative" cooking and its "relaxed" atmosphere. / **Sample dishes:** goats cheese with char-grilled vegetables; pan-fried beef & mushrooms with pepper sauce; warm pear frangipane flan. **Details:** off town square; 9 pm; closed Mon & Sun; no credit cards; no smoking in dining room. **Accommodation:** 3 rooms, from £70.

FLEET, DORSET   2–4B

Moonfleet Manor £ 37

DT3 4ED   (01305) 786948

"The kids sleep soundly upstairs, while you eat a 'proper' dinner" — though family-friendliness is the USP of this Georgian manor house hotel (overlooking Lyme Bay) its "fresh, modern cooking" is pretty "reasonable" too. / **Sample dishes:** duck liver & foie gras parfait; confit duck with olive mash & cherry sauce; caramelised rice pudding. **Value tip:** set 3-crs Sun L £15. **Details:** www.moonfleetmanor.com; from Weymouth, B3157 then follow signs; 9.30 pm; D only, except Sun open L & D; no smoking; children: before 7.30 pm only. **Accommodation:** 39 rooms, from £100.

FLETCHING, EAST SUSSEX   3–4B

The Griffin Inn £ 33   𝔸 ★

TN22 3SS   (01825) 722890

This "old but stylish" inn attracts pretty consistent praise for its "excellent food and drink" and "great atmosphere" (and a "garden that's ideal for kids"); there are one or two continued gripes that it's "not as good as it was". / **Sample dishes:** grilled sardines with chilli & wild garlic; roast lamb with Mediterranean vegetables; rhubarb, honey & saffron tart. **Details:** www.thegriffininn.co.uk; off A272; 9.30 pm; closed Sun D (in winter only); no smoking area. **Accommodation:** 8 rooms, from £70.

sign up for the survey at www.hardens.com

FORD, WILTSHIRE   2–2B
White Hart Inn   £ 33
SN14 8RP   (01249) 782213
"Worth finding" – especially for visitors to nearby Castle Coombe
– this attractive boozer, by a stream, offers a "limited menu,
but one that's well prepared and presented". / **Sample dishes:** chilli
beef carpaccio with oriental pickles; roast duck & chicory in pearl barley broth;
chocolate & raspberry tart. **Details:** on A420 between Chippenham & Bristol;
9.30 pm; no smoking area. **Accommodation:** 11 rooms, from £84.

FORT WILLIAM, HIGHLAND   9–3B
Crannog   £ 34   Ⓐ★★
Town Pier PH33 7NG   (01397) 705589
"Stunning" seafood and a "wonderful" setting generate few
reports short of rapture on this former smokehouse overlooking
the loch; it can be "filled with tourists", though, and "booking is
essential". / **Sample dishes:** surf clams & mussels with lemon mayonnaise;
pistachio-crusted halibut with risotto; treacle toffee pudding.
Details: www.crannog.net; 10 pm (9 pm Dec-Mar); no Amex; no smoking area.

Inverlochy Castle   £ 64   Ⓐ
Torlundy PH33 6SN   (01397) 702177
With its "magnificent" setting, this "impressive" Victorian pile in
the foothills of Ben Nevis wins majority approval for its "superb"
(if unsurprisingly "expensive") cooking, and also for the
"best service ever". / **Sample dishes:** wild mushroom tart with veal kidneys;
roast duck with vanilla mash & pickled cherries; orange crème brûlée with lemon &
lime sorbet. **Value tip:** set 3-crs L £28.50. **Details:** www.inverlochy.co.uk; off A82;
9.15 pm; closed Jan & part of Feb; no Amex; jacket & tie required; no smoking;
children: 12+. **Accommodation:** 17 rooms, from £255.

FOWEY, CORNWALL   1–4B
Food For Thought   £ 33
4 Town Quay PL23 1AT   (01726) 832221
Fans of this "well-located" quayside restaurant say it offers
"very good local fish, interestingly prepared"; it does have its
critics, though, for whom it "promises much, and doesn't deliver".
/ **Sample dishes:** pan-fried scallops; roasted shellfish with garlic olive oil; chocolate
marquise. **Details:** 10 pm; D only, closed Sun; no smoking; children: 10+.

FOWLMERE, CAMBRIDGESHIRE   3–1B
Chequers   £ 28   ★
SG8 7SR   (01763) 208369
"Delicious" food ensures that this "nice" pub, not far from
Cambridge, is often "crowded"; "arrive early" to get the best of
the "sometimes unreliable" service. / **Sample dishes:** Spinach & walnut
risotto; Calves liver with horseradish mash & spinach; rhubarb & almond crumble.
Details: on B1368 between Royston & Cambridge; 10 pm; no smoking area.

FRITHSDEN, HERTFORDSHIRE   3–2A
Alford Arms   £ 31
HP1 3DD   (01442) 864480
"Very popular in a gastronomic desert" – this "friendly" gastropub
offers "above-average" cooking; the press of custom, however,
can lead to service becoming "over-stretched".
/ **Sample dishes:** Dolcelatte & fig tart; roast cod & chorizo with spinach; lemon
crème brûlée. **Details:** near Ashridge College, by vineyard; 10 pm; booking: max 12.

FRODSHAM, CHESHIRE   5–2A
Netherton Hall   £27
Chester Rd WA6 6UL (01928) 732342
A "friendly and easy-going" pub/restaurant offering an
"interesting" selection of "good-quality" dishes.
/ **Sample dishes:** tomato & basil soup with gin; pot-roast lamb with fried cabbage
mash; Mars bar cheesecake. **Details:** 4m from Stanlow service station on A56;
9 pm; mainly non-smoking.

GANTS HILL, ESSEX   3–2B
Elephant Royale   £32
579-581 Cranbrook Rd IG2 6JZ (020) 8551 7015
There were no actual words this year from reporters, but their
ratings indicated ongoing satisfaction with this rather grimly-
located suburban Thai; it has a twin on the tip of the Isle of Dogs.
/ **Value tip:** set 3-crs L £9.50. **Details:** 11.15 pm; children: 2+.

GLANWYDDEN, CONWY   4–1D
Queen's Head   £28
Llandudno Junction LL31 NJP (01492) 546570
It's "best to book", "especially on Sunday", if you want to enjoy
lunch or dinner at this converted wheelwright's cottage – a
destination that's "always reliable" in a not over-provided area.
/ **Sample dishes:** asparagus & mushroom risotto; char-grilled chicken with chilli
glaze; fruit pavlova. **Details:** 9 pm; no Amex; no smoking area; no booking, Sat D;
children: 7+.

GLASGOW, CITY OF GLASGOW   9–4C

It's difficult to avoid the feeling that the Glasgow restaurant
scene has suffered a loss of momentum of late. A few years
ago it looked as if it might become the UK's number 2
restaurant city. That status now seems elusive.

As in London, the best restaurant is presided over by
Gordon Ramsay. Amaryllis at One Devonshire Gardens is the
most commented-upon place in town and generates
outstanding feedback. The fact that its famed owner is non-
resident, however, perhaps robs the city of a true culinary
standard-bearer.

This situation is reinforced by the fact that Glasgow's two
other great culinary institutions, Rogano and the Ubiquitous
Chip both seem to be suffering from some complacency
nowadays. What's more, celeb chef Nick Nairn has never
quite established Nairns as an unqualified success, and the
city has this year lost one of its most innovative chefs Ferrier
Richardson – of first Yes!, then Eurasia, both RIP – to rural
Renfrewshire.

Real contemporary highlights are thin on the ground. Gamba
– a notable destination for fish-lovers – and the less
ambitious Air Organic are two honourable exceptions. The
commendable Stravaigin – now with two locations – put in a
more variable performance this year.

Glasgow scores highly for well-established atmospheric
insititutions. In addition to the Chip and Rogano (above),
examples include Sarti's, Babbity Bowster and Café Gandolfi.

The city boasts a good range of Indian restaurants (*Ashoka* and *Mother India*), and there are also a number of good oriental options (*Amber Regent*, *Ichiban* and *Thai Fountain*).

Air Organic £ 26 ★
36 Kelvingrove G3 7SA (0141) 564 5200
The "pretentious" setting may "make you feel like an extra in Blake's 7", but most reporters find consolation in the "simple" and "delicious" organic food, which comes in "great variety" at this "friendly" Kelvingrove spot. / **Sample dishes:** *roast tomato & Mozzarella crostini; beef fillet bento box; white chocolate & lemon cheesecake.* **Details:** *near Kelvingrove art galleries; 10 pm; no smoking area; booking: max 10 at weekends.*

Amaryllis
One Devonshire Gardens £ 62 ★★
1 Devonshire Gardens G12 0UX (0141) 337 3434
Most reporters feel "in the hands of a master" at the city's grandest dining room — Gordon Ramsay's home town outpost — and hail "fabulous" cooking from chef David Dempsey; atmosphere can be "lacking" though, and service is sometimes "erratic". / **Sample dishes:** *lobster & langoustine ravioli in lobster bisque; venison with red cabbage & bitter chocolate sauce; chocolate fondant tart.* **Value tip:** *set 3-crs L £21.* **Details:** *1.5m from M8, J17; 11 pm; closed Mon, Tue & Sat L.* **Accommodation:** *35 rooms, from £145.*

Amber Regent £ 38
50 West Regent St G2 2RA (0141) 331 1655
This "dark" city-centre Chinese may be "a touch expensive"; it's "reliable", though, and probably "the best in town". / **Value tip:** *set 3-crs L £9.95.* **Details:** *10.45 pm; closed Sun.*

Arthouse £ 35
129 Bath St G2 2SZ (0141) 221 6789
This "trendy city-centre venue" still strikes some reporters as something of "a let down" (particularly on the service front), but it does maintain a fan club, especially for its fish and seafood dishes. / **Sample dishes:** *melon with Roquefort & Parma ham; smoked haddock mornay with spring onion mash; chilled coconut soufflé.* **Value tip:** *set 3-crs L £11.50.* **Details:** *www.arthousehotel.com; 11 pm.* **Accommodation:** *65 rooms, from £100.*

Ashoka £ 22 ★
19 Ashton Ln G12 8SJ (0800) 454817
There are many Ashokas in Glasgow, and not all even under the same ownership (the best-known bearer of the name at 108 Elderslie St, tel 0141 221 1761 is run separately from the rest); fortunately — not least for your editors — they're all "easy-going" places, whose curries can prove "addictive". / **Value tip:** *set 2-crs pre-theatre £7.95.* **Details:** *www.harlequin-leisure.co.uk; behind Hillhead station; midnight; closed Sun L.*

Babbity Bowster £ 29 Ⓐ
16-18 Blackfriar's St G1 1PE (0141) 552 5055
"A great place for traditional Scottish fayre" — this famed Merchant City pub (occupying a James Adam building) offers dependable bar food ("brilliant oysters" and so on), plus more substantial options in its 'Schottische' restaurant, upstairs. / **Sample dishes:** *poached Scottish oysters; beef with port & foie gras sauce; chocolate terrine with Glayva.* **Details:** *11 pm; closed Sat L & Sun.* **Accommodation:** *6 rooms, from £70.*

Café Gandolfi £26 *A* ★
64 Albion St G1 1NY (0141) 552 6813
This "affable" Merchant City institution has a "lovely" setting with its "eccentric" woody interior, and offers an "eclectic" menu – from snacks to full meals – that's "a modern take on traditional Scottish food". / **Sample dishes:** warm potato & chorizo salad; polenta with wild mushrooms & Gorgonzola; rhubarb summer pudding. **Details:** near Tron Theatre; 11.30 pm; no smoking area.

Café India £35
171 North St G3 7DA (0141) 248 4075
It has its ups and downs, but fans of this cavernous city-centre curry house still hail it as "the best". / **Value tip:** set 3-crs L £8.95. **Details:** www.cafeindia-glasgow.com; next to Mitchell Library; midnight; no smoking area.

Café Mao £26
84 Brunswick St G1 1ZZ (0141) 564 5161
This "modern, bright and airy" joint still wins praise from most reporters for its "great" simple, fusion fare; it can be so "busy" it's "frenetic", though, at which time standards seemingly suffer as a result. / **Value tip:** set 2-crs L £7.95. **Details:** www.cafemao.com; 11 pm; no smoking area.

Chardon D'Or £38
176 West Regent St G2 4RL (0141) 248 3801
Some claim you get "Glasgow's best food" at this "seemingly blighted" city-centre site near Blythswood Square (formerly the City Brasserie, RIP); reports are inconsistent, though, and service can be too "Weegie" for some tastes – if you don't understand the term, your Edinburgh friends will be pleased to explain. / **Sample dishes:** salmon with cucumber & dill dressing; coley with warm celery & lentil salad; roast pears with caramel sauce. **Details:** www.lechardondor.com; 10 pm; closed Sat L & Sun; no smoking in dining room.

City Merchant £34
97-99 Candleriggs G1 1NP (0141) 553 1577
For the most part reporters praised the "impressive and wide-ranging Franco-Scottish cuisine" (and "good seafood" in particular) at this "unusual and relaxed" Merchant City fixture; the odd disappointment, however, is not unknown. / **Sample dishes:** smoked duck & bacon salad; venison with black pudding mousse & apple jus; cranachan ice cream. **Value tip:** set 2-crs L & pre-theatre £9.25. **Details:** www.citymerchant.co.uk; 10.30 pm; closed Sun L; no smoking area.

Crème de la Crème £26
1071 Argyle St G3 8LZ (0141) 221 3222
In a part of town that's "devoid of good eating places", what may well be "the biggest Indian in Scotland" – an "interesting" venture occupying a converted cinema – provides a surprisingly "good-value" destination. / **Value tip:** set 3-crs L £6.95. **Details:** near Scottish Exhibition Centre; 11 pm; closed Sun L; no smoking area.

Fusion £24
41 Byres Rd G11 5RG (0141) 339 3666
Reporters are pretty forgiving of the occasional "bungle" at this West End Japanese – it's a "relaxed" place, and "cheap" by the standards of the cuisine. / **Value tip:** set 2-crs L £4.95. **Details:** at very end of Byres Rd, at Dunbarton Road intersection; 10 pm, Thu-Sat 11 pm; closed Mon & Sun L; no Amex; no smoking.

Gamba £41 ★
225a West George St G2 2ND   (0141) 572 0899
"Cooked with skill, and presented with flair" – the fish dishes at this *"cosy"* and *"peaceful"* central basement attract nothing but praise. / **Sample dishes:** mackerel with potato & horseradish salad; roast cod with mussel & thyme stew; pannacotta with strawberries & mint syrup. **Value tip:** set 2-crs pre-theatre £12.95. **Details:** www.gamba.co.uk; 10.30 pm; closed Sun; children: 14+.

Gordon Yuill & Company £34
257 West Campbell St G2 4SQ   (0141) 572 4052
Gordon Yuill's long stint at Rogano (where he was maître d') has helped win much PR for his fledgling mini-chain (GY & Co West is at 2 Byres Rd, tel 0141 337 1145); of the limited feedback it generates, though, too many reporters are deeply unimpressed (especially by service, ironically), and "can't understand why it's rated by all the guides"; that said, they can be useful meeting places, and make a feature of "great breakfasts" (served all day). / **Sample dishes:** crispy duck & watercress salad; sea bass with braised fennel; triple chocolate marquise. **Details:** www.gordonyuillandcompany.co.uk; 10.30 pm; children: 14+.

Ichiban £17 ★
50 Queen St G1 3DS   (0141) 204 4200
"Budget bowls of noodles (slurp)" and *"top-class sushi"* win many admirers for this *"simple and inspiring"* café, with its *"helpful"* staff; it's a *"fun"* place, too, if *"rather too loud"*. (A second branch has opened at 184 Dumbarton Rd, tel 0141 334 9222.) / **Details:** www.ichiban.co.uk; 9.45 pm, Thu-Sat 10.45 pm; no smoking; no booking at weekends.

Kama Sutra £25 Ⓐ
331 Sauchiehall St G2 3HW   (0141) 332 0055
"It takes Indian food to another dimension", say fans of this *"contemporary"* subcontinental, which is done out in splendidly OTT style; this year's feedback was limited, but confirmed the continuation of good all-round standards. / **Details:** www.kama-sutra-restaurant.com; midnight; closed Sun L.

Killermont Polo Club £25 Ⓐ
2022 Maryhill Rd G20 0AB   (0141) 946 5412
This pukka, colonial-themed Maryhill Indian generally wins praise for its "great atmosphere" and "superb food"; the occasional reporter, however, considers it "overspiced and overpriced". / **Details:** www.killermont-polo-club.co.uk; near Maryhill station; 10.30 pm; closed Sun L; no smoking area.

Mitchell's £34
157 North St G3 7DA   (0141) 204 4312
"Consistently reliable and good value", Angus Boyd's bistro duo (formerly a trio) continues to create general satisfaction; the Carmunnock branch is at 107 Waterside Rd (tel 0141 644 2255). / **Sample dishes:** grilled squid with chorizo; Scottish beef with crispy potatoes & mustard lentils; coconut tart with orange sorbet. **Value tip:** set 2-crs L £9.95. **Details:** 10.30 pm; closed Mon & Sun; smoking discouraged; children: 12+.

Mother India £ 28 *A* ★
28 Westminster Ter G3 7RU (0141) 221 1663
"Aromatic curries which are a delight to the senses" have made
this *"truly fun and democratic"* fixture south of Kelvingrove Park a
very popular destination; some continue to fear it's *"going
downhill"*, though. / *Value tip:* set 3-crs L £8.50. **Details:** beside Kelvingrove
Hotel; 10.30 pm, Fri & Sat 11 pm; closed Mon L, Tue L, Sat L & Sun L.

Mr Singh's India £ 25
149 Elderslie St G3 7JR (0141) 204 0186
"Variations on standard Indian cuisine" delivered by kilted waiters
offer *"something different"* on a visit to this Kelvingrove Park
subcontinental. / **Sample dishes:** pan-fried prawns with lime; south Indian
garlic spiced chicken; toffee pudding. **Details:** 11.30 pm.

Nairns £ 43
13 Woodside Cr G3 7UL (0141) 353 0707
TV-chef Nick Nairn's *"romantic"* Kelvingrove Park townhouse
restaurant has had its ups and downs over the years, and the
cooking *"is still not living up to the name"*; that said, this year's
reports suggested considerable improvement. / **Sample dishes:** crispy
duck with oriental lentils; rib-eye steak with herb mash; chocolate & banana mousse.
Value tip: set 2-crs L £12. **Details:** www.nairns.co.uk; 9 pm; closed Mon & Sun;
no smoking at D; children: 10+ at D.

Number 16 £ 31 ★
16 Byres Rd G11 5JY (0141) 339 2544
The setting is *"tiny, too tiny"*, but the accomplished cooking at this
"relaxed" bistro seems to have survived its recent change of
ownership pretty well; local produce remains *"to the fore"*.
/ **Sample dishes:** hot cheese fritters with apple & port sauce; roast venison with
spiced red cabbage; sticky toffee pudding. **Value tip:** set 2-crs pre-theatre £10.50.
Details: 10 pm; closed Sun; no Amex; no smoking at D.

Parmigiana £ 28
447 Great Western Rd G12 8HH (0141) 334 0686
With its *"traditional"*, rather *"old-fashioned"* approach, this *"small
and friendly family-run Italian restaurant"* just outside the city
centre goes down well with practically all reporters.
/ **Sample dishes:** lobster ravioli; fish & shellfish soup with bruschetta; lemon tart
with cherries. **Value tip:** set 3-crs pre-theatre £11.50.
Details: www.laparmigiana.co.uk; at Kelvinbridge station; 11 pm; closed Sun.

Puppet Theatre £ 40 *A*
11 Ruthven Ln G12 9BG (0141) 339 8444
The *"extremely original setting"* – a warren of *"intimate spaces"*
– is the highlight at this *"romantic"* West End fixture; reports on
the cooking, though, were very mixed this year.
/ **Sample dishes:** fricassée of scallops & courgettes; lamb with fennel & potato
purée; orange flower & cardamom tart. **Details:** 10.30 pm; closed Mon & Sat L;
no smoking area; children: 12+.

Rogano £ 50 *A*
11 Exchange Pl G1 3AN (0141) 248 4055
The *"wonderful Art Deco surroundings"* still help make this
"elegant" fish and seafood restaurant *"an institution worth
visiting"*, so far as most reporters are concerned; *"standards are
declining"*, though, and – given the *"high prices"* – the cooking
can seem *"ordinary"*. / **Sample dishes:** smoked salmon with quails eggs &
caperberries; sea bream with cabbage & bacon; chocolate & ginger snap
cheesecake. **Value tip:** set 3-crs L £16.50. **Details:** www.rogano.co.uk; 10.30 pm;
no smoking before 10 pm.

Saint Judes £37 Ⓐ
190 Bath St G2 4HG (0141) 352 8800
This Caledonian spin-off from the famous Soho media club (formerly known as Groucho St Judes) is "not cheap", but its stylish dining room generally wins praise as a "fun and unpretentious" venue, and for interesting cooking "with a Scottish twist". / **Sample dishes:** duck liver mousse in Madeira aspic; John Dory with asparagus & lime mayonnaise; dark chocolate & cherry fudge cake. **Value tip:** set 2-crs L £11.50. **Details:** www.grouchosaintjudes.com; 10.30 pm; closed Sat L & Sun L. **Accommodation:** 6 rooms, from £115.

Sarti's £21 Ⓐ
121 Bath St G2 2SZ (0141) 204 0440
"Bath Street is probably the favourite" branch of this celebrated Italian deli/café mini-chain (there's also a deli/bistro around the corner and a further branch at 42 Renfield St, tel 0141 572 7000) — it's "renowned" for its "lively", "warm" and "authentic" atmosphere and "great" simple dishes ("perfect" thin-crust pizzas in particular); there is the odd gripe of "complacent" standards, though. / **Sample dishes:** minestrone soup; four cheese pizza; tiramisu. **Details:** 11 pm; no smoking area; no booking at L.

78 St Vincent £38 Ⓐ
78 St Vincent's St G2 5UB (0141) 248 7878
A "smart" setting in an "amazing" former banking hall wins many nominations for this city-centre establishment as a good business venue — its standards are "good enough if someone else pays". / **Sample dishes:** rainbow trout with sweet pepper butter; halibut with braised fennel & rocket; white chocolate praline tart. **Value tip:** set 2-crs L £9.50. **Details:** www.78stvincent.com; 2 mins from George Sq; 10 pm, Fri & Sat 10.30 pm; closed Sun L; no smoking area.

Shish Mahal £24
66-68 Park Rd G4 (0141) 339 8256
"Still one of the best" — this long-established BYO Indian earns praise for its "reliable", "traditional" cooking. / **Details:** www.shishmahal.co.uk; 11.30 pm; closed Sun L; no smoking area.

Stravaigin £37
28 Gibson St G12 8NX (0141) 334 2665
"Huge portions of great food at low prices" help make Colin Clydesdale's "imaginative" establishment near the University a "buzzy" destination; satisfaction remains generally high, but this year's reports were spiced with the odd 'disappointment' — perhaps it was the strain of opening Stravaigin 2 nearby (8 Ruthven Lane, tel 0141 334 2665). / **Sample dishes:** roasted artichoke & garlic broth; chicken stuffed with red pepper & pesto; Belgian chocolate & ginger truffle tart. **Details:** www.stravaigin.com; 11 pm; closed Mon, Tue L, Wed L & Thu L; no smoking before 10 pm.

Thai Fountain £35
2 Woodside Cr G3 7UL (0141) 332 1599
It's "a bit pricey" and "service is no more than OK" at this large, well-established (and quite smart) oriental; most (but not all) reporters praise its "sumptuous" cooking. / **Value tip:** set 2-crs L £7.80. **Details:** www.thai-fountain.com; 11 pm, Fri & Sat midnight; closed Sun; children: 7+.

for updates visit www.hardens.com

Two Fat Ladies　　　　　　　**£ 34**
88 Dumbarton Rd G11 6NX   (0141) 339 1944
*This quirky, small fish restaurant was sold in early 2002 – and no
reports have yet been filed on the new regime; let's hope the old
high standards are being maintained. / **Sample dishes:** asparagus spears
with hollandaise; lemon sole & salmon roulade with spinach; strawberry pavlova.
Value tip: set 2-crs L £10.95. **Details:** 10.30 pm; closed Mon & Sun L.*

Ubiquitous Chip　　　　　　**£ 46**　　　　𝔸
12 Ashton Ln G12 8SJ   (0141) 334 5007
*After 30 successful years, it's no great surprise that this famous
West Ender strikes some as a "fading star" nowadays;
its "characterful setting" still has a "great atmosphere", though,
and "Scottish fare at its best" (plus a "big and interesting" wine
list) continues to win the place many fans. / **Sample dishes:** vegetarian
haggis & neeps; Loch Fyne herrings with tapenade mash & aubergine caviar;
Caledonian oatmeal ice cream. **Details:** www.ubiquitouschip.co.uk; behind Hillhead
station; 11 pm.*

University Café　　　　　　　**£ 13**
87 Byres Rd G11 5HM   (0141) 339 5217
*This now somewhat "run-down" Art Deco institution is
"an essential part of any visit to Glasgow", say its supporters;
it's as a popular breakfast destination that it's most notable.
/ **Sample dishes:** chicken noodle soup; lasagne & salad; pistachio ice cream.
Details: 10 pm; closed Tue; no credit cards.*

GODALMING, SURREY　　　　　　　　3–3A

Bel & The Dragon　　　　　　**£ 41**　　　𝔸
Bridge St GU7 3DU   (01483) 527333
*This "astonishing renovation" of a former church (part of a small
chain of lavish pubs) provides a "splendid" and "interesting"
setting – shame the food tends to be "overpriced and
uninteresting". / **Sample dishes:** Thai crab & spring onion dumplings;
Cumberland sausages with cabbage & bacon mash; apricot & honeycomb
cheesecake. **Details:** www.belandthedragon.co.uk; 10 pm.*

GOLCAR, WEST YORKSHIRE　　　　　　5–1C

The Weavers Shed　　　　　　**£ 37**　　★
Knowl Rd HD7 4AN   (01484) 654284
*"Don't let the name put you off" – the "interesting" menu is
"well prepared" at this "pleasant" and "friendly" former mill,
now converted to a restaurant with rooms. / **Sample dishes:** potted
crab & avocado with egg mayonnaise dressing; rib-eye steak with potato wedges;
sticky toffee pudding. **Value tip:** set 2-crs L £9.95.
Details: www.weaversshed.co.uk; 9 pm, Sat 10 pm; closed Mon, Sat L & Sun;
no smoking in dining room. **Accommodation:** 5 rooms, from £55.*

GORING, BERKSHIRE　　　　　　　　2–2D

Leatherne Bottel　　　　　　**£ 38**
Bridleway RG8 OHS   (01491) 872667
*A "perfect riverside location" has long made this "discreet"
Thames Valley destination a "stunning summer venue"; the food is
"lovingly prepared", but even fans concede it's "rather pricey".
/ **Sample dishes:** flat mushrooms on black olive toast; steak with chilli onions &
deep-fried cabbage; sticky toffee pudding. **Details:** www.leathernebottel.co.uk;
0.5m outside Goring on B4009; 9 pm; closed Sun D; children: 8+.*

---

sign up for the survey at www.hardens.com

GRAMPOUND, CORNWALL   1–4B

Eastern Promise   £ 28   ★
1 Moor View TR2 4RT   (01726) 883033
*"A find in this part of the country"; a recent change of hands has
only caused a minor blip in the high level of enthusiasm for this
"consistently good classic Chinese", improbably located in a small
Cornish village. / Details: between Truro & St Austell on A390; 10 pm; D only,
closed Wed; no smoking.*

GRANGE MOOR, WEST YORKSHIRE   5–1C

Kaye Arms   £ 29   ★
29 Wakefield Rd WF4 4BG   (01924) 848385
*"A great wine list, very reasonably priced" adds to the appeal of
this "very popular" gastropub, where "a good standard of cooking
is maintained"; "booking essential". / Sample dishes: smoked duck with
sweetcorn & walnuts; Cheddar cheese soufflé with stuffed peppers; coconut tart.
Details: 7m W of Wakefield on A642; 9.30 pm; no Amex; no smoking area;
no booking on Sat; children: 14+ at D.*

GRASMERE, CUMBRIA   7–3D

Lancrigg Country House Hotel   £ 35   ★
Easedale Rd LA22 9QN   (01539) 435317
*The "lovely" vegetarian cooking "never fails", say supporters of
this "friendly" establishment, just outside the village; the organic
wine list is also approved. / Sample dishes: Parmesan & pine kernel soufflé;
chestnut, wild mushroom & cranberry tart; orange, sultana & pecan pudding.
Details: www.lancrigg.co.uk; 8 pm; D only (bar meals only at L); no smoking in
dining room. Accommodation: 12 rooms, from £100, incl D.*

GREAT BARROW, CHESHIRE   5–2A

The Foxcote   £ 31   ★
Station Ln CH3 7JN   (01244) 301343
*A "marvellous fish selection" helps make this a "brilliant"
gastropub, so far as most – if not quite all – locals are concerned;
some, though, find the setting rather "old-fashioned".
/ Sample dishes: battered haggis with mustard; Thai red snapper with sticky rice;
sticky toffee pudding. Details: www.thefoxcote.com; 10 pm; no Amex; mainly
non-smoking.*

GREAT DUNMOW, ESSEX   3–2C

Starr   £ 34   ★
Market Pl CM6 1AX   (01371) 874321
*An "always-reliable" standard of "first-class" food has made this
beamed village inn a popular destination; service is usually highly
"professional", but there were a couple of complaints this year of
a "snooty" attitude. / Sample dishes: smoked salmon with marinated
vegetables; roast guinea fowl & celery with grapes; aniseed parfait. Details: 8m E of
M11, J8 on A120; 9.30 pm; closed Sun D; no smoking. Accommodation: 8
rooms, from £110.*

GREAT GONERBY, LINCOLNSHIRE   5–3D

Harry's Place   £65   ★★
17 High St NG31 8JS   (01476) 561780
*Harry Hallam's "original and fantastic cooking using top-quality
ingredients" makes a visit to his family's "tiny" (10 seats) cottage
dining room a "sublime" (if notably "expensive") experience;
the atmosphere some find "so intimate" is "lacking" to others.*
/ **Sample dishes:** mushroom soup with truffle oil; roe deer fillet with black
pudding & Madeira sauce; cherry brandy jelly. **Details:** on B1174 1m N of
Grantham; 9.30 pm; closed Mon & Sun; no Amex; no smoking; booking essential;
children: 5+.

GREAT MILTON, OXFORDSHIRE   2–2D

Le Manoir aux Quat' Saisons   £109   Ⓐ★
Church Rd OX44 7PD   (01844) 278881
*Raymond Blanc's "fantabulous" modern French cooking and the
"magnificent country setting" of his "divine" medieval manor
house again make it England's (and reporters') Number One
'destination' restaurant; even some fans, though, think prices are
"over the top".* / **Sample dishes:** quail egg ravioli with Parmesan & truffles;
roast Trelough duck with vinegar & tamarind sauce; pistachio soufflé with bitter
cocoa sorbet. **Value tip:** set 3-crs L £45. **Details:** from M40, J7 take A329;
9.30 pm; no smoking. **Accommodation:** 32 rooms, from £245.

GREAT TEY, ESSEX   3–2C

The Barn Brasserie   £26
Dicken Barn, Brook Rd CO6 1JE   (01206) 212345
*"Good food" is the general (but not invariable) drift of
commentary on this popular local destination; a pianist nightly
(except Sun) contributes to the ambience.* / **Sample dishes:** grilled
garlic mushrooms; crispy duck on sea-spiced aubergine; deep-fried chocolate ravioli
with raspberries. **Details:** www.thebarnbrasserie.co.uk; 10 pm; no smoking in dining
room.

GREAT YELDHAM, ESSEX   3–2C

White Hart   £38   Ⓐ
Poole St CO9 4HJ   (01787) 237250
*This half-timbered old inn is often "very busy", and many tip it as
a "great Sunday lunch place"; doubters find it "over-rated".*
/ **Sample dishes:** wild mushroom & pigeon salad; steamed venison & onion
pudding; raspberry & Amaretto trifle. **Details:** between Haverhill & Halstead on
A1017; 9.30 pm; no smoking.

GUERNSEY, CHANNEL ISLANDS

La Frégate   £32   Ⓐ
Les Cotils, St Peter Port GY1 1UT   (01481) 724624
*You get "stunning views" (over St Peter Port) from this manor
house hotel; most reporters award its dining room top marks for
"fabulous fish" and "professional" service, but one or two think
"it's lost appeal in its recent revamp", or find it a mite
"pretentious".* / **Sample dishes:** lobster bisque; stir-fried beef with ginger &
garlicblack beans; chocolate terrine with caramel sauce.
Details: lafregate.guernsey.net; 9.30 pm.

sign up for the survey at www.hardens.com

GUILDFORD, SURREY   3–3A

Café de Paris   £33

35 Castle St GU1 3UQ (01483) 534896

*For fans, this long-established brasserie and restaurant offers "good traditional Gallic food" and "a real French environment"; as ever, though, there are those who say it's "mediocre" and "expensive". / **Sample dishes:** onion & anchovy tartlet; guinea fowl casserole with tarragon sauce; lemon tart. **Value tip:** set 3-crs L & pre-theatre £16.50 (Mon-Thu). **Details:** www.cafedeparisguildford.co.uk; 10.30 pm, Fri & Sat 11 pm; closed Sun.*

Cambio   £40   ★

10 Chapel St GU1 3UH (01483) 577702

*"Classic Italian cooking in a beamed setting" wins 'local hero' status for this "friendly" fixture, in an historic house near the Castle. / **Sample dishes:** black lasagne with crab; veal with Parma ham & sage; Amaretto mousse. **Value tip:** set 2-crs L £11.50. **Details:** www.cambiorestaurant.co.uk; by Guildford Castle; 10.30 pm, Fri & Sat 11 pm; closed Mon L, Sat L & Sun; no smoking in dining room.*

fish!   £26   ✗

Rooftop, Sydenham Rd Car Pk GU1 3RT (01483) 532230

*It attracts much commentary, but it's difficult to avoid the conclusion that this is the worst member of this (over-)expanded chain of fish diners – "fantastic views of Guildford and the Cathedral" offer insufficient compensation for "dull" cooking and "perfunctory" service. / **Sample dishes:** devilled whitebait; grilled monkfish with olive oil dressing; bread & butter pudding. **Value tip:** set 2-crs weekday menu £10. **Details:** www.fishdiner.co.uk; 10.30 pm; closed Sun D; no smoking area.*

Rumwong   £29   ★

16-18 London Rd GU1 2AF (01483) 536092

*"Consistently very good" cooking has made this "big", "busy" and "friendly" – but "cramped" – Thai a long-running, and continuing, success story. / **Details:** www.rumwong.com; 10.30 pm; closed Mon; no Amex or Switch; no smoking area.*

GULLANE, EAST LOTHIAN   9–4D

La Potinière   £46

Main St EH31 2AA (01620) 843214

*Hilary & David Brown made this small dining room perhaps Scotland's top culinary destination – new owners (from August 2002) Mary Runciman & Keith Marley have quite an act to follow. / **Sample dishes:** crispy salmon with vierge sauce; honey-roast venison; lemon tart. **Details:** 20m E of Edinburgh, off A198; 9 pm; closed Mon, Tue L, Sat L & Sun D; no Amex; no smoking.*

GULWORTHY, DEVON   1–3C

Horn of Plenty   £54   ★

PL19 8JD (01822) 832528

*"A wonderful outlook over the Devon hills" helps create "a real sense of occasion" at Peter Gorton's "courteous" and "stylish" restaurant with rooms; it's "pricey" and not everyone is 'wowed' by the ambience, but, all-in-all, many "excellent" meals are reported. / **Sample dishes:** millefeuille of smoked salmon & crab; roast lamb with mint & pesto tagliatelle; cappuccino parfait & coffee meringue. **Value tip:** set 3-crs L £23.50. **Details:** www.thehornofplenty.co.uk; 3m W of Tavistock on A390; 9 pm; closed Mon L; no smoking; children: 13+. **Accommodation:** 10 rooms, from £115.*

HALE, CHESHIRE   5–2B

Amba   £ 27
106-108 Ashley Rd WA14 2UN   (0161) 928 2343
*This very à la môde successor to the Hale Wine Bar offers tapas
and snacks all day, as well as more substantial fare; it opened just
as our survey for the year was closing – the only reporter who
made it in time was impressed.* / **Sample dishes:** *sweet & sour stir-fried
prawns; Mexican char-grilled chicken; lemon & lime brulée tart.*
Details: *www.amba.uk.com; 0.5m SE of Altrincham; 10.30 pm.*

HALIFAX, WEST YORKSHIRE   5–1C

Design House   £ 30
Dean Clough HX3 5AX   (01422) 383242
*This stylish venue in a mill-conversion – a well-established and
superior local – changed hands in 2002, too late for meaningful
reports on the new regime.* / **Sample dishes:** *smoked salmon & saffron
risotto; pork belly with noodles & tempura vegetables; pear & cinnamon fritters.*
Value tip: *set 2-crs D £13.95.* **Details:** *www.designhouserestaurant.co.uk;
from Halifax follow signs to Dean Clough Mills; 9.30 pm; closed Mon D, Sat L &
Sun; no Amex; no smoking.*

HAMBLETON, RUTLAND   5–4D

Finch's Arms   £ 29
Oakham Rd LE15 8TL   (01572) 756575
*"Spectacular views over Rutland Water" (best enjoyed from the
large outside area) are the highpoint at this characterful
gastropub; reports vary, but its simple fare gets a mainly positive
press.* / **Sample dishes:** *artichoke tagliatelle; steamed beef with marrow & thyme
dumplings; pannacotta with glazed kumquats.* **Details:** *www.finchsarms.co.uk;
9.30 pm; no Amex; no smoking in dining room.* **Accommodation:** *6 rooms,
from £65.*

Hambleton Hall   £ 65   Ⓐ ★
LE15 8TH   (01572) 756991
*"Fantastic views from the terrace" set the tone at this "top-class"
country house hotel, overlooking Rutland Water, where the
"gorgeous" (if "expensive") modern French cooking attracts
consistent praise; one or two reporters find the atmosphere
"stilted", but more commonly it's held to be "serene".*
/ **Sample dishes:** *langoustine cannelloni; roast pigeon with foie gras ravioli & truffle
sauce; pavé of white & dark chocolate.* **Value tip:** *set 2-crs L £17.50.*
Details: *www.hambletonhall.com; 9.30 pm; no smoking; children: 7+.*
Accommodation: *17 rooms, from £205.*

HAROME, NORTH YORKSHIRE   8–4C

Star Inn   £ 34   Ⓐ ★★
YO62 5JE   (01439) 770397
*"Simply the best pub I have ever been to"; reporters do not stint
in their praise for the "wonderful" and "innovative" cooking
("all from local produce") at Andrew & Jacquie Pern's "super-
friendly" thatched 14th-century inn; it has an "exceptional
ambience", too.* / **Sample dishes:** *Yorkshire gammon terrine with fried quails
eggs; braised rabbit with pea & mint risotto; lemon tart with blueberry sauce.*
Details: *3m SE of Helmsley off A170; 9.30 pm; closed Mon & Sun D; no Amex;
no smoking in dining room.* **Accommodation:** *3 rooms, from £90.*

sign up for the survey at www.hardens.com

HARPENDEN, HERTFORDSHIRE 3–2A

Chef Peking £28
5-6 Church Grn AL5 2TP (01582) 769358
"Consistently good food" (and in *"generous portions"*) is the
theme of all reports on this Chinese local favourite; it's *"quite
pricey"* – at least for the area – but *"worth it"*. / **Details:** *just off the
High Rd; 10.45 pm; no smoking area.*

HARROGATE, NORTH YORKSHIRE 5–1C

Attic £33
62 Union St HG1 1BS (01423) 524400
*"A newish restaurant that's working hard to build up custom"; it is
generally hailed as a "welcome addition" to the town, but initial
reports are a little uneven.* / **Sample dishes:** *pigeon salad with beetroot &
sour cream; roast duck with caramelised bananas & pak choy; passion fruit tart
with mascarpone ice cream.* **Value tip:** *set 2-crs pre-theatre £11.50 (Mon-Thu).*
Details: *www.attic-harrogate.co.uk; 10 pm; closed Sun.*

Bettys £26 Ⓐ
1 Parliament St HG1 2QU (01423) 877300
*For "an expensive treat", this "beautiful" '30s tearoom –
the original of the eminent Yorkshire chain – remains an
extremely popular destination (with queues an ever-present
hazard); bread and cakes are "fantastic", but other fare can taste
"mass-produced".* / **Sample dishes:** *Yorkshire rarebit; sausages & mash; fresh
fruit tart.* **Details:** *www.bettysandtaylors.co.uk; 9 pm; no Mastercard or Amex;
no smoking; no booking.*

The Boar's Head £27 Ⓐ★
Ripley Castle Estate HG3 3AY (01423) 771888
*It's "well worth the drive", say fans of this grand but "not overly
pretentious" coaching inn, just outside the town; some reporters
prefer the "terrific atmosphere" in the bistro to the panelled
dining room, but "quality cuisine at very reasonable prices" is
reported throughout.* / **Sample dishes:** *rabbit with caramelised apples;
duck with summer vegetable risotto; hot strawberry soufflé.*
Details: *www.boarsheadripley.co.uk; off A61 between Ripon & Harrogate; 9 pm;
no smoking; booking essential.* **Accommodation:** *25 rooms, from £120.*

Cutlers on the Stray £26
19 West Pk HG1 1BL (01423) 524471
*Some dismiss it as "ordinary", but the "modern bistro" at this
"interesting" old central coaching inn wins a fair number of
mentions for its "good, reasonably-priced" cooking and its
"airy and pleasant" setting.* / **Sample dishes:** *warm crispy bacon salad with
pine kernels; salmon & crab sushi with avocado wasabi; sticky toffee pudding.*
Details: *www.cutlersonthestray.activehotels.com/TUK; 9.30 pm.*
Accommodation: *19 rooms, from £85.*

Drum & Monkey £27 ★★
5 Montpellier Gardens HG1 2TF (01423) 502650
*"Only the freshest fish, cooked to perfection and so reasonably
priced"* – its many fans do not stint in their praise for this *"great-
value"* Victorian bar; perhaps unsurprisingly, it can sometimes
seem *"cramped and crowded"*. / **Sample dishes:** *lobster delice; smoked
haddock florentine; crème brûlée.* **Details:** *10.15 pm; closed Sun; no Amex;
booking: max 8.*

Rajput £20 ★★
11 Cheltenham Pde HG1 1DD (01423) 562113
"An ordinary exterior belies a marvellous Indian" at Mrs Perveen Khan's "plain-looking" but "lively" subcontinental; its "gorgeous" cooking comes at "incredible-value" prices, with fish and veggie curries the top attractions. / **Details:** midnight; D only, closed Mon; no Amex.

Villu Toots
Balmoral Hotel £33
Franklin Mount HG1 5EJ (01423) 705805
"Good food in a modern atmosphere" is proving a winning formula for this emerging local success story, whose "interesting and different" fare is consistently approved. / **Sample dishes:** game terrine with chicory & apple salad; tuna teriyaki with mango, lychee & red chard salad; apple & cinnamon crumble tart. **Value tip:** set 2-crs L £6. **Details:** www.villutoots.co.uk; 9.45 pm; closed Sat L. **Accommodation:** 20 rooms, from £84.

HARROW, MIDDLESEX 3–3A

Golden Palace £26 ★
146-150 Station Rd HA1 2RH (020) 8863 2333
Some of "the best dim sum in the UK" ("comparable to central London's best"), served until 5pm daily, is the highlight of this "buzzy" family-run oriental; the "range and quality of other dishes is special, too". / **Details:** 11.30 pm.

Kaifeng £50 Ⓐ★
51 Church Road NW4 4DU (020) 8203 7888
"Worth re-mortgaging the house for" say fans of this "excellent" but "astronomically-pricey" suburban fixture – the cooking wins a very high rating, but it's as the only kosher Chinese in Greater London that it's most noteworthy. / **Details:** www.kaifeng.co.uk; 10.30 pm.

HASCOMBE, SURREY 3–3A

White Horse £35 ★
The Street GU8 4JA (01483) 208258
This "cosy" 16th-century inn comes complete with a "pretty garden", and it's praised for its "gourmet pub food"; the "great-value bar menu" is sometimes tipped in preference to the "reliably good" restaurant. / **Sample dishes:** Thai fishcakes; roast rack of lamb; sticky toffee pudding. **Details:** 10 pm.

HASTINGS, EAST SUSSEX 3–4C

The Mermaid Café £20 ★★
2 Rock-a-Nore Rd TN34 3DW (01424) 438100
"The best fish and chips in the world" are hailed by the many fans of this "legendary" seaside chippy; unsurprisingly it's rather "busy". / **Sample dishes:** prawn salad; skate & chips; spotted dick & custard. **Details:** 7.30 pm; no credit cards; no booking, except D in winter.

sign up for the survey at www.hardens.com

HATCH END, GREATER LONDON 3–3A

Rotisserie £27
316 Uxbridge Rd HA5 4HR (020) 8421 2878
"Good food, not overpriced" commends this *"unpretentious"*
steakhouse (an outpost of a small London chain) to almost all
who comment on it. / **Sample dishes:** char-grilled spare ribs; ostrich with red
wine & garlic sauce; maple & pecan bread pudding.
Details: www.therotisserie.co.uk; 10.30 pm; D only, except Sun open L & D.

Sea Pebbles £22 ★
348-352 Uxbridge Rd HA5 4HR (020) 8428 0203
"Wonderful fish and chips" – and in *"large portions"* – make it
well worth seeking out this *"out-of-the-way"* chippy.
/ **Sample dishes:** calamari rings; deep-fried scampi & chips; bread & butter
pudding. **Details:** 9.45 pm; closed Mon L & Sun; only Switch; need 10+ to book.

HATFIELD PEVEREL, ESSEX 3–2C

Blue Strawberry £34 🄰
The Street CM3 2DW (01245) 381333
"A beautiful old building divided into smallish rooms" provides the
setting for this *"busy bistro"*, hailed by fans as *"one of the best-
kept secrets in Essex"*; overall, though, the food was only rated
"average-plus" this year. / **Sample dishes:** Colchester oysters; duck with
prune & pistachio stuffing; dark chocolate & raisin pudding. **Value tip:** set 2-crs L
£12.50. **Details:** 3m E of Chelmsford; 10 pm; closed Sat L & Sun D.

HATHERSAGE, DERBYSHIRE 5–2C

The Plough Inn £32
Leadmill Bridge S32 1BA (01433) 650319
The *"wide range of interesting dishes"* – *"way beyond normal pub
food"* – wins universal praise for this ancient riverside inn, inside
the Peak District National Park. / **Sample dishes:** wild mushroom & leek
tart; Hungarian pork hot pot with leeks & saffron rice; bread & butter pudding.
Details: www.theploughinn-hathersage.com; 9.30 pm; no Amex; no smoking in
dining room; booking: max 10; children: 5+. **Accommodation:** 5 rooms,
from £69.50.

HAWORTH, WEST YORKSHIRE 5–1C

Weavers £33 🄰★
15 West Ln BD22 8DU (01535) 643822
Praise is unanimous for the *"wonderful"* food, *"attentive"* service
and *"lovely"* atmosphere at this *"cosy"* fixture (occupying
converted cottages) which fans say is *"under-rated"*; the place is a
favourite for couples – *"if only the men of the world were as
reliable and romantic as Weavers…"* / **Sample dishes:** monkfish,
scallops & prawns; seared pork with wilted greens; sticky toffee pudding.
Value tip: set 2-crs pre-theatre £12.50. **Details:** www.weaversmallhotel.co.uk;
1.5m W on B6142 from A629, near Parsonage; 9.15 pm; D only, closed Mon &
Sun; no smoking. **Accommodation:** 3 rooms, from £75.

HAYWARDS HEATH, WEST SUSSEX   3–4B

Jeremys at Borde Hill   £ 36   A★★

Balcombe Rd RH16 1XP   (01444) 441102

"Lovely fresh ingredients and a bit of imagination" come together
to produce some "amazing results" at Jeremy Ashpool's
"cheerfully-decorated bar and restaurant"; the atmosphere is
enhanced by the "beautiful gardens". / **Sample dishes:** prawn bisque
with prawn & coriander dumplings; rabbit with bubble 'n' squeak; apple & rhubarb
tart. **Details:** www.homeofgoodfood.co.uk; 15m S of M23, J10a; 9.30 pm; closed
Mon & Sun D; no smoking.

HAZLEWOOD, NORTH YORKSHIRE   5–1C

1086
Hazlewood Castle Hotel   £ 44

Paradise Ln LS24 9NJ   (01937) 535354

The dining room at this ancient castle is on an upward curve –
serious criticisms were absent this year and the cooking was
generally thought "good"; it still, however, doesn't quite live up to
the "lavish" setting, and some say the bistro is "better value".
/ **Sample dishes:** hot smoked salmon with dried fruit chutney; salmon with oriental
greens; 'predictable' cheese & biscuits. **Details:** www.hazlewood-castle.co.uk;
signposted off A64; 9.30 pm; closed Mon, Tue-Sat D only, closed Sun D; no smoking;
children: before 7 pm only. **Accommodation:** 21 rooms, from £125.

HELMSLEY, NORTH YORKSHIRE   8–4C

Black Swan   £ 44

Market Pl YO62 5BJ   (01439) 770466

This "old-fashioned" market town hotel is a "graceful" and
"relaxing" destination; its traditional fare didn't inspire much
commentary this year – such as we got was mainly (if not quite
unanimously) complimentary. / **Sample dishes:** poached egg & smoked
salmon with caviar hollandaise; duck breast & confit leg with raspberry jus; vodka &
lime parfait. **Details:** www.macdonaldhotels.co.uk; 9 pm; no smoking.
Accommodation: 45 rooms, from £118.

HEREFORD, HEREFORDSHIRE   2–1B

Café at All Saints   £ 17   A★

All Saints Church, High St HR4 9AA   (01432) 370415

"Dramatically" situated in part of a (functioning) medieval church,
this "friendly" veggie café makes a handy stand-by, even for
carnivores. / **Sample dishes:** mushroom bisque; smoked Cheddar & spring onion
quiche; chocolate brownies. **Details:** near Cathedral; L only; closed Sun; no Amex;
no smoking; no booking; children: 6+ upstairs.

La Rive at Castle House
Castle House Hotel   £ 51

Castle St HR1 2NW   (01432) 356321

Some "intriguing" and ambitious modern cooking won more-than-
local recommendations for this dining room, which forms part of a
(listed) townhouse hotel. / **Sample dishes:** Thai risotto with tempura frogs
legs; salmon & crab brandade with lobster won tons; Pimm's jelly with cucumber ice.
Details: www.castlehse.co.uk; 10 pm; no smoking. **Accommodation:** 15 rooms,
from £155.

HERSHAM, SURREY   3–3A

Dining Room   £ 28   𝔸 ★

10 Queens Rd KT12 5LS (01932) 231686

"Solid British food (with a few twists)" is served at this "old-style", "knick-knacky" establishment, where some liken a visit to "being invited into someone's home". / **Sample dishes:** Double Gloucester, ale & mustard pot; lamb & mint pie; spotted dick. **Details:** www.the-dining-room.co.uk; just off A3, by village green; 10.30 pm; closed Sat L & Sun D; no smoking area.

HERSTMONCEUX, EAST SUSSEX   3–4B

Sundial   £ 50   𝔸 ★

Gardner St BN27 4LA (01323) 832217

Some find it "pricey", but this "classy" fixture in a 17th-century cottage generally wins enthusiastic praise for its "immaculate French cooking" and its "quiet and private" ambience. / **Sample dishes:** langoustine tails with vegetable tempura; sea bass with stuffed courgette flowers; Breton shortbread with lime & basil sorbet. **Details:** 9.30 pm; closed Mon & Sun D; no smoking in dining room. **Accommodation:** 1 room, at about £85.

HETTON, NORTH YORKSHIRE   5–1B

The Angel   £ 37   𝔸 ★★

BD23 6LT (01756) 730263

"A wonderful treat" that's "worth the journey"; this "sophisticated" dining pub in a "lovely" remote Dales location remains the most popular in the UK thanks to its "consistently high-quality" bar meals ("get there early"), the "fabulous" food in the restaurant (where fish is the highlight) and a wine list which offers notably "good value". / **Sample dishes:** black pudding with lentils & pancetta; rack of lamb with thyme mash; sticky toffee pudding. **Value tip:** set 3-crs 'earlybird' menu £15. **Details:** www.angelhetton.co.uk; 5m N of Skipton off B6265 at Rylstone; 9 pm; D only, except Sun when L only; no smoking area.

HINDON, WILTSHIRE   2–3C

The Lamb   £ 27

High St SP3 6DP (01747) 820573

A "gracious old pub in a beautiful unspoilt village" – "good, simple" food is served in a setting that makes you "feel at home". / **Sample dishes:** asparagus with butter; roast lamb with redcurrant sauce; chocolate truffle cake. **Details:** www.youngs.co.uk; 8.45 pm; no Amex; no smoking.

HINTLESHAM, SUFFOLK   3–1C

Hintlesham Hall   £ 48

IP8 3NS (01473) 652334

"Imposing" and "spacious", or "ostentatious" and "pretentious" – the debate about this "very grand" country house hotel (made famous by Robert Carrier) remains very evenly balanced. / **Sample dishes:** smoked haddock, mussel & roast vegetable salad; lamb chump with harissa mash; iced raspberry parfait. **Value tip:** set 3-crs L £21. **Details:** www.hintleshamhall.com; 4m W of Ipswich on A1071; 9.30 pm; closed Sat L; jacket & tie required; no smoking; no booking; children: 12+. **Accommodation:** 33 rooms, from £120.

HINTON CHARTERHOUSE, BATH/NE SOMERSET 2–3B

Homewood Park £55

BA2 7TB (01225) 723731

Some find a meal "a deliciously indulgent and comfortable experience" at this part-Georgian country house hotel, a short drive from Bath; both service and ambience, however, receive a lukewarm overall response from reporters. / **Sample dishes:** smoked salmon & apple salad; roast chicken with confit cabbage; chocolate fondant with orange sorbet. **Value tip:** set 2-crs L £19.50. **Details:** www.homewoodpark.com; 6m from Bath on A36 to Warminster; 9.30 pm; no smoking. **Accommodation:** 19 rooms, from £139.

HISTON, CAMBRIDGESHIRE 3–1B

Phoenix £26 ★

20 The Green CB4 4JA (01223) 233766

The "super" Chinese food at this village green oriental makes it of more-than-local note; service, though, can be "grumpy". / **Details:** 10.30 pm; no Amex or Switch; no smoking area.

HOCKLEY HEATH, WARWICKSHIRE 5–4C

Nuthurst Grange £65

Nuthurst Grange Ln B94 5NL (01564) 783 972

Off the M40 – about half-way between Birmingham and Stratford – this "welcoming" establishment provides a classic country house hotel experience; fans say the cooking can be "very good". / **Sample dishes:** tomato, red pepper & olive oil soup; smoked sirloin steak with artichokes & wild mushrooms; Victoria plum & ginger soufflé. **Details:** www.nuthurst-grange.com; J4 off M42, A3400; 9.30 pm; smart appearance; no smoking area. **Accommodation:** 15 rooms, from £159.

HOGNASTON, DERBYSHIRE 5–3C

Red Lion £28

Main St DE6 1PR (01335) 370396

"A blackboard menu and scrubbed pine tables" set a "homely" tone to this pub on the fringe of the Peak District; its varied menu is approved by most, if not all, reporters. / **Sample dishes:** New Zealand green-lipped mussels; warm smoked chicken salad; whisky bread & butter pudding. **Details:** www.lionrouge.com; 8.45 pm; closed Mon & Sun D; no smoking area; no booking; children: 5+. **Accommodation:** 3 rooms, from £75.

HOLKHAM, NORFOLK 6–3C

Victoria Hotel £24

Park Rd NR23 1RG (01328) 711008

"The food's enjoyable, but avoid weekends, with London visitors and their children" is one local's best advice on this "off-beat" and "chilled-out" new gastropub with rooms, "opposite the famous beach"; some, though, think it "over-hyped". / **Sample dishes:** smoked eel with apple & horseradish vinaigrette; venison with creamed cabbage & chocolate sauce; tarte Tatin with green apple sorbet. **Details:** www.victoriaatholkham.co.uk; 9.30 pm; no Amex; no smoking.

HOLT, NORFOLK 6–3C

Yetman's £46   Ⓐ ★
37 Norwich Rd NR25 6SA   (01263) 713320
"Top London-standard food at non-scary prices", and "friendly" service in a "delightful" cottage setting win nothing but praise for Alison & Peter Yetman's "simple" and "informal" ("cramped") venture. / **Sample dishes:** *Louisiana crabcakes with red pepper mayonnaise; char-grilled duck with spiced figs; passion fruit & mango bombe.* **Details:** *www.yetmans.net; on A148, 20m N of Norwich; 9.30 pm; D only, except Sun when L only (open Sun D Jul & Aug); no smoking in dining room.*

HONLEY, WEST YORKSHIRE 5–2C

Mustard & Punch £30
6 Westgate HD9 6AA   (01484) 662066
New owners (the existing head chef and his brother) are making quite a go of this "cosy" village restaurant; initial reports – though not numerous – are all very complimentary. / **Sample dishes:** *veal sweetbread ravioli with langoustine consommé; venison with oxtail macaroni & chanterelles; white chocolate tart.* **Value tip:** *set 3-crs L £10.95.* **Details:** *www.mustardandpunch.com; 10 pm; closed Sat L & Sun D; no Amex.*

HOOK, HAMPSHIRE 2–3D

Tylney Hall £53   Ⓐ ★★
Rotherwick RG27 9AZ   (01256) 764881
"Outstanding in every way", this 18th-century country house hotel – where "everything is done properly" – is beginning to make a (deserved) name for itself; praise for its "amazing food" and its "rare and special" wines is unanimous. / **Sample dishes:** *goats cheese & sweet pepper terrine; lamb with roast Mediterranean vegetables; chocolate & Grand Marnier soufflé.* **Details:** *www.tylneyhall.com; 9.45 pm; jacket and/or tie required; no smoking in dining room.* **Accommodation:** *112 rooms, from £159.*

HORNDON ON THE HILL, ESSEX 3–3C

The Bell Inn £32   ★
High Rd SS17 8LD   (01375) 642463
"Imaginative" and sometimes "adventurous" cooking – "consistent over many years" – continues to distinguish this olde worlde village pub; it can be "difficult to book". / **Sample dishes:** *sweet potato & garlic soup; roast duck with stuffed squid & parsnips; apple crumble with praline ice cream.* **Value tip:** *set 2-crs L £14.* **Details:** *www.bell-inn.co.uk; signposted off B1007, off A13; 10 pm; no smoking in dining room.* **Accommodation:** *15 rooms, from £50.*

HOUGHTON CONQUEST, BEDFORDSHIRE 3–2A

Knife & Cleaver £32
The Grove MK45 3LA   (01234) 740387
Perhaps it was just a 'wobble' – despite some praise, the food at this well-established country restaurant with rooms was overall judged "nothing special" this year, and some reporters left "disappointed, after previous good experiences". / **Sample dishes:** *salt cod Spanish tortilla with black olive sauce; beef with wild mushrooms, Stilton & crispy onions; chocolate marquise with raspberry coulis.* **Value tip:** *set 2-crs L £12.95.* **Details:** *www.knifeandcleaver.com; off A6, 5m S of Bedford; 9.30 pm; closed Sat L & Sun D; no smoking.* **Accommodation:** *9 rooms, from £49.*

HOYLAKE, MERSEYSIDE 5–2A
Linos £28 ★
122 Market St CH47 3BH (0151) 632 1408
"Always a pleasure" – "consistently excellent" cooking makes the Galantini family's small restaurant a popular local "haunt". / **Sample dishes:** three cheese & onion tartlet; roast duck with bitter sweet orange sauce; nut, rum & raisin chocolates. **Details:** www.linos-restaurant.co.uk; 3m from M53, J2; 10 pm; closed Mon & Sun; closed Aug; no Amex.

HUDDERSFIELD, WEST YORKSHIRE 5–1C
Bradley's £24 ★
84 Fitzwilliam St HD1 5BB (01484) 516773
"A real find", this "cosy" town-centre spot attracts nothing but praise for its "good choice of well-cooked food at reasonable prices", and its "friendly and efficient" service; there are "excellent jazz nights", too. / **Sample dishes:** chicken fritters with peanut & lime dip; roast lamb with cherry tomato couscous; mango tart with caramel ice cream. **Value tip:** set 3-crs L £6.95. **Details:** www.bradleysrestaurant.co.uk; 10 pm; closed Sat L & Sun L; no Amex; no smoking area.

Nawaab £26 ★
35 Westgate HD1 1NY (01484) 422775
Thanks to the almost invariably "good" cooking, it can be "hard to get a table" at this "upmarket" curry house, which is part of a small local chain. / **Details:** www.nawaab.com; between bus & railway stations; 11 pm, Fri & Sat midnight; D only.

HULL, KINGSTON UPON HULL 6–2A
Hitchcocks £16 Ⓐ★
1 Bishop Ln HU1 1PA (01482) 320233
"Excellent value and service" makes this quirky (mainly vegan) veggie – "in a dilapidated old warehouse building" – well worth seeking out; they only open if they've received a booking – if you're first to book, you can call the culinary tune for the night; BYO. / **Sample dishes:** guacamole & bean dip; veggie satay with fried noodles; pecan pie. **Details:** follow signs to Old Town; 8.30 pm; D only; no credit cards; booking essential.

HUNTINGDON, CAMBRIDGESHIRE 3–1B
Old Bridge Hotel £35 Ⓐ★
1 High St PE29 3TQ (01480) 424300
"Excellent wines and lovely food" are the theme of pretty much all reports on this "classy" hotel dining room, in an 18th-century building beside the River Ouse. / **Sample dishes:** garlic & mushroom risotto with parsley; roast salmon with Swiss chard & mussels; lemon tart. **Details:** www.huntsbridge.com; off A1, off A14; 10.30 pm; no smoking in dining room. **Accommodation:** 24 rooms, from £90.

Pheasant Inn £35
Loop Rd PE28 0RE (01832) 710241
The cooking is "satisfying" but "not outstanding", say most reporters on this popular thatched tavern, which has a "pleasant" village location; there's a "great wine list", too, and it's "sensibly priced". / **Sample dishes:** spinach soup with nutmeg cream; crab & mussel tagliatelle with Parmesan; moist chocolate cake with cherries. **Value tip:** set 2-crs L £11.75. **Details:** 1m S of A14 between Huntingdon & Kettering; 9.30 pm; no smoking area.

ILKLEY, WEST YORKSHIRE   5–1C

Bettys   £26
32-34 The Grove LS29 9EE   (01943) 608029
"Long queues at weekends" attest to the "reliable" standards of this "atmospheric but expensive" tearoom; it's "good for lunch or tea", with "delicious cakes" a highlight. / **Sample dishes:** Swiss potato rosti; Yorkshire rarebit with apple chutney; fresh fruit tart.
Details: www.bettysandtaylors.com; L & afternoon tea only; no smoking; no booking.

The Box Tree   £45   ✕
35-37 Church St LS29 9DR   (01943) 608484
"We keep trying, but have never yet had a good experience!"; "snotty", "unwelcoming", "rude" and "hectoring" service features in a remarkably high proportion of reports on this "vastly overpriced" establishment, which "seems to trade on its good name of 20 years ago". / **Sample dishes:** roast quail & hazelnut salad; sea bass with lobster & fennel; honey & lime crème brûlée. **Value tip:** set 2-crs meal £19.50. **Details:** www.theboxtree.co.uk; on A65 near town centre; 9.30 pm; closed Mon & Sun D; closed 2 weeks in Jan; no smoking in dining room.

Far Syde   £29
back of The Grove LS29 9EE   (01943) 602030
"It can get noisy", but most reporters like the "good buzz" and "reliably good" grub at this "crowded" local wine bar/brasserie favourite. / **Sample dishes:** chicken & prawn risotto; lamb wrapped in Mozzarella & aubergine; cappuccino cup. **Value tip:** set 3-crs L £11.95. **Details:** 10 pm; closed Mon & Sun (open Sun brunch Oct-May); no Amex; no smoking area.

Negreskis   £31
1 New Brook St LS29 8DQ   (01943) 605900
Critics think that "big prices" for what is offered put off a wider following for this small town bistro; fans, though, laud the "sensible wine list" and quality cooking. / **Sample dishes:** prawn, saffron & sweetcorn risotto; braised oxtail & potato pie; pineapple crumble with lychee ice cream. **Details:** 9.30 pm; closed Mon L, Wed D & Sun; no Amex; no smoking area.

ILMINGTON, WARWICKSHIRE   2–1C

The Howard Arms   £30   𝔸
Lower Grn CV36 4LT   (01608) 682226
"A welcoming free house", on the edge of the Cotswolds, that's "very popular" thanks to its "busy and friendly" ambience, its "good wine list" and its "interesting but, thankfully, not over-long menu". / **Sample dishes:** avocado, French bean & bacon salad; beef, ale & mustard pie; pear, plum & apple flapjack crumble. **Details:** www.howardarms.com; 8m SW of Stratford-upon-Avon off A4300; 9 pm, Fri & Sat 9.30 pm; no Amex; no smoking in bar. **Accommodation:** 3 rooms, from £78.

IPSWICH, SUFFOLK   3–1D

Baipo   £23
63 Upper Orwell St IP4 1HP   (01473) 218402
A "long-standing but consistent" town-centre Thai – useful in an area without a huge number of such attractions. / **Details:** www.baipo.co.uk; 10.45 pm; closed Mon L & Sun.

The Galley £33 ★
25 St Nicholas St IP1 1TW (01473) 281131
"Interesting" (British) food from a Turkish chef makes this "busy and trendy town-centre" bistro of more than usual note, even if the setting is a mite "cramped". / **Sample dishes:** crispy feta & parsley filo pastry; Norfolk smoked trout; Belgian chocolate delice. **Details:** www.galley.uk.com; 10 pm (11 pm in summer); closed Sun; no smoking area.

Mortimer's Seafood Restaurant £31
1 Duke St IP3 0AE (01473) 230225
Ken Ambler's popular fish-specialist of many years standing recently decamped from the quayside to the street behind; the old place always had a 'star' for its "excellent seafood", but we've removed its rating pending reports on what's effectively a new restaurant. / **Sample dishes:** Brittany sardines with garlic butter; swordfish & tuna kebab with smoked paprika; baked apple & almond pudding. **Details:** 9.15 pm; closed Sat L & Sun; no smoking area.

IRON BRIDGE, SHROPSHIRE 5–4B
Malthouse £28
The Wharfage TF8 7NH (01952) 433712
With its "frequent live music", this "lively" country "pub and wine bar" makes a "groovy" destination (for these parts, anyway); the menu stretches from "wicked burgers" to the quite exotic. / **Sample dishes:** confit chicken with pineapple salsa; roast lamb with bubble & squeak polenta; lemon pudding with ginger fudge sauce. **Details:** www.malthousepubs.co.uk; 500 metres from the Iron Bridge; 9.45 pm; no smoking area. **Accommodation:** 9 rooms, from £65.

IVINGHOE, BEDFORDSHIRE 3–2A
Kings Head £49
Station Rd LU7 9EB (01296) 668388
The setting is still a bit of a "time warp", but a take-over by long-serving staff members seems to be pepping up the cooking at this "'70s-kitsch" restaurant in an ancient timber-framed pub; "simply the best Aylesbury duck in the UK" remains a highlight. / **Sample dishes:** tomato, Mozzarella & chorizo tartlet; pink bream with lobster risotto & fennel; lemon tart with berry compote. **Value tip:** set 3-crs L £15.25. **Details:** 3m N of Tring on B489 to Dunstable; 9.45 pm; closed Sun D; jacket & tie required at D; no smoking in dining room.

JERSEY, CHANNEL ISLANDS
Jersey Pottery Restaurant £38 𝔸★
Jersey Pottery JE3 9EP (01534) 851119
"Fresh fish, simply cooked, at good-value prices" is the gastronomic highlight of this popular conservatory-restaurant; there is now also a spin-off in St Helier (tel 01534 725115). / **Sample dishes:** pan-fried scallops in lemon & lime sauce; grilled fish platter; cassata ice cream. **Details:** www.jerseypottery.com; signposted from St Helier; L only; closed Mon; no smoking area.

Longueville Manor £63 𝔸★
Longueville Rd, St Saviour JE2 7WF (01534) 725501
Reports regarding this grand (Relais & Châteaux) dining room are thin on the ground; those who did make the trip say it matches its reputation as "the best in the Channel Islands", with "superb local seafood" receiving special praise. / **Sample dishes:** foie gras terrine with orange salad & brioche; brill & calamari with aromatic noodles; mint & white chocolate soufflé. **Value tip:** set 3-crs L £17.50. **Details:** www.longuevillemanor.com; 9.30 pm; no smoking area. **Accommodation:** 30 rooms, from £200.

Suma's £ 42 A★
Gorey Hill, Gorey JE3 6ET (01534) 853291
"Beautiful in every sense"; "refined" Mediterranean cooking, service with "attention to detail" and a "wonderful view" of Gorey Harbour make this a very consistent all-rounder.
/ **Sample dishes:** *goats cheese tart with shallot confit; sea bass with scallop & lobster gratin; selection of mini desserts.* **Value tip:** *set 2-crs L £12.50.*
Details: *underneath castle in Gorey Harbour; 9.45 pm; booking: max 12.*

JEVINGTON, EAST SUSSEX 3–4B

Hungry Monk £ 35 A
BN26 5QF (01323) 482178
If you're looking for "olde England", you won't do much better than this "cosy" 'chocolate box' cottage, praised by fans for its "fabulous, if quite rich" cooking (appropriate, as they claim to have invented banoffi pie here); for doubters, though, "such fine surroundings call for a more imaginative menu".
/ **Sample dishes:** *crab & avocado tian; lamb with Moroccan spiced crust & butternut squash; baked chocolate & raspberry Alaska.*
Details: *www.hungrymonk.co.uk; 5m W of Eastbourne; 9.30 pm; D only, except Sun open L & D; no smoking in dining room; children: 5+.*

KENILWORTH, WARWICKSHIRE 5–4C

Bosquet £ 41 ★★
97a Warwick Rd CV8 1HP (01926) 852463
Bernard Lignier's "classy" and "consistently innovative" Gallic cooking makes his family's "homely" restaurant a first rate foodie destination; service is "friendly", but it can be "slow".
/ **Sample dishes:** *watercress soup with caviar; roast veal with chive & cream sauce; blueberry & almond tart.* **Value tip:** *set 3-crs meal £26 (Tue-Fri).* **Details:** *10 pm; closed Mon, Sat L & Sun; closed Aug.*

Simpsons £ 47 ★
101-103 Warwick Rd CV8 1HL (01926) 864567
"The best all-rounder in the area" — Andreas Antona's town-centre fixture is a "very professional" outfit indeed, and its cooking is "first class". / **Sample dishes:** *Salcombe crab tart with smoked salmon; roast brill with spring vegetables; turron parfait with marinated pineapple.* **Value tip:** *set 2-crs L £15.* **Details:** *www.simpsons-restaurant.co.uk; 10 pm; closed Mon & Sun; no smoking area.*

KINCLAVAN, PERTH & KINROSS 9–3C

Ballathie House £ 49 A
PH1 4QN (01250) 883268
Overlooking the River Tay, this "grand" country house hotel provides a "lovely" setting and a good all-round experience, which combines "friendly staff", enjoyable cooking and a "great" wine list. / **Sample dishes:** *game sausage with lentils & bacon; seared scallops with chilli polenta & pesto; citrus tart.* **Details:** *www.ballathiehousehotel.com; off B9099,take right form 1m N of Stanley; 9 pm; jacket & tie; no smoking.* **Accommodation:** *42 rooms, from £170.*

KINGUSSIE, HIGHLAND 9–2C

The Cross £ 48 𝔸 ★

Tweed Mill Brae, Ardbroilach Rd PH21 ITC
(01540) 661166

*"Fantastic attention to detail" characterises preparation of the
(limited, set) menu at Ruth & Tony Hadley's restaurant with
rooms, in a former mill; "excellent" wines and cheeses – all non-
Gallic – are a highlight. / **Sample dishes:** scallop & prawn sausage with
fennel; saddle of lamb with rosemary & red wine sauce; lime cheesecake.
Details: www.thecross.co.uk; head uphill on Ardbroilach Rd, turn left into private
drive after traffic lights; 8.30 pm; D only, closed Tue; no Amex; no smoking; children:
8+. **Accommodation:** 9 rooms, from £115.*

KIRKBY LONSDALE, CUMBRIA 7–4D

Snooty Fox Hotel £ 26 ✕

Main St LA6 2AH   (01524) 271308

*"Not the same since the change" – though some say it's still a
"good traditional pub", this well-known town-centre hostelry has
"really gone downhill" since it moved into group ownership a few
years ago. / **Sample dishes:** duck & pistachio parfait; smoked haddock risotto;
sticky toffee pudding. **Value tip:** set 2-crs L £7.95.
Details: www.mortal-man-inns.co.uk; off A65, 6m from M6, J36; 10 pm;
no smoking area. **Accommodation:** 9 rooms, from £56.*

KNIGHTWICK, WORCESTERSHIRE 2–1B

Talbot £ 30

WR6 5PH   (01886) 821235

*Mixed reports this year on this riverside coaching inn and
brewery; supporters praise its "delicious", home-made food
(with a local organic emphasis) and "good choice of ale and wine"
– critics say it's just "dull" and "over-hyped". / **Sample dishes:** warm
game liver salad; roast sea bass with pesto; sticky toffee pudding. **Value tip:** set
2-crs L £11.95. **Details:** www.the-talbot.co.uk; 9m from Worcester on A44; 9 pm;
no smoking area. **Accommodation:** 10 rooms, from £69.50.*

KNUTSFORD, CHESHIRE 5–2B

Belle Epoque £ 37 𝔸

King St WA16 6DT   (01565) 633060

*This aptly-named Art Nouveau building provides a "delightful"
venue; its prices, though, "have rocketed" of late and even some
former fans say that its "plain bistro fare" is now "overpriced".
/ **Sample dishes:** Tuscan spring salad; sea bass with red onion salsa; apricot fritters
with Cointreau mousse. **Value tip:** set 3-crs Sun L £15. **Details:** 1.5m from M6,
J19; 10.30 pm; closed Mon L & Sat L; no smoking area. **Accommodation:** 6
rooms, from £60.*

LACOCK, WILTSHIRE 2–2C

At the Sign of the Angel £ 37 𝔸

6 Church St SN15 2LB   (01249) 730230

*It's the "14th-century setting in a beautiful National Trust village"
which makes this ancient inn – with its "open fires and
flagstones" – such a "diverting" location; that said, the grub is
also enjoyable, if "a bit unoriginal". / **Sample dishes:** Stilton & walnut
pâté; steak & kidney pudding; crème brûlée. **Details:** www.lacock.co.uk; close to
M4, J17; 9 pm; closed Mon L. **Accommodation:** 10 rooms, from £99.*

LANCASTER, LANCASHIRE   5–1A

Bay Horse   £31   ★
Bay Horse Ln LA2 0HR (01524) 791204
A "pleasant", small village pub, just off the M6, which fans praise
for its "excellent" (and quite contemporary) cooking.
/ **Sample dishes:** potted Morecambe Bay shrimps; braised lamb with ale & thyme
sauce; lemon tart & lemon fruit ice. **Value tip:** set 3-crs Sun L £14.95.
Details: www.bayhorseinn.com; 0.75m S of A6, J33 M6; 9.30 pm; closed Mon &
Sun D; no smoking.

Simply French   £23   🅐
27a St Georges Quay LA1 1RD (01524) 843199
It's "a real gem", say fans of this "small riverside brasserie", which
is praised for its simple but "good-value" Gallic fare.
/ **Sample dishes:** baked courgette stuffed with spinach & salmon mousse; chicken
marinated in lemon & olive oil; apricot tart. **Details:** 9.30 pm; closed Mon, Tue &
Wed L; no Amex.

Sultan of Lancaster   £15   🅐 ★
Old Church, Brock St LA1 1UU (01524) 61188
A "fantastic conversion of a Baptist church" provides the
"impressive setting" for this "lovely" subcontinental; fans say its
"fresh and delicately prepared food" makes it "the best Indian in
north Lancashire or south Cumbria" ("no booze"
notwithstanding). / **Details:** 11 pm; D only; no Amex; no smoking area.

Sun Café   £32   ★
Sun Street Studios, 25 Sun St LA1 1EW (01524) 845599
Adjoining an art gallery, this "trendy" licensed café, near the
station has quite a local following for its "good-value" simple fare.
/ **Sample dishes:** asparagus & poached egg with Parmesan; scallops & shrimps
with teryaki dressing; cheesecake with pistachios & honey. **Details:** 9.30 pm; closed
Mon D.

LANGAR, NOTTINGHAMSHIRE   5–3D

Langar Hall   £38   🅐
NG13 9HG (01949) 860559
"Idiosyncratic management" helps create a "charming" and
"quirky" ambience at this "rustic" country house hotel, where the
cooking is generally "interesting". / **Sample dishes:** asparagus & pea
soup; roast duck with citrus sauce; banana parfait with caramel ice. **Value tip:** set
2-crs L £12.50. **Details:** off A52 between Nottingham & Grantham; 9.30 pm,
Sat 10 pm; no smoking area. **Accommodation:** 10 rooms, from £130.

LANGHO, LANCASHIRE   5–1B

Northcote Manor   £56   ★★
Northcote Rd BB6 8BE (01254) 240555
"A serious contender as the North West's best" – Nigel Haworth's
food is an "excellent combination of local and traditional cuisines"
and the "quiet, spacious and comfortable" dining room of this
Victorian villa in the Ribble Valley wins nothing but praise.
/ **Sample dishes:** black pudding & pink trout with nettle sauce; Pendle lamb with
lemon marmalade & chive mash; apple crumble soufflé with Lancashire cheese ice
cream. **Value tip:** set 3-crs Sun L £18.50. **Details:** www.northcotemanor.com;
M6, J31 then A59; 9.30 pm; closed Sat L; no smoking. **Accommodation:** 14
rooms, from £130.

LANGTON GREEN, KENT   3–4B
The Hare   £ 26   𝔸 ★
Langton Rd TN3 0JA   (01892) 862419
"Book well ahead", if you want to eat in the (preferred) main dining room of this consistently-applauded village green boozer; it offers *"great pub food"*, *"freshly prepared"* and *"in huge variety"*. / **Sample dishes:** bacon, lentil & goats cheese tart; seared salmon with sweetcorn fritters; Malibu roulade with pineapple. **Details:** on A264 to East Grinstead; 9.30 pm.

LAPWORTH, WARWICKSHIRE   5–4C
The Boot   £ 35
Old Warwick Rd B94 6JU   (01564) 782464
This *"very popular"* pub (with *"great gardens"*) got a rather mixed press this year – fans say the food's *"interesting and tasty"*, while critics say it's *"living on its reputation"* and *"expensive"*.
/ **Sample dishes:** rustic bread with olive oil; chicken with goats cheese & saffron; Bailey's cheesecake. **Details:** www.thebootatlapworth.co.uk; off A34; 10 pm.

LAVENHAM, SUFFOLK   3–1C
Great House   £ 37   𝔸 ★
Market Pl CO10 9QZ   (01787) 247431
"Why go to France?"; the Crépy family's *"individualistic"* medieval house on the market square is a *"friendly"* place, and the cuisine is *"excellent"*. / **Sample dishes:** moules marinière; venison in red wine with duck foie gras sauce; saffron crème brûlée. **Value tip:** set 2-crs L £13.95. **Details:** www.greathouse.co.uk; follow directions to Guildhall; 9.30 pm; closed Mon & Sun D; closed Jan; no smoking in dining room. **Accommodation:** 5 rooms, from £70.

Swan Hotel   £ 40   ✗
High St CO10 9QA   (01787) 247477
"Trading on its history and location", this *"wonderful"* Tudor landmark has a *"lovely setting"*, but it has been let down in recent times by *"poor value"* cooking and *"disappointing"* service; let's hope the arrival of a new head chef heralds an improvement.
/ **Sample dishes:** scallops & Parma ham with green bean salad; sea bass with salt crust & lemon sauce; peach & thyme ice cream. **Details:** www.macdonaldhotels.com; 9 pm; no smoking. **Accommodation:** 51 rooms, from £146.

LEEDS, WEST YORKSHIRE   5–1C

Towards the higher end of the market, Leeds seems to specialise in restaurants which are almost quite good. It has a raft of places of moderate to high ambition – *Pool Court at 42* and *Leodis*, for example – which continually seem to fall just short of achieving what they ought to. The most commented-on place in town is *Sous le Nez en Ville* – a good-hearted place with no great culinary pretensions.

Gueller looked set to be an exception to this rather glum general rule. However, the eponymous chef departed soon before this guide went to press, to pursue a new venture in outside catering, leaving the long-established *Darbar* and newish Italian *Brio* as the only city-centre restaurants receiving anything like an unequivocal endorsement.

sign up for the survey at www.hardens.com

Stars away from the city centre incude Chapel Allerton's modestly-priced *Casa Mia Grande* and the self-explanatory *Shogun Teppanyaki*.

Aagrah £21

Aberford Rd LS25 1BA   (0113) 287 6606

The best-known of an "excellent chain of out-of-town Indians", this "massive" subcontinental delivers a "great selection" of "consistently good" dishes in a "plush" setting.
/ **Details:** www.aagrah.co.uk; from A1 take A642 Aberford Rd to Garforth; 11.30 pm; D only; no smoking area.

Amigos £19

70 Abbey Rd LS5 3JG   (0113) 228 3737

"Cheap" and "fun" – this family-run tapas bar is a continuingly "popular" Kirkstall destination. / **Sample dishes:** meatballs in chilli & tomato sauce; paella; Manchego cheese with apple. **Details:** on A65 in Kirkstall; 11 pm; no Amex.

Art's Bar (Café) £26   Ⓐ

42 Call Ln LS1 6DT   (0113) 243 8243

With its "relaxed, Bohemian atmosphere", this "lively" Continental-style café/bar in the Exchange Quarter makes a "good and informal" rendezvous; "delicious and filling lunch plates" are a top culinary attraction. / **Sample dishes:** roast garlic & thyme risotto; crispy duck with halloumi & herb salad; Belgian chocolate cake. **Details:** www.artscafe.co.uk; near Corn Exchange; 11 pm.

Bibis £35   Ⓐ

Minerva Hs, 16 Greek St LS1 5RU   (0113) 243 0905

This "big and bustling" (and campily flashy) city-centre Italian is a "reliable" favourite for many reporters – even those who find the food "nothing special" applaud the "great buzz".
/ **Sample dishes:** beef tomatoes with basil oil dressing; pigeon & foie gras terrine; chocolate & Amaretto cake. **Details:** www.bibisrestaurant.com; off Park Row ; 11.15 pm; no booking, Sat.

Brasserie Forty Four £35

44 The Calls LS2 7EW   (0113) 234 3232

It's certainly "buzzy" and serves "reasonable food", but there's a feeling that this early-'90s brasserie is "rather ordinary in every way" nowadays; canalside tables are something of a "redeeming feature". / **Sample dishes:** home-made corned beef with beetroot relish; smoked cod with leeks & Gorgonzola; Toblerone & Amaretto fondue. **Value tip:** set 2-crs L & pre-theatre £12.50. **Details:** www.dine-services.com; 10.30 pm, Fri & Sat 11 pm; closed Sat L & Sun.

Brio £33   ★

40 Great George St LS1 3DL   (0113) 246 5225

"Very popular and rightly so" – this "smart" and "welcoming" Italian offers superior cooking in a "modern and fresh" environment. / **Sample dishes:** haricot beans in chilli & wine sauce; seared tuna niçoise; pannacotta. **Details:** www.brios.co.uk; 10.30 pm; closed Sun.

Browns £29   Ⓐ

The Light, The Headrow LS1 8EQ   (0113) 243 9353

"A fantastic building" (a converted banking hall) and the group's trademark "buzz" help win praise for this "enormous" city-centre outpost of the well-known brasserie chain; the food is too often "dull", though, and service "inattentive". / **Sample dishes:** smoked salmon & watercress salad; pan-fried bream with wilted spinach; hot fudge brownie with vanilla ice cream. **Details:** www.browns-restaurants.com; 11 pm; no smoking area.

Bryan's £26

9 Weetwood Ln LS16 5LT   (0113) 278 5679

Opinions divide sharply on this famed Headingley chippy; fans say it's "in a league of its own" – critics say it's "not as good as the old days" and "can't understand its popularity".
/ **Sample dishes:** *chicken goujons with spicy BBQ dip; Jumbo deep-fried haddock & chips; treacle sponge & custard.* **Details:** *9.30 pm; no Amex; no smoking; need 8+ to book.*

The Calls Grill £29

Calls Landing, 38 The Calls LS2 7EW   (0113) 245 3870

A "great position", by a canal, adds much to the appeal of these warehouse conversion premises; the food is "variable", but "brilliant" steaks are a highlight. / **Sample dishes:** *smoked tuna with Spanish omelette; Dover sole with citrus butter; rice pudding bavarois.* **Value tip:** *set 2-crs D £9.95.* **Details:** *opp Tetleys brewery on waterfront; 10.30 pm; D only, closed Sun; booking: max 6, Sat.*

Casa Mia Grande £24 *A*★

33-35 Harrogate Rd LS7 3PD   (0113) 239 2555

The growing fame of this "hugely popular" Chapel Allerton Italian (and of its more informal and "authentic" sibling Casa Mia, at 10-12 Stainbeck Ln, tel 0113 239 2555) have led to expansion and refurbishment all round; the pressure is beginning to tell somewhat on the ratings, but this remains an "excellent", "lively" destination for most reporters. / **Sample dishes:** *smoked chicken salad with mango vinaigrette; honey-roasted salmon with spinach & lemon sauce; tiramisu.* **Details:** *www.casa-mia.co.uk; 10.30 pm; D only, except Sun open L & D (Casa Mia open L & D every day); no Amex; no smoking area.*

Clock Café £19

16a Headingley Ln LS6 2AS   (0113) 294 5464

"Good food" – on an East-meets-West theme – at "reasonable prices" makes this "relaxed" venture quite a popular destination. / **Sample dishes:** *moules marinière; Malaysian chicken; fruit crêpes.* **Details:** *10 pm, Fri & Sat 10.30 pm; no Amex.*

Darbar £30 *A*★

16-17 Kirkgate LS1 6BY   (0113) 246 0381

The "unprepossessing" entrance does nothing to prepare the eye for the "sumptuous" interior of this city-centre Indian; a visit here is certainly "an experience", and the food is usually "really tasty". / **Details:** *www.darbar.co.uk; 11.30 pm; closed Sun.*

Dare Café £19

49 Otley Rd LS6 3AB   (0113) 230 2828

"Cheap but good Mexican food" (plus all-day breakfasts) is the proposition at this "laid-back" and "lively" Headingley café. / **Sample dishes:** *tomato & Mozzarella salad; chicken fajitas; chocolate fudge cake.* **Details:** *10 pm; no Amex; no smoking area.*

The Fat Cat Café Bar £24 *A*

8 South Pde LS1 5BY   (0113) 245 6288

"A great place to read, eat tasty snacks and watch the world go by" – this city-centre branch of the growing café/bar chain provides "comfy sofas" in which to enjoy "big portions" of "reasonably-priced" fare (including breakfast). / **Sample dishes:** *smoked salmon salad; pork & tiger prawn stir-fry with mange tout; apple crumble.* **Details:** *www.fatcat.to; 10 pm; no smoking area; children: 18+ only.*

Flying Pizza £28

60a Street Ln LS8 2DQ   (0113) 266 6501

"You might see Jimmy Saville" – or even *"Premier League footballers"* – at this Roundhay *"institution"*, which is usually *"full of the local glitterati"*; the only question is: *"why?"*
/ **Sample dishes:** rolled Italian ham with Mozzarella; chicken with farfalle in spicy tomato sauce; tiramisu. **Details:** www.theflyingpizza.co.uk; just off A61, 3m N of city centre; 11 pm, Thu-Sat 11.30 pm; no smoking area; no booking at D.

Fourth Floor Café
Harvey Nichols £34

107-111 Briggate LS1 6AZ   (0113) 204 8000

"Not as good as it thinks it is" – though some see this Harvey Nic's outpost as the ultimate in *"northern chic"* (and a top venue for a *"brilliant brunch"*), even some of its fans find it rather *"pretentious"*. / **Sample dishes:** smoked chicken with pears & Roquefort; rib-eye steak with sweet potato mash; passion fruit mousse. **Value tip:** set 2-crs L £14. **Details:** 10 pm; L only, except Thu-Sat when L & D; no smoking area; no booking, Sat L.

Fuji Hiro £16 ★

45 Wade Ln LS2 8NJ   (0113) 243 9184

The *"stark"* setting may be *"basic"*, but *"lovely big plates of noodles"* and other *"good, simple fare"* makes this *"very cheap"* oriental an *"always dependable"* choice. / **Details:** 10 pm, Fri & Sat 11 pm; no credit cards; no smoking; need 5+ to book.

La Grillade £29

Wellington St LS1 4HJ   (0113) 245 9707

This *"typical Gallic bistro"* is a *"popular business lunch venue"*, in a city-centre cellar; it's pretty *"authentic"*, as you'd hope for somewhere that's *"French-owned and run"*. / **Sample dishes:** French onion soup; char-grilled rib-eye steak; bread & butter pudding. **Details:** 10.30 pm; closed Sat L & Sun.

Hansa's £17

72-74 North St LS2 7PN   (0113) 244 4408

For most reporters, the *"really original"* and *"delicious"* Gujerati vegetarian food at this *"idiosyncratic"* family-run fixture delivers an *"excellent"* experience; some *"disappointing"* experiences this year have, however, robbed it of its 'star' rating.
/ **Details:** www.hansas.co.uk; 10.30 pm; closed Sun D; no Amex; no smoking area; children: under 5s eat free.

Leodis £39

Victoria Mill, Sovereign St LS1 4BJ   (0113) 242 1010

This *"large"* and *"airy"* canalside brasserie is a *"favourite lunchtime hang-out for local suits"*, and – with its *"busy"* ambience – some find it a destination that *"never fails"*; others, though, *"can't see what the fuss is about"*, and knock it as *"pompous"* and *"overpriced"*. / **Sample dishes:** warm bacon & poached egg salad; steak & kidney sausages with mash; chocolate nut brownie. **Value tip:** set 3-crs L £15.95. **Details:** www.leodis.co.uk; 10 pm, Sat 11 pm; closed Sat L & Sun.

Lucky Dragon £24

Templar Ln LS2 7LP   (0113) 245 0520

"Where the Chinese eat, especially for dim sum"; this *"bustling"* but *"unatmospheric"* city-centre basement is quite *"authentic"*, but it can also seem *"complacent, in the absence of decent local competition"*. / **Details:** www.luckydragon.co.uk; 11.30 pm.

Malmaison £33
Sovereign Quay LS1 1DQ (0113) 398 1000
Even those who say that the cooking at this design-hotel brasserie is "reliable" concede that it's "predictable" – too many, though, just find it "unexciting and expensive". / **Sample dishes:** *pear, walnut & Pecorino salad; pot-roasted chicken with celeriac mash; crème brûlée.* **Value tip:** *set 2-crs L £9.95.* **Details:** *www.malmaison.com; 11.45 pm.* **Accommodation:** *100 rooms, from £120.*

Maxi's £26
6 Bingley St LS3 1LX (0113) 244 0552
This "massive" Chinese restaurant on the fringe of the city-centre can seem a bit of a "barn"; it remains "very popular", but the cooking is only "average", and the approach rather "impersonal". / **Details:** *www.maxi-s.co.uk; 11.30 pm; no smoking area.*

Millrace £29 ★
2-4 Commercial Rd LS5 3AQ (0113) 275 7555
Even some praising the "gorgeous" dishes at this "imaginative" organic venture admit that prices are on the "fancy" side – the overall view, though, is that they are "worth it". / **Sample dishes:** *seared Cornish scallops; roast ham with smoked Cheddar hash; triple chocolate cheesecake.* **Details:** *www.themillrace-organic.com; near Kirkstall Abbey; 11 pm; closed Mon & Sun; no Amex; no smoking in dining room.*

No 3 York Place £38
3 York Pl LS1 2DR (0113) 245 9922
Shortly before this guide went to press, and just as "fabulous" cooking was helping – after a rather rocky start – to re-establish this city-centre townhouse restaurant (then known as Guellers), the chef/patron departed; his protégé Martel Smith (who in recent times has had his own establishment in Gateforth) has now stepped into his former master's shoes. / **Sample dishes:** *lobster, mango & avocado salad with basil oil; pigs trotter stuffed with ham hock & morels; blood orange mousse.* **Value tip:** *set 2-crs L & pre-theatre £14.50.* **Details:** *www.guellers.com; 10 pm; closed Mon & Sun; no smoking in dining room; children: 5+.*

Olive Tree £26
55 Rodley Ln LS13 1NG (0113) 256 9283
For a bit of "Greek hospitality", this long-established, family-run fixture (on the city's main ring road) continues to win recommendations; some think the "simple" fare "overpriced", but it generally finds favour. / **Sample dishes:** *calamari with garlic sauce; lamb stuffed with apricots & prunes; custard tart.* **Value tip:** *set 2-crs L (incl Sun) £6.95.* **Details:** *at junction of A6120 & A657; 11 pm.*

Paris £33
Calverley Bridge LS13 1NP (0113) 258 1885
"A pleasant experience, but could be better" – one reporter neatly summarises the overall experience of this "reliable, if not outstanding" Gallic bistro in Rodley (a sibling of Leodis). / **Sample dishes:** *pork & apple terrine with pear chutney; Paris mixed grill; cherry meringue parfait.* **Details:** *www.paris-restaurant.co.uk; on outskirts of Leeds, off A657; 10.30 pm; closed Sat D.*

Pool Court at 42   £55
42 The Calls LS2 7EW   (0113) 244 4242
This "small and select" establishment in a canalside boutique hotel still wins general support for its "dependable" cooking and its "quiet and decorous" atmosphere; given the high prices, though, some reports are rather less rapturous than one might hope for. / **Sample dishes:** Scotch beef tartare with quail eggs; roast sea bass with anchovy-stuffed squid; chilled pineapple & lemongrass soup.
Details: www.dine-services.com; 10 pm; closed Sat L & Sun; no smoking; children: no babies.

Sala Thai   £25
13-17 Shaw Ln LS6 4DH   (0113) 278 8400
This "crowded" Headingley oriental owes its local popularity to its "welcoming" service and its "elegantly presented" dishes.
/ **Details:** www.salathaileeds.com; just off Otley Rd, near Arndale Centre; 10.30 pm; closed Sat L & Sun; no smoking area.

Salvo's   £30
115 Otley Rd LS6 3PX   (0113) 275 5017
"Get there early", if you want to avoid the queues at this "popular" and "noisy" Headingley Italian – "a fast and efficient place, with good food, too". / **Sample dishes:** deep-fried Brie with raspberry vinaigrette; veal with field mushrooms & Parma ham crisps; Malteser mousse.
Value tip: set 2-crs L £5. **Details:** www.salvos.co.uk; 2m N of University on A660; 10.45 pm, Fri & Sat 11 pm; closed Sun; no smoking area; no booking at D.

Sheesh Mahal   £19   ★
346-348 Kirkstall Rd LS4 2DS   (0113) 230 4161
"Consistently assured" cooking and "a warm welcome" (from the jovial Azram) maintains the strong local following of this "good-value" Indian (which has a handy pre-cinema location, by the Warner Village). / **Details:** www.sheeshmahal.co.uk; next to Yorkshire TV centre; midnight; D only; no smoking area.

Shogun Teppanyaki   £36   𝔸★
Unit V-W, Granary Whf LS1 4BN   (0113) 245 1856
"Not just great food, but a 'variety' show as well"; this "entertaining" Japanese makes a "fun" and "different" destination, offering teppan-yaki ("fresh ingredients cooked by your own chef at the table"), conveyor-belt sushi and other dishes all at "bargain" prices (relatively speaking).
/ **Details:** www.shogunteppanyaki.com; in arches under railway station; 11 pm; closed Mon L & Sun; no smoking.

Simply Heathcote's   £32
Canal Whf, Water Ln LS11 5BB   (0113) 244 6611
The eponymous North Western restaurateur has somersaulted over the Pennines to rescue an ambitious, but ultimately failed canalside restaurant (Rascasse, RIP); as the survey year spanned the transition, it's unsurprising that reports are very mixed, but at least one reporter says the place is "better now".
/ **Sample dishes:** warm black pudding & poached egg salad; herb-roasted chicken with oyster mushrooms; Heathcote's bread & butter pudding. **Value tip:** set 2-crs L & pre-theatre £13.50. **Details:** www.heathcotes.co.uk; off M621, J3, behind Granary Wharf; 9.30 pm; no smoking.

Sous le Nez en Ville £31

Quebec House, Quebec St LS1 2HA   (0113) 244 0108

"A good early-bird menu" is a highlight of this *"bustling"* city-centre basement of long standing; *"during the daytime, it's mainly business"* but the *"reliable"* Anglo-French cooking and *"interesting"* wine list commend it at any time.

/ **Sample dishes:** deep-fried Brie with pepper & mango sauce; rib of beef with béarnaise sauce; white chocolate pâté. **Value tip:** set 3-crs pre-theatre menu £18. **Details:** 10 pm, Fri & Sat 10.30 pm; closed Sun.

Tampopo £23

15 South Pde LS1 5QS   (0113) 245 1816

"Noodles served fast 'n' fresh in a minimalist setting" is proving a popular formula for this two-year-old oriental; critics, though, say it's like *"a factory"*. / **Sample dishes:** vegetable gyoza; prawns with coconut & Asian basil sauce; mango sorbet. **Details:** 11 pm; no smoking; need 7+ to book.

Thai Siam £27

68 New Briggate LS1 6NU   (0113) 245 1608

The Thai cooking is *"not bad"* at this city-centre oriental; its ambience, though, inspires little affection.

/ **Details:** www.thai-siam.co.uk; 11 pm; closed Mon.

Whitelocks Luncheonette £18   A

Turk's Head Yd, off Briggate LS2 6HB   (0113) 245 3950

This *"old-fashioned central refuge"* has *"a real buzz"* and its *"time warp"* appeal ensures it's *"always crowded"*; it serves *"classic"*, *"hearty"*, *"cheap and cheerful"* fare – *"hot beef sarnies with gravy"*, for example. / **Sample dishes:** crispy haddock fingers; steak & Stilton pie; jam roly-poly with custard. **Details:** 7.30 pm; children: 18+ only.

LEICESTER, LEICESTER CITY   5–4D

Bobby's £15   ★

154-156 Belgrave Rd LE4 5AT   (0116) 266 0106

A *"legendary"* fixture of the famous Curry Mile that's *"always busy"* on account of its *"wonderful"* and cheap veggie thalis and sweets; its décor couldn't be more *"unpretentious"*.

/ **Details:** www.eatatbobbys.com; 10 pm; closed Mon; no Amex; no smoking.

Case £30   A

4-6 Hotel St LE1 5AW   (0116) 251 7675

With its *"trendy"*, *"London-comes-to-Leicester"* styling, this local *"benchmark"* by St Martins – which has become the most talked-about place in town – scores best for its *"overall atmosphere"*; *"it has 'off' dishes occasionally, but is generally reliable"*.

/ **Sample dishes:** red onion & goats cheese tart; turkey escalope with roasted polenta; brioche pudding. **Details:** www.thecase.co.uk; near the Cathedral; 10.30 pm; closed Sun; no smoking area.

Friends Tandoori £23   ★

41-43 Belgrave Rd LE4 6AR   (0116) 266 8809

Most (if not quite all) reporters agree with the local fame accorded to this comfortable curry house on the Golden Mile, saying its *"excellent"* cooking is *"a real treat"*. / **Details:** 11.30 pm; closed Sat L & Sun; no smoking in dining room.

sign up for the survey at www.hardens.com   235

Jones Cafe £27
93 Queens Rd LE2 1TT (0116) 270 8830
This Clarendon Park café is "as good as many restaurants", say its fans, and comes recommended as "a great brunch or lunch venue". / **Sample dishes:** warm duck salad with Thai dressing; coriander-crusted chicken with red onion confit; Malteser tiramisu. **Details:** 9.30 pm; closed Mon; no smoking area; children: before 7.30 pm only.

Opera House £41
10 Guildhall Lane LE1 5FQ (0116) 223 6666
The "romantic" charm of this intriguingly-situated town-centre restaurant (originally part of St George's Hall) make it a popular local destination; even those 'wowed' by the setting, though, may acknowledge that "for the price, the food is average and the service poor". / **Sample dishes:** twice-baked Cheddar soufflé; plaice with herb risotto & lobster sauce; chocolate tart with praline ice cream. **Value tip:** set 2-crs L £11.75. **Details:** 10 pm; closed Sun; no Amex; no smoking.

Stones £33
29 Millstone Ln LE1 5JN (0116) 291 0004
Some reporters say that this centrally-located restaurant, in a converted Victorian mill, enjoys an "inflated local reputation"; it's a "lively" place, though, and "worthy of note" for serving some of the best non-Asian food in town. / **Sample dishes:** antipasto platter; harissa-glazed salmon with saffron fettucini; chocolate pudding. **Details:** midnight; closed Sun; smoking discouraged.

The Tiffin £27
1 De Montfort St LE1 7GE (0116) 247 0420
An "enjoyable evening-out" destination near the station – this "popular" (perhaps too much so, on occasions) Indian provides a less challenging experience than a trip to the Golden Mile, and one that's enhanced by notably "friendly" service. / **Details:** www.the-tiffin.co.uk; near railway station; 10.45 pm; closed Sat L & Sun; no smoking area.

Watsons £27
5-9 Upper Brown St LE1 5TE (0116) 222 7770
"Things are looking up in Leicester", as evidenced by this trendy factory-conversion; though some say it's "gone downhill since opening", for the most part it's hailed as a "reliable venue", with "OK" food (particularly the "good-value" lunches) and a "lively" ambience. / **Sample dishes:** fish soup with rouille; salmon with wok-fried greens; strawberry millefeuille. **Value tip:** set 2-crs L £8.95. **Details:** next to Phoenix Art Theatre; 10.30 pm; closed Sun.

LEIGH ON SEA, ESSEX 3–3C

Boat Yard £40
8-13 High St SS9 2EN (01702) 475588
It has a "fantastic location" (especially on a sunny day), but this ambitious yearling "has still not got its act together" – even some who report "excellent food" say "I won't go back, the cost is excessive". / **Sample dishes:** seared tuna with pickled vegetables; Australian beef with green peppercorn sauce; chocolate tart with clotted cream. **Value tip:** set 3-crs L £14.95. **Details:** www.theboatyardrestaurant.co.uk; near railway station; 10.30 pm; closed Mon, Tue L & Sun D; no Amex.

LEMSFORD, HERTFORDSHIRE   3–2B

Auberge du Lac
Brocket Hall   **£56**
AL8 7XG   (01707) 368888
"Wonderfully-situated by the lake at Brocket Hall", this grand
venture can be "idyllic on summer evenings"; it's "very pricey"
though ("apart from the excellent-value set lunch"), and some
find it a "stuffy" place that's just "trying too hard".
/ **Sample dishes:** foie gras terrine with Szechuan pepper; brill with endives & red
wine sauce; frozen vanilla soufflé with rhubarb compote. **Value tip:** set 3-crs L £25
(incl wine), Sun £30. **Details:** www.brockethall.co.uk; on B653 towards Harpenden;
10 pm; closed Mon & Sun D. **Accommodation:** 16 rooms, from £170.

LENHAM, KENT   3–3C

Lime Tree   **£55**
8-10 The Limes, Lenham Sq ME17 2PQ   (01622) 859509
"A lovely location in a village square" helps win fans for this "cosy"
(some say "twee") establishment – part of a small hotel – which
is praised for its "good" cooking. / **Sample dishes:** rabbit rilletes with
raspberry vinaigrette; lobster, tiger prawns & monkish flambéed in Pernod;
hot chocolate soufflé. **Details:** 9 pm; closed Mon & Sun D; children: only at L.
Accommodation: 8 rooms, from £65.

LEWDOWN, DEVON   1–3C

Lewtrenchard Manor   **£45**   Ⓐ
EX20 4PN   (01566) 783256
There were again limited reports this year on this charmingly-
located Elizabethan manor house on the fringe of Dartmoor;
on balance, reporters rated the cooking "good" rather than
remarkable. / **Sample dishes:** langoustine cappuccino with truffled leeks;
sautéed liver with garlic mash & crispy bacon; apricot bread & butter pudding.
Value tip: set 2-crs L £10. **Details:** www.lewtrenchard.co.uk; off A30 between
Okehampton & Launceston; 9 pm; no smoking in dining room; children: 8+.
Accommodation: 9 rooms, from £130.

LEWES, EAST SUSSEX   3–4B

Circa   **£36**
145 High St BN7 1XT   (01273) 471777
"London-quality food" – especially "East Asia-meets-Italy in a
fusion that actually works!" – is an unlikely find in this sleepy
town, and has stirred instant interest in this "classy" newcomer;
even those who find the place "fussy" or "pretentious" may
concede that it has its good points. / **Sample dishes:** Thai buttnernut
squash soup; tandoori trout with potatoes & tzatziki; red gooseberry crème brûlée.
Details: www.circacirca.com; 10 pm; closed Mon & Sun D; no smoking area.

LICKFOLD, WEST SUSSEX   3–4A

Lickfold Inn   **£33**
GU28 9EY   (01798) 861285
This "revamped village boozer" in the South Downs (with a
"smart restaurant upstairs, and pub food downstairs") is generally
praised for its "above-average" cooking; not all reporters, however,
were impressed. / **Sample dishes:** grilled goats cheese with red pepper relish;
pan-fried saea bass with black olive mash; white chocolate crème brûlée.
Details: 3m N of A272 between Midhurst & Petworth; 9.30 pm.

LIDGATE, SUFFOLK   3–1C

Star Inn   £33   Ⓐ
The Street CBY 9PP   (01638) 500275
"Solid Spanish home cooking" served *"in old pub surroundings"*
may be an unlikely formula, but it seems to please most visitors to
this *"out-of-the-way"* establishment. / **Sample dishes:** *Catalan salad;
paella Valenciana; treacle tart.* **Value tip:** *set 2-crs L £10.50.* **Details:** *on B1063
6m SE of Newmarket; 10 pm; closed Sun D; no smoking.*

LIFTON, DEVON   1–3C

Arundell Arms   £39   ★
Fore St PL16 0AA   (01566) 784666
"Excellent Anglo-French food, well served" makes this *"old-
fashioned"* country hotel (nicely situated on the River Tamar)
consistently popular; it's *"a pricey destination"*, says one reporter,
but *"worth it"*. / **Sample dishes:** *spiced potted chicken with apricot chutney;
roast monkfish with scallop & lentil fricassée; passion fruit delice.* **Value tip:** *set
3-crs L £23.* **Details:** *0.5m off A30, Lifton Down exit; 9.30 pm; no smoking.*
Accommodation: *28 rooms, from £110.*

LINCOLN, LINCOLNSHIRE   6–3A

Browns Pie Shop   £26   ★
33 Steep Hill LN2 1LU   (01522) 527330
A *"splendid and simple"* traditional-ish menu (with *"good pies"*
the star attraction) is served in *"huge portions"* at this *"friendly"*
fixture; it *"can get very busy"*. / **Sample dishes:** *Yorkshire pudding with
spiced onion gravy; Grimsby Market fish pie; Bailey's cheesecake.* **Value tip:** *set
2-crs L £6.50.* **Details:** *near the Cathedral; 10 pm; no smoking area.*

Jew's House   £39
15 The Strait LN2 1JD   (01522) 524851
"You're possibly paying for the location", at this smart
establishment, which occupies one of the city's oldest buildings
(and which moved into new ownership last year); its *"cosy"*
ambience and *"good"* cooking, however, find general approval.
/ **Sample dishes:** *wild mushroom vol-au-vents; braised monkfish with spinach; white
chocolate cheesecake.* **Details:** *halfway down Steep Hill from Cathedral; 9.30 pm;
closed Sun D; no smoking.*

The Wig & Mitre   £35
30-32 Steep Hill LN2 1TL   (01522) 535190
Some say it's *"starting to improve again"*, but support for this
popular pub, in the shadow of the Cathedral, is still suffering from
its move a few years ago; on balance, though it's still judged
"worth the climb up the hill". / **Sample dishes:** *wild mushroon & Madeira
soup; chicken in Parma ham with pistachio & lemon stuffing; baked vanilla
cheesecake.* **Value tip:** *set 3-crs L £12.75.* **Details:** *between Cathedral & Castle;
11 pm; no smoking in dining room.*

LINLITHGOW, WEST LOTHIAN 9–4C

Champany Inn £54
EH49 7LU (01506) 834532

"The best steak in the UK?" – it *"must come close"*, say fans of this legendary inn (in a beautiful location not far from Edinburgh), and *"what a wine list"* (one of the largest in the country); dining here is *"very costly"*, though, and not everyone is impressed (although you can eat in the adjoining Chop & Ale House for around half the price.) / **Sample dishes:** quail with bacon & tarragon stuffing; Boerewors sausages with mash & onion gravy; hazelnut meringues. **Value tip:** set 2-crs L £16.75. **Details:** www.champany.com; 2m NE of Linlithgow on junction of A904 & A803; 10 pm; closed Sat L & Sun; jacket & tie required; children: 8+ in restaurant. **Accommodation:** 16 rooms, from £95.

LITTLE SHELFORD, CAMBRIDGESHIRE 3–1B

Sycamore House £34 ★
1 Church St CB2 5HG (01223) 843396

"Very capable" cooking and an *"interesting wine list"* make the Sharpes' *"straightforward"*, *"friendly"* and *"quiet"* restaurant a top local destination. / **Sample dishes:** Stilton & celery soup; steamed prawns with sour cream & sweet chilli; Campari & orange sorbet. **Details:** 1.5m from M11, J11 on A10 to Royston; 9 pm; D only, closed Sun-Tue; no Amex; no smoking; children: 12+.

LIVERPOOL, MERSEYSIDE 5–2A

Atmosphere on a budget (or at least at relatively reasonable cost) is the general theme of most of the city's more satisfactory places, including two good all-rounders – *Everyman Bistro* and *Pod* – as well as *L'Alouette*, *Jalons Wine Bar*, *Keiths Wine Bar* and the *Living Room*.

The city remains thinly provided with quality restaurants. The best remains the appropriately-named *60 Hope Street*, while in the Albert Dock, Paul Heathcote's new venture *Simply Heathcote's* has generated a lot of interest, and is perhaps the best of that North Western group.

L'Alouette £34 Ⓐ
2 Lark Ln L17 8US (0151) 727 2142

Some find this *"lovely"* Sefton Park fixture – now in business for nearly two decades – a *"romantic"* destination, and its Gallic cooking is *"as good as ever"*. / **Sample dishes:** snails & frogs legs in garlic; steak with Roquefort; lemon tart. **Value tip:** set 2-crs meal £12.50. **Details:** 10 pm; closed Mon.

Casa Italia £21
40 Stanley St L1 6AL (0151) 227 5774

It's *"rough and ready, noisy and lively"* and – if you like that sort of thing – *"great value"*, say fans of this *"colourful"* Italian, housed in a former warehouse. / **Sample dishes:** smoked & cured meat platter; Ventresca bacon & olive pizza; cassata ice cream. **Details:** off Victoria St; 10 pm; closed Sun; no Amex; need 8+ to book.

sign up for the survey at www.hardens.com

Everyman Bistro £18 A ★
5-9 Hope St L1 9BH   (0151) 708 9545
A real "Liverpool institution" – this "crowded" and "lively" self-service bistro under the Everyman Theatre has earned its stripes for three decades now with "wholefoody" fare of "consistent" quality, "great beer" and a decent wine selection, all at "budget" prices. / **Sample dishes:** nutty parsnip soup; red chilli chicken with yellow rice; apricot & almond cobbler. **Details:** www.everyman.co.uk; midnight, Fri & Sat 2 am; closed Sun; no Amex; no smoking area.

Far East £23
27-35 Berry St L1 9DF   (0151) 709 3141
The "cooking is better than the surroundings", at this large and popular Chinese, authentically-located over an oriental cash & carry. / **Details:** by church on Berry St; 11.15 pm; no smoking area.

Gulshan £24
544-548 Aigburth Rd L19 3QG   (0151) 427 2273
In the absence of any decent local competition, this "solid" Indian – with its "OTT", "old-fashioned" décor – is reporters' tip as the "best in town"; perhaps unsurprisingly, it can seem rather "complacent". / **Details:** www.gulshan-liverpool.com; 10.45 pm; D only; no smoking area.

Jalons Wine Bar £30 A
473-475 Smithdown Rd L15 5AE   (0151) 734 3984
Live music (nightly) "makes the atmosphere" at this popular spot near Penny Lane, which some find quite a romantic destination. / **Sample dishes:** chicken liver pâté; pot-roasted lamb in red wine & port; apple pie. **Details:** 10 pm; D only, closed Mon; children: before 7 pm.

Keiths Wine Bar £15 A
107 Lark Ln L17 8UR   (0151) 728 7688
"There's something for everyone", say those who recommend this "unpretentious" and "Bohemian" wine bar, near Sefton Park. / **Sample dishes:** grilled halloumi with pitta bread; Spanish-style chicken with rice; sticky toffee pudding. **Details:** 11 pm; no Amex.

Left Bank £33 ★
1 Church Rd L15 9EA   (0151) 734 5040
A "cramped" but popular Gallic bistro, heartily praised for its dependable cooking at "reasonable" prices. / **Sample dishes:** tomato & Mozzarella tart; roast duck with honey & thyme glaze; crème brûlée. **Value tip:** set 3-crs L £7.95. **Details:** www.leftbankfrenchrestaurant.co.uk; off Penny Lane; 10 pm; closed Sat L.

The Living Room £28 A
Victoria St, Victoria Buildings 15 L2 5QS   (0870) 442 2535
A "thriving bar/restaurant, serving interesting food day or night" – this "trendy" city-centre outpost of a cool piano-bar chain has no great culinary aspirations, but it does what it does very well. / **Sample dishes:** duck spring rolls with shitake salsa; Cumberland bangers & mash; Belgian waffles. **Details:** www.thelivingroom.co.uk; 11 pm; no smoking area at L.

Number 7 Café £22
7-11 Falkner St L8 7PU   (0151) 709 9633
"A great little deli in the University Quarter" which, with its "imaginative" menu, makes a superior destination for a snack. / **Sample dishes:** tuna & olive salad; lemon & chilli chicken ragoût; chocolate mousse. **Details:** between the Cathedrals; 7 pm; closed Sun; no credit cards; no smoking area; need 6+ to book.

The Other Place £28
141-143 Allerton Rd L18 2DD   (0151) 724 1234
*"A good choice for students, families and couples", this classily
rustic-looking Mossley Hill spot offers an "interesting" and
"always-changing" menu; the place is "always busy",
with breakfast especially popular.* / **Sample dishes:** goats cheese & red
pepper spring rolls; grilled cod with hazelnut & herb potato cake; passion fruit &
coconut tart. **Details:** 10 pm; closed Mon & Sun D; no Amex; appreciated if guests
try to refrain from smoking.

Pod £18   𝔸★
137-139 Allerton Rd L18 2DD   (0151) 724 2255
*A "cool" and "buzzing" wine/tapas bar in Allerton; the modern
European snacks can be "excellent", and a "lovely brunch" is a
highlight.* / **Sample dishes:** prawn & squid tempura with wasabi mayonnaise;
chicken stuffed with chorizo & coriander; sticky toffee pudding. **Details:** 9.30 pm;
booking: max 6 at weekends.

Siam Garden £24
607 Smithdown Rd L15 5AG   (0151) 734 1471
*You "must book", if you want to experience the "authentic"
charms of this unpretentious Thai restaurant, in Sefton Park.*
/ **Details:** 11.45 pm; closed Sun L.

Simply Heathcote's £30
Beetham Plaza 25, The Strand L2 0XJ   (0151) 236 3536
*"The best Paul Heathcote establishment I've been to" –
this "busy" new brasserie in Albert Dock is a good all-round
performer, especially by the standards of the 'Conran of the
North'; even so, some find it "cold", "pretentious" and
"overpriced".* / **Sample dishes:** pan-fried sardines with tomato salsa; char-grilled
chicken Caesar salad; bread & butter pudding. **Details:** www.heathcotes.co.uk;
10 pm; no smoking in dining room.

60 Hope Street £40   𝔸★
60 Hope St L1 9BZ
(0151) 707 6060
*"A lovely modern eatery in the heart of the University Quarter";
this "stylish" but "unpretentious" bar/café/restaurant hits just the
right note; the "cheery basement" wins particular praise –
book ahead.* / **Sample dishes:** fishcakes with smoked pepper aioli; lamb with
crispy spinach risotto; peanut butter brûlée. **Value tip:** set 2-crs L £10.95.
Details: www.60hopestreet.com; between the Cathedrals; 10.30 pm; closed Sat L &
Sun; no Amex; no smoking area.

Tabac £19   𝔸
126 Bold St L1 4JA   (0151) 709 9502
*"A fine stop-off in town on a busy day" – this city-centre café has
recently been refurbished; it offers a wide-ranging menu, and is
particularly popular as a breakfasting spot.* / **Sample dishes:** roast
aubergine & red pepper pâté; shepherds pie; chocolate espresso mousse.
Details: 10 pm; no Amex; no smoking area.

Tai Pan £21
WH Lung Building, Gt Howard St L5 9TZ   (0151) 207 3888
*This "huge barn of a place, above a Chinese supermarket" is
"always busy" (and "too noisy" for some tastes); it makes an
authentic Sunday dim sum destination, but the scoff falls some
way short of being remarkable.* / **Value tip:** set 2-crs L £5.45.
Details: 11.30 pm.

sign up for the survey at www.hardens.com

Yuet Ben £ 20 ★
1 Upper Duke St L1 9DU (0151) 709 5772
"Superb" service adds gloss to this Chinatown stalwart of over
three decades' standing, which serves *"good-quality"*
(and inexpensive) grub, (including *"excellent veggie options"*).
/ **Details:** www.yuetben.co.uk; 11 pm; D only, closed Sun.

Ziba £ 27
Hargreaves Building, Chapel St (0151) 236 6676
*This popular restaurant was closed at press time, in preparation
for a move to the ground floor of the former Racquet Club –
look out for a re-opening in late 2002.* / **Sample dishes:** seared tuna
with aubergine chutney; suckling pig with dauphinoise potatoes; white chocolate &
mango terrine. **Details:** 10 pm; closed Sat L & Sun; no smoking area.

LLANDDEINIOLEN, GWYNEDD 4–1C

Ty'n Rhos £ 32 ★
LL55 3AE (01248) 670489
"Beautiful views of the Menai Strait" add to the romantic appeal
of this hotel occupying a converted farmhouse; the cooking rarely
disappoints. / **Sample dishes:** crab tart with crab bisque dressing; lamb with
bean & rosemary casserole; gooseberry & elderflower tart.
Details: www.tynrhos.co.uk; 8.30 pm; closed Mon L; no smoking; children: 6+.
Accommodation: 14 rooms, from £80.

LLANDEGLA, DENBIGHSHIRE 5–3A

Bodidris Hall Hotel £ 40 𝔸★
LL11 3AL (01978) 790434
*This ancient medieval manor house has an "excellent" setting
with fine views; its fairly traditional cooking can be "very good".*
/ **Sample dishes:** confit duck terrine with Cumberland sauce; lamb with leek &
mint mousse; roast pear & almond tart. **Value tip:** set 3-crs L £14.95.
Details: www.bodidrishall.com; on A5104 from Wrexham; 9 pm; no smoking in
dining room; children: 18+ on Sat. **Accommodation:** 9 rooms, from £99.

LLANDUDNO, CONWY 4–1D

Bodysgallen Hall £ 51 𝔸
Pentywyn Rd LL30 1RS (01492) 584466
"Fantastic views of Snowdonia" are a highlight of this *"lovely"*
country house hotel, which, though it can seem *"hushed"*,
is *"not excessively formal"*; reports on the cooking run the gamut
from *"excellent"* to *"somewhat disappointing"*. / **Sample dishes:** roast
tomato soup with pesto tortellini; Welsh lamb with bacon potato cake & mint jus;
grape & grenadine jelly. **Value tip:** set 3-crs L £18. **Details:** www.bodysgallen.com;
2m off A55 on A470; 9.30 pm; no Amex or Switch; jacket & tie required at D;
no smoking in dining room; children: 8+. **Accommodation:** 35 rooms, from £160.

Richards £ 35 ★
7 Church Walks LL30 2HD (01492) 877924
*Richard Hendey's often "excellent" cooking (and his selection of
wines) makes this well-established bistro/restaurant a continuing
success; it's a destination some find "romantic".*
/ **Sample dishes:** chicken, venison & pistachio terrine; Welsh pork with Bramley
apple sauce; Caribbean rum, raisin & coffee ice cream. **Details:** 11 pm; D only,
closed Mon & Sun.

St Tudno Hotel £ 45 ★
Promenade LL30 2LP   (01492) 874411
Rare indeed are seaside-town hotel restaurants with standards as good as this small dining room (quite near the pier); though there is the odd report of "ordinary" results, most rate their meals here as "exceptional". / **Sample dishes:** crab risotto with parmesan; Welsh lamb with cabbage & oatmeal; warm chocolate fondant with coconut ice cream. **Value tip:** set 2-crs L £13. **Details:** www.st-tudno.co.uk; 9.30 pm; no smoking; children: no babies or toddlers at D. **Accommodation:** 19 rooms, from £90.

LLANGAMMARCH WELLS, POWYS 4–4D

Lake Country House £ 50 ★
LD4 4BS   (01591) 620202
"A gem of a place, in the middle of nowhere", this "quiet" Edwardian country house offers "wonderful, wonderful food", say its supporters, and "beautifully served", too. / **Sample dishes:** roast Mediterranean vegetable soup; confit duck & foie gras terrine; rum & mango crème brûlée. **Value tip:** set 3-crs L £18.50. **Details:** off A483 at Garth, follow signs; 9 pm; jacket & tie required; no smoking; children: 7+. **Accommodation:** 19 rooms, from £130.

LLANGOLLEN, DENBIGHSHIRE 5–3A

Bryn Howel Hotel £ 34
LL20 7UW   (01978) 860331
It's not the local destination it once was, but this comfortable hotel dining room (with views over the Vale of Llangollen) can still deliver "good" results. / **Sample dishes:** smoked rabbit terrine with apricot chutney; salmon delice in lemon butter sauce; Welsh pudding with roasted plums. **Details:** on A539 towards Ruabon; 9 pm; no smoking. **Accommodation:** 36 rooms, from £95.

Corn Mill £ 26 Ⓐ
Dee Ln LL20 8PN   (01978) 869555
"A superb setting on the River Dee", is the highlight at this intriguingly-converted mill in the heart of this pretty little town; its "good pub food" is universally approved. / **Sample dishes:** melon, feta & pine kernel salad; aubergine & goats cheese with red pepper dressing; bara brith bread & butter pudding. **Details:** 9.30 pm; no smoking area; children: before 5.30 pm only.

LLANWDDYN, POWYS 4–2D

Lake Vyrnwy Hotel £ 40 Ⓐ★
Lake Vyrnwy SY10 0LY   (01691) 870692
It's not just the "superb location" which makes this Victorian hotel dining room (overlooking a huge reservoir) rather out of the ordinary; the cooking – much of it using meat and game from the hotel's own estate – is "excellent", too. / **Sample dishes:** tuna carpaccio with smoked quails eggs; pot-roasted pork with sage mash; lime pannacotta with peppered strawberries. **Value tip:** set 3-crs L £15.95. **Details:** www.lakevyrnwy.com; on B4393 at SE end of Lake Vyrnwy; 9.15 pm; no smoking. **Accommodation:** 35 rooms, from £115.

sign up for the survey at www.hardens.com

LLANWRTYD WELLS, POWYS 4–4C

Carlton House Hotel £ 42 ★
Dolecoed Rd LD5 4RA (01591) 610248
*Some say it's "hyped", but fans are in the majority when it comes
to this "somewhat eccentric", family-run venture, lauding its
"remarkable-value" Welsh cooking.* / **Sample dishes:** seared king
scallops; warm peppered beef salad; apple & Calvados sorbet.
Details: www.carltonrestaurant.com; 8.30 pm; D only, closed Sun; no Amex;
no smoking in dining room. **Accommodation:** 5 rooms, from £65.

LLYSWEN, POWYS 2–1A

Griffin Inn £ 29 🄰★
LD3 0UR (01874) 754241
*"For bar food by a log fire, you won't do better" – this ancient inn
gets only positive reports for its "simple" but "consistent" fare
served in a "cosy and friendly" setting.* / **Sample dishes:** hot smoked
salmon salad; braised lamb shank with roasted garlic; treacle tart.
Details: www.griffin-inn.co.uk; on A470; 9 pm; closed Sun D; no smoking area;
children: only at L. **Accommodation:** 7 rooms, from £70.

Llangoed Hall £ 54
LD3 0YP (01874) 754525
*"Good enough for Bill Clinton, and fine for me", says one reporter,
but otherwise this country house hotel owned by the family of the
late Laura Ashley attracts few and rather muted reports.*
/ **Sample dishes:** butternut squash velouté with smoked chicken; herb-crusted lamb
with pea purée; seared pineapple with tarragon sorbet. **Value tip:** set 3-crs L
£28.50 (Sun £25). **Details:** www.llangoedhall.com; 11m NW of Brecon on A470;
9.30 pm; jacket & tie required; no smoking in dining room; children: 8+.
Accommodation: 23 rooms, from £145.

LOCH LOMOND, WEST DUNBARTONSHIRE 9–4B

Cameron House £ 61
G83 8QZ (01389) 755565
*"Elegant surroundings" and "excellently-sourced produce"
contribute to "a superb experience" for fans of this silver service
dining room on the banks of Loch Lomond; some reporters have
their reservations, though, and the place is undoubtedly
"very expensive".* / **Sample dishes:** asparagus, leek & mushroom terrine;
lobster & langoustine with black olive pasta; banana tarte Tatin with pineapple
sorbet. **Details:** www.cameronhouse.co.uk; over Erskine Bridge to A82, follow signs
to Crianlarich; 9.45 pm; D only, closed Mon; jacket & tie required; no smoking;
children: 12+. **Accommodation:** 96 rooms, from £185.

LOCKINGTON, EAST RIDING OF YORKSHIRE 6–1A

Rockingham Arms £ 41
52 Front St YO25 9SH (01430) 810607
*A "reliable" family-run former pub, which benefits from a
"beautiful" village location.* / **Sample dishes:** spiced crab cakes; roast
Gressingham duck; glazed cherry sabayon. **Details:** between Beverley & Gt Driffield
on A164; 9.30 pm; D only, closed Mon & Sun; no Amex; children: 10+.
Accommodation: 3 rooms, from £110.

LOCKSBOTTOM, KENT   3–3B

Chapter One   £ 38   ★
Farnborough Common BR6 8NF   (01689) 854848
"It's hard to book a table at short notice", at this very popular
suburban favourite, thanks to its *"beautifully presented"* modern
cooking and its chic, metropolitan-style setting.
/ **Sample dishes:** smoked goose, walnut & raspberry salad; provençale salmon,
clam & mussel confit; apple tart & thyme ice cream. **Value tip:** set 2-crs L £16.
Details: www.chaptersrestaurants.co.uk; 2m E of Bromley on A21; 10.30 pm.

LONG CRENDON, BUCKINGHAMSHIRE   2–2D

Angel   £ 35
Bicester Rd HP18 9EE   (01844) 208268
"More a restaurant than a pub nowadays", this (rare) rural fish
specialist (*"in a quaint Chilterns village"*) can sometimes deliver
"surprisingly good" results; most – but not all – reporters find a
visit *"an extremely pleasant experience"*. / **Sample dishes:** feta,
tomato & olive gateau; duck & smoked bacon with blueberry sauce; cranberry toffee
tart. **Value tip:** set 3-crs Sun L £17.95. **Details:** 2m NW of Thame, off B4011;
9.30 pm; closed Sun D; no Amex; no smoking area. **Accommodation:** 3 rooms,
from £65.

LONG MELFORD, SUFFOLK   3–1C

Scutchers Bistro   £ 34
Westgate St CO10 9DP   (01787) 310200
"Simple" and *"consistent"* cooking, *"always using good
ingredients"*, makes this *"rather '80s-looking"* bistro a *"reliable"*
destination. / **Sample dishes:** seared scallops; roast lamb with stuffed tomatoes;
crêpes Suzette. **Details:** www.scutchers.com; 9.30 pm; closed Mon & Sun;
no smoking in dining room.

LONGRIDGE, LANCASHIRE   5–1B

The Longridge Restaurant   £ 56
104-106 Higher Rd PR3 3SY   (01772) 784969
In early autumn 2002, Paul Heathcote removed his name from
this rural restaurant, whose Michelin star 'made' him as a
northern celebrity; a much more informal approach is now
promised, together with a major refurb of the interior.
/ **Sample dishes:** herb polenta with char-grilled vegetables; crispy pork belly with
spinach & red wine; iced apricot & gingerbread parfait. **Value tip:** set 3-crs L
£16.50. **Details:** www.heathcotes.co.uk; follow signs for Jeffrey Hill; 9.30 pm; closed
Mon, Tue & Sat L; no smoking.

LONGSTOCK, HAMPSHIRE   2–3D

Peat Spade Inn   £ 29
SO20 6DR   (01264) 810612
"Much more than bar food" (including *"good vegetarian fare"*) is
served by the *"helpful and polite"* staff of this *"hospitable"* pub-
conversion, which enjoys a *"lovely"* setting in the Test Valley.
/ **Sample dishes:** creamed celeriac soup; Moroccan lamb with cumin couscous;
lemon cheesecake. **Details:** 1.25m from Stockbridge; 9 pm; closed Mon & Sun D;
no credit cards; no smoking area. **Accommodation:** 2 rooms, from £58.75.

sign up for the survey at www.hardens.com   245

LOUGHBOROUGH, LEICESTERSHIRE 5–3D

Thai House £26
5a High St LE11 2PY (01509) 260030
*"Nice for a change" – "authentic Thai fare at reasonable prices"
makes this high street oriental a consistently popular local
destination. / Details: 11 pm.*

LOW FELL, TYNE & WEAR 8–2B

Eslington Villa Hotel £32 Ⓐ
8 Station Rd NE9 6DR (0191) 487 6017
*No one doubts the "top-quality service" or the "lovely setting"
(particularly the glazed-in terrace) of this Victorian country house
hotel; by comparison, some find the food a "let-down" – perhaps
new chef David Kennedy will pep it up. / Sample dishes: smoked
haddock & chive risotto; pork & pancetta with sage & onion mash; British cheeses
with quince jelly. Value tip: set 2-crs L £11.50. Details: A1 exit for Team Valley
Retail World, then left off Eastern Avenue; 9.30 pm; closed Sat L & Sun D;
no smoking. Accommodation: 18 rooms, from £50.*

LOWER ODDINGTON, GLOUCESTERSHIRE 2–1C

The Fox Inn £27 Ⓐ
GL56 OUR (01451) 870555
*This "lovely", "picturesque" Cotswolds pub makes a "useful eating
option near Stow"; there were some gripes about the cooking this
year (mostly minor), but, on balance, "wholesome ale and food"
won continued support. / Sample dishes: smoked haddock & watercress
tart; braised lamb shank with lemon zest; steamed treacle sponge.
Details: www.foxinn.net; on A436 near Stow on the Wold; 10 pm; no Amex.
Accommodation: 3 rooms, from £58.*

LOWER PEOVER, CHESHIRE 5–2B

Bells of Peover £24
The Cobbles WA16 9PZ (01565) 722269
*A "beautiful" setting – by the church of a charming village –
has long made this "busy" inn a local destination; its "varied"
menu is still approved by most reporters, but some feel that the
place has "deteriorated" since Scottish & Newcastle took over a
couple of years ago. / Sample dishes: pâté & toast; steak & Theakstons pie;
plum & apple crumble. Details: opp St Oswald's church, off B5081; 10 pm;
no smoking area; no booking; children: before 7 pm.*

LOWER SLAUGHTER, GLOUCESTERSHIRE 2–1C

Lower Slaughter Manor £63
GL54 2HP (01451) 820456
*This "pampering" hotel has long been of note, and it can still
make an "impressive" Cotswolds destination; recent commentary
on all aspects of its operation, however, was very mixed.
/ Sample dishes: tomato tarte Tatin with scallops; pork with sage risotto & ginger
jus; plum & port jelly with rosemary ice cream. Value tip: set 3-crs L £19.95.
Details: www.lowerslaughter.co.uk; 2m from Burton-on-the-Water on A429;
9.30 pm; no smoking; children: 12+. Accommodation: 16 rooms, from £220.*

LOWER WOLVERCOTE, OXFORDSHIRE 2–2D

Trout Inn £24   🅐
195 Godstow Rd OX2 8PN (01865) 302071
"Service, what service?" – "they need more staff" at this
"very busy", "olde worlde pub", whose regular appearances on
'Inspector Morse' add to the intrinsic appeal of its "wonderful"
setting, by the Thames; the pub grub is realised to an "OK"
standard. / **Sample dishes:** salmon & broccoli fishcakes; Mediterranean chicken
with new potatoes; toffee apple bread & butter pudding. **Details:** 2m from junction
of A40 & A44; 9 pm, Fri & Sat 9.30 pm; no smoking area; no booking.

LUDLOW, SHROPSHIRE 5–4A

Ego Café Bar £26
Quality Square SY8 1AR (01584) 878000
"Delicious food" makes this "friendly" wine bar an ideal "cheap
and cheerful" stand-by. / **Sample dishes:** pork kebabs with satay sauce;
baked trout with rhubarb mayonnaise; pan-fried bananas in rum. **Details:** off Castle
Square, through timber arches; 9.30 pm; closed Sun D; no Amex; no smoking area.

Hibiscus £46   ★★
17 Corve St SY8 1DA (01584) 872325
Sometimes "phenomenal" Gallic cooking has quickly made a big
name for the most recently-established of this celebrated town's
'heavy hitters'; reservations include sometimes "small" portions,
though ("we left hungry, after seven courses"), and some find the
setting, in a 17th-century inn, rather "lifeless". / **Sample dishes:** white
onion & lime ravioli with broad beans; roast turbot with tarragon & orange; chocolate
tart with star anise. **Details:** 9.30 pm; closed Mon L, Tue L & Sun; management
declined to provide further information.

Koo £25   ★
127 Old St SY8 1NU (01584) 878462
"A hidden gem in the backstreets of Ludlow" – the "subtle and
beautiful" cooking at this "friendly" oriental can make it
"an agreeable introduction to Japanese cuisine". / **Details:** 9.45 pm;
closed Mon & Sun; no Amex.

Merchant House £40   ★★
Lower Corve St SY8 1DU (01584) 875438
"Absolutely stunning cooking worth going any distance for" has
made Shaun Hill's townhouse restaurant – and, in its wake,
the whole town – a famous foodie Mecca; the general "absence of
fuss" is a plus for most reporters, but for some a "cool" reception
contributes to a "lack of atmosphere". / **Sample dishes:** grilled sea bass
with allspice; roast pigeon with morels; Hungarian apricot trifle. **Details:** 9 pm;
closed Mon & Sun; no Amex or Switch; no smoking in dining room.

Mr Underhill's £42   ★
Dinham Wier SY8 1EH (01584) 874431
"First-rate food, even if there is no choice" (with "exceptional
puddings" attracting particular praise) wins much support for
Chris & Judy Bradley's riverside hotel and restaurant; (it also
makes "a beautiful setting for an overnight stay").
/ **Sample dishes:** smoked haddock with confit tomatoes; Perigord duck with
olives & honey; Italian bread & butter pudding. **Details:** www.mr-underhills.co.uk;
8.30 pm; closed Tue; no Amex; no smoking. **Accommodation:** 6 rooms, from £75.

Overton Grange   **£51**
Hereford Rd SY8 4AD   (01584) 873500
*Let's hope that new owners (as of July 2002) can reinvigorate the
cooking at this Edwardian house – despite its reputation,
and (some would say) "wonderful" cuisine, too many reporters
have judged it "rather dull all round" for some time.*
/ **Sample dishes:** roast scallops & langoustines with truffles; seared turbot with
salsify & roast shallots; chocolate cup with pistachio ice cream.
Details: www.overtongrangehotel.co.uk; 9.30 pm; D only; no Amex; no smoking
area. **Accommodation:** 14 rooms, from £95.

LYDFORD, DEVON   1–3C

The Dartmoor Inn   **£32**   ★
EX20 4AY   (01822) 820221
*Nowadays, this revamped ancient boozer is arguably more like "a
restaurant with a bar attached"; whatever you call it, Philip &
Karen Burgess's establishment is "an oasis" hereabouts
(the western side of the Dartmoor National Park) with "excellent"
modern cooking.* / **Sample dishes:** artichoke purée tart with baby onions;
grilled mixed fish with courgette flower fritters; Bramley apple ice cream with roasted
cob nuts. **Details:** 9 pm; closed Mon & Sun D; no Amex; no smoking in dining
room; children: 5+ at weekends.

LYDGATE, GREATER MANCHESTER   5–2B

White Hart   **£33**   ★
51 Stockport Rd OL4 4JJ   (01457) 872566
*"Both the setting and the grub are superb", at this popular
gastropub up on the moors near Oldham; "simple dishes are
cooked to perfection" (with a "wide range" of "excellent"
sausages the speciality).* / **Sample dishes:** grilled tandoori chicken with
cucumber yoghurt; calves liver with pickled cabbage & thyme; lime & raspberry
cheesecake. **Value tip:** set 3-crs L £13.95. **Details:** 2m E of Oldham on A669,
then A6050; 9.30 pm; no smoking area. **Accommodation:** 12 rooms, from £90.

LYMINGTON, HAMPSHIRE   2–4C

Egan's   **£38**   ★
Gosport St SO41 9BE   (01590) 676165
*"Good, reliable food", "well presented" and at "reasonable
prices", is already winning quite a following for John Egan's
"friendly" new bistro.* / **Sample dishes:** seafood tempura; rack of lamb with
leeks; strawberries & ice cream. **Details:** 10 pm; closed Mon & Sun; no smoking in
dining room; booking: max 6, Sat.

LYNDHURST, HAMPSHIRE   2–4C

Le Poussin at Parkhill   **£49**
Beaulieu Rd SO43 7FZ   (023) 8028 2944
*"Excellent inventive cuisine" justifies the eminent reputation of this
Georgian country house hotel for most reporters; doubters,
though, say "it's not as good as when it was located in
Brockenhurst", and complain of high prices and a rather "flat"
atmosphere.* / **Sample dishes:** salmon with cucumber salad & Avruga caviar;
rare beef with red wine sauce; hot chocolate fondant. **Details:** 9.30 pm; no smoking
in dining room; children: 10+ at D.

for updates visit www.hardens.com

MADINGLEY, CAMBRIDGESHIRE 3–1B

Three Horseshoes £37

CB3 8AB (01954) 210221

"Imaginative" (if rather "variable") cooking of the "ambitious pub" variety and a "splendid wine list" maintains the large following of this "airy" and "lively" village boozer – long a classic destination for Cambridge undergraduates and their parents. / **Sample dishes:** leek & morel tortellini with leek mousse; venison with star anise noodles & pak choy; lemon tart with cherry vodka sorbet. **Details:** 2m W of Cambridge, off A14 or M11; 9.30 pm, Fri & Sat 10 pm; closed Sun D; no smoking area.

MALMESBURY, WILTSHIRE 2–2C

Old Bell £43 Ⓐ

Abbey Rw SN16 0AG (01666) 822344

The 'oldest hotel in England' still extends the "warm" welcome its storybook charms would suggest (and children are put at their ease, too); its "old-fashioned, and atmospheric" dining room provides an enjoyable, if not a particularly gastronomic, experience. / **Sample dishes:** chicken liver crostini; Cotswold lamb shepherds pie; chocolate fondant with pistachio ice cream. **Value tip:** set 2-crs L £10. **Details:** www.oldbellhotel.com; next to Abbey; 9.30 pm; no smoking. **Accommodation:** 31 rooms, from £110.

MANCHESTER, GREATER MANCHESTER 5–2B

Manchester's restaurant scene is something of a curate's egg.

When it comes to European cooking, the city still lacks anywhere of high ambition, with the possible exceptions of the long-established Moss Nook (which is located near the Airport on the way to leafy Cheshire) and nearby Altrincham's Juniper (which has put in an uneven performance in recent years).

In the middle price ranges, however, the city centre is improving fast, and there are now three top choices. These could not be more different in style – the Restaurant Bar & Grill (slick contemporary), Lounge 10 (intimate-rococo-contemporary) and the idiosyncratic Market (happily stuck somewhere in the '70s). Many Mancunians in search of a good-quality, atmospheric venue still make the journey to West Didsbury's impressive Lime Tree. El Rincon and Croma are popular city-centre stand-bys.

Many of the city-centre outlets – Simply Heathcote's, The Lincoln, The Reform and Stock – really could be better, and there are some spectacularly awful outlets of national 'quality' chains. There are also some not-bad ones – Le Petit Blanc and Livebait are amongst the most commented-upon places in town, and mostly attract positive feedback.

The city has an impressive range of ethnic restaurants. For top-notch oriental fare, the Yang Sing – the country's most famous Chinese restaurant, and justifiably so – is supported by Little Yang Sing, New Emperor, Pacific, Pearl City, Tai Pan and Wong Chu. In Koh Samui, the city again has an excellent Thai restaurant (and a worthy successor to Chiang Rai).

Fans of the Indian subcontinent are well catered for –
but only at the cheaper end of the market – not just with
Rusholme's curry strip (*Lal Haweli*, *Punjab Tandoori*, *Tandoori
Kitchen*), but also with the likes of West Didsbury's *Great
Kathmandu* or *Gurkha Grill*.

A huge number of students helps to support a growing
number of fun and/or affordable places (*Cachumba*, *Cafe Pop*,
The Mark Addy) as well as some good veggies (most notably
Green's). The institutionalised alternative lifestyle of the Gay
Village sustains what is perhaps the UK's best gay
bar/restaurant, *Velvet*.

The Bridgewater Hall   £ 28
Lower Mosley St M2 3WS   (0161) 950 0000
*"An excellent prelude to a concert"; the menu may not have great
ambitions – "super soups and open sandwiches", for example –
but the catering at this concert hall café generally hits the right
note.* / **Sample dishes:** shredded chicken salad; roast cod with pesto gnocchi;
chocolate marquise with poached apricots. **Details:** www.bridgewater-hall.co.uk;
10.30 pm; openings affected by concert times; no smoking.

Cachumba   £ 15   ★
220 Burton Rd M20 2LW   (0161) 445 2479
*"Superb", "consistently spicy" fusion fare at very "affordable"
prices makes it worth putting up with the sometimes "grumpy"
service at this "hippified" West Didsbury BYO café.* / **Details:** 9 pm;
closed Sun D; no credit cards.

Café Pop   £ 9   A★
34-36 Oldham St M1 1JN   (0161) 237 9688
*"Huge veggie breakfasts" (including "the infamous Scooby Snack"
– served all day) are the highpoint at this "great", "time-warp"
café, in the gritty Northern Quarter.* / **Sample dishes:** tomato &
Mozzarella salad; triple-decker veggie breakfast sandwich; chocolate fudge cake.
Details: off Piccadilly Gardens; L & afternoon tea only; no credit cards; no smoking
area.

Chez Gérard   £ 29
43a Brown St M2 2JJ   (0161) 214 1120
*The "reasonable, if formulaic" northern outpost of London's
steak/frites chain has attractive basement premises in the city-
centre; its "cosy booths" are ideal for business (and even,
some find, for romance).* / **Sample dishes:** toasted goats cheese salad;
corn-fed chicken with chips; chocolate cake. **Details:** www.santeonline.co.uk; 11 pm;
closed Sun.

Croma   £ 22   A
1 Clarence St M2 4DE   (0161) 237 9799
"A cut above PizzaExpress" – comparisons between this *"busy"*
yearling and the national chain are inevitable as the owners of the
former used to be the local franchisees of the latter; a *"smart and
trendy vibe"* is the highlight, here, but *"imaginative pizzas"* are
also consistently praised.* / **Sample dishes:** goats cheese bruschetta; chicken
Caesar salad pizza; crème brûlée cheesecake. **Details:** off Albert Square; 11 pm;
no smoking area; need 6+ to book.

Darbar £18
65-67 Wilmslow Rd M14 5TB (0161) 224 4392
*"Well-executed" cooking was more consistently praised this year at this well-established Rusholme Indian; it's still not going to win any prizes for décor, though. / **Details:** 11.30 pm; no Amex; no smoking area.*

Dimitri's £31 Ⓐ
1 Campfield Avenue Arc M3 4FN (0161) 839 3319
*"Buzzing" and "lively", this "reliable" taverna — with its semi-alfresco tables in a Victorian arcade — "just keeps on going"; its "Greek tapas" are "nice to share", and "good with friends" (or children). / **Sample dishes:** chorizo salad; ribs with vegetable couscous; baklava. **Details:** www.dimitris.co.uk; near Museum of Science & Industry; 11.30 pm.*

Dukes 92 £26 Ⓐ
19-25 Castle St M3 4LZ (0161) 839 8646
*"A great choice of amazing ploughmans" — "I've never seen that much cheese on a plate" — makes this "lively" canalside Castlefield pub a top place for a not-so-light bite. / **Sample dishes:** roast tomato soup; ciabatta with bacon & pesto; hot fudge cake. **Details:** off Deansgate; 8 pm; no Amex.*

East £23
52-54 Faulkner St M1 4SH (0161) 236 1188
*Raymond Wong opened this conventionally-styled Chinatown Chinese in the summer of 2002 — he's also the man behind the Pacific, so this new place could well be one to watch. / **Details:** www.theeastrestaurant.co.uk; 11 pm; no smoking area.*

Eighth Day Café £10
Sidney St M1 7DU (0161) 273 4878
*This "original" "veggie haven", near the University, is set to move into swanky new premises in 2003; for the present, it's squatting in temporary digs, just round the corner. / **Sample dishes:** Armenian lentil soup; vegan pâté with pitta bread & salad; vegan chocolate cake. **Details:** www.eighth-day.co.uk; 6.15 pm; closed Sat D & Sun; no smoking.*

Francs £28
2 Goose Grn WA14 1DW (0161) 941 3954
*"Never brilliant, never bad" — this "uncomplicated" Altrincham fixture provides a "lively" setting for some "tasty French grub"; a Salford Quays branch opened in 2002 (tel 0161 877 7702). / **Sample dishes:** salmon dauphinoise; chicken in coconut & lime; chocolate praline tartlet. **Value tip:** set 3-crs L £8.50. **Details:** www.francs-altrincham.com; 10.30 pm, Fri & Sat 11 pm; no smoking area.*

French Restaurant £27
25 The Downs WA14 2QD (0161) 941 3355
*This comfortable, suburban establishment has "slipped" in recent years; it remains an "old favourite" for some, though, and fans praise its "good-value" set menus. / **Sample dishes:** wild mushrooms in garlic; spicy penne with chicken; crème brûlée. **Value tip:** set 2-crs pre-theatre £7. **Details:** 10 pm; closed Mon, Tue-Sat D only, Sun open L & D; no smoking in dining room.*

Great Kathmandu £20 ★
140 Burton Rd M20 1JQ (0161) 434 6413
*"More distinctive than your average Indian, and very cheap" — this West Didsbury Nepalese does "the most original curry in town", according to its loyal and widespread fan club. / **Details:** near Withington hospital; midnight.*

Green's £ 27 ★
43 Lapwing Ln M20 2NT   (0161) 434 4259
*The "consistently high" standards of "the best veggie in town"
draw "many meat-eaters" to this café-like BYO West Didsbury
destination – across the board, it's one of the most satisfactory
places in town. / **Sample dishes:** feta, watermelon & cucumber salad;
aubergine & potato Massaman curry; chocolate & honeycomb mocha pot.
Value tip: set 2-crs L £6.95. **Details:** 4m S of city centre; 10.30 pm; closed
Mon L & Sat L; no Amex.*

The Greenhouse £ 17
331 Great Western St M14 4AN   (0161) 224 0730
*"An amazing choice of very tasty and hearty vegetarian and
vegan dishes" is praised by fans of this "cosy and friendly" fixture,
occupying a front room in a Rusholme end-of-terrace house.
/ **Sample dishes:** houmous & pitta bread; peppers stuffed with cashews & pilau
rice; knickerbocker glory. **Details:** www.dineveggie.com; 9.30 pm; closed Aug;
no Amex; no smoking area at L, no smoking at D.*

The Grinch £ 24 🐀
5-7 Chapel Walks, off Cross St M2 1HN   (0161) 907 3210
*"An old favourite that doesn't disappoint" – this "groovy" (going-
on-grungy) city-centre café bar is a small but "buzzy" haven,
whose "safe" snacks include some "good pizza".
/ **Sample dishes:** crispy duck & Japanese cucumber salad; grilled chilli chicken
Caesar salad; marshmallow ice cream & chocolate fudge sauce.
Details: www.grinch.co.uk; 10.30 pm; no smoking area.*

Gurkha Grill £ 18 ★★
198 Burton Rd M20 1LH   (0161) 445 3461
*"It's shabby but nothing beats the Gurkha" – this "exceptional"
Didsbury Nepalese may be "small", but it offers "brilliant
subcontinental food" that's "a match for any of its better-known
competitors". / **Details:** 11.30 pm, Fri & Sat 12.30 am; D only; no Amex.*

Hard Rock Café £ 29 ✗
Corporation St M4 2BS   (0161) 831 6700
*Perhaps it is "good for kids", but this "corny" theme-joint
continues to attract criticism for its "in yer face" service and
sometimes "atrocious" food – it's not a patch on the London
original. / **Sample dishes:** nachos & dips; hickory BBQ bacon cheeseburger &
fries; hot fudge brownie. **Details:** www.hardrock.com; 11 pm; no smoking area;
no booking.*

Jamfish £ 30 ✗
28-32 Greenwood St WA14 1RZ   (0161) 928 6677
*"Their motto should be, 'Pretentious? Moi?'" – this "cool"-looking
Altrincham bar/restaurant (featuring regular live music) takes flak
from most reporters for its "disappointing" standards.
/ **Sample dishes:** tomato risotto cakes; deep-fried cod with pesto butter; rhubarb
crumble. **Value tip:** set 2-crs L £9.50. **Details:** www.jamfish.co.uk; 10 pm;
closed Mon.*

Juniper £ 47
21 The Downs WA14 2QD   (0161) 929 4008
*"It's on the up again", say advocates of Paul Kitching's "low-key"
Altrincham foodie haunt, which is hailed as "Greater Manchester's
best restaurant" by some reporters; portions are rather nouvelle
for some tastes, though, as are the sometimes "clever, clever"
combinations. / **Sample dishes:** scallops with curried pea sauce; lamb with
raisins & sweetbreads in espresso sauce; lemon tart with Florida fruit cocktail.
Value tip: set 2-crs L £14. **Details:** 10 pm; closed Mon, Sat L & Sun; no smoking.*

Koh Samui £26 ★★
16 Princess St M1 4NB (0161) 237 9511
"Undoubtedly Manchester's finest Thai restaurant", this Didsbury
newcomer has been a worthy successor to Chiang Rai (RIP),
and its "excellent" cooking attracts notably consistent reports.
/ **Details:** www.kohsamuirestaurant.co.uk; opp City Art Gallery; 11.30 pm; closed
Sat L & Sun L.

Kro Bar £18
325 Oxford Rd M1 7ED (0161) 274 3100
"The best breakfast in Manchester, served all day" is a highlight
at this "lively" and "pleasant" spot, near the University –
"a Danish bar serving a varied menu at bargain prices"; Kro 2
(also on Oxford Rd, tel 0161 236 1048) opened in May 2002,
and there's a third branch in the Manchester Museum.
/ **Sample dishes:** smoked fish chowder; African-spiced chicken with coconut rice;
hot chocolate fudge cake. **Details:** www.kro.co.uk; 11 pm; no Amex;
children: 18+ only.

Lal Haweli £20 ★
68-72 Wilmslow Rd M14 (0161) 248 9700
"It gets very busy and cramped", but this lesser-known Rusholme
Indian pleases a small fan club, for whom it's a curry strip
favourite. / **Details:** 1.30 am; no smoking area.

Lead Station £24
99 Beech Rd M21 9EQ (0161) 881 5559
"Still going strong"; "good food" that's "interesting enough for
adults and obvious enough for children", and a "lively"
atmosphere make this "stylish" Chorlton café/bar an ever-popular
destination, particularly for breakfast and brunch.
/ **Sample dishes:** baked goats cheese with honey; Spanish lamb casserole with
chorizo & mash; Belgian chocolate cheesecake. **Value tip:** set 2-crs pre-theatre
£7.95. **Details:** 9.30 pm, Thu-Sat 10 pm ; no booking.

Lemongrass £28
19 Copson St M20 3HE (0161) 434 2345
Enthusiasm for this "quirky" Withington oriental is ebbing;
some still praise its "wide range of authentic Thai food", but there
were too many reports this year of lacklustre cooking, and of
service that's sometimes plain "abusive". / **Details:** 10.30 pm; D only;
no Amex.

The Lime Tree £32 𝔸★
8 Lapwing Ln M20 2WS (0161) 445 1217
"Happy", "relaxing" and "unassuming"; this mega-popular
Didsbury restaurant manages to be both "lovely and romantic"
and "formal enough for business" – as a consistent all-rounder,
it is without compare in Manchester and its environs.
/ **Sample dishes:** peppered tuna carpaccio; fillet steak with black pepper & cream
sauce; Baileys cheesecake with honeycomb ice cream. **Value tip:** set 2-crs L &
pre-theatre £10.95. **Details:** www.thelimetree.com; near Withington hospital;
10.30 pm; closed Mon L & Sat L; no smoking area.

The Lincoln £40
1 Lincoln Sq M2 5LN (0161) 834 9000
This "popular business lunch venue" continues to divide opinion –
fans say it's an all-round "enjoyable" destination, while critics find
it a "stuffy" place, whose "standard" modern brasserie fare is
"pricey" for what it is. / **Sample dishes:** Moroccan beef salad; tandoori
monkfish with spinach & raita; spotted dick with custard ice cream. **Value tip:** set
2-crs L & pre-theatre £12.50. **Details:** opp Manchester Evening News building;
10.30 pm, Fri & Sat 11 pm; closed Sat L & Sun D.

Little Yang Sing £ 25 ★★

17 George St M1 4HE (0161) 228 7722

"Newly refurbished, and better than ever", says one of the many supporters of this (now much expanded) oriental, on the Chinatown site of the original Yang Sing; its standards – including "great dim sum" – are broadly on a par with Big Brother, though some do find it a touch "impersonal". / **Details:** 11.30 pm.

Livebait £ 29

22 Lloyd St M2 5WA (0161) 817 4110

"There's a lack of competition for fish restaurants in Manchester", and a large number of locals report "surprisingly good" results ("for a group") at this city-centre chain outpost; the setting, though, is rather "cold". / **Sample dishes:** *Mediterranean fish soup; lobster with new potato salad; pannacotta & strawberries.* **Value tip:** *set 2-crs L £11.50.* **Details:** *www.santeonline.co.uk; 10.30 pm; closed Sun; no smoking area.*

Lounge 10 £ 32 A★

10 Tib Ln M2 4JB
(0161) 834 1331

Décor whose opulence "defies belief" has allowed this "very intimate" newcomer to make a big splash; appearances might lead you to think that "it's a place to be seen, not eat", but the cooking is surprisingly "imaginative". / **Sample dishes:** *goats cheese with seaweed & chilli dressing; salt & pepper duck with onion bhaji & plum sauce; white chocolate mousse.* **Details:** *www.lounge10manchester.com; 11 pm.*

Love Saves The Day £ 21 A★

Smithfield Buildings, Tib St M4 1LA (0161) 832 0777

This "lovely little deli" is applauded for bringing some "New York style" to downtown Manchester; "lovely home-made soups" and "consistently good coffee" get a particular thumbs-up.
/ **Sample dishes:** *Cheshire ham & cheeses with picalilli; sausages with bacon bubble 'n' squeak; sticky toffee pudding.* **Details:** *www.lovesavestheday.co.uk; 7 pm; closed Sun; no smoking.*

The Lowry £ 28

Pier 8, Salford Quays M50 3AZ (0161) 876 2121

Reports on the restaurant in the impressive new Salford Quays arts centre remain very mixed; it's undoubtedly "convenient", though, "if you're going to the theatre". / **Sample dishes:** *sea bass & salmon millefeuille; venison sausages with herb mash; praline crème brûlée.* **Value tip:** *set 2-crs L £10.95.* **Details:** *www.thelowry.com; 10 pm; closed Mon D & Sun D; no smoking.*

Malmaison £ 33

Piccadilly M1 3AQ (0161) 278 1000

"Sometimes good, sometimes poor, sometimes very noisy" – this fashionable boutique-hotel brasserie can deliver "impressive" results, but it can also seem "overhyped" and "boring" too.
/ **Sample dishes:** *smoked salmon with lemon; roast spring lamb with Dijon crust; bitter chocolate tart.* **Details:** *www.malmaison.com; near Piccadilly Station; 10.45 pm; no smoking area.* **Accommodation:** *167 rooms, from £120.*

The Mark Addy £ 16 ★

Stanley St M3 5EJ (0161) 832 4080

"Unpretentious but brilliant" – the "cheese, cheese and cheese" formula (plus the odd bit of pâté) makes this simple subterranean spot, with river views, a unanimously popular destination.
/ **Sample dishes:** *chive & onion cheese with bread; duck pâté & salad; no puddings.* **Details:** *9.30 pm; no Amex.*

The Market £ 34   A ★
104 High St M4 1HQ (0161) 834 3743
"Always good, always changing, always welcoming"; this "quirky" and "homely" city-centre "gem" – where "huge" portions of "interesting" English fare are served on ancient china – remains a much-loved local favourite. / **Sample dishes:** *potato ravioli with mint; Parmesan turkey with red pepper confit; banana & passion fruit pavlova.* **Details:** *www.market-restaurant.com; 10 pm; open only Wed-Sat for D; closed for a week at Easter & Xmas.*

Metropolitan £ 25   A
2 Lapwing Ln M20 2WS (0161) 374 9559
"Packed most nights, but usually worth the wait" – this large but "cosy" Withington gastropub serves up "tasty food" (including "the best burgers") to a "trendy" crowd. / **Sample dishes:** *Stilton fritters with lemongrass dressing; pork & leek sausages with apple mash; sticky toffee pudding.* **Details:** *near Withington hospital; 9.30 pm.*

Le Mont
Urbis Science Museum £ 43
Cathedral Gdns M4 (0161) 605 8282
Given that it's not only in a museum but also has a view, one expects the worst, culinarily speaking, of this impressively-sited new restaurant, which opened in the summer of 2002; somewhat surprisingly however, a post-survey correspondent speaks of initially "excellent" results. / **Sample dishes:** *creamy white onion & cider soup with cheese croutons; grilled & roasted Cumbrian lamb with vegetables; cinnamon poached pear with ice cream.* **Details:** *www.urbis.org.uk; 10.30 pm; closed Sat L & Sun; no smoking area.*

Moss Nook £ 50   ★
Ringway Rd M22 5WD (0161) 437 4778
Celebrating three decades in the same ownership (two of them with the same chef), this "cosy" and "old-fashioned, but not stuffy" establishment near Manchester Airport provides "surprisingly" "excellent" (if pricey) cooking.
/ **Sample dishes:** *twice-baked cheese & chive soufflé; beef with foie gras pâté & rosti; crème brûlée.* **Value tip:** *set 3-crs L £18.50.* **Details:** *on B5166, 1m from Manchester airport; 9.30 pm; closed Mon, Sat L & Sun; children: 11+.*

Mr Thomas's Chop House £ 31   A
52 Cross St M2 7AR (0161) 832 2245
This "amazing, unspoilt Victorian chophouse" – an impressively tiled bar/restaurant – offers "traditional and solid lunchtime fare" that's a great favourite with the business community; on Saturdays, it becomes quite a "cool" destination.
/ **Sample dishes:** *black pudding, egg & smoked bacon salad; roast cod with bubble 'n' squeak; jam sponge with custard.* **Details:** *L only; closed Sun.*

Mumbo £ 25   A
35a King St M2 (0161) 834 8871
"The tea-house with everything" – this sophisticated café in the heart of Manchester's trendy shops does indeed have it all, including a sweet (and wholly unexpected) top-floor terrace.
/ **Sample dishes:** *smoked salmon blinis; goats cheese bruschetta with Caesar salad; bread & butter pudding.* **Details:** *www.mumbos.com; 6.45 pm; no booking, Sat & Sun.*

New Bouchon £ 26
63 Bridge St M3 3BQ (0161) 832 9393
This "authentic" and very "traditional" Gallic bistro, not far from Kendal's, is an "intimate" place offering "well-made" dishes; its standards come as "a pleasant surprise" to most first-time reporters. / **Sample dishes:** Burgundy snails with garlic confit; beef with Applewood dauphinoise; profiteroles. **Value tip:** set 2-crs L £11.95. **Details:** 10 pm; closed Mon & Sun; no smoking.

New Emperor £ 23 ★★
52-56 George St M1 4HF (0161) 228 2883
"Excellent dim sum" – and "exquisite" cuisine generally – is hailed by the small but enthusiastic fan club of this Chinatown spot; service is "first-class" too. / **Details:** www.newemperor.co.uk; 11.30 pm.

Nico Central £ 35 ✗
2 Mount St M60 2DS (0161) 236 6488
"Appalling" – this celebrity-branded city-centre brasserie was again slammed by a majority of reporters for its "poor and pretentious" standards. / **Sample dishes:** marinated tuna with beetroot tartare; breaded pork with caramelised apple mash; pineapple tarte Tatin with coconut ice cream. **Value tip:** set 2-crs L & pre-theatre £11.50. **Details:** www.trpplc.com; opp St Peter's Square; 10.30 pm; closed Sat L & Sun; no smoking area.

The Nose £ 20
6 Lapwing Ln M20 8WS (0161) 445 3653
"Great soups and sandwiches" or "simple, well-prepared breakfasts" are the kinds of "snacky" food this "busy" and "happy" West Didsbury bar/restaurant does well; there's also a "great selection of wines". / **Sample dishes:** Welsh rarebit; mixed fish kebabs; sticky toffee pudding. **Details:** between Palatine Road & Withington hospital; 9.30 pm; no smoking area; need 10+ to book.

The Ox £ 25
71 Liverpool Rd M3 4NQ (0161) 839 7740
"Above-average pub food" in "huge portions", plus a "wide selection of beers", wins enduring popularity for this "busy" but "relaxing" Castlefield boozer. / **Sample dishes:** teriyaki beef; roast rack of lamb; toffee & pecan cheesecake. **Details:** www.theox.co.uk; 10.30 pm; no Amex; no smoking area. **Accommodation:** 9 rooms, from £44.95.

Pacific £ 29 A★
58-60 George St M1 4HF (0161) 228 6668
This "next-generation" Chinatown two-year-old continues to make waves with its "sophisticated", "light" and "modern" setting and "high-quality" cooking; the Thai upstairs attracts a fraction more attention than the Chinese section below. / **Value tip:** set 2-crs L £7.50. **Details:** www.pacific-restaurant-manchester.co.uk; 10.45 pm; no smoking area; children: 3+.

Palmiro £ 27
197 Upper Chorlton Rd M16 OBH (0161) 860 7330
Cooking which "used to be fantastic" made this "very minimalist and unusual", two-year-old Italian (in Whalley Range) a huge hit on opening; it seems to be "getting cocky", though, and there is a clear feeling that "it's not been so good of late". / **Sample dishes:** slow-roasted tomato risotto; char-grilled sea bass with salmoriglio sauce; poached pears & caramel with polenta. **Details:** www.palmiro.net; 10.30 pm; D only.

Pearl City £ 22 ★

33 George St M1 4PH (0161) 228 7683
"The best everyday Chinese in Chinatown"; the cooking at this vast "old favourite" is "consistently of a high standard".
/ **Details:** *3 am, Fri & Sat 4 am, Sun midnight.*

Le Petit Blanc £ 31

55 King St M2 4LQ (0161) 832 1000
"High standards" of brasserie fare and "friendly" service have made Raymond Blanc's city-centre yearling one of the top options in town (particularly for business); for heretics though, it is "relying on a famous name". / **Sample dishes:** *snail & spinach fricassée; roast chicken with braised leeks & morels; lemon tart with raspberry sorbet.*
Value tip: *set 2-crs L & pre-theatre £12.50.* **Details:** *www.lepetitblanc.co.uk; 11 pm; no smoking area.*

Punjab Tandoori £ 18 ★★

177 Wilmslow Rd M14 5AP (0161) 225 2960
"Dosas to die for" are a highlight of the "wonderful vegetarian choice" (meat dishes are also available) at what reporters rate as "the best restaurant on the Curry Mile"; staff "friendliness" (including to children) is a highlight. / **Details:** *11.45 pm; no Amex.*

The Reform £ 47 ✕

Spring Gdns, King St M2 4ST (0161) 839 9966
"Popular with Man U footballers and Coronation Street actors", it may be, but this kitsch city-centre restaurant – housed in an impressive Victorian club building – strikes too many reporters as simply "awful" and "overpriced". / **Sample dishes:** *king prawn, pancetta & artichoke salad; fillet steak with Madeira jus; pannetone bread & butter pudding.* **Value tip:** *set 3-crs L £14.50.* **Details:** *11 pm; closed Sun.*

The Restaurant Bar & Grill £ 32 Ⓐ★

14 John Dalton St
M2 5JR (0161) 839 1999
A "trendy vibe" has helped establish this "buzzing" city-centre yearling as "without doubt the best place in town for people-watching"; the cooking doesn't aim to push the culinary frontiers too far, but it is "enjoyable" and "well-prepared".
/ **Sample dishes:** *spicy shrimp risotto; crispy duck with pear & watercress salad; bread & butter pudding.* **Details:** *10.45 pm; no smoking area; booking: max 8 at weekends.*

Rhodes & Co £ 35

Waters Reach M17 1WS (0161) 868 1900
It's handy enough for Old Trafford, but what Gary Rhodes is doing putting his name to this "clinical" venture – with its "unexceptional" fare and its "poor" service – remains something of a mystery. / **Sample dishes:** *stuffed Piedmont red peppers; salmon fishcakes with lemon butter sauce; lemon rice pudding.* **Details:** *next to Golden Tulip Hotel at Old Trafford; 9.45 pm; closed Sat L & Sun L; booking: max 8.*

El Rincon £ 26 Ⓐ

Longworth St, off St John's St M3 4BQ (0161) 839 8819
"Bueno! – an authentic piece of Spain in heart of Manchester"; this "friendly" and "well-run" basement tapas bar near Deansgate attracts nothing but praise for its "solid" cooking and its "very lively" atmosphere. / **Sample dishes:** *prawns 'pil-pil'; grilled sea bass with lemon; cheesecake.* **Details:** *off Deansgate; 11.30 pm.*

River Room Marco Pierre White
Lowry Hotel £ 37 ✕
50 Dearman's Pl, Chapel Wharf M3 5LH (0161) 827 4041
*This northerly outpost of the MPW-branded empire has stylish
quarters in a new luxury hotel; standards, however, are "ordinary"
in the extreme.* / **Sample dishes:** *lobster minestrone; grilled calves liver &
bacon; almond & fig ice cream.* **Details:** *www.roccofortehotels.com; 10.30 pm.*
Accommodation: *165 rooms, from £209.*

Sangam £ 14
13-15 Wilmslow Rd M14 5TB (0161) 257 3922
*This "consistent" subcontinental undoubtedly offers "good-value",
"tasty" scoff – for some it's the favourite destination on
Rusholme's street of a thousand curries.* / **Details:** *www.sangam.co.uk;
midnight; no smoking area.*

Shere Khan £ 19
52 Wilmslow Rd M14 5TQ (0161) 256 2624
*"Production-line service at the weekend" – when the place is
"absolutely packed" – is the chief gripe about this bright
establishment, prominently located on the Curry Mile; it may not
be the best, but it is very "consistent".* / **Details:** *www.skrestaurant.com;
midnight; no smoking area.*

Shimla Pinks £ 28
Dolefield, Crown Sq M3 3EN (0161) 831 7099
*"A bit classier than your usual curry house" – food standards have
recovered somewhat at this city-centre Indian, known (like others
in the chain) for its "new approach to Indian cooking".*
/ **Value tip:** *set 3-crs L £8.95.* **Details:** *opp Crown Courts; 11 pm, Sat & Sun
11.30 pm; closed Sat L & Sun L.*

Siam Orchid £ 26
54 Portland St M1 4QU (0161) 236 1388
*"Good Thai food, well served" makes it worth remembering this
oriental stand-by, behind Piccadilly station.* / **Value tip:** *set 2-crs L £6.*
Details: *11.30 pm; closed Sat L & Sun L.*

Simply Heathcote's £ 30 ✕
Jackson Row, Deansgate M2 5WD (0161) 835 3536
*"Great expectations are left wanting" at Paul Heathcote's
"seriously disappointing" city-centre brasserie – it received a
thorough drubbing from reporters for its "poncy and overpriced"
cooking, its "soulless" décor and its "we-know-best" service.*
/ **Sample dishes:** *ham hock terrine; roast lamb with couscous; rice pudding with
vanilla ice cream.* **Details:** *near Opera House; 10 pm, Sat 11 pm; no smoking in
dining room.*

Stock £ 39 🅐
4 Norfolk St M2 1DW (0161) 839 6644
*If you're looking for a setting with "elegant sophistication",
this "beautiful" building – the city's former stock exchange –
may well be the place; even some of those who say the Italian
cooking is "good", though, feel it's "not worth the prices".*
/ **Sample dishes:** *linguine with crayfish tails; calves liver in balsamic vinegar sauce;
caramelised peach tartlet.* **Value tip:** *set 2-crs L £9.*
Details: *www.stockrestaurant.co.uk; 10.30 pm; closed Sun.*

Tai Pan   £ 24   ★

81-97 Upper Brook St M13 9TX   (0161) 273 2798
This vast oriental some way from the city-centre is "always full of Chinese families"; "the food's great" (with dim sum especially commended), but some find the setting rather "hangar-like". / **Details:** 11 pm.

Tampopo   £ 23   ★

16 Albert Sq M2 5PF   (0161) 819 1966
"Manchester's original noodle bar" makes an ideal city-centre pit stop for a "cheap", "reliable" and "tasty" south east Asian meal, "swiftly" served; it now has a sibling in the Trafford Centre (tel 0161 747 8878). / **Value tip:** set 2-crs L £5.95. **Details:** 11 pm; no Amex; no smoking; need 7+ to book.

Tandoori Kitchen   £ 18   ★

131-133 Wilmslow Rd M14 5AW   (0161) 224 2329
"Some dreamy Persian dishes" add interest to the mainly Indian menu at this "old favourite" of the curry mile; even some who say "it used to be better" think it's still "the best", and it is "very inexpensive" (especially as you can BYO). / **Details:** midnight; no smoking area.

That Café   £ 34   ★

1031-1033 Stockport Rd M19 2TB   (0161) 432 4672
This cosy and well-established fixture comes as a surprise in its unpromising Levenshulme location; it's a "special little haunt" according to its dedicated fan club, on account of its "consistent" and "interesting" cooking. / **Sample dishes:** pan-fried squid & king prawn salad; beef fillet with celeriac rosti; passion fruit tart. **Value tip:** set 2-crs pre-theatre & Sun L £9.95. **Details:** www.thatcafe.co.uk; on A6 between Manchester & Stockport; 10.30 pm; closed Mon, Tue-Sat D only, closed Sun D; no Amex; no smoking area.

This & That   £ 5   ★

3 Soap St M4 1EW   (0161) 832 4971
You get "excellent food" at "bargain prices" – you "couldn't spend a fiver", if you tried – at this "shabby" but "fantastic-value" Indian canteen; the "rice-plus-three" (doled out "cafeteria-style") is the top tip. / **Details:** 5 pm; closed Sun D; no credit cards.

Velvet   £ 23   Ⓐ ★

2 Canal St M1 3HE   (0161) 236 9003
"Still the best the Gay Village has to offer"; this "funky" fixture is not just notable for "the fish in the floor" and the "TV in the toilets" – its "interesting" snacks are "always good". / **Sample dishes:** soup of the day; steak with pepper sauce & chips; chocolate fudge cake. **Value tip:** set 2-crs Sun L £7.95. **Details:** 10 pm, Fri & Sat midnight; children: not permitted.

Wong Chu   £ 19   ★

63 Faulkner St M1 4FF   (0161) 236 2346
"No frills, no dragons, no tacky pictures, just fantastic big bowls of noodle soup and so on"; some find it "off-putting" from the outside, but this Chinatown chowhouse is a top "cheap and cheerful" recommendation. / **Details:** midnight; no Amex.

sign up for the survey at www.hardens.com

Woodstock Tavern £23
139 Barlow Moor Rd M20 2DY   (0161) 448 7951
"Interesting" dishes (including exotic meats, for example) add interest to a visit to this *"lively"* Chorlton-cum-Hardy boozer. / **Sample dishes:** salt & pepper chicken wings; kangaroo steak with port & mushroom sauce; strawberry daquiri cheesecake. **Value tip:** set 2-crs Sun L £10. **Details:** 7.30 pm; no Amex; no smoking area; no booking; children: weekends only (until 8 pm).

Yang Sing £29 ★★
34 Princess St M1 4JY   (0161) 236 2200
The *"extraordinary tastes, textures and combinations"* of Harry Yeung's Cantonese cuisine continue to earn this large and flashy Chinatown veteran acclaim as *"the best Chinese in the UK"*; *"amazing banquets"* win particular praise – *"it's a good idea to have them design them for you"*. / **Details:** www.yang-sing.com; 11.45 pm, Fri & Sat 12.15 am; smoking discouraged.

Zinc Bar & Grill £36 ✗
The Triangle, Hanging Ditch M4 3ES   (0870) 333 4333
"A triumph of style over content"; this branch of Conran's depressingly lacklustre nationwide chain of brasseries – in the Triangle shopping mall – predictably *"doesn't live up to the hype"*, and offers a *"very poor"* all-round experience. / **Sample dishes:** fried squid with chilli; lamb kebabs with bulgar wheat salad; lemon tart. **Value tip:** set 2-crs L £12.50. **Details:** www.conran.com; 10 pm.

MANNINGTREE, ESSEX 3–2C

Stour Bay Café £30
39-43 High St CO11 1AH   (01206) 396687
This popular bistro continues to win majority support for its decent cooking, *"cosy"* atmosphere and *"personal"* approach; some fans of its previous regime (which ended two or three years ago) find it *"disappointing, by comparison"*, though. / **Sample dishes:** crab bisque with whisky; seared tuna with bean & tomato salad; pecan pie. **Value tip:** set 2-crs L £10.50. **Details:** www.allaboutessex.co.uk; 9.30 pm; closed Mon & Sun D; no Amex; no smoking.

MARKET HARBOROUGH, LEICESTERSHIRE 5–4D

Han's £28 ★
29 St Mary's Rd LE16 7DS   (01858) 462288
"Very good food" and a *"smart"* ambience continue to make this town-centre Chinese a cut above the norm. / **Details:** 11 pm; closed Sat L & Sun.

MARLOW, BUCKINGHAMSHIRE 3–3A

Compleat Angler £57 ✗
Marlow Bridge SL7 1RG   (0870) 400 8100
"Afternoon tea in the garden overlooking the Thames still impresses visitors", but otherwise too many reporters find this famous (and *"stuffy"*) hotel something of a *"rip-off"*; *"terrible"* service is a particular bugbear. / **Sample dishes:** smoked haddock & potato terrine; roast duck with marinated white cabbage; Baileys & honey parfait. **Value tip:** set 3-crs L £26.50. **Details:** www.macdonald-hotels.co.uk; 10.30 pm; no smoking area. **Accommodation:** 64 rooms, from £225.

Danesfield House Hotel £60
Henley Rd SL7 2EY (01628) 891010
"Beautiful surroundings" commend this wedding cake-style
Victorian country house hotel to some reporters; prices are very
high though, and the food is *"good… but not that good"*.
/ **Sample dishes:** cauliflower pannacotta with oysters; venison with artichoke &
shallot fricassée; apricot & ginger crème brûlée. **Value tip:** set 2-crs L £18.50.
Details: www.danesfieldhouse.co.uk; 3m outside Marlow on the A4155; 10 pm;
no smoking. **Accommodation:** 87 rooms, from £205.

The Vanilla Pod £37 ★
31 West St SL7 2LS
(01628) 898101

"Off to a good start" – chef Michael Macdonald has quite a CV,
and his *"new and exciting"* venture delivers *"very good quality"*
modern French cuisine that's served in a small, attractively
decked-out dining room. / **Sample dishes:** scallops with vanilla-poached
pears; sea bass with Szechuan sauce; bitter chocolate fondant.
Details: www.thevanillapod.co.uk; 10 pm; closed Mon L & Sun; smoking in bar only.

MASHAM, NORTH YORKSHIRE 8–4B
Floodlite £28 ★
7 Silver St HG4 4DX (01765) 689000
"A superb range of seasonal dishes" – including *"excellent gamey
game"* and *"exceptional puds"* – wins consistent praise for
Charles Flood's Dales fixture. / **Sample dishes:** Arbroath smokie soufflé;
chicken stuffed with banana & curry sauce; strawberry shortbread. **Value tip:** set
2-crs L £11.50. **Details:** 9 pm; closed Mon, Tue L, Wed L, Thu L & Sun D;
no Switch; no smoking area; booking essential, Sun.

MATFEN, TYNE & WEAR 8–2B
Matfen Hall, Library Restaurant £37 Ⓐ
NE20 0RH (01661) 886500
This *"grand"* country house hotel is just a short drive from
Newcastle; even its critics agree the setting is *"lovely"*, but the
cooking – generally *"competent"* – can sometimes misfire.
/ **Sample dishes:** seafood & saffron chowder; char-grilled steak with sautéed
mushrooms; plum & thyme crème brûlée. **Details:** www.matfenhall.com; 9.30 pm;
D only, except Sun open L & D; no smoking; booking: max 10.
Accommodation: 31 rooms, from £120.

MAWDESLEY, LANCASHIRE 5–1A
Red Lion £22
68 New St L40 2QP (01704) 822999
"Pub food with a bit of panache" makes this a boozer of some
note, in spite of standards which can be rather *"variable"*.
/ **Sample dishes:** scallops in pancetta with pesto risotto; rack of lamb with black
pudding & Guinness sauce; Bakewell tart with clotted cream. **Details:** 9 pm; closed
Mon & Tue; no smoking.

MELBOURNE, DERBYSHIRE 5–3C
Bay Tree £35
4 Potter St DE73 1DW (01332) 863358
"Good food in pleasant surroundings" is the upshot of most
commentary on this *"consistent"* restaurant, in an ancient former
coaching inn; by local standards, though, it is *"quite expensive"*.
/ **Sample dishes:** minted melon with lemongrass granita; pork tenderloin with goats
cheese gnocchi; Canadian pancakes with maple syrup. **Value tip:** set 3-crs L £16.50
(Sun £18.50). **Details:** www.baytreerestaurant.co.uk; 10 pm; closed Mon & Sun D;
no smoking area.

Ruskins £ 34 Ⓐ ★
2 Blanchcroft DE73 1GG (01332) 864170
"An amazing choice of food, and all of it amazing" — it's hardly surprising that it is becoming "harder and harder to get a table" at Penny Lee's "small" and "cosy" cottage-restaurant, whose BYO policy helps make it "great value". / **Sample dishes:** *crab thermidor; crispy duck in plum & ginger sauce; summer pudding.* **Details:** *9.30 pm; closed Mon, Tue, Wed, Thu L & Sun; no credit cards; booking essential.*

MELBOURN, CAMBRIDGESHIRE 3–1B

Pink Geranium £ 53
25 Station Rd SG8 6DX (01763) 260215
Following Mark Jordan's succession to Steven Saunders at this pretty, thatched restaurant, reporters' esteem for the place has declined — even some who say his new regime is "very good" note that it's "very expensive", and others say the place is simply "over-rated". / **Sample dishes:** *niçoise vegetable terrine with tapenade dressing; boudin of lobster with new potatoes; crème brûlée with raspberry coulis.* **Value tip:** *set 3-crs Sun L £22.50.* **Details:** *www.pinkgeranium.co.uk; off A10, 2nd exit (opp church); 10 pm; closed Mon & Sun D; no smoking.*

Sheene Mill £ 45
Station Rd SG8 6DX (01763) 261393
It has a "very pretty setting", but there are rather too many reports of "average" cooking and lacklustre service at this converted riverside mill, where TV chef Steven Saunders now presides. / **Sample dishes:** *crispy duck spring rolls with sweet chilli sauce; wild venison with mushroom risotto; banana tarte Tatin.* **Details:** *www.sheenemill.co.uk; off A10, 10m S of Cambridge; 10 pm; closed Sun D; no smoking before 9.30 pm.* **Accommodation:** *9 rooms, from £70.*

MELLOR, CHESHIRE 5–2B

Oddfellows Arms £ 25
73 Moor End Rd SK6 5PT (0161) 449 7826
This "old inn" with "good ales" is praised by local fans for its "extensive menus" of "superb" fare; it can be "variable", though. / **Sample dishes:** *soused herrings with mustard sour cream; Catalan pork tenderloin with basil ragu; frosted peach schnapps cheesecake.* **Details:** *7m S of Stockport; 9.30 pm; closed Mon D & Sun D; no Amex; no smoking in dining room; book for D & Sun L only.*

MELMERBY, CUMBRIA 8–3A

Shepherd's Inn £ 21 Ⓐ ★
CA10 1HF (0870) 745 3383
"A real gem"; after over 20 years, the word's well and truly out about Martin Baucutt's "super country pub", whose "consistently good" all-round standards continue to draw the crowds. / **Sample dishes:** *dill-marinated herrings; breaded wholetail scampi; lemon cheesecake.* **Details:** *www.shepherdsinn.net; 9.45 pm; no smoking area; no booking.*

Village Bakery £ 23 ★
CA10 1HE (01768) 881515
"High-quality organic fare" ("truly fantastic breakfasts" in particular) win praise for these tearoom-like premises — part of a Lakeland bakery that's on the way to becoming a well-known brand. / **Sample dishes:** *vegetable soup; grilled trout with herb butter; upside down pear & ginger pudding.* **Details:** *www.village-bakery.com; 10m NE of Penrith on A686; 5 pm; L only; no Amex; no smoking; need 6+ to book.*

MERTHYR TYDFIL, MERTHYR TYDFIL   4–4D

Nant Ddu Lodge   £ 29   ★
Brecon Rd CF48 2HY   (01685) 379111
A "really friendly welcome" and a "good varied menu" are
highlights at this old hunting lodge (now an hotel, where you can
eat in either the bar or the bistro); it has a "nice setting", too, by a
river. / **Sample dishes:** duck mousse with caramelised oranges; ham hock with
mustard mash & parsley sauce; plum crumble. **Details:** www.nant-ddu-lodge.co.uk;
6m N of Merthyr on A470; 9.30 pm; closed Sun D; no smoking; booking: max 8.
Accommodation: 28 rooms, from £69.50.

MICKLEHAM, SURREY   3–3A

King William IV   £ 25   ★
Byttom HI RH5 6EL   (01372) 372590
"Pleasant" and "dependable" – this rural ale house may not seek
the heights, but its "satisfying" cooking wins nothing but praise.
/ **Sample dishes:** garlic bread with Mozzarella; steak & kidney pie; treacle tart.
Details: www.king-williamiv.com; off A24; 9.30 pm; no Amex; no booking in
summer; children: 12+.

MIDDLESBROUGH, MIDDLESBROUGH   8–3C

Purple Onion   £ 32
80 Corporation Rd TS1 2RF   (01642) 222250
It's the "best hereabouts", but there's a feeling that this trendy
Mediterranean bistro is "getting too big for its boots", and some
think its prices "ridiculous" by local standards.
/ **Sample dishes:** seared king scallop & crab fritters; honey-glazed pork with
courgettes; char-grilled peaches in Cointreau. **Details:** by law courts; 10.30 pm;
closed Sun D; no Amex.

MILTON KEYNES, MILTON KEYNES   3–2A

Jaipur   £ 25
599 Grafton Gate East MK9 1AT   (01908) 669796
An "impressive Taj Mahal-esque building" – which claims to be
Europe's largest purpose-built Indian – is the new home for this
long-established subcontinental; the cooking is generally held to be
"of a very high standard", but "a bit pricey" for what it is.
/ **Details:** www.jaipur.co.uk; 11 pm; no smoking in dining room.

MORSTON, NORFOLK   6–3C

Morston Hall   £ 45   𝔸★★
Main Coast Rd NR27 7AA   (01263) 741041
"Good old-fashioned cooking served the old-fashioned way by staff
who know their stuff" elicits a continuing hymn of praise for this
"wonderful", 17th-century country house hotel, a couple of miles
from the coast. / **Sample dishes:** Milanese risotto with deep-fried leeks; roast
lamb with buttery mash; sticky toffee pudding with butterscotch sauce.
Details: www.morstonhall.com; between Blakeney & Wells on A149; 8 pm; D only,
except Sun open L & D; no smoking at D. **Accommodation:** 6 rooms, from £210,
incl D.

MOULSFORD, OXFORDSHIRE   2–2D
Beetle & Wedge   £43   A
Ferry Ln OX10 9JF (01491) 651381
The "beautiful" setting (the inspiration for 'The Wind in the Willows') is the highlight of a visit to this charming Thames-side fixture; the "pleasantly rustic" boathouse (with its grill-based menu) is a more popular choice than the relative formality of the dining room proper. / **Sample dishes:** onion tart with foie gras & truffle sauce; monkfish & surf clams in champagne & saffron sauce; Cointreau soufflé with raspberry coulis. **Details:** www.beetleandwedge.co.uk; on A329 between Streatley & Wallingford, take Ferry Lane at crossroads; 9.45 pm; closed Mon & Sun D, Boathouse open daily; no smoking in dining room. **Accommodation:** 10 rooms, from £165.

MOULTON, NORTH YORKSHIRE   8–3B
Black Bull   £38   A★
DL10 6QJ (01325) 377289
"One of the best pub restaurants in the north of England"; "beautiful seafood" and a "fantastic atmosphere" (especially in the converted Pullman railway carriage, but also in the "nice conservatory") make this "unique" fixture a "consistently good" choice. / **Sample dishes:** shellfish bisque; lemon sole in prawn, leek & cheese sauce; pancakes with lemon sauce. **Value tip:** set 3-crs L £15.50. **Details:** 1m S of Scotch Corner; 10.15 pm; closed Sun; children: 7+.

MYLOR BRIDGE, CORNWALL   1–4B
Pandora Inn   £30   A
Restronguet Creek TR11 5ST (01326) 372678
A "wonderful position on the water's edge" (complete with a pontoon out on the creek) is the hard-to-match attraction of this remote thatched inn; it serves "competent and hearty pub grub" which is better value in the bar than the upstairs restaurant. / **Sample dishes:** avocado, mango & smoked salmon salad; turbot with fresh greens; lemon ricotta cheesecake. **Details:** signposted off A390, between Truro & Falmouth; 9 pm; closed Sun D (in winter only); no Amex; no smoking; children: 12+.

NAILSWORTH, GLOUCESTERSHIRE   2–2B
Calcot Manor   £41   ★
GL8 8YJ (01666) 890391
This "excellent country hotel" – in a converted farmhouse – is hailed by most reporters for its "very good food" and "friendly service"; there's a choice of eating either in the dining conservatory, or the cheaper 'Gumstool Inn'. / **Sample dishes:** scallops with spiced couscous; roast pork confit with lardons & red onion; bread & butter pudding. **Value tip:** set 2-crs L £13.95 (Sun £19). **Details:** www.calcotmanor.co.uk; junction of A46 & A4135; 9.30 pm; no smoking area; booking essential; children: only at L. **Accommodation:** 28 rooms, from £145.

NAYLAND, SUFFOLK   3–2C
White Hart   £32   ★
11 High St C06 4JF (01206) 263382
Michel Roux's "delightful pub run by ex-Waterside Inn staff" is – after a rather mixed start – winning ever-greater acclaim as "an oasis of Gallic charm and quality" in "deepest Suffolk", where the "light and subtle" cooking generally offers "good value". / **Sample dishes:** rock fish soup; roast suckling pig with sweet potato pureé; ginger & lemon gateau. **Value tip:** set 3-crs L £13. **Details:** www.whitehart-nayland.co.uk; off A12, between Colchester & Sudbury; 9.30 pm. **Accommodation:** 6 rooms, from £82.

NETHER ALDERLEY, CHESHIRE   5–2B

Wizard   £ 35   𝔸 ★

Macclesfield Rd SK10 4UB   (01625) 584000
"More restaurant than pub", this *"secluded establishment in the leafy Cheshire countryside"* is a *"sophisticated"* place, and its cooking is *"always good"*. / **Sample dishes:** baby spinach, avocado & Gorgonzola salad; herb-crusted cod with pea pureé; rice pudding with stem ginger & maple syrup. **Value tip:** set 2-crs L £10 (Sun £16). **Details:** from A34, take B5087; 9.30 pm; closed Mon & Sun D; no smoking area.

NETTLEBED, OXFORDSHIRE   2–2D

White Hart   £ 55   ★

High St RG9 5DD   (01491) 641245
It's early days for this modernistically made-over ancient boozer, where the cooking has high ambitions – even a reporter who had a "fantastic" meal, though, complained of "woeful" service and an environment reminiscent of a "wind tunnel".
/ **Sample dishes:** pan-fried scallops with roast fennel & orange salad; Gressingham duck with white bean cassoulet; iced chestnut parfait with rum sauce. **Value tip:** set 3-crs weekday D (in bistro) £15. **Details:** www.whitehartnettlebed.com; 9 pm; closed Mon & Sun (bistro open every day for L & D); no smoking in dining room; booking essential; children: 14+ in dining room. **Accommodation:** 12 rooms, from £105.

NEW BARNET, GREATER LONDON   3–2B

Mims   £ 25

63 East Barnet Rd EN5 8RN   (020) 8449 2974
This curious Barnet destination continues to win praise for its "excellent" (if sometimes "inconsistent") cooking that some think "amazing value"; even ardent fans note the "very slow" service, though, and the fact that there's "no ambience".
/ **Sample dishes:** deep-fried tomato & onion salad; roast duck with roast vegetables; banana crêpes. **Details:** between Cockfosters & High Barnet; 11 pm, Sat 10.30 pm; closed Mon; no Amex or Switch; no smoking area.

NEW MILTON, HAMPSHIRE   2–4C

Chewton Glen   £ 55   𝔸 ★

Christchurch Rd BH25 6QS   (01425) 275341
As long as you go for that Relais & Châteaux experience, it's "hard to beat the ambience" of this "plush" New Forest-fringe country house; the cooking has "got better again" of late, and the "charming" staff includes a "fantastic sommelier".
/ **Sample dishes:** tiger prawn ravioli with white truffle sauce; Angus beef with green pepper hollandaise; caramelised apples with cinnamon ice cream. **Value tip:** set 3-crs Sun L £36. **Details:** www.chewtonglen.com; on A337 between New Milton & Highcliffe; 9.30 pm; jacket required at D; no smoking; children: 6+.
Accommodation: 59 rooms, from £275.

NEWARK, NOTTINGHAMSHIRE   5–3D

Café Bleu   £ 29   𝔸 ★

14 Castle Gate NG24 1BG   (01636) 610141
"A real find"; "good food and atmosphere" is the tenor of all feedback on this *"lovely"* modern brasserie by the river, and fans say it offers *"excellent value"*, too. / **Sample dishes:** sardines with saffron couscous; braised Aberdeen beef with baby carrots; lemon posset with champagne sorbet. **Details:** www.cafebleu.co.uk; 9.30 pm; closed Sun D; no Amex; no smoking area.

sign up for the survey at www.hardens.com

NEWCASTLE UPON TYNE, TYNE & WEAR 8–2B

Newcastle is famously a going-out sort of place, and the city sustains a fair number of interesting places. Most of the action is around the Quayside — an area utterly transformed over the past decade where *Café 21* and a couple of notable upmarket Indians (*Leela's, Vujon*) lead the pack.

In the centre of town, *Barn Again Bistro* remains a great favourite as an informal venue. A short taxi-ride from the centre, the city's grandest restaurant, *Fisherman's Lodge*, enjoys a particularly picturesque situation in the leafy Jesmond Dene.

For diners on a budget, such Italians as *Francesca's, Pani's* and *Paradiso* offer a number of options with character, as does the Indian *Valley Junction*, housed in an old railway carriage. A new café/brasserie, the *Café Royal*, has quickly acquired quite a following.

Barn Again Bistro £34 🄺
21a Leazes Park Rd NE1 4PF   (0191) 230 3338
"Unique offbeat décor" has long made this *"bright"* and *"noisy"* spot — which does indeed occupy a converted barn — *"the best"* city-centre destination for many reporters; its *"exciting"* and *"varied"* menu still delivers *"more hits than misses"*, but the recent enlargement of the premises has garnered rather unsettled reports. / **Sample dishes:** *wild garlic leaf risotto with Parmesan; Arabic-spiced lamb with aubergine & Mozzarella; fallen chocolate soufflé.* **Value tip:** *set 3-crs L £15.* **Details:** *near St James's Park football ground; 10 pm; closed Sun.*

Blake's £10
53 Grey St NE1 6QH   (0191) 261 5463
"A huge range of excellent and unusual sandwiches" is the top culinary feature at this *"studenty"* café, which is *"always busy"*; service, though, can be *"dopey"*. / **Details:** *9.45 pm; no credit cards; no smoking area; no booking.*

Café 21 £35 ★
21 Queen St, Princes Whf NE1 3UG   (0191) 222 0755
It's *"still Newcastle's best place to eat out by far"*, say fans of the former '21 Queen Street', acclaiming its *"consistent and enterprising"* cuisine; the place is certainly *"busier and noisier"* than in its grander former incarnation, but — even allowing for its lower ambitions — a shade less rapturously received.
/ **Sample dishes:** *duck & green peppercorn pâté; sirloin with parsley butter & chips; crème brûlée.* **Value tip:** *set 3-crs L £14.50.* **Details:** *10.30 pm; closed Sun; no smoking area.*

Café Royal £26 ★
8 Nelson St NE1 5AW   (0191) 261 4298
It's as a venue for *"gorgeous cakes and pastries"* that this airy new all-day venture — *"busy at lunch, cosy in the evenings"* — attracts most support; however, the more ambitious fare served upstairs is *"tasty and good value"*, too. / **Sample dishes:** *crispy duck & watercress salad; Café Royal beefburger; Irish chocolate cake.* **Details:** *www.sjf.co.uk; 7 pm; closed Mon D, Tue D & Sun D; no smoking.*

Dragon House £24
30-32 Stowell St NE1 4XQ   (0191) 232 0868
Newcastle – first-time visitors may be surprised to know – boasts a Chinatown, where this particular establishment is one of the best of a pretty average bunch of restaurants. / Value tip: set 3-crs L £5.50. Details: 11 pm; no Amex.

Fisherman's Lodge £50
Jesmond Dene NE7 7BQ   (0191) 281 3281
Despite a recent change of ownership, standards at this "beautifully-located" fish-specialist (in an "unusual" location in the wooded Jesmond Dene valley) remain pretty "sound" all round, and it's still a top destination locally; as ever, though, it can seem rather "pricey" for what it is. / Sample dishes: assiette of crab; trio of salmon with langoustine sauce; chocolate ganache tart. Value tip: set 3-crs L £19.50. Details: www.fishermanslodge.co.uk; 2m from city centre on A1058, follow signposts to Jesmond Dene; 10.45 pm; closed Sat L & Sun; no smoking in dining room; children: 8+.

Francesca's £20   Ⓐ
Manor House Rd NE2 2NE   (0191) 281 6586
A "great", "noisy" atmosphere and "friendly" staff make this family-run institution – majoring in "cheap" and "authentic" pizza – "the best Italian in the north" for its loyal fans; the queues are part of the "fun". / Sample dishes: garlic king prawns; mixed fish grill; tiramisu. Value tip: set 1-crs weekday pre-theatre £3.70. Details: 9.30 pm; closed Sun; no Amex; no booking.

King Neptune £41   ★
34-36 Stowell St NE1 4XQ   (0191) 261 6657
"Invariably good food" is the theme of reports on this "popular" and "friendly" Chinese – reporters favourite in Chinatown. / Details: 10.45 pm.

Leela's £29   ★★
20 Dean St NE1 1PG   (0191) 230 1261
"Leela herself presides, and talks you through the menu" at this "lovely" (if "modestly decorated") city-centre fixture; it has a big reputation for its "really different and lovingly prepared" South Indian vegetarian dishes. / Details: 11.30 pm; closed Sun; no Switch; no smoking area at L.

Malmaison £33
104 Quayside NE1 3DX   (0191) 245 5000
"Exceptional views of the vibrant quayside" add interest to a visit to this "trendy" boutique hotel brasserie; the cooking, though, is decidedly "average". / Sample dishes: artichokes & asparagus with walnut oil; steamed sea bass with radish & aubergine salad; English cheese platter. Value tip: set 2-crs L £12. Details: www.malmaison.com; 10.30 pm. Accommodation: 116 rooms, from £120.

McCoys at the Baltic
Baltic £40
South Shore Rd N38 3BA   (0191) 440 4949
This vast new contemporary arts centre, converted from a grain warehouse (and actually in Gateshead), is home to two restaurants – the glazed 'Rooftop' (price shown), which offers panoramic views of the Tyne, and the cheaper first-floor 'Riverside' (£28); both sites are run by the McCoys, of Tontine fame. / Sample dishes: langoustine ravioli with shellfish reduction; braised pork wrapped in Parma ham with potato rosti; chocolate bread pudding. Details: www.balticmill.com; 10 pm; closed Sun D; no smoking in dining room.

sign up for the survey at www.hardens.com

Pani's £20   𝔸★

61-65 High Bridge NE1 6BX (0191) 232 4366

"Amazing value, and authentic" – this "friendly", "cosy" and "genuine" bistro attracts nothing but praise for its "Naples-come-to-Newcastle" charms; unsurprisingly, it's often "very busy". / **Sample dishes:** bruschetta; chicken stuffed with Dolcelatte; tiramisu. **Details:** www.paniscafe.com; off Gray Street; 10 pm; closed Sun; no Amex; no booking at L.

Paradiso £26   𝔸★

1 Market Ln NE1 6QQ (0191) 221 1240

A "young and stylish café/bar/restaurant" that makes a "chilled location for a light snack or full meal"; its "Mediterranean-style" cooking rarely disappoints. / **Sample dishes:** goats cheese & courgette lasagne; Indian-spiced cod with couscous & roast vegetables; egg custard tart. **Value tip:** set 2-crs L £6.95. **Details:** www.paradiso.co.uk; opp fire station; 10.45 pm; closed Sun; no Amex; no smoking area.

Sachins £25

Forth Banks NE1 3SG (0191) 261 9035

"High standards for 20 years" have won a devoted fan club for this Punjabi "stalwart" behind Central Station; it is liked for its "amusing" service, and its "spicy" dishes served in "huge portions". / **Details:** behind Central Station; 11.15 pm; closed Sun.

Valley Junction 397 £24   𝔸★

Old Jesmond Station, Archbold Ter NE2 1DB
(0191) 281 6397

"The good reputation is deserved", say fans of this restaurant, intriguingly-located "in an old rail carriage"; it has a "fabulous atmosphere and fabulous staff" and its "standard Indian fare" is "very good", too. / **Value tip:** set 3-crs L £6.75. **Details:** near Civic Centre, off Sandyford Rd; 11.15 pm; closed Mon; no smoking area.

Vujon £30   ★

29 Queen St NE1 3UG (0191) 221 0601

The "subtle" cuisine at this "reliable" and "welcoming" Quayside "oasis" puts it "a cut above your average Indian", and makes it one of "the best in the North East". / **Details:** 10.30 pm; closed Sun L.

Junction 28 £29   ★

Station Approach NP10 8LD (01633) 891891

This "bustling" joint in a converted station takes some flak from reporters for its "dated" décor; its "surprisingly good cooking", though, is consistently approved. / **Sample dishes:** mushroom & pancetta risotto; Thai red monkfish & prawn curry; chilled melon soup with mint sorbet. **Value tip:** set 2-crs L £8.95. **Details:** www.junction-28.co.uk; off M4, J28 towards Caerphilly; 9.30 pm; closed Sun D; smoking discouraged.

Crooked Billet £34   ★★

2 Westbrook End MK17 0DF (01908) 373936

"A superb wine list at very realistic prices" and "very good food" (in "big portions") generate glowing feedback for this two-year-old venture in a country pub, whose style is "rather metropolitan". / **Sample dishes:** watercress soup with goats cheese crostini; rack of lamb with coriander couscous & tapenade jus; roasted peaches with thyme ice cream. **Details:** www.the-crooked-billet-pub.co.uk; 10 pm; closed Mon & Sun D; no smoking; no booking at L.

NEWTON-ON-THE-MOOR, N'HUMBERLAND   8–2B

Cook & Barker   **£ 26**
NE65 9JY   (01665) 575234
*A reputation for "above-average pub grub" helps make this well-known country inn "very crowded", and some think it rather "over-rated". / **Sample dishes:** avocado, tandoori chicken & rocket salad; pot roast lamb with bubble 'n' squeak; Belgian chocolate truffle cake. **Value tip:** set 2-crs weekday L £10. **Details:** 12m N of Morpeth, just off A1; 9 pm; no smoking area. **Accommodation:** 4 rooms, from £70.*

NORTON, SHROPSHIRE   5–4B

Hundred House   **£ 44**
Bridgnorth Rd   TF11 9EE   (01952) 730353
*Reports are not only fewer than we would like about this intriguing-looking pub-cum-restaurant, but also rather mixed – the bar, therefore, praised for "the best pub food in the area", seems to be a rather safer bet than the restaurant.
/ **Sample dishes:** shallot, fennel & goats cheese tartlet; wild boar with white bean casserole & chorizo; raspberry & meringue ice cream.
Details: www.hundredhouse.co.uk; on A442 between Bridgnorth & Telford; 9.30 pm; closed Sun D; no smoking. **Accommodation:** 10 rooms, from £99.*

NORWICH, NORFOLK   6–4C

Adlards   **£ 44**   ★
79 Upper Giles St   NR2 1AB   (01603) 633522
*This locally-celebrated establishment will always be just too small for some people ("don't go if you mind the whole place being able to eavesdrop"); some sense a recent "reinvigoration", however, and results from the "carefully balanced" menu are "consistently good". / **Sample dishes:** foie gras in cumin with toasted brioche; veal with mash & roast parsnips; banana tarte Tatin. **Value tip:** set 2-crs L £15. **Details:** www.adlards.co.uk; near the Roman Catholic Cathedral; 10.30 pm; closed Mon L & Sun; no smoking at D.*

Brummells   **£ 43**   𝔸 ★
7 Magdalen St   NR3 1LE   (01603) 625555
*"Very good fish" and "a wide selection of seafood" are unanimously endorsed at this "atmospheric" venture in an ancient building, even if it's "expensive", by local standards.
/ **Sample dishes:** seafood pancakes with aniseed sauce; sea bass & leeks with prawn butter; apple & wild mushroom crumble with cider sorbet.
Details: www.brummells.co.uk; 10.30 pm.*

By Appointment   **£ 38**   𝔸 ★
25-29 St George's St   NR3 1AB   (01603) 630730
*It doesn't generate a huge amount of commentary, but this "unusual and intimate" townhouse wins praise for its "great Edwardian atmosphere" and for its "delicious" cooking.
/ **Sample dishes:** tuna carpaccio with capers; guinea fowl, chorizo & mushrooms with basil sauce; pineapple tarte Tatin with cardamom ice cream. **Details:** in a courtyard off Colegate; 9 pm; D only, closed Mon & Sun; no Amex; no smoking in dining room; children: 12+. **Accommodation:** 4 rooms, from £95.*

Delia's City Brasserie £31
Norwich City Football Ground, Carrow Rd NR1 1JE
(01603) 218705
"I could cook the same at home with her recipe books" –
this football-themed dining room at the Canaries' HQ (named
after the club's most famous director) generates limited feedback,
much of it uncomplimentary. / **Sample dishes:** *Thai fishcakes with*
sesame & lime sauce; roast salmon with Pecorino & pesto topping; chocolate crème
brûlée. **Details:** *www.canaries.co.uk; 9.30 pm; open Sat D only; no Amex;*
no smoking area; booking: max 12.

Tatlers £36 ★
21 Tombland NR3 1RF (01603) 766670
"Sensitively-prepared food" and *"a high standard of service"* make
this *"good city-centre restaurant"* a *"reliable"* (and *"relaxing"*)
destination for all who comment on it. / **Sample dishes:** *salad Lyonnaise;*
rib-eye steak with red wine & mushroom sauce; lemon tart. **Value tip:** *set 2-crs L*
£12.50. **Details:** *www.tatlers.com; near Cathedral, next to Erpingham Gate; 10 pm;*
closed Sun; no smoking area.

The Tree House £18 ★
14-16 Dove St NR2 1DE (01603) 763258
"Wonderful, fresh vegetarian food" – from *"fantastic salads to*
winter warmers" – is served at this simple café (run as a workers'
co-op); *"go early to beat the queues".* / **Sample dishes:** *spicy tomato &*
lentil soup; potato & cauliflower curry with rice; blueberry tofu cheesecake.
Details: *9 pm; L only Mon-Wed, closed Sun; no credit cards; no smoking;*
no booking at L.

NOTTINGHAM, CITY OF NOTTINGHAM 5–3D

Nottingham is surprisingly under-rated as a dining
destination. For its size it boasts a very good range of quality
mid-price restaurants, of which *Hart's* is the undoubted star
(having now eclipsed its chief rival, the longer-established
Sonny's). A little way from the centre, *La Toque* and in a
different idiom, *Hotel des Clos*, are starting to make quite a
name.

Eye-catching design has helped *World Service* become the
place locally to see and be seen, even if it has no claims to
being a foodie hot spot.

The city boasts a number of very acceptable ethnic
restaurants, with good examples of both Thai (*Royal Thai*,
Siam Thani) and Indian establishments (*Saagar*, *Shimla Pinks*).

Atlas £9 ★
9 Pelham St NG1 2EH (0115) 950 1295
"Excellent coffee and great sandwiches" – *"delicious and*
imaginative, and using fantastic breads" – put this central
café/deli in a class of its own locally. / **Sample dishes:** *no starters;*
ciabatta with tuna, basil & plum tomatoes; Danish pastry. **Details:** *5 pm; L only;*
no Amex or Switch; no smoking.

Bees Make Honey £29
12 Alfreton Rd NG7 3NG (0115) 978 0109
"Comforting home cooking" wins much praise for Michael
Walton's *"laid-back"* BYO café. / **Sample dishes:** *cuttlefish tagliatelle;*
sea bass with ackee & okra; white chocolate cheesecake. **Details:** *5 mins from*
Playhouse & Theatre Royal; 10.15 pm; D only, closed Mon & Sun; no credit cards.

Fashion £ 27 _A_

10 Middle Pavement NG1 7DW (0115) 950 5850

"No children" is either a big plus or a big minus for visitors to this – yes – "fashionable" bar/restaurant, hailed by reporters as a reasonably-priced place for a light meal, or for breakfast. / **Sample dishes:** sole goujons with mango & avocado; chicken in Seville orange sauce; red cherry frangipane tart. **Details:** 9.30 pm; no Amex; children: not permitted.

French Living £ 24 ★

27 King St NG1 2AY (0115) 958 5885

"Good for Francophiles", this "unpretentious" and "reasonably-priced" fixture wins all-round praise for its "real French staff", its "down-to-earth" Gallic cooking and its "cosy" atmosphere. / **Sample dishes:** Burgundy snails with garlic & parsley butter; venison with peppered blueberry sauce; white chocolate bavarois. **Value tip:** set 2-crs L £6.90. **Details:** near Market Square; 10 pm; closed Sun; booking: max 10, Sat pm.

Hart's £ 34 _A_ ★

Standard Ct, Park Row NG1 6GN (0115) 911 0666

Tim Hart's "chic", "classy" and extremely successful brasserie near the Castle – with its "interesting" modern British cooking – offers "a superb all-round eating experience" for most reporters; there is the odd gripe that it is a little "snooty" and "sterile", though. / **Sample dishes:** courgette tart with goats cheese; veal with spinach & Parmesan risotto; tarte Tatin with caramel ice cream. **Value tip:** set 2-crs L £11. **Details:** www.hartsnottingham.co.uk; near Castle; 10.30 pm; no smoking area. **Accommodation:** 34 rooms, from £100.

Hotel des Clos   £ 51 _A_ ★

Old Lenton Ln NG7 2SA
(0115) 986 6566

"A real find" – it's not a newcomer, but chef Sat Bains's "superb" cooking is starting to win greater recognition for this "small and cosy" dining room – part of a small hotel that occupies converted farm buildings a little out of the city centre (on the banks of the Trent). / **Sample dishes:** roast scallops with Indian-spiced cauliflower; Goosnargh duck with apple & foie gras; apple tart with Granny Smith sorbet. **Details:** www.hoteldesclos.com; 9.30 pm; closed Sat L & Sun; no smoking; children: 8+. **Accommodation:** 8 rooms, from £89.50.

Loch Fyne £ 30

17 King St NG1 2AY (0115) 950 8481

Fair quality seafood at "good value" prices has made this (well-established) branch of the expanding national seafood chain one of the most talked-about places in town; it has its critics, though, for whom it's totally "forgettable". / **Sample dishes:** lobster bisque with garlic rouille; rosemary-infused bream with tomatoes & black olives; lemon sorbet. **Details:** www.loch-fyne.com; 9 pm; no smoking area.

Mem Saab £ 28

12-14 Maid Marian Way NG1 6HS (0115) 957 0009

This "designer" curry house made a more uneven showing this year; many locals still praise its "fresh-flavoured food" and "modern style", but there were a couple of reporters who dismissed it as an "overpriced" "canteen". / **Value tip:** set 2-crs D £12.50. **Details:** near Castle; 10.3 pm, Fri & Sat 11 pm; D only, closed Sun; no smoking in dining room; children: 5+.

Merchants
Lace Market Hotel   £ 33   ✗
29-31 High Pavement NG1 1HE   (0115) 852 3232
*This city-centre brasserie (part of a designer hotel) "tries hard" for
a cutting edge modern style; even some fans concede its
standards "can vary", however, and for critics it's "overblown" and
"at best mediocre".* / **Sample dishes:** aubergine, smoked Mozzarella &
chorizo tart; tuna steak with cherry tomato salad; vanilla & blackcurrant bavarois.
Value tip: set 3-crs L £9.90. **Details:** www.lacemarkethotel.co.uk; 10.30 pm;
closed Sat L & Sun D. **Accommodation:** 42 rooms, from £99.

Mr Man's   £ 25   ★
Wollaton Park NG8 2AD   (0115) 928 7788
*"Great food at reasonable prices" makes this large, flashily
decked-out Cantonese, prominently located at the entrance of
Wollaton Park, a consistent hit with reporters.* / **Value tip:** set 3-crs L
£9.50. **Details:** 11 pm.

Petit Paris   £ 27
2 Kings Walk NG1 2AE   (0115) 947 3767
*"A real lively bistro ambience" contributes to the popularity of this
"busy and noisy" Gallic city-centre fixture; the cooking can be a bit
"predictable".* / **Sample dishes:** smoked chicken & mushroom pancake;
veal with mushroom & brandy flambé; profiteroles with hot chocolate sauce.
Details: near Theatre Royal; 10.30 pm; closed Sun; no smoking area.

Pretty Orchid   £ 29
12 Pepper Street NG1 2GH   (0115) 958 8344
*"Fresh, tasty food" and a "friendly" approach win a loyal local fan
club for this well-established city-centre Thai.* / **Details:** 11 pm; closed
Sun; no Amex.

Royal Thai   £ 23   ★
189 Mansfield Rd NG1 3FS   (0115) 948 3001
*"Great service" and "lovely presentation" add to the attractions of
this popular oriental, especially as "a good lunch venue".*
/ **Details:** 11 pm; closed Sun L; no Amex; no smoking area; children: 5+.

Saagar   £ 25   ★
473 Mansfield Rd NG5 2DR   (0115) 962 2014
*"The wafts of curry draw you in" to this "slightly upmarket"
Sherwood subcontinental, where rather "different" cooking is
served in "very big portions".* / **Details:** 1.5m from city centre; midnight;
closed Sun L; no smoking area; children: 5+.

Shimla Pinks   £ 29   ★
38-46 Goosegate NG1 1FF   (0115) 958 9899
*Some find its modern setting "cheesy", but this trendy Indian still
"surprises" its fans with "interesting" and "well-prepared" dishes.*
/ **Value tip:** set 3-crs L £7.95. **Details:** www.shimlapinks.bite2enjoy.com; 11 pm;
closed Sat L & Sun L; no smoking area.

Siam Thani   £ 23   ★
16-20a Carlton St NG1 1NN   (0115) 958 2222
*With its "very good" Thai food, "gracious" service and "elegant",
surroundings, reporters find little to criticise at this airy, modern
restaurant in the Lace Market.* / **Details:** www.siamthani.co.uk; 10.30 pm;
closed Sun L; no Amex; no smoking area.

Sonny's £ 33

3 Carlton St NG1 1NL   (0115) 947 3041

"Complacency has set in" at this modernistic city-centre brasserie; its *"sophisticated food and décor"* still makes it *"a favourite"* for many reporters, but satisfaction is diluted by those who now find it *"over-rated and overpriced."*. / **Sample dishes:** tomato linguine with roasted peppers; roast lamb with Daphne potatoes; blueberry & almond tart. **Value tip:** set 2-crs L £10 (Sun £15). **Details:** near Victoria Centre; 10.30 pm, Fri & Sat 11 pm; no smoking area.

La Toque £ 39 𝔸 ★

61 Wollaton Rd NG9 2NG   (0115) 922 2268

Recent *"radical refurbishment"* has now given Mattias Karlsson's oddly-located bistro the setting that his Gallic cooking deserves, and results can be *"outstanding"*. / **Sample dishes:** quail consommé & toasted brioche; lemon sole with green bean fricassée; baked prune soufflé. **Value tip:** set 2-crs L £13.95. **Details:** off A52 towards Beeston; 10.30 pm; closed Sun; no smoking area; children: 6+.

Travellers Rest £ 27

Mapperley Plains, Plains Rd NG3 5RT   (0115) 926 4412

"A massive choice (with a great veggie selection)" enables *"all generations"* to be catered for at this *"good-value"* Mapperley boozer. / **Sample dishes:** black pudding tower; lamb en croûte; chocolate muffin sundae. **Details:** off B684 between Nottingham & Woodborough; 10 pm; no smoking area; no booking.

Victoria Hotel £ 20 ★

Dovecote Ln NG9 1JG   (0115) 925 4049

"The quality of the food keeps improving" at this *"lively local pub"*, which was converted a few years ago from a former railway hotel by Beeston station; *"the real ales come highly recommended"*, too. / **Sample dishes:** spinach & apple soup; herb-crusted rack of lamb; Mars bar cheesecake. **Details:** www.tynemill.co.uk/nottm/vic.htm; by Beeston railway station; 8.45 pm; no Amex; no smoking; need 6+ to book; children: before 8 pm only.

World Service £ 37

Newdigate Hs, Castle Gate NG1 6AF   (0115) 847 5587

"Designer décor" and an *"interesting menu"* have helped this *"stylish"* yearling gather a very large local following; the less star-struck describe its style as *"enjoyably pretentious"*.
/ **Sample dishes:** salt & pepper squid with orange salad; roast lamb with braised fennel & crispy garlic; pear & cinnamon tarte Tatin. **Value tip:** set 2-crs L £9.50. **Details:** www.worldservicerestaurant.com; 10 pm; no smoking.

Nicks
Lord Nelson's House £ 38 ★

11 Marketplace LE15 6DT   (01572) 723199

"Plain and unspoilt food" that's *"simple and well-cooked"* wins much approval for this beamed restaurant in the corner of the marketplace. / **Sample dishes:** roast goats cheese with poached pears; steak with rosti & caramelised onions; walnut & ginger steamed pudding. **Details:** www.nelsons-house.com; 9.30 pm; closed Mon & Sun; no Amex; no smoking. **Accommodation:** 4 rooms, from £80.

sign up for the survey at www.hardens.com

OAKMERE, CHESHIRE   5–2B

Nunsmere Hall   **£50**
Tarporley Rd   CW8 2ES   (01606) 889100
*If you want to hang out with the "Cheshire Set", this "plush"
country house hotel (complete "with its own lake"), is just the
place; the food has generally been pretty unremarkable in recent
times, but perhaps the new chef (2002) will help it hit the
heights.* / **Sample dishes:** *roast lobster consommé with herb dumplings;
peppered duck with white beans & pancetta; pear, apricot & papaya crumble.*
Details: *www.nunsmere.co.uk; off A49, 4m SW of Northwich; 10 pm; no smoking;
children: 12+.* **Accommodation:** *36 rooms, from £175.*

OBAN, ARGYLL & BUTE   9–3B

The Fish Café (Ee-Usk)   **£31**   ★★
104 George St PA34 5NS
(01631) 565666
*"Superb fresh fish in an out-of-the-way location" – this "brilliant"
newcomer receives top marks from all who comment on it for
delivering no-nonsense seafood dishes to an "excellent" standard;
plans are already afoot as we go to press for building swanky new
premises nearby.* / **Sample dishes:** *mussels with garlic butter; monkfish with
mornay sauce & savory mash; bread & butter pudding with Irish cream.*
Details: *10 pm; no Amex; no smoking area.*

OCKLEY, SURREY   3–4A

Bryce's at the Old School House   **£35**   ★
RH5 5TH   (01306) 627430
*"Original" dishes that are "well prepared" have made quite a
name for this "fish restaurant in a pub"; it can seem "a little
pricey", though, for what it is.* / **Sample dishes:** *coconut crab cakes with
sweet & sour scallops; plaice with brioche herb crust; butterscotch & honeycomb
cheesecake.* **Details:** *www.bryces.co.uk; 8m S of Dorking on A29; 9.30 pm; closed
Sun D in Nov, Jan & Feb; no Amex; no smoking in dining room.*

ODIHAM, HAMPSHIRE   2–3D

The Grapevine   **£33**
121 High St RG29 1LA   (01256) 701122
*"The early-bird menu is very good value" at this "relaxed" cute
little bistro, in the heart of the village.* / **Sample dishes:** *scallops with
lentils & bitter leaf salad; beef with wild mushroom & Gorgonzola risotto; basil crème
brûlée.* **Value tip:** *set 2-crs L £9, set 3-crs pre-theatre menu £15.*
Details: *www.grapevine-gourmet.com; follow signs from M3, J5; 10 pm; closed
Sat L & Sun.*

OLD DALBY, LEICESTERSHIRE   5–3D

Crown Inn   **£32**
7 Debdale Hill LE14 3LF   (01664) 823134
*A "charming" pub whose "excellent" victuals are unanimously
praised; it can seem a touch "expensive" for what it is.*
/ **Sample dishes:** *asparagus, spinach & poached egg salad; slow-roasted rib-eye
beef; oranges in Cointreau cream.* **Value tip:** *set 3-crs L £11.95.*
Details: *www.old-dalby.org; 5m N of Melton Mowbray; 9.30 pm; closed Sun D;
no Amex; no smoking area; children: 5+ at L, 10+ at D.*

OLDHAM, GREATER MANCHESTER   5–2B

Ho Ho's   £ 30   ★
57-59 High St OL4 3BN   (0161) 620 9500
*No reporter actually gave us any words to describe this Lees
cottage-oriental – the stellar ratings they award, however, confirm
that this rather unlikely destination remains one of the best
Chinese restaurants in these parts.* / **Details:** www.hohos.co.uk; follow
signs from M62, J20; 11 pm.

OMBERSLEY, WORCESTERSHIRE   2–1B

Kings Arms   £ 27   𝔸
Main Rd WR9 0EW   (01905) 620142
*This "upmarket" half-timbered pub is a "buzzy" (and sometimes
"crowded") place, that serves "plain but well-cooked food" from a
"varied menu"; a nice walled garden is a special sunny-day
attraction.* / **Sample dishes:** black pudding, bacon & quails egg salad; calves
liver & bacon with mash; chocolate praline brûlée.
Details: www.kingsarmsombersley.co.uk; 10.15 pm; no smoking area.

ONGAR, ESSEX   3–2B

Smiths Brasserie   £ 39   𝔸
Fyfield Rd CM5 0AL   (01277) 365578
*"It's great to find such a good place out-of-town", say advocates of
this "converted boozer" whose menu majors in fish and seafood
(not least, "quality fish and chips").* / **Sample dishes:** asparagus with
hollandaise; Scotch salmon fillet cake with parsley; roasted pineapple with
butterscotch sauce. **Value tip:** set 3-crs L £17.50. **Details:** left off A414 towards
Fyfield; 10.30 pm; closed Mon; no Amex; children: 12+.

ORFORD, SUFFOLK   3–1D

Butley Orford Oysterage   £ 31   ★
Market Hill IP12 2LH   (01394) 450277
*After four decades in business, the "no-frills" décor at this ever-
popular "one-off" is "in need of a revamp"; "good cheap
seafood" and "the freshest fish, simply cooked", however, provide
ample compensation for practically all who comment on it.*
/ **Sample dishes:** smoked salmon pâté; hot smoked mackerel with mustard sauce;
run baba. **Details:** 9 pm; closed Mon D-Thu D & Sun D in winter; no Amex;
no smoking.

The Crown & Castle   £ 34
IP12 2LJ   (01394) 450205
*"Interesting" cooking has made this Victorian hotel – rejuvenated
under new ownership since 1999 – a destination of some note
(and to some, a "perfect get-away"); service can be "very poor",
though, and the atmosphere is thought rather "sterile" by some.*
/ **Sample dishes:** cockle, bacon & endive salad; crispy pork with spiced lentils &
gingered greens; hot bitter chocolate mousse.
Details: www.crownandcastlehotel.co.uk; 9 pm; closed Sun D in winter; no Amex;
mainly non-smoking; booking: max 6; children: under 8s L in Parlour only.
Accommodation: 18 rooms, from £80.

ORKNEY ISLANDS, ORKNEY ISLANDS

The Creel　　　　　**£38**　　　🅐★
Front Rd, St Margaret's Hope, South Ronaldsay KW17 2SL
(01856) 831311
"*Beautifully sited, overlooking the waterfront*", Allan Craigie's
esteemed restaurant with rooms evokes a hymn of praise from
reporters for its "*very imaginative cooking, using fresh
ingredients*". / **Sample dishes:** shore crab bisque; supreme of cod; Drambuie
pannacotta. **Details:** www.thecreel.co.uk; off A961 S of town, across Churchill
barriers; 9 pm; D only; closed Jan-Mar; no Amex; no smoking. **Accommodation:** 3
rooms, from £70.

ORPINGTON, KENT　　　　　　　　　　3–3B

Xian　　　　　　　　**£22**　　　★
324 High St BR6 0NG　(01689) 871881
"*London standards in the suburbs*" – this "*very busy*" Chinese
"*never fails to please*"; "*booking essential*". / **Details:** 11.15 pm, Fri &
Sat 11.45 pm; closed Sun L.

OSMOTHERLEY, NORTH YORKSHIRE　　　8–4C

Golden Lion　　　　　**£28**　　　🅐
6 West End DL6 3AA　(01609) 883526
The "*lovely*" ambience is the highpoint at this popular, rustically-
furnished pub, where the cooking is "*reliable*", but doesn't aim to
set the world on fire. / **Sample dishes:** spaghetti with clams; pork & Parma
ham with sage mash; lemon & passion fruit pavlova. **Details:** 10.30 pm; no Amex;
no smoking area.

Three Tuns　　　　　　**£34**
9 South End DL6 3BN　(01609) 883301
"*Imaginative*" cooking is served in the modern surroundings of this
converted brewery, at the heart of an "*interesting Yorkshire
village*". / **Sample dishes:** crab & salmon fishcakes; Dover sole with lemon &
chive butter; mini croque-em-bouche. **Value tip:** set 3-crs Sun L £13.95.
Details: www.lifeandstyle.co.uk; 6m NE of Northallerton; 9.30 pm; no smoking in
dining room. **Accommodation:** 7 rooms, from £65.

OSWESTRY, SHROPSHIRE　　　　　　　5–3A

Sebastians　　　　　　**£39**　　　★
45 Willow St SY11 1AQ　(01691) 655444
"*Amazingly good for somewhere like Oswestry*"; Mark Sebastian
Fisher's "*slick*" Gallic operation (part of a small hotel) attracts
little but praise. / **Sample dishes:** seafood cassoulet with bacon & cannellini
beans; roast duck with caramelised apples & sage sauce; cinnamon cream with
spiced rhubarb. **Details:** www.sebastians-hotel.co.uk; near town centre, follow signs
towards Selattyn; 9.45 pm; closed Mon & Sun; no smoking. **Accommodation:** 8
rooms, from £60.

OTFORD, KENT　　　　　　　　　　　3–3B

Bull　　　　　　　　　**£23**　　　★
High St TN14 5PG　(01959) 523198
*Reporters speak only well of the food at this "friendly" country
pub, which generally offers a "good experience".*
/ **Sample dishes:** spinach & Roquefort tart; beef & Theakston's pie; banana toffee
crumble. **Details:** 10 pm; children: before 5 pm only.

OTLEY, WEST YORKSHIRE 5–1C

Korks £ 28 Ⓐ

40 Bondgate LS21 1AD (01943) 462020
"Really impressive" all-round standards make this cosy wine bar a *"good-value"* troughing spot as well as a superior watering hole; let's hope that Monsieur Poli, the new chef, maintains the same high standards. / **Sample dishes:** *tandoori chicken with coriander noodles; pork with cauliflower & turmeric jus; summer berry pavlova.* **Value tip:** *set 3-crs D £12.95.* **Details:** *www.korks.com; 10 pm, Fri & Sat 11 pm; closed Sat L & Sun.*

OUNDLE, NORTHANTS 3–1A

Falcon Inn £ 35 ★

Fotheringay PE8 5HZ (01832) 226254
This old stone hostelry in the middle of the village attracts little but praise, not least for its "good-value" Mediterranean cooking. / **Sample dishes:** *pea & mint soup with Parma ham; curried pork with fruity rice & poppadums; sticky toffee pudding.* **Value tip:** *set 2-crs L £11.* **Details:** *just off A605; 9 pm; no smoking.*

OVER PEOVER, CHESHIRE 5–2B

Dog Inn £ 27

Well Bank Ln WA16 8UP (01625) 861421
A "busy" country pub, worth knowing about for its "large portions" of dependable scoff. / **Sample dishes:** *smoked chicken with melon & orange salad; spinach & mushroom lasagne; sticky toffee pudding.* **Details:** *off A50; 9.30 pm; no Amex; no smoking.* **Accommodation:** *6 rooms, from £75.*

OVINGTON, HAMPSHIRE 2–3D

The Bush Inn £ 32

SO24 0RE (01962) 732764
"Lovely surroundings" add to the appeal of this *"old-fashioned rural pub"*, which – though not a foodie destination – is *"one of the best places in the area"*; it can seem *"overpriced"*, though. / **Sample dishes:** *chicken liver pâté with brandy & port; soinach & wild mushroom lasagne; chocolate & black cherry bread & butter pudding.* **Details:** *just off A31 between Winchester & Alresford; 9.30 pm; closed Sun D; no smoking area.*

OXFORD, OXFORDSHIRE 2–2D

The fact which says most about the Oxford dining scene is that the two top restaurants are both Thai. Admittedly *Chiang Mai* and *Bangkok House* are two of the country's best Thai all-rounders, but the fact remains that the best food in Oxford is largely ethnic. Indian restaurants, in particular, are well represented at most price-levels (*Aziz, Bombay, Chutney's* and *Jamals*).

Oxford's best restaurant is in fact in nearby Great Milton, in the shape of the Raymond Blanc's Manoir aux Quat' Saisons – the best-known restaurant in the UK outside London. Those who settle for Monsieur Blanc's much-frequented spin-off brasserie in Jericho, *Le Petit Blanc* may find that its performance does not really do justice to the Blanc name.

Equally, the city's other European restaurants – *Cherwell Boathouse*, *Gees*, *The Old Parsonage* and *Quod* – generally seem to rely on the charm of their location, offering food that is no more than satisfactory. Though still well-known, *Browns* is a shadow of its former self. The only European star is the modestly-ambitious newcomer, *Savannah*.

Al Shami   £ 23   ★
25 Walton Cr OX1 2JG   (01865) 310066
Thanks to its "appetising" Lebanese food, "sensible" prices and "friendly" service, this "plain and unadorned" Jericho favourite is "always busy". / **Details:** www.al-shami.co.uk; 11.45 pm; no Amex; no smoking area. **Accommodation:** 12 rooms, from £45.

Aziz   £ 30   ★
228-230 Cowley Rd OX4 1UH   (01865) 794945
"Consistently good" cooking (with an "unusual selection" of dishes) makes this "friendly" and "elegant" fixture the best-known – and many would say "the best" – of the local curry houses. / **Value tip:** 3-crs Sun buffet £8.90. **Details:** www.aziz.uk.com; 10.45 pm; closed Fri L; no smoking area.

Bangkok House   £ 23   𝔸★
42a High Bridge St OX1 2EP   (01865) 200705
This "lovely" central oriental continues to deliver all-round satisfaction, thanks to its "very attractive" setting, its "charming" staff and its "good choice" of "reasonably-priced" Thai food. / **Details:** 10.45 pm; closed Mon.

Bombay   £ 18   ★
82 Walton St OX2 6EA   (01865) 511188
"Great curries plus the fact you can BYO make this a great budget night out", say fans of this "award-winning" Jericho Indian. / **Details:** 11.45 pm; closed Fri L; no Amex.

Branca   £ 27
111 Walton St OX2 6AJ   (01865) 556111
Oxford's "new kid on the block" has made quite a splash, but reports on it are all over the place – a 'middle view' would be that it's a "pricey" but "standard" Brit-Italian brasserie, where service is "nice" but "slow", and whose "bright" setting is "hip, but noisy and echoey". / **Sample dishes:** summer minestrone soup; linguine with tiger prawns & chilli; tiramisu. **Details:** www.branca-restaurants.com; 11 pm.

Browns   £ 29   ✗
5-11 Woodstock Rd OX2 6HA   (01865) 319655
Some still say it's a "good stand-by", but dismay is widespread about how this once-loved varsity favourite has "gone to seed" under Six Continents (formerly called Bass) – "this place used to be lively, fun and reliable, now it's dreadful in every way". / **Sample dishes:** grilled goats cheese salad; confit duck with plum relish; bread & butter pudding. **Details:** www.browns-restaurants.com; 11.30 pm; no smoking area; no booking at D.

Café Coco   £ 21   𝔸
23 Cowley Rd OX4 1HP   (01865) 200232
This "trendy pizza place" is "popular" all day long (from the "infamous" breakfast pizza onwards). / **Sample dishes:** houmous & garlic bread; Greek wine, sausage & ham pizza; tiramisu. **Details:** 11 pm; no Amex; no booking.

Cherwell Boathouse   £29   A

Bardwell Rd OX2 6ST   (01865) 552746

A "charming waterside location (you can arrive by punt)",
"considerate" service and "a staggering wine list" are the
highlights at this long-established riverside destination;
the cooking, though, is a "let down". / **Sample dishes:** sweetcorn &
spring onion risotto; chicken in bacon with cranberry confit; Key lime pie.
Value tip: express 1-crs L £9.75. **Details:** www.cherwellboathouse.co.uk; 10 pm;
no smoking.

Chiang Mai   £31   A★★

Kemp Hall Pas, 130a High St OX1 4DH   (01865) 202233

"Very authentic" cuisine – rather oddly served in the "fantastic"
setting of a "beautiful" 14th-century building, just off the High
Street – makes this mega-popular Thai restaurant a "sensational"
success. / **Details:** 10.30 pm; no smoking area.

Chutney's   £23   ★

36 St Michaels St OX1 2EB   (01865) 724241

"Popular with all ages", this "airy", "loud" and "cheerful" central
spot offers "vibrant" south Indian cooking at modest prices;
veggies are well catered for. / **Value tip:** buffet L £7.50.
Details: www.chutneysoxford.co.uk; 11 pm; closed Mon.

Edamame   £18   ★

15 Holywell St OX1 3SA   (01865) 246916

"Friendly, relaxed, quick and efficient" – this "tiny"
(and "cramped") "hole in the wall" inspires nothing but praise,
especially as regards its "good and authentic" Japanese
"home cooking". / **Details:** www.edamame.co.uk; opp New College; 8.30 pm;
L only, except Fri & Sat when L & D, closed Mon; no Amex; no cards at L;
no smoking; no booking.

Elizabeth's   £43

82 St Aldates OX1 1RA   (01865) 242230

Mr Lopes the owner is set to retire, so the days of this "glorious
time warp" (est. 1966) may soon be up; hurry along if you're
looking for the ultimate in "traditional" Gallic restaurant
experiences – they really don't make 'em like this any more.
/ **Sample dishes:** seafood mousse; roast wood pigeon; champagne sorbet.
Value tip: set 3-crs L £17. **Details:** www.restaurant-elizabeth.com; 10.30 pm;
closed Mon; no smoking.

Fishers   £35

36-37 St Clements OX4 1AB   (01865) 243003

"Good fresh fish, sympathetically cooked" wins quite a following
for this cramped, nautically-themed bistro; doubters find the
cooking "variable", though, and service is very iffy.
/ **Sample dishes:** king prawns with garlic mayonnaise; seared tuna with aubergine
salsa & herb oil; sticky toffee pudding. **Value tip:** set 2-crs L £9.50.
Details: www.fishers-restaurant.com; by Magdalen Bridge; 10.30 pm; closed Mon L;
no Amex; no smoking area.

Gees   £38   A

61 Banbury Rd OX2 6PE   (01865) 553540

A "lovely" Victorian conservatory setting (complete with "twinkly
fairy lights") underpins the "romantic" appeal of this north Oxford
"old favourite"; the cooking is rather "unexciting", though,
and service can be "amateurish". / **Sample dishes:** king scallops with
leeks; roast lamb with borlotti beans & tapenade; chocolate soufflé with pistachio
sauce. **Value tip:** set 2-crs L £9.50. **Details:** 11 pm; no smoking.

The Gourmet Pizza Co   £26
100-101 Gloucester Grn OX1 2BU (01865) 793146
An "interesting pizza selection" helps make this outpost of the
London chain (now owned by PizzaExpress) a useful destination.
/ **Sample dishes:** Caesar salad; Mexican lime chicken pizza; banoffi pie.
Details: 11 pm; no smoking area.

Jamals   £18   ★
108 Walton St OX2 6XJ (01865) 310102
"The best Indian in Oxford, if not the cheapest", say fans of this
large but "personable" curry house, near the Phoenix Cinema.
/ **Details:** 11.15 pm.

Joe's   £26
21 Cowley Rd OX4 1HP (01865) 201120
"An excellent full English breakfast" (served all day) is a highlight
at this "quality local restaurant"; it's also "a great place to sit
outside on a sunny day". / **Sample dishes:** deep-fried Brie; burger with
cheese & bacon; sticky toffee pudding. **Details:** 11 pm; no Amex.

Kazbah   £19   𝔸
25-27 Cowley Rd OX4 1HP (01865) 202920
"Amazing Spanish/Moroccan décor" helps set an upbeat tone at
this "fun" "hang-out", not far from the city centre, where "tasty"
and "original" tapas come in "smallish portions".
/ **Sample dishes:** anchovies cured in vinegar; chicken & olive tajine with preserved
lemon; baklava. **Details:** 11 pm; no Amex; no booking.

Loch Fyne   £33
55 Walton St OX2 6AE (01865) 292510
It says much about Oxford's restaurants that this new chain outlet
– albeit one fêted by some as an "all-round good fish restaurant"
– is currently one of the most popular places in town; critics say
the cooking is only "OK to variable", and find the setting "a bit
bleak". / **Sample dishes:** lobster bisque with garlic rouille; rosemary-infused
bream with tomatoes & black olives; lemon sorbet. **Details:** www.loch-fyne.com;
10 pm; no smoking area.

The Old Parsonage   £34   𝔸
1 Banbury Rd OX2 6NN (01865) 310210
The setting is "dignified" and "tranquil", and "so close to the
centre of town", but the simple fare at this "romantic" medieval
townhouse-hotel is really rather "variable". / **Sample dishes:** seared
smoked salmon; rare marinated beef & salad; New York style cheesecake.
Details: www.oxford-hotels-restaurants.co.uk; 0.5m N of city centre; 10.30 pm.
Accommodation: 30 rooms, from £155.

Le Petit Blanc   £31
71-72 Walton St OX2 6AG (01865) 510999
"Not bad, but could do better" – ambivalence is something of a
watchword when it comes to Raymond Blanc's much talked-about
Jericho brasserie; it can be quite a "fun" place, but "amateurish"
service, in particular, can let the side down. / **Sample dishes:** foie
gras & chicken liver pâté; confit of guinea fowl with wild mushrooms; 'floating island'
dessert. **Value tip:** set 2-crs L & pre-theatre £12.50.
Details: www.lepetitblanc.co.uk; 11 pm; no smoking in dining room.

for updates visit www.hardens.com

Quod
Old Bank Hotel £31
92-94 High St OX1 4BN (01865) 202505

An "interesting" setting and a "busy, buzzy atmosphere" underpin the success of this Italian two-year-old (a new venture from the creator of Browns); "it's difficult to see why it is so popular", though, given food that's often "poorly prepared" and service which can be "unaccommodating". / **Sample dishes:** crab salad with sweet chilli; confit duck with caramelised prunes & lardons; chocolate marble brownie. **Value tip:** set 2-crs L £8.75. **Details:** www.quod.co.uk; opp All Souls College; 11 pm; no smoking area; no booking at L, Fri-Sun. **Accommodation:** 42 rooms, from £155.

Radcliffe Arms £11
67 Cranham St OX2 6DE (01865) 514762

"Sunday lunch is recommended" at this "student stalwart pub"; some cavil at its standards, but prices are of the "I-don't-know-how-they-do-it-so-cheap" variety. / **Sample dishes:** tomato soup; lasagne & salad; chocolate fudge cake. **Details:** 9 pm; no Amex.

Randolph £35
Beaumont St OX1 2LN (01865) 203100

This grand city-centre hotel once again attracted very mixed commentary this year; it recently changed hands, was refurbished and now has a new chef – an early report gives some cause for optimism. / **Sample dishes:** clam chowder; spiced duck with red cabbage; walnut tart with maple syrup ice cream. **Value tip:** set 3-crs L & pre-theatre £11. **Details:** www.macdonaldhotels.com; opp Ashmolean Museum; 10 pm; no smoking. **Accommodation:** 119 rooms, from £99.

Savannah
Royal Oxford Hotel £25 ★
17 Park End St OX1 1HU (01865) 793793

"Basic but good-quality steak or fish", "a good wine list" (from which "diners are invited to taste three before choosing") and a "trendy" setting come together to make this "minimalist" newcomer, near the railway station, a "neat concept". / **Sample dishes:** beef carpaccio; sirloin steak with hollandaise; lemon tart. **Details:** www.savannah.co.uk; 11 pm; no smoking area.

White House £30
2 Botley Rd OX2 0AB (01865) 242823

"It looks awful outside, but it's a treasure inside" – fans insist that "flashes of brilliance" illuminate the cooking at this well-established 'lounge bar and restaurant', near the station. / **Sample dishes:** sizzling red mullet & spring onions; beef medallions with sweet chilli sauce; tarte Tatin. **Details:** www.thewhitehouseoxford.co.uk; 9.30 pm; no Amex.

PADSTOW, CORNWALL 1–3B

Margot's £33 ★
11 Duke St PL28 8AB (01841) 533441

"Excellent service from the friendly owners" distinguishes this "tiny" seafood bistro; "really great food at a great price" is the tenor of nearly all reports. / **Sample dishes:** sardines with watercress & radish salad; rack of lamb with spring onion crust; saffron poached pears with shortbread. **Details:** www.margots.co.uk; 9.30 pm; closed Mon & Tue; closed Jan; no smoking.

No 6 Café   £ 37   ★
6 Middle St PL28 8AP   (01841) 532093
*News reached us before we went to press of the sale of this fish
bistro – apparently there are no plans for sweeping changes,
but fans of previous owners Karen & Peter Scott's "genuinely
innovative cooking" might like to know that they're adding to
Padstow's ever-growing restaurant scene by opening at 1 The
Strand (tel 01841 532565) in April 2003. / **Sample dishes:** Cornish
scallops with sweet chilli sauce; sea bass with lemongrass risotto; chocolate pot with
Tia Maria cream. **Details:** 10.30 pm (9.30 pm in winter); D only, closed Tue;
no Amex; no smoking; children: 12+. **Accommodation:** 2 rooms, from £65.*

Rick Stein's Café   £ 32
10 Middle St PL28 8AP   (01841) 532777
*'Great value for money' is the stated aim of Mr Stein's latest
outlet – a useful destination for those who wish to worship at the
altar of TV celebrity at relatively reasonable cost; it's a B&B,
so you can stay, too. / **Sample dishes:** Thai fishcakes with sweet & sour
cucumber dressing; char-grilled steak with tomato & red onion salad; lime posset
with balsamic strawberries. **Details:** www.rickstein.com; 10 pm; closed Sun;
no Amex; no smoking; booking essential at D. **Accommodation:** 3 rooms,
from £75.*

Seafood Restaurant   £ 62   ★
Riverside PL28 8BY   (01841) 532700
*Rick Stein's phenomenally popular HQ is once again delivering
standards to match its reputation (and the "personable" service,
in particular, is much improved on recent years); for such a "laid-
back" place, it's undoubtedly now "very pricey" but the fish is
"cooked to perfection". / **Sample dishes:** cuttlefish salad; shark & Dover sole
vindaloo; pannacotta with stewed rhubarb. **Details:** www.rickstein.com; 10 pm;
no Amex; no smoking in dining room; booking: max 14; children: 3+.
Accommodation: 19 rooms, from £95.*

St Petroc's House Bistro   £ 42
4 New St PL28 8BY   (01841) 532700
*Some find Rick Stein's secondary operation – the dining room of a
small hotel just off the seafront – a "relaxed and cheerful"
offshoot that's "nearly as good" as his main venture; misfires tend
to be serious, though, and a small but vociferous minority left
"deeply disappointed". / **Sample dishes:** poached egg, bacon & crouton
salad; lemon sole with sea salt & lemon; Gorgonzola with honey & walnuts.
Details: www.rickstein.com; 9.30 pm; closed Mon (in winter only); no Amex;
no smoking. **Accommodation:** 10 rooms, from £100.*

PAINSWICK, GLOUCESTERSHIRE   2–2B

Painswick Hotel   £ 46   A
Kemps Ln GL6 6YB   (01452) 812160
*"A grand country house, with cooking to match" is the theme of
most feedback on this "glorious" hotel, "beautifully located" in the
Cotswolds; a couple of disgruntled reporters, though, spoilt its
otherwise unblemished record. / **Sample dishes:** smoked quail ravioli;
Cornish monkfish wrapped in Parma ham & basil; rhubarb & custard upside-down
crème brûlée. **Details:** www.painswickhotel.com; 9.30 pm; no smoking in dining
room. **Accommodation:** 19 rooms, from £120.*

for updates visit www.hardens.com

PARK GATE, HAMPSHIRE   2–4D

Kam's Palace   **£32**   𝔸 ★

I Bridge Rd SO31 7GD (01489) 583328

"Over the top, but as good a Chinese as you'll find" – this pagoda-style spot is praised for both its "wonderful" food and its "marvellous" ambience. / Details: 10.30 pm, Fri & Sat 11 pm.

PARKGATE, CHESHIRE   5–2B

Marsh Cat   **£26**

I Mostyn Sq CH64 6SL (0151) 336 1963

With its "lovely estuary views", this popular bistro "tries hard" and offers a "very unusual" menu; it's a "good-value" destination (especially if you go for "the Sunday lunch or the early-bird"), but this year's reports were rather variable. / Sample dishes: crab claws & monkfish in Thai coconut sauce; Cajun-blackened swordfish & cat fish; nutty torte with raspberries. Value tip: set 2-crs weekday L £7.95. Details: www.marshcat.com; 10.30 pm; smoking discouraged.

PAXFORD, GLOUCESTERSHIRE   2–1C

Churchill Arms   **£30**   ★

GL55 6XH (01386) 594000

"Sophisticated and delicious pub food" (if "at restaurant prices") has made a big name for this ambitious Cotswold boozer – "thank heavens you can't book, or we'd never get a table!" / Sample dishes: duck with grapefruit & fennel salad; guinea fowl in Madeira & mushroom cream sauce; sticky toffee pudding. Details: www.thechurchillarms.com; off Fosse Way; 9 pm; no Amex; no booking. Accommodation: 4 rooms, from £70.

PENSHURST, KENT   3–3B

Spotted Dog   **£28**   𝔸 ★

Smarts Hill TN11 8EP (01892) 870253

"Beautiful views over west Kent" and an "adventurous" menu – dispensed by "friendly" staff in "generous" portions – help make this a country pub of more than usual note. / Sample dishes: crispy seafood platter; chicken in tarragon & garlic sauce; chocolate Bailey's mousse. Details: near Penshurst Place; 9.15 pm; no Amex; no smoking area.

PERTH, PERTH & KINROSS   9–3C

63 Tay Street   **£37**   ★

63 Tay St PH2 8NN (01738) 441451

Jeremy & Shona Wares "have got it together" on the food front at their minimally-decorated two-year-old venture in the heart of the city, which is praised for its "precise cooking using high-quality ingredients". / Sample dishes: smoked trout salad with lardons; Angus beef with spring onion mash; date & fig pudding. Details: www.63taystreet.co.uk; on city side of River Tay, 1m from Dundee Rd; 9 pm; closed Mon & Sun; no smoking; children: 10+ at D.

Let's Eat   **£35**   𝔸 ★

77-79 Kinnoull St PH1 5EZ (01738) 643377

"Great local produce" cooked to "a consistently high standard", and "super service" win this "very pleasant" bistro unanimous recommendations. / Sample dishes: smoked salmon with spiced prawns & avocado; herb-crusted lamb with rosemary jus; steamed ginger pudding with rhubarb. Details: www.letseatperth.co.uk; opp North Inch Park; 9.45 pm; closed Mon & Sun; no smoking area.

PETERSFIELD, HAMPSHIRE 2–3D

River Kwai £27
16-18 Dragon St GU13 4JJ (01730) 267077
Rarity value helps make this Thai notable in the area (though metropolitans may sniff that the cooking rises no higher than "good provincial" standard). / **Details:** *10.30 pm; closed Mon L & Sun L; no smoking area.*

PHILLEIGH, CORNWALL 1–4B

Roseland Inn £27 Ⓐ
TR2 5NB (01872) 580254
A picturesque and "atmospheric" old country pub (where dining outside is the preferred course); top marks this year go to the "seafood platter for 2 (order 24 hrs ahead) — it's fantastic in size and quality". / **Sample dishes:** *duck liver pâté; rump steak with potatoes & salad; chocolate bread & butter pudding.* **Details:** *near King Harry ferry; 9 pm; no Amex; no smoking area.*

PICKERING, NORTH YORKSHIRE 8–4C

White Swan £35 ★
Market Pl YO18 7AA (01751) 472288
Disappointments are not unknown, but the cooking at this town-centre coaching inn generally gets a good rep — "great bar lunches" (and a "fantastic French wine list") are among the highlights. / **Sample dishes:** *chicken liver & foie gras terrine; rack of lamb with aubergine & tomato caviar; grilled figs & Amaretto cream.* **Details:** *www.white-swan.co.uk; 9 pm; no smoking.* **Accommodation:** *12 rooms, from £90.*

PINNER, GREATER LONDON 3–3A

Friends £36
11 High St HA5 5PJ (020) 8866 0286
Local fans are generous in their praise of Terry Farr's well-established restaurant, which is housed in a "beautiful Tudor building"; it is world-famous in Pinner for the "sophisticated French cuisine" served in its "cosy" setting. / **Sample dishes:** *leek & goats cheese strudel; lamb steak with bubble 'n' squeak; Bramley apple crumble.* **Details:** *www.friendsrestaurant.co.uk; near Pinner Underground station; 10 pm; closed Sun D; no smoking area.*

La Giralda £18
66-68 Pinner Grn HA5 2AB (020) 8868 3429
This long-established Spanish stalwart is a well-run and "very reasonably priced" local destination, and as a result is usually "busy"(-going-on-"crowded"). / **Sample dishes:** *melon with Serrano ham; pink trout with nut butter; poached pears with syrup.* **Details:** *A404 to Cuckoo Hill Junction; 10 pm; closed Mon & Sun D.*

PLUMTREE, NOTTINGHAMSHIRE   5–3D

Perkins   £ 29
Old Railway Station NG12 5NA   (0115) 937 3695
It has an "interesting location in an old railway station", but even
fans (and there are many) of this "relaxed" bistro concede that it's
"not exciting" – what they like is that it's very "reliable" and that
"the people still care". / **Sample dishes:** spicy tomato & oatmeal soup; fillet
steak with pickled walnut sauce; lime torte with dark chocolate pastry.
Value tip: set 2-crs L £9.75. **Details:** www.perkinsrestaurant.co.uk; off A606
between Nottingham & Melton Mowbray; 9.30 pm; closed Mon & Sun D;
no smoking area.

PLYMOUTH, DEVON   1–3C

Chez Nous   £ 46   ★
13 Frankfort Gate PL1 1QA   (01752) 266793
"Very good traditional French cuisine" generally enables this
"classic" restaurant to transcend its setting "in a dreadful '60s
shopping district"; the odd "dull" meal, however, is not unknown.
/ **Sample dishes:** crab & orange salad; fillet steak with wild mushrooms; tarte Tatin.
Details: www.business.thisisplymouth.co.uk/cheznous; near Theatre Royal;
10.30 pm; closed Mon, Sat L & Sun; closed 3 weeks in Feb & Sep.

Platters   £ 26   ★
12 The Barbican PL1 2LS   (01752) 227262
"Imagine a transport caff serving generous portions of wickedly
fresh fish plainly and well cooked" – that's the picture painted by
all the feedback on this "cheap and cheerful" Barbican fixture.
/ **Sample dishes:** steamed mussels; deep-fried cod & chips; tiramisu.
Details: 10 pm; no Amex.

Thai Palace   £ 25
3 Elliot St, The Hoe PL1 2PP   (01752) 255770
"Spicy and genuine (well almost)" cooking makes this "pleasant"
and "consistent" oriental worth knowing about in this
underprovided city. / **Details:** 11 pm; D only, closed Sun.

PONTELAND, NORTHUMBERLAND   8–2B

Café 21   £ 32   ★
35 The Broadway, Darras Hall NE20 9PW   (01661) 820357
It's "small" and "rather noisy" (and not particularly nicely situated,
near Newcastle airport), but this offshoot of Terry Laybourne's
locally-eminent group is "always a great place to go" on account
of its "lovely staff" and super Mediterranean cooking.
/ **Sample dishes:** goats cheese bruschetta; fishcakes with buttered spinach &
parsley cream; lime pannacotta with rhubarb. **Details:** 1m past Newcastle Airport,
off A1; 10 pm; D only, closed Sun.

The Smithy   £ 32
3 Bell Villas NE20 9BD   (01661) 820020
A short drive from Newcastle airport, this bistro attached to a
large inn is praised for its "consistent" cooking.
/ **Sample dishes:** seared scallops in leek & ginger broth; duck confit & puy lentils
with blackberry jus; roast peaches with nougatine. **Details:** 10 pm; closed Sat L &
Sun D; no Amex; no smoking in dining room.

POOLE, DORSET   2–4C

Mansion House   £37   A
Thames St BH15 1JN   (01202) 685666
*"A lovely panelled dining room" creates a "classic", "clubby"
ambience at this Georgian townhouse hotel; the "interesting
modern cooking", generally praised, can be "variable".*
/ **Sample dishes:** *mackerel terrine; scallops with lentils & Indian spices; bread &
butter pudding.* **Value tip:** *set 3-crs Sun L £17.50.*
Details: *www.themansionhouse.co.uk; follow signs for Ferry, turn left onto quayside;
9 pm; closed Sat L & Sun D; no smoking in dining room; children: 5+.*
Accommodation: *32 rooms, from £120.*

PORT APPIN, ARGYLL & BUTE   9–3B

Airds Hotel   £62
PA38 4DF   (01631) 730236
*Under the Allen family, this lochside hotel was "a real haven of
tranquillity and excellence"; they've now relocated to Perthshire,
and the new owners (from summer 2002) have quite an act to
follow.* / **Sample dishes:** *seared scallops with slow-cooked fennel; salmon with
deep-fried capers & bean salad; caramel parfait with toasted almonds.*
Details: *www.airds-hotel.com; 20m N of Oban; 8.30 pm; closed part of Dec & Jan;
no Amex; no smoking; children: 8+.* **Accommodation:** *12 rooms, from £194.*

Pier House Hotel   £37   A ★
PA38 4DE   (01631) 730302
*"Fantastic views", "attentive" service and "superb fresh seafood"
(in "generous portions") can make a visit to this remote dining
room, on the shores of Loch Linnhe, a "memorable" experience.*
/ **Sample dishes:** *scallops with rice; beef stroganoff; death by chocolate.*
Details: *www.pierhousehotel.co.uk; just off A828 by pier; 9.15 pm; no Amex;
no smoking.* **Accommodation:** *12 rooms, from £70.*

PORTAFERRY, COUNTY DOWN   10–2D

The Narrows   £35
8 Shore Rd BT22 1JY   (028) 4272 8148
*"Wonderful fresh fish" was the highlight of reports on this
somewhat "crowded" restaurant-with-rooms, which has "lovely
views" over Strangford Lough; let's hope new chef Paul Graham
can maintain his predecessor's high standards.*
/ **Sample dishes:** *lobster & marinated tomato salad; grilled turbot with tarragon
cream; strawberries with hazelnut meringue.* **Details:** *www.narrows.co.uk; opposite
the marina; 9 pm; no smoking area.* **Accommodation:** *13 rooms, from £85.*

Portaferry Hotel   £35   A ★
10 The Strand BT22 1PE   (028) 4272 8231
*"Superb seafood" is the culinary highlight of a visit to this
"romantic" ferryside hotel, which overlooks Strangford Lough.*
/ **Sample dishes:** *warm goats cheese, Parma ham & fig salad; salmon & champ
with prawn cream; double chocolate torte with coconut ice cream.*
Details: *www.portaferryhotel.com; on shore front, opposite ferry slipway; 9 pm.*
Accommodation: *14 rooms, from £90.*

PORTHGAIN, PEMBROKESHIRE   4–4B

Harbour Lights   £38   *A* ★
SA62 5BL   (01348) 831549
An "atmospheric quayside shed", where "fish straight from the rod" is prepared by "a chef who allows ingredients to speak for themselves". / **Sample dishes:** French onion soup; grilled Dover sole with prawn butter; strawberry & cream meringues. **Details:** www.art2by.com; 7.5m NE of St Davids; 8.30 pm; open only Thu-Sat D (open for L in Jul & Aug); no Amex; no smoking area; children: 12.

PORTMEIRION, GWYNEDD   4–2C

Portmeirion Hotel   £41   *A* ★
LL48 6ER   (01766) 770000
"A magical setting" – in the midst of Sir Clough Williams-Ellis's fantasy Mediterranean village – contributes to the "wonderful" ambience of this romantic dining room "overlooking the sea"; the "excellent, traditional cuisine" does not let the side down. / **Sample dishes:** crab & smoked salmon potato cake; chicken & pancetta with wild mushroom tartlet; Barabrith & butter pudding. **Value tip:** set 2-crs L £11.50. **Details:** off A487 at Minffordd; 9 pm; closed Mon L; no smoking. **Accommodation:** 51 rooms, from £125.

PORTPATRICK, DUMFRIES & GALLOWAY   7–2A

Crown Hotel   £28
North Cr DG9 8SX   (01776) 810261
"A lovely harbourside setting" is the special attraction of this comfortable hotel dining room; its fish and seafood dishes generally please, but some find them "over-ambitious". / **Sample dishes:** herring & prawn platter; venison in pepper & brandy sauce; strawberry shortcake. **Details:** 10 pm; no smoking area. **Accommodation:** 12 rooms, from £72.

PORTREATH, CORNWALL   1–4A

Tabb's   £31   ★
Tregea Ter TR16 4LD   (01209) 842488
"Fresh fish, vibrantly cooked" is the culinary highlight at Nigel Tabb's converted granite forge – a "special" find in an area without many competing culinary attractions. / **Sample dishes:** smoked mackerel & vegetable pâté; baked chicken with shredded leeks; dark chocolate marquise. **Details:** 9 pm; D only (except Sun open L & D), closed Tue; no Amex; no smoking in dining room.

PORTRUSH, COUNTY ANTRIM   10–1C

Ramore   £24   *A* ★
The Harbour BT56 8D3   (028) 7082 4313
The "wide-ranging clientèle" creates a "buzzy atmosphere" at this stylish bar/canteen; it's known for "interesting, freshly-cooked" Mediterranean fare (including pizza) that's "always very good value". / **Sample dishes:** tortilla chips with guacamole; pizza with spicy meatballs & peppers; tiramisu. **Details:** 10 pm; no Amex; need 10+ to book; children: before 8 pm only.

sign up for the survey at www.hardens.com   287

PRESTBURY, CHESHIRE   5–2B

White House   £ 37   A ★
New Rd SK10 4DG   (01625) 829376
*"Good sound modern food", "friendly" service and an "airy"
ambience have helped make this popular village restaurant
"the best hereabouts"; it now has a new sibling, Amba, in Hale.*
/ **Sample dishes:** Caesar salad with sautéed tiger prawns; Dover sole with sea
salt & lime; strawberry brûlée with roast rhubarb. **Value tip:** set 3-crs L £14.50.
Details: 2m N of Macclesfield on A538; 10 pm; closed Mon L & Sun D.
Accommodation: 11 rooms, from £70.

PRESTEIGNE, POWYS   5–4A

Hat Shop   £ 25
7 High St LD8 2BA   (01544) 260017
*"A limited menu, but one that's good value" is the unanimous
verdict on the "tasty" nosh at this "quirky" local favourite, which is
liked for its "easy, relaxed and unpretentious" approach.*
/ **Sample dishes:** aubergine & sweet potato samosas; chicken with bacon & walnut
stuffing; chocolate charlotte. **Details:** 9 pm; closed Sun; no credit cards; no smoking
area.

PRESTON BAGOT, WARWICKSHIRE   5–4C

The Crabmill   £ 36   A ★
B95 5DR   (01926) 843342
*A "very unusual and innovative menu", with a Mediterranean
slant, makes this "really smart pub/restaurant" – "brilliantly
converted from an old house" – a pretty-much-unanimous local
recommendation.* / **Sample dishes:** roast veal with tuna confit & lemon
mayonnaise; char-grilled pork with sage & lemon polenta; pannacotta with
honeycomb biscuits. **Details:** on main road between Warwick & Henley; 9.30 pm;
closed Sun D; no smoking area.

PRESTON, LANCASHIRE   5–1A

Bruccianis   £ 5
91 Fishergate PR1 2NJ   (01772) 252406
*A "busy", long-established (1935) café near the station that
serves "very fresh sandwiches, soup, coffee and so on" in a "'50s-
style" setting.* / **Sample dishes:** no starters; baguette with chicken, bacon &
salad; cheesecake. **Details:** 5.30 pm; no credit cards.

Simply Heathcote's   £ 35
23 Winckley Sq PR1 3JJ   (01772) 252732
*Paul Heathcote is undoubtedly a "renowned" local chef, but this
"clinical" town-centre brasserie attracts very mixed reviews,
and some reporters think it an unduly "expensive" place that
"trades on its reputation"; the basement is being reformatted in
late-2002, and is to be relaunched as a pizzeria called The Olive
Press.* / **Sample dishes:** grilled mackerel with sour cream; wild mushroom linguine
with Parmesan & basil; rum & raisin parfait. **Value tip:** set 2-crs L £12.50.
Details: www.heathcotes.co.uk; 10 pm, Sat 10.30 pm; no smoking in dining room.

PRESTWOOD, BUCKINGHAMSHIRE   3–2A
Polecat   £ 25
170 Wycombe Rd HB16 0HJ   (01494) 862253
*"Always busy, particularly on sunny evenings and for lunch" –
this large, but "overcrowded", roadside tavern is a local hit,
praised for its "great-value" menu. / **Sample dishes:** baked field
mushrooms with melted cheese; walnut-crusted pork with spring onion salsa; coconut
meringues with mango syllabub. **Details:** on A4128 between Great Missenden &
High Wycombe; 9 pm; closed Sun D; no credit cards; no smoking area; children: not
permitted in dining room.*

PRIORS HARDWICK, WARWICKSHIRE   2–1D
Butchers Arms   £ 41   ★
Church End CV47 7SN   (01327) 260504
*A "welcoming" attitude helps win fans for this "pleasant" poshed-
up boozer; the menu is on the "traditional" side (including
puddings from the trolley). / **Sample dishes:** mushroom & Stilton tart;
beef stroganoff; profiteroles. **Value tip:** set 3-crs L £17.
Details: www.thebutchersarms.com; 9.30 pm; closed Sat L & Sun D; no smoking in
dining room.*

PURTON, WILTSHIRE   2–2C
Pear Tree at Purton   £ 42
SN5 4ED   (01793) 772100
*Reports on this "quiet", luxuriously-converted rectory are fewer
than we would like; the food is "good", though, by all accounts.
/ **Sample dishes:** creamed leek & smoked haddock broth; roast lamb with olive
mash & pesto gravy; pear & hazelnut tart with fudge ice cream.
Details: www.peartreepurton.co.uk; 9.15 pm; closed Sat L. **Accommodation:** 18
rooms, from £110.*

PWLLHELI, GWYNEDD   4–2C
Plas Bodegroes   £ 46   Ⓐ★★
Nefyn Rd LL53 5TH   (01758) 612363
*"Just a magical place, with food to match" – Chris Chown's
country house hotel offers "simply brilliant cooking" in a
"beautiful" and "peaceful" setting. / **Sample dishes:** cod with
Carmarthen ham & laverbread; roast spiced lamb with couscous; cardamom crème
brûlée. **Value tip:** set 3-crs Sun L £15.50. **Details:** www.bodegroes.co.uk; on A497
1m W of Pwllheli; 9.30 pm; closed Mon, Tue-Sat D only, Sun open L & D; no Amex;
no smoking. **Accommodation:** 11 rooms, from £70.*

RAMSGILL-IN-NIDDERDALE, NORTH YORKSHIRE 8–4B
Yorke Arms   £ 46   ★
HG3 5RL   (01423) 755243
*Frances Atkins has quite a reputation as a chef, and her cooking
can now be enjoyed at this "beautiful country inn"; the food is
"excellent" – but it comes at "London prices", and some find the
surroundings rather "jaded". / **Sample dishes:** lobster ravioli; lamb wrapped
in parsley crust; warm pear & butterscotch tart. **Details:** www.yorke-arms.co.uk;
4m W of Pateley Bridge; 9.15 pm; no smoking; booking: max 6.
Accommodation: 14 rooms, from £105.*

READING, BERKSHIRE   2–2D
Bens Thai   £ 24
Royal Ct, Kings Rd RG1 4AE   (0118) 959 6169
*"Extremely welcoming" service is a highlight at this "no-frills"
riverside Thai, which offers "consistent cooking that's well priced".
/ **Details:** 10 pm; closed Sun.*

London Street Brasserie £ 39
2-4 London St RG1 4SE   (0118) 950 5036
A "great riverside setting" and "good, if pricey" cooking win quite
a following for this "slick" modern brasserie; it's "rather cramped",
though, and service is notably "unreliable". / *Sample dishes:* foie
gras & duck terrine with raisin toast; sea bass with baby squid & saffron dressing;
Bakewell tart & custard. *Value tip:* set 2-crs L & pre-theatre £12.95.
Details: www.londonstbrasserie.co.uk; 10.30 pm.

Nino's £ 26
46 Market Pl RG1 2DT   (0118) 958 8966
A simple central Italian; it's praised for its "good-value" cooking
and its "sympathetic" staff. / *Sample dishes:* avocado salad; fillet steak
with Dolcelatte cream; Sicilian ice cream. *Details:* www.ninos-restaurants.co.uk;
10 pm; closed Sun L.

Old Siam £ 29
Kings Wk, Kings St RG1 2HG   (0118) 951 2600
It has an "odd location", in a shopping mall, but "reliable" food
helps make this popular Thai a "value-for-money" destination.
/ *Value tip:* set 2-crs L £9.50. *Details:* www.oldsiam.co.uk; 10 pm; closed Sun;
no smoking in dining room.

Standard Nepalese Tandoori £ 22 ★
141-143 Caversham Rd RG1 8AU   (0118) 959 0093
This "reliable", long-established Indian "continues to be of high
quality"; it's "always busy", even though service "tends to be
slow". / *Details:* 11 pm; no smoking area.

REIGATE, SURREY   3–3B

La Barbe £ 40
71 Bell St RH2 7AN   (01737) 241966
Some think "it's getting a bit pricey", but this "really decent,
suburban French place" of over twenty years standing still
commands widespread support, thanks to its "reliable and
friendly" approach and its "classic, brasserie-style" food.
/ *Sample dishes:* Roquefort mousse with poached pears; chicken, apple & cider
casserole; iced coffee mousse with lavender sauce. *Value tip:* set 2-crs L £15.95.
Details: www.labarbe.co.uk; 9.30 pm; closed Sat L & Sun; no smoking area.

Tony Tobin @ The Dining Room £ 47
59a High St RH2 9AE   (01737) 226650
Too many uncharacteristically poor reports – including "tired"
cooking and "barely adequate" service – marred this year's
feedback on TV-chef Toby Tobin's "cramped" and increasingly
"overpriced" town-centre dining room; perhaps it was the strain –
after 8 years at the stoves – of preparing to take over the
ownership, which was finally effected in the summer of 2002,
and which has also been marked by a major expansion.
/ *Sample dishes:* crispy squid with fried green tomatoes; crispy duck with melted
onions; banana tart with vanilla ice cream. *Value tip:* set 2-crs L £13 (not Sun).
Details: 10 pm; closed Sat L & Sun D; no smoking.

for updates visit www.hardens.com

REYNOLDSTON, SWANSEA   1–1C

Fairyhill   £41   A★★
SA3 1BS   (01792) 390139
"A magical place in the heart of the Gower"; with its "sensational
and inventive" food (largely "locally sourced"), this "top-notch but
unstuffy" country house hotel dining room, has arguably
"done more to modernise Welsh cooking than any other
restaurant". / **Sample dishes:** Gower crab bisque; chicken supreme with
mustard risotto cake; banana soufflé pancakes with fudge sauce. **Value tip:** set
2-crs L £14.95. **Details:** www.fairyhill.net; 20 mins from M4, J47 off B4295; 9 pm;
no smoking; children: 8+. **Accommodation:** 8 rooms, from £125.

RIDGEWAY, SOUTH YORKSHIRE   5–2C

Old Vicarage   £46   ✕
Ridgeway Moor S12 3XW   (0114) 247 5814
"Living on a reputation earned many years ago"; perhaps it's
because the "hushed" style is just what Michelin inspectors seem
to like, they seem not to have noticed that the cooking here often
"fails to deliver". / **Sample dishes:** spinach frittata with dill-marinated salmon;
calves liver & foie gras with sping onion mash; baked chocolate pudding with fudge
sauce. **Details:** www.theoldvicarage.co.uk; 10 mins SE of city centre; 10 pm; closed
Mon & Sun D; no smoking in dining room.

RIPLEY, SURREY   3–3A

Michels   £46
High St GU23 6AQ   (01483) 224777
Despite a change of ownership (with a more Mediterranean slant
to the Gallic menu), the verdict on this "comfortable" restaurant,
prettily housed on a cobbled street, is largely unchanged –
"decent food in a staid atmosphere". / **Sample dishes:** potato pancake
with smoked salmon & caviar; roast sea bass with artichoke hearts; rhubarb &
strawberry terrine. **Value tip:** set 2-crs Sun L £18. **Details:** 9.15 pm; closed Mon,
Tue-Sat D only, closed Sun D; no smoking.

ROADE, NORTHANTS   3–1A

Roade House   £39   ★
16 High St NN7 2NW   (01604) 863372
A "consistently high standard" of "well-executed simple fare" wins
endorsements for the dining room at this comfortable,
but unpretentious, hotel. / **Sample dishes:** tomato & basil tartlet with
prosciutto; sea bass with ginger & lime sauce; apple & blackcurrant crumble.
Details: www.roadehousehotel.co.uk; 9.30 pm; closed Mon L & Sun; no smoking in
dining room. **Accommodation:** 10 rooms, from £67.

ROCKBEARE, DEVON   1–3D

Jack in the Green Inn   £30   ★
London Rd EX5 2EE   (01404) 822240
The interior "lacks atmosphere a bit", but everyone agrees that
the "good, short menu" at this "busy" pub, just off the old A30,
delivers some "excellent" results. / **Sample dishes:** smoked seafood
mousse; roast pigeon with salsify & pink peppercorns; rice pudding with pralines.
Value tip: set 2-crs Sun L £13.25. **Details:** www.jackinthegreen.uk.com; 9.30 pm;
no Amex; no smoking in dining room; children: Sun L only.

sign up for the survey at www.hardens.com   *291*

ROMALDKIRK, COUNTY DURHAM 8–3B

The Rose & Crown £ 34 Ⓐ
DL12 9EB (01833) 650213
*Despite the odd gripe regarding "average" cooking,
this "wonderful" country pub – "beautifully located on the village
green" – generally wins praise for its "consistent" traditional fare.
/ **Sample dishes:** Cotherstone cheese fritters with sweet & sour aubergines; roast
lamb with puy lentils & minto pesto; baked chocolate cheesecake.
Details: www.rose-and-crown.co.uk; 6m NW of Barnard Castle on B6277; 9 pm;
D only, except Sun when L only; no Amex; no smoking; children: 6+.
Accommodation: 12 rooms, from £86.*

ROMSEY, HAMPSHIRE 2–3D

Old Manor House £ 40
21 Palmerston St SO51 8GF (01794) 517353
*"The Bregolis are a dream, especially if they like you" – those not
so favoured may find "abysmal" service and a "cold" and "stiff"
atmosphere at this long-established Italian; the food, however,
is often "great". / **Sample dishes:** carpaccio of foie gras; chicken with wild
mushrooms; ice cream. **Details:** 9.30 pm; closed Mon & Sun D.*

ROTHWELL, NORTHANTS 5–4D

The Thai Garden £ 29
3 Market HI NN14 6EP (01536) 712345
*"Very good food" and "lovely cheerful service" combine to make
this an above-average oriental destination; it's "great with
children", too. / **Details:** off A14 near Kettering; 11 pm; no smoking area.*

ROWDE, WILTSHIRE 2–2C

George & Dragon £ 36 ★
High St SN10 2PN (01380) 723053
*"An excellent choice of superb fresh fish" is the highlight of the
"imaginative" menu at this "relaxed" and "convivial" backwoods
boozer. / **Sample dishes:** spinach & watercress soup; curried smoked haddock
pancakes; baked orange custard. **Value tip:** set 2-crs L £10. **Details:** on A342
between Devizes & Chippenham; 10 pm; closed Mon & Sun; no Amex; no smoking.*

ROYAL LEAMINGTON SPA, WARWICKSHIRE 5–4C

Emperors £ 26
Bath Pl CV31 3BP (01926) 313666
*"Above-average" Chinese cooking makes this a popular
destination hereabouts – it's "always busy". / **Details:** 10.45 pm; closed
Sun.*

Thai Elephant £ 30
20 Regent St CV32 5HQ (01926) 886882
*It's quite pricey by the standards of provincial orientals, but –
thanks to its "good" food and its "pleasant", slightly unusual
setting – this "busy" basement spot maintains a strong local
following. / **Details:** 10.30 pm; closed Sat L.*

RYE, EAST SUSSEX   3–4C

Landgate Bistro   £ 25
5-6 Landgate TN31 7LH   (01797) 222829
A "low-key", long-established English bistro, which continues to win
acclaim as a "good-value", "pleasant local eatery"; it's a shame,
though, that "mediocre service seems almost a point of principle".
/ **Sample dishes:** broad bean & pecorino tart; lambs kidneys with grain mustard
sauce; Jamaican chocolate cream. **Details:** www.landgatebistro.co.uk; 9.30 pm,
Sat 10 pm; D only, closed Mon & Sun; no smoking in dining room.

Mermaid   £ 51   A
Mermaid St TN31 7EY   (01797) 223065
"Ignore the inevitable tourists", say fans, and this "beautiful
ancient inn" – with its "real Tudor dining room" – can offer a
"lovely" experience; the cooking is "expensive", though,
and "rather ordinary". / **Sample dishes:** pan-fried scallops & langoustines;
lobster thermidor; crème brûlée. **Value tip:** set 3-crs L £18.50.
Details: www.mermaidinn.com; 9.15 pm; no smoking. **Accommodation:** 31
rooms, from £150.

SALISBURY, WILTSHIRE   2–3C

Jade   £ 28   ★
109a Exeter St SP1 2SF   (01722) 333355
"Salisbury's best Chinese restaurant" – is perhaps rather more
notable than that description might suggest; "very good lobster"
and "reasonably-priced seafood platters" are among the
highlights. / **Details:** near the Cathedral; 11.30 pm; closed Sun; no Amex.

LXIX   £ 40   ★
69 New St SP1 2PH   (01722) 340000
"The best food in Salisbury by far" is to be found at this modern
venture (also incorporating a bar and bistro); it's unanimously
praised for its "interesting" modern British menu and "cracking"
service. / **Sample dishes:** blue fin tuna with chilli salsa; roast cod with lime oil &
noisette butter; chocolate marquise. **Details:** adjacent to Cathedral Close; 10 pm;
closed Sat L & Sun; no smoking; children: 12+.

SALTAIRE, WEST YORKSHIRE   5–1C

Salts Diner   £ 22   A
Salts Mill, Victoria Rd BD18 3LB   (01274) 530533
This "interesting converted mill space" makes a "lovely", "breezy",
"family-orientated" destination that's extremely popular with the
locals; the cooking is not the main attraction, but "maintains a
good standard". / **Sample dishes:** garlic bread; confit duck leg; sticky toffee
pudding. **Details:** 2m from Bradford on A650; 5 pm; L only; no Amex; no smoking
area.

SAWLEY, LANCASHIRE   5–1B

Spread Eagle   £ 24   A ★
BB7 4NH   (01200) 441202
"Gloriously unfashionable in every respect other than the stylish
food" – this "wonderful" old hostelry offers an "excellent-value"
package, which includes "magnificent views" over the River
Ribble. / **Sample dishes:** fish hors d'oeuvres; braised lamb with root vegetable
sauce; tarte Tatin. **Value tip:** set 2-crs L £8.50.
Details: www.the-spreadeagle.co.uk; NE of Clitheroe off A59; 9 pm; closed Mon &
Sun D; no smoking.

SCAWTON, NORTH YORKSHIRE 8–4C

Hare Inn £29 𝔸★

YO7 2HG (01845) 597289

A "classic isolated country pub", serving "good-value", "farmhouse" cooking; it's "very busy, but efficiently run".
/ **Sample dishes:** *warm smoked duck & bacon salad; deep-fried Whitby haddock; strawberry pavlova.* **Details:** *off A170; 9.30 pm; closed Mon; no Amex; no smoking area.*

SEAHAM, COUNTY DURHAM 8–2B

Seaham Hall 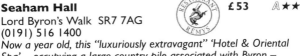 £53 𝔸★★

Lord Byron's Walk SR7 7AG
(0191) 516 1400

Now a year old, this "luxuriously extravagant" 'Hotel & Oriental Spa' – occupying a large country pile associated with Byron – is becoming the most exciting location in the North East; in its "designer" restaurant, chef John Connell provides "proper cuisine, of a type normally found in London". / **Sample dishes:** *assiette of foie gras; venison with chocolate & coffee jus; chocolate & orange tart with citrus confit.* **Details:** *www.seaham-hall.com; 9.30 pm; no smoking in dining room.* **Accommodation:** *19 rooms, from £145.*

SEAVIEW, ISLE OF WIGHT 2–4D

Seaview Hotel £32 𝔸★

High St PO34 5EX (01983) 612711

"The place to eat if on the Isle" – this "civilised" family-run hotel is our reporters most commented-on venture hereabouts, not least due to its "interesting" cooking and "cosy and informal" atmosphere; the "traditional" dining room and the modern Sunshine Room both share the same menu – there's "good bar food", too. / **Sample dishes:** *hot crab ramekin; monkfish wrapped in Parma ham with crab bisque; blackcurrant sorbet with forest fruits.* **Details:** *www.seaviewhotel.co.uk; 9.30 pm; closed Sun D; no smoking area; children: 5+ at D.* **Accommodation:** *16 rooms, from £95.*

SEDGEFIELD, COUNTY DURHAM 8–3B

Dun Cow £27 ★

43 Front St TS21 3AT (01740) 620894

Quality pub grub is "matched by a good selection of real ales" at this popular fixture, by the village green. / **Sample dishes:** *freshwater prawns with lime dressing; medallions of pork with apple sauce; cheesecake.* **Details:** *www.mortal-man-inns.co.uk; 9.30 pm.* **Accommodation:** *6 rooms, from £65.*

SELLACK, HEREFORDSHIRE 2–1B

The Lough Pool Inn £29 ★

HR9 6LX (01989) 730236

"Stephen Bull has really found his feet in Herefordshire", say fans of this returning local son's 17th-century inn, where "sophisticated" modern cooking can be enjoyed at "very un-metropolitan prices"; some prefer the "rough and ready" ambience in the bar to that in the more low-key restaurant. / **Sample dishes:** *butternut squash risotto; roast monkfish with curried red lentil salsa; warm ginger cake with brown bread ice cream.* **Details:** *9.30 pm; closed Mon; no smoking; children: 14 (unless eating).*

SHEFFIELD, SOUTH YORKSHIRE   5–2C

Bahn Nah   £ 25   ★
19-21 Nile St S10 2PN   (0114) 268 4900
*"An excellent Thai restaurant, even if it's very small" – Mrs Low's
"friendly" oriental has been "consistently good for many years
now". / **Details:** on A57 from Sheffield to Manchester; 11 pm; D only, closed Sun;
no Switch; no smoking.*

Everest   £ 25
59-61 Chesterfield Rd S8 0RL   (0114) 258 2975
*"A good Indian in a nice setting" – nothing remarkable, but worth
knowing about in this under-provided city.
/ **Details:** www.everest-restaurant.co.uk; close to Newbridge; 12.45 am,
Thu 1.45 am, Fri & Sat 2.45 am; D only.*

Kashmir Curry Centre   £ 12   ★
123 Spital Hill S4 7LD   (0114) 272 6253
*"Cheap and authentic" curry wins high praise at this "bright" and
"basic" subcontinental; "getting your beer from the pub across the
road" only adds to the "excellent value for money" experience.
/ **Details:** midnight; D only; no credit cards; no smoking area.*

Marco @ Milano   £ 33   ★
Archer Rd S8 0LA   (0114) 235 3080
*"Excellent food and range, good service, a little overpriced" –
one reporter says it all about this stylish modern Italian.
/ **Sample dishes:** spicy mussel & cannelloni bean soup; lamb with bell pepper
sauce & Gorgonzola polenta; chocolate fudge cake with raspberry sorbet.
Value tip: set 2-crs D £15. **Details:** 11.30 pm; D only, closed Sun; no Amex.*

Nirmals   £ 21
189-193 Glossop Rd S10 2GW   (0114) 272 4054
*After two decades in business, Mrs Gupta's famous curry house
seems to be hitting a rough patch; fans still say "the food is great,
and Mrs Gupta will tell you what to order", but critics perceive a
"can't be bothered" attitude. / **Details:** near West St; midnight, Fri & Sat
1 am; closed Sun L; no smoking area.*

Nonna's   £ 33   ★
539-541 Eccleshall Rd S11 8PR   (0114) 268 6166
*"Sheffield's most Italian Italian" is a "fun" and "friendly" deli,
espresso bar and enoteca (wine bar) in the heart of the city,
where the "authentic" and "inventive" dishes rarely disappoint.
/ **Sample dishes:** chilli tuna carpaccio with rocket; polenta with Italian sausage &
roast tomatoes; vanilla & lemon cream with plums. **Value tip:** set 2-crs L £13.
Details: www.nonnas.co.uk; M1, J33 towards Bakewell; 9.45 pm; no Amex;
no smoking area.*

Rafters   £ 35   ★
220 Oakbrook Rd, Nether Green S11 7ED
(0114) 230 4819
*The Bosworth family's ambitious local restaurant will soon be
celebrating ten years in business; its "original" dishes deliver some
"great" tastes. / **Sample dishes:** twice-baked Cheddar soufflé; rack of lamb
with smoked aubergine caviar; baked apple bread & butter pudding.
Details: www.raftersrestaurant.co.uk; 10 pm; D only, closed Tue & Sun; children:
7+.*

sign up for the survey at www.hardens.com

Richard Smith at Thyme £36 ★

32-34 Sandygate Rd S10 5RY (0114) 266 6096

Richard Smith's "good, honest cooking" shows "great attention to detail", and has made his restaurant (formerly called Smiths of Sheffield) by far the most commented-on in town; the "café-like" setting, however, "lacks atmosphere". / Sample dishes: smoked salmon & haddock with cucumber gazpacho; Tuscan veal casserole with polenta mash; sticky toffee pudding & toffee sauce. *Details:* www.thymeforfood.co.uk; 10 pm; closed Sun D; smoking in bar only.

Slammers £33 ★

625a Ecclesall Rd S11 8PT (0114) 268 0999

"Good, for Sheffield" – this simple fish restaurant newcomer is enthusiastically hailed by a local fan club for its quality cooking; it can already seem "packed". / Sample dishes: roast cod spring rolls with lemongrass; smoked salmon & prawn tagliatelle with truffle oil; apple galette with vanilla ice cream. *Details:* www.slammersseafood.co.uk; 10 pm; closed Mon L & Sun; no Amex; no smoking.

SHELLEY, WEST YORKSHIRE 5–2C

Three Acres £38 Ⓐ★★

Roydhouse HD8 8LR (01484) 602606

"Well worth the drive up to Emley Moor"; you may pay "London prices", but results are "always exceptional" at this "busy and vibrant gastropub" – "an absolute gem tucked away near the TV transmitter"; "the only downside is having to book weeks ahead". / Sample dishes: oxtail & spring vegetable terrine; chicken with pak choi in sweet & sour sauce; meringue with muscat poached fruits. *Details:* near Emley Moor TV tower; 9.45 pm; closed Sat L. *Accommodation:* 20 rooms, from £75.

SHEPPERTON, SURREY 3–3A

Edwinns £33

Church Rd TW17 9JT (01932) 223543

Consistently praised for its "pleasant" environment (and "passable" food), this founder member of a small chain of comfy Home Counties brasseries offers "reliably good value", in a thin area. / Sample dishes: char-grilled artichoke with Parmesan crisps; crispy duck with Thai vegetables; lemon & ginger steamed sponge. *Value tip:* set 2-crs L £11.50. *Details:* www.edwinns.co.uk; opp church & Anchor Hotel; 10.15 pm, Fri & Sat 10.45 pm; closed Sat L & Sun D; no smoking area.

SHEPTON MALLET, SOMERSET 2–3B

Charlton House £55 Ⓐ★

Charlton Rd BA4 4PR (01749) 342008

The décor at this grand country house hotel is "very Mulberry", which is unsurprising really, as it's owned by the marque's founding family; its "graceful" style and its "interesting and well-presented" cooking win all-round praise. / Sample dishes: salt beef terrine with cumin seed bread; bream with smoked salmon & leek tart; raspberry tart with spicy praline mousse. *Value tip:* set 2-crs L £14.50. *Details:* www.charltonhouse.com; on A361 towards Frome; 9.30 pm; no smoking. *Accommodation:* 16 rooms, from £155.

SHERE, SURREY   3–3A

Kinghams   £36   A★
Gomshall Ln GU5 9HB   (01483) 202168
*Paul Baker's "consistently high standard" cooking wins all-round
praise for this "cosy" thatched restaurant; service is "friendly" and
"attentive", too. / **Sample dishes:** seared scallops with pea & bacon patties;
roast lamb with sweet potato mash; chocolate pudding with espresso sauce.
Value tip: set 2-crs L £13.95. **Details:** www.kinghams-restaurant.co.uk; off A25
between Dorking & Guildford; 9.30 pm; closed Mon & Sun D; no smoking.*

SHINCLIFFE, COUNTY DURHAM   8–3B

Seven Stars   £29
High St DH1 2NU   (0191) 384 8454
*"If you're in Durham, and want to avoid the students",
this "upmarket" pub (just a few miles out of the city) is tipped as
"the best and most comfortable local" in the area; it offers "good"
food, "imaginatively served". / **Sample dishes:** king prawns & bean sprouts;
oriental-spiced pork with pak choy stir-fry; sticky toffee pudding & butterscotch
sauce. **Details:** off A177; 9.30 pm; no Amex; no smoking. **Accommodation:** 8
rooms, from £50.*

SHINFIELD, BERKSHIRE   2–2D

L'Ortolan   £56   A★★
Church Ln RG2 9BY
(0118) 988 8500
*Alan Murchison has made "a most impressive start" in the former
rectory made famous by John Burton-Race; this is "a serious
improvement on JB-R" (and "better value" too), say a number of
reporters, and there are universal plaudits for the "fabulous"
creative cooking and "wonderful" atmosphere. / **Sample dishes:** crab
blinis & caviar; roast sea bass with Thai shellfish; passion fruit tart with mango
sorbet. **Details:** www.lortolan.com; 11 pm; closed Sun D; no smoking.*

SHIPLEY, WEST YORKSHIRE   5–1C

Aagrah   £23   A★
4 Saltaire Rd BD18 3HN   (01274) 530880
*"Great interior design" at the "airy" new premises contributes to
the continuing popularity of this "busy" subcontinental;
most reporters say the food is still "great", too.
/ **Details:** www.aagrah.com; midnight, Fri & Sat 1 am; no smoking area.*

SHIPSTON-ON-STOUR, WARWICKSHIRE   2–1C

The Old Mill   £56
8 Mill St CV36 4AW   (01608) 663888
*As we went to press it's all change at Mark Maguire's esteemed
venture (previously known as Chavignol) – chef Marcus Ashenford
has gone, a former Fat Duck director has joined the team, and
the operation is being re-badged and re-launched with an
adjacent brasserie (along similar lines to what was the Chav
Brasserie)./ **Sample dishes:** wood pigeon with apple salad; braised pigs cheek
with parsley mash; chocolate delice & raspberry jelly. **Details:** www.chavignol.co.uk;
9.45 pm; closed Mon, Tue & Sun D; no smoking. **Accommodation:** 5 rooms,
from £190.*

SHREWSBURY, SHROPSHIRE 5–3A

Cromwells Hotel £ 30
11 Dogpole SY1 1EN (01743) 361440
"Good food combinations" and the odd "unusual dish" (including for veggies) make this town-centre boozer a handy destination.
/ **Sample dishes:** baked aubergine & goats cheese; Cajun seafood sausages; rhubarb tart with ginger custard. **Value tip:** set 2-crs pre-theatre £7.50.
Details: opp Guildhall; 10 pm; no smoking in dining room. **Accommodation:** 7 rooms, from £45.

Floating Thai Restaurant £ 23
Welsh Bridge SY3 8JQ (01743) 243123
A "different setting" – on the River Severn – and a "lovely view" add spice to a visit to the dependable family-run oriental.
/ **Details:** www.floatingthairestaurant.co.uk; 10.30 pm; D only.

Sol £ 41 ★
82 Wyle Cop SY1 1UT (01743) 340560
The Michelin star awarded to this promising, cheery town-centre restaurant risks going to its head – the Mediterranean cooking is still widely praised, but there were one or two gripes this year about a "snobby" atmosphere. / **Sample dishes:** roast pigeon with foie gras; beef galette with wild mushroom sauce; passion fruit parfait with blackcurrant jelly. **Details:** www.solrestaurant.co.uk; 9.30 pm; closed Mon & Sun; no Amex; no smoking; children: 8+ at D.

SKENFRITH, MONMOUTHSHIRE 2–1B

Bell £ 38 🄰★
NP7 8UH (01600) 750235
Tranquilly-situated on the Welsh border, this riverside inn – recently revamped as an hotel – wins all-round praise for its "perfect" ambience and for its "fresh and imaginative" cuisine.
/ **Sample dishes:** whole globe artichoke with hollandaise; pork tenerloin with shallot mash; cherry & cashew frangipane tart. **Details:** on B4521, 10m NE of Abergavenny; 9.30 pm; closed Mon (Nov-Mar only); no smoking area.
Accommodation: 8 rooms, from £85.

SLAUGHAM, WEST SUSSEX 3–4B

Chequers £ 40 ★
RH17 6AQ (01444) 400239
The occasional reporter thinks it "expensive for what it is", but this hotel dining room is praised by the most for its "great" fish and seafood, delivered in "large portions".
/ **Sample dishes:** prawn cocktail; smoked haddock rarebit with creamed spinach; banoffi pie. **Details:** 8.30 pm; closed Sun D; no smoking area; children: discouraged.
Accommodation: 5 rooms, from £80.

SLEAT, ISLE OF SKYE 9–2A

Kinloch Lodge £ 45 🄰★
IV43 8QY (01471) 833333
"Fantastic local produce, cooked to perfection and served among the silver and mahogany, and the family portraits" – that's the picture at Lord Macdonald of Macdonald's former hunting lodge, which offers a "top-quality" overall experience.
/ **Sample dishes:** smoked Skye salmon with lime & cucumber; roast rack of lamb with oatmeal stuffing; ginger steamed sponge. **Details:** www.kinloch-lodge.co.uk; D only (closed weekdays in winter); no smoking; booking essential.
Accommodation: 14 rooms, from £50.

SNAPE, SUFFOLK 3–1D

The Crown Inn £30 ★
Bridge Rd IP17 1SL   (01728) 688324
"An atmospheric old pub with an interesting menu and very good food"; its "nice rural setting" is convenient for the Maltings too.
/ **Sample dishes:** coarse game pâté with chutney; scallops with lemon couscous & spiced sauce; sticky toffee pudding. **Details:** off A12 towards Aldeburgh; 9 pm; no Amex; no smoking in dining room; children: 14+. **Accommodation:** 3 rooms, from £65.

SOLIHULL, WEST MIDLANDS 5–4C

Beau Thai £31 ★
761 Old Lode Ln   B92 8JE   (0121) 743 5355
"Excellent traditional Thai food" is unanimously acclaimed by the local fan club of this congenial, family-run favourite.
/ **Details:** www.beauthai.co.uk; 10 pm; closed Mon L, Sat L & Sun; no smoking area.

SONNING ON THAMES, WOKINGHAM 2–2D

Bull Inn £30
High St   RG4 6UP   (0118) 969 3901
A quaint and "friendly" old-worlde inn, picturesquely located near the Thames; its "traditional pub grub" isn't hugely ambitious, but comes in "large portions". / **Sample dishes:** smoked salmon with Thai prawns; lambs liver & bacon casserole; blueberry tortellini with coconut ice cream. **Details:** off A4, J10 between Oxford & Windsor; 9 pm; no smoking area; no booking. **Accommodation:** 7 rooms, from £85.

The French Horn £57 🄰
RG4 6TN   (0118) 969 2204
"Still the same after 30 years"; this "pretty", "old-school" Gallic restaurant – with "lovely views" over the Thames – has long been a favourite "special occasion" destination; "the best spit roast duck" and "great Sunday lunches" play to its culinary strengths.
/ **Sample dishes:** scallops in bacon with creamed pea soup; rack of lamb with olive jus; poached pear with chocolate sorbet. **Value tip:** set 2-crs L £20. **Details:** www.thefrenchhorn.co.uk; M4, J8 or J9, then A4; 9.30 pm. **Accommodation:** 21 rooms, from £110.

SOUTHAMPTON, SOUTHAMPTON 2–3D

Kuti's £26
37-39 Oxford St   SO14 3DP   (023) 8022 1585
"Very popular, and always busy" – this "consistent" Indian remains the most commented-on place in town (though it thrives "in the absence of much competition"). / **Value tip:** set 2-crs L £8.50. **Details:** www.kutis.co.uk; near Ocean Village; midnight.

SOUTHEND-ON-SEA, ESSEX 3–3C

Pipe of Port £26 🄰★
84 High St   SS1 1JN   (01702) 614606
"Sawdust on the floor and candles" help fuel the atmosphere at this long-established cellar; it serves some "tasty", "traditional" fare ("great pies" in particular), accompanied by "a good variety of wines and ports". / **Sample dishes:** herrings with creamed Stilton dressing; pork, plum & celery pie; ginger cheesecake with orange syrup. **Details:** 10.30 pm; closed Sun; children: 16.

SOUTHPORT, MERSEYSIDE   5–1A

Auberge Brasserie   £31
1b Seabank Rd PR9 0EW   (01704) 530671
*What was a "cosy little backstreet Gallic bistro" has been
enlarged of late and adopted more of a brasserie style; some slate
the change, but for the most part reporters praise the "relaxed"
ambience and "good-value" cuisine. / **Sample dishes:** hot duck & apple
salad; lemon sole with prawn & dill mousse; chocolate & basil marquise.
Value tip: set 2-crs L £5.95. **Details:** www.auberge-brasserie.com; 10.30 pm.*

Hesketh Arms   £20
Botanic Rd PR9 7NA   (01704) 509548
*"Good-quality food in good portions" makes this popular boozer a
useful local stand-by (and one which was saved from
'chainification' this year by campaigning locals).
/ **Sample dishes:** potted shrimps; steak & kidney pie; bread & butter pudding.
Details: near Botanical Gardens; 8 pm; closed Mon D & Sun D; no smoking area;
children: before 9 pm.*

Warehouse Brasserie   £32   ★
30 West St PR8 0DP   (01704) 544662
*"By far the best place to eat in this part of the world" –
this surprisingly "modern" brasserie delivers "good all-round
standards". / **Sample dishes:** Lebanese mezze; grilled chicken with smoked
cheese & leek risotto; chocolate & honeycomb torte. **Value tip:** set 2-crs L £7.95.
Details: www.warehouse-brasserie.co.uk; 10.15 pm; closed Sun.*

SOUTHWOLD, SUFFOLK   3–1D

The Crown   £35   𝔸★
High St IP18 6DP   (01502) 722275
*The "bustling" bar of this celebrated hostelry gets "too busy" for
some tastes, thanks to its "delicious" and "reasonably-priced"
cooking, washed down with "excellent Adnams ales" and an
"amazing variety of wine by the glass"; the small and cosy dining
room attracts relatively little comment. / **Sample dishes:** Norfolk crab
with potato salad; cod tempura with sweet potato chips; apple & cinnamon tart.
Details: www.adnams.co.uk; 9.30 pm; no smoking. **Accommodation:** 13 rooms,
from £92.*

The Swan   £39
The Market Pl IP18 6EG   (01502) 722186
*"Serene", "old-world" charm and "genuinely pleasant"
(if sometimes "amateurish") service are enduring attractions of
Adnams' grand hotel on the market square; even fans, though,
say the traditional-ish cooking is "not as good as it was a couple
of years ago". / **Sample dishes:** seared tuna with Niçoise style salad; roasted
lemon chicken; caramelised lemon tart. **Value tip:** set 2-crs L £18.
Details: www.adnams.co.uk; 9 pm; open L&D all week (D only Nov-Easter);
no smoking; children: 5+ at D. **Accommodation:** 4 rooms, from £110.*

SOWERBY BRIDGE, WEST YORKSHIRE   5–1C

Gimbals   £28   𝔸★
Wharf St HX6 2AF   (01422) 839329
*"Small, friendly and family-run", this "accommodating" bistro
offers "a varied menu" that's "very well cooked and presented".
/ **Sample dishes:** Dolcelatte & mushroom open lasagne; mustard-glazed pork with
parsnip mash; bread & butter pudding. **Details:** 9.15 pm; D only, closed Tue;
no Amex; no smoking at D.*

Java £17 ★
75 Wharf St HX6 2AF (01422) 831654
"Adventurous" Indonesian cooking not being that easy to find in
these parts, this "authentic" spot is "well worth a try".
/ **Sample dishes:** king prawns in filo pastry; chicken in spicy tomato sauce;
coconut & chocolate crêpes. **Details:** 11 pm; D only; no Amex; no smoking.

The Millbank £33
Millbank HX6 3DY (01422) 825588
"Good food in a lovely setting" has made quite a name for this
stylish gastropub; if new chef Glen Futter maintains the high
standards of the former regime, this place will have a 'star' next
year. / **Sample dishes:** pea soup with potato & ham dumplings; lamb with
artichoke & chestnuts in pastry; Yorkshire parkin with toffee apple mousse.
Value tip: set 3-crs L £13.50 (Sun £15). **Details:** www.themillbank.com; 9.30 pm;
closed Mon & Tue L; no Amex; no smoking in dining room; book only at weekends.

SPARSHOLT, HAMPSHIRE 2–3D
Plough Inn £31
SO21 2NW (01962) 776353
"It still has a pubby atmosphere", but "hardly anyone just goes for
a drink" at this "consistent" country inn, liked for its
"wide selection" of pub grub. / **Sample dishes:** grilled goats cheese with
herb croutons; roast pork in smoked bacon, apricot & ginger sauce; pear Condé with
chocolate sauce. **Details:** 9 pm, Fri & Sat 9.30 pm; no Amex; no smoking area.

SPEEN, BUCKINGHAMSHIRE 3–2A
Old Plow £43
HP27 OPZ (01494) 488300
This converted country pub wins praise for its "good but rich"
Gallic cooking; the food in the "relaxed" bistro-style bar is "just as
good" (and similarly priced) as that in the "smart" adjoining
restaurant. / **Sample dishes:** game terrine with redcurrant & beetroot preserve;
goats cheese, leek & Stilton tart; caramel tart with coffee sauce. **Details:** 20 mins
from M40, J4 towards Princes Risborough; 8.45 pm; closed Mon, Sat L & Sun D;
smoking in bar only.

ST ALBANS, HERTFORDSHIRE 3–2A
La Cosa Nostra £22
62 Lattimore Rd AL1 3XR (01727) 832658
"Bustling and cramped", this traditional Italian restaurant is
nominated by locals as a useful "cheap and cheerful" option in a
thin area. / **Sample dishes:** grilled aubergine salad; spaghetti with garlic &
parsley; tiramisu. **Details:** near railway station; 11 pm; closed Sat L & Sun.

Sukiyaki £21
6 Spencer St AL3 5EG (01727) 865009
"Why is it never in your guide – it's the only decent place in
town", says one fan of this "minimalist" establishment, which
demonstrates that "Japanese cooking isn't just about sushi";
critics, though, say it's "boring". / **Details:** 10 pm; closed Mon & Sun.

Thai Rack £24
13 George St AL3 4ER (01727) 850055
You can "eat in or take-away" at this "not-bad local" – one of the
better options in this underserved town. / **Details:** 10.30 pm; no Amex;
no smoking area.

The Waffle House
Kingsbury Water Mill   £ 20   A
Kingsbury Water Mill, St Michael's St AL3 4SJ
(01727) 853502
"Waffles sweet and savoury, served in an olde-worlde setting"
(plus some "lovely outdoor seating") make this old mill a
destination that's particularly "good with kids".
/ **Sample dishes:** chunky vegetable soup; ham, cheese & mushroom waffle;
banana & butterscotch waffle. **Details:** near Roman Museum; 6 pm (5 pm in
winter); L only; no Amex; no smoking in dining room; no booking.

ST ANDREWS, FIFE   9–3D

Vine Leaf Garden   £ 33   ★
131 South St KY16 9UN   (01334) 477497
The Hamilton family's "nice and cosy place, down a lane" delivers
"outstanding" but "rich" Scottish fare – "imaginative fish and
veggie dishes" are singled out for particular praise.
/ **Sample dishes:** Indian-spiced prawns with mini poppadoms; venison with
mushroom, brandy & peppercorn soup; brown sugar pavlova with strawberries.
Details: 9.30 pm; D only, closed Mon & Sun; no smoking.

ST IVES, CORNWALL   1–4A

Alfresco   £ 32   A ★
Harbourside Wharf Rd TR26 1LF   (01736) 793737
"Slow service" bugs some reporters, but otherwise this
"charming" (mainly) fish restaurant by the harbourside "maintains
high standards", and most find dining here a "memorable"
experience. / **Sample dishes:** steamed crab dumplings; red mullet tart with
basil; strawberry pavlova with raspberry coulis. **Details:** www.stivesharbour.com;
on harbour front; 9.30 pm; no Amex.

Blue Fish   £ 30   ★
Norway Ln TR26 1LZ   (01736) 794204
"Perfect holiday eating" is the gist of all reports on this
"attractive" restaurant, nicely located above a crafts centre;
the cooking can be "surprisingly good". / **Sample dishes:** shrimps in
garlic; chicken & goats cheese salad; chocolate ganache. **Details:** behind the Sloop
Inn; 10.30 pm (9 pm in winter).

Josephs   £ 29   ★
39a Fore St TR26 1HE   (01736) 796514
This "super modern café, by the harbour" is praised for its
"superb" fish; it's also a popular breakfast destination.
/ **Sample dishes:** scallops with chilli jam; grilled Dover sole with lemon butter;
lemon & almond pudding. **Details:** 9.30 pm; closed Sun; no Amex;
children: 8+ at D.

Porthminster Café   £ 35   A ★
Porthminster Beach TR26 2EB   (01736) 795352
"Gorgeous food" (with a Mediterranean slant) and a "great view"
make this "modern seafront café/restaurant" an "idyllic" location
for many reporters – "on a sunny day, the terrace is the best
place in England". / **Sample dishes:** grilled scallops & goats cheese; turbot
with braised leeks; chocolate pudding with orange ice cream.
Details: www.porthminstercafe.co.uk; near railway station; 10 pm; closed Nov-Mar;
no Amex; no smoking in dining room.

The Seafood Café £ 26 ★

45 Fore St TR26 IHE
(01736) 794004
"An excellent way of serving fresh fish" – "you choose the food at the counter" and it arrives "superbly cooked" and "beautifully presented" at this simple, but effective new café, which fans "can't rate highly enough". / **Sample dishes:** *Cornish shellfish; catch of the day with seasonal vegetables; sticky toffee pudding.* **Details:** *www.seafoodcafe.co.uk; 10.30 pm; no smoking area.*

Tate Gallery £ 24 Ⓐ

Porthmeor Beach TR26 ITG (01736) 796226
This stylish café – with "amazing views" from its "lovely open roof terrace" – is "not as overpriced as some gallery eateries"; it wins widespread support as a "classy and reliable" venue offering "tasty", "home-made" food. / **Sample dishes:** *roast red pepper & aubergine soup; grilled sea bass with fennel sauce; raspberry cheesecake.* **Details:** *www.tate.org.uk; L & afternoon tea only; no Amex; no smoking.*

ST KEYNE, CORNWALL 1–3C

The Well House £ 44 ★

PL14 4RN (01579) 342 001
Tranquilly-located in the Looe valley, this agreeable country house hotel has a "very pleasant" dining room, where chef Matthew Corner produces some accomplished modern cuisine; there's also an "excellent" wine list. / **Sample dishes:** *ham terrine with pineapple tart; vanilla-seared bream with Swiss chard; pecan tart with coffee bean ice cream.* **Details:** *www.wellhouse.co.uk; half way between Liskeard & Looe off the B3254; 8.30 pm; booking essential at L; children: 8+ at dinner.* **Accommodation:** *9 rooms, from £115.*

ST MARGARETS AT CLIFFE, KENT 3–3D

Walletts Court £ 50

Westcliffe CT15 6EW (01304) 852424
Overlooking the North Downs, the Oakley family's country house hotel has provided a "smart eating place" for over 25 years now; it's hard to avoid the conclusion, though, that the "solid", "provincial" cooking is just not up to the "arm-and-a-leg" pricing. / **Sample dishes:** *grilled squid with blackened green peppers; partridge stuffed with game parfait; crème brûlée with raspberries.* **Value tip:** *set 3-crs L £17.50.* **Details:** *www.wallettscourt.com; on B2058 towards Deal, 3m NE of Dover; 9 pm; closed Mon L & Sat L; no smoking.* **Accommodation:** *16 rooms, from £90.*

ST MAWES, CORNWALL 1–4B

Hotel Tresanton £ 46 Ⓐ

Lower Castle Rd TR2 5DR (01326) 270055
The "magical view from the terrace" is the 'crown jewel' feature of Olga Polizzi's (née Forte) "stylish all-round" design-hotel dining room; the consensus on the cooking (dominated by fish and seafood) is that it's "good but expensive". / **Sample dishes:** *Gorgonzola & spinach tart; roast John Dory with saffron gnocchi; honey fritters with lemon ricotta.* **Value tip:** *set 2-crs L £20.* **Details:** *www.tresanton.com; near Castle; 9.30 pm; no smoking at D.* **Accommodation:** *26 rooms, from £235.*

STADDLEBRIDGE, NORTH YORKSHIRE 8–4C

McCoys at the Tontine £40

DL6 3JB (01609) 882671

A "brilliant" ambience and "top-notch" cooking makes this celebrated bistro and restaurant something of an "oasis" for many reporters; it has its critics, though, for whom it's gone "off the boil". / **Sample dishes:** grilled black pudding with beetroot sauce; salmon & mussels with langoustine butter; sticky toffee pudding. **Value tip:** set 2-crs L £10.95. **Details:** www.mccoysatthetontine.co.uk; junction of A19 & A172; 10 pm; bistro L & D all week; restaurant Sat D only. **Accommodation:** 6 rooms, from £95.

STADHAMPTON, OXFORDSHIRE 2–2D

Crazy Bear £42 𝔸

Bear Ln OX44 7UR, (01865) 890714

It may sound an odd concept – "nice Thai food, in a country hotel setting" – but this "funky" venue with a "pretty garden" attracts nothing but praise; upstairs, the more conventional modern British brasserie also finds favour. / **Sample dishes:** Roquefort soufflé with pears & walnuts; roast duck with cider braised potatoes; warm chocolate cake. **Value tip:** set 2-crs L £10 (not Sun). **Details:** www.crazybearhotel.co.uk; 10 pm; closed Sun L. **Accommodation:** 13 rooms, from £120.

STAFFORD, STAFFORDSHIRE 5–3B

Julians £36

21 High St ST21 6BW (01785) 851200

Julian Ankers's "friendly" bistro continues to receive a slightly mixed press, but fans praise it as an island of "sophistication" in this very thin area; a new chef arrived in spring 2002 as the survey was drawing to a close. / **Sample dishes:** pan-fried scallops with tempura beans; fillet steak with duck ravioli & tarragon sauce; egg custard tart with nutmeg ice cream. **Details:** 9.30 pm; closed Mon & Sun; no smoking in dining room; children: 8+ at D.

STAITHES, NORTH YORKSHIRE 8–3C

Endeavour £32

1 High St TS13 5BH (01947) 840825

A change of ownership halfway through the surveying year gave rise to contradictory reports on this popular "fisherman's cottage in a picturesque village"; we've removed ratings pending next year's survey results. / **Sample dishes:** parsnip & orange soup; fillet steak with foie gras butter; iced Drambuie mousse. **Details:** 10m N of Whitby, off A174; 9.45 pm; closed Mon & Sun; no smoking area; booking essential. **Accommodation:** 3 rooms, from £55.

STAMFORD, LINCOLNSHIRE 6–4A

The George Hotel £46 𝔸

71 St Martins PE9 2LB (01780) 750750

"Rather expensive, but full of character"; this famous and "historic" coaching inn boasts a "beautiful" panelled dining room (which serves "OK" food) and offers an impressive wine list; there's also a "great outdoor brasserie in summer", which comes highly recommended. / **Sample dishes:** chicken & wild mushroom sausage with lentils; pork & tarragon mustard in filo pastry; British cheeses. **Value tip:** set 2-crs L £16.50. **Details:** www.georgehotelofstamford.com; off A1, 14m N of Peterborough, onto B1081; 10.30 pm; jacket & tie required; no smoking before 10 pm. **Accommodation:** 47 rooms, from £105.

STANTON, SUFFOLK
3–1C

Leaping Hare Vineyard
£34   A★

Wyken Vineyards IP31 2DW   (01359) 250287

"A great barn" houses this "superb" all-rounder, where the "simple cooking emphasises the quality of the local ingredients"; the wine (even the red) is produced on the premises. / **Sample dishes:** tempura courgette flowers stuffed with Thai crab; vine-smoked guinea fowl with bacon mash; apricot sorbet. **Details:** 9m NE of Bury St Edmunds; follow tourist signs off A143; 9 pm; L only, except Fri & Sat open L & D; no Amex; no smoking.

STAPLEFORD, LEICESTERSHIRE
5–3D

Stapleford Park
£50

LE14 2EF   (01572) 787522

This "relaxed" and "romantic" country house enjoys a "beautiful parkland setting"; some say the cooking is "picking up" under new owners, but even fans concede it is still "not always the best", and its overall ratings remain humdrum. / **Sample dishes:** tomato tarte Tatin; fillet steak with foie gras sauce; soufflé. **Details:** 4m from Melton Mowbray on B676; 9.30 pm, Fri & Sat 10.30 pm; jacket required; no smoking. **Accommodation:** 51 rooms, from £175.

STOCKCROSS, BERKSHIRE
2–2D

Vineyard at Stockcross
£61

RG20 8JU   (01635) 528770

Perhaps the new chef (installed in early-2002) will finally push this "formal" but "friendly" California-style restaurant-with-rooms in to the front-rank position it has always so obviously craved; in the meantime, the "unending" wine list remains an "amazing" attraction. / **Sample dishes:** pressed chicken & foie gras terrine; roast sea bass with butter bean purée; warm chocolate fondant. **Value tip:** set 3-crs L £23. **Details:** www.the-vineyard.co.uk; from M4, J13 take A34 towards Hungerford; 9 pm; no smoking area. **Accommodation:** 31 rooms, from £219.

STOKE BRUERNE, NORTHANTS
2–1D

Bruerne's Lock
£37

5 The Canalside NN12 7SB   (01604) 863654

An "interesting" menu that's "well cooked and presented" and an "attractive canalside setting" make this a uniformly popular destination; it can seem a touch pricey for what it is, though. / **Sample dishes:** deep-fried quails eggs with pancetta; beef Wellington with port jus; apple & cinnamon crumble. **Value tip:** set 3-crs L £12.95. **Details:** www.bruerneslock.co.uk; 0.5m off A508 between Northampton & Milton Keynes; 9.45 pm; closed Mon & Sat L; no smoking in dining room.

STOKE BY NAYLAND, ESSEX
3–2C

Angel Inn
£28

Polstead St CO6 4SA   (01206) 263245

It's "absolutely essential to book at weekends", if you want to enjoy the "perfectly-cooked fresh fish" which has made quite a name for this elegant old boozer – "too many customers", though, can put pressure on standards across the board. / **Sample dishes:** mushroom & pistachio pâté; roast pork with apple mousse & red cabbage; raspberry bavarois. **Details:** 5m W of A12, on B1068; 9 pm; no Amex; no smoking area; children: 14+. **Accommodation:** 6 rooms, from £67.50.

STOKE HOLY CROSS, NORFOLK   6–4C
Wildebeest   £34
Norwich Rd NR14 8QJ (01508) 492497
*"Down-to-earth, but high-quality" – this "old pub on the city's outskirts" offers a surprisingly "modern" menu, and one which generally goes down well. / **Sample dishes:** sautéed calamari with squid ink risotto; roast lemon & thyme pork fillet; passion fruit tart & rhubarb sorbet. **Value tip:** set 2-crs L £9.95 (Sun £10.95). **Details:** from A140, turn left at Dunston Hall, left at T-junction; 10 pm; no smoking area.*

STOKE ROW, OXFORDSHIRE   2–2D
The Crooked Billet   £38   A★
Newlands Ln RG9 5PU (01491) 681048
*"Good cooking with interesting dishes and immense portions" helps make this "cosy" country boozer a "good family destination" (especially for Sunday lunch); jazz nights are an occasional attraction. / **Sample dishes:** onion & pepper tartlet with Roquefort glaze; gammon hock with Polish sausage & sauerkraut; Bakewell tart & custard sauce. **Value tip:** set 2-crs L £11.95. **Details:** www.thecrookedbillet.co.uk; on A4130; 10 pm; no Amex or Switch.*

STOKE SUB HAMDON, SOMERSET   2–3B
The Priory House   £50   ★★
1 High St TA14 6PP (01935) 822826
*This "very personal" establishment is the latest perch of (recently) peripatetic chef Martin Hadden (formerly of London's Halcyon and then Ockendon Manor); some find the décor rather "bland", but otherwise early reports are a hymn of praise to the "quite exceptional" cooking, and to the "personal" and "unobtrusive" service. / **Sample dishes:** mushroom risotto with Parmesan; grilled cod with black olive tapenade & mash; burnt lemon cream with raspberry sorbet. **Details:** 9 pm; closed Mon, Wed D & Sun; closed 2 weeks in Aug & Dec; no Amex; no smoking.*

STOKESLEY, NORTH YORKSHIRE   8–3C
Y-Thai   £28
4 High St TS9 5DQ (01642) 710165
*"A jewel in this small market town" – a "lovely" Thai restaurant that's unanimously well received. / **Details:** 9.30 pm; no smoking.*

STONEHAVEN, ABERDEEN   9–3D
Lairhillock Inn   £27   A★
Netherley AB39 3QS (01569) 730001
*This "very cosy" pub – a prime destination for Aberdonians – offers "the same attention to food as in the classy restaurant next door" (the Crynoch fine dining room, £37), and "excellent" service too. / **Sample dishes:** chunky seafood chowder; wild boar sausage with musatrd mash; sticky toffee pudding. **Details:** www.lairhillock.co.uk; 7m S of Aberdeen; 9.30 pm; no smoking area.*

Tolbooth   £36   A
Old Pier Rd AB39 2JU (01569) 762287
*Not just because it's "an oasis in a desert", Chris McCarrey's fish and seafood restaurant is found "quite memorable" by some reporters – especially those who can bag "the romantic table by the window". / **Sample dishes:** smoked salmon with Parma ham & pesto; wolf fish with champagne & watercress sauce; sticky toffee pudding. **Details:** www.tolboothrestaurant; 9.30 pm; D only, closed Mon & Sun; no Amex; children: 8+.*

STONY STRATFORD, MILTON KEYNES 2–1D
Peking £ 27
117 High St MK11 1AT   (01908) 563120
*No reporter was actually inspired to write any words about this
long-established oriental – the ratings they awarded, however,
confirm that it remains a useful stand-by in a thin area.*
/ **Details:** off A5; 11.30 pm; no smoking area.

STORRINGTON, WEST SUSSEX 3–4A
Fleur de Sel £ 49 A★
Manley's Hill RH20 4BT   (01903) 742331
*"A warm welcome from le patron" sets the tone at this "very
French" establishment (which has an "out-of-the-way" rural
location); the "elegant" cooking is undoubtedly "expensive", bu
most reporters think it's "superb", too.* / **Sample dishes:** roasted prawns
with French bean salad; Gressingham duck with honey & ginger sauce; mango tarte
Tatin. **Value tip:** set 2-crs L £15.50. **Details:** W of Storrington on A283; 9.30 pm;
closed Mon, Sat L & Sun D; no smoking in dining room; children: 12+.

STOURBRIDGE, WORCESTERSHIRE 5–4B
French Connection £ 31 ★
3 Coventry St DY8 1EP   (01384) 390940
*"A gem in a culinary wasteland", this cosy, family-run restaurant is
voted "very good value" by its local supporters.* / **Sample dishes:** chicken liver, brandy & garlic pâté; baked pesto-crusted cod;
brioche bread & butter pudding. **Value tip:** set 3-crs L £8.95.
Details: www.frenchconnectionbistro.co.uk; 9.30 pm; closed Mon, Tue D & Sun;
mainly non-smoking.

STOW ON THE WOLD, GLOUCESTERSHIRE 2–1C
The Royalist (947AD)
Eagle & Child £ 30
Digbeth St GL54 1BN   (01451) 830670
*"The ex-755 Fulham Road team, now decamped to the
Cotswolds" run this two-year-old venture in what claims to be the
oldest inn in England; the ambitious cooking attracts rather mixed
reviews.* / **Sample dishes:** avocado & pine nut salad; crab & cod cakes with
tomato & ginger sauce; caramelised orange & pineapple pancake.
Details: www.theroyalisthotel.co.uk; 10 pm; no smoking area; need 6+ to book.
Accommodation: 8 rooms, from £90.

STRATFORD UPON AVON, WARWICKSHIRE 2–1C
Desports £ 39
13-14 Meer St CV37 6QB   (01789) 269304
*Some (but not all) reporters praise "superb" dishes from the
ambitious, trendy menu served in this brightly-decorated first-floor
dining room, above a deli/café.* / **Sample dishes:** cashew & herb risotto;
Dover sole with curry sauce & big chips; cherry custard tart with cherry ice cream.
Value tip: set 2-crs L £5. **Details:** www.desports.co.uk; 9.30 pm; closed Mon &
Sun; closed Jan; no smoking area.

Lambs £ 29 A
12 Sheep St CV37 6EF   (01789) 292554
*"Still the favourite pre-theatre" destination – this "cramped"
fixture remains the most commented-on place in town, thanks to
its "consistently good" cooking and "relaxing atmosphere";
service, though, can be "off-hand".* / **Sample dishes:** crispy duck &
watercress salad; roast chicken & mango in lime butter; banoffi pie. **Value tip:** set
2-crs L £11.50. **Details:** 9.30 pm.

Opposition £ 28
13 Sheep St CV37 6EF (01789) 269980
"Always good, and quite imaginative" – this long-established wine
bar vies with its better-known neighbour Lambs as *"a lovely
destination before the theatre"*. / **Sample dishes:** *Greek salad with
deep-fried halloumi; chorizo & red pepper pizza; tiramisu.* **Details:** *10.30 pm;
no Amex; booking: max 12.*

Russons £ 30 ★
8 Church St CV37 6HB (01789) 268822
"A good find for a pre-theatre supper" – this town-centre spot
provides a decent standard of cooking *(with fish and ice cream
receiving special mention)*. / **Sample dishes:** *snails in garlic butter with
spiced croutons; monkfish, salmon & bacon brochettes; sticky toffee cheesecake.*
Details: *9.45 pm; closed Mon & Sun; no smoking area; booking: max 8; children:
8+ after 7pm.*

Thai Kingdom £ 27 ★
11 Warwick Rd CV37 6YW (01789) 261103
"Even the set meals are exciting", claim fans of this *"authentic"*
oriental, where *"above-average"* cooking comes in *"generous
portions"*. / **Details:** *10.45 pm; closed Sun; no smoking area.*

Three Lions £ 44 ★
Stuckton Rd SP6 2HF (01425) 652489
"Pricey but excellent" cooking using *"wonderful"* ingredients wins
many enthusiastic recommendations for the Womersleys'
converted pub, on the fringe of the New Forest. / **Sample dishes:** *crab
bisque with shrimps; roasted roe buck with ceps; hot chocolate pudding.*
Value tip: *set 2-crs L £14.75.* **Details:** *1m E of Fordingbridge off B3078; 9.30 pm;
closed Mon & Sun D; no smoking in dining room.* **Accommodation:** *3 rooms,
from £65.*

Plumber Manor £ 34
DT10 2AF (01258) 472507
A *"delightful"*, family-run country house hotel whose fairly
traditional culinary attractions include *"proper Sunday lunches"*
and *"wonderful puds"*. / **Sample dishes:** *wild mushroom millefeuille with
brandy cream; peppered sirloin steak with mustard sauce; lemon meringue pie.*
Details: *www.plumbermanor.com; off A357 towards Hazelbury Bryan; 9.30 pm;
D only, except Sun open L & D; closed Feb; booking essential.*
Accommodation: *16 rooms, from £100.*

Red Onion Bistro £ 23
57 Ballingdon St C010 2DA (01787) 376777
"Standard bistro fare" is served here with *"no frills"* but at
"reasonable prices", making this town-centre fixture a useful
"cheap and cheerful" destination. / **Sample dishes:** *crab & creamed leek
tart; winter lamb casserole with caper dauphinoise; raspberry & vanilla cheesecake.*
Value tip: *set 2-crs menu £8.* **Details:** *on A131; 9.30 pm; closed Sun D.*

SUNDERLAND, TYNE & WEAR 8–2C

throwingstones
National Glass Centre £24 A ★
Liberty Way SR6 0GL   (0191) 565 3939
"A lovely setting, overlooking the River Wear" is just one of the
features which raises this *"incredible building"* far above the
standards of your typical museum café; *"the menu is limited,
but all the options are fabulous"*. / **Sample dishes:** *roast pepper &
Mozzarella salad; salmon with rocket & orange salad; brandy snap with toffee ice
cream.* **Details:** *A19 to Sunderland, follow signs for National Glass Centre; 9 pm;
L only, except Fri & Sat when L & D; no Amex; no smoking.*

SURBITON, SURREY 3–3B

The French Table £36 ★
85 Maple Rd KT6 4AW   (020) 8399 2365
"Wow!" – *"a super find in this area"* – this *"intimate"* (if *"rather
cramped"*) new Gallic establishment provides an *"oasis"* in the
suburban desert; *"ambitious cooking that comes off"* looks set to
make it quite a destination. / **Sample dishes:** *mushroom cannelloni with
truffle oil; pork stuffed with chorizo mousse & endive; lemon curd ice cream.*
Value tip: *set 3-crs L £15.* **Details:** *10 pm; closed Mon, Tue-Sat D only, closed
Sun D; no Amex; no smoking.*

SUTTON COLDFIELD, WEST MIDLANDS 5–4C

New Hall £58 A
Walmley Rd B76 1QX   (0121) 378 2442
The setting – the oldest manor house in England – is *"wonderful"*,
but there's something of the *"production line"* about the cooking
at this pricey hotel, not far from Brum. / **Sample dishes:** *saffron risotto
with confit tomatoes; canon of lamb with cucumber noodles; cinnamon & apple
parfait.* **Value tip:** *set 3-crs L £18.* **Details:** *www.newhallhotel.net; from A452, right
onto B4148, past Walmley; 9.30 pm; closed Sat L; no smoking; booking essential.*
Accommodation: *60 rooms, from £153.*

SWANSEA, SWANSEA 1–1D

La Braseria £33
28 Wind St SA1 1DZ   (01792) 469683
"You know what you are going to get" from this large and long-
established Spanish-themed joint – it's a basic, *"good-value"*
formula, where you choose your steak or seafood for them to
prepare for you. / **Sample dishes:** *Diablos chicken livers; halibut mornay;
crème caramel.* **Value tip:** *set 2-crs L £7.50.* **Details:** *www.labraseria.com;
11.30 pm; closed Sun; need 6+ to book; children: 6+.*

Dermotts
Morgans Hotel £51
Somerset Pl SA1 1RR   (01792) 466664
Dermott Slade – the city's top chef – now has a swankier home
than his former High Street location, with a move to the city's first
five-star hotel (opening as we go to press in the old Associated
British Ports building); the whole operation will be a larger and
more ambitious affair, and there is also to be a cheaper brasserie,
Plimsoll Line. / **Sample dishes:** *seared scallops with butternut squash; roast
goose with sweet onion couscous; citrus tart with gin & tonic sorbet.*
Details: *www.morganshotel.co.uk; 9.30 pm; closed Mon, Tue L, Wed L, Sat L &
Sun D; no Amex; no smoking area.* **Accommodation:** *20 rooms, from £100.*

sign up for the survey at www.hardens.com

Moghul Brasserie £25
81 St Helen's Rd SA1 4BQ (01792) 475131
*A popular curry house, which continues to win praise for
"good food at reasonable prices". / Details: midnight, Fri & Sat 2 am;
no Amex.*

Opium Den £22
20 Castle St SA1 1JF (01792) 456160
*"Nice vibes" and "good food" make this "intimate" central
Chinese a useful stand-by. / Details: 11.30 pm; closed Sun L.*

Patricks £30 Ⓐ
638 Mumbles Rd SA3 4EA (01792) 360199
*This "lively" bistro (part of a restaurant with rooms on the
Mumbles seafront) wins praise for its "friendly" service, and for its
"appealing range" of modern British dishes; however, "run-of-the-
mill" results are not unknown. / Sample dishes: feta sorbet with
char-grilled watermelon; sesame-crusted pork with satay sauce; cappuccino &
chocolate terrine. Details: www.patricks-restaurant.co.uk; in Mumbles, 1m before
pier; 9.50 pm; closed Sun D; no smoking in dining room. Accommodation: 8
rooms, from £85.*

SWINTON, SCOTTISH BORDERS 8–1A

Wheatsheaf Inn £30 ★
Main St TD11 3JJ (01890) 860257
*"The best place for miles" – this popular Borders pub offers
"good-value" traditional cooking, served by "friendly" staff in a
"comfortable" setting. / Sample dishes: chicken, spring vegetable & herb
broth; Scotch beef in claret & cep oil sauce; iced Drambuie parfait.
Details: www.wheatsheaf-swinton.co.uk; between Kelso & Berwick-upon-Tweed,
by village green; 9.15 pm; closed Mon & Sun D (to non-residents); no Amex;
no smoking. Accommodation: 7 rooms, from £85.*

TADCASTER, NORTH YORKSHIRE 5–1D

Aagrah £23
York Rd LS24 8EG (01937) 530888
*"Authentic décor and cuisine" win nothing but praise for this
branch of the leading chain of Yorkshire Indians.
/ Details: www.aggrah.com; 7m from York on A64; 11.30 pm; D only; no smoking
area.*

TALSARNAU, GWYNEDD 4–2C

Maes y Neuadd £31 Ⓐ★
LL47 6YA (01766) 780200
*This "wonderful country house hotel", parts of which go back to
the 14th century, is hailed by its fans as "truly unique"; it boasts a
"good outlook" (to Snowdonia), and the cooking – from home-
grown produce – is "consistently very good". / Sample dishes: soused
mackerel with Waldorf salad; chicken with bacon & garlic risotto; strawberry & mint
delice. Value tip: set 3-crs Sun L £15.25. Details: www.neuadd.com; 3m N of
Harlech off B4573; 9 pm; no smoking in dining room. Accommodation: 16
rooms, from £141, incl D.*

TAPLOW, BERKSHIRE 3–3A

Waldo's at Cliveden £ 83 A
Berry Hl SL6 0JF (01628) 668561
The Astors' former palazzo provides a "beautiful and magical"
setting for this subterranean dining room; some do say that
"everything is looking up, with the arrival of a new chef"
(Mark Dodson), but quite a few reports continue to dwell on the
"poor" service and "exorbitant" prices. / **Sample dishes:** sea bass
poached in champagne; roast partridge with blackcurrant vinegar; fig tartlet with
honey ice cream. **Details:** www.clivedenhouse.co.uk; M4, J7 then follow National
Trust signs; 9.30 pm; D only, closed Mon & Sun; jacket & tie required; no smoking;
booking: max 6; children: 12+. **Accommodation:** 38 rooms, from £385.

TAUNTON, SOMERSET 2–3A

Brazz
Castle Hotel £ 30
Castle Bow TA1 3NF (01823) 252000
"Fair-to-middling standards" characterise reports on this "trendy"
brasserie spin-off from the neighbouring Castle Hotel (the first
member of what's now a growing West Country chain).
/ **Sample dishes:** walnut & blue cheese salad; sirloin steak with sauce béarnaise;
Eton Mess. **Value tip:** set 3-crs L £12.95.
Details: www.the-castle-hotel.com/brazz.htm; 10 pm.

The Castle Hotel £ 49 A
Castle Grn TA1 1NF (01823) 272671
Even some for whom it's an "old favourite" say the "creative"
British cooking is "not up to its old standard" at this "lovely old
wisteria-clad" institution; service is "excellent", and there's an
"exceptional wine list". / **Sample dishes:** rabbit pie with mustard dressing;
sea bass with truffled macaroni cheese; golden raisin soufflé. **Value tip:** set 2-crs L
£16.95. **Details:** www.the-castle-hotel.com; follow tourist information signs; 9 pm;
closed Sun D; no smoking. **Accommodation:** 44 rooms, from £170.

TEFFONT EVIAS, WILTSHIRE 2–3C

Howards House Hotel £ 40 A ★
SP3 5RJ (01722) 716392
The "delightful location" – "a charming" 17th-century house in a
"picturebook village" – adds to the atmosphere of this small hotel,
whose "high culinary standards" are consistently praised.
/ **Sample dishes:** crab bisque with sour chive cream; venison with cabbage,
bacon & foie gras; sorbet with raspberry purée.
Details: www.howardshousehotel.com; 9m W of Stonehenge off A303; 9.30 pm;
D only, except Sun L only; no smoking in dining room. **Accommodation:** 9 rooms,
from £145.

TETBURY, GLOUCESTERSHIRE 2–2B

Trouble House Inn £ 32
Cirencester Rd GL8 8SG (01666) 502206
"Well-prepared and well-presented dishes" win praise for this
"pretty old inn"; some feel, though, that "the dining area could be
improved". / **Sample dishes:** wild mushroom casserole; lemon sole with braised
leeks & mussels; white chocolate cheesecake with lemon ice cream.
Details: www.troublehouse.co.uk; 1.5m from Tetbury on A433 towards Cirencester;
9.30 pm; closed Mon; closed 2 weeks in Jan; no smoking area; booking: max 8;
children: 14+ in bar.

THORNBURY, GLOUCESTERSHIRE 2–2B

Thornbury Castle £ 57
Castle St BS35 1HH (01454) 281182
*Perhaps the new chef will pep up the cooking at this Tudor
landmark, where, in the past, reporters have felt you "pay for the
historic surroundings".* / **Sample dishes:** pan-fried French quail with tomato
confit; grilled halibut with tomato fondue & caviar cream; pecan & maple chocolate
brownie. **Value tip:** set 3-crs L (incl Sun) £22.50.
Details: www.thornburycastle.com; near intersection of M4 & M5; 9.30 pm,
Sat 10 pm; no smoking in dining room. **Accommodation:** 24 rooms, from £130.

THORNHAM, NORFOLK 6–3B

Lifeboat Inn £ 29
PE36 6LT (01485) 512236
*"A wonderful setting" near the harbour and beach, and "generous
portions of fresh, local produce" have won high popularity for this
ancient boozer; it's become "a victim of its own success", though,
and reports of "sloppy" results are now all too common.*
/ **Sample dishes:** Thai crab cakes with capsicum chutney; lemon sole with crisp
capers & prawns; fruit crumble. **Details:** www.lifeboatinn.co.uk; 20m from Kings
Lynn on A149 coast road; 9.30 pm; no Amex. **Accommodation:** 12 rooms,
from £80.

THORPE LANGTON, LEICESTERSHIRE 5–4D

Bakers Arms £ 30   Ⓐ
Main St LE16 7TS (01858) 545201
*"A great relaxing atmosphere" helps underpin the popularity of
this "busy village eatery", praised for its "restaurant-quality"
cooking.* / **Sample dishes:** fresh mussels; sea bass with sweet potato mash;
chocolate tart with caramelised bananas. **Details:** near Market Harborough off the
A6; 9.30 pm; open only Tue-Fri for D, all day Sat & Sun L; no smoking area;
children: 12+.

TILE HILL, WEST MIDLANDS 5–4C

Rupali £ 27
337 Tile Hill Ln CV4 9DU (024) 7642 2500
*"The food and service never let you down", say local fans of this
large, well-established Indian restaurant; "visitors seem to enjoy it,
too".* / **Details:** 10.30 pm; no smoking area.

TITLEY, HEREFORDSHIRE 2–1A

Stagg Inn £ 32   ★
HR5 3RL (01544) 230221
*Steven Reynolds trained at Le Gavroche, and his "superb" cooking
has created a deserved reputation for this "welcoming" country
pub; the idea, though, that this is prime Michelin territory
(this having been the first pub in the country honoured with a
gong from the tyre men) is "ridiculous".* / **Sample dishes:** mussel &
saffron risotto; braised lamb with tomato & tarragon gravy; treacle tart with clotted
cream. **Value tip:** set 3-crs Sun L £12.50. **Details:** www.thestagg.co.uk; on B4355,
NE of Kington; 9.30 pm; closed Mon (& 2 weeks in Nov); no Amex; no smoking
area. **Accommodation:** 2 rooms, from £60.

TODMORDEN, WEST YORKSHIRE 5–1B

The Old Hall Restaurant £36 🄰

Hall St OL14 7AD (01706) 815998

"Stone flags and roaring fires" and a "hospitable" attitude generate strong satisfaction with Nick & Madeleine Hoyle's charmingly-restored 17th-century country house, which is praised for its "enjoyable" cooking. / **Sample dishes:** grilled mackerel with potato cakes; crispy duck & watercress salad; winter berry pavlova. **Value tip:** set 2-crs L £7.50 . **Details:** 15 mins from M62; 9 pm, Sat 9.45 pm; closed Mon & Sun D; no Amex; no smoking in dining room.

TONBRIDGE, KENT 3–3B

Bottle House £29

Sharts Hill TN11 8ET (01892) 870306

A picturesque Kent pub, delivering a "huge" menu to a "good" standard. / **Sample dishes:** breaded lemon & pepper scallops; spicy Cajun chicken with salsa; banoffi pie. **Details:** SW of Penshurst on B2188; 10 pm; no Amex; no smoking area.

TOPSHAM, DEVON 1–3D

The Galley £44

41 Fore St EX3 0HU (01392) 876078

Many reporters recommend this quirky, Buddhist-influenced restaurant (with views over the estuary), saying it's "just the best for superb fish"; there are doubters, though, who feel "you pay for the philosophy", rather than the "average" food.
/ **Sample dishes:** deep-fried Thai fishcakes; roast salmon with blinis & mango; meringues with iced Turkish Delight. **Details:** www.galleyrestaurant.co.uk; 11 pm; closed Mon L, Tue L & Wed L; no smoking; booking essential; children: 12+. **Accommodation:** 4 rooms, from £75.

TREBURLEY, CORNWALL 1–3C

Springer Spaniel £28 ★

PL15 9NS (01579) 370424

"Interesting dishes, by the standards of the area" – and at "reasonable prices" – win numerous nominations for this "friendly" and "reliable" pub/restaurant.
/ **Sample dishes:** Mediterranean tart; sirloin steak with garlic butter; brandy snap basket with raspberries. **Details:** 4m S of Launceston on A388; 9 pm; no Amex; no smoking before 10 pm.

TREEN, CORNWALL 1–4A

Gurnards Head £31 ★

TR26 3DE (01736) 796928

It's "worth the drive", say fans of this "true English pub" which offers "gorgeous views" over the coast between St Ives and Land's End; its fish and seafood dishes – "huge crab claws" and a "wonderful trio of Cornish fish" for instance – win particular praise. / **Sample dishes:** Cornish seafood broth; seared pigeon with bacon & mushrooms; bread & butter pudding. **Details:** www.gurnardshead.fsnet.co.uk; on coastal road between Land's End & St Ives, near Zennor; 9.15 pm; no smoking area. **Accommodation:** 6 rooms, from £55.

TROON, SOUTH AYRSHIRE 9–4B

Lochgreen House £ 40

Lochgreen Hs, Monktonhill Rd KA10 7EN   (01292) 313343

For a "spoiling" experience, this "beautiful" (some might say OTT) Edwardian golf hotel has long been a popular destination; given the recent arrival of a new chef, Andrew Costley – and plans for serious expansion – a rating is not appropriate.
/ **Sample dishes:** *scallops with celeriac & mustard oil; horseradish-crusted lamb with rosemary noodles; hot chocolate & cherry pudding.* **Details:** *www.lochgreenhouse.co.uk; 9.30 pm; no smoking.* **Accommodation:** *40 rooms, from £195, incl D.*

The Oyster Bar £ 32   𝔸 ★

The Harbour, Harbour Rd KA10 6DH   (01292) 319339

"Delicious" fish, "fresh from the sea" is the highpoint of the "wonderful" cuisine at this former mill; it has an "excellent location", overlooking the harbour. / **Sample dishes:** *roast scallops & tomatoes with prosciutto; baked turbot with mushrooms, leeks & truffles; lemon Mascarpone with blueberry coulis.* **Details:** *follow signs for Sea Cat Ferry Terminal, past shipyard; 9.30 pm; closed Mon & Sun D; no Amex.*

TROUTBECK, CUMBRIA 7–3D

Queen's Head £ 27   𝔸 ★

Townhead LA23 1PW   (01539) 432174

"Very fine pub grub" ensures that this 17th-century coaching inn, "beautifully situated" in the Lakes, is often "very busy" – "there's no booking, so get there early". / **Sample dishes:** *wild mushroom, Stilton & black olive terrine; supreme of chicken with mash; bread & butter pudding.* **Details:** *www.queensheadhotel.com; A592, on Kirkstone Pass; 9 pm; D only; no Amex; no smoking area.* **Accommodation:** *15 rooms, from £70.*

TRURO, CORNWALL 1–4B

Numberten £ 31   ★

10 Kenwyn St TR1 3DU   (01872) 272363

"Original and interesting food" helps make this Aussie-run café/bistro a "pleasant surprise" for first-time visitors, and it attracts only complimentary reports. / **Sample dishes:** *prawn & chick pea fritters; chicken with sweet potato mash; lemon tart.* **Details:** *9.30 pm; closed Sun L (& Sun D in winter); no smoking in dining room.*

TUNBRIDGE WELLS, KENT 3–4B

Hotel du Vin et Bistro £ 42

Crescent Rd TN1 2LY   (01892) 526455

This impressively stripped-down Victorian hotel building is not the sparkiest member of this superior chain; fans do praise the "lovely" setting and "outstanding" wine list, but the food is only "competent", and service can really let the side down.
/ **Sample dishes:** *salt cod brandade with peppers; chicken with creamed leeks & black pudding; pineapple crème brûlée.* **Details:** *www.hotelduvin.com; 9.30 pm; booking: max 10.* **Accommodation:** *36 rooms, from £85.*

Signor Franco £ 40

5a High St TN1 1UL   (01892) 549199

"A good welcome" helps win praise for the swankiest Italian in these parts; it's rather "cramped", though, and even fans find it "a little expensive" for what it is. / **Sample dishes:** *smoked sturgeon; pasta filled with white truffles; pancakes with crème pâtissière.* **Details:** *11 pm; closed Sun; no Amex.*

Thackeray's House £41 🄰
85 London Rd TN1 1EA (01892) 511921
"New management is trying hard" at this modishly revamped townhouse (once the residence of the novelist), where they've spent "over a million on a wonderful face-lift"; the "unexpectedly modern" approach includes cooking that's "excellent", if – unsurprisingly in the circumstances – "pricey" for what it is.
/ **Sample dishes:** roast quail salad; grilled tuna with potatoes; banana tarte Tatin. **Details:** www.thackeraysrestaurant.co.uk; 10.30 pm; closed Mon & Sun D; no smoking area.

TUNSTALL, LANCASHIRE 7–4D
Lunesdale Arms £24
LA6 2QN (01524) 274203
"A converted pub, now incorporating a light and airy bistro"; its "creative" cooking is served at "affordable" prices in a "lively" atmosphere. / **Sample dishes:** tomato bruschetta with pesto; lime & lemongrass chicken with rice; cappuccino mousse. **Details:** 9 pm; closed Mon; no Amex.

TURNBERRY, SOUTH AYRSHIRE 7–1A
Turnberry Hotel £65 🄰
KA26 9LT (01655) 331000
The views from this famous hotel are "stunning" (and "the golf is OK" too); the impressive dining room has its fans, but the cooking doesn't always live up to the very high prices.
/ **Sample dishes:** oak-smoked Scottish salmon; seared monkfish with basil polenta; raspberries & mango. **Details:** www.turnberry.co.uk; A77, 2m after Kirkswald turn right, then right again after 0.5m; 9.30 pm; closed Sun L. **Accommodation:** 221 rooms, from £170.

TUTBURY, STAFFORDSHIRE 5–3C
Olde Dog & Partridge £27
High St DE13 9LS (01283) 813030
You can eat in either the brasserie or the carvery at this large half-timbered inn – both have their fans; given the recent arrival of a new chef, we've left the place unrated.
/ **Sample dishes:** twice-baked Dovedale cheese soufflé; mustard-glazed ham with celeriac mash; Knickerbocker glory. **Value tip:** set 2-crs L & pre-theatre £6.95. **Details:** www.dogandpartridge.net; 9.45 pm; no smoking in dining room. **Accommodation:** 20 rooms, from £70.

TWICKENHAM, MIDDLESEX 3–3A
Brula £31
43 Crown Rd TW1 3EJ (020) 8892 0602
"Good bistro-style food" wins consistent praise from the locals for this "friendly" and "intimate" venture, in St Margarets.
/ **Sample dishes:** pork & veal terrine with onion marmalade; roast duck with courgette & basil cream sauce; baked chocolate pot. **Details:** 50 yards from St Margarets station; 10.30 pm; closed Sun; no Amex; booking: max 8.

TYNEMOUTH, TYNE & WEAR 8–2B
Sidney's £24 🄰★
3-5 Percy Park Rd NE30 4LZ (0191) 257 8500
They're "trying to please" at this "small, modern and busy" bistro, where the locals are generous in their praise for the "reliable" realisation of its "imaginative" menu. / **Sample dishes:** honey-roast duck with noodles & plum salad; Moroccan-braised lamb with couscous; chocolate-stuffed prune tart. **Value tip:** set 3-crs L £9.95. **Details:** www.sidneys.co.uk; 10 pm; closed Sun D; no smoking before 9 pm.

---

sign up for the survey at www.hardens.com

ULLINGSWICK, HEREFORDSHIRE   2–1B
The Three Crowns Inn   £ 32   ★
HR1 3JQ   (01432) 820279
"Expert cooking of high-quality ingredients" distinguishes this superior town-centre pub; "the pricing is high" (at least by local standards) but "the food is worth it." / **Sample dishes:** smoked salmon with cucumber & lovage vinaigrette; rack of lamb with shallots & spinach; chocolate tart. **Value tip:** set 2-crs L £10. **Details:** www.threecrownsinn.com; 1.5m from A417; 9.30 pm; closed Mon; no Amex; no smoking area.

ULLSWATER, CUMBRIA   7–3D
Sharrow Bay   £ 61   Ⓐ★★
CA10 2LZ   (01768) 486301
Messrs Coulson and Sacks may have departed, but their "lovely" Lakeland legacy lives on – the country house hotel they founded remains simply "the best in England" for many reporters; "for the non-calorie-conscious", it offers "the ultimate gourmet treat in a gorgeous setting". / **Sample dishes:** crab & scallop pancake with crayfish oil; lamb with herb brioche crust & thyme jus; Old English Regency syllabub. **Details:** www.sharrow-bay.com; on Pooley Bridge Rd towards Howtown; 8 pm; jacket & tie required; no smoking; children: 13+. **Accommodation:** 26 rooms, from £300, incl D.

ULVERSTON, CUMBRIA   7–4D
Bay Horse   £ 47   Ⓐ
Canal Foot LA12 9EL   (01229) 583972
"Lovely views over the estuary" are a highlight of this "quaint" hotel (where "they still have a gong for dinner"); the food is "consistent", even if it's "safe" rather than exciting. / **Sample dishes:** chilled tomato & redcurrant soup; guinea fowl with grape & chestnut stuffing; Irish coffee meringues. **Value tip:** set 3-crs L £18. **Details:** www.thebayhorsehotel.co.uk; after Canal Foot sign, turn left & pass Glaxo factory; 7.30 pm; closed Mon L & Sun L; no Amex; no smoking; children: 12+. **Accommodation:** 9 rooms, from £75, incl D.

UPPER SLAUGHTER, GLOUCESTERSHIRE   2–1C
Lords of the Manor   £ 61   Ⓐ
GL54 2JD   (01451) 820243
One or two early reports on the new (early-2002) regime at this formerly "cracking" Cotswolds hotel were rather discouraging; let's hope that ex-Box Tree chef Toby Hill was just settling in. / **Sample dishes:** quail ravioli with morels; roast John Dory with Parma ham & foie gras; pistachio soufflé. **Value tip:** set 2-crs L £16.95. **Details:** www.lordsofthe manor.com; 2m W of Stow on the Wold; 9.30 pm; no smoking; children: 7+. **Accommodation:** 27 rooms, from £149.

UPPINGHAM, RUTLAND   5–4D
The Lake Isle   £ 35
16 High Street East LE15 9PZ   (01572) 822951
This simply-decorated fixture (part of a small hotel near the market square) is "renowned in the area"; fans say that the "well-prepared" cooking has "held up under new owners", but there's also a school which says it's "gone off the boil". / **Sample dishes:** asparagus & Parmesan tart with hollandaise; chicken with tarragon & cranberry risotto; bread & butter pudding with cherry custard. **Value tip:** set 3-crs L £10 (Sun £13.50). **Details:** www.lakeislehotel.com; 9.30 pm; closed Mon L; no smoking. **Accommodation:** 13 rooms, from £69.

WADDESDON, BUCKINGHAMSHIRE   3–2A

Five Arrows   £34   ★
High St HP18 OJE   (01296) 651727
*As you might expect – as it's owned by the Rothschilds –
this "beautifully-run pub/hotel" is a cut above the norm; a wine list
including vintages from their neighbouring Waddesdon Manor
estate complements an "interesting menu" of "very good" food.*
/ **Sample dishes:** beetroot & cumin soup; Moroccan lamb stew with cardamom
rice; bourbon mousse with mango & raspberry coulis.
Details: www.waddesdon.org.uk; on A41; 9.30 pm; no Amex; no smoking area;
children: special area for under 10s. **Accommodation:** 11 rooms, from £80.

WAKEFIELD, WEST YORKSHIRE   5–1C

Aagrah   £21   ★
Barnsley Rd WF1 5NX   (01924) 242222
*"Newly refurbished to a high standard", this outpost of the
Yorkshire chain of upmarket Indians offers a "varied menu" of
"very good food".* / **Details:** www.aagrah.com; from M1, J39 follow Denby Dale
Rd to A61; 11.30 pm; D only; no smoking area. **Accommodation:** 13 rooms,
from £40.

WALKINGTON, EAST RIDING OF YORKSHIRE   6–2A

The Manor House   £41   𝔸
Northlands HU17 8RU   (01482) 881645
*"Set in grounds of some splendour", this family-run Wolds country
house usually displays a "high standard" of cooking "to match its
elegant interior"; it attracts the odd complaint, though, that it's
"stuffy", or "resting on its laurels".* / **Sample dishes:** Chinese crispy
lamb & poached egg salad; roast guinea fowl with bramble sauce; chocolate tart with
white & dark chocolate ice cream. **Value tip:** set 3-crs weekday D £15.
Details: www.the-manor-house.co.uk; between Walkington & Bishop Burton;
9.15 pm; D only, closed Sun; no smoking; children: 6+ (hotel guests excluded).
Accommodation: 7 rooms, from £80.

WAREHAM, DORSET   2–4C

Priory   £45   𝔸
Church Grn BH20 4ND   (01929) 551666
*"A summer's day lunch in the garden is a delight", say fans of this
long-running fixture on the River Frome (which has a vaulted
dining room in the old undercroft for less clement times);
it maintains a "good" standard of cooking.* / **Sample dishes:** seared
scallops with rhubarb butter; lamb with herb polenta & roast garlic jus; ginger crème
brûlée. **Value tip:** set 4-crs Sun L £21.50. **Details:** 10 pm; no Amex; no smoking
area; children: 8+. **Accommodation:** 18 rooms, from £135.

WARHAM ALL SAINTS, NORFOLK   6–3C

Three Horseshoes   £19   𝔸
Bridge St NR23 1NL   (01328) 710547
*"Like going back in time" – this "old inn" makes an
"atmospheric" location in which to enjoy "traditional" pub food
and "great beer".* / **Sample dishes:** shellfish & cheese bake; Norfolk beef pie;
ice cream & sorbet. **Details:** 1m off A148; 8.30 pm; no credit cards; no smoking
area; no booking. **Accommodation:** 6 rooms, from £24.

WARMINSTER, WILTSHIRE
Bishopstrow House   £ 43   2–3B

BA12 9HH   (01985) 212312

This impressive Georgian country house hotel (which has an attractive dining conservatory) recently changed hands; long-serving chef Chris Suter remains – in recent times, his "adventurous" cooking has won majority, if not unanimous, praise. / **Sample dishes:** *carpaccio of tuna with herb salad; roast rabbit wrapped in Parma ham; raspberry & orange gratin.* **Details:** *www.slh.com/bishopst; 1m from town centre on A36 to Salisbury; 9 pm; no smoking.* **Accommodation:** *32 rooms, from £199.*

WATH-IN-NIDDERDALE, NORTH YORKSHIRE   8–4B
Sportsman's Arms   £ 34

HG3 5PP   (01423) 711306

With its "lovely" Dales location, this long-established restaurant (under the same chef/patron for a quarter of a century) pleases most, if not quite all, reporters with its "good" standard of cooking. / **Sample dishes:** *goats cheese with caramelised red onions; duck with rosti, prunes & oranges; summer pudding.* **Details:** *take Wath Road from Pateley Bridge; 9 pm; D only, closed Sun; no Amex; no smoking.* **Accommodation:** *13 rooms, from £80.*

WATTON AT STONE, HERTFORDSHIRE   3–2B
George & Dragon   £ 26   Ⓐ★

82 High St SG14 3TA   (01920) 830285

Consistency across the board is the striking feature of reports on this 16th-century village pub, with its "fresh" cooking and "friendly" staff; "the only problem is getting in". / **Sample dishes:** *potted crab with ginger; fillet steak stuffed with oysters; lemon & passion fruit tart.* **Details:** *www.georgeanddragon-watton.co.uk; A602 from Stevenage; 10 pm; closed Sun D; no smoking; children: before 9pm.*

WEST HALLAM, DERBYSHIRE   5–3C
The Bottle Kiln   £ 11   Ⓐ

High Lane West DE7 6HP   (0115) 932 9442

"I'm not sure I want you to mention it" – fans prize their seats at this "art gallery buttery", recommended for a coffee or a "cheap and cheerful" bite. / **Sample dishes:** *no starters; Stilton & walnut quiche with salad; cheesecake.* **Details:** *L & afternoon tea only; closed Mon; no smoking; children: not permitted in garden.*

WEST WICKHAM, KENT   3–3B
Prima Donnas   £ 32   Ⓐ★

1-2 Red Lodge Rd BR4 0EL   (020) 8777 8433

This "very popular" Italian, near the station, is praised by the locals for its "lively", "Continental" ambience and its "wide-ranging" menu of "good-value" dishes. / **Sample dishes:** *Spanish oysters; roast rack of lamb; tiramisu.* **Details:** *www.primadonnas.co.uk; 11 pm; no Amex; no smoking area.*

WESTERHAM, KENT   3–3B
Tulsi   £ 26   ★

20 London Rd TN16 1BD   (01959) 563397

"The best Indian for miles around" is a "welcoming" place with "tasteful" décor; it's "always busy". / **Value tip:** *set 3-crs L £8.95.* **Details:** *11.30 pm.*

WESTFIELD, EAST SUSSEX   3–4C

Wild Mushroom   £33   ★

Westfield Ln TN35 4SB   (01424) 751137

"Book early", if you want to enjoy the "wonderful", if fairly straightforward, cuisine on offer at this "friendly" modern restaurant. / *Sample dishes: red pepper & tomato soup; chicken with mushrooms, capers & mash; tropical fruit sorbets with jasmine syrup.* ***Details:*** *www.wildmushroom.co.uk; 9.30 pm; closed Mon & Sun D; closed 3 weeks in Jan; no smoking in dining room; children: 8+ prefered in evening.*

WEYBRIDGE, SURREY   3–3A

Colony   £33   ★

3 Balfour Rd KT13 8HE   (01932) 842766

Food which "never lets you down" makes this "really good" and "professional" Chinese restaurant a continuing success; it can get "too hectic" at the weekends. / ***Details:*** *on A317; 10.30 pm.*

WEYMOUTH, DORSET   2–4B

Perry's   £33

4 Trinity Rd, The Old Harbour DT4 8TJ   (01305) 785799

With its "lovely location on the quay", this "tea shop-style" bistro serves a dependable menu (in particular, "fine fish") in "unhurried" style. / *Sample dishes: chicken & bacon terrine with apple chutney; fillet steak with tarragon cream sauce; pear sorbet & brandy snaps.* ***Details:*** *www.perrysrestaurant.co.uk; 9.30 pm; closed Mon L & Sat L (& Sun D in winter); no smoking area; children: 5+.*

WHITBY, NORTH YORKSHIRE   8–3D

Magpie Café   £22   ★★

14 Pier Rd YO21 3PU   (01947) 602058

"The best fish and chips in the world" – not to mention other "marvellously-fresh seafood" and "sensational sweets" – make it "worth the inevitable queue" to enter this "unsurpassable" café (which attracted more survey commentary than anywhere else in North East England). / *Sample dishes: grilled tuna with courgette fritters; Whitby cod & chips; sticky sultana loaf.* ***Details:*** *www.magpiecafe.co.uk; opp Fish Market; 9 pm; open L & D all week; closed part of Jan & Feb; no Amex; no smoking.*

The White Horse & Griffin   £34   Ⓐ

Church St YO22 4AE   (01947) 604857

This "old and genuine" coaching inn is consistently praised for its "intimate and candlelit" setting that creates a "quaint bistro-style" atmosphere; its hearty traditional-ish fare is "generally good", but can disappoint. / *Sample dishes: Caesar salad; char-grilled steak & chips; plum & almond pizza.* **Details:** *centre of old town, on Abbey side of river; 9.30 pm; no Amex.* **Accommodation:** *11 rooms, from £55.*

WHITCHURCH, HAMPSHIRE   2–3D

Red House Inn   £29   ★

21 London St RG28 7LH   (01256) 895558

"A really super little spot"; "inventive" and "consistently good" cooking – from Californian chef Shannon Wells – is making this "modern" but "unpretentious" inn a destination of growing note. / *Sample dishes: Parmesan-crusted langoustine; fillet steak in bacon with Stilton sauce; lemon tart & strawberry coulis.* ***Details:*** *9.30 pm; no Amex; no smoking; booking essential; children: 12+.*

WHITEBROOK, MONMOUTHSHIRE   2–2B
The Crown at Whitebrook   £ 38   ★
NP25 4TX   (01600) 860254
*It may be "hard to find", but most reporters reckon the "interesting and delicious" menu served in this "olde-worlde" restaurant-with-rooms in the Wye Valley makes the search worthwhile. / **Sample dishes:** venison carpaccio; roast monkfsh & foie gras wirh red lentil purée; caraway parfait with fig sponge. **Value tip:** set 3-crs Sun L £17.50. **Details:** www.crownatwhitebrook.co.uk; 2m W of A466, 5m S of Monmouth; 8.45 pm; closed Mon L & Sun D; no smoking in dining room; children: 12+. **Accommodation:** 10 rooms, from £85.*

WHITEHAVEN, CUMBRIA   7–3C
Zest   £ 31   ★
Low Rd CA28 9HS   (01946) 692848
*"Worth a trip up North, just to work through the menu", says a (Chelsea) fan of this lively modern brasserie, where some tip "special" puddings as the highlight of the "faultless" dishes. / **Sample dishes:** chicken liver & whisky cream pâté; spice-coated chicken with curried new potatoes; apple tarte Tatin with green apple sorbet. **Details:** 9.30 pm; D only, closed Sun-Tue; no Amex; no smoking in dining room.*

WHITLEY, WILTSHIRE   2–2B
The Pear Tree Inn   £ 35   Ⓐ
Top Ln SN12 8QX   (01225) 709131
*A "cosy", rustic hostelry, which wins consistent all-round praise for its "lovely" pub grub. / **Sample dishes:** wild mushroom & tarragon risotto; lamb cutlets with creamed leeks & caper jus; green fig tarte Tatin with pannacotta. **Details:** 9.30 pm; no Amex; no smoking.*

WHITSTABLE, KENT   3–3C
Crab & Winkle   £ 33   ★
South Quay, Whitstable Harbour CT5 1AB
(01227) 779377
*With its "great view over the harbour", this popular (and "noisy") fish restaurant is praised by most, if not quite all, reporters for its "excellent, fresh seafood". / **Sample dishes:** oysters; baked crab with garlic butter & Cheddar; treacle sponge & custard. **Details:** www.crab-winkle.co.uk; 9.45 pm; no Amex.*

Wheeler's Oyster Bar   £ 29   ★★
8 High St CT5 1BQ   (01227) 273311
*"Keep it to yourself", but there's "amazing" fish to be had in this "bizarre 'front room'", which "only seats a tiny number of people". / **Sample dishes:** skate ravioli; baked cod with spinach & curried mussels; date & chocolate sponge. **Details:** 7.30 pm; closed Wed; no credit cards.*

Whitstable Oyster Fishery Co.   £ 37   Ⓐ★
Horsebridge Beach CT5 1BU   (01227) 276856
*"Simple seafood, beautifully cooked", in a spot "overlooking the sea" has made a big name for this unpretentious fixture, where "London prices (and clientèle)" have long been a defining feature; the cooking is back on form of late, although "aloof" service is still a bit of a bugbear. / **Sample dishes:** rock oysters; char-gilled mackerel with roast tomato sauce; chocolate truffle cake with raspberries. **Details:** www.oysterfishery.co.uk; 9 pm, Sat 10 pm; closed Mon (& Sun D Sep-May). **Accommodation:** 30 rooms, from £40.*

WILMSLOW, CHESHIRE   5–2B
Chili Banana
Kings Arms Hotel   £ 28   ★
Alderley Rd SK9 IPZ   (01625) 539100
"Beautiful food" at *"good prices"* wins local acclaim for this
"relaxed" Thai, *"slightly oddly located at the back of a pub"*.
/ **Value tip:** set 3-crs L £9.45. **Details:** 11 pm; closed Mon, Tue L, Wed L & Thu L.

WINCHCOMBE, GLOUCESTERSHIRE   2–1C
Wesley House   £ 40   A★
High St GL54 5LJ   (01242) 602366
A characterful half-timbered building provides an *"intimate"*
setting for this highly-rated all-rounder, where *"good and
unobtrusive"* staff deliver *"interesting"* dishes. / **Sample dishes:** red
snapper terrine with saffron potatoes; seared duck with pickled apples & Calvados
cream; iced toffee & pistachio parfait. **Value tip:** set 2-crs L £10.
Details: www.wesleyhouse.co.uk; next to Sudeley Castle; 9.30 pm; closed Sun D;
no smoking in dining room. **Accommodation:** 5 rooms, from £65.

WINCHESTER, HAMPSHIRE   2–3D
Hotel du Vin et Bistro   £ 43   A
14 Southgate St SO23 9EF   (01962) 841414
"An eclectic style with candles and mirrors" creates an *"excellent
buzzy atmosphere"* at this *"relaxed"* boutique-hotel dining room;
the *"superb wine list"* is the highlight – the cooking tends to be a
mite *"predictable"*. / **Sample dishes:** moules marinière; salmon pavé with
mussel ragoût; lime pannacotta with melon. **Details:** www.hotelduvin.com; 9.45 pm.
Accommodation: 23 rooms, from £99.

Old Chesil Rectory   £ 52   ★★
1 Chesil St SO23 OHU   (01962) 851555
Philip Storey's *"impressive and very well presented"* dishes make it
well worth seeking out this *"low-key but uniformly excellent"*
establishment, housed in an historic Tudor building.
/ **Sample dishes:** twice-baked Roquefort soufflé; duck with parsnip purée & lime
vanilla sauce; melon sorbet with ginger shortbread. **Value tip:** set 2-crs L £22.
Details: 8.45 pm, Sat 9.15 pm; closed Mon & Sun; no smoking area.

Wykeham Arms   £ 34   A
75 Kingsgate St SO23 9PE   (01962) 853834
"A wonderfully warm and genial atmosphere" has long been the
special strength of this celebrated pub, next to the college; its wine
list is the key gastronomic highlight, to which the *"wholesome"*,
"traditional" cooking plays an honourable supporting rôle.
/ **Sample dishes:** mushroom, wlanut & Stilton pâté; roast monkfish with red
onion & cherry tomato salad; orange & maple cheesecake. **Value tip:** set 2-crs
Sun L £14.50. **Details:** between Cathedral and College; 8.45 pm; closed Sun D;
no smoking area; booking: max 8; children: 14+. **Accommodation:** 14 rooms,
from £79.50.

WINDERMERE, CUMBRIA   7–3D
Gilpin Lodge   £ 40   A★★
Crook Rd LA23 3NE   (01539) 488818
"You are made to feel like favoured guests", at this splendid
Lakeland country house hotel; some find the fare *"too rich"*,
but most reporters can't speak highly enough of the *"top-quality"*
cooking. / **Sample dishes:** smoked haddock pavé; roast lamb with truffled
potato & garlic sauce; Greek yoghurt sorbet. **Details:** www.gilpin-lodge.co.uk; 9 pm;
no smoking in dining room; children: 7+. **Accommodation:** 14 rooms, from £150,
incl D.

sign up for the survey at www.hardens.com

Holbeck Ghyll £ 57 A

Holbeck Ln LA23 ILU (01539) 432375

This "beautiful country house hotel" enjoys a "glorious position" overlooking Lake Windermere; some reporters praise its Gallic cooking as "excellent", but those who find the place "pretentious" and "overpriced" are also quite vociferous. / **Sample dishes:** veal ravioli with morels; salmon with tomato fondue; pear & praline parfait. **Value tip:** set 2-crs L £19.50. **Details:** www.holbeckghyll.com; 3M N of Windermere, towards Troutbeck; 9.30 pm; no smoking; children: 8+. **Accommodation:** 20 rooms, from £170.

Jerichos £ 37 ★

Birch St LA23 IEG (01539) 442522

"They try hard to please", at this "friendly" town-centre restaurant, where "quality" ingredients are used to produce "consistently good" results. / **Sample dishes:** smoked haddock, spring onion & Cheddar risotto; pork tenderloin with roast parsnips & Madeira jus; butterscotch toffee crème brûlée. **Details:** 9.30 pm; D only, closed Mon; no Amex; no smoking; children: 12+.

WINDSOR, WINDSOR & MAIDENHEAD 3–3A

Al Fassia £ 26 ★

27 St Leonards Rd SL4 3BP (01753) 855370

"A great local couscous house", which numbers "friendly and accommodating service" and "interesting Moroccan wines" among its attractions; "prices are creeping up", though. / **Details:** 10.30 pm, Fri & Sat 11 pm; closed Sun.

Bel & The Dragon £ 37

Thames St SL4 IPQ (01753) 866056

This outpost of a small chain of heavily-themed pubs, offers a "lively" atmosphere and a sometimes "innovative" menu; the realisation of the latter tends to be "mediocre", though, and "these are not really pub prices". / **Sample dishes:** curried lamb with Bombay potatoes; char-grilled tuna with caperberry salsa; honeycomb cheesecake. **Details:** www.belandthedragon.co.uk; 10.30 pm, Sun 8.30 pm; no smoking area.

WINKLEIGH, DEVON 1–2D

Pophams £ 32 A★

Castle St EX19 8HQ (01837) 83767

"Almost unique" – this lunchtime-only, BYO 10-seater (for which you must book ahead) is "exceptionally small, but so very friendly"; fans say the cooking is "excellent". / **Sample dishes:** baked goats cheese with spicy chutney; lamb in puff pastry with mushroom pâté; orange tart with apricot sauce. **Details:** off A377 between Exeter & Barnstaple; L only; open only Wed-Fri for L & D; closed Feb; no credit cards; no smoking; children: 14+.

WINTERINGHAM, NORTH LINCOLNSHIRE 5–1D

Winteringham Fields £ 66 A★★

DN15 9PF (01724) 733096

"The absolute best"; "cuisine that could not be bettered anywhere" wins Annie & Germain Schwab's "exceptional" 16th-century manor house the highest food rating in the survey – "sheer professionalism in every way" can make a visit here "an awesome experience". / **Sample dishes:** pan-fried langoustines; veal with wild mushrooms & veal jus; chocolate & macadamia mousse. **Value tip:** set 2-crs L £22. **Details:** www.winteringhamfields.com; 4m SW of Humber Bridge; 9.30 pm; closed Mon & Sun; no smoking. **Accommodation:** 10 rooms, from £90.

WITHERSLACK, CUMBRIA　　　　　　　7–4D

Old Vicarage　　　　　　　　　**£40**　　　Ⓐ ★
Church Rd LA11 6RS   (01539) 552381
*"A limited menu of well-cooked food" (making "excellent use of
local produce") commends this "dark and ancient" but "relaxing"
country house hotel to most reporters. /* **Sample dishes:** *oyster tempura
with horseradish cream; seared smoked venison with sweet potato purée; star anise
syrup sponge.* **Value tip:** *set 2-crs L & pre-theatre £12.50.*
Details: *www.oldvicarage.com; from M6, J36 follow signs to Barrow on A590; 9 pm;
D only, except Sun open L & D; no smoking.* **Accommodation:** *14 rooms,
from £65.*

WOBURN, BEDFORDSHIRE　　　　　　3–2A

Birch　　　　　　　　　　　　**£34**
20 Newport Rd MK17 9HX   (01525) 290295
*It's "an oasis in the desert", so "booking is essential" at this "light
and airy" and "very friendly" establishment, where a "modern grill
menu" is dependably realised. /* **Sample dishes:** *cod carpaccio with
gazpacho sauce; pork with apple & black pudding stuffing; honey crème brûlée with
orange shortbread.* **Details:** *9.30 pm; closed Sun D; no smoking in dining room;
booking: max 8, Fri & Sat.*

Paris House　　　　　　　　　**£63**
Woburn Pk MK17 9QP   (01525) 290692
*This rather old-fashioned French restaurant (two decades in the
same ownership) boasts a "wonderful" setting – a half-timbered
house in a deer park; all-in-all the cooking was judged "enjoyable
but outrageously expensive". /* **Sample dishes:** *prawn & crayfish with
mango; roasted brill with Noilly Prat sauce; raspberry soufflé.* **Value tip:** *set 2-crs L
£20 (Sun £28).* **Details:** *www.parishouse.co.uk; on A4012; 9.30 pm; closed Mon &
Sun D; no smoking area.*

WOKINGHAM, WOKINGHAM　　　　　3–3A

Rose Street　　　　　　　　　**£44**
6 Rose St RG40 1XU   (0118) 978 8025
*This may indeed be "Wokingham's best restaurant by far", but –
given its modest, if cosy, quarters – it really is quite pricey for
what it is. /* **Sample dishes:** *Thai fishcakes with seared scallops; roast beef with
bourgignonne tart; iced lemon verbena parfait.* **Value tip:** *set 2-crs L £14.*
Details: *9.30 pm; closed Sun; no Amex; no smoking.*

WOLVERHAMPTON, WEST MIDLANDS　5–4B

Bilash　　　　　　　　　　　**£36**　　　★
2 Cheapside WV1 1TU   (01902) 427762
*"It will change your view of 'Indian' cooking", say fans of Sitab
Khan's "superb" Bangladeshi cuisine, who hail this town-centre
curry house as "the best in the West Midlands". /* **Value tip:** *set 2-crs
L £7.50.* **Details:** *www.bilash-tandoori.co.uk; opp Civic Centre; 11 pm; closed Sun;
no smoking area.*

sign up for the survey at www.hardens.com

WOODBRIDGE, SUFFOLK   3–1D

Captains Table   £ 28
3 Quay St IP12 1BX   (01394) 383145
*Though some think it "pretentious" or "overpriced",
most reporters praise the "surprisingly accomplished" cooking at
this misleadingly-named venture (there's no longer any great
emphasis on fish) in a "quaint town". / **Sample dishes:** twice-baked
spinach soufflé; slow-roasted duck with red wine sauce; hot toffee pudding.
Details: www.captainstable.co.uk; 100 yds from theatre; 9.30 pm, Fri & Sat 10 pm;
closed Mon & Sun D; closed 2 weeks in Jan; no Amex; smoking in bar only.*

Seckford Hall Hotel   £ 30   𝔸 ★
IP13 6NU   (01394) 385678
*An "excellent all-round package" – this Elizabethan house in
Constable Country comes complete with "stately home"
ambience, and offers quality food and wines "at very competitive
prices". / **Sample dishes:** salmon roulade; monkfish with pasta & wilted greens;
champagne mousse with strawberries. **Details:** www.seckford.co.uk; 9.30 pm;
closed Mon L; no smoking; children: 6+ after 7 pm. **Accommodation:** 32 rooms,
from £120.*

WOODSTOCK, OXFORDSHIRE   2–1D

The Feathers Hotel   £ 54
Market St OX20 1SX   (01993) 812291
*"Superb" food in the restaurant – "or try the bar or garden for a
cheaper meal in lovely surroundings" – commends this "civilised"
luxury hotel to its fans; some find the atmosphere "a little
hushed", though, and the whole set-up "slightly pretentious and
overpriced". / **Sample dishes:** confit chicken with fig marmalade; lemon sole
with rocket soufflé; nougat glacé with mango & chocolate sauce. **Value tip:** set 2-crs
L £15.50. **Details:** www.feathers.co.uk; 8m N of Oxford on A44; 9.15 pm;
no smoking. **Accommodation:** 21 rooms, from £115.*

WOOTTON WAWEN, WEST MIDLANDS   2–1C

Bulls Head   £ 30
Stratford Rd B95 6BD   (01564) 792511
*A "beautiful setting", not far from Stratford, is part of the appeal
of this "casual" pub/restaurant; the period during which a new
chef has been installed has seen reports ranging from "stunningly
different" to "not exceptional". / **Sample dishes:** pan-fried scallops with
onion jam; pan-fried chicken with cherry tomato jam; Bailey's crème brûlée.
Details: on A3400, N of Stratford, near Wootton Hall; 10 pm; no smoking.*

WORCESTER, WORCESTERSHIRE   2–1B

Brown's   £ 43   𝔸
24 Quay St WR1 2JJ   (01905) 26263
*"An oasis in the Worcester desert" – this "spacious room with
river views" makes a "reliable" destination (not to be confused
with the chain of brasseries); a "nice selection of fish" is the
highlight of the "professional" cooking. / **Sample dishes:** devilled lambs
kidneys with polenta; roast duck with minted pea mousseline; bitter chocolate ice
cream. **Value tip:** set 3-crs L £21.50. **Details:** near the Cathedral; 9.45 pm; closed
Mon, Sat L & Sun D; no smoking; children: 8+.*

Glass House £36 Ⓐ
Church St WR1 2RH (01905) 611120
"Wonderful outdoor seating" is part of the formula which has
made this ambitious operation – housed in a 16th-century school
house – quite a local *"favourite";* compared to the charms of the
setting, though some find the rest of the performance rather
"amateurish". / **Sample dishes:** *crab & red mullet tabbouleh; roast lamb with
pearl barley risotto & haggis; macadamia nut parfait.* **Details:** *10 pm; closed
Mon & Sun; no smoking.*

Lemon Tree £31
12 Friar St WR1 2LZ (01905) 27770
*It's still quite early days for the new owners of this "welcoming"
and "colourful" little restaurant; some misfires were reported this
year, but for the most part the "reliable" Mediterranean cooking
appears to have survived the transition.* / **Sample dishes:** *Mozzarella,
mint, Peach & prosciutto salad; roast cod with bean & chorizo broth; spiced apple &
sultana spring rolls.* **Details:** *www.thelemontree.co.uk; 2 mins walk from Guildhall;
10 pm; closed Mon, Tue D, Wed D & Sun; no Amex; no smoking.*

WREXHAM, WREXHAM 5–3A

Pant Yr Ochan £27 Ⓐ
Old Wrexham Rd LL12 8TY (01978) 853525
*An "unusual" choice of dishes in "ample" portions helps secure a
big local following for this "friendly" pub/restaurant; it's hailed as
"a great destination for families and couples" alike.*
/ **Sample dishes:** *mushroom ravioli; red bream & olive potatoes with asparagus;
apple tart with cider custard.* **Details:** *1m N of Wrexham; 9.30 pm; no smoking
area; children: before 6 pm only.*

WRIGHTINGTON BAR, LANCASHIRE 5–1A

Mulberry Tree £36 ★
9 Wrightington Bar WN6 9SE (01257) 451400
*A classically-trained chef produces "some exceptional food",
at this "relatively new" pub/restaurant; the atmosphere, though,
is "not great" (Sunday lunch seems to be something of a
weakness), and service "could be better".* / **Sample dishes:** *pea & ham
soup with Parmesan croutons; baked cod with cheese & basil crust; rice pudding with
apricots.* **Details:** *2m along Mossy Lea Rd, off M6, J27; 10 pm; no Amex;
no smoking.*

WYE, KENT 3–3C

Wife of Bath £36
4 Upper Bridge St TN25 5AF (01233) 812540
*"French cooking comes with a fusion twist from a Kiwi chef",
at this well-established country fixture (occupying an old house in
the village); results "can be good or can be average".*
/ **Sample dishes:** *goats cheese & pickled quail egg salad; sea bass with lime &
coriander slasa; sticky toffee pudding.* **Value tip:** *set 2-crs L £11.50.*
Details: *www.wifeofbath.com; off A28 between Ashford & Canterbury; 10 pm;
closed Mon & Sun.* **Accommodation:** *5 rooms, from £75.*

YARMOUTH, ISLE OF WIGHT   2–4D

George Hotel   £41   A
Quay St PO41 0PE   (01983) 760331
"*Wonderful outdoor seating*" *adds much to the appeal of the
brasserie at this* "*favourite*" *harbourside hotel, overlooking the
Solent; there's also a grander, more formal restaurant (formula
price £56).* / **Sample dishes:** trio of duck starters; braised pork with Morteau
sausage & parsnip purée; rum baba with Earl Grey syrup.
Details: www.thegeorge.co.uk; 10 pm; D only, closed Mon & Sun; booking: max 8;
children: 8+. **Accommodation:** 17 rooms, from £205.

YARM, STOCKTON ON TEES   8–3C

D P Chadwicks   £35   A★
104b High St TS15 9AU   (01642) 788558
"*Consistently good cooking and ambience*" *make David Brown-
Less's* "*friendly*" *modern café/brasserie a very popular local
destination.* / **Sample dishes:** Catalan seafood salad; calves liver & bacon with
onion rings; baked cherry cheesecake. **Details:** www.chadwicksrestaurant.com;
just after Yarm Bridge; 9.30 pm; closed Mon & Sun (open 1 Sun a month); no Amex;
no smoking area; no booking.

YATTENDON, BERKSHIRE   2–2D

Royal Oak Hotel   £40
The Square RG18 0UG   (01635) 201325
"*'Vaut le voyage' from the M4*", *say fans of this impressive village
inn, who praise* "*wonderful food in a lovely setting*"; *critics feel it's
*"*rather overpriced*", *however, and* "*fails to live up to its
ambitions*". / **Sample dishes:** lobster ravioli on seasoned spinach; roast lamb
with celeriac gratin; praline soufflé. **Details:** www.trpplc.com; 5m W of Pangbourne,
off B4009; 9.30 pm; closed Sun D; no smoking; children: 6+. **Accommodation:** 5
rooms, from £120.

YORK, CITY OF YORK   5–1D

Bettys   £24   A
6-8 St Helen's Sq YO1 8QP   (01904) 659142
"*Unalloyed pleasure*" *is the theme of most reports on this
*"*excellent old-style tearoom*" (*formerly Taylor's, but now an
outpost of the famous Harrogate institution*); "*wonderful*" *coffee
and* "*marvellous*" *cakes primarily create the queues,
but* "*all manner of snacks*" *are favourably commented on.*
/ **Sample dishes:** Swiss rosti with bacon & cheese; Yorkshire rarebit with apple
chutney; Yorkshire curd tart. **Details:** www.bettysandtaylors.com; down Blake St
from York Minster; 9 pm; no Amex; no smoking area; no booking.

Blue Bicycle   £38
34 Fossgate YO1 9TA   (01904) 673990
"*The busiest place is town*" *is* "*very inconsistent*" *nowadays –
some still find a visit to this (*"*mainly fish*") *restaurant a* "*fun*" *and
*"*romantic*" *experience, but it is* "*hit-and-miss*", *and even fans say
it's* "*expensive*". / **Sample dishes:** spicy salmon hash with lime salsa; Aberdeen
Angus beef with green bean stir-fry; passion fruit & Campari rice pudding.
Details: www.bluebicyclerestaurant.com; 10 pm; no smoking; booking: max 6;
children: 12+. **Accommodation:** 2 rooms, from £150.

Café Concerto   £ 28   𝔸 ★
21 High Petergate YO1 7EN (01904) 610478
*"Consistently good for years now"; this "busy", "bistro-style"
fixture by the Minster delivers "admirable and simple" cooking,
"friendly" service and a "fun" atmosphere; "the shame is that it's
not bigger" (there's "often a queue"). / **Sample dishes:** grilled halloumi
with pomegranate molasses; pork chops with root vegetable mash; Irish coffee jelly
with amaretti biscuits. **Details:** by the W entrance of York Minster; 9.30 pm, Fri &
Sat 10 pm; no Amex; no smoking; no booking at L.*

City Screen Café Bar   £ 16   𝔸 ★
Coney St YO1 9QL (01904) 541144
*On the top floor of a "fantastic" modern cinema, this glazed café
makes a very popular all-day destination, serving "interesting",
"bistro-type" food. / **Sample dishes:** Parma ham & Mozzarella salad; smoked
salmon & scrambled eggs; lemon cheesecake. **Details:** 9 pm; no Amex; no smoking
area; no booking; children: before 7 pm only.*

Melton's   £ 34   ★
7 Scarcroft Rd YO23 1ND (01904) 634341
*"Innovative cooking that always hits the spot" attracts consistent
praise for this "friendly" and "unassuming" shop-conversion,
and – for some – a "limited mark-up on good wines" contributes
to an impression of "unbeatable value". / **Sample dishes:** Jerusalem
artichoke soup with truffle oil; braised oxtail with chervil mash; apple crêpes with
cider sorbet. **Value tip:** set 2-crs L £13.50. **Details:** www.meltonsrestaurant.co.uk;
10 mins walk from Castle Museum; 10 pm; closed Mon L & Sun; no Amex;
no smoking area.*

Melton's Too   £ 27
25 Walmgate YO1 9TX (01904) 629222
*"A sympathetic conversion of an old saddlery" provides the setting
for this "new and welcome bistro-style" offshoot of Melton's;
its cooking, in the early days at least, doesn't seem to be anything
special (but an "extensive brunch menu" is particularly approved).
/ **Sample dishes:** pork rillettes with Cumberland sauce; Merguez sausage with
couscous & lemon oil; Yorkshire curd tart. **Details:** www.meltonstoo.co.uk;
10.30 pm; no smoking in dining room.*

Middlethorpe Hall   £ 48   𝔸
Bishopthorpe Rd YO23 2GB (01904) 641241
*A glorious location – part of a country house hotel and spa, in a
200-acre estate right on the fringe of the city – is the undisputed
attraction of this "smart" and "intimate" dining room; feedback
on both food and service is, however, more mixed.
/ **Sample dishes:** oxtail terrine with horseradish cream; pike fillet with Bayonne
ham; aniseed parfait with roast pears. **Value tip:** set 3-crs L £19.50 (Sun £22.50).
Details: www.middlethorpe.com; next to racecourse; 9.45 pm; no Amex; jacket &
tie required; no smoking in dining room; children: 8+. **Accommodation:** 30 rooms,
from £160.*

Rish   £ 34
7 Fossgate YO1 9TA (01904) 622688
*Some still say it's a "welcome find", but – after a promising start
– this "trendy" yearling seems on the slide; many note its "toppish
prices" and some find the atmosphere a turn-off.
/ **Sample dishes:** beetroot-scented gravadlax; roast lamb with olive mash & salsify;
pear Bakewell tart with Calvados sorbet. **Value tip:** set 2-crs L & pre-theatre £11.
Details: www.rish-york.co.uk; 10 pm, Fri & Sat 10.30 pm; no smoking area.*

UK MAPS

10

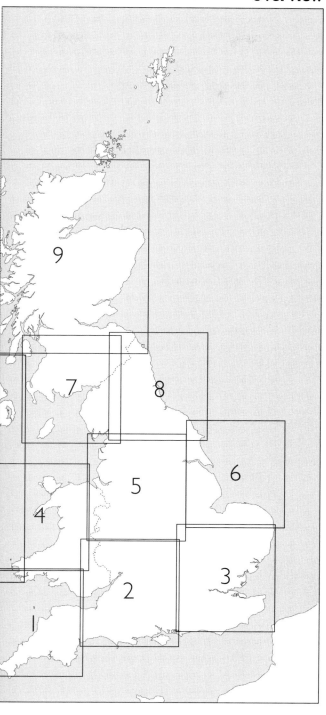

Map 1

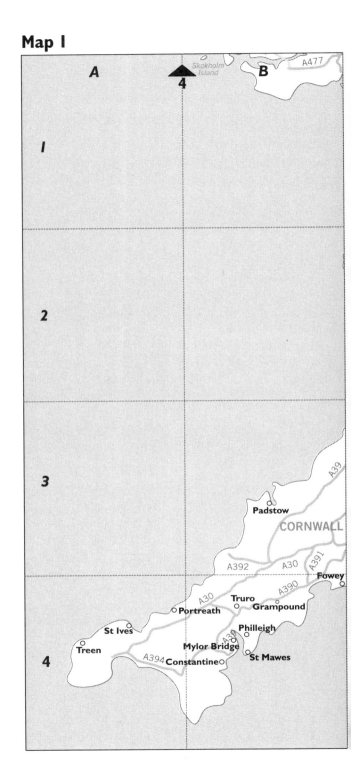

A   ▲**4** *Skokholm Island*   B   *A477*

I

2

3

Padstow○

CORNWALL

A392 *A30* *A391*

Fowey●

A30 Truro○ *A390*

Portreath○ **Grampound**

St Ives○ **Philleigh**○

Treen○ **Mylor Bridge**○

4 *A394* **Constantine**○ **St Mawes**

Map I

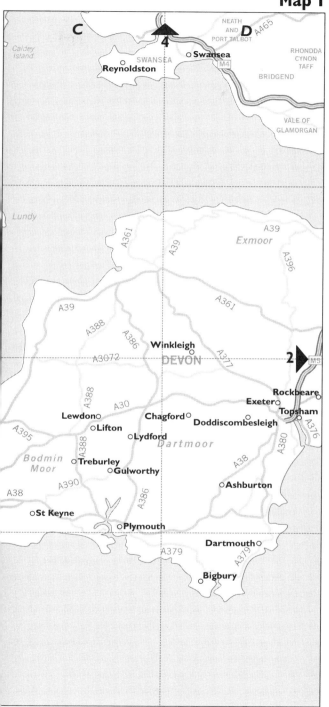

Map 2

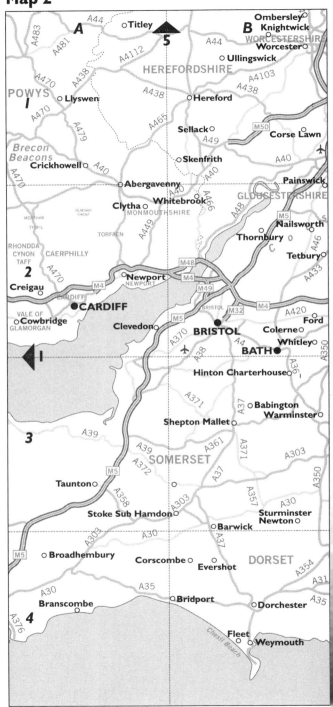

Map 2

Map 3

Map 3

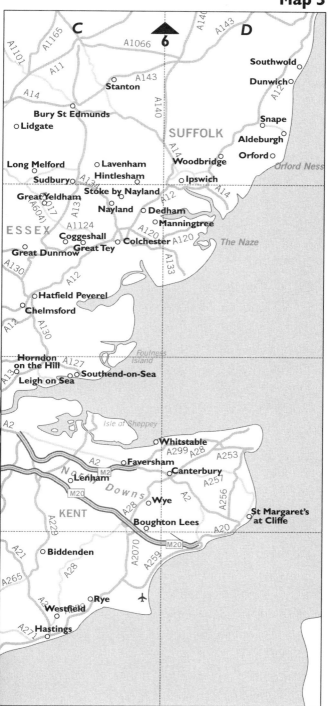

Map 4

A

B

I

Holy Island

2

Bardsey
Island

3

4

Fishguard
○ Porthgain

Ramsey
Island

PEMBROKESHIRE

Broad Haven

Skomer
Island

Skokholm
Island

A487

A40

A4076

A40

A478

A477

Map 4

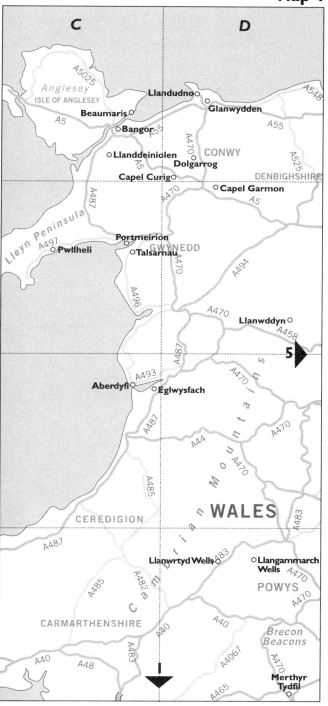

Map 5

Map 5

Map 6

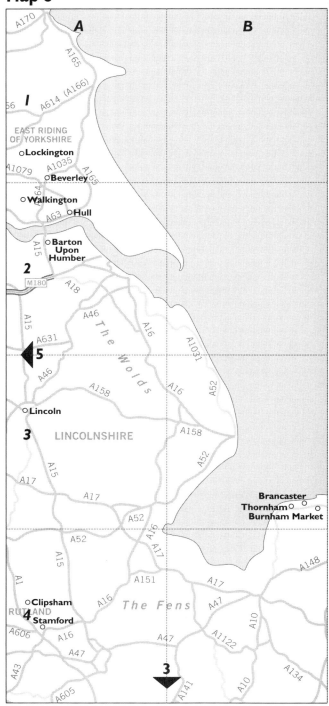

Map 6

C

D

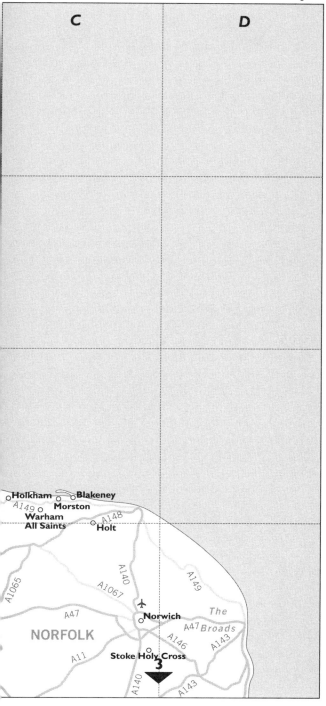

Holkham Blakeney
A149 Morston
Warham
All Saints Holt A148

A140
A1065 A1067 A149

A47 Norwich The
A47 Broads
NORFOLK A146 A143

A11 Stoke Holy Cross
A140 3 A143

Map 7

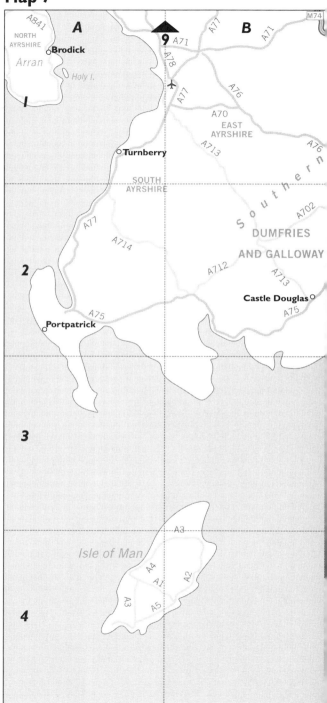

Map 7

A721 **C**
A73
9
U p l a n d s
A72
D
A697

S. LANARKSHIRE
A702
A708
BORDERS

A701
A74(M)
A7
A68

A74

The Borders

A701
A74(M)

A76
A75

✈

A689

A596
8

A598
M6
A6
A686

CUMBRIA

Cockermouth
A66
A5086
A66 **Applethwaite**

o**Troutbeck**
o**Ullswater**

Whitehaven

Lake District
A591

Grasmereo
Elterwatero **Ambleside**o
A685

Windermereo
Bowness

A595

o**Crosthwaite**

Cartmel Fello
M6

A590
Witherslacko
Kirkby Lonsdaleo

Ulverstono **Cartmel**o
Beethamo

A590
A6
Tunstallo

Isle of Walney
A683

5

M6

Map 8

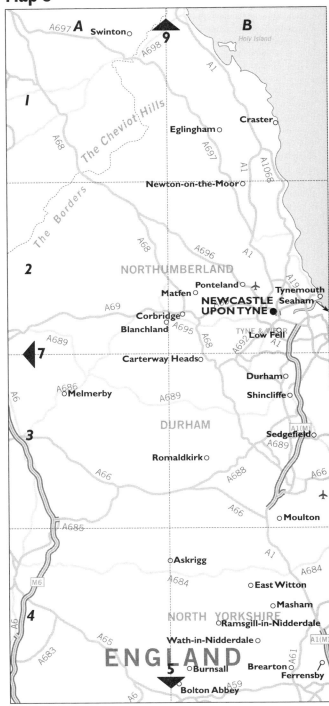

Map 8

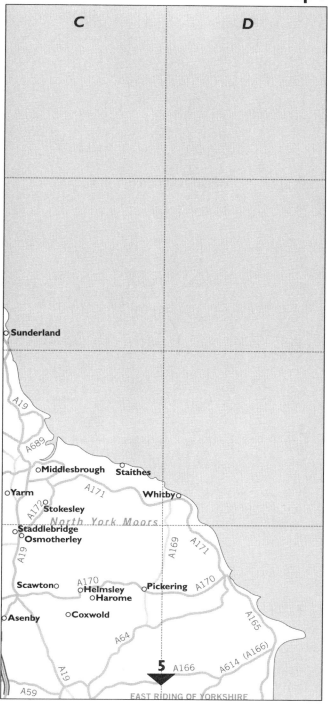

C

D

Sunderland

A19

A689

Middlesbrough   Staithes

Yarm   A171

A172   Whitby

Stokesley

North York Moors

Staddlebridge

Osmotherley   A169   A171

A19

A170

Scawton   Helmsley   Pickering   A170

Harome

Asenby   Coxwold   A165

A64

5   A166   A614 (A166)

A19

A59

EAST RIDING OF YORKSHIRE

Map 9

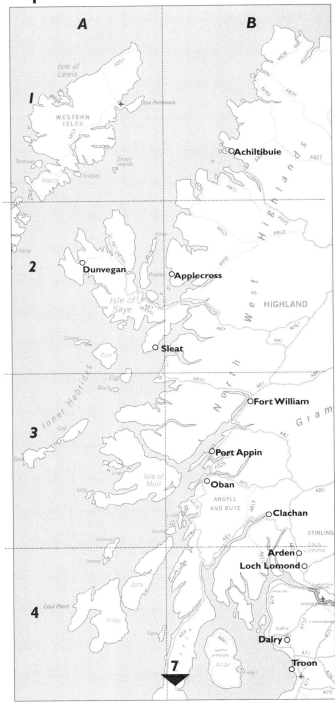

Map 9

Map 10

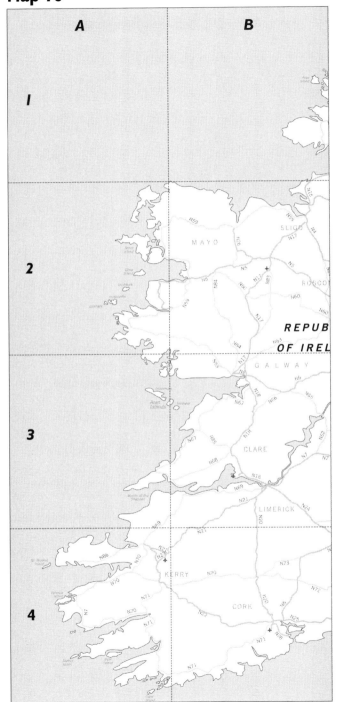

Map 10

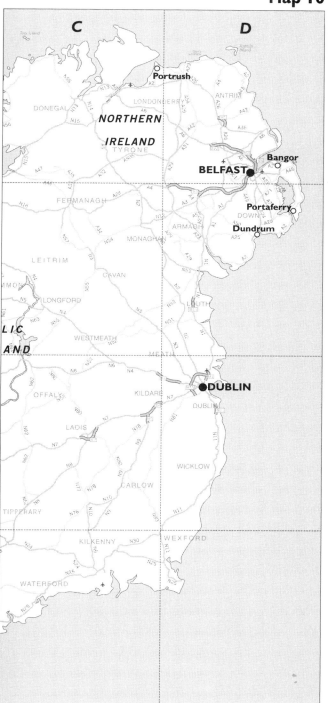

ALPHABETICAL INDEX

ALPHABETICAL INDEX

ALPHABETICAL INDEX

ALPHABETICAL INDEX

ALPHABETICAL INDEX

ALPHABETICAL INDEX

To get into your clients' good books, get on to one of ours.

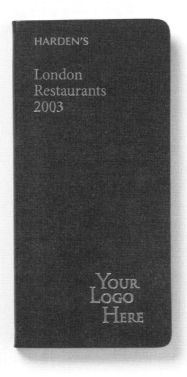

Harden's restaurant guides make perfect presents. Embossed with your logo, our guides provide a visual reminder every time your client chooses a place to dine. In short, Harden's titles provide an extremely flexible way of promoting your corporate image at a reasonable cost.

Call us now for a copy of our corporate brochure, or visit our website.
Telephone (020) 7839 4763 Website www.hardens.com

Further publications from Harden's

Harden's London Restaurants 2003

ISBN: 1-873721-50-1
Price: £8.99
280pp

"Gastronome's Bible" *Evening Standard*
Contributions from over 7,000 ordinary diners
help review over 1,200 restaurants.

Harden's Good Cheap Eats in London 2003

ISBN: 1-873721-54-4
Price: £5.99
154pp

How to eat well in London, but keep costs
down – 500 of the best places to eat out for
under £20 per head.
Published in Nov. (2002 edition out now)

Harden's London Food Shops 2002/03

ISBN: 1-873721-48-X
Price: £6.99

The first survey driven guide to London's
food shops

Harden's Bars & Pubs

ISBN: 1-873721-47-1
Price: £5.99

Featuring over 1000 establishments, this is
the only truly pocket-sized guide to
London's bars and pubs. (Published in Nov.)

Please visit www.hardens.com for further details or call
(020) 7839 4763